Lecture Notes in Business Information Processing   422

More information about this series at http://www.springer.com/series/7911

Boris Shishkov (Ed.)

Business Modeling and Software Design

11th International Symposium, BMSD 2021
Sofia, Bulgaria, July 5–7, 2021
Proceedings

 Springer

Editor
Boris Shishkov
University of Library Studies
and Information Technologies
Sofia, Bulgaria

Delft University of Technology
Delft, The Netherlands

BAS - Institute of Mathematics
and Informatics
Sofia, Bulgaria

IICREST
Sofia, Bulgaria

ISSN 1865-1348   ISSN 1865-1356 (electronic)
Lecture Notes in Business Information Processing
ISBN 978-3-030-79975-5   ISBN 978-3-030-79976-2 (eBook)
https://doi.org/10.1007/978-3-030-79976-2

This Springer imprint is published by the registered company Springer Nature Switzerland AG
The registered company address is: Gewerbestrasse 11, 6330 Cham, Switzerland

Preface

This book contains the *proceedings* of **BMSD 2021** (the 11th International Symposium on **B**usiness **M**odeling and **S**oftware **D**esign), held in *Sofia, Bulgaria*, on 5-7 July (http://www.is-bmsd.org). BMSD is an annual event that brings together researchers and practitioners interested in enterprise modeling and its relation to software specification.

The BMSD Community is inspiring! Many of us met *physically* in Berlin last year, for the 10th edition of the symposium, being so very happy about that. Probably few of us would have imagined how special such a physical meeting would be, in the current pandemic period. It is marked not only by huge stress among most people (in Europe and beyond) but also by an increasing pressure over many systems: Hospitals were burdened by too many patients in their intensive-care units; Border police officers were pressed, pushed to control again the EU-internal borders; Police were not only expected to fight crime but also to control the population by enforcing the imposed restrictions; Universities had to go online, with no time to prepare; Travel companies were excessively burdened to also consider the health status of their customers; Logistics was severely affected by numerous travel restrictions; Banks had to accommodate new (credit) schemes for the benefit of "problematic" customers; and so on. Unfortunately, *Information and Communication Technology* (ICT) did not bring benefits in this regard as much as we all hoped for. This concerns an *expectations mismatch* between Society and *Big Tech* (BT): (i) Society expected that BT would truly aim to meet user needs (especially during the pandemic), rather than re-branding and imposing existing technology-driven solutions; (ii) BT expected from Society more trust and cooperativeness rather than suspicion. We argue that very few existing IT solutions have undergone essential developments in response to the changing and increasing societal needs during the pandemic, neither have we seen cutting-edge IT innovations in the 2020-21 period. But what we see instead is an increasing *power* of BT, that goes beyond the boundaries of ICT, entering the territory of *politics*. Some top BT representatives seem to be less interested in stimulating the creation of new ICT-related solutions for the benefit of people, being at the same time more interested in entering healthcare-related discussions and stating opinions about how people should live. Last but not least, BT has accumulated abundant wealth in the abovementioned period, and this raises questions. Can we speak of a delivery of ICT-related solutions in response to user needs, for the benefit of Society, and in concert with human values and public values? Do we observe BT doing things that normally politicians should do? Are users "the King" whose needs are to be identified and reflected in REQUIREMENTS that in turn "govern" the ICT developments or is it the case that BT "determines" what the user needs SHOULD be? We have very simple examples from the last several years: (i) A laptop purchased several years ago is very similar (as it concerns its key features) to the corresponding model of today; (ii) Some big operating systems are enforcing updates almost every week but what we get as users remains nearly the same; (iii) The platforms we are using for routing, e-banking, and so on are mainly changing their fancy banners and colors but essentially what we benefit from using them remains the same. Those examples indicate that often a new ICT project is realized just for the sake of realizing yet another ICT project. USER NEEDS and REQUIREMENTS are not seen on the horizon. More and more we observe R&D projects realized by huge interdisciplinary teams where there is a HUGE GAP between the work of domain specialists and the work of technology developers. Domain specialists have their attitudes but are often unable to judge how a proposed ICT solution is relevant to particular domain-specific needs and whether at all the ICT-system-to be would contribute to any relevant improvements. This gives "unlimited power" in the hands of ICT developers who would often "massage" some of their existing products and re-shape +re-brand them as "new" products. The funding is provided and a "new product" is delivered. If in several years it would appear that the product is not good enough, this may just lead to yet another project. Is this what we want? Is this what we need? Probably we should all be listening to the WIND OF CHANGE! We should bring back ICT DEVELOPMENT and SOFTWARE DESIGN to its CREATIVE ROOTS and SENSITIVITY to USER NEEDS. Not always BOTTOM-UP (technology-driven) solutions are the best for Society, especially if it is very difficult for other stakeholders to adequately perceive the relevance and utility of the proposed technical and technological solution(s). Often a USER-CENTRIC approach would be better in this regard, especially if the demands of domain specialists are properly codified in MODELS that in turn would "fuel" the technical specifications. And this all should be essentially driven by the goal of satisfying user needs, as stated in the preface of the BMSD 2020 Proceedings. As also mentioned in the BMSD 2020 preface, THE way of achieving this is to methodologically align business (enterprise) modeling and software design, this bringing the BMSD Community together, inspired to contribute to the area of **ENTERPRISE INFORMATION SYSTEMS**.

Since 2011, we have enjoyed **ten successful BMSD editions**. The first BMSD edition (**2011**) took place in **Sofia, Bulgaria**, and the theme of BMSD 2011 was: "Business Models and Advanced Software Systems." The second BMSD edition (2012) took place in **Geneva, Switzerland**, with the theme: "From Business Modeling to Service-Oriented Solutions." The third BMSD edition (**2013**) took place in **Noordwijkerhout, The Netherlands**, and the theme was: "Enterprise Engineering and Software Generation." The fourth BMSD edition (**2014**) took place in **Luxembourg, Grand Duchy of Luxembourg**, and the theme was: "Generic Business Modeling Patterns and Software Re-Use." The fifth BMSD edition (2015) took place in **Milan, Italy**, with the theme: "Toward Adaptable Information Systems." The sixth BMSD edition (**2016**) took place in **Rhodes, Greece**, and had the theme: "Integrating Data Analytics in Enterprise Modeling and Software Development." The seventh BMSD edition (2017) took place in **Barcelona, Spain**, and the theme was: "Modeling Viewpoints and Overall Consistency." The eighth BMSD edition (**2018**) took place in **Vienna, Austria**, with the theme: "Enterprise Engineering and Software Engineering - Processes and Systems for the Future." The ninth BMSD edition (**2019**) took place in **Lisbon, Portugal**, and the theme of BMSD 2019 was: "Reflecting Human Authority and Responsibility in Enterprise Models and Software Specifications". The tenth BMSD edition (**2020**) took place in **Berlin, Germany**, and the theme of BMSD 2020 was: "Towards Knowledge-Driven Enterprise Information Systems". The current edition brings BMSD back to where it once started – Sofia, Bulgaria. BMSD 2021 marks the **ELEVENTH EVENT**, with the theme: "**Towards Enterprises and Software that are Resilient Against Disruptive Events**."

We are proud to have attracted distinguished guests as keynote lecturers, who are renowned experts in their fields: **Manfred Reichert**, *Ulm University*, Germany (2020), **Mathias Weske**, *HPI - University of Potsdam*, Germany (2020), **Jose Tribolet**, *IST - University of Lisbon*, Portugal (2019), **Jan Mendling**, *WU Vienna*, Austria (2018), **Roy Oberhauser**, *Aalen University*, Germany (2018), **Norbert Gronau**, *University of Potsdam*, Germany (2017), **Oscar Pastor**, *Polytechnic University of Valencia*, Spain (2017), **Alexander Verbraeck**, *Delft University of Technology*, The Netherlands (2017), **Paris Avgeriou**, *University of Groningen*, The Netherlands (2016), **Jan Juerjens**, *University of Koblenz-Landau*, Germany (2016), **Mathias Kirchmer**, *BPM-D*, USA (2016), **Marijn Janssen**, *Delft University of Technology*, The Netherlands (2015), **Barbara Pernici**, *Politecnico di Milano*, Italy (2015), **Henderik Proper**, *Public Research Centre Henri Tudor*, Grand Duchy of Luxembourg (2014), **Roel Wieringa**, *University of Twente*, The Netherlands (2014), **Kecheng Liu**, *University of Reading*, UK (2013), **Marco Aiello**, *University of Groningen*, The Netherlands (2013), **Leszek Maciaszek**, *Wroclaw University of Economics*, Poland (2013), **Jan L. G. Dietz**, *Delft University of Technology*, The Netherlands (2012), **Ivan Ivanov**, *SUNY Empire State College*, USA (2012), **Dimitri Konstantas**, *University of Geneva*, Switzerland (2012), **Marten van Sinderen**, *University of Twente*, The Netherlands (2012), **Mehmet Aksit**, *University of Twente*, The Netherlands (2011), **Dimitar Christozov**, *American University in Bulgaria – Blagoevgrad*, Bulgaria (2011), **Bart Nieuwenhuis**, *University of Twente*, The Netherlands (2011), and **Hermann Maurer**, *Graz University of Technology*, Austria (2011).

The high quality of the BMSD 2021 technical program is enhanced by two keynote lectures delivered by outstanding guests and previous BMSD keynote speakers: **Norbert Gronau**, *University of Potsdam*, Germany (the title of his lecture is: "The Socio-Technical Factory of the Future: How AI and Human Can Work Together") and **Alexander Verbraeck**, *Delft University of Technology*, The Netherlands (the title of his lecture is: "Resilient Enterprise Information Systems"). Also, the presence (physically or distantly) of former BMSD keynote lecturers is much appreciated: *Roy Oberhauser* (2018), *Mathias Kirchmer* (2016), *Marijn Janssen* (2015), and *Marten van Sinderen* (2012). The technical program is further enriched by a panel discussion (featured by the participation of some of the abovementioned outstanding scientists) and also by other discussions stimulating *community building* and facilitating possible *R&D project acquisition initiatives*. Those special activities are definitely contributing to maintaining the event's high quality and inspiring our steady and motivated Community.

The BMSD 2021 Technical Program Committee consists of a Chair and 106 Members from 36 countries (*Australia, Austria, Brazil, Bulgaria, Canada, China, Colombia, Denmark, Egypt, Estonia, Finland, France, Germany, Greece, India, Indonesia, Italy, Lithuania, Grand Duchy of Luxembourg, Malaysia, Mexico, New Zealand, Palestine, Poland, Portugal, Russia, Singapore, Slovak Republic, Slovenia, Spain, Sweden, Switzerland, Taiwan, The Netherlands, UK,* and *USA,* listed alphabetically) – all of them competent and enthusiastic representatives of prestigious organizations.

In organizing BMSD 2021, we have observed **highest ethical standards**: We guarantee *at least two reviews per submitted paper* (assuming reviews of adequate quality), under the condition that the paper fulfills the BMSD 2021 requirements. In assigning a paper for reviewing, it is our responsibility to *provide reviewers that have relevant expertise*. Sticking to a **double-blind review process**, we guarantee that a reviewer would not know who the authors of the reviewed paper are (we send anonymized versions of the papers to the reviewers) and an author would not know who has reviewed his/her paper. We require that a reviewer *respects the content of the reviewed paper* and does not disclose (parts of) its content to third parties before the symposium (and also after the symposium in case the manuscript gets rejected). We *guarantee against conflict of interests*, by not assigning papers for reviewing by reviewers who are immediate colleagues of any of the co-authors. In our decisions to accept/reject papers, we **guarantee against any discrimination based on age, gender, race, or religion**. As it concerns the EU data protection standards, **we stick to the GDPR requirements**.

We have demonstrated for a 11th consecutive year a high quality of papers. We are proud to have succeeded in establishing and maintaining (for many years already) a high scientific quality (as it concerns the symposium itself) and a stimulating collaborative atmosphere; also, our Community is inspired to share ideas and experiences.

As mentioned already, BMSD is essentially leaning toward **ENTERPRISE INFORMATION SYSTEMS** (EIS), by considering the **MODELING OF ENTERPRISES AND BUSINESS PROCESSES** as a basis for **SPECIFYING SOFTWARE**. Further, in the broader EIS context, BMSD 2021 addresses a large number of research areas and topics, as follows:

› **BUSINESS PROCESSES AND ENTERPRISE ENGINEERING** - *enterprise systems; enterprise system environments and context; construction and function; actor roles; signs and affordances; transactions; business processes; business process coordination; business process optimization; business process management and strategy execution; production acts and coordination acts; regulations and business rules; enterprise (re-) engineering; enterprise interoperability; inter-enterprise coordination; enterprise engineering and architectural governance; enterprise engineering and software generation; enterprise innovation.*

› **BUSINESS MODELS AND REQUIREMENTS** - *essential business models; re-usable business models; business value models; business process models; business goal models; integrating data analytics in business modeling; semantics and business data modeling; pragmatics and business behavior modeling; business modeling viewpoints and overall consistency; business modeling landscapes; requirements elicitation; domain-imposed and user-defined requirements; requirements specification and modeling; requirements analysis and verification; requirements evolution; requirements traceability; usability and requirements elicitation.*

› **BUSINESS MODELS AND SERVICES** - *enterprise engineering and service science; service-oriented enterprises; from business modeling to service-oriented solutions; business modeling for software-based services; service engineering; business-goals-driven service discovery and modeling; technology-independent and* *platform-specific service modeling; re-usable service models; business-rules-driven service composition; web services; autonomic service behavior; context-aware service behavior; service interoperability; change impact analysis and service management; service monitoring and quality of service; services for IoT applications; service innovation.*

› **BUSINESS MODELS AND SOFTWARE** - *enterprise engineering and software development; model-driven engineering; co-design of business and IT systems; business-IT alignment and traceability; alignment between IT architecture and business strategy; business strategy and technical debt; business-modeling-driven software generation; normalized systems and combinatorial effects; software generation and dependency analysis; component-based business-software alignment; objects, components, and modeling patterns; generic business modeling patterns and software re-use; business rules and software specification; business goals and software integration; business innovation and software evolution; software technology maturity models; domain-specific models; croscutting concerns - security, privacy, distribution, recoverability, logging, performance monitoring.*

› **INFORMATION SYSTEMS ARCHITECTURES AND PARADIGMS** - *enterprise architectures; service-oriented computing; software architectures; cloud computing; autonomic computing (and intelligent software behavior); context-aware computing (and adaptable software systems); affective computing (and user-aware software systems); aspect-oriented computing (and non-functional requirements); architectural styles; architectural viewpoints.*

› **DATA ASPECTS IN BUSINESS MODELING AND SOFTWARE DEVELOPMENT** - *data modeling in business processes; data flows and business modeling; databases, OLTP, and business processes; data warehouses, OLAP, and business analytics; data analysis, data semantics, redundancy, and quality-of-data; data mining, knowledge discovery, and knowledge management; information security and business process modeling; categorization, classification, regression, and clustering; cluster analysis and predictive analysis; ontologies and decision trees; decision tree induction and information gain; business processes and entropy; machine learning and deep learning - an enterprise perspective; uncertainty and context states; statistical data analysis and probabilistic business models.*

› **BLOCKCHAIN-BASED BUSINESS MODELS AND INFORMATION SYSTEMS** - *smart contracts; blockchains for business process management; blockchain schemes for decentralization; the blockchain architecture - implications for systems and business processes; blockchains and the future of enterprise information systems; blockchains and security/privacy/trust issues.*

› **IoT AND IMPLICATIONS FOR ENTERPRISE INFORMATION SYSTEMS** - *the IoT paradigm; IoT data collection and aggregation; business models and IoT; IoT-based software solutions; IoT and context-awareness; IoT and public values; IoT applications: smart cities, e-Health, smart manufacturing.*

BMSD 2021 received 61 paper submissions from which 27 papers were selected for publication in the symposium proceedings. Of these papers, 14 were selected for a 30-minute oral presentation (full papers), leading to a **full-paper acceptance ratio of 23%** (compared to 22% in 2019 and 19% in 2018, and exactly the same as in the previous year) - an indication of our intention to preserve a high-quality forum for the next editions of the symposium. The BMSD 2021 keynote lecturers and authors come from: Austria, Bulgaria, China, Colombia, Finland, Germany, Indonesia, Italy, Norway, Pakistan, Portugal, Serbia, Sweden, Switzerland, The Netherlands, and USA (listed alphabetically); that makes a total of 16 countries (compared to 10 in 2019, 15 in 2018, 20 in 2017, 16 in 2016, 21 in 2015, 21 in 2014, 14 in 2013, 11 in 2012, 10 in 2011, and exactly the same as in the previous year) to justify a strong international presence. Three countries have been represented at all eleven BMSD editions so far – **Bulgaria**, **Germany**, and **The Netherlands** – indicating a strong European influence.

Clustering BMSD papers is always inspiring because this gives different perspectives with regard to the challenge of **adequately specifying software based on enterprise modeling**. As it concerns the BMSD 2021 full papers, some of them are directed towards BUSINESS MODELING while others are touching upon CONTEXT-AWARENESS; some papers address issues concerning SECURITY and PRIVACY while others are leaning towards KNOWLEDGE MANAGEMENT and GOVERNANCE; finally, there are papers addressing software development, by considering ARCHITECTURES and DESIGN. As it concerns the BMSD 2021 short papers, some of them are more CONCEPTUAL, touching upon information systems, the digital transformation, and enterprise architectures, while others are leaning towards REQUIREMENTS; some papers are directed towards SOFTWARE ENGINEERING while others are touching upon issues related to DATA, and still others are considering PROJECT TIME ANALYSIS and SMART CONTRACTING; finally, there are application-oriented papers featuring INTERNET-of-THINGS and SMART CITIES.

BMSD 2021 was organized and sponsored by the *Interdisciplinary Institute for Collaboration and Research on Enterprise Systems and Technology (IICREST)* and technically co-sponsored by *BPM-D*. Cooperating organizations were *Aristotle University of Thessaloniki (AUTH)*, *Delft University of Technology (TU Delft)*, the UTwente *Digital Society Institute (DSI)*, the *Dutch Research School for Information and Knowledge Systems (SIKS)*, and *AMAKOTA Ltd.*

Organizing this interesting and successful symposium required the dedicated efforts of many people. First, we thank the *authors*, whose research and development achievements are recorded here. Next, the *Program Committee members* each deserve credit for the diligent and rigorous peer reviewing. Further, we would like to mention the excellent organization provided by the *IICREST team* (supported by its *logistics partner, AMAKOTA Ltd.*) – the team (words of gratitude to *Aglika Bogomilova*!) did all the necessary work for delivering a stimulating and productive event, supported by the *Hilton-Sofia team* (words of gratitude to *Katia Kovacheva*!) and also by Christoph Hartmann. We are grateful to *Springer* for their willingness to publish the current proceedings and we would like to especially mention *Ralf Gerstner* and *Christine Reiss*, appreciating their professionalism and patience (regarding the preparation of the symposium proceedings). We are certainly grateful to our *keynote lecturers, Prof. Gronau* and *Prof. Verbraeck*, for their invaluable contribution and for their taking the time to synthesize and deliver their talks. I take the opportunity to also personally address them: Alexander, Norbert, your continuing support to BMSD in so many ways is more than appreciated!

We wish you inspiring reading! We look forward to meeting you next year in *Fribourg, Switzerland*, for the *12th International Symposium on Business Modeling and Software Design (BMSD 2022)*, details of which will be made available on http://www.is-bmsd.org.

June 2021   Boris Shishkov

Organization

Chair

Boris Shishkov
University of Library Studies and Information Technology, Bulgaria
Delft University of Technology, The Netherlands
BAS - Institute of Mathematics and Informatics, Bulgaria
IICREST, Bulgaria

Program Committee

Marco Aiello	University of Stuttgart, Germany
Mehmet Aksit	University of Twente, The Netherlands
Amr Ali-Eldin	Mansoura University, Egypt
Apostolos Ampatzoglou	University of Macedonia, Greece
Paulo Anita	Delft University of Technology, The Netherlands
Juan Carlos Augusto	Middlesex University, UK
Paris Avgeriou	University of Groningen, The Netherlands
Saimir Bala	WU Vienna, Austria
Jose Borbinha	University of Lisbon, Portugal
Frances Brazier	Delft University of Technology, The Netherlands
Bert de Brock	University of Groningen, The Netherlands
Barrett Bryant	University of North Texas, USA
Cinzia Cappiello	Politecnico di Milano, Italy
Kuo-Ming Chao	Coventry University, UK
Michel Chaudron	Chalmers University of Technology, Sweden
Samuel Chong	Fullerton Systems, Singapore
Dimitar Christozov	American University in Bulgaria - Blagoevgrad, Bulgaria
Jose Cordeiro	Polytechnic Institute of Setubal, Portugal
Robertas Damasevicius	Kaunas University of Technology, Lithuania
Ralph Deters	University of Saskatchewan, Canada
Claudio Di Ciccio	Sapienza University of Rome, Italy
Jan L. G. Dietz	Delft University of Technology, The Netherlands
Aleksandar Dimov	Sofia University St. Kliment Ohridski, Bulgaria
Teduh Dirgahayu	Universitas Islam Indonesia, Indonesia
Dirk Draheim	Tallinn University of Technology, Estonia
John Edwards	Aston University, UK
Hans-Georg Fill	University of Fribourg, Switzerland
Chiara Francalanci	Politecnico di Milano, Italy
Veska Georgieva	Technical University – Sofia, Bulgaria

J. Paul Gibson	Telecom & Management SudParis, France
Rafael Gonzalez	Javeriana University, Colombia
Paul Grefen	Eindhoven University of Technology, The Netherlands
Norbert Gronau	University of Potsdam, Germany
Clever Ricardo Guareis de Farias	University of Sao Paulo, Brazil
Jens Gulden	Utrecht University, The Netherlands
Ilian Ilkov	IBM, The Netherlands
Ivan Ivanov	SUNY Empire State College, USA
Marijn Janssen	Delft University of Technology, The Netherlands
Gabriel Juhas	Slovak University of Technology, Slovak Republic
Dmitry Kan	Silo AI, Finland
Stefan Koch	Johannes Kepler University Linz, Austria
Vinay Kulkarni	Tata Consultancy Services, India
John Bruntse Larsen	Technical University of Denmark, Denmark
Peng Liang	Wuhan University, China
Kecheng Liu	University of Reading, UK
Claudia Loebbecke	University of Cologne, Germany
Leszek Maciaszek	University of Economics, Poland
Somayeh Malakuti	ABB Corporate Research Center, Germany
Jelena Marincic	ASML, The Netherlands
Raimundas Matulevicius	University of Tartu, Estonia
Hermann Maurer	Graz University of Technology, Austria
Heinrich Mayr	Alpen-Adria-University Klagenfurt, Austria
Nikolay Mehandjiev	University of Manchester, UK
Jan Mendling	WU Vienna, Austria
Michele Missikoff	Institute for Systems Analysis and Computer Science, Italy
Dimitris Mitrakos	Aristotle University of Thessaloniki, Greece
Ricardo Neisse	European Commission Joint Research Center, Italy
Bart Nieuwenhuis	University of Twente, The Netherlands
Roy Oberhauser	Aalen University, Germany
Olga Ormandjieva	Concordia University, Canada
Paul Oude Luttighuis	Le Blanc Advies, The Netherlands
Mike Papazoglou	Tilburg University, The Netherlands
Marcin Paprzycki	Polish Academy of Sciences, Poland
Jeffrey Parsons	Memorial University of Newfoundland, Canada
Oscar Pastor	Universidad Politecnica de Valencia, Spain
Krassie Petrova	Auckland University of Technology, New Zealand
Prantosh K. Paul	Raiganj University, India
Barbara Pernici	Politecnico di Milano, Italy
Doncho Petkov	Eastern Connecticut State University, USA
Gregor Polancic	University of Maribor, Slovenia
Henderik Proper	LIST, Grand Duchy of Luxembourg
Mirja Pulkkinen	University of Jyvaskyla, Finland
Ricardo Queiros	Polytechnic of Porto, Portugal

Jolita Ralyte	University of Geneva, Switzerland
Julia Rauscher	University of Augsburg, Germany
Stefanie Rinderle-Ma	University of Vienna, Austria
Werner Retschitzegger	Johannes Kepler University Linz, Austria
Jose-Angel Rodriguez	Tecnologico de Monterrey, Mexico
Wenge Rong	Beihang University, China
Ella Roubtsova	Open University, The Netherlands
Irina Rychkova	University Paris 1 Pantheon-Sorbonne, France
Shazia Sadiq	University of Queensland, Australia
Ronny Seiger	University of St. Gallen, Switzerland
Andreas Sinnhofer	Graz University of Technology, Austria
Valery Sokolov	Yaroslavl State University, Russia
Richard Starmans	Utrecht University, The Netherlands
Hans-Peter Steinbacher	FH Kufstein Tirol University of Applied Sciences, Austria
Janis Stirna	Stockholm University, Sweden
Coen Suurmond	Cesuur B.V., The Netherlands
Adel Taweel	Birzeit University, Palestine
Bedir Tekinerdogan	Wageningen University, The Netherlands
Ramayah Thurasamy	Universiti Sains Malaysia, Malaysia
Jose Tribolet	IST - University of Lisbon, Portugal
Roumiana Tsankova	Technical University - Sofia, Bulgaria
Martin van den Berg	Utrecht University of Applied Sciences, The Netherlands
Willem-Jan van den Heuvel	Tilburg University, The Netherlands
Han van der Aa	Humboldt University of Berlin, Germany
Marten van Sinderen	University of Twente, The Netherlands
Damjan Vavpotic	University of Ljubljana, Slovenia
Alexander Verbraeck	Delft University of Technology, The Netherlands
Hans Weigand	Tilburg University, The Netherlands
Roel Wieringa	University of Twente, The Netherlands
Dietmar Winkler	Vienna University of Technology, Austria
Shin-Jer Yang	Soochow University, Taiwan
Benjamin Yen	University of Hong Kong, China
Fani Zlatarova	Elizabethtown College, USA

Invited Speakers

Norbert Gronau	University of Potsdam, Germany
Alexander Verbraeck	Delft University of Technology, The Netherlands

Abstracts of Keynote Lectures

The Socio-Technical Factory of the Future: How AI and Human Can Work Together

Norbert Gronau

University of Potsdam, Germany
norbert.gronau@wi.uni-potsdam.de

Abstract. We are in the midst of the 4th industrial revolution. Small inexpensive computers with very high processing ability are more and more used in factories and logistical networks to increase the competitive ability of participating companies. The keynote of Prof. Gronau, member of the German Academy of Technical Sciences ACATECH and director of the 4IR research center Potsdam, Germany, will provide an overview about these achievements and will address the question, which position belongs to the humans in the factory of the future? As Artificial Intelligence (AI) is also enlarging its capabilities, it is possible to create a joint AI-human team in the factory. The keynote will show the elements of such a factory system, how to achieve it and its benefits for humans and the company as well.

Resilient Enterprise Information Systems

Alexander Verbraeck

Delft University of Technology, The Netherlands
a.verbraeck@tudelft.nl

Abstract. Crises such as cyber-attacks and the Corona pandemic have unfortunately demonstrated that many of the important information systems in businesses and Government are not resilient. After disruptive events, these systems have long periods of reduced service levels, and it takes major efforts to restore the systems to their normal state of operation. After a brief introduction into the topic of resilience, we will discuss how risk management frameworks, originating from the project management field and the safety sciences field, can help to assess the vulnerability of information systems or their components. Combined with an evaluation of the criticality of the components, a decision can be made to invest in either reducing their vulnerability or their criticality, or both. Techniques for improving the resilience of information systems are readily available from systems engineering and range from decoupling important parts so they can function independently to duplication of subsystems that provide critical services. Many of these are already being used as part of the design of complex information systems but the deployment is often not based on a structured assessment to make the entire information system more resilient. The presentation will illustrate the usage of risk assessment methods and architectural solutions with a number of examples.

Contents

Short Papers

Full Papers

Extending Business Model Development Tools with Consolidated Expert Knowledge

Sebastian Gottschalk[✉], Jonas Kirchhoff, and Gregor Engels

Software Innovation Lab, Paderborn University, Paderborn, Germany
{sebastian.gottschalk,jonas.kirchhoff,gregor.engels}@uni-paderborn.de

Abstract. Business Model Innovation (BMI) is a creative process that often needs collaboration between different stakeholders with the support of domain experts. Instead of innovation workshops where the domain experts need to be physically present, software-based tools allow reusing the knowledge of many domain experts independent of their actual presence. This reusing of expert knowledge, which improves the quality of the developed business models, is currently not supported by existing Business Model Development Tools (BMDTs). To address this shortcoming, we present an approach to support BMDTs with consolidated knowledge of different experts. In our approach, domain experts formalize their knowledge about business models for particular domains in expert models to make them useable within and transferable between different tools. Business developers can subsequently choose the expert models they need, consolidate the knowledge, and use it within the BMI process. With this approach, we provide a three-fold contribution to the research of BMDTs: First, we design a modeling language to store the business model knowledge of individual experts. Second, we develop a concept to consolidate expert knowledge and detect possible knowledge conflicts. Third, we provide blueprints to add expert knowledge into existing BMDTs. We demonstrate the technical feasibility of our approach with an open-source BMDT implementation and show the applicability with an exemplary instantiation of a local event platform.

Keywords: Business domain knowledge · Business Model Development Tool · Expert knowledge · Business Model Innovation

1 Introduction

An essential task for a company to stay competitive is the continuous innovation of its business models, defined by Osterwalder et al. as "the rationale of how the

---

This work was partially supported by the German Research Foundation (DFG) within the CRC "On-The-Fly Computing" (CRC 901, Project Number: 160364472SFB901) and the European Regional Development Fund (ERDF, Funding Code: EFRE-0801186).

B. Shishkov (Ed.): BMSD 2021, LNBIP 422, pp. 3–21, 2021.
https://doi.org/10.1007/978-3-030-79976-2_1

organization creates, delivers, and captures value" [27]. The high complexity of this task is also one of the results of the GE Innovation Barometer 2018 [15], a study with over 2000 business executives, in which 64% of these executives have mentioned the "difficulty to define an effective business model to support new ideas and make them profitable" [15]. By comparing the results with a previous study of 2015, the challenge is getting even larger (59% of over 3000 executives). An important reason for this is that customers expect solutions for perceived needs rather than just products [34]. These perceived needs result in the business model potentially being more important than the latest technology of the product [6].

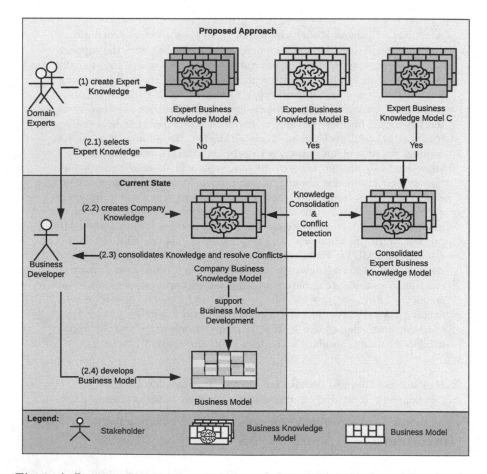

Fig. 1. A *Business Developer* can develop better business models by building upon existing domain knowledge provided by multiple *Domain Experts*

One challenge in Business Model Innovation (BMI) is that the process of BMI is a creative task that often requires the collaboration of different internal and external stakeholders [11]. One group of these stakeholders are so-called domain experts who provide deep knowledge in a particular domain. Instead of collaborating directly with these experts, it is also possible to use their expert knowledge in the form of business model taxonomies (e.g., [19,23]) or business model patterns (e.g., [13,31]). Advantages of this expert knowledge are its cost-effect reusability independent from the actual presence of the expert. Consequently, software-based Business Model Development Tools (BMDTs) and the business developer as users can benefit from this expert knowledge to innovate their business models. Nevertheless, this reusing of expert knowledge is not covered by existing BMDTs in practice [33], and their underlying modeling languages [20].

In this paper, we present an approach that consolidates the knowledge of different experts to support business model development (see Fig. 1). For this purpose, we provide a modeling structure based on the concept of feature models [3], and the Business Model Canvas [27] where *Domain Experts* can store their knowledge about different business domains as shown in Fig. 1 *(1)*. The *Business Developer* selects the expert knowledge *(2.1)* he wants to use for innovating his business model. Moreover, he captures the business domain knowledge of the company *(2.2)*. Because the experts and the company may use different vocabulary and contrary ideas, the knowledge of the experts needs to be consolidated, and conflicts in the knowledge between the experts and the company need to be resolved. For this, we present a concept to consolidate expert and company knowledge and detect conflicts. Out of this consolidating process, the *Business Developer* receives a homogeneous knowledge base *(2.3)* with all knowledge relevant to him. This homogeneous knowledge base, in turn, will support him in developing new business models for his company *(2.4)*. This can be done by discovering business elements, suggesting business patterns, and comparing business models.

Our approach provides a threefold contribution to the research of software-based business model development. First, we provide a ready-to-use modeling language for expert knowledge that can be implemented and used in existing tools. Second, we develop concepts for the consolidation of different expert knowledge and the handling of conflicts between them. Third, we provide blueprints on how expert knowledge can support the process of business model development in BMDTs. Moreover, we implement our concept in an open-source BMDT and apply it with an exemplary instantiation for the development of a business model of a local event platform.

The rest of the paper is structured as follows: Sect. 2 provides the background in terms of business model development and feature models. Section 3 explains the solution concept for the modeling language, the concept, and the blueprints. Their technical implementations are shown in Sect. 4. The application of the approach is shown in Sect. 5. Section 6 presents the related work of our approach. Finally, we conclude our paper in Sect. 7.

2   Background

In this section, we show the background of our work which can be divided into the process of business model development (Sect. 2.1) and the usage of feature models (Sect. 2.2).

2.1   Business Model Development

The process of business model development is a creative task that often requires creativity and collaboration between different stakeholders [11], together with a deep analysis of the market, existing competitors, and potential customers [34]. A common setting to develop new business models are workshops [14]. In these workshops, different stakeholders try to understand the current needs of the customers and develop possible solutions, often with the help of expert knowledge like patterns [13] or taxonomies [22].

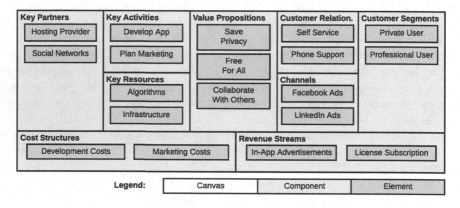

Fig. 2. Structure of the Business Model Canvas with *Components* and *Elements* based on the example of a mobile to-do app

In these workshops, the structuring of insights can be supported by business model modeling languages (BMMLs) like the e3-Value Model [16] or the Business Model Canvas (BMC) [27]. While many languages have been developed over the years [20], the BMC [27] is the de-facto standard for business modeling. The BMC divides the business model into the nine components of *Customer Segments*, *Value Propositions*, *Channels*, *Customer Relationships*, *Key Activities*, *Key Resources*, *Key Partners*, *Revenue Streams*, and *Cost Structure*. An example of the BMC for the business model of a to-do app can be seen in Fig. 2. The example consists of different customer segments (e.g., *Private User*) from which money can be generated through different revenue streams (e.g., *In-App Advertisements*). While, in practice, the structuring of different elements in a single canvas is done with different colored sticky notes [12], the underlying work [26] also introduced a Business Model Ontology (BMO) for formalizing the relationships between the different components. This, in turn, can be used to understand the dependencies between the modeled elements. This ontology can be directly used in an editor [12] but is also the basis for the concepts of dynamic business models [8] and meta-modeling [24]. To cover the maturity of the different BMMLs, Alberts et al. [1] present a meta-model for BMMLs based on the Meta-Object Facility (MOF). Moreover, to support the modeling and comparison of different business models, Osterwalder et al. [29] provide the idea to model different types of business models as taxonomies so that concrete businesses can be interpreted as instances of these taxonomies. These taxonomies can also be represented through feature models [17]. Moreover, the business model development can be supported by software-based tools.

These software-based tools are often called Business Model Development Tools (BMDT) and provide different guidance levels to develop new and improve existing business models [33]. Here, earlier examples of these tools in the literature focus on the visualization of the business model [12] or simple financial assessments [16]. An analysis of business modeling tools in practice [33] shows that those tools focus on the design of business modeling but not on the actual decision support. Nevertheless, a shift from simple design support of business modeling to real decision support by these tools needs to be done [28].

2.2 Feature Models

The concept of feature models is part of Software Product Lines (SPLs) that can be defined as "a set of software-intensive systems sharing a common, managed set of features that satisfy the specific needs of a particular market segment or mission and that are developed from a common set of core assets in a prescribed way" [7]. Here, feature models are used to structure this common, managed set of features in a hierarchical model. An example for a feature model, which we applied to the business modeling in [17], can be seen in Fig. 3. Here, the hierarchy refines the top feature of the *Canvas* (e.g., *Business Model Canvas*) into the sub-features of the *Components* (e.g., *Customer Segments*). Next, these features are refined to *Elements* (e.g., *Private User*) and could be further refined to sub-elements.

Features can be *Mandatory* (e.g., *Value Propositions*) or *Optional* (e.g., *Customer Segments*) for the model instances. Moreover, there can be *Or* (at least one sub-feature is selected/e.g., *Save Privacy* or *Collaborate with Others*), and *Xor* (exactly one sub-feature is selected/e.g., *Private User* xor *Professional User*) relationships between a parent and a child feature. To refine the model instance, cross-tree constraints for *requiring* (e.g., *Professional User* requires to *Save Privacy*) and *excluding* (e.g., *Save Privacy* is excluded from *Free for All*) dependencies can be made. A big issue in SPL development, which also exists in modeling the expert knowledge of business models, is to find the right granularity for the features [21].

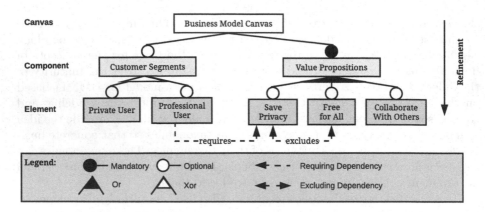

Fig. 3. Structure of feature models with an refinement to the *Components* and *Elements* of the Business Model Canvas

3   Solution Concept

In this section, we describe the solution concept to add the support of consolidated expert knowledge to Business Model Development Tools. For that, we first define a modeling language to store expert knowledge (Sect. 3.1). Based on that, we introduce concepts for knowledge consolidation and conflict detection (Sect. 3.2) together with blueprints on how expert knowledge can be used in BMDTs to support the development process (Sect. 3.3).

3.1   Modeling of Expert Knowledge

To allow the consolidation of expert knowledge, the *Domain Experts* need to store their knowledge into distinct *Expert Business Knowledge Models*. For this, we use the concept of feature models [3] that we already transferred to business modeling in the past [17]. The structure of these business models, based on the Business Model Canvas [27], can be seen in Fig. 3. While these models can cover the basic information of the business models, we need to cover additional information from the domain expert to allow a reusing of the knowledge. These additional information include knowledge about the model itself, the meaning of the possible features and the relationships between different business model elements. Moreover, we want to store possible instance sets of the features that can be either the elements for an exemplary company or patterns used in successful business models.

The meta-model for storing expert knowledge can be seen in Fig. 4. It consists of all constraints and relationships which are previously shown in Fig. 3. Moreover, we add additional information about the *FeatureModel* itself (*name, description, version, copyright*) and the *Author* (*name, company, email, website*) to give the *Business Developer* initial information about the *Domain Expert* and the application domain of the model. Additionally, we add a *description* to the

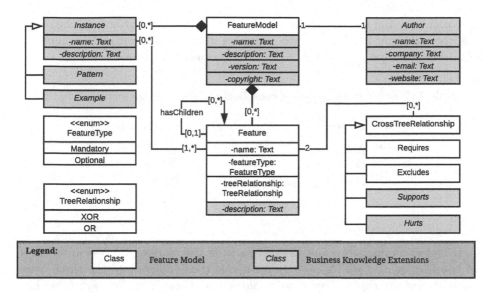

Fig. 4. Meta-Model of the *Business Knowledge Model* which is based on feature models and is extended with additional information

Feature to provide a uniform understanding of the feature between the *Domain Expert* and all *Business Developer* who use the model. In addition to the hard *CrossTreeRelationships* of *Requires* and *Excludes*, we add some softer constraints in the form of *Supports* and *Hurts* as relationships between the features. These softer constraints, which are also used in requirements engineering [35], can be used by the *Domain Expert* to model recommendations between the elements (e.g., if the *Business Developer* considers this feature he should/should not also consider this feature). Moreover, we explicitly model sets of these features as *Instances*. Here, *Patterns* are describe good combination of features (e.g., combining *Freemium* and *Mass-Market* for a gaming app) and *Examples* describe used combinations by existing companies (e.g., features of the business model of a particular gaming app). For both of them, we add a *name* and an additional *description* to ensure an unified understanding.

3.2 Knowledge Consolidation and Conflict Detection

After the *Domain Experts* have stored their knowledge into the *Expert Business Knowledge Models*, the knowledge needs to be consolidated so that it can be used by the *Business Developer*. For that, we are using the nine components (e.g., *Value Propositions*, *Customer Segments*) of the Business Model Canvas [27] as a starting point to merge the different knowledge models that the *Business Developer* wants to use. From this point, we provide the *Business Developer* assistance in merging the elements of the business knowledge model with the expert knowledge models into the homogeneous knowledge base. Here, the developer can add new elements of the expert models, merge elements with the same namings, and merge elements with different naming. For both of the mergings, merging conflicts between the different models can occur. These conflicts need to be detected so that the *Business Developer* can resolve them.

Table 1. Possible conflicts in the consolidation of knowledge models A and B

Conflict between	Characteristic A	Characteristic B
Feature types	Mandatory	Optional
Tree relationships	XOR	OR
Cross-tree relationships	Requires	Excludes
	Supports	Hurts

To detect conflicts, we analyze the model in the merging process in terms of the conflicts mentioned in Table 1. We divide the conflicts into the three categories of *Feature Types*, *Tree Relationships*, and *Cross-Tree Relationships*. The conflicts in *Feature Types* and *Tree Relationships* can be easily detected by comparing the single features in the merging process. The detection of conflicts in *Cross-Tree Relationships* is more computation-intensive as it requires the traversal of the whole feature model tree. Nevertheless, this effort is justified as faulty *Cross-Tree Relationships* can lead to impossible business model instances. To resolve the knowledge conflicts, the *Business Developer* can store his preferred decisions into his *Company Business Knowledge Model* because these elements will overwrite the knowledge of the *Domain Experts* at the development of the business model.

3.3   Integrating Expert Knowledge into BMDTs

After the *Business Developer* has selected the expert knowledge and resolved potential conflicts, the *Consolidated Expert Business Knowledge Model* needs to be integrated into the business model development process. For this, we provide three blueprints how developers of BMDTs could use those expert knowledge in their corresponding tools:

– **Discover Business Elements:** During the design of new business models, expert knowledge can be used as a library to discover possible business model elements that the *Business Developer* can use. By providing descriptions for all elements, the library ensures a common understanding between different *Business Developers*. Moreover, expert knowledge can be used to check the designed business model against the recommendation of experts, which supports the *Business Developer* in building effective business models.
– **Suggesting Business Patterns:** The existing expert knowledge can also be used to suggest possible business model improvements to the *Business Developer*. For this, the tool can suggest possible business model patterns if parts of the patterns are already used in the business model. Moreover, the tool

can analyze the strength (modeled as support-relationship) and weaknesses (modeled as hurt-relationship). This can support the *Business Developer* in focusing on the most critical parts of the business model.

– **Comparing Business Models:** Finally, the *Business Developer* can compare their designed business models with examples of expert knowledge. Here, it is possible to directly choose competitors' business models to analyze competitive advantages by differences in the selected elements. Moreover, it is possible to search for similar existing business models in the whole library. These companies, in turn, can be analyzed by the *Business Developer* to gather more insights for his own business.

4   Technical Implementation

In this section, we show the technical implementation of our approach. For this, we create a ready-to-use *Expert Business Domain Knowledge* modeling language[1] and integrate the concept of the knowledge consolidation together with the blueprints in a Business Model Development Tool called *BMDL Feature Modeler*[2].

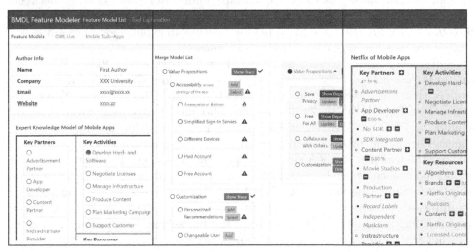

Fig. 5. Overview of the BMDT with examples on *(a) Adding Expert Knowledge, (b) Merging Knowledge Sources* and *(c) Comparing Business Models*

The *BMDL Feature Modeler*, which is shown in Fig. 5, is based on an existing tool that we already presented in [18]. Here, we introduced the concept of combining the engineering process of Software Product Lines with the structure of

---

[1] Language Specification: https://github.com/sebastiangtts/bmdl-feature-modeler/tree/master/specification/.

[2] Online Version: https://sebastiangtts.github.io/bmdl-feature-modeler/.

the Business Model Canvas to model business models. In this paper, we extend the tool for modeling expert knowledge (see Fig. 5 (a) for creating an expert knowledge model), consolidate the knowledge models, and detect conflicts (see Fig. 5 (b) for detecting knowledge conflicts) together with the blueprint of how the knowledge can be used (see Fig. 5 (c) for a comparing business models). In the following subsection, we give details on the implementations behind these concepts. Moreover, the publish the source code of our tool[3] so that it is usable and extensible by the whole information systems community.

4.1   Modeling of Expert Knowledge

The modeling of the *Business Knowledge Model* is based on the JavaScript Object Notation (JSON). JSON is a lightweight file format that uses simple key-value pairs and arrays. We use JSON as it is a wide-accepted standard for data transmission in web applications. Moreover, the file easy to read and write for humans and easy to parse and generate for software. To support the structuring of those data, we use JSON Schema. JSON Schema[4] provides a vocabulary that allows the annotation and validation of JSON documents. This standardization, in turn, allows us to provide compatibility and data exchange between different BMDTs. The JSON can be created with a graphical editor inside the *BMDL Feature Modeler* (see Fig. 5 (a) for creating an expert model) or any other text editor (see Fig. 6 (b) for a textual document).

A fragment of our schema and a valid model is shown in Fig. 6. While the *Business Knowledge Schema* (see Fig. 6 (a)) provides formalization for valid models that are based on our meta-model in Fig. 4, the *Business Knowledge Model* (see Fig. 6 (b)) shows a possible valid model of an expert. Inside the schema, which is based on the meta-model in Fig. 4, we define a unique identifier together with the properties of general model information, the corresponding author, the features of the model, and possible instances. The features, which are nested in each other, have an identifier, a name, properties, and relationships to other features (based on their identifiers). The instances have a name, a type (example or pattern), and a list of feature identifiers the instance is using. While the modeling is possible within our tool, the full schema and exemplary model together with a detailed explanation can be accessed in our repository.

4.2   Knowledge Consolidation and Conflict Detection

After modeling the expert knowledge, we need to consolidate this knowledge with the business knowledge to make it usable within the business model development process. For this, we need to merge the features and relationships of both models (see Fig. 5 (b) for merging the business knowledge and the expert knowledge). Instead of physically merging those features, we create virtual trace links between the models in the *BMDL Feature Modeler*. Virtual trace links are additional links

---

[3] Source Code: https://github.com/sebastiangtts/bmdl-feature-modeler/.

[4] Website of JSON Schema: https://json-schema.org/.

```
"$schema": "https://json-schema.org/draft/20
"$id": "http://github.com/...",
"title": "Business Knowledge Model Schema De
"description": "This schema defines the supp
"properties": {
    "name": {
        "description": "Name of the Business
        "type": "string"
    },
    //...
    "features": {
        "description": "The list of features
        "type": "object",
        "additionalProperties": {
            "$ref": "#/definitions/feature"
        }
    },
    "instances": [
        "description": "The list of patterns
        "type": "array",
        "items": {
            "$ref": "#/definitions/instance"
        },
        "uniqueItems": true
```

```
"name": "ToDo List Knowledge",
"description": "Knowledge from the analy
"author": {
    "name": "First Author",
    "email": "first-author@university.tl
},
"features": {
    "value-propositions": {
        "name": "Value Propositions",
        "type": "mandatory",
        "subfeatures": {
            //...
        }
    },
    //...
},
"instances": [
    {
        "name": "Todoist",
        "description": "Todoist as a pre
        "type": "example",
        "usedFeatures": [
            "private-user",
            "facebook-ads",
```

a) Excerpt of the Business Knowledge Schema   **b) Excerpt of the Business Knowledge Model**

Fig. 6. Excerpts of the *Business Knowledge Schema* and developed *Business Knowledge Model* based on code snippets

between both knowledge bases. This, in turn, simplifies adding, modifying, and removing the different expert models. An example of using these trace links can be seen in Fig. 7. While in this section, we describe the merging of the *Business Knowledge Model* with a single *Expert Business Knowledge Model*, the steps can be repeated for every other *Expert Business Knowledge Models* to create a homogeneous knowledge base.

At the beginning of the step, all nine *Components* of the models are automatically merged because they exist in both models (see *Customer Segments* in Fig. 7). After that, the *Business Developer* manually selects the *Elements* he wants to use. If the *Element* does not exist within the *Company Business Knowledge Model*, it can directly be added to the hierarchy of the model (see removing of *One-Sided Market* in Fig. 7). Otherwise, the attributes (*Type, TreeRelationship*) of both *Elements* need to be compared to detect possible conflicts. Moreover, the *Business Developer* can link *Elements* of the *Expert Business Knowledge Model* directly to *Elements* of the *Business Knowledge Model*. This is used to overcome the restrictions of the hierarchy and merge equal *Elements* with different namings (see trace link from *Private User* to *User* in Fig. 7). After all *Elements* have been added to the *Company Business Knowledge Model*, the *Business Developer* also needs to add the *CrossTree-Relationships* between both models. Here, we need to check all *CrossTree-Relationships* where both *Ele-*

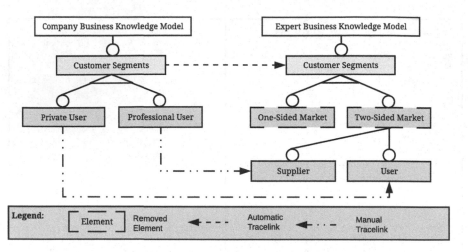

Fig. 7. Example of the Knowledge Consolidation based on Automatic and Manual Trace Links

ments are merged with the *Business Knowledge Model* for potential conflicts (e.g. conflict of hurts- and supports-relationships). To avoid following cycles in the *CrossTree-Relationships*, the whole traversing of the model is needed. The whole step, which is used for a single expert model, is now repeated for all expert models.

4.3   Integrating Expert Knowledge into BMDTs

After consolidating the knowledge of the different experts, we have a single *Business Knowledge Model*, which can be used to support the business model development process. For this, we have conceptualized three different blueprints in the last section.

In *Discover Business Elements*, we want to show the business developer the business elements he can use. For that, we provide at each component and element a button to open a list of subfeatures with a name and explanations. Moreover, we check the business model against the relationships in the *Business Knowledge Model* to show conformance errors between both.

In *Suggesting Business Patterns*, we want to suggest business model improvements to the developer. For that, we compare the elements in the patterns with the elements in the business models to show existing patterns and provide recommendations for patterns where single elements are missing. Moreover, we highlight strengths and weaknesses in the business model according to the hurts- and supports-relationships.

The last blueprint is *Compare Business Models*, where we compare our own business model with other business models based on a heatmap (see Fig. 5 (c) for a comparing business models). For that, we provide Algorithm 1 to calculate the distance between the features sets OF (Own Features) and CF (Comparison Fea-

---

Algorithm 1. Comparison of different business models

```
 1: function COMPAREMODELS(FM, OF, CF)              ▷ Compare Business Models
 2:     similarityCounter, similarityScore ← 0
 3:     for feature in FM.features do
 4:         similarityScore ← COMPAREFEATURE(feature, OF, CF)
 5:         similarityCounter ← similarityCounter + similarityScore
 6:         print feature.name+ ": "+similarityScore          ▷ Component Similarity
 7:     end for
 8:     print "Business Model Canvas: "+ similarityCounter/9  ▷ Canvas Similarity
 9: end function
10:
11: function COMPAREFEATURE(F, OF, CF)                 ▷ Compare Business Elements
12:     similarityCounter, similarityScore, featureCounter ← 0
13:     for subfeature in F.subfeatures do
14:         if subfeature in OF and subfeature in CF then
15:             featureCounter ← featureCounter + 1
16:             similarityScore ← 0.5+0.5× COMPAREFEATURE(subfeature, OF, CF)
17:             similarityCounter ← similarityCounter + similarityScore
18:             print subfeature.name+ ": "+similarityScore     ▷ Element Similarity
19:         else if subfeature in OF or subfeature in CF then
20:             featureCounter ← featureCounter + 1
21:         end if
22:     end for
23:     return featureCounter > 0 ? similarityCounter/featureCounter : 1
24: end function
```

---

tures) based on a feature model FM. In COMPAREMODELS(FM, OF, CF), we sum up the similarities of each component to get the overall similarity of the business models. In COMPAREFEATURE(F, OF, CF), we compare the similarity of a single feature with all its subfeatures. Here, we halved the similarity weight in each hierarchy level because elements in lower levels are less important than the upper ones.

5 Application to Local Event Platform

In this section, we show how the approach can be applied to a concrete usage scenario. For this, we first instantiate our approach on top of business models for a local event platform (Sect. 5.1) and second discuss the current limitations of the approach (Sect. 5.2).

5.1 Instantiation

We show the applicability of our approach by providing an instantiation on OWL Live. OWL Live is a local event platform created in the OWL culture portal's research project[5]. This research project aims to establish a local area

---

[5] Project Website: https://www.sicp.de/en/projekte/owlkultur-plattform.

event platform that the project partners should sustainably operate. The value of the platform is to aggregate event information from different sources based on machine learning algorithms. OWL Live is a two-sided market between event providers and event visitors that both have to be considered during business model development. At the beginning of the instantiation, we interview the responsible project manager to gather information about the platform. According to Teece [34], we ask questions about the market, the possible competitors, and the own niche. After the interview, we use the information to create different *Expert Business Knowledge Models* and the *Company Business Knowledge Models*. After consolidating that knowledge, we derive three possible *Business Models* for the platform.

We use the *Expert Business Knowledge Models* to store the information about the market and the possible competitors. For the market, we first cover mobile applications in general. Here, we use our existing feature model for business models of mobile applications as introduced in [17]. Because the model allows just standard feature models relationships, we add hurts- and supports-relationships (e.g., In-App Ads hurts Privacy) to the model. Moreover, we add existing patterns (e.g., Low-Price Strategy) and the existing models as examples (e.g., Spotify) to the model. After that, we create additional expert models for application fields related to the platform's concept. We gather our information by analyzing the business model of a subset of existing companies in that field. The analyzed fields were content aggregations (e.g., Rotten Tomatoes), which aggregate content from different sources, social media networks (e.g., Instagram), which provide interactions of a mass amount of users, and trending apps (e.g., Clubhouse), which should provide us information about current usage trends. For the possible competitors, we analyze event apps (e.g., Eventim), which act in a broader range than the platform, and local competitors (e.g., local newspaper), which provide an alternative to the usage of the platform. In total, we created six expert knowledge models.

We use the *Company Business Knowledge Model* to store information about the niche that the platform should have. This information is mostly obtained from the project manager. It contains ideas for specialized customer segments (e.g., culture enthusiasts), new customer relationships (e.g., customer contact over culture offices), new revenue streams (e.g., usage of sponsorships), and enhanced value propositions (e.g., route approximation to event).

After consolidating that knowledge, we use it to derive three different *Business Models*. First, we derive a type of content aggregator, where a mass amount of local events is crawled to gain interest for a mass market of users. Based on that, revenue streams of personalized advertisements and affiliate links to existing ticket sellers could be established. Second, we derive a type of ticker seller, where the focus is mainly on small local events. The customer relationships could be arranged personally, and a commission fee could generate revenue. Third, we derive a type of sponsored platform, where revenue is gained from private and public sponsorships. Based on that, value propositions of privacy-friendly usage and independent prioritization could be established. Using our tool, all developed business models can be directly compared to the event app and the local competitors to analyze a competitive advantage.

5.2 Discussion

With the implementation and its instantiation, we show the applicability of our approach. Nevertheless, while conducting the instantiation, we found some limitations with respect to the *Business Knowledge Generalization*, the *Business Process Modeling* and the *Instantiation Restrictions*.

For the *Business Knowledge Generalization*, we currently based our *Business Knowledge Model* on the Business Model Canvas (BMC). While the BMC is widely used for business model innovation, other canvas structures support other steps of the innovation process (e.g., Value Proposition Canvas for identifying the needs of the customer) or special types of business models (e.g., Platform Canvas for platform business models). Therefore, we want to improve our *Business Knowledge Model* by supporting freely definable canvas structures in the future.

For *Business Process Modeling*, we currently allow the execution of steps of the innovation process (e.g., adding expert knowledge, develop business model) concurrent with each other, which increases the complexity of the approach. Moreover, it provides the business developer less guidance about methods to derive the knowledge of the business knowledge model. Therefore, we want to extend our approach by providing a stepwise creation and validation of business models.

For *Instantiation Restrictions*, we applied our approach to the development of business models of a local event platform. Although this allowed us to demonstrate and evaluate all steps of our approach, it has the limitation that we combined the domain expert and the business developer in one person. This results in less knowledge to consolidate and conflicts to detect. Therefore, we want to conduct workshops where business developers must use existing expert knowledge to validate our approach further.

6   Related Work

In this section, we show the related work of our approach. We divide this work into *Knowledge Modeling* and *Business Model Development Tools*.

In the area of *Knowledge Modeling*, current languages for business modeling do not support the meta-modeling of business model knowledge [20]. Therefore, we look into the similar topic of requirements engineering which also provides the foundation for feature models. In goal-oriented requirements engineering [35], the different user needs are modeled as goals with relationships between them. Here, languages like iStar [9] or KAOS [35] provide different semantic relationships like decompositions and contributions types (e.g. help, hurt) between the goals to structure them. Because these requirements can come from many sources, tools for requirements consolidation have already been developed [25]. Moreover, this consolidation is also used in Software Product Lines with the merging of feature models [2]. Nevertheless, these approaches are built for requirements engineering and cannot directly be transferred to the different contexts of business modeling (e.g. modeling business pattern). Moreover, they are not used to reuse gained expert knowledge.

In the area of *Business Model Development Tools*, current tools in practice do not support the usage of expert knowledge [33]. Therefore, we look into current research which mostly develops design principles for future BMDTs. The Business Model Assistance System [10] uses a reference database of existing business models for comparison with the own business model. The Business Model Developer [5] is a domain-specific approach with a shared vocabulary based on a taxonomy and uses semantic relationships between the elements for financial calculations. The concept of semantic relationship is also used by Business Model Analyzer [4] to support the business model comprehension. The Green Business Model Editor [32] uses existing schemas to provide patterns for sustainable business models. The idea of the sustainable business pattern, which is modeled through a taxonomy, is also implemented by the Smart Business Modeler [22]. The Computer-Aided Business Model Design [30] introduces a concept for bringing different business developer experience levels into account. Here, novices are supported in coherent modeling, experts model the interactions of business model elements, and masters aim to evaluate different business model alternatives. Nevertheless, these approaches are made for knowledge models that are made by a single expert and do not support multiple knowledge sources and a corresponding knowledge consolidation.

7   Conclusion and Outlook

Business model innovation is a creative task that often requires the external knowledge of experts. While this expert knowledge is easily accessible in workshops, current BMDTs do not support reusing this knowledge. This expert knowledge, in turn, could improve the quality of the developed business models. In this paper, we present an approach to consolidate the knowledge of different experts to support the business model innovation process. With our approach, different domain experts can model their expert knowledge based on a ready-to-use modeling language. Business developers, in turn, can model the company knowledge and consolidate that knowledge with expert knowledge. This consolidated knowledge can then be used in various ways during the business model development. For this, we develop different blueprints to extend existing business model development tools. We implement the whole approach in an open-source tool and show the applicability with an exemplary instantiation for a local event platform.

Our future work is threefold and deals with improving the current limitations in the discussion of our instantiation. First, we want to improve the current limitations in terms of business knowledge generalization by providing support for different canvas structures. This will ensure a broader usage of the modeling language and tooling. Second, we want to improve business process modeling by providing stepwise execution methods for developing and validating business models. This will provide business developers additional support in the business model development. Third, we want to work on the instantiation restrictions by conducting workshops with business developers to derive their own business models. This will increase the validity of our approach in real-life settings.

References

1. Alberts, B.T., Meertens, L.O., Iacob, M.-E., Nieuwenhuis, L.B.J.M.: A meta-model perspective on business models. In: Shishkov, B. (ed.) BMSD 2012. LNBIP, vol. 142, pp. 64–81. Springer, Heidelberg (2013). https://doi.org/10.1007/978-3-642-37478-4_4
2. Alves, V., et al.: An exploratory study of information retrieval techniques in domain analysis. In: 12th International Software Product Product Line Conference (SPLC), pp. 67–76. IEEE (2008)
3. Apel, S., Batory, D., Kästner, C., Saake, G.: Feature-Oriented Software Product Lines. Springer, Heidelberg (2013). https://doi.org/10.1007/978-3-642-37521-7
4. Augenstein, D., Fleig, C., Maedche, A.: Development of a data-driven business model transformation tool. In: Chatterjee, S., Dutta, K., Sundarraj, R.P. (eds.) DESRIST 2018. LNCS, vol. 10844, pp. 205–217. Springer, Cham (2018). https://doi.org/10.1007/978-3-319-91800-6_14
5. Boßelmann, S., Margaria, T.: Guided business modeling and analysis for business professionals. In: Pfannstiel, M.A., Rasche, C. (eds.) Service Business Model Innovation in Healthcare and Hospital Management, pp. 195–211. Springer, Cham (2017). https://doi.org/10.1007/978-3-319-46412-1_11
6. Chesbrough, H.: Business model innovation: it's not just about technology anymore. Strategy Leadersh. **35**(6), 12–17 (2007)
7. Clements, P., Northrop, L.: Software Product Lines: Practices and Patterns, 7th edn. Addison-Wesley, Boston (2009)
8. Cosenz, F., Noto, G.: A dynamic business modelling approach to design and experiment new business venture strategies. Long Range Plan. **51**(1), 127–140 (2018)
9. Dalpiaz, F., Franch, X., Horkoff, J.: iStar 2.0 Language Guide (2016)
10. Di Valentin, C., Emrich, A., Werth, D., Loos, P.: Business modeling in the software industry: conceptual design of an assistance system. In: Harmsen, F., Proper, H.A. (eds.) PRET 2013. LNBIP, vol. 151, pp. 34–45. Springer, Heidelberg (2013). https://doi.org/10.1007/978-3-642-38774-6_3
11. Ebel, P., Bretschneider, U., Leimeister, J.M.: Leveraging virtual business model innovation: a framework for designing business model development tools. Inf. Syst. J. **26**(5), 519–550 (2016)
12. Fritscher, B., Pigneur, Y.: Supporting business model modelling: a compromise between creativity and constraints. In: England, D., Palanque, P., Vanderdonckt, J., Wild, P.J. (eds.) TAMODIA 2009. LNCS, vol. 5963, pp. 28–43. Springer, Heidelberg (2010). https://doi.org/10.1007/978-3-642-11797-8_3
13. Gassmann, O., Frankenberger, K., Csik, M.: The Business Model Navigator: 55 Models that Will Revolutionise Your Business. Pearson, Harlow (2014)
14. Geissdoerfer, M., Bocken, N.M., Hultink, E.J.: Design thinking to enhance the sustainable business modelling process - a workshop based on a value mapping process. J. Clean. Prod. **135**, 1218–1232 (2016)

15. General Electric Inc: GE Global Innovation Barometer 2018. https://www.ge.com/reports/innovation-barometer-2018/
16. Gordijn, J., Akkermans, H.: Designing and evaluating e-business models. IEEE Intell. Syst. **16**(4), 11–17 (2001)
17. Gottschalk, S., Rittmeier, F., Engels, G.: Intertwined development of business model and product functions for mobile applications: a twin peak feature modeling approach. In: Hyrynsalmi, S., Suoranta, M., Nguyen-Duc, A., Tyrväinen, P., Abrahamsson, P. (eds.) ICSOB 2019. LNBIP, vol. 370, pp. 192–207. Springer, Cham (2019). https://doi.org/10.1007/978-3-030-33742-1_16
18. Gottschalk, S., Rittmeier, F., Engels, G.: Hypothesis-driven adaptation of business models based on product line engineering. In: International Conference on Business Informatics (CBI). IEEE (2020)
19. Hartmann, P.M., Zaki, M., Feldmann, N., Neely, A.: Capturing value from big data - a taxonomy of data-driven business models used by start-up firms. Int. J. Oper. Prod. Manag. **36**(10), 1382–1406 (2016)
20. John, T., Kundisch, D., Szopinski, D.: Visual languages for modeling business models: a critical review and future research directions. In: Proceedings of the 38th International Conference on Information Systems (ICIS). AIS (2017)
21. Kästner, C., Apel, S., Kuhlemann, M.: Granularity in software product lines. In: 13th International Conference on Software Engineering (ICSE), p. 311. ACM (2008)
22. Lüdeke-Freund, F., Bohnsack, R., Breuer, H., Massa, L.: Research on sustainable business model patterns: status quo, methodological issues, and a research agenda. In: Aagaard, A. (ed.) Sustainable Business Models. PSSBIAFE, pp. 25–60. Springer, Cham (2019). https://doi.org/10.1007/978-3-319-93275-0_2
23. Lüdeke-Freund, F., Carroux, S., Joyce, A., Massa, L., Breuer, H.: The sustainable business model pattern taxonomy–45 patterns to support sustainability-oriented business model innovation. Sustain. Prod. Consumption **15**, 145–162 (2018)
24. Meertens, L.O., Iacob, M.E., Nieuwenhuis, L., van Sinderen, M.J., Jonkers, H., Quartel, D.: Mapping the business model canvas to ArchiMate. In: Proceedings of the 27th Annual ACM Symposium on Applied Computing (SAC). ACM (2012)
25. Nagappan, M., Shihab, E.: Future trends in software engineering research for mobile apps. In: 23rd International Conference on Software Analysis, Evolution, and Reengineering (SANER), pp. 21–32. IEEE (2016)
26. Osterwalder, A.: The Business Model Ontology: A Proposition in a Design Science Approach. Dissertation, University of Lausanne, Lausanne (2004)
27. Osterwalder, A., Pigneur, Y.: Business Model Generation: A Handbook for Visionaries, Game Changers, and Challengers. Wiley, Hoboken (2010)
28. Osterwalder, A., Pigneur, Y.: Designing business models and similar strategic objects: the contribution of IS. J. Assoc. Inf. Syst. **14**(5), 237–244 (2013)
29. Osterwalder, A., Pigneur, Y., Tucci, C.L.: Clarifying business models: origins, present, and future of the concept. Commun. Assoc. Inf. Syst. **16** (2005)
30. Pigneur, Y., Fritscher, B.: Extending the business model CanvasA dynamic perspective. In: Proceedings of the Fifth International Symposium on Business Modeling and Software Design, pp. 86–95. SCITEPRESS (2015)
31. Reman, G., Hanelt, A., Tesch, J., Kolbe, L.: The business model database - a tool for systematic business model innovation. Int. J. Innov. Manag. **21**(01) (2017)
32. Schoormann, T., Behrens, D., Knackstedt, R.: Design principles for leveraging sustainability in business modelling tools. In: Twenty-Sixth European Conference on Information System. AIS (2018)

33. Szopinski, D., Schoormann, T., John, T., Knackstedt, R., Kundisch, D.: Software tools for business model innovation: current state and future challenges. Electron. Mark. **60**(11), 2794 (2019)
34. Teece, D.J.: Business models, business strategy and innovation. Long Range Plan. **43**(2–3), 172–194 (2010)
35. van Lamsweerde, A.: Goal-oriented requirements engineering: a guided tour. In: International Symposium on Requirements Engineering, pp. 249–262. IEEE (2001)

Disruption and Images of Organisation

Coen Suurmond[(⊠)]

Cesuur B.V., Velp, The Netherlands
coen@cesuur.info

Abstract. The short answer to the question "what is needed to make enterprises and software less vulnerable against disruptive events?" is: eliminate the disruptive character of events. Disruption, defined as a violent dissolution of continuity (OED), is not a property of an event as such, but is about the disruptive effect that some events can have on enterprises or software systems. The better enterprises and their systems are able to deal with disturbances in their environments, the less they will be disrupted. How enterprises are viewed and organised is important in this regard. One view is to approach enterprises as machines, cf. the concept of enterprise engineering. Viewed as a machine, an enterprise will be modelled and structured as primarily driven by events causing sequences of predefined processes. Another view is the enterprise as an organism, flexibly acting to achieve its goals, using instruments and adapting to never fully predictable circumstances. This paper will argue that enterprises seeing and structuring themselves along the organism metaphor will be less vulnerable than enterprises seeing and structuring themselves along the machine metaphor.

Keywords: Disruption · Organisation metaphor · Semiotics · Final causation · Business modelling

1 Introduction

Organisations operate in environments that are exhibiting recurring patterns of behaviour, sometimes interrupted by irregular events, possibly disruptive. Process efficiency requires standardisation and is focused on dealing with the regular patterns. Exceptions to the regular patterns can disturb the processing flows because the normal processing rules are not applicable and/or they result in irregular outcomes that affect downstream processes. Vulnerability of organisations to disruption is linked to its capability for processing exceptional situations. The subject of this paper is how the way organisations see and structure themselves impacts their vulnerability for disruption.

In exploring this question, theories and metaphors will be discussed first. The discussion starts with semiotics and the process of creating meaning in problematic circumstances; followed by an examination of the essential business nature of the firm and the role of signs and sign systems in organisational information systems. The next section discusses the machine and organism metaphor for the organisation, and two different concepts of causality that are implicated by those metaphors. The two theoretical sections are followed by two section oriented on business practice. Examples will be

© Springer Nature Switzerland AG 2021
B. Shishkov (Ed.): BMSD 2021, LNBIP 422, pp. 22–39, 2021.
https://doi.org/10.1007/978-3-030-79976-2_2

provided first of coping with disturbance in real-world situations; this is followed by a discussion of some principles for business modelling and the development of enterprise information systems. A concluding section ends the paper.

2 Demarcation

It is good to draw a few lines first, making clear what this paper is about, and what not. First of all, business as such and society in which business is embedded are out of scope. Disruptive events, either of biological character (COVID-19) or of political character (Brexit), are "just happening" from the viewpoint of this paper. Information specialists are not tasked to change business and even less to change society, they are tasked to develop instruments (information systems) that support business processes in the context of society.

That being said, it should be clear that the development of information systems that are both useful and reliable requires an understanding of the circumstances in which such systems could be used. Robert Musil wrote in the Man without Qualities: "If there is a sense of the real, then there must be a sense of the possible". Musil continues by telling us that someone endowed with a sense of the possible will not be engaged with what has happened, will happen or must happen, but he will be imagining what could happen [1]. Such "possibility thinking" should be part of the understanding that an information specialist develops in analysing business processes, should be represented in business modelling and must be part of the considerations in software design. Why this is necessary, and how to approach these issues, will be subject of this paper.

In this paper I will not differentiate between "unforeseen" and "unforeseeable" events. As an escape from accountability it is a fairly common human trait to dub unforeseen events as unforeseeable. An example is the reaction of many politicians to the COVID-19 pandemic. They pictured this threat as unforeseeable ("nobody could have expected this") while this threat was perfectly described in previous years. Examples from 2018 are an article entitled The Next Plague published in The Atlantic and also a description of the influence of a flu pandemic on business continuity in a book about risk management [2, 3]. However, as business as such and society are out of scope in this paper, and also because preparation for all possible foreseeable disruptive events is simply not economically feasible, this distinction between unforeseen and unforeseeable will not be made in this paper. The challenge for business modelling is to represent the business processes in such a way that it helps business to shape their reaction to unforeseen events (regardless whether they could have been foreseen), and to design software systems in such a way that unexpected events will have only local effects and will not lead to the breakdown of whole systems, business processes, and business itself.

3 Theories

3.1 Semiotics

Semiotics is the study of signs. The modern semiotic tradition that started with Peirce is essentially about the study of using signs in the world, as opposed to the structuralist tradition studying relations between signs in a linguistic system [4]. An often cited Peircean definition of the sign is "A sign, or representamen, is something which stands to somebody for something in some respect or capacity" [5]. This definition suggests the role of context in the interpretation of a sign, the same sign can stand for different things, depending on both the "somebody" and the "respect or capacity" involved. An example: where the haulier perceives a wrapped pallet as a physical unit to be transported (content not of interest), a producer perceives product in crates (packaging not of prime interest), and a fire insurer perceives packaging material that is either combustible wood or incombustible plastic. Another example: the Serial Shipping Container Code is just a unique reference number without further meaning for the purpose of electronic exchange of logistical data, a domain expert can derive additional information such as country and producer of origin of the shipping unit.

Barend van Heusden has taken this idea further in his article Trias Semiotica [6]. He analyses signs as consisting of "a *form* we perceive, the *meaning* or content it conveys, and the *object* it is about", and thus differentiates between the sign-as-a-process and the sign-as-a-form. The latter is something physical that we perceive (either conventional codes such as letters and digits, physical artefacts such as pallets and crates, cultural artefacts such as music or paintings, or natural objects such as smoke and footprints), the former is the action of interpreting something as sign in a context. Meaning is "not a thing, but something we do […] is active, it is an event, it is work – meaning is in the making". A further essential element in Van Heusden's semiotics is the analysis of the difference between the generality of the form and the individuality of the object. "A distinctive trait of the human brain resides in the way in which it processes perceptual information […] Perceptual stimuli can be processed simultaneously, and in parallel, by two (sub)systems […] Together the two systems are responsible for the deeply dialectical nature of human cultural cognition and for our experience of reality as being always different from what we already know". In perception, we can be simultaneously processing the situation as an example of something we already know, and as an individual case. We perceive blue plastic pallets as belonging to some pallet pool, to be collected and returned to some depot. In the process of collecting and stacking emptied pallets we will just perceive "pallets", not being aware of either material or colour, and put them on their stack. However, when we must distinguish between pallets of different owners, marked by a grey or blue colour, we will be aware of the vague bluish-greyish colour of an individual pallet. Once we have decided about the colour of the pallet, the pallet is classified and stacked as either blue or grey and the problem is solved. This example brings us to a third major point in the theory. In an unproblematic situation a general form is coupled to a typical action (stacking of pallets without a further thought). The form causes a reaction, it works out as a signal. Van Heusden writes "A signal is a form that calls for a reaction which can be innate, or learned. But it lacks aboutness and, as such, it is not a semiotic phenomenon. … Aboutness is what distinguishes signs from signals, and the semiotic from stimulus-response reactions". To recapitulate the three points above in one sentence: interpretation is triggered by the awareness of the difference between general form and individual perception (both simultaneously present in perception), and is about the response (action) to the problematic perception in a given context.

T.L. Short has analysed Peirce's semiotics and process philosophy in his book entitled Peirce's Theory of Signs [7]. Short discusses how Peirce used and adapted the Aristotelian concepts of efficient causation (think of the collision of billiard balls and Newtonian mechanics) and final causation. For Peirce, final causation does not require intention or purpose (think of "blind" directed and irreversible processes such as in thermodynamics and in Darwinian evolution theory). Interpretation, taken as a response to a sign, is taken as essentially a purposeful action. Interpretation is partly determined by a conventional reaction to the sign as "standing for an object" (this part could be called a causal reaction), and partly determined by an intentional movement towards a future state (this part could be called final causation because that intended future state explains the action). This approach to interpretation matches very well the description of an organism by Peirce's contemporary Wheeler (see further discussion below).

Routine processes exhibit mostly habitual reactions to predefined situations. In non-routine situations we notice a difference between an automatic and a human response. An algorithm would have no other possibility than to apply predefined rules automatically to the situation, reducing the situation to a predefined form and reacting accordingly. The sign is reduced to a signal triggering a predefined (habitual) response. The individuality of the problematic object is lost (note: machine learning is about developing the general rule, and not about awareness of the individuality of the case). A knowledgeable human would interpret the situation and choose an action accordingly, possibly creating new meaning.

3.2 Theory of the Firm

The raison d'être of the company is its capability to produce products (including services) for its customers at a healthy margin. The function of the primary business processes is to bring forth those products in an efficient and effective way. Non-primary processes manage and facilitate the primary processes, or are managing relations, markets, products or resources. Business processes are structured in both a formal and an informal way, contributing to the efficiency and effectiveness of the processes. What is stated above for companies, can also be applied to governmental organisations, mutatis mutandis: their raison d'être is to serve the citizens, they have internal processes to provide meaningful products or services for the citizen in combination with managing processes, and the combination of formal organisational and informal habits structure the internal processes.

In the 1950s Arrow and Debreu proved mathematically the effectiveness of competitive markets, working in the tradition of classical economics. Some decades before Coase asked the question why firms would be able to exist, when the market would provide optimal solutions for all economic exchanges [8]. The difference between the neoclassical assumption of competitive markets and Coase's approach is that the former leaves out the cost of information required for trading on markets. As Coase writes: "The main reason why it is profitable to establish a firm would seem to be that there is a cost of using the price mechanism". Transactions between the firm and its environment (customers, suppliers, employees) are mostly based on longer term contracts. This avoids the cost of settling a separate contract for each and every exchange. After Coase's critique on the fiction of optimal markets, McNeil attacked the fiction of fully specified legal contracts. He argued that all legal contracts are to some degree relational contracts [9, 10]. A contract is a formalised representation of a business agreement, specifying promises of the business partners to each other to deliver something at some point in the future. When the agreement is challenged and the contract parameters are discussed (either directly between the business partners or in court), the interpretation of the language in the contract is open for discussion, and, much more importantly, the contract parameters are discussed against the background of the original intentions of the business partners in relation to the possible change of relevant circumstances. The concept of the relational contract is central in the work of John Kay in analysing firms. Mentioning relationships of the firm with business partners, employees, governments and competitors Kay writes: "It is the totality of these relationships which defines the individual firm and creates its distinctive identity" [11]. In another book Kay writes about the Arrow-Debreu model that "it is a framework for understanding more clearly the nature of competitive markets, not a description of a complex modern economy" [12].

Real world business is not about spot-exchanges in an ideal market where all relevant information is readily available, but about enduring social commitments and their fulfilment under sometimes difficult circumstances. Fulfilment of the business agreements requires that all relevant information about those agreements should be available for business processes, e.g. whether a certain customer attaches more importance to delivery on time (but incomplete) or to a complete delivery (but late). To a high degree business agreements are standardised and a few parameters are sufficient (Who? What? When? Amount? Price?), but their fulfilment requires additional "soft" information for processing whenever applicable (e.g.: atypical terms and conditions, awareness of customer habits and values, atypical circumstances).

3.3 Information, Signs, Information Systems

Information is carried by signs (Stamper 1973 [13]). Semiotics differentiates between the sign itself (which is directly perceived), what is stands for (its absent object), and what it does (its interpretation, its meaning in the context in which the sign is perceived. Signs belong to sign systems. Sign systems are either social or formal (other classifications are possible of course). Social sign systems come into being by practical use in the social world, with emerging rules, conventions, habits. Formal sign systems are defined by a formally defined set of operators and syntax (e.g. Jensen & Wirth, Pascal User Manual and Report [14]). Formal sign systems are closed, social sign systems are open. In social sign systems meaning is open for interpretation and debate, and sensitive to its use in context (striving towards some future state, considering social values). Habermas' theory of communicative action is based on the open character of social sign systems [15, 16], IT systems are examples of closed formal sign systems [14].

IT systems are embedded in the social world, and its users can be creative. When a customer orders "everything you've got", there is no equivalent sign available in the IT system. Human convention, however, quickly settles such issues by inputting "99999" as ordered amount, and everyone in the organisation knows this means "everything". The IT system, being a formal sign system devoid of meaning, might later on classify the fulfilment of such orders as deficient because the customer did not get the 99999 pieces he had ordered.

Enterprise information systems are tasked with supporting the business and the business processes with relevant information. Much information can be categorised in general form and processed automatically; natural language is required for periodic routine information exchanges in face-to-face meetings as well as ad-hoc encounters where problematic situations needing mutual adjustment are considered. Enterprise information systems should organise multiple information channels, both natural language based and IT-based. The need for such multiplicity of information channels was recognised in the early '80's of last century in the seminal paper on the Language Action Perspective approach by Goldkuhl and Lyttinen where they wrote "the formal and closed nature of information systems implies a need for information channels side by side the formalized information systems" [17], but the LAP approach seems not to have followed up on this.

4 Metaphors: Organisation as Machine or as Organism?

4.1 Gareth Morgan: Images of Organisation

In his well-known book "Images of Organization" Gareth Morgan analysed the nature of the metaphor and its role in the understanding of organisation and management [18]. Morgan writes that "the use of metaphor implies *a way of thinking* and *a way of seeing* that pervade how we understand our world generally" (italics in the original), that metaphor "in highlighting certain interpretations [...] tends to force others into a background role" and that "metaphor *always* creates distortions" (italics in the original). Morgan points out that he will not present an exhaustive list of metaphors of organisation, for there is no limit to finding images usable as metaphor. He does discuss eight images: machine, organism, brain, culture, political system, psychic prison, flux & transformation, instrument of domination. For analysis of the impact of disruption on organisations, I will focus on the images of the machine and the organism.

4.2 Machines

Morgan writes "Anyone who has observed work in the mass-production factory or in any of the large "office factories" processing paper forms such as insurance claims, tax returns, or bank checks will have noticed the machinelike way in which such organizations operate [...] employees are in essence expected to behave as if they were parts of a machine" [18]. He discusses both Taylor's assembly line and Weber's bureaucracy in his history of the machine metaphor, and mentions that in Weber's work "we find the first comprehensive definition of bureaucracy as a form of organization that emphasizes precision, speed, clarity, regularity, reliability, and efficiency achieved through the creation of a fixed division of tasks, hierarchical supervision, and detailed rules and regulations". Consistent with this line of thinking is the branding of the people that populate the organisation (to borrow a term from the organism metaphor) as "human resources". This is an apt expression for looking at people as functional units, not as persons.

It is important to be aware of the difference between a bureaucracy as a metaphorical machine and an IT system as a real machine. A bureaucracy uses a form of specialised natural language with differs from common language but which is still a social sign system interpreted by humans. An IT system, however, is an implementation of a formal sign system, is driven by logical rules and is not capable of interpretation. That is why a computer could be described as the ideal-typical bureaucrat, not susceptible to human "weaknesses" such as having an own mind.

4.3 Organisms

Arie de Geus, building on the organism metaphor in his book "The Living Company", identified four factors common in long-lived companies: (1) sensitivity to their environment, (2) coherence with a strong sense of identity, (3) ability to build constructive relationships with other entities, within and outside itself, and (4) ability to govern its own growth and evolution effectively [19]. The organism metaphor presents an organisation as a coherent whole, interacting with its environment, and continuously adapting and evolving for the sake of the continuity of the organism. The metaphor suggests that organisations, like organisms, strive as individuals for continuity, mature in time, and adapt to circumstances. The entomologist Wheeler described in 1911 an organism as "neither a thing nor a concept, but a continual flux of process, and hence forever changing and never complete" [20]. More than the view of an organism as, for example, "an organized body, consisting of mutually connected and dependent parts constituted to share a common life" (OED) [21], Wheeler's definition emphasises the dynamic aspects of an organism: always processing, and always changing, and De Geus's analysis of the living company fits Wheeler's definition well.

The same Wheeler provided another biological concept, possibly suitable for metaphorical use. In studying insect societies he designated the individual ant-colony as superorganism because (1) it behaves as a unit; (2) it shows some idiosyncrasies in behaviour; (3) it undergoes a cycle of growth and reproduction that is clearly adaptive; and (4) it is differentiated into queens and workers [22]. It is certainly alluring to investigate the superorganism concept as metaphor for an organisation, because of the characteristics mentioned above, and also because of the essential difference between the unitary control system of the organism (some form of a central nervous system) and the individual control systems of the organisms that together constitute the superorganism. As biological concept it can account for individual agency, a phenomenon that is discussed as a shortcoming of the organism metaphor [23]. However, for this paper I want to limit myself to just this observation and not delve deeper into this idea.

4.4 Efficient and Final Causation

Peirce has written: "The signification of the phrase "final cause" must be determined by its use in the statement of Aristotle that all causation divides into two grand branches, the efficient, or forceful; and the ideal, or final [...] Final causation does not determine in what particular way it is to be brought about, but only that the result shall have a certain general character. Efficient causation, on the other hand, is a compulsion determined by the particular condition of things, and is a compulsion acting to make that situation begin to change in a perfectly determinate way; and what the general character of the result may be in no way concerns the efficient causation" [5]. The efficient/causal causation was mentioned earlier in this paper when discussing interpreting signs as opposed to merely reacting to signs, here the two kinds of causation return for our understanding of a fundamental distinction between machines and organisms.

The "behaviour" of a machine is determined by nothing but the laws of physics, its movements are only driven by efficient causation. Its future state is determined by its construction and its history, not by some awareness of that future state. The "behaviour" of a logical machine (the computer) is similarly determined by efficient causation. Given its structure of logical rules (program), its initial state (data), and some triggering event the logical transformations on the data are fully determined by the laws of logic (the fact that mechanical and logical machines are designed and deployed for realising future states is discussed in the next subsection). Note: the observation that humans, including software engineers, are not always fully able to understand and explain the way the computer system "behaves" does not alter the fact that computers just follow logical rules.

All living organisms exhibit a combination of homeostasis (dynamically keeping a stable state in a variable environment) and development from an initial state to a mature state. Higher organisms also display intentional behaviour that guides its actions towards a desired future state. The phenomenon that the development and behaviour of an organism is explained by some future state is the final causation described above by Peirce: the organism strives to bring about (causes) the future state, along a not fully determinate way. Of course organisms are not completely free to choose and realise future states. As material beings they are subject to the laws of physics and chemistry; social organisms inhabiting their social world are also subject to the constraints of rules and habits formed in the history of the individual interacting with its social environment.

Organisms, driven by final causation (their desires, intentions, plans), use instruments. Humans use their practical and theoretical knowledge of efficient causation to construct physical and logical machines as instruments for the realisation of their goals. A machine in operation is driven by efficient causation, the process of design and use of a machine is driven by final causation. The final state of design is represented in abstract models, the final state of construction is represented by the building plan.

The term enterprise engineering borrows from the machine metaphor. Individual behaviour and individual choices are ignored and the organisation is considered as a machine driven by efficient causation. The term suggests that the enterprise engineer aspires to design the enterprise as an instantiation of the Weberian ideal-typical bureaucracy. It is intriguing to think about the question of the place of the "operator" of such an organisation-as-machine: is the operator outside or inside? If outside, then he is not part of the organisation. If inside, then the machine is self-steering and more like an organism.

4.5 Efficient and Final Causation in the Application of Rules

When confronted with an irregular situation in a standardised routine process, one issue is to determine what is going on (classification), another issue is how to proceed (action). Sometimes classification and action are obvious. It gets disturbing when there is no obvious proper way to proceed. Either it is not clear what is going on (and still less how to proceed, think of the first stages of the COVID pandemic in early 2020), or the situation is clear but applicable rules are either lacking or conflicting. This problem is extensively discussed in law. In interpreting problematic cases in court, a judge has several methods at his disposal (which are not mutually exclusive in their effects, but overlapping). Different methods can result in different conclusions, giving preference either to the exact words of written law (grammatical); to customary interpretation (historical); to consistency across applications (systematic); or to the original aims the makers of the law had in mind (teleological).

In business, as in law, matters must be decided by interpreting general rules in a concrete case (cf the earlier section about semiotics), choosing between the interpretation methods mentioned above. Given the relational nature of business, the preference should be for the systematic and teleologic methods of interpretation. Systematic, because the business should be a reliable and predictable partner and behave consistently in its interactions with customers, suppliers, employees, and other stakeholders. Teleologic, because the business should act according to the spirit of its contracts and agreements, respecting the agreed purposes of its commitments and promises. Traditionally, however, bureaucratic tendencies in larger organisations with its formalised language favour verbal meaning and historical interpretation. The proliferation of IT systems with its formal languages have the tendency to reinforce bureaucratic interpretation. The machine metaphor, leaning towards verbal (mechanic) interpretation, can therefore be considered as a risk for fulfilling business agreements under non-standard circumstances.

4.6 Cybernetics

Of course, machines (either mechanical or logical) are not just dumb mechanisms. Bennett describes in his book "A history of control engineering" how centuries ago practical engineers invented and improved feedback mechanisms, "often being far ahead of the theoretical understanding of what they were trying to achieve" [24]. Feedback mechanisms in the world of organisms and in the world of machines were studied simultaneously. The parallel between organisms and machines was recognised by Norbert Wiener in his seminal work about cybernetics, where he wrote "We see that for an effective action on the outer world, it is not only essential that we possess good effectors, but that the performance of these effectors be properly monitored back to the central nervous system, and that the readings of these monitors be properly combined with other information coming in from the sense organs to produce a properly proportioned output to the effectors. Something quite similar is the case in mechanical systems" [25]. Such feedback mechanisms are instruments for controlling proper behaviour of the organism and the movements of the machine. Sometimes the control is about homeostasis (keeping the state in the organism or machine within bounds), sometimes it is about controlling transitions from state to state.

Notwithstanding the significant parallelisms between feedback mechanisms in organisms and in machines, some cybernetic mechanisms in higher organisms are fundamentally different from machines: (1) only higher organisms can consciously develop (invent, experiment with) new reactions on perception and feedback, (2) only higher organisms are able to formulate goals, and (3) only higher organisms can understand and weigh goals depending on social circumstances. The cybernetic differences between machine and organism are reflected in Stafford Beer's Viable System Model, where Systems 1 and 2 are about the execution of processes, System 3 is about establishing rules, resources, rights and responsibilities, and Systems 4 and 5 are about monitoring the environment and policy decisions [26, 27]. While Systems 1 and 2 could be formalised and executed by machines, Systems 3, 4 and 5 are necessarily based on the flexibility of human perception and interpretation, as well as human value judgements. The lower systems might be mechanical, the higher systems must be social.

4.7 Machine Metaphor or Organism Metaphor?

It goes without saying that modern society with its modern organisations is based on standardised processes, often high volume, and processing flexibility is ever increasing. The machine metaphor is apt to guide our thinking about such processes. However such machine-like processes are embedded in the organisation as a whole, supporting the dynamic and evolving business relations of the organisation. For the latter the organism metaphor is much more suitable. Like organisms, in case of unforeseen events organisations must be able to interpret and act in creative ways in order to continue and achieve its goals. Machines are subservient to (super)organisms. In the next sections examples of disturbance will be discussed first, and methods to prevent disruption next.

5 Examples of Disturbing Events

5.1 Examples from Business Processes

I will start with a story about the capabilities of gulls. At the University of Bristol, a research group in the field of Aerodynamics and Aeroelasticity was engaged with the improvement of the flight capabilities of drones in cities. One of the challenging problems was flying drones in fiercely turbulent air around high buildings. The researchers had noted that gulls could move very smoothly there, and they wanted to learn from the gulls. Hence, they invited the Dutch marine biologist Kees Camphuysen, a specialist on gulls, in order to discuss this issue. Camphuysen writes about his visit to Bristol: "what impressed the researchers most was the sensitivity of birds. In flight, all feathers appeared to play a role, if it was not for floating on the air, then for steering, braking, or simply sensing the differences in air pressure. Each feather turned out to be a sensor and the information transmitted through the nerves could immediately be used to continuously adjust the position of the tail and wings, as well as the position of the rest of the body, to the varying airflow and the desired manoeuvre in the air". He contrasts this fine-tuned capability of birds (already existing some 120–130 million years ago) to the relative clumsiness of the drones build by humans, at that time having some dozens of sensors [28].

It is interesting to compare Camphuysen's rendition of the sensoric-motoric capabilities of gulls to an example of organised information channels in a company, as told to me by the owner of a meat processing company. His company used to provide smaller supermarket chains with pre-packaged meat. He owned about 20 delivery vans for distributing the products to the stores. The owner told me that he repeatedly had been advised to outsource transport, because that would be much cheaper. However, he had a clear motivation for having his own distribution: his drivers visited all his customers multiple times each week, having a chat and a peek at the unloading and storing area at each store, possibly noticing changes in the behaviour of the customer. This "sensing system" provided him (as a hands-on owner) with hugely valuable information for doing his business. Account managers would never be able to provide such information from their conversations with customers in meeting rooms.

A second example of organising the "sensing system" in an organisation is also from meat processing, this time from the production area for deboning the meat. The person responsible for bringing the meat into the area was physically located at the weighing scale at the entrance to the area, having a good view on the deboning lines in the area, on the cold buffer area in his back, on the production lines beyond the buffer area, and on the weighing scales registering their output. Together this created a good and highly capable low-level "sensoric-motoric" coordination system on the work floor regulating the flows of meat to and from the deboning area, monitoring both production pace and yield in real-time and 'real-place'. This man was also the key information channel between planner and production, both for adjusting planning to actual production results, for assessing possible planning changes, and for communicating planning changes to the work floor. In later years, I could compare the operation of the deboning department of this plant with deboning departments of other plants (some of them belonging to the same parent company). I learned to appreciate the difference between various implementations of exactly the same business processes. When people of different departments are operating in isolation from each other and communicating only via formalised information in IT systems (production orders, production records), monitoring and coordination is slower and of lower quality than in companies where people in different departments interact directly with each other. It is the capability to perceive, process and convey information about irregularities that make the difference.

These two examples, one from the commercial environment and one from the production environment, indicate the importance of using "thick descriptions" in business modelling [29, 30]. Process schemata are lifeless, as are "thin" descriptions that represent processes by means of rigidly formalised and formatted schemata. The latter type of process representations form a very convenient input for configuring IT systems, but it is poor in providing context to the business processes. Thick process descriptions, by contrast, are outcome oriented and provide context information about why the process is what it is. Thin descriptions make clear how the process is structured, thick descriptions are needed to understand why it is running the way it is. Thick descriptions can also explain the difference between processes that are the result of their history (the accumulation over a longer period of time of small adaptations, each being rational, can sometimes result in suboptimal processes), the result of a specific configuration of resources (availability of key employees with specific capabilities), or the result of a deliberate design. Thick business models show place and function of human interpretation, allow for purposeful ('teleological') interpretation in case of irregularity in processes and are prerequisite for achieving stability of the processes under unforeseen circumstances.

5.2   Examples from IT Support

A good example of business continuity under disturbing circumstances was provided by a middle manager in a plant where I was doing a project a few years ago. More than 10 years earlier the centralised ERP system of the multinational parent company broke down and was not available for more than a week. She noticed that very soon all over Europe production facilities halted their operations as a consequence. Much to her pride she recounted that "her" plant was able to keep running for the whole breakdown period, reducing production loss to a minimum. They were able to do this because of the combination of a heterogeneous IT landscape, with loose couplings between the central system and process control, and knowledgeable and experienced shift leaders in each production department. This allowed them to sustain production during the ERP breakdown by focussing on long runs of a choice of fast-moving simple products.

A similar example of flexible IT support was the request by one of our customers for a new shop floor IT system in a revitalised plant, to be realised within a few weeks. The request was triggered by winning a tender for producing a rather large volume of products for a major retailer. This very short implementation could be realised by focussing on the really essential processes: firstly, the reliable registration of ordered, shipped and invoiced product quantities (fulfilling the business agreement with the customer), and secondly (and much less critical) the reliable registration of ordered, received and invoiced incoming goods (checking the business agreements with the suppliers).

A contrasting example is something that happened as a consequence of the selling off of a production plant by a multinational company. The plant produced branded products for the parent company, in combination with products for third parties (the latter flow is irrelevant for this example). Output of the production lines was shipped directly to the warehouses of the parent company, the production plant was not allowed to keep stocks of end products. The weekly production plan of the plant was initiated by a product demand from the parent company. The plant would then produce the indicated demand, with some variability (production is not an exact science). Part of the deal with the new owner was that all information flows and material flows regarding the finished products of the plant would remain unchanged. Of course, all necessary commercial contracts about performance and finance were arranged, especially regarding the payment of shipped delivered products. So far, so good. But during the transition period a very tenacious problem emerged regarding administrative procedures and IT systems of the parent company. Receipt of the finished product in their warehouses changed from "internal transfer" from an internal supplier to "purchase" from an external supplier. A hard condition for receiving goods from an external supplier in the ERP system was an exact match in the ERP system between ordered quantity and received quantity. Without such a match the delivery would be rejected. This condition clearly did not match the business agreement, and could never be fulfilled in practice. Adapting this condition in the ERP system was apparently a no-go, possibly because of the complexity of the centralised IT system and the difficulty to assess the impact of such an adaptation to other purchase processes in this large company. Much time over a long period was spent looking for a solution, involving many people. One of the proposals was to have the shipping department of the production plant enter a purchase order after loading a truck, impossible to implement because of the 24/7 flow of goods. The IT system was not capable of supporting such a perfectly normal business agreement and frustrated business relations with a strategic supplier.

6 How to Prevent Disruption in Business Processes

6.1 Rosenhead's Robustness Analysis and Its Application to Business Modelling and Software Design

Jonathan Rosenhead has analysed planning as a form of decision making under uncertainty, and his analysis could fruitfully be used for our subject. He contrasts classical planning methodology with his so-called robustness methodology. In the classical approach all steps and commitments from current state to future state ("target configuration") via intermediate states are defined in the planning stage, which is followed by the execution of the plans. Chances are that plans must be revised during execution due to uncontrolled external circumstances and deviations in intermediate outcomes, leading to unrest and extra costs. Rosenhead pleads for a robustness methodology, which "declines to identify a future decision path or target. The only firm commitments called for are those in the initial decision package – possible future commitments are of interest principally for the range of capability to respond to unexpected developments in the environment that they represent" [31]. This methodology is about step-by-step decision making, working towards a not fully defined future situation. A primary criterion for each step is how many "good" future states are made possible by the decision, and how many "bad" future states are closed down. The more a decision opens up desirable (or acceptable) future states, the more a decision closes down undesirable (or unacceptable) future states, the more a decision is preferred. In other words, in an uncertain environment you are making piecemeal steps towards not fully specified goals, always checking the environment and the actual situation, and always prepared to change the path towards those goals according to the given situation.

Rosenhead's approach could be viewed as simply a form of incremental planning in the sense that one should not bite off more than one can chew. Although this view would not be entirely wrong, for the purposes of this paper his argument could better be viewed as the contraposition of the two different forms of causation. To repeat part of the earlier citation of Peirce: "Final causation does not determine in what particular way it is to be brought about, but only that the result shall have a certain general character. Efficient causation, on the other hand, is a compulsion determined by the particular condition of things [...] what the general character of the result may be in no way concerns the efficient causation". Rosenhead's methodology is about final causation (focus on outcome, flexible path), conventional planning about efficient causation (path is fixed, outcome is at risk).

Reading Rosenhead's analysis as a method to eliminate the disrupting character of unforeseen events, his ideas can be used for thinking about disturbances in operational processes and putting a check on their disruptive effects. His argument could be summarised in three questions: (1) where do I want to go? (2) what is my current position? and (3) which choices will bring me be nearer to a desired (or at least acceptable) position? Translated into the world of operational business processes, his line of thinking is not about process history (which led to your current position), but about process future (how to get to a desired position). When normal process flow is disrupted beyond immediate repair, you need to look for available alternative processing routes.

One way of facilitating this kind of operational choice is by breaking up business process flows in more or less autonomous processes (or process chains) with explicitly specified entry and exit conditions. Please note that such conditions are not restricted to informational issues, but about all sorts of material and immaterial conditions. For example, suppose that an initial condition for a process is "clean material". Any material that is deemed to be clean (whatever the operational meaning of "clean" might be) can be processed, any not-clean material must be cleaned first (pre-processed). In irregular circumstances, the business can decide about alternative routes considering the extra costs (money, time) of the required pre-processing.

This idea is not new, of course. Business has always operated this way, searching for and finding alternatives when need arose. But the idea is a reversal of the modern approach of highly integrated and tightly coupled process chains. It is a plea for loose and clearly defined couplings between business processes. As a by-product, it enhances the flexibility of the business to contract out (or in) part of its processes, for example by hiring an external packager to relieve a temporary bottleneck on its own packaging lines, or for packaging products for a special contract.

6.2 "Thick" Information Systems

Continuing along the line of thought in the subsection above and focusing on informational issues (emphatically no restriction to an IT perspective here), two very basic questions could be asked as a starting point in process analysis. The first question is about initial informational conditions: "which information is required by the process to do a proper job". The second question is about the exit condition: "which information must be the result from the process, enabling possible downstream processes to do their jobs properly". Theoretically, an exhaustive analysis along such lines would render a complete map of information links between processes. Any information that is used in a process could be traced back to its originating process. Any information that is not used in a downstream process is redundant and should be eliminated (the latter is an application of a major principle of lean production). Practically, the questions help to discuss business processes as understood by its practitioners themselves because it is about their world and it does not exclude any form of information. As an example of the impartiality of this approach to the kind of information, suppose a fork-lift truck driver must fetch material from an internal warehouse required by a production line. As a generic process, several pieces of information are required: what? – when? – where from? – where to? – how many? In one company with a few experienced drivers and a manually fed production line, such information is mostly available in the form of background knowledge and mutual understanding. In another company, with temporary drivers and an automatically fed production line, most of the information must be explicit and in understandable language for the driver. In a third company the process is fully automated, the fork-lifts are driverless automatic guided vehicles and all information must be coded in IT systems (and must probably be interfaced between heterogeneous IT systems, having their own interpretation issues). The abstract process is clearly definable in a few variables applicable independent the local circumstances; while real processes are highly variable and require very different solutions for a supporting information system.

Analogous to the distinction in anthropology between "thick" and "thin" descriptions as mentioned in the last paragraph of Sect. 5.2, we could differentiate between "thick" and "thin" information systems. "Thin information systems" are restricted to IT systems and their immediate functional relations with their environment (users, processes, IT-engineers). "Thick" information systems are about all information used and produced by business processes, regardless their form.

6.3 Autonomy of Registration

The German 19th century historian Leopold von Ranke is famous for his statement that history must show what actually happened ("wie es eigentlich gewesen ist"). The same criterion should apply to the capturing of business data, which must show users "what actually happened", undistorted by ideas of what ought to have happened. An implication is that information must not be restricted to predefined (foreseen) possible events. Whatever happened, was evidently possible and should be appropriately recorded (giving operational meaning to "appropriate" will be one of the challenges in system development). Information should not be restricted to predefined formats.

Specifically, irregular circumstances that have disturbed business processes must not prohibit proper registration of business data, just because the planning was not realised or an order was modified by telephone. Or, the fact that my colleague has entered a wrong item code at stock-in, should not prohibit me in entering the right item code at stock out, even when this results in negative stock in the IT system. In designing an IT system, the registration functions should be conceived first and independent of orders and planning. In critical circumstances a business will find creative ways to continue its operations. A relatively autonomous registration function in IT systems allows much more support in such circumstances.

6.4 Business Modelling and Information System Design

Three principles for business modelling and information systems design were discussed in this section: (1) the "possibility principle": allow alternative routes in business processing (manually pre-processing material and information when necessary); (2) the "thick information principle": design encompassing information systems where all relevant information exchange in business processes is covered; and (3) the "autonomy principle": design registration functions for capturing "what really happened", not as feedback on "what should have happened".

Business modelling in an existing organisation is both about modelling the "official" process landscape as well as identifying and investigating existing "goat paths" in the organisation. The latter often are important informal patterns of adjustment between processes. The official process landscape runs the risk of being too abstract and will sometimes be representing a "fair-weather" model how the organisation thinks it should operate, the goat paths can reveal much about the real operation and makes a discussion possible about strengths and risks of such informal patterns.

Once I noticed production managers taking their morning coffee break at the planner's office at the time the planner was about to finish his rescheduling of the afternoon shift. When I asked about it they told me this was habitual. It provided an opportunity for comparing views about the actual situation on the shop floor (late or ahead of schedule, overshoots and undershoots of output, smooth flows or hiccups) and about the intended changes. This face-to-face communication exemplifies informal mutual adjustment, making quantities, sequences and times in the planning schedule meaningful. The planned order "Produce 100 pieces X output 1600 kg input Y between 10am and 11am" can mean that 1600 kg Y must be produced (100 pieces Y being the normative output), or that 100 pieces X must be produced (1600 kg Y being the normative input), or produce X out of Y until 11am sharp (expected 100 pieces X output, 1600 kg Y input).

Informal patterns in an organisation are an important element in the distinctive capabilities as described by John Kay [11]. They constitute part of the "sensoric-motoric" system of the organisation. Under normal operational circumstances this contributes to the smooth operation of the organisation, detecting and solving the small irregularities that are part and parcel of our real world. When bigger irregularities occur, potentially resulting in a "violent dissolution of continuity" (i.e., disruption), this "sensoric-motoric" system is called on to find solutions by creatively adapting and reconfiguring business processes.

7 Conclusion

At the end I want to return once more to Short's analysis of the concepts of efficient and final causation in Peirce. Referring to Peirce, he writes: "in this passage, two sorts of process are distinguished by their form, one involving variable steps with constant type of result, the other, constant rule by which one step follows another but with variable result" [7]. The latter process is mechanistic, driven by efficient causation. Under normal operational circumstances, having input and transformation under control in routine processes, efficient causation will result in intended output. Obtaining intended output in irregular circumstances must "[involve] variable steps with a constant type of result". Which steps are chosen will be guided by the idea of the "constant type of result", hence driven by final causation. This is essentially a semiotic process, interpreting the situation while being aware of desired future states. This process might involve improvisation and creativity, as noticed by Short: "One advantage Peirce's conception has over Aristotle's is that the cooperation it assigns to chance and selection accounts for the emergence of novel forms of order". This last citation links very well with De Geus's observation that long-lived companies are "particularly tolerant of activities in the margin: outliers, experiments and eccentricities within the boundaries of the cohesive firm, which kept stretching their understanding of possibilities". Improvisation and creativity is required under disturbing conditions (the primary theme of this paper), but can also be induced by new forms of business commitments (resulting from business strategy, from particular opportunities, or from ill-considered acceptance in a business contract of customer specifications and conditions).

To repeat the first sentence of the abstract: The short answer to the question "what is needed to make enterprises and software less vulnerable against disruptive events?"

is: eliminate the disruptive character of events. As argued in this paper, this should entail both a "thick" approach to business processes, explaining the role of processes in the fulfilment of business agreements, and a "thick" approach to information systems, allowing the use of different kinds of information and information channels. Developing an organisation like this will enhance both the "sensing" and the "motoric" capabilities of the organisation (respectively scanning the environment for upcoming disturbances, and executing business agreements under non-standard circumstances as well as executing non-standard business agreements). Disturbing irregularities will then cause "solvable disorder" in an organisation, instead of real disruption and breakdowns. Vulnerability of organisations to disruption is diminished by enhancing its capabilities for processing exceptional situations.

References

1. Musil, R.: Der Mann ohne Eigenschaften. Rowohlt, Hamburg (1981)
2. Yong, E.: When the next plague hits. In: Murphy, C. (ed.) The American Crisis. Simon and Schuster, New York (2020)
3. Hopkin, P.: Fundamentals of Risk Management, 5th edn. Kogan Page, London (2018)
4. De Saussure, F.: Course in General Linguistics. McGraw-Hill, New York (1966)
5. Hartshorne, C., Weiss, P. (eds.): Collected Papers of Charles Sanders Peirce. Thoemmes Press, Bristol (1998)
6. Heusden, B.P.: The Trias Semiotica (in press)
7. Short, T.L.: Peirce's Theory of Signs. Cambridge University Press, Cambridge (2007)
8. Coase, R.: The nature of the firm. In: Williamson, O.E., Winter, S.G. (eds.) The Nature of the Firm. Oxford University Press, Oxford (1993)
9. MacNeil, I.R.: The New Social Contract. Yale University Press, New Haven (1980)
10. MacNeil, I.R.: Reflections on relational contract theory after a neo-classical seminar. In: Campbell, D., Collins, H., Wightman, J. (eds.) Implicit Dimensions of Contract. Hart Publishing, Portland (2003)
11. Kay, J.: Foundations of Corporate Success. Oxford University Press, Oxford (1993)
12. Kay, J.: The Truth about Markets. Allen Lane, London (2003)
13. Stamper, R.: Information in Business and Administrative Systems. Wiley, New York (1973)
14. Jensen, K., Wirth, N.: Pascal User Manual and Report. Springer, New York (1985). https://doi.org/10.1007/978-1-4684-0261-2
15. Habermas, J.: The Theory of Communicative Action, vol. 1. Polity Press, Cambridge (1986)
16. Habermas, J.: The Theory of Communicative Action, vol. 2. Polity Press, Cambridge (1987)
17. Goldkuhl, G., Lyytinen, K.: A language action view of information systems. In: Ginzberg, M., Ross, C.A. (eds.) Proceedings of the 3rd International Conference on Information Systems, TIMS/SMIS/ACM, pp. 13–29 (1982)
18. Morgan, G.: Images of Organization, 2nd edn. Sage, Thousands Oaks (1997)
19. De Geus, A.: The Living Company. Nicholas Brealey Publishing, London (1997)
20. Wheeler, W.M.: The Ant-Colony as Organism. https://www.semanticscholar.org/paper/The-ant%E2%80%90colony-as-an-organismWheeler/317fd0b833e1ed391ed72bf170af25bfd75cd21e. Accessed 22 Nov 2020
21. OUP: The Oxford English Dictionary. Oxford University Press, Oxford (1989)
22. Wilson, E.O.: The Insect Societies. Harvard University Press, Cambridge (1971)
23. Kerr, R., Robinson, R.K., Elliott, C.: Developing metaphors in light of the visual and digital turns in organizational studies. In: Örtenblad, A., Trehan, K., Putnam, L.L. (eds.) Exploring Morgan's Metaphors. Sage Publications, Thousand Oaks (2017)

24. Bennett, S.: A History of Control Engineering. The Institution of Electrical Engineers, London (1979)
25. Wiener, N.: Cybernetics or Control and Communication in the Animal and the Machine. Wiley, New York (1948)
26. Beer, S.: Brain of the Firm, 2nd edn. Wiley, Chichester (1994)
27. Beer, S.: Diagnosing the System for Organisations. Wiley, Chichester (1985)
28. Camphuysen, K.: De Zilvermeeuw. Atlas, Amsterdam (2018)
29. Ryle, G.: Thinking and reflecting. In: Ryle, G.: Collected Essays 1929–1968. Routledge, Abingdon (2009)
30. Geertz, C.: Thick description: toward an interpretative theory of culture. In: Geertz, G. (ed.) The Interpretation of Cultures – Selected Essays. Basic Books, New York (1973)
31. Rosenhead, J.: Robustness analysis: keeping your options open. In: Rosenhead, J., Mingers, J. (eds.) Rational Analysis for a Problematic World Revisited. Wiley, Chichester (2001)

VR-UML: The Unified Modeling Language in Virtual Reality – An Immersive Modeling Experience

Roy Oberhauser[(✉)] [iD]

Department of Computer Science, Aalen University, Aalen, Germany
`roy.oberhauser@hs-aalen.de`

Abstract. Software models in the Unified Modeling Language (UML) can been created or automatically reverse-engineered and used for quickly gaining structural insights into larger, legacy, or unfamiliar software. But as the size, structural complexity, and interdependencies between software components in larger systems grows, two-dimensional viewing and modeling has limitations, and new ways of visualizing larger models and numerous associated diagrams of different types are needed to intuitively convey structural and relational insights. To investigate the feasibility of using Virtual Reality (VR) to create an immersive UML-based software modeling experience, this paper contributes a VR solution concept for visualizing, navigating, modeling, and interacting with software models using UML notation. An implementation shows its feasibility while an empirical evaluation highlights its potential.

Keywords: Virtual Reality · Unified Modeling Language · Software modeling · UML tools · Visualization

1 Introduction

Aristotle once stated "thought is impossible without an image," and F. P. Brooks, Jr. asserted that the invisibility of software remains an essential difficulty of software construction - because the reality of software is not embedded in space [1]. Text-based program comprehension remains the norm in our day, despite the obvious limitations for this form of software comprehension, as evidenced in the low code review reading rates of around 200 lines of code per hour [2].

In general, modeling provides an abstracted or simplified representation of a system that can assist with understanding relationships between elements or concepts of interest. Typically, views are used to address stakeholder concerns and portray relevant aspects of a model. For visualizing the structural design of a software system, UML [3] has provided a unified and standard modeling notation. UML tools can support software developers via visualization, diagramming, model-based code generation, reverse engineering (from code to models), round-trip engineering, model transformation, and support for XML Metadata Interchange (XMI) [4] for transferring models between tools.

© Springer Nature Switzerland AG 2021
B. Shishkov (Ed.): BMSD 2021, LNBIP 422, pp. 40–58, 2021.
https://doi.org/10.1007/978-3-030-79976-2_3

Commonly available 2D modeling depictions in standard modeling tools have limitations, and one can lose insight into the interrelationships across views, diagrams, and relevant model elements as the size of the model and views grows. Evidence includes [5], who concluded a network graph in VR was three times as good as a 2D diagram. For 3D UML, X3D-UML [6] determined a clear and measurable benefit in 3D UML software visualization, while a 3D UML tool case study [7] showed that a 3D perspective was intuitive and improved model comprehension. A VisAr3D experimental study with 18 participants [8] showed positive evidence for 3D for UML model understanding when many elements were present (and the third dimension's contribution), while showing that precision, efficacy, and time were not negatively affected.

VR could potentially assist with visualizing large and complex software models and their interrelationships simultaneously while also providing an immersive experience in the software models. VR is defined as a "real or simulated environment in which the perceiver experiences telepresence" [9], a mediated visual environment which is created and then experienced. VR has made inroads in various domains and become readily accessible as hardware prices have dropped and capabilities improved, increasing the accessibility and ubiquity of VR-based model visualization. VR-based visualization of *software* models for insights could rejuvenate the interest with software models in general and UML modeling in particular. In their study with 99 participants, [10] showed that VR resulted in better overall learning performance and higher engagement than textbook or video modes. A new approach via software model immersion could help rejuvenate the software modeling area and help transition from source-code only comprehension to more integrative use of visual models where it makes sense. VR offers a unique advantage in the unconstrained 3D space for visualizing, conveying, navigating, and analyzing complex and heterogeneous models simultaneously. As software models grow in complexity, an immersive environment could provide an additional visualization capability to comprehend the "big picture" for structurally and hierarchically complex and interconnected software diagrams, while providing an immersive experience for the UML models in a 3D space viewable from different perspectives. The sensory immersion of VR can support task focus during model comprehension while limiting the visual distractions that typical 2D display surroundings incur.

In prior work, [11] demonstrated the use of various metaphors for a VR immersion in software structures without the use of UML. VR-BPMN [12] described our solution concept for visualizing Business Process Model and Notation (BPMN) [13] models in VR. Next, VR-EA [14] presented a VR solution concept for visualizing, navigating, annotating, and interacting with ArchiMate [15] Enterprise Architecture (EA) models, while also describing our generalized VR modeling framework (VR-MF). Subsequently, VR-EAT [16] integrated EA tool visualizations into VR, in particular dynamically generated diagrams from the EA tool Atlas and its meta-model [17]. VR permits the extent of large models to be depicted and navigated visually, while overall interrelationships within and between heterogeneous elements, models, and diagrams can be indicated and considered. This paper extends our prior contributions with our solution concept VR-UML, which provides a way to visually depict and immersively navigate, model, and interact with UML-based software models in VR, enhancing these diagrams with

3D depth, color, and inter-diagram element followers, while supporting heterogenous hypermodels in VR.

The remainder of this paper is structured as follows: Sect. 2 discusses related work. Section 3 presents our solution concept VR-UML. Section 4 then provides details on our prototype implementation that demonstrates its feasibility. In Sect. 5 VR-UML is empirically evaluated, and a conclusion follows in Sect. 6.

2   Related Work

Work on combining VR and UML includes Ozkaya & Erata [18], who propose their intent for a research framework of a conceptual modeling tool, Virtual Reality Unified Modeling Language (VRUML), but no VR realization details could be found. That VR features are not yet commonplace in UML tools is evidenced by Ozkaya [19], who systematically analyzed 58 different UML modeling tools without any mention of VR, and Ozkaya & Erata [20] who surveyed 109 practitioners to determine their UML preferences without any mention of VR. Related 3D (non-VR) UML visualization includes the aforementioned X3D-UML [6], VisAr3D [8], and the case study by Krolovitsch & Nilsson [7].

As to VR-based non-UML software model visualization, besides our own aforementioned prior software modeling in VR [11, 12, 14, 16], various metaphors in VR have been attempted. Schreiber & Misiak [21] and Nafeie & Schreiber [22] use an island metaphor in VR to represent components, packages, classes, and dependencies. Vincur et al. [23] applies a city metaphor to software analysis. Schreiber & Brüggemann [24] use a modular electrical component system metaphor in VR to visualize software components.

Regarding hypermodeling work, besides our own prior work, the survey by Bork et al. [25] comprehensively analyzed eleven visual modeling languages, including UML, ArchiMate, and BPMN, revealing heterogeneity in the specified modeling language concepts and techniques employed for concept specification. They found a lack of a common visual metamodel across various visual modeling languages, incompleteness, and thus difficulties in providing an overarching metamodel that could be used to simplify the specification and interrelations between various model types.

In contrast, the VR-UML solution concept realizes a VR-centric visualization of and immersive experience in UML models, providing automatic layout of views as stacked 3D hyperplanes, visualizing the reality of inter-view relations and recurrence of elements, and enabling interactive modeling in VR. Its support for hypermodeling, e.g., such that UML, ArchiMate, BPMN, and EA tool (Atlas) models can be visualized simultaneously in the same virtual space supports deeper cross-model analysis across various diagram types and stakeholder concerns. This capability may grow in importance with increasing digitalization as (automatically extracted) UML-based software models become more relevant to the business and EA and text-based code analysis (by non-developers) is no longer efficient or viable.

3 Solution Concept

With the upcoming challenges that increasing digitalization and IT infrastructure will bring to enterprise architecture, rather than viewing models in isolation and in separate tools, we envision the future of (software) modeling as integrative and holistic, utilizing and accessing various available models concomitantly. VR provides a unique medium of unlimited space and an immersive environment to support this modeling vision. Thus, the foundation for our VR-UML solution (shown in blue in Fig. 1) is our generalized VR Modeling Framework (VR-MF) [14]. It provides a VR-based domain-independent *hypermodeling* framework supporting multiple heterogeneous models while addressing three primary aspects of modeling in VR: visualization, navigation, interaction, and data retrieval. Relationships between elements can be shown in 3D space, and related elements can be grouped in 3D layers or views as appropriate. The capability to simultaneously visualize multiple heterogenous models in VR is a key principle of our solution concept as realized via VR-MF. As depicted in Fig. 1, prior work based on VR-MF addressed enterprise architecture (EA) modeling with Archimate in VR called VR-EA [14], business process modeling in VR called VR-BPMN [12], and integrated EA tool data and visualizations demonstrated with VR-EAT [16] using the EA tool Atlas. ArchiMate models use a graphical notation consisting of a collection of concepts (approximately 50) to portray a wide scope of EA elements and relationships. On the other hand, BPMN models focus on business processes and consist of Business Process Diagrams (BPDs) composed of graphical elements consisting of flow objects, connecting objects, swim lanes, and artifacts. To meet commercial EA needs, Atlas, as a representative EA tool, provides access to diverse EA-related data in a coherent repository and meta-model and is not restricted to certain standards or notations. Thus, while UML is focused on modeling software structural aspects, ArchiMate, BPMN, and other EA models and views can convey other non-software aspects that may also be of importance to various stakeholders depending on their context and concern, especially as software becomes an integral part of the overall digital organizations and their processes. Thus, our *hypermodeling* principle as detailed in our prior work plays a fundamental role towards supporting heterogenous VR model visualization with regard to our VR-UML solution concept.

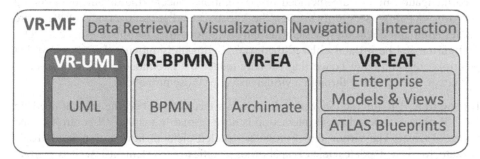

Fig. 1. Solution concept showing our new VR-UML solution concept within our VR-MF modeling framework, with VR-EAT, VR-EA, and VR-BPMN support.

Visualization. UML models use a graphical notation consisting of a collection of concepts to portray a wide scope of software elements and relationships. The diagram types can be categorized as structural diagrams (Class, Component, Composite structure, Deployment, Object, Package, and Profile) and behavioral diagrams (Activity, Communication, Interaction overview, Sequence, State, Timing, and Use case). These diagrams can participate in views used to convey information addressing concerns of specific stakeholders. While many visual options and metaphors can be considered for VR, diverging too far from the 2D diagrams and UML notations familiar to UML tool users would reduce diagram comprehension. Yet placing 2D UML images like flat screens in front of users would provide little added value in the 3D VR space. For visualizing and differentiating diagrams, planes are used to take advantage of the 3D space, with each plane representing a diagram. *Stacked hyperplanes* support viewing multiple diagrams at once, while allowing the user to quickly see an overview of how many diagrams of what type are available. Furthermore, stacked hyperplanes allow us to utilize the concept of a common transparent or invisible backplane to indicate common elements across diagrams via multi-colored inter-diagram *followers*. Stacked diagrams are a scalable approach for larger projects (compared to side-by-side) since the distance to the VR camera is shorter, and multiple stacks can be used to group diagrams or delineate heterogeneous models. Diagrams are of interest can be viewed side-by-side by moving them from the stack via an affordance on a diagram corner we call *anchor spheres*, which can also hide or collapse diagrams to reduce visual clutter.

To distinguish UML elements types, generic (customizable) UML icons are placed on upper right and lower left of the top of the element. Rather than graphically modeling each element type separately, this enables us to quickly support many different element types using a common shallow box approach.

Due to the current lack of a common metamodel and/or inter-model specification language that can be used when visualizing heterogenous models (cf. [25] in Sect. 2), we resort to a pragmatic approach of providing a basic inter-model annotation capability in VR.

Navigation. The immersion afforded by VR requires addressing how to intuitively navigate the space while reducing the likelihood of potential VR sickness symptoms. Two navigation modes are included in the solution concept: the default uses gliding controls, enabling users to *fly through* the VR space and get an overview of the entire model from any angle they wish. Alternatively, teleporting permits a user to select a destination and be instantly placed there (i.e., by instantly moving the camera to that position); this can be disconcerting but may reduce the likelihood of VR sickness that can occur when moving through a virtual space for those prone to it.

Interaction. VR interaction with VR elements has not yet become standardized. In our VR concept, user-element interaction is done primarily via the VR controllers and a virtual tablet. The virtual tablet provides detailed element information with CRUD (Create, Retrieve, Update, Delete) capabilities specific to each element as well as a virtual keyboard for text entry via laser pointer key selection. The aforementioned corner anchor sphere affordance supports moving/hiding/displaying diagrams. Inter-diagram element *followers* can be displayed, hidden, or selected (emphasized).

4 Realization

The VR-UML implementation architecture for our prototype is shown in Fig. 2. Due to its multi-platform support, direct VR integration, popularity, and cost, the Unity game engine 2020.2.0b4 is used with the SteamVR plugin v2.6.0b4. As shown, Unity uses various assets such as Models, Scenes, and Scripts, which in turn access external model files via our plugin adapter interface that parses and converts various model file formats (e.g., UML, BPMN, ArchiMate) to our internal generic object representation.

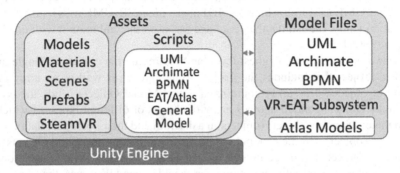

Fig. 2. VR-UML implementation architecture.

For text readability, an aspect that is irrelevant for 2D but which VR needs to consider is that the viewing angle from the user to the element (camera angle) can be dynamic based on the VR camera position in space (which is what is actually moved to "navigate"), thus the recognition and readability of elements must be considered from various angles. Thus, in VR-UML the diagrams and any elements they contain are raised slightly for a 3D effect and these visible side edges utilized for text placement to permit the text to be read from all sides in addition to the top. To support element delineation in space, rather than using clear elements with border outlines - as is typically done in 2D UML representations, in VR-UML a texture/color/material is used on all sides of an element to give it substance. However, in 3D space if the elements are opaque, then another element or relation could become hidden (and the user unaware of this), so a certain degree of transparency for diagram planes and for certain elements is used to ensure that relations and elements do not completely "disappear" within or behind other elements. Furthermore, a customizable color scheme, e.g., Coad et al. [26] or the colored layers used in the ArchiMate specification can be used to help distinguish UML diagrams and elements as models grow, since, in contrast to 2D, many elements can be depicted visually in VR.

One unexpected challenge in the UML visualization area is support for a common UML diagram interchange format between UML tools that contains positioning and layout data. While a mechanism for UML model exchange had been specified for UML 1.x using XMI, it only provides information on the model elements while lacking support for exchanging diagram and element positioning and layout information. This limitation is due to the UML metamodel lacking a standard way of representing diagram definitions. While UML Diagram Interchange (UMLDI) [27] was published in 2006, few UML tool vendors appear to implement and support it. At the time UML 2.0 was published in 2005, UMLDI was unavailable for another year, so vendors may have ignored it and continued with their own proprietary format for maintaining diagram layout information. Most web-based UML tools and various desktop tools we tried support exporting only common image file formats, while some support exporting the model in XMI but lack any positional information. As XML can readily be converted into a JSON format, rather than relying on the older common XML format in UML, we wanted to investigate utilizing the newer and more efficient JSON format for UML model files. Various popular UML tools were analyzed to determine if they already used or supported a JSON format for UML. As StarUML uses JSON in their MDJ model files, VR-UML uses its UML JSON file format. In Unity, the JsonDotNet package was used in combination with quicktype to parse the JSON model file.

As shown in Fig. 3, at the highest level, an MDJ model file contains a single object of the type Project that includes the project name and ID as well as an array of the next level of objects. This array contains all saved Model Objects inside the project. These Model Objects contain another array of objects of different types, of which we focus on three: Diagram Objects (objects in a diagram and their positional data), Model Data Objects (objects and their model data including relations and Child Objects), and Collaboration Objects (all diagram data for sequence diagrams). While further objects for diagram types such as activity or flowchart would expand the types, they are similar to the sequence diagram in another object tree branch.

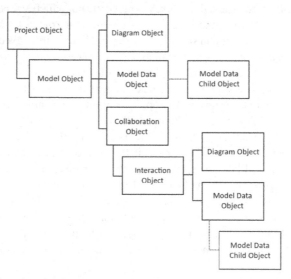

Fig. 3. Model file structure in JSON format.

To evaluate the practicality of the VR-UML solution concept and implementation prototype, a case study was used. Support is initially limited to the common UML diagram types: use case, class, sequence, and deployment. The travel agency example project provided by UML Designer [28] was used as a UML model basis and then imported to StarUML in order to get an MDJ model in JSON format. The model provides the basic UML diagram types known in the 4+1 view model [29]: a use case diagram depicting requirements in the scenario view (Fig. 4 left), a sequence diagram (Fig. 4 right) depicting runtime behavior in the dynamic or process view, a class diagram for depicting the internal structure in the logical view (Fig. 5), and a deployment diagram (Fig. 6) for depicting the physical view.

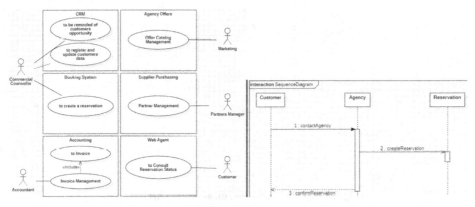

Fig. 4. Travel agency use case (left) and sequence (right) diagrams in StarUML.

The VR_UML visualization of the travel agency model is shown in Fig. 7, depicting *stacked hyperplanes* for this model. Colors help differentiate diagram types. Here the top grey plane shows a sequence diagram, the second purple plan the use case diagram, the third plane the deployment diagram in green, and the bottom a class diagram in red. Random colored *followers* along the invisible backplane (currently closest to the camera) are automatically generated between recurring elements across diagrams to follow participating elements across views (e.g., Customer (purple), Reservation (aqua) and Customer (light green), which recur in the class and sequence diagrams with details shown later), and can be used to quickly recognize recurring elements in other diagrams. *Anchor spheres* on the corner of each diagram act as affordances that supports expanding, collapsing, and moving a diagram.

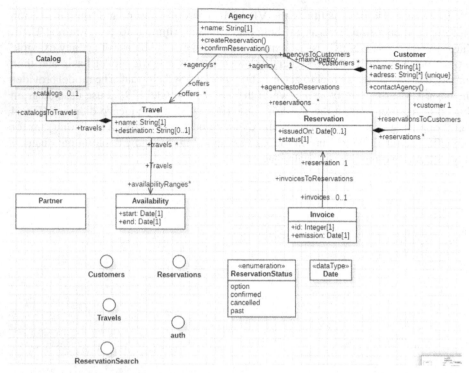

Fig. 5. Travel agency class diagram in StarUML.

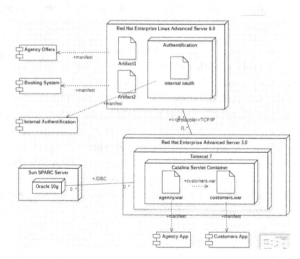

Fig. 6. Travel agency deployment diagram in StarUML.

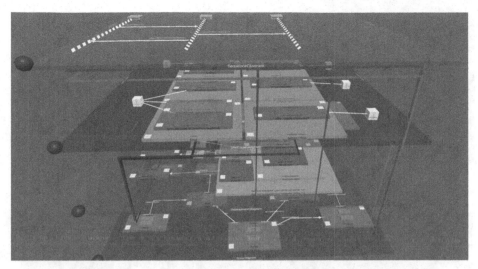

Fig. 7. VR-UML stacked hyperplane visualization of travel agency model.

A virtual tablet is provided in VR-UML to support interaction and modeling and to provide detailed information about an element. We chose this method since tablet usage is common and intuitive (less VR training needed), and other VR-based affordances are not yet standardized for providing detailed context-specific information for an element. Figure 8 shows the ability to add a new class to a diagram including a keyboard where each key is picked via a virtual laser pointer. Figure 9 shows the interface for creating a new relation and indicating the type of relation (e.g., association, aggregation, etc.) and its multiplicity. Figure 10 shows the ability to edit class attributes, e.g., the type, multiplicity, and visibility.

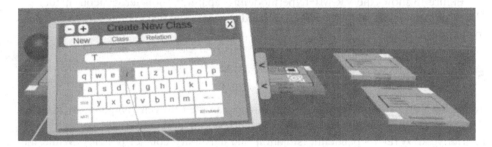

Fig. 8. VR-UML create class modeling support with virtual tablet and virtual keyboard.

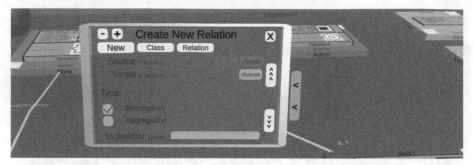

Fig. 9. VR-UML create relation modeling support with virtual tablet.

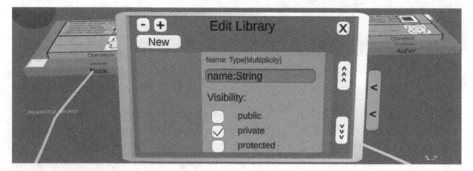

Fig. 10. VR-UML attribute modeling support via virtual tablet.

As exemplified in Fig. 11, visual clutter can be reduced via the anchor sphere affordance to collapse (hide) a diagram (which then displays the hidden diagram type).

Figure 12 shows side-by-side and offset diagram placement via anchor spheres.

Figure 13 shows the VR-MF hypermodeling capability for heterogeneous models in VR (e.g., here UML and ArchiMate); related elements can be annotated across models to support analysis.

5   Evaluation

To assess VR-UML empirically, a convenience sample of seven computer science students from sophomore through master students participated, despite the currently very restrictive COVID-19 pandemic situation and university contact policies. While the group is not large enough to be statistically significant, the results can provide insights to inform and guide future research. The subjects used an HTC Vive room scale VR set with a head-mounted display and two wireless handheld controllers tracked by two base stations. Each subject worked individually with a supervisor who provided instructions and timed the tasks. A Likert five-point scale was used for range-based responses. All had some familiarity with UML and had used Sparx Systems Enterprise Architect before; only two had used StarUML, and all but one had used VR.

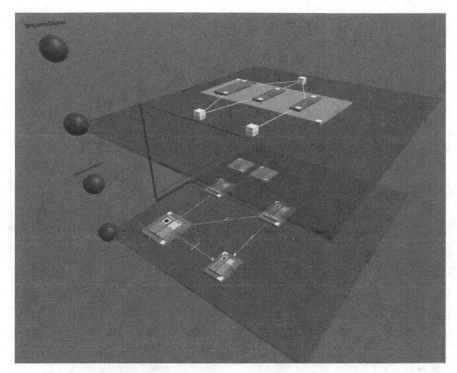

Fig. 11. VR-UML stacked plane view with two hidden/collapsed diagrams.

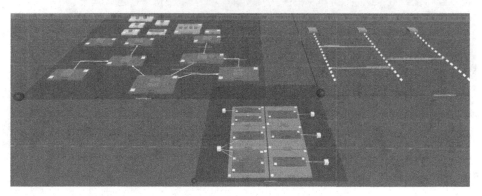

Fig. 12. VR-UML side-by-side and offset diagram placement.

The hypotheses that guided our tasks and questions were: while VR-UML will likely be less efficient than 2D modeling in general, (1) VR-UML is advantageous and efficient for more complex and multi-diagram models; and (2) users will subjectively enjoy the VR immersion experience in UML models more that the 2D models.

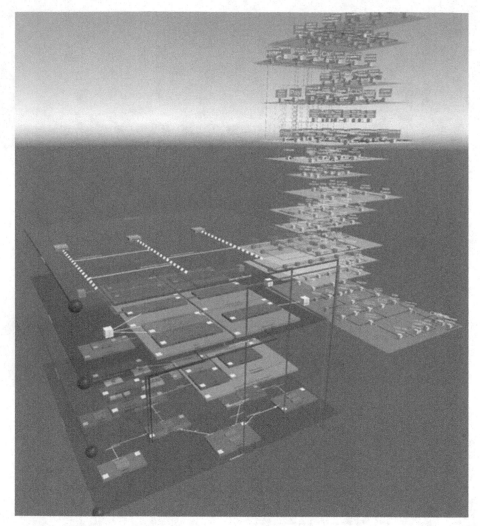

Fig. 13. Hypermodeling example showing a VR-UML and VR-EA ArchiMate model.

5.1 Quantitative Analysis

The subjects were timed for the following tasks in non-VR (using StarUML) and VR-UML:

1. Multi-diagram elements: which elements with the same name recur in multiple diagrams and how often?
2. Change the attribute "email" in the Customer class from public to private.
3. Change the relation multiplicity between Customer to Shopping Cart to 1-1.
4. Create the Model-View-Controller (MVC) pattern in the class diagram in non-VR (see Fig. 14) and VR-UML (Fig. 15). In non-VR a paper copy was accessible as a

reference, in VR they had to remember or verbally ask questions while wearing the headset.

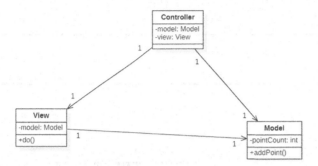

Fig. 14. MVC pattern task example in StarUML.

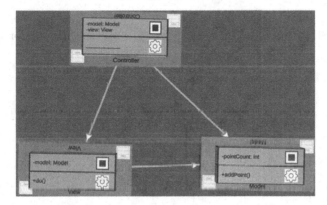

Fig. 15. MVC pattern task example in VR-UML.

Figure 16 shows the task duration results. On average, VR took 344% longer for Task 1, 141% longer for Task 2, and 43% longer for Task 4. For Task 3, when dealing with multi-diagram elements, VR was 14% more efficient on average - because VR-UML's ability to visualize multiple diagrams and highlight inter-diagram elements. We see this result as providing support for hypothesis (1). Note that for Task 2, 3, and 4, the ranges show a large degree of overlap, which can be interpreted that VR can perform better than non-VR to depending on the user's UML and VR competency.

Three possible reasons for the longer VR results are: 1) the VR interface is more cumbersome to control for modeling vs. a 2D mouse-based interface with which the subjects have been trained, 2) text entry via virtual laser pointer keypad selection (resembling one finger typing using a laser pointer) instead of the non-VR physical keyboard (enabling touch typing), and 3) time spent in VR navigating through 3D space to see or interact with the object of interest (vs. in 2D moving the mouse on a screen). As VR keyboards become commonplace, this could reduce this factor's efficiency influence.

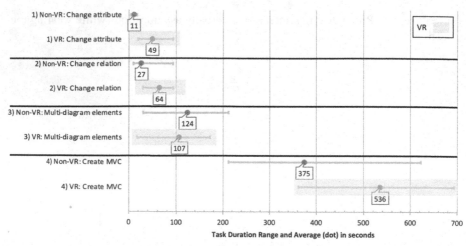

Fig. 16. VR and Non-VR task duration range and average (blue dot) in seconds. (Color figure online)

Table 1. UML familiarity (1 to 5, 5 = very familiar, 1 = unfamiliar) vs. error frequency.

UML familiarity	Non-VR errors	VR errors	Total errors
2	1	3	4
3	0	0	0
3	2	0	2
4	0	2	2
4	0	0	0
4	0	2	2
4	0	5	5

Table 1 shows the errors made. We note that in two cases no errors were made in either mode, in one case fewer errors were made in VR, while in four cases errors increased in VR. Since VR relied on subjects' memory of the pattern and subjects could not compare their model to a reference model on paper as they did in non-VR, we do not weight VR errors strongly. Due to the relatively minor error rate differences, we interpret the results to indicate that with additional training and familiarity with VR-UML, the error rate in VR could be equivalent to that of 2D and that it is not inherently more error prone for all cases and all subjects.

5.2 Qualitative Analysis

In the qualitative responses shown in Fig. 17, all agreed VR-UML to be intuitive and 43% more so than non-VR. 86% agreed that VR-UML provided a clear model structure.

As to changing an element, 71% found them equivalent while 29% found non-VR easier. For finding recurring elements across diagrams, 86% strongly agreed that it was easy in VR-UML compared to 43% for non-VR. In general, VR did not fare worse than non-VR on these qualitative aspects, and often even better.

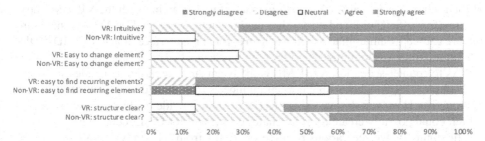

Fig. 17. Qualitative comparison of VR and Non-VR.

Additionally, 71% stated that they liked VR-UML better than non-VR. We interpret this as support for hypothesis (2). VR-UML advantages explicitly mentioned included: VR provided a better overview of diagrams and how they relate to each other, the layered 3D hyperplane stack makes comprehension of architecture easier, better visualization in general - and specifically for relations, VR is more intuitive, the VR user interface simpler than a menu system, and VR provides better focus due to immersion. Disadvantages mentioned included: efficiency to perform tasks, text input takes much longer via virtual keyboard with laser pointer, and the potential for VR sickness for sensitive users. Suggested improvements included: voice input or other text input alternative for VR.

5.3 Discussion

While our small sample size is not statistically significant, we believe there is still sufficient value from the results to infer trends and to inform future research. The study showed evidence that VR can indeed support modeling for certain scenarios. We hypothesized that VR would be advantageous relative to 2D for more complex structures or inter-diagram scenarios which VR can better depict simultaneously due to its 3D nature. As shown in Fig. 16, recurring elements across multiple diagrams were indeed found more quickly (16% on average), due primarily to our VR-based support for visually depicting these same elements, supporting hypothesis (1).

Factors that affected our study included: the COVID-19 policies to reduce interactions and interaction time, such that no preparation, training, or warm-up was given (no VR training nor VR-UML app training). In contrast, all participants had used 2D UML tools beforehand. Furthermore, VR app interaction and controls are not yet standardized and familiar, so subjects may not automatically know how to achieve some goal in VR – compared with professional 2D tools where common expectations exists as to where one will likely find menu items to achieve some task. Another aspect is cognitive stimulus: VR visualization takes up much more visual processing that is still relatively new and unfamiliar as yet to these subjects and can be disconcerting or initially affect efficiency (i.e., a new world to explore effect).

Threats to validity include: the small convenience sample size; the self-assessed UML competency (vs. a UML competency test); lack of experienced software developer UML competency or certification; VR tasks were performed directly rather than after a VR warm-up phase; users lacked a MVC reference image in VR (non-VR had a paper copy), thus subjects had to recall the MVC pattern from memory - which some may be better at than others - or verbally ask questions; lack of prior training with the VR-UML app, leading to inefficiencies and errors that may not actually depend on VR as a medium, but are caused by unfamiliarity with such an app and its interface (due to COVID-19 the evaluation time was minimized and training time cancelled).

As to counter-scenarios, VR-UML is likely not suitable or recommended for small and simple UML models or single-diagram models from and efficiency or effectiveness perspective. However, despite this, VR-UML could provide qualitative improvements which could possibly create (or rejuvenate) excitement for UML modeling.

In summary, we see various positive indicators from this study that VR-UML can show advantages where more complex and multi-diagram models are involved (and by inference hypermodeling); that the immersive experience of UML models in VR adds qualitative aspects that users prefer; and that any task inefficiencies in VR are probably tolerable (as shown be the task duration range overlap). VR-UML efficiency could be improved with explicit VR-UML training and text entry alternatives.

6 Conclusion

With our VR-UML contribution we have provided an immersive UML model experience for visually depicting and navigating UML diagrams of software models in VR. The solution concept and guiding principles were described, and its feasibility demonstrated with a VR prototype, with which we empirically evaluated our solution. Based on our VR hyperplane principle, it enhances UML diagrams with 3D depth, color, and automatically generated inter-diagram element followers based on our backplane concept. Modeling and interaction are supported via a virtual tablet and virtual keyboard. By leveraging the unlimited space in VR, the overall extent of multiple diagrams and large models can be depicted and navigated visually, while overall interrelationships within and between heterogeneous elements, diagrams, and models can be indicated and analyzed. Furthermore, our VR modeling framework VR-MF contributes a generalized hypermodeling approach for loading and visualizing different model types in VR whereby UML and EA-related models such as ArchiMate, BPMN, and Atlas can be visualized and analyzed simultaneously. The sensory immersion of VR can support task focus during model comprehension and increase modeling enjoyment, while limiting the visual distractions that typical 2D display surroundings incur. Most subjects preferred VR-UML overall.

Various UML tools support reverse-engineering models directly from the code (Ozkaya 2019). By leveraging today's processors and cloud computing, they can rapidly provide just-in-time reverse-engineered models to document and visually convey the real software model based on the actual codebase both efficiently and without model-to-code inconsistencies. In combination with VR-UML, visualization, analysis, and immersion in software models could rejuvenate UML-based software modeling in the face of rapidly evolving codebases and in support of software maintenance of legacy systems. Future work includes adding support for additional UML diagram and elements types, enhancing the VR interface, adding additional inter-model annotation and informational capabilities, optimizing the model storage format, and a comprehensive empirical study.

Acknowledgements. The authors would like to thank Marie Baehre and Stefan Wehrenberg for their assistance with the implementation and evaluation.

References

1. Brooks Jr., F.P.: The Mythical Man-Month. Addison-Wesley Longman Publication Co., Inc., Boston (1995)
2. Kemerer, C.F., Paulk, M.C.: The impact of design and code reviews on software quality: an empirical study based on PSP data. IEEE Trans. Softw Eng **35**(4), 534–550 (2009). https://doi.org/10.1109/TSE.2009.27
3. OMG: Unified modeling language version 2.5.1 (2019)
4. OMG: XML Metadata Interchange (XMI) Specification Version 2.5.1 (2015)
5. Ware, C., Franck, G.: Viewing a graph in a virtual reality display is three times as good as a 2D diagram. In: Proceedings of 1994 IEEE Symposium on Visual Languages, pp. 182–183. IEEE (1994). https://doi.org/10.1109/VL.1994.363621
6. McIntosh, P.: X3D-UML: user-centered design, implementation and evaluation of 3D UML using X3D. Ph.D. dissertation, RMIT University (2009)
7. Krolovitsch, A., Nilsson, L.: 3D Visualization for Model Comprehension: A Case Study Conducted at Ericsson AB. University of Gothenburg, Sweden (2009)
8. Rodrigues, C.S.C., Werner, C.M., Landau, L.: VisAr3D: an innovative 3D visualization of UML models. In: 2016 IEEE/ACM 38th International Conference on Software Engineering Companion (ICSE-C), pp. 451–460. IEEE (2016)
9. Steuer, J.: Defining virtual reality: dimensions determining telepresence. J. Commun. **42**(4), 73–93 (1992). https://doi.org/10.1111/j.1460-2466.1992.tb00812.x
10. Allcoat, D., von Mühlenen, A.: Learning in virtual reality: effects on performance, emotion and engagement. Res Learn Technol **26** (2018). https://doi.org/10.25304/rlt.v26.2140
11. Oberhauser, R., Lecon, C.: Virtual reality flythrough of program code structures. In: Proceedings of the Virtual Reality International Conference-Laval Virtual 2017, pp. 1–4. ACM (2017). https://doi.org/10.1145/3110292.3110303
12. Oberhauser, R., Pogolski, C., Matic, A.: VR-BPMN: visualizing BPMN models in virtual reality. In: Shishkov, B. (ed.) BMSD 2018. LNBIP, vol. 319, pp. 83–97. Springer, Cham (2018). https://doi.org/10.1007/978-3-319-94214-8_6
13. OMG: Business Process Model and Notation (BPMN) Version 2.0.2 (2014)
14. Oberhauser, R., Pogolski, C.: VR-EA: virtual reality visualization of enterprise architecture models with ArchiMate and BPMN. In: Shishkov, B. (ed.) BMSD 2019. LNBIP, vol. 356, pp. 170–187. Springer, Cham (2019). https://doi.org/10.1007/978-3-030-24854-3_11
15. Open Group: ArchiMate 3.1 Specification. The Open Group (2019)
16. Oberhauser, R., Sousa, P., Michel, F.: VR-EAT: visualization of enterprise architecture tool diagrams in virtual reality. In: Shishkov, B. (ed.) BMSD 2020. LNBIP, vol. 391, pp. 221–239. Springer, Cham (2020). https://doi.org/10.1007/978-3-030-52306-0_14
17. Sousa, P., Leal, R., Sampaio, A.: Atlas: the enterprise cartography tool. In: 18th Enterprise Engineering Working Conference Forum, vol. 2229. CEUR-WS.org (2018)

18. Zhang, B., Chen, Y.S.: Enhancing UML conceptual modeling through the use of virtual reality. In: Proceedings of the 38th Annual Hawaii International Conference on System Sciences, p. 11b. IEEE (2005). https://doi.org/10.1109/HICSS.2005.239
19. Ozkaya, M.: Are the UML modelling tools powerful enough for practitioners? A literature review. IET Softw. **13**, 338–354 (2019). https://doi.org/10.1049/iet-sen.2018.5409
20. Ozkaya, M., Erata, F.: A survey on the practical use of UML for different software architecture viewpoints. Inf. Softw. Technol. **121**, 106275 (2020). https://doi.org/10.1016/j.infsof.2020.106275. ISSN 0950-5849
21. Schreiber, A., Misiak, M.: Visualizing software architectures in virtual reality with an island metaphor. In: Chen, J.Y.C., Fragomeni, G. (eds.) VAMR 2018. LNCS, vol. 10909, pp. 168–182. Springer, Cham (2018). https://doi.org/10.1007/978-3-319-91581-4_13
22. Nafeie, L., Schreiber, A.: Visualization of software components and dependency graphs in virtual reality. In: Proceedings of the 24th ACM Symposium on Virtual Reality Software and Technology, pp. 1–2. ACM (2018). https://doi.org/10.1145/3281505.3281602
23. Vincur, J., Navrat, P., Polasek, I.: VR city: software analysis in virtual reality environment. In: 2017 IEEE International Conference on Software Quality, Reliability and Security Companion (QRS-C), pp. 509–516. IEEE (2017). https://doi.org/10.1109/QRS-C.2017.88
24. Schreiber, A., Brüggemann, M.: Interactive visualization of software components with virtual reality headsets. In: 2017 IEEE Working Conference on Software Visualization (VISSOFT), pp. 119–123. IEEE (2017). https://doi.org/10.1109/VISSOFT.2017.20
25. Bork, D., Karagiannis, D., Pittl, B.: A survey of modeling language specification techniques. Inf. Syst. **87**, 101425 (2020). https://doi.org/10.1016/j.is.2019.101425
26. Coad, P., Lefebvre, E., De Luca, J.: Java Modeling in Color with UML: Enterprise Components and Process. Prentice Hall (1999) ISBN 0-13-011510-X
27. OMG: UML Diagram Interchange (UMLDI) 1.0 (2006)
28. UML Designer (2021). http://www.umldesigner.org
29. Kruchten, P.: Architectural blueprints - the "4+1" view model of software architecture. IEEE Softw. **12**(6), 42–50 (1995). https://doi.ieeecomputersociety.org/10.1109/52.469759

A Reference Architecture for Enhanced Design of Software Ecosystems

Sanket Kumar Gupta, Bahar Schwichtenberg$^{(\boxtimes)}$, and Gregor Engels

Paderborn University, Paderborn, Germany
{bahar.schwichtenberg,gregor.engels}@upb.de,
skgupta@mail.uni-paderborn.de

Abstract. Software ecosystems have become a novel architectural approach to extend software development to the outside of companies, where third-party providers develop applications on top of a common platform. While designing software ecosystems, platform providers face an overwhelming design space of business and technical architectural decisions. Usually, enterprise architecture modeling languages such as ArchiMate are used to design the ecosystem around the platforms. Despite a body of work studying architecture of software ecosystems, there is still a lack of a reference architecture that captures both business and technical aspects, which can be followed by platform providers to design these systems.

In this paper, we develop a reference architecture by using different sources of information such as existing ecosystems and the literature. After identifying the shortcomings of the ArchiMate language to design software ecosystems, we extend the language using the reference architecture to enable direct and enhanced modeling of ecosystem-specific concepts. The extended ArchiMate has been implemented in a tool that we use to design a real-world ecosystem called F-Droid. Our results show the reference architecture captures the F-Droid ecosystem architecture. Bad architectural smells are detected, and improvement suggestions are made. Our work will assist platform providers to improve architectural decision-making by making informed design decisions.

Keywords: Software ecosystems · Reference architecture · Business modeling · ArchiMate · F-Droid

1 Introduction

Today, leading software companies open up their software development processes to the third-party provider to adapt to the continuously increasing demand for innovative and changing software solutions and, at the same time, to address business needs [1]. This novel approach is termed as software ecosystem [2], which is inspired by the idea of natural ecosystems, where organisms interact with each other and live as a unit [3]. An example of software ecosystems is the ecosystem around the *Google Android* platform[1], where the *Google* company is

---

[1] https://www.android.com, Last Access: 1 June 2021.

© Springer Nature Switzerland AG 2021
B. Shishkov (Ed.): BMSD 2021, LNBIP 422, pp. 59–77, 2021.
https://doi.org/10.1007/978-3-030-79976-2_4

the platform provider offering the platform and a repository of in-house and third-party mobile applications called *Play Store*[2].

Designing software ecosystems is a complex and challenging task. Firstly because the platform providers have to face a broad and overwhelming range of interrelated business and technical design decisions [4]. Opening a platform requires exposing internal resources to the third-party providers, which has critical security implications and business risks for the platform providers [5]. Although a body of work in literature has already studied architectural characteristics of software ecosystems, there is still a lack of a reference architecture that provides a unified picture of the business-related and technical architectural building blocks. In the absence of a reference architecture, platform providers have to rely on arbitrary architectural decision-making. As a result, the providers' time and budget are invested in mistake-prone development processes, which miss informed architectural decision-making. In this situation, the resulting ecosystems can be too restrictive, making the ecosystems less attractive for third-party providers or the ecosystems are overly exposed, which threatens the platform providers' intellectual property [6]. Another challenge related to the development of software ecosystems is to use enterprise modeling languages like ArchiMate[3] to design the ecosystem architecture. Such languages are too generic. Thus, platform providers fail to capture some critical ecosystem-specific aspects such as openness policies using these languages. To overcome these challenges, systematic architectural support is needed that provides the required knowledge to enhance architectural decision-making and a modeling language that enables platform providers to apply that knowledge.

In this paper, we propose a reference architecture for software ecosystems by using the knowledge that we extract from various sources such as the literature and existing ecosystems, and based on our previous work [7]. The reference architecture span across organizational, business, and technical aspects. It provides a template solution to address key quality attributes of software ecosystems. Besides, we extend the ArchiMate language with the ecosystem-specific concepts from the reference architecture. Our solution has been implemented in a tool using which platform providers can automatically generate an initial architecture based on the reference architecture and further tailor the architecture by using the extended ArchiMate. Furthermore, we model and analyze a real-world ecosystem called F-Droid using our solution. F-Droid is a platform for the development of open-source Android Apps. We detect architectural smells and deficiencies in the F-Droid ecosystem and suggest design decisions to overcome them. Our work helps establish a solid knowledge base. It assists platform providers in informed architectural decision-making.

The remainder of the paper is structured as follows: Sect. 2 elaborates the research steps that we apply to develop the reference architecture. In Sect. 3 we propose a reference architecture to facilitate the systematic designing of software

---

[2] https://play.google.com/store, Last Access: 1 June 2021.
[3] https://www.opengroup.org/ArchiMate-forum/ArchiMate-overview, Last Access: 1 June 2021.

ecosystems. Section 4 present our approach to extend the ArchiMate language for ecosystem modeling that is followed by Sect. 5, where we describe our case study. Section 6 discusses related work. Section 7 concludes the paper and addresses future research directions.

2 Design Steps

We design the reference architecture for software ecosystems by following the approach of systematically creating an empirically-grounded reference architecture proposed by Galster et al. [8]. The procedure for designing the reference architecture comprises six steps. Following, we explain each of these steps concerning the development of reference architecture for software ecosystems.

Step 1: Decision on Type of Reference Architecture. The first step of designing a reference architecture is to select an appropriate type of reference architecture that would clearly state its main objectives [8]. At first, we determine the type of reference architecture that we aim to create by using a classification framework presented by Angelov et al. [9]. As per this classification framework, reference architecture can be classified into five types. As a result, we conclude that the proposed reference architecture of software ecosystems whose goal is to *facilitate* multiple organizations in systematic creation of ecosystem is developed by a *research center* loosely falls under *Type 3*. The following steps are aligned with the selected *Type 3* reference architecture type.

Step 2: Selection of Design Strategy. There are two possible design strategies associated with designing a reference architecture. First, it can be created from scratch. Second, it can be designed based on existing research work and architectures available in the problem domain [8]. We choose the second strategy of using existing research work and literature available in the software ecosystem domain. In the next step, we illustrate the literature and research papers used to gather information to design the reference architecture.

Step 3: Empirical Acquisition of Data. The next step is to accumulate information available in the target domain of the reference architecture. For this, we refer to the set of descriptive and analytical requirements presented by Sadi et al. [5], raised while designing software ecosystems. We used these requirements as guiding principles to define software ecosystem ontology and identify the architectural building blocks of the designed reference architecture. These design principles are comprehensively explained in Sect. 3. In addition, we refer to our previous work presented by Jazayeri et al. [7], where we identify three architectural patterns for software ecosystems called *resale software ecosystems*, *partner-based software ecosystem*, and *OSS-based ecosystem*. We complement this knowledge by identifying relevant sources of knowledge by investigating the developer and technical forums of the existing ecosystems.

Step 4: Construction of Reference Architecture. As per the decided *Type 3* category, we construct an informal basic design of the designed reference architecture expressing the business, organizational, and technological aspects of a software ecosystem. The previously mentioned elements in Step 3 are arranged in conceptually similar groups of architectural building blocks. These architectural building blocks are the smallest composing element of the reference architecture and are based on the performance drivers as quality attributes described by Mhamdia et al. [10] and Jazayeri et al. [11].

Step 5: Enabling Reference Architecture with Variability. Variability refers to the possible range of concrete architectures based on the context which can be designed using the reference architecture. One of the ways to enable variability in a reference architecture is through annotation of the architectural element. Annotation refers to attaching additional information about the variability [8]. In our case, we enable the proposed reference architecture with variability by attaching additional information using attributes to relevant elements. We identified the elements which need to be annotated based on the design decisions of three architectural design patterns developed by Jazayeri et al. [11]. The annotated elements of the proposed reference architecture are: *revenue generation system, third-party developer, context, openness* and *platform*.

Step 6: Evaluation of Reference Architecture. Evaluation of the proposed reference architecture is out of scope for the study of this paper. Although, we have used an actual world case study of an existing software ecosystem named F-droid to show how the proposed reference architecture can be used in the systematic designing of a software ecosystem. Furthermore, as a result of the instantiation, we pointed out the features missing from the F-Droid ecosystem.

3   A Reference Architecture for Software Ecosystems

In this section, we present a reference architecture for software ecosystems. The reference architecture aims at capturing interdisciplinary design decisions of software ecosystems to facilitate the systematic design of these systems. As mentioned in Sect. 2, we designed the reference architecture based on the design principles, which we also used to identify its architectural building blocks and determine software ecosystem ontology.

Two primary elements of software ecosystems are a software *platform* on top of which different stakeholders of an ecosystem interact to develop end-user applications and a *store* where these applications are marketed. In the following, we elaborate on architectural building blocks of the reference architecture.

Collaborators: As per the definition, the stakeholders of an ecosystem could be classified into three types, i.e., *Platform Providers, Third-party developers,* and, *Users. Third-party developers* can further be classified as *Trusted Partners* and *Independent Developers* based on the contractual agreement between them and the platform provider.

Interactions: Platform providers are responsible for establishing an interaction between various stakeholders as a part of *Orchestration* [2]. At tactical and operational level, connectedness between various stakeholders are established through *Community Building, Knowledge Sharing,* and *Support & Services.* A platform provider can put constraints on the platform's usage and extension by defining a set of rules or guidelines, deciding on the degree of *openness* and imposing entry barriers to make sure only the right third-party developers can enter the ecosystem [12].

Incentives and Motivations of Collaborators: To encourage third-party developers to participate and contribute to the platform, platform providers can decide on an appropriate level of openness and entry barriers to ease the process of application development. A good *Marketing & Sales* strategy helps platform providers in improving the profit margin for third-party developers [12]. Other motivating factors include *vision* through which platform providers can clearly state the future state of their ecosystem, to help collaborators decide on their participation [12]. *Feedback loop facilitator* helps collaborator in collecting feedbacks from users to track their satisfaction and using *Market Analytics,* which is another type of feedback technique, gives an insight into the market growth, in turn, helping platform providers enhance their profit margin [7].

Trust and Reliability: *Contract management* which can be used to regulate their contribution or decide the type of agreement with the collaborators and their share of profit in the revenue generated [13]. Using *License Management,* platform providers can control the redistribution of its software and regulate the usage of its intellectual property to ensure the development activities are carried out responsibly [3].

Risk, Vulnerability and Tolerance: Risk, vulnerability & tolerance in a software ecosystem can be controlled by deciding the degree of openness of the software platform and its entry barriers. A software platform too open and with a relaxed entry barrier may result in loss of quality and an increase in uncontrolled growth of an ecosystem [12], thereby making it vulnerable to outside attacks. Risk, vulnerability, and tolerance can also be managed by *Security, Openness, License Management, and Privacy.* **Costs and Benefits** of opening up a software platform for external development is managed through a *Revenue Generation System* which includes *Platform fee, Service fee, Entrance fee or donation. Marketing & Sales* is another way through which benefits of opening up a software platform can be provided to the collaborators.

Distributing and Decentralizing Responsibilities and Resources: Platform providers can provide common platform boundary resources such as *Technical & Social boundary resources* offering different technical development toolkits such as APIs and social resources such as documentation and guidelines to facilitate development activities for collaborators [14].

Distributing Control, Authority, Decision Making, and Access: Platform providers manage *Orchestration* which involves developing strategies, specifying entry barriers, setting quality standards, defining guidelines for development activities, etc. [3,15].

Security and Privacy: Security and privacy concerns can be addressed through *Access & Identity Management* which facilitates identity-based access to the platform and its resources, and *Security & Privacy policies* which is are legal documents to precisely define what is acceptable and what is not in the development activities carried out by the external developers.

Health, Productivity, Robustness and Performance: *Health* of an ecosystem is influenced by the *Productivity, Robustness and Niche Creation* of a software ecosystem [12]. The quality attributes, i.e., productivity, sustainability, robustness, interoperability, modifiability, stakeholder satisfaction, and creativity, are the performance drivers in an ecosystem [10].

Alignment and Conflict Resolution: Platform providers can resolve conflicts among stakeholders and enhance sustainability by establishing a solid relationship among third-party developers through improving connectedness.

Figure 1 illustrates the visual structure of the designed reference architecture for software ecosystems. It consists of architectural building blocks grouped in similar conceptual groups depicting the organizational, technological, and business aspects of a software ecosystem. These conceptual groups are as follows.

Actors: Actors in software ecosystems can be broadly classified into three types. Firstly, *platform providers* who represent a software vendor of a leading software company, someone who is the provider of the ecosystem and is responsible for the orchestration of the whole software ecosystem. Secondly, *third-party developers* who are the external entities that extend the technological platform to provide a wide variety of applications for the ecosystem users. Third-party developers can be further classified into two types 1) *Trusted Partners*, which is a type of extender with expertise in a particular domain. They collaborate with the platform providers to develop domain-specific applications, which are later marketed jointly. 2) *Independent Developers* who work independently in collaboration with platform providers to provide various innovative solutions to the users.

Business Management: Business management groups together business activities and tasks, influencing the whole ecosystem and its performance. Some of these business activities are *revenue generation system, marketing & sales, community building, support & services, knowledge sharing, market analytics, and contract management.* The ecosystem provider performs these business activities and tasks to ensure the resources are optimally used, and the ecosystem performs well.

Organizational Management: Organizational management groups together the cross-cutting organizational aspects of a software ecosystem. Platform providers are primarily responsible for managing the ecosystem. Some of these organizational management activities are taking care of the *health, security and communication & coordination* of an ecosystem, deciding the *context* of an ecosystem by planning ecosystem's *domain criticality, targeted market, and commerciality* and performing the operational activities such as *orchestration, policy & license management.*

Platform: The platform group represents the software-based platform and the resources to support third-party development activities through its extension. Platform providers are now providing resources, i.e., software tools and knowledge base, to third-party developers to assist them in developing a wide variety of innovative applications. These resources are referred to as platform boundary resources. These resources can be further classified into technical boundary resources and social boundary resources. Technical boundary resources are the technical resources that help third-party developers extend the software-based platforms and application development. Social boundary resources are the resources that are used to transfer knowledge about the development process. It is concerned with providing documentation on how to extend the platform using the available resources [14].

Store: A store is an online repository of end-user applications where a user can find paid or unpaid applications. It consists of search functionality, an application catalog, a feedback loop facilitator, and a backup repository.

User Interface: The constituent architectural building blocks of the User Interface group acts as one of the access points to the software ecosystem's users. Platform providers offer an online store of applications to their users. These online stores are part of a user interface of the software platform, which can be a web-based application or a stand-alone application, or an operating system [16].

Computing Hardware: This group includes the architectural building blocks representing the deployment aspect of a software ecosystem. Each architectural building block in this group represents a computing unit on which the technological platform is deployed. The software platform can be deployed on **Portable Devices**, or it can be a web-based application or a stand-alone application.

Additionally, we enable the proposed reference architecture with variability by attaching additional information using attributes to relevant elements. We identified the elements which need to be annotated based on the design decisions of three architectural design patterns, i.e., *Resale Software Ecosystem, partner-based Ecosystem* and *OSS-based Ecosystem* developed in [7]. The annotated elements of the proposed reference architecture are: *revenue generation system, third-party developer, context, openness* and *platform*. These elements are marked with a star for distinction in Fig. 1.

4   ArchiMate Extended with Ecosystem-Specific Concepts

To facilitate model-based designing of software ecosystems, we studied ArchiMate as a modeling language to design a comprehensive software ecosystem model capturing its various aspects. ArchiMate is a meta-model-based graphical modeling language that provides an extensive set of symbols to model different aspects of an enterprise architecture [17]. However, it lacks the semantic strength to model domain-specific concepts because of its high level of abstractness [18].

As a part of our acquisition of empirical data, while designing the reference architecture, we first established the architectural building blocks of the designed

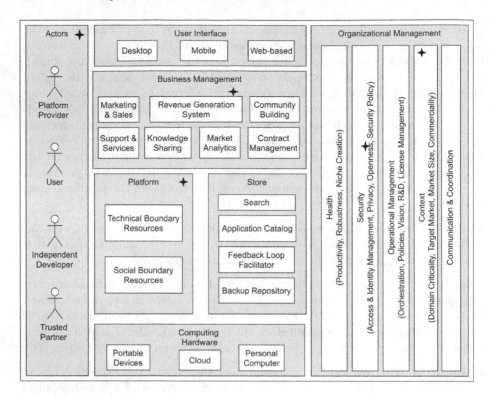

Fig. 1. Reference architecture for software ecosystems

reference architecture such as *platform, store, platform provider*, etc., as software ecosystem ontology. A software ecosystem ontology consists of a minimum set of domain-specific concepts to describe the software ecosystem domain. Modeling languages should provide these concepts specific to the software ecosystem domain to describe a software ecosystem. However, there is a gap between the graphical and analytical requirements of designing a software ecosystem and the current model-based approaches [5]. Hence, to create a comprehensive software ecosystem model, additional domain-specific concepts are needed. In the following, we illustrate the ArchiMate modeling language's extension with concepts specific to the software ecosystem's domain.

4.1   Mapping ArchiMate to Domain of Software Ecosystem

We integrate the software ecosystem ontology with the domain-independent ontology of ArchiMate using model transformation technique, which includes defining a mapping strategy [19,20]. This mapping strategy involves mapping the concepts of software ecosystem ontology with the concepts of the domain-independent ontology of ArchiMate.

The mapping of concepts is done based on the closeness of their semantic description of elements from both ontologies. For instance, the stakeholders of the software ecosystems, i.e., *Platform Provider*, *Trusted Partner*, *Independent Developer* and *User* in a very abstract way can be described as actors who perform numerous activities and have some responsibility towards the ecosystem. A *Business Actor* is capable of doing some action and has some responsibility. Hence, we can conclude that an ecosystem's stakeholders can be mapped to the *Business Actor* modeling element of ArchiMate.

4.2 Identifying Missing Concepts for Designing Software Ecosystems

Mapping of the elements explained in the previous section results in identifying different sources of challenges that makes modeling software ecosystems using the Archimate language complicated. We categorize these challenges into three groups as listed in Table 1. In the following, we discuss them.

- **Overload**: It defines the situation, where the source concepts can be mapped to more than one destination concept. For instance, the software ecosystem concept *platform* refers to the software application, which third-party developers extend. This software application can be a web-based, a stand-alone application, or an operating system. A platform that is an operating system can be modeled using *System Software* whereas, in the other two cases of a stand-alone application and web-based application, it can be modeled using *Application Component* modeling element of ArchiMate. We have addressed this ambiguity by introducing a new modeling element, i.e., *Platform* with an additional attribute to describe the type of technological platform. The *Type* attribute can have three possible values to represent the category of the platform, i.e. *Operating System*, *Web-based Application* and *Stand-alone Application*.
- **Redundancy**: It describes a situation when more than one source concept can be mapped to one destination concept. Apart from these outcomes, we found that the mapped ArchiMate concept's definition is too abstract to describe the software ecosystem concept and requires more expressiveness. For instance, there can be two types of third-party developers, i.e., *Trusted Partners* and *Independent Developers* depending on the type of collaborative commitment they have with the platform provider. To model such a stakeholder of an ecosystem, the modeling element needs additional information about their contractual agreement with the platform provider and their responsibilities within the ecosystem.
- **Deficiency**: It concerns the situation in which the source concept can not be mapped to any of the destination concepts. For instance, after carefully going through the semantic description of every ArchiMate element from its specification [21], we found out that no modeling element can be used to model the organizational setting, i.e., *Context* of an ecosystem. To address this deficiency, we added a new element *Context* with additional attributes *Domain*

Criticality, Target Market, and *Commerciality* to model the organizational setting of a software ecosystem.

As a result of the mapping, we conclude that the third-party developers could be modeled using the *Business Actor* modeling element of ArchiMate. The primary drawback of representing a *Third-party developer* using *Business Actor* is that the *Business Actor* fails to express the contractual agreement *Third-party developers* have with the platform provider. Since ArchiMate does not provide any attribute to describe additional information about *Business Actor*, a new element is needed to describe the required information.

Table 1. Three groups of missing concepts in Archimate

	Ecosystem-Specific Concepts	Archimate Concepts
Overload Concepts	Platform	System Software
		Application Component
	Openness	Capability
		Constraint
Redundancy of Concepts	Trusted Partner	Business Actor
	Independent Developer	
	Rating	Application Process
	Ranking	
	Reviewing	
	Technological Boundary Resources	Resource
	Social Boundary Resources	
Deficiency of Concepts	Context	— (No match is found.)

4.3   Extending ArchiMate

Domain-specific concepts in meta-model-based enterprise architecture modeling language such as ArchiMate can be introduced through language extension, also termed as language re-use mechanism. It provides two extension mechanisms to facilitate language customization to add domain-specific concepts, namely, adding attributes and specialization.

The first extension mechanism allows users to attach additional information to the modeling elements using attributes either when modeling or initially configuring the modeling tool. On the other hand, using specialization enables the addition of specialized elements of the existing modeling elements and relationships through inheritance. Specialization of generalized concepts (elements and relationships) provides modelers extra freedom to define domain-specific concepts without manipulating the language's core concepts. It also enables the analysis and visualization procedures applicable to the core concepts to be applied to the specialized concepts too [21].

ArchiMate language and its concepts are defined through meta-models using a meta-modeling approach [22]. The meta-modeling approach of designing a modeling language involves defining its abstract and concrete syntax using meta-models [22]. A meta-model defines the concepts and their attributes, relationships between the concepts, and the rules and constraints to unite the concepts and relationships to design a model. In a graphical modeling language such as ArchiMate, a meta-model helps a modeling language define its abstract syntax by specifying modeling elements such as concepts, relations, and constraints. Additionally, the ArchiMate framework defines a graphical representation for every element and relationship in its initial meta-model, which belongs to its concrete syntax [22].

Figure 2 shows the domain-specific concepts of the software ecosystem with respective graphical notations which we have identified. Out of these concepts, we have added attributes to a few of them. For instance, the new modeling element to express the *Revenue Generation System*, we attached additional information regarding the source of revenue using four attributes, each capturing *Platform Fee, Service Fee, Entrance Fee* and *Donation*.

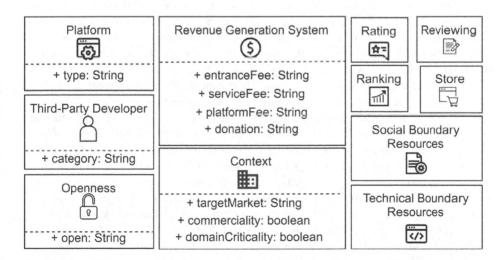

Fig. 2. Identified concepts specific to software ecosystem domain

To implement the extension of the ArchiMate language, we choose the Archi tool. Archi is an open-source graphical modeling tool based on the ArchiMate framework. In the Archi tool, the ArchiMate framework's meta-model is defined using Eclipse Modeling Framework' Ecore language. Ecore is used to describe models and provide runtime support for models, including change notifications, persistence support, APIs for manipulating EMF objects [23].

We add the identified software ecosystem concepts by extending the initial meta-model of the ArchiMate framework. We create specialized classes for each of the identified domain-specific concepts. In addition, additional attributes are added for *Revenue Generation System, Context, Third-party Developer, Platform* and *Openness*. Moreover, we develop a plugin to facilitate future platform providers in generating a pre-designed software ecosystem model based on our reference architecture. The implemented plug-in can be found on our Git repository[4].

5   Case Study: F-Droid

To demonstrate the application of the reference architecture to create a concrete ecosystem architecture in practice, we used the F-Droid ecosystem as our case study. F-Droid Limited is a UK "private company" that provides an ecosystem around Google's Android mobile operating system and provides Free and Open Source Software (FOSS) applications to the Android users[5]. We imagined a scenario where F-Droid wants to create an ecosystem using our software ecosystem reference architecture.

As a future platform provider, F-Droid can use the extended ArchiMate and developed utility to create the architecture of its software ecosystem by using the reference architecture as a base and make changes as per their requirement. As shown in Fig. 3, *FOSS Community Developers* and their consultants named *COTECH* and *IzzySoft* extends the *Android platform* and develop end-user applications which are further published on *F-Droid store*. To extend the Android platform, F-Droid provides *Technological Boundary Resources* tools aggregated with *Android Studio, Testing Suit* as an instance of *Technological Boundary Resources* and *Android APIs* as an instance of *Application Interface*. Additionally, it provides *Social Boundary Resources* aggregated with *F-Droid Docs* as an instance of type *Artifact, F-Droid Forum, Repositories (Client, Server, Data, Website)* and *F-Droid FAQs* as an instance of type *Social Boundary Resources*.

Furthermore, F-Droid manages ecosystem's business processes named *Support & Services* which is aggregated with instances of type capability named *Consultancy Services* and *Support through Email (team@f-droid.org), Community Building* aggregated with instances of type social boundary resources of social network activities on platforms named *Fediverse, Matrix, Freenode* and *F-Droid Forum, Contract Management* aggregated with instances of type contract named *Inclusion Policy* and *Terms of Service*, generating revenue through instance of type revenue generation system named *Donation via OpenCollective,*

---

[4] https://git.cs.uni-paderborn.de/bahareh/SecoArc_Runtime, Last Access: 1 June 2021.

[5] https://f-droid.org/en/about/, Last Access: 1 June 2021.

knowledge sharing is done through *F-Droid Docs* which is an instance of type artifact.

Vision of the ecosystem is a set, i.e., *"provide free and open source (FOSS) software for the Android platform users"*, which also influences its *health* driven by *Productivity, Robustness* and *Niche Creation*. F-Droid models the *Context* of its ecosystem by setting the attributes of modeling instance of element type *Context* as false for *Domain Criticality*, false for *Commerciality* since all the applications on F-Droid repository are free and open source, and *Targeted Market* as *"develop end-user applications for Android portable device users"*.

Context of an ecosystem influences the *Organizational Management* of an ecosystem done by the F-Droid as a platform provider. *Organizational Management* aggregates various capabilities such as *R&D, Orchestration, License Management, Security,* and *Communication & Coordination*. The capability of *License Management* further have access relationship with instances of type contract named *CC BY-NC-SA 3.0* for user contribution, *GNU Public License* for applications and *GNU Free Documentation License* for documentations. The capability of *Security* aggregates *Security Model* of type principle and instance of capability named *Contributor Identity Management*. Furthermore, capability named *Communication & Coordination* is aggregated with *F-Droid* instance of type social boundary resource. *Operational Management* has access relationship with a type of contract named *Inclusion policy, Copyright Infringement, DMCA Policy*.

F-Droid provides an ecosystem around Google's Android, which is an open-source technology. Hence, the *Openness* is set as open using the attribute with the same name. *Openness* has an influence relationship with the *Organizational Management*. F-Droid Limited as a platform provider, provides an online store of end-user applications named *F-Droid* which has an access relationship with two user interfaces, one is a mobile application named *F-Droid*, and another one is a web-based application with URL *f-droid.org*.

Improvement Suggestions

Based on our case study, we make suggestions to improve the quality of the F-Droid ecosystem by introducing the features that are missing in the architecture. During the case study, we could identify three unavailable features in the F-Droid ecosystem architecture, which include *Market Analytics, Marketing & Sales,* and *Feedback Loop Facilitator*.

Market analytics helps contributors analyze the market and provide better applications to the ecosystem users. The reason F-Droid does not offer download statistics as it is against its policy to track a user or their device[6]. However, the statistics related to the usage of applications can be obtained in a privacy-preserving way[7]. The absence of market analytic hinders the robustness and productivity of an ecosystem.

---

[6] https://f-droid.org/en/about/, Last Access: 1 June 2021.
[7] https://guardianproject.info/2017/06/08/tracking-usage-without-tracking-people, Last Access: 1 June 2021.

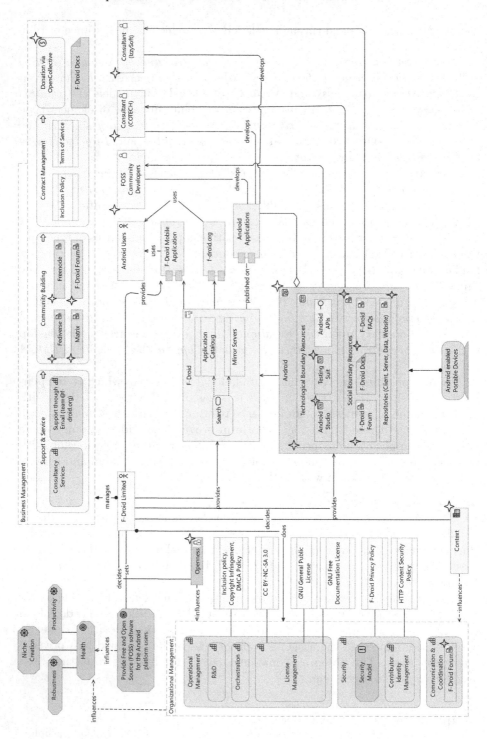

Fig. 3. F-Droid ecosystem architecture modeled using the extended archimate

Furthermore, the architecture of F-Droid is missing marketing & sales strategy defined by F-Droid to promote applications on its online store. The absence of marketing and sales strategies results in degradation of the ecosystem's health as the applications are not sold and marketed well, which means less profit margin. Finally, feedback loop facilitator is another missing feature. Specifically, there is no possibility that users can directly rate, review, or rank applications on F-Droid. Users can rate the source code of the Apps by referring to the Git repository, where the Apps are stored. Feedback can help platform providers and third-party developers in determining user satisfaction. Without a feedback loop facilitator, it would be hard to find out applications that adversely affect the ecosystem.

6 Related Work

Out of numerous research areas in software ecosystems, there are two crucial research areas relevant to our work done under this article. Firstly, systematic designing of software ecosystem architectures. Secondly, modeling techniques to describe and create software ecosystem models.

Christensen et al. [24] describes software ecosystem architecture as the composition of software, business, and organizational structure. Using the concept of software ecosystem architecture, authors have identified improvement in an existing software ecosystem named Danish Telemedicine of the healthcare domain and demonstrated how it could systematically create a new Danish Telemedicine software ecosystem. However, their study of software ecosystem architecture does not provide a deep perspective on the essential concerns of the collaboration between platform providers and third-party providers. Kruize et al. [25] proposes a reference architecture for farm software ecosystems created around an object system comprising production units and resources. Authors in their study have focused on the interoperability between information and communication technology components in a farm software ecosystem developed by different actors on top of an object system. However, they have addressed the collaboration, business, and technological aspect of farm ecosystems dealing with information and communication technology products and services [25].

The Open Platform[8] provides an enterprise reference model which focuses on enterprises' ecosystem or a more comprehensive business ecosystem [26]. However, the enterprise reference model is business ecosystem-oriented. At the same time, software ecosystems can be thought of as an instance of business ecosystem [27]. Authors of [28] have developed a vendor and technology-neutral reference architecture for a digital ecosystem, which provides a set of guidelines to design a digital ecosystem systematically. Like business ecosystems, software ecosystems can also be considered an instance of digital ecosystems [27]. Having said that, a reference architecture for a digital ecosystem is too generic for designing software ecosystems.

---

[8] http://www.opengroup.org/openplatform3.0/op3-snapshot/, Last Access: 1 June 2021.

The work of Sadi et al. [5] mentions two primary procedures for model-based description of software ecosystems. Firstly, by developing a new modeling technique. Secondly, using or extending an existing modeling technique. In the work of Boucharas et al. [29], the authors have developed a new modeling technique using met-modeling. In the work of Yu et al. [30], authors have used the *I* modeling technique* which is a modeling technique to model the intended relationship between the actors from business, technical and organizational perspective [31]. The authors have demonstrated a strategic modeling approach from the I* modeling framework to describe a software ecosystem and represent the dependencies between platform providers, third-party developers, and the end-users. Christensen et al. [24], have demonstrated the use of *Business Model Canvas* (BMC) to model the business view of a software ecosystem and its collaborators. Additionally, to model their proposed software ecosystem architecture's software structure, the authors have used different UML viewpoints. For instance, to model the hardware and software development, they have used *development view*, to model the behavior of software they have used *functional view*.

In the work of Hara et al. [32], authors have demonstrated the modeling of digital enterprise ecosystem with ArchiMate. In their study, authors have illustrated the inappropriateness of existing enterprise modeling approaches in comprehensive model-based designing of digital enterprise ecosystems. Furthermore, they proposed a domain-specific extension of ArchiMate using its specialization extension mechanism by extending it with additional domain-specific modeling classes. Chiprianov et al. [22] proposed a telecommunications profile with domain-specific concepts to model telecommunication-specific tasks named service creation. A similar approach of language extension was taken in the work of Sayeb et al. [33] to extend enterprise architecture language ArchiMate. In their study, the authors added two urbanization concepts with graphical notations by extending the meta-model of ArchiMate.

7   Conclusion and Future Work

In this paper, we propose a reference architecture for software ecosystems. The reference architecture provides architectural support to future platform providers in making knowledgeable and informed design decisions for the systematic design of these systems. It provides guidelines and a blueprint with essential software features and activities concerning the software ecosystem's organizational, technical, and business aspects. The proposed reference architecture also contains elements that can enhance the quality attributes such as productivity, sustainability, robustness, interoperability, modifiability, stakeholder satisfaction, and creativity. Furthermore, we extended the ArchiMate language to facilitate direct modeling of ecosystem-specific concepts. Using our solution concept, we analyzed the architecture of a real-world ecosystem, i.e., F-Droid. We identified the critical features that are currently missing in the architecture.

In the future, design processes to use the reference architecture should be developed. The reference architecture needs be applied in an industrial context and real projects to improve its practice-related aspects. Furthermore, by enabling automatic generation of code out of the reference architecture, the platform provider can save a considerable amount of time and effort. However, the gap between the high-level ecosystem architecture discussed in this paper and the code should be considered and handled during the processes of code generation.

References

1. Gottschalk, S., Yigitbas, E., Engels, G.: Model-based hypothesis engineering for supporting adaptation to uncertain customer needs. In: Shishkov, B. (ed.) BMSD 2020. LNBIP, vol. 391, pp. 276–286. Springer, Cham (2020). https://doi.org/10.1007/978-3-030-52306-0_18
2. Manikas, K., Hansen, K.M.: Software ecosystems-a systematic literature review. J. Syst. Softw. **86**(5), 1294–1306 (2013)
3. Jansen, S., Finkelstein, A., Brinkkemper, S.: A sense of community: a research agenda for software ecosystems. In: International Conference on Software Engineering Companion. IEEE Computer Society, Los Alamitos (2009). https://doi.ieeecomputersociety.org/10.1109/ICSE-COMPANION.2009.5070978
4. Boudreau, K.: Open platform strategies and innovation: granting access vs. devolving control. Manag. Sci. **56**(10), 1849–1872 (2010). https://doi.org/10.1287/mnsc.1100.1215
5. H. Sadi, M., Yu, E.: Designing software ecosystems: how can modeling techniques help? In: Gaaloul, K., Schmidt, R., Nurcan, S., Guerreiro, S., Ma, Q. (eds.) CAISE 2015. LNBIP, vol. 214, pp. 360–375. Springer, Cham (2015). https://doi.org/10.1007/978-3-319-19237-6_23
6. 5 mistakes to avoid when deploying an enterprise app store—cio. https://cio.com/article/2394413. Accessed 16 Aug 2020
7. Jazayeri, B., Zimmermann, O., Engels, G., Küster, J., Kundisch, D., Szopinski, D.: Design options of store-oriented software ecosystems: an investigation of business decisions. In: Shishkov, B. (ed.) BMSD 2018. LNBIP, vol. 319, pp. 390–400. Springer, Cham (2018). https://doi.org/10.1007/978-3-319-94214-8_30
8. Galster, M., Avgeriou, P.: Empirically-grounded reference architectures: a proposal. In: Proceedings of the Joint ACM SIGSOFT Conference - QoSA and ACM SIGSOFT Symposium - ISARCS on Quality of Software Architectures - QoSA and Architecting Critical Systems - ISARCS, QoSA-ISARCS 2011, pp. 153–158. Association for Computing Machinery, New York (2011). https://doi.org/10.1145/2000259.2000285
9. Angelov, S., Grefen, P., Greefhorst, D.: A classification of software reference architectures: analyzing their success and effectiveness. In: 2009 Joint Working IEEE/IFIP Conference on Software Architecture (WICSA) & 3rd European Conference on Software Architecture (ECSA). IEEE Computer Society, Los Alamitos (2009). https://doi.ieeecomputersociety.org/10.1109/WICSA.2009.5290800
10. Mhamdia, A.B.H.S.: Performance measurement practices in software ecosystem. Int. J. Prod. Perform. Manag. (2013)
11. Jazayeri, B., Zimmermann, O., Küster, J., Engels, G., Szopinski, D., Kundisch, D.: Patterns of store-oriented software ecosystems: detection, classification, and analysis of design options. Latin American PLOP (2018)

12. van den Berk, I., Jansen, S., Luinenburg, L.: Software ecosystems: a software ecosystem strategy assessment model. In: Proceedings of the Fourth European Conference on Software Architecture: Companion Volume, ECSA 2010, pp. 127–134. Association for Computing Machinery, New York (2010) https://doi.org/10.1145/1842752.1842781

13. Axelsson, J., Papatheocharous, E., Andersson, J.: Characteristics of software ecosystems for federated embedded systems: a case study. Inf. Softw. Technol. **56**(11), 1457–1475 (2014). https://doi.org/10.1016/j.infsof.2014.03.011

14. Ghazawneh, A.: Towards a boundary resources theory of software platforms. Ph.D. dissertation, Jönköping International Business School (2012)

15. Alves, C., Oliveira, J., Jansen. S.: Software ecosystems governance - a systematic literature review and research agenda. In: Proceedings of the 19th International Conference on Enterprise Information Systems, ICEIS, INSTICC, vol. 1, pp. 215–226. SciTePress (2017)

16. Bosch, J.: From software product lines to software ecosystems. In: Proceedings of the 13th International Software Product Line Conference, SPLC 2009. Carnegie Mellon University, USA, pp. 111–119 (2009)

17. Atkinson, C., Kühne, T.: A deep perspective on the archimate enterprise architecture modeling language. Enterp. Model. Inf. Syst. Archit. Int. J. Concept Model. **15**, 2:1–2:25 (2020)

18. Lankhorst, M., et al.: Enterprise Architecture at Work, vol. 352. Springer, Heidelberg (2009). https://doi.org/10.1007/978-3-642-01310-2

19. Guizzardi, G.: Ontological foundations for structural conceptual models. Ph.D. dissertation, University of Twente (2005)

20. Rosemann, M., Green, P., Indulska, M.: A reference methodology for conducting ontological analyses. In: Atzeni, P., Chu, W., Lu, H., Zhou, S., Ling, T.-W. (eds.) ER 2004. LNCS, vol. 3288, pp. 110–121. Springer, Heidelberg (2004). https://doi.org/10.1007/978-3-540-30464-7_10

21. T Group: ArchiMate® 3.0.1 Specification. Van Haren Publishing (2017). https://books.google.de/books?id=Jmo3DwAAQBAJ

22. Chiprianov, V., Kermarrec, Y., Rouvrais, S., Simonin, J.: Extending enterprise architecture modeling languages for domain specificity and collaboration: application to telecommunication service design. Softw. Syst. Model. **13**(3), 963–974 (2014). https://doi.org/10.1007/s10270-012-0298-0

23. Ecore - eclipsepedia. https://wiki.eclipse.org/Ecore. Accessed 13 Jan 2021

24. Christensen, H.B., Hansen, K.M., Kyng, M., Manikas, K.: Analysis and design of software ecosystem architectures-towards the 4s telemedicine ecosystem. Inf. Softw. Technol. **56**(11), 1476–1492 (2014)

25. Kruize, J., Wolfert, J., Scholten, H., Verdouw, C., Kassahun, A., Beulens, A.: A reference architecture for farm software ecosystems. Comput. Electron. Agric. **125**(C), 12–28 (2016). https://doi.org/10.1016/j.compag.2016.04.011

26. Open platform 3.0 snapshotÂ - enterprise ecosystems. http://www.opengroup.org/openplatform3.0/op3-snapshot/p3.htm#fig_ent_ecosystem_rm. Accessed 22 Jan 2021

27. Jansen, S., Cusumano, M.A.: Defining software ecosystems: a survey of software platforms and business network governance. In: Software Ecosystems. Edward Elgar Publishing (2013)

28. Averian, A.: A reference architecture for digital ecosystems. Internet Things, J. Sen, Ed. ch. 6. IntechOpen, Rijeka (2018). https://doi.org/10.5772/intechopen.77395

29. Boucharas, V., Jansen, S., Brinkkemper, S.: Formalizing software ecosystem modeling. In: Proceedings of the 1st International Workshop on Open Component Ecosystems, IWOCE 2009, pp. 41–50. Association for Computing Machinery, New York (2009). https://doi.org/10.1145/1595800.1595807
30. Yu, E., Deng, S.: Understanding software ecosystems: a strategic modeling approach. In: CEUR Workshop Proceedings, vol. 746, p. 01 (2011)
31. Eric, S., Giorgini, P., Maiden, N., Mylopoulos, J.: Social Modeling for Requirements Engineering. MIT Press, Cambridge (2011)
32. Pittl, B., Bork, D.: Modeling digital enterprise ecosystems with archimate: a mobility provision case study. ICServ 2017. LNCS, vol. 10371, pp. 178–189. Springer, Cham (2017). https://doi.org/10.1007/978-3-319-61240-9_17
33. Sayeb, Y., Ayba, M., Ghezela, H.B.: Extending enterprise architecture modeling languages: application to requirements of information systems urbanization. In: Lecture Notes on Information Theory, vol. 3, no. 1 (2015)

Managing Knowledge of Intelligent Systems
The Design of a Chatbot Using Domain-Specific Knowledge

Marcus Grum[1(✉)], David Kotarski[1], Maximilian Ambros[2], Tibebu Biru[2], Hermann Krallmann[2], and Norbert Gronau[1]

[1] University of Potsdam, Potsdam, Germany
mgrum@lswi.de
[2] Krallmann AG, Berlin, Germany

Abstract. Since more and more business tasks are enabled by Artificial Intelligence (AI)-based techniques, the number of knowledge-intensive tasks increase as trivial tasks can be automated and non-trivial tasks demand human-machine interactions. With this, challenges regarding the management of knowledge workers and machines rise [9]. Furthermore, knowledge workers experience time pressure, which can lead to a decrease in output quality. Artificial Intelligence-based systems (AIS) have the potential to assist human workers in knowledge-intensive work. By providing a domain-specific language, contextual and situational awareness as well as their process embedding can be specified, which enables the management of human and AIS to ease knowledge transfer in a way that process time, cost and quality are improved significantly. This contribution outlines a framework to designing these systems and accounts for their implementation.

Keywords: Domain-specific language · Morphologic box · Explainability

1 Introduction

The capabilities of intelligent systems are increasing with regard to data gathering and analysis. They tap numerous data sources provided in digitized economics contexts, such as business processes and Industry 4.0 environments, and increasingly use AI-based techniques to analyze this data and learn from it [17]. The interplay between humans and machines becomes essential, as all intelligent systems are based on either knowledge representations from AI-based algorithms, by externalized human experiences or a combination of both [9]. Thus the knowledge transfer between machines and human process participants as well as among process participants is key for an optimal business process and demands for management.

© Springer Nature Switzerland AG 2021
B. Shishkov (Ed.): BMSD 2021, LNBIP 422, pp. 78–96, 2021.
https://doi.org/10.1007/978-3-030-79976-2_5

Faced with the task of reducing costs, Ducker even argues knowledge is the only meaningful resource today [4]. Yet, the potential of the adaptability and information processing power of intelligent systems to act as knowledge carrier has not be considered or assessed thus far: If it was possible to design intelligent systems to align with a certain role as process participant in specific knowledge transfer situations and intervene by management-induced interventions, the business processes efficiency can increase, e.g. by means of reduced time or increased quality of process outcomes. For the situational awareness and the selection of interventions, influencing factors need to be known and incorporated into intelligent systems. Further, their behavior needs to be controlled throughout the process. Therefore, the following paper outlines the systematical examination of tools for the creation of Artificial Intelligence-based systems (AIS), which refer in an example case to a chatbot response to online customer requests, and the design of a domain-specific language specifying the intelligent system for the optimization of knowledge transfer.

Hence, the following research will focus on optimization of knowledge transfer with the help of modeling techniques that can answer the following research question: *"How can intelligent systems be managed with the aid of a domain-specific language?"* This paper intends not to draw an all-embracing description of concrete, technical realizations of those novel management attempts. It intends to set a first step to a clarification of non-transparent knowledge use and controlling. Hence, sub research questions are:

1. "How can an adequate foundation for the construction of intelligent chatbots be identified systematically?"
2. "How can domain-specific knowledge be integrated with AI based systems?"

In accordance with the Design Science Research Methodology (DSRM) [13], this research has been initiated by a problem-centered entry focusing the research questions presented and the remainder of this paper is structured as follows. The second section presents a theoretical foundation of knowledge use and managing intelligent systems. The third section identifies requirements for the problem of modeling intelligent systems and a methodological proceeding. These are realized by a design with which this research problem shall be overcome. The fourth section demonstrates the design's functioning in a real-world case study, which is evaluated in the fifth section. The final section summarizes the extent to which the initial problem has been solved and to what extent the research questions can be answered.

2   Theoretical Foundation and Underlying Concepts

The first sub-section works out an AIS definition, so that an interpretation for modeling chatbots as intelligent systems can be established. Then, knowledge modeling approaches are collected, so that a foundation for the meta-model design is available.

2.1 Chatbots and Artificial Intelligent-Based Systems

Intelligent systems are able to sense their environment, to process environmental information, such as with the aid of AI-based algorithms, and to respond accordingly by different forms of actuators [7]. The key differentiators of the AI-based Systems (AIS) mentioned here are the ways how they sense their environment (e.g. through sensors), which kind of powerful AI algorithms are applied (e.g. deep neuronal networks) and how they react to it (e.g. by a certain motion or speech).

Chatbots are a prominent example of AIS these days, which have become increasingly popular for end users as well as businesses. A chatbot is a program that simulates a conversation between a human conversation partner and itself [2]. For example, the chatbot receives an input query from the user (e.g. a question, such as "what is your name?"). Then, it applies different kinds of AI-based algorithms for processing its perception and finally responds via its verbalizing actuators by presenting text (e.g. "My name is chatbot." or "Call me chatbot"). In order to understand and interpret the question as well as be creative to create the response, the chatbot uses some form of internal and external knowledge. In addition, the chatbot incorporates many more complex components for recognizing the conversation partner's intention, translating queries, considering the business' motivation. All these components are subsumed under the term of *processing* in the AIS definition presented.

The emergence of chatbots and other intelligent systems powered by machine learning and AI triggered humans to question how such systems process and make decisions. Out of this, the need for explainability emerged [12,20] i.e. explaining the decisions in human terms.

Interim Conclusion: The approach worked out in the following differentiates from contemporary attempts for explaining the behavior of AIS as it focuses on the visualization of knowledge provided by external systems of a certain process context and make it accessible for AIS. Its significance is present because it enables human to control input and output of AIS such as chatbots.

2.2 Modeling Knowledge

To make the most out of the conversations, chatbots need to be able to access knowledge that is distributed within organizations. Typically, it is stored in different silos, such as product catalogues, price lists in Product Information Management (PIM) systems, knowledge about customers in Customer Relationship Management (CRM) systems, and product knowledge or process knowledge in Knowledge Management (KM) systems. So far, the following attempts for modeling knowledge are present.

First, knowledge can be modeled by *propositional logic* or *predicate logic* that evaluate the content of truth of a statement and corresponding predicates [1]. As dialogues surpass the information content of statements to be true and false in everyday life, this knowledge modeling approach is not very attractive for chatbots.

Second, knowledge can be modeled by *rule-based systems* that are able to deal with logical dependencies and relations. These consist of a *factual basis* such as databases, a *rule base* that is probably expert made and provides conditional clauses, as well as an *interpretation engine*, which executes rules on the factual basis [8]. While simple rules-based systems are easy to implement, they lack the level of detail that is necessary to send a high-quality response by AIS, such as the chatbot to be designed.

Third, knowledge can be modeled by *semantic nets* that consider objects, their properties, relations among different kinds of objects and their instances. Here, *frames* extend semantic networks, so that data of these objects are stored by uniform schemes at the corresponding object-specific frame description [15]. Although these networks can be associated with the silos mentioned above, these lack in a clear and human readable visualization.

In this sense, *domain-specific languages* (DSL) can be considered as a form of frames referring to high-level software implementation languages that support concepts and abstractions that are related to a particular (application) domain [16]. Since this kind of approach represents organizational knowledge, so that the chatbot can directly process it, the following focuses on the construction of an adequate DSL.

Fourth, *process-oriented knowledge modeling* intends to visually model knowledge with its creation as well as its use along knowledge-intensive processes [6]. While these have strengths in visualization, they lack the ability to provide object information, so that the chatbot can process it directly.

Interim Conclusion: The approach worked out in the following differentiates from contemporary attempts for modeling knowledge as it focuses on the combination of DSL and process-oriented description languages to make knowledge accessible for AIS. Its significance is present because it enables human to control AIS such as chatbots.

3 Objectives and Methodology

Following the DSRM approach [13], this section identifies objectives independent from a design. Then, a methodology is presented that satisfies methodological objectives. These are separated from the design and its demonstration so that artifacts can be created before, the fulfillment of requirements can be evaluated. Following a methodological foundation, designed artifacts give evidence in a demonstration in regard to their functioning.

3.1 Objectives

The aim is to design an intelligent chatbot whose knowledge can be managed with the help of a DSL. Therefore, this section presents a set of requirements that have to be considered at the artifact realizations.

1. An adequate foundation of tools required for the development of a chatbot needs to be systematically and methodically identified.
2. Different organizational knowledge sources are to be considered for the chatbot's dialogues. As such, we can find silos of PIM, CRM and KM systems.
3. Knowledge of intelligent systems which is intended to be managed needs to be visualized so that human managers are able to comprehend the effect of their management activities on systems managed.
4. Data and information required for the performing of intelligent systems need to be integrated on a common technical level so that a chatbot can process it directly.

Based on these requirements, a methodological foundation that focuses on a morphological analysis and a design-oriented artifact creation is considered.

3.2 Morphological Analysis

Following Zwicky, in order to explore all the possible solutions to a multi-dimensional, non-quantified complex problem for various domains, the *morphological analysis* is a suitable tool [19, p. 34]. It is accepted in various domains, such as anatomy, geology, botany and biology, and Ritchey summarizes the history of morphological methods [14].

By proceeding with the general morphological analysis, the morphologic box, the so called *Zwicky box*, is constructed in five iterative steps [18]: The problem *dimensions* are properly defined first. Since these probably refer to relevant issues, a practical applicability is supported. Then, *parameters* are defined as a spectrum of values for the dimensions. Usually, these refer to different solution approaches for that dimension. Third, by setting the parameters against each other in an n-dimensional matrix, the morphological box is created. Since each cell of the n-dimensional box represents one parameter of the problem, the selection of one parameter per dimension marks a particular state or condition of the problem complexity. The selection is called *configuration* and represents one solution of the complex problem. In our case, an empirical survey has been realized to identify the best configuration which has the widest acceptance. A fourth step scrutinizes and evaluates possible solutions in regard to the intended purpose. In our case, this refers to the identification of the best foundation for the chatbot construction. In a fifth step, the optimal solution, which is the morphologic box, is practically applied. The necessary insights from the application are considered in previous steps.

4   Design

In accordance with the DSRM of Peffers [13], this section presents artifacts that are designed in order to overcome the problem of modeling AIS. Here, the first sub-section presents the design of the systematic selection of tools which is

Dim. Category	Dimension	Guiding Question	Scale
			Finally Selected
Technical Dimensions	Presence of digital representation of systems	Does the system provide a digital representation?	Yes/No
	Live access to systems	Is the system able to deal with real-time data?	Real-time data
	Ability of systems to communicate (technique)	Is the system able to communicate?	Yes/No
	Ability of systems to communicate (standard)	Is the system able to communicate?	Yes/No
	Ability of systems to communicate (interfaces)	Is the system able to communicate?	Yes/No
	Ability of systems to sense	Is the system able to sense its environment?	Yes/No
	Ability of systems to carry out actions	Is the system able to interact with its environment?	Yes/No
	Ability of systems to process	Is the system able to process data?	Yes/No
	Requiredness of additional setup	Do we need any additional setup (e.g. client application, third-party connections, etc.)?	Yes/No
	Presence of API	Can we access the data via an API?	Yes/No
Knowledge Dimensions	Availability of data	Is the system able to interact with its environment?	Yes/No
	Availability of explicit knowledge	Is the data easily available?	Yes/No
	Availability of tacit knowledge	Hard to identify? Structured form?	Yes/No
	Role as knowledge carrier in process	Does the system participate in the process, so that it uses its knowledge? Does it have a role in the process?	Yes/No
	Degree of articulation [German: Artikulationsgrad]	Is it hard to explain the function?	Numeric Scale of KMDL3.0
	Degree of generality [German: Allgemeinheitsgrad]	How general is the knowledge? Can it be used in multiple dialogues?	Numeric Scale of KMDL3.0
	Competence [German: fachliche Einsicht]	Does the system address competences for the dialog?	Yes/No
	Experience	Does the system address experiences for the dialog?	Yes/No
	Documentation availability	Is the product completed by a great documentation?	Wiki pages
	Sample data availability	Can we access sample data?	Yes/No
AI Dimensions	Input data availability	Does the system support unsupervised learning?	Explicitly indicated
	Unsupervised functional approaches	Does the system support unsupervised learning?	Yes/No -> Availability
	Input data availability	Does the system support supervised learning?	Explicitly/Implicitly/Not indicated at all
	Output data availability	Does the system support supervised learning?	Explicitly/Implicitly/Not indicated at all
	Supervised functional approaches	Does the system support supervised learning?	Availability / Not Available
	State data availability	Does the system support reinforced learning?	Explicitly/Implicitly/Not indicated at all
	Action data availability	Does the system support reinforced learning?	Explicitly/Implicitly/Not indicated at all
	Reward data availability	Does the system support reinforced learning?	Explicitly/Implicitly/Not indicated at all
	Punishment data availability	Does the system support reinforced learning?	Yes/No
	Reinforced functional approaches	Does the system support reinforced learning?	Availability/ Not available
Customer Dimensions	Perceptability in dialog system	How can data be perceived in the dialog system?	Obviousness / Questionable
	Usefulness of data	How might this data be useful in a conversation with the chatbot?	Yes/No
	SME relevance	How relevant is this software for SMEs (KMUs)?	Yes/No
	Expected relevance	What future relevance for this software do we predict?	Yes/No
Vendor Dimensions	System costs	What is the cost of the system (license, consulting, maintenance, infrastructure)?	Total costs
	Paid access	Do we need to pay for (API) access?	Total costs
	Vendor market share	What is the market share of the vendor? How many of the clients are SMEs in Germany? How many companies use this kind of software?	Revenue
	Vendor reputation	What is the vendor reputation?	Target group fit
	Vendor business model uniqueness	How is the vendor's business model unique?	Long term advantage from software (huge / medium / small)
	Trial version	Is there a trial developer account?	Cost
	Technical support	What is the level of tech support by the vendor?	Community based
	Vendor technique advantage	What is the vendor's technological advantage?	USP in market availability (huge / medium / small / qualitative)
Financial Dimensions	Presence of data structure	Does the system provide a data structure, so that the implementation is not expensive?	Yes/No
Political Dimensions	Limitations by laws	Does the use of system-specific data correspond to contemporary laws?	Yes/No
Ethical Dimensions	Limitations by labor unions	Does the use of system-specific data correspond to contemporary ethical understanding?	Yes/No

Fig. 1. Morphologic box with best parameters.

relevant for the implementation of an AIS. Then, the draft for a DSL is presented, with which the technical understanding of AIS is described. The third sub-section designs a human-readable form of visualization for the DSL.

4.1   Design of a Morphologic Box

In order to systematically identify the requirements in different dimensions, a morphological box was constructed. The dimensions examined during this process were: Technology, Knowledge, AI, Customers, Vendors, Finance, Politics,

Ethics. For each dimension, the corresponding properties were compiled and concretized by appropriate guiding questions. Subsequently, different scales per dimension were recorded and evaluated by means of a consensus to determine whether there are conditions that are mutually exclusive. Finally, the possible scales were examined by means of a survey of experts. On the basis of 12 complete survey entries, the best configuration of the morphological box has been identified with the aid of the widest acceptance per dimension. Figure 1 visualizes best scales per dimension only.

4.2   Design of a DSL

In order to enable a dialogue-based system to answer queries in high quality, it must have access to operational knowledge, such as product, customer and process knowledge. This knowledge is available in various sources; Parts of this knowledge are found in product catalogues, price lists and CRM systems as well as in various ontological levels, such as departments, sales and service staff. It is therefore necessary to bring together the extensive operational knowledge by means of knowledge engineering and make it available in the dialog system.

The necessary linguistic knowledge for dialogue design and the situation-specific knowledge should be prepared and made available for a dialogue-based query. For this purpose, a suitable representation should be developed that enables optimal dialogue-based processing. One possibility of representation is a DSL. A DSL is a suitable linguistic knowledge representation that targets a situation-specific problem, instead of general software problem [5]. Then, the dialogue-based system uses the data from the DSL to answer complex questions in dialogue with the customer and can be seamlessly integrated in the operational context.

There are a number of open source tools to design DSLs. Some of these tools include *JetBrains MPS*, *Xtext*, and *TextX*. In this work, the language used for the DSL specification is *TextX* [3] per design decision, which is a meta-language model suitable for defining grammar descriptions and its rules to build a textual language in Python. Based on the grammar definition, it generates a metal-model and a parser for the language. The expressions of the new language are parsed by the parser and a graph of Python objects which corresponds to the meta-model is built. The main objective is to create and realize the design of a DSL for the specification of complex dynamic linguistic knowledge and complex context-dependent knowledge to be used in a dialog-based system as well as its interactive visualization. Then, a sustainable and methodically secured knowledge acquisition and knowledge utilization can be achieved.

The following words in Table 1 are list of terms that are important for the construction of the DSL grammar. Moreover, the function of each term is explained by the definition provided.

Table 1. List of terms used in DSL grammar definition.

Term	Definition
Actions	List of things the bot can do or say
Aliases	Alternate name for an entity
Dialogues	Conversation turns between user and bot
Intents	Things we expect the user to say
Products	List of items with properties or other attributes
Responses	Hard-coded values or messages the bot can respond with
Slots	User-defined variables which need to be tracked in a conversation

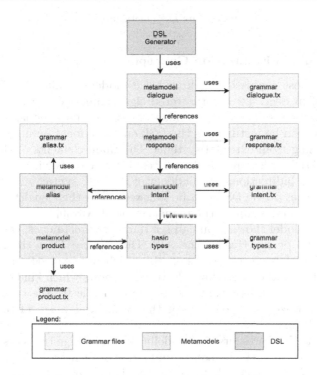

Fig. 2. Generator that combines all defined grammar rules to construct the DSL.

As for illustration, Fig. 2 presents the construction of a simple DSL that is initiated by the DSL generator. The grammar definition of each entity or rather component that makes up part of the overall DSL is combined with the remaining ones to generate the full structure. Each grammar definition is used to interpret and parse the corresponding DSL file.

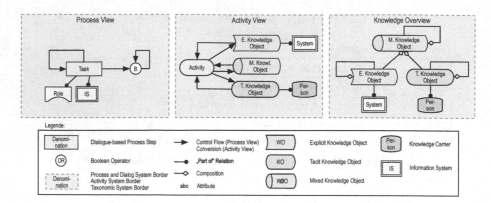

Fig. 3. The DSL meta-model.

4.3 Design of a Visualization Concept

Following the most sophisticated knowledge modeling called NMDL [10], the DSL described in Sect. 4.2 is interpreted algorithmically and transcoded to a visualization variant, which corresponds to its subset meta-model of Fig. 3. The subset selection can be justified, as the DSL ought to focus on input and output knowledge coming from external systems. The main elements of the DSL thus refer to the NMDL's elements of the process view, activity view and knowledge overview. Since a bidirectional dependency of the DSL syntax and the visualization exists, changes of the DSL can be followed up at the visualization and vice versa. By this, it shall support the management of AIS [9].

In the meta-model shown, you can see three gray rectangles, each representing an individual perspective on the AIS. The *Process View* characterizes the sequential order of business process tasks which are realized with the aid of boolean operators and control flows. Further, it shows which kind of system and which kind of process participants have a certain role for the task realization. Thus, it characterizes the behavior of the procedural range of processes and process networks [9].

The *Activity View* presents the modeling of knowledge transfers among persons and systems. Here, the person-bound forms of tacit knowledge, the person-unbound form of explicit knowledge as well as their combination in mixed knowledge forms is issued so that knowledge conversions can be clarified in accordance with Nonaka and Takeuchi [11]. The *Knowledge Overview* characterizes the hierarchical decomposition of modeled knowledge objects in order to enable a comfortable dealing with numerous modeling items. It also supports the creation of clean and clear models that are easy to interpret.

5 Case Study - The Chatbot as AIS

Following the DSRM, this sections applies the artifacts designed to demonstrate their use and evaluate if the initial research problem has been answered. The first sub-section demonstrates the morphologic box in order to identify a best tool foundation. The second sub-section demonstrates the interaction of the DSL and corresponding visualization mechanisms to manage the chatbot knowledge base.

5.1 Identification of an Ideal Chatbot Foundation

In accordance with the fifth step of the morphological analysis described in Sect. 3.2, the previously established best configuration of the morphologic box has been applied for the identification of a best tool foundation for the case of a chatbot construction. The better a parameter of a tool performs at a certain dimension, the more suitable the tool is for being an adequate foundation of the chatbot construction. The case thus prepares the knowledge management of AIS.

In a workshop session with 12 research and consulting experts of the domains of knowledge management, artificial intelligence, process management and business applications, the guidance questions were answered individually for the software tools that were identified by the workshop participants. In total 22 tools were divided into four clusters, which namely are CRM tools with 5 systems, PIM tools with 9 systems, KM tools with 3 systems and AI tools with 5 systems.

As a consensus of the experts, best tools for each cluster were then determined in the final stage. Preferring the tools that are closest to the previously determined optimum, the detailed analysis can be seen in Fig. 7 and Fig. 8 at Appendix 7 and the suitability has been visualized by the color range from red (bad) to green (good).

For the chatbot construction, the systems in the CRM, PIM and KM clusters were classified as knowledge sources that provide required information to the chatbot easily. AI tools rather are used to support the construction of the chatbot. For the CRM cluster, *Hubspot* and *Pipedrive* were chosen because they have a good API and adequate test data availability. In the PIM cluster, *PimCore* was chosen as a priority and extended by *Plytix* because of the vendor business model uniqueness and open source license or price model. In the KM cluster, *Confluence* was chosen because of its price model. In the AI cluster, *TensorFlow* and *PyBrain* have been chosen because of the possibility to explicitly consider data at different learning approaches. All these systems thus serve as knowledge base to support the basic function of the chatbot.

5.2 Controlling the Chatbot's Knowledge

The demonstration of the DSL and its visualization refers to the construction of an AI-based chatbot. Its task refers to dealing with first contact of customers on a homepage. The case thus shows the visual knowledge management of AIS. Although numerous purposes for customer requests on homepages exist, for the purpose of presenting a clear model, the following focuses on requests about price information of bags.

DSL Example: In order to demonstrate a simple DSL construction based on grammar rules depicted in Fig. 2, an example of a simple conversation exchange between the customer and the chatbot has been prepared by the DSL file definitions in Listing 1.1 up to Listing 1.7. The most illustrative entry point can be found in Listing 1.1, which shows the dialog DSL construct.

```
1  dialog: ask_for_product  # name: dialog_name
2      -> intent: greet
3      <- response: utter_greet
4      <- response: utter_how_can_i_help
5      -> intent: ask_for_bag:
6         slot:
7               product:  bag
8      <- response: utter_price_information
9         slot:
10              price_information:  900
11     -> intent: goodbye
```

Listing 1.1. dialogs.dsl example

The different elements used to construct the "dialogs" DSL are as follows:

- *"ask_for_product"* name of dialog guided by intent
- *"->"* symbol to identify user utterance
- *"<-"* symbol to identify bot utterance
- *"intent:greet"* user utterance with intent 'greet'
- *"response:utter_greet"* bot utterance with response 'utter_greet'
- *"response:utter_how_can_i _help"* bot utterance with response 'utter_help'
- *"intent:ask_for_bag"* user utterance with intent 'ask_for_bag'
- *"slot: product: bag"* keeps the context of the conversation by storing important piece of information
- *"response:utter'price'information"* bot utterance with response of price information
  - *"slot: price_information: 900"* keeps track of context of conversation by storing the customized 'price_information'
- *"intent:goodbye"* user utterance with intent 'goodbye'

All the remaining separate DSL file definitions shown in Listing 1.2 up to Listing 1.7 are interwoven with this listing and complement the dialog presented by the provision relevant knowledge from PIM, CRM and KM systems selected (see Sect. 5.1). Further, they store the knowledge acquired in the conversation via slots directly in the DSL so that the chatbot's operational knowledge is also accessible.

Visualization Examples: Following the meta-model design presented in Fig. 3, the following presents the modeling of the AI-based chatbot. It is based on the DSL files just issued. Figure 4 clarifies the behavior of the chatbot which is derived from the underlying DSL file of Listing 1.1. Although the following

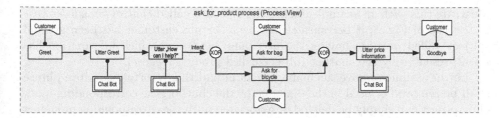

Fig. 4. The process view of the chatbot example.

focuses on the DSL visualization, because of the direct dependencies of both, modifications at the visualization are projected on the DSL and vice versa.

In the figure, one can see that the conversation with the chatbot is started by the customer (task called *Greet*). Having uttered the greeting by the chatbot (task called *Utter Greet*), it aims to find out the reason for the customer's visit (task called *Utter 'How can I help?'*). In the case the customer asks for a bag (task called *Ask for bag*, the chatbot first presents the corresponding price information (task called *Utter price information*).

The detailed knowledge transfers have been specified by the activity views of Fig. 5, which have been derived from the underlying DSL files as follows:

- *Activity View 1* mainly gets information on the basis of Listing 1.4,
- *Activity View 2* considers information of the Listings 1.3, 1.4 and 1.7,
- *Activity View 3* obtains information of Listing 1.5,
- *Activity View 4* mainly bases on Listing 1.2 and 1.5.

Since the system borders of activity views provide the same naming than the associated task, each activity view specifies the knowledge transfers of a certain task. As the bold written attributes of the four activity views show, the concrete values of process instances are assigned via slots. By this, the concrete process instance of each customer - chatbot - conversation can be visualized. Further, it becomes clear how different systems interact. To illustrate this with an example, facing the activity called *Utter price information* in the bottom right of Fig. 5, it becomes clear that three kinds of systems interact in order to deal with the customer's request. The CRM system provides information about the current offer, the PIM system provides the original price information of the bag requested, and the chatbot provides the concrete product request and presents the response for the customer request. So, the customer gets to know relevant, customized properties regarding the initial request called *desires of bag*, which is 900 *Euro* less than the standard price of 1.000 *Euro*.

The complete knowledge overviews can be seen at Fig. 6. Since the knowledge objects provide the same naming as the activity views, the concrete knowledge, data and information used at each activity and its corresponding task becomes clear. As the bold written attributes of the three knowledge overviews show, the concrete values of process instances are taken from the activity views. By this, the knowledge base of the chatbot presents the knowledge about each customer. To illustrate this with an example, facing the overview called *chatbot knowledge base* in the top of Fig. 6, it becomes clear how a certain customer has been greeted (object called *greeting* having the attribute 'hey') and which information has been presented by the chatbot (object called *product request*).

Let us assume to have the management intend that a certain goodbye phrase shall be removed or used in the dialogue by the chatbot, the corresponding modeling object can simply be deleted or associated with the corresponding modeling object of the knowledge base Fig. 6, which is in this case the object called *goodbye*. Further management attempts refer to the modification of the dialog flow of Fig. 4 and shall be oriented to the symbiotic knowledge management approach of human and artificial knowledge bearers [9].

6   Evaluation

In accordance with the DSRM of Peffers [13], this section evaluates the demonstration issued in the previous section, if requirements are fulfilled, that have been presented in Sect. 3.1.

– Req. 1 has been satisfied because the methodology of a morphological analysis has been realized in order to create a tool for analyzing different kinds of tools for their suitability to be a foundation of the chatbot creation. By applying the empirically verified morphologic box and identifying a consensus on the evaluation of attractive tools from the viewpoint of practical experts, an adequate foundation has been systematically and methodically identified.
– Req. 2 has been satisfied because the silos *Hubspot* (CRM system), *PimCore* (PIM system) and *Confluence* (KM system) have been considered as organizational knowledge sources and they have been considered in the chatbot dialogue realization using the AI tools called *PyBrain* and *TensorFlow*.
– Req. 3 has been satisfied because the visualization concept and the DSL directly depend on each other. Since the modification of the DSL is directly visualized at the human readable knowledge visualization, and human modifications are directly transformed to the DSL, the effect of management activities on the chatbot becomes comprehensible.
– Req. 4 has been satisfied because the different knowledge sources have been projected onto the DSL, which functions as a common technical level. So, the chatbot can directly process on the DSL for insuring AI-based components realize the dialogue.

Since requirements have been jointly satisfied, and the demonstration has shown the practical application of the artifacts designed, the modeling and management of AI-based intelligent systems has shown exemplary result in a simple dialogue situation. Next implementation steps will address more complex situations and prove the functioning of sophisticated conversation flow versions.

7   Conclusion

The first research question (*"How can an adequate foundation for the construction of intelligent chatbots be identified systematically?"*) can be answered by conducting a morphological analysis. On the basis of an empirical research, most relevant parameters of the identification of an adequate foundation for the chatbot construction have been identified. By using the morphologic box constructed, best tools as knowledge sources and as AI tools have been identified, which refer to *Hubspot* (CRM system), *PimCore* (PIM system), *Confluence* (KM system) as well as *PyBrian* and *TensorFlow* (AI system).

The second research question (*"How can domain-specific knowledge be integrated with AI-based systems?"*) can be answered by the concrete DSL design, the visualization concept and the integration of both. This is achieved as follows: domain-specific knowledge is directly codified at the DSL. Then, the DSL is imported or rather extracted from the knowledge sources, such as *Hubspot*, *PimCore* and *Confluence*, so that it can be processed directly by the chatbot and its AI components. Since the modeling language visualizes the DSL foundation, the chatbot and its AI-based components can be manipulated directly by human readable modeling objects and drag and drop mechanisms.

Thus, the main research question (*"How can intelligent systems be managed with the aid of a domain-specific language?"*) can be answered by the specified way to integrate domain-specific knowledge at DSL. By making it visual, the knowledge use becomes manageable and the behavior of AIS can be controlled. Since the design is independent from the specific AI approach, different kinds of AI algorithms can operate on the DSL specified.

Although managing knowledge of AIS has been considered in a practical validation with researchers, the real-world case study presented has not been validated in everyday situations facing end customers. Thus, the controlling of arbitrary complex disturbances has not been issued, yet.

Next steps of this research will focus on the examination of the chatbot by end customers. Here, the refinement of modeling objects is evaluated so that intents, aliases, products, types, responses and dialogue objects can be differentiated. Further, extending the collection of the tool base of the morphological analysis is attractive.

Appendices

1 Domain-Specific Language Listings

```
1  action:get_product # action:action_name
2  action:get_reclamation_protocol
3  action:get_invoice
4  action:get_offer
```

Listing 1.2. actions.dsl example

```
1  alias:member # alias:alias_name
2      Member
3      client
4      customer
```
Listing 1.3. aliases.dsl example

```
1  intent:greet # intent:intent_name
2      hey
3      hello
4      hi slot:first_name # alias:first_name
5      good morning
6      good evening
7      hey there
8  intent:goodbye
9      bye
10     goodbye
11     see you around
12     see you later
```
Listing 1.4. intents.dsl example

```
1  product:15495 # product:product_identifier
2      family: accessories
3      category:
4      supplier_zaro
5      print_accessories
6      master_accessories_bags
7      name: Bag
8      attributes:
9        ean: 1234
10       weight: 500.00
11       price: 1000.00
```
Listing 1.5. products.dsl example

```
1  response:utter_greet   # response:response_name
2      nice to meet you
3      hi there
4      hi slot:first_name # slot:first_name
5  response:utter_how_can_i_help
6  responce:utter_price_information
```
Listing 1.6. responses.dsl example

```
1  slot:first_name # slot:slot_name
2      name: John
```
Listing 1.7. slots.dsl example

2 Visualization of Listings

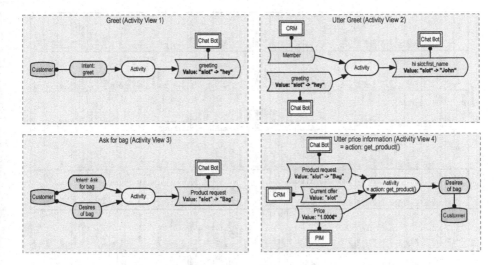

Fig. 5. The activity views of the chatbot example.

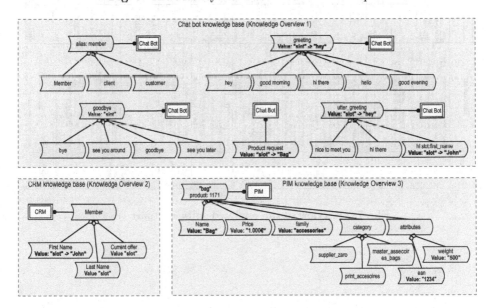

Fig. 6. The knowledge overviews of the chatbot example.

3 Overview of the Tools Analyzed

Dim. Category	Dimension	Tool Selection							
		Knowledge Management			AI Library / Platforms				
		Confluence	Tallium	Comaround	Tensor Flow	PyTorch	Google Dialog Flow	Amazon LEX	Pybrain
Technical Dimensions	Presence of digital representation of systems	Yes	Yes	Yes	No	No	Yes	Yes	No
	Live access to systems	Real-time data	Real-time data	Real-time data	Real-time data	Real-time data	Real-time data	Real-time data	Real-time data
	Ability of systems to communicate (technique)	Yes	Yes	Yes	No	No	Yes	Yes	No
	Ability of systems to communicate (standard)	Yes	Yes	Yes	No	No	Yes	Yes	No
	Ability of systems to communicate (interfaces)	No	No	No	Yes	Yes	Yes	Yes	Yes
	Ability of systems to sense	No	No	No	No	No	No	No	No
	Ability of systems to carry out actions	Yes(changes)	Yes(changes)	Yes(changes)	Yes	Yes	Yes	Yes	Yes
	Ability of systems to process	No	No	No	Yes	Yes	Yes	Yes	Yes
	Requiredness of additional setup	Yes	Yes	Yes	Yes	Yes	Yes	Yes	Yes
	Presence of API	No	No	No	No	No	No	No	No
Knowledge Dimensions	Availability of data	Yes	Yes	Yes	Yes	Yes	Yes	Yes	Yes
	Availability of explicit knowledge	Yes	Yes	Yes	No	No	No	No	No
	Availability of tacit knowledge	No	No	No	No	No	No	No	No
	Role as knowledge carrier in process	Yes	Yes	Yes	No	No	Yes	Yes	No
	Degree of articulation [German: Artikulationsgrad]	0	0	0	0	0	0	0	0
	Degree of generality [German: Allgemeinheitsgrad]	1	1	1	0	0	0	0	0
	Competence [German: fachliche Einsicht]	Yes	yes	yes	No	No	Yes	No	No
	Experience	Yes	Yes	Yes	No	No	Yes	Yes	No
	Documentation availability	Yes	Yes	Yes	Yes	Yes	Yes	Yes	Yes
	Sample data availability	Yes	Yes	Yes	Yes	Yes	Yes	Yes	Yes
AI Dimensions	Input data availability	Explicitly	Explicitly	Explicitly	Explicitly	Explicitly	Explicitly	Explicitly	Explicitly
	Unsupervised functional approaches	Not Avail.	Not Avail.	Not Avail.	Available	Available	Available	Available	Available
	Input data availability	Explicitly	Explicitly	Implicitly	Explicitly	Explicitly	Explicitly	Explicitly	Explicitly
	Output data availability	Implicitly	Implicitly	Available	Explicitly	Explicitly	Available	Explicitly	Explicitly
	Supervised functional approaches	Not Avail.	Not Avail.	Available	Available	Available	Available	Available	Available
	State data availability	N.i.a.a.	N.i.a.a.	N.i.a.a.	Explicitly	Explicitly	N.i.a.a.	N.i.a.a.	Explicitly
	Action data availability	N.i.a.a.	N.i.a.a.	N.i.a.a.	Explicitly	Explicitly	N.i.a.a.	N.i.a.a.	Explicitly
	Reward data availability	N.i.a.a.	N.i.a.a.	N.i.a.a.	Explicitly	Explicitly	N.i.a.a.	N.i.a.a.	Explicitly
	Punishment data availability	N.i.a.a.	N.i.a.a.	N.i.a.a.	N.i.a.a.	N.i.a.a.	N.i.a.a.	N.i.a.a.	No
	Reinforced functional approaches	Not Avail.	Not Avail.	Not Avail.	Available	Available	Not Avail.	Not Avail.	Available
	Perceptability in dialog system	Questionable	Questionable	Questionable	Questionable	Questionable	Obvious	Obvious	Questionable
Customer Dimensions	Usefulness of data	Yes	Yes	Yes	No	No	Yes	Yes	No
	SME relevance	Yes	Yes	Yes	No	No	Yes	Yes	No
	Expected relevance	Yes	No	No	Yes	No	Yes	Yes	No
Vendor Dimensions	System costs	free (up to 10 user)	365$/user/year	5405$/User/Year	0 (No costs)	0 (No costs)	0 (No costs)	$0.00075 /request text & $0.004 speech	0 (No costs)
	Paid access	0 (No costs)	0 (No costs)	660$/User/Year	0 (No costs)	0 (No costs)	$0.002/request	$0.00075 /request text & $0.004 speech	0 (No costs)
	Vendor market share	<1%	<1%	<1%	0 (Open Source)	0 (Open Source)	0,01%	184 companies	0 (Open Source)
	Vendor reputation	Fit	Fit	Fit	Fit	Fit	Fit	Fit	Fit
	Vendor business model uniqueness	Small	Small	Small	Huge	Small	Medium	Medium	Small
	Trial version	0 (free up to 10 User)	0 (Trial)	0 (Trial)	0 (Open Source)	0 (Open Source)	0 (Open Source)	0 (Open Source)	0 (Open Source)
	Technical support	Community	Community	Community	Community	Community	Community	Community	Community
	Vendor technique advantage	small	small	small	huge	medium	medium	medium	huge
Financial Dimensions	Presence of data structure	Yes	Yes	Yes	Yes	Yes	Yes	Yes	Yes
Political Dimensions	Limitations by laws	Yes	Yes	Yes	Yes	No	No	No	No
Ethical Dimensions	Limitations by labor unions	Yes	Yes	Yes	No	No	No	No	No

Fig. 7. Overview of the analyzed software (part I).

Dim. Category	Dimension	Tool Selection													
		CRM					PIM								
		Hubspot	Salesforce	Zoho	Pipedrive	Insightly	Akeneo	Plytix	Salsify	Ircooy	Perfion	sales layer	Pimcore	Productsup	Pimberly
Technical Dimensions	Presence of digital representation of systems	Yes	Yes	Yes	Yes	Yes	Yes	Yes	Yes	Yes	Yes	Yes	Yes	Yes	Yes
	Live access to systems	Real-time data	Real-time data	Real-time data	Real-time data	Real-time data	Real-time data	Real-time data	Real-time data	Real-time data	Real-time data	Real-time data	Real-time data	Real-time data	Real-time data
	Ability of systems to communicate (technique)	Yes	Yes	Yes	Yes	Yes	Yes	Yes	Yes	Yes	Yes	Yes	Yes	Yes	Yes
	Ability of systems to communicate (standard)	Yes	Yes	Yes	Yes	Yes	Yes	Yes	Yes	Yes	Yes	Yes	Yes	Yes	Yes
	Ability of systems to communicate (interfaces)	Yes	Yes	Yes	Yes	Yes	Yes	Yes	Yes	Yes	Yes	Yes	Yes	Yes	Yes
	Ability of systems to sense	No	No	No	No	No	No	No	No	No	No	No	No	No	No
	Ability of systems to carry out actions	No	Yes(changes)	Yes(changes)	Yes(changes)	Yes(changes)	No	No	No	No	No	No	No	No	No
	Ability of systems to process	Yes(changes)	Yes(changes)	Yes(changes)	Yes(changes)	Yes(changes)	No	No	No	No	No	No	No	No	No
	Requiredness of additional setup	No	Yes	No	Yes	No	No	No	No	No	No	No	No	No	No
	Presence of API	Yes	Yes	Yes	Yes	Yes	Yes	Yes	Yes	Yes	Yes	Yes	Yes	Yes	Yes
Knowledge Dimensions	Availability of data	Yes	Yes	Yes	Yes	Yes	Yes	Yes	Yes	Yes	Yes	Yes	Yes	Yes	Yes
	Availability of explicit knowledge	No	No	No	No	No	No	No	No	No	No	No	No	No	No
	Availability of tacit knowledge	Yes	Yes	Yes	Yes	Yes	Yes	Yes	Yes	Yes	Yes	Yes	Yes	Yes	Yes
	Role as knowledge carrier in process	0	0	0	0	0	0	0	0	0	0	0	0	0	0
	Degree of articulation [German: Artikulationsgrad]	1	1	1	1	1	1	1	1	1	1	1	1	1	1
	Degree of generality [German: Allgemeinheitsgrad]	Yes	Yes	No	No	No	No	No	No	No	No	No	No	No	No
	Competence [German: fachliche Einsicht]	No	No	No	No	No	No	No	No	No	No	No	No	No	No
	Experience	Yes	Yes	Yes	Yes	Yes	Yes	Yes	Yes	Yes	Yes	Yes	Yes	Yes	Yes
	Documentation availability	Yes	Yes	Yes	Yes	Yes	Yes	Yes	Yes	Yes	Yes	Yes	Yes	Yes	Yes
	Sample data availability	Explicitly	N.i.a.a.	Explicitly	Explicitly	Explicitly	Explicitly	Explicitly	Explicitly	Explicitly	Explicitly	Explicitly	Explicitly	Explicitly	Explicitly
AI Dimensions	Input data availability	Not Avail.	Not Avail.	Not Avail.	Not Avail.	Not Avail.	Available	Available	Available	Available	Available	Available	Available	Available	Available
	Unsupervised functional approaches	Explicitly	Explicitly	Explicitly	Explicitly	Explicitly	Explicitly	Explicitly	Explicitly	Explicitly	Explicitly	Explicitly	Explicitly	Explicitly	Explicitly
	Input data availability	Implicitly	Implicitly	Implicitly	Implicitly	Implicitly	Explicitly	Explicitly	Explicitly	Explicitly	Explicitly	Explicitly	Explicitly	Explicitly	Explicitly
	Output data availability	Not Avail.	Not Avail.	Not Avail.	Not Avail.	Not Avail.	Not Avail.	Not Avail.	Not Avail.	Not Avail.	Not Avail.	Not Avail.	Not Avail.	Not Avail.	Not Avail.
	Supervised functional approaches	N.i.a.a.	N.i.a.a.	N.i.a.a.	N.i.a.a.	N.i.a.a.	N.i.a.a.	N.i.a.a.	N.i.a.a.	N.i.a.a.	N.i.a.a.	N.i.a.a.	N.i.a.a.	N.i.a.a.	N.i.a.a.
	State data availability	N.i.a.a.	N.i.a.a.	N.i.a.a.	N.i.a.a.	N.i.a.a.	N.i.a.a.	N.i.a.a.	N.i.a.a.	N.i.a.E.	N.i.a.a.	N.i.a.a.	N.i.a.a.	N.i.a.a.	N.i.a.a.
	Action data availability	N.i.a.a.	N.i.a.a.	N.i.a.a.	N.i.a.a.	N.i.a.a.	N.i.a.a.	N.i.a.a.	N.i.a.a.	N.i.a.a.	N.i.a.a.	N.i.a.a.	N.i.a.a.	N.i.a.a.	N.i.a.a.
	Reward data availability	Not Avail.	Not Avail.	Not Avail.	Not Avail.	Not Avail.	Not Avail.	Not Avail.	Not Avail.	Not Avail.	Not Avail.	Not Avail.	Not Avail.	Not Avail.	Not Avail.
	Punishment data availability	Obvious	Obvious	Obvious	Obvious	Obvious	Obvious	Obvious	Obvious	Obvious	Obvious	Obvious	Questionable	Questionable	Questionable
	Reinforced functional approaches	Yes	Yes	Yes	Yes	Yes	Yes	Yes	Yes	Yes	Yes	Yes	Yes	Yes	Yes
	Perceptibility in dialog system	Yes	Yes	Yes	Yes	Yes	Yes	Yes	Yes	Yes	Yes	Yes	Yes	Yes	Yes
Customer Dimensions	Usefulness of data	No	Yes	Yes	Yes	Yes	No	No	No	No	No	No	No	No	No
	SME relevance														
	Expected relevance	500€/year/User (Free for basic functions)	150€/year/User	250€/year/User	From 12.50€ per user per month	From $29 per user per month	-	$830/mo	-	-	-	-	Open Source to managed cloud	enterprise access 1500€ per month	24-72k per year depending on plan
Vendor Dimensions	System costs	0 (No costs)	yes	250€/year/User	0 (No costs)	0 (No costs)	0-10%	$830/mo	-	3.32%	-	-	0 (No costs)	0 (No costs)	<1%
	Paid access	Fit	Fit	Fit	Fit	Fit	45 in Germany	Fit	Fit	Many	13 in Germany	1 in Germany	<1%	<1%	Fit
	Vendor market share	Small	Small	Small	Small	Medium	Small	Small	Small	Small	Small	Small	Fit	Fit	Small
	Vendor reputation	0 (free for 30 days)	0 (Yes)	0 (Yes)	0 (Yes)	0 (Yes)	0 (Free)	0 (Free)	0 (No.)	0 (No.	0 (No)	0 (30 day trial version)	Huge	Small	0 (No)
	Vendor business model uniqueness	paid vendor / community free	paid vendor / community free	paid vendor / community free	Community	Community	Community	Community	Community	?	?	Community	0 (Open Source)	Community	Community
	Trial version	small	medium	small	small	huge	small	small	small	small	small	small	Community	huge	small
	Technical support	Yes	Yes	Yes	Yes	Yes	Yes	Yes	Yes	Yes	Yes	Yes	small	Yes	Yes
	Vendor technique advantage	Yes	Yes	Yes	Yes	Yes	Yes	Yes	Yes	Yes	Yes	Yes	Yes	Yes	Yes
Financial Dimensions	Presence of data structure	Yes	Yes	Yes	Yes	Yes	Yes	Yes	Yes	Yes	Yes	Yes	Yes	Yes	Yes
Political Dimensions	Limitations by laws														
Ethical Dimensions	Limitations by labor unions														

Fig. 8. Overview of the analyzed software, (continued, part II).

References

1. Ali, A., Khan, M.A.: Selecting predicate logic for knowledge representation by comparative study of knowledge representation schemes. In: 2009 International Conference on Emerging Technologies, Islamabad, Pakistan, pp. 23–28 (2009)
2. Dahiya, M.: A tool of conversation: chatbot. Int. J. Comput. Sci. Eng. **5**, 158–161 (2017)
3. Dejanović, I., Vaderna, R., Milosavljević, G., Vuković, Z.: TextX: a python tool for domain-specific languages implementation. Knowl.-Based Syst. **115**, 1–4 (2017)
4. Drucker, P.F.: Post-Capitalist Society. Butterworth-Heinemann, Oxford (1994)
5. Fowler, M.: Domain-Specific Languages. Pearson Education, Lomdon (2010)
6. Gronau, N.: Modeling and Analyzing Knowledge Intensive Business Processes with KMDL: Comprehensive Insights Into Theory and Practice, p. 7. GITOmbh, Berlin (2012)
7. Gronau, N., Grum, M., Bender, B.: Determining the optimal level of autonomy in cyber-physical production systems. In: IEEE 14th International Conference on Industrial Informatics (INDIN), pp. 1293–1299 (2016)
8. Grosan, C., Abraham, A.: Rule-Based Expert Systems. In: Grosan, C., Abraham, A. (eds.) Intelligent Systems: A Modern Approach, vol. 17, pp. 149–185. Springer, Heidelberg (2011). https://doi.org/10.1007/978-3-642-21004-4_7
9. Grum, M.: Managing human and artificial knowledge bearers. In: Shishkov, B. (ed.) BMSD 2020. LNBIP, vol. 391, pp. 182–201. Springer, Cham (2020). https://doi.org/10.1007/978-3-030-52306-0_12
10. Grum, M.: CoNM Repository (2020). https://github.com/MarcusGrum/CoNM. Accessed October 2020
11. Nonaka, I., Takeuchi, H.: The Knowledge-Creating Company: How Japanese Companies Create the Dynamics of Innovation. Oxford University Press, Oxford (1995)
12. Olah, C., Mordvintsev, A., Schubert L.: Feature visualization. In: Distill (2017). https://distill.pub/2017/feature-visualization
13. Peffers, K., et al.: The design science research process: a model for producing and presenting information systems research. In: 1st International Conference on Design Science in Information Systems and Technology (DESRIST), vol. 24, no. 3, pp. 83–106 (2006)
14. Ritchey, T.: Problem structuring using computer-aided morphological analysis. J. Oper. Res. Soc. Spec. Issue Prob. Struct. Methods **57**(7), 792–801 (2006)
15. Tanwar, P., Prasad, T.V., Aswal, M.S.: Comparative study of three declarative knowledge representation techniques. Int. J. Comput. Sci. Eng. **2**(07), 2274–2281 (2010)
16. Visser, E.: Generative and Transformational Techniques in Software Engineering (GTTSE 2007). In: Lammel, R., Saraiva, J., Visser, J. (eds.) Lecture Notes in Computer Science. Springer, Heidelberg (2008). https://doi.org/10.1007/978-3-540-88643-3
17. Waibel, M.W., Steenkamp, L.P., Moloko, N., Oosthuizen, G.A.: Investigating the effects of smart production systems on sustainability elements. Proc. Manuf. **8**(1), 731–737 (2017)
18. Zwicky, F.: Entdecken, Erfinden, Forschen im morphologischen Weltbild. D. Knaur, California (1966)
19. Zwicky, F.: Discovery, Invention, Research - Through the Morphological Approach. The Macmillan Company, Toronto (1969)
20. Yu, R., Lei, S.: A user-based taxonomy for deep learning visualization. Vis. Inf. **2**(03), 147–154 (2018)

From Elementary User Wishes and Domain Models to SQL-Specifications

Bert de Brock[(✉)] [ID]

Faculty of Economics and Business, University of Groningen,
PO Box 800, 9700 AV Groningen, The Netherlands
E.O.de.Brock@rug.nl

Abstract. In the development of (software) systems, new user wishes must usually be implemented very quickly. This poses a real challenge for system development. This challenge led from *waterfall* to *incremental, agile,* and even *continuous* development. In this paper we treat the research question how to come from elementary user wishes and simple domain models all the way to concrete SQL-specifications in a quick, straightforward, and traceable way.

We will follow the classical distinction between the *static* part (i.e., the *data structures*) and the *dynamic* part (i.e., the *processes*) of the system under development. We also explain how these different aspects are coordinated. Moreover, we will distinguish between the *Problem Analysis* part and the *Software Design* part of system development. We introduce the notions of _elementary User Wish_ and _textual System Sequence Description_, which help us to start in an early phase of development, to align our subsequent development steps, and to consider and treat a sequence of SQL-executions as one whole.

Keywords: Model driven engineering · Business model · Software development · Statics · Domain model · Conceptual data model · Database model · Dynamics · User wish · User story · Use case · System sequence description · MVC-pattern · (Stored) procedure

1 Introduction

Nowadays new user wishes must be implemented very quickly. Over the last decades, their 'time-to-market' had to become shorter and shorter. This 'need for speed' poses a real challenge and an increasing problem for system development. It led from *waterfall* to *incremental, agile,* and even *continuous* development. Moreover, in the beginning of a software project requirements are seldom clear, unambiguous, complete, etc. Therefore, we treat the challenging research question how to come from elementary user wishes and simple domain models all the way to concrete SQL-specifications in a quick, straightforward, and also traceable way [1, 2]. The essence of the answer to our question will be: By *stepwise clarification, stepwise refinement* and *stepwise specification.* To speed up development, the development steps should be carefully chosen and be well-aligned.

© Springer Nature Switzerland AG 2021
B. Shishkov (Ed.): BMSD 2021, LNBIP 422, pp. 97–117, 2021.
https://doi.org/10.1007/978-3-030-79976-2_6

We follow the classical distinction between the *static* part and the *dynamic* part of the system under development. The *static* part refers to the *data structures* and the *dynamic* part to the *processes*. They can be considered as the two sides of the same coin.

To answer the old question '*Should we be Data-oriented or Process-oriented?*': You should do both, concurrently! The data structures and the processes must be (and stay) mutually consistent. But the data structures are usually more stable than the processes.

Furthermore, we will distinguish between the *Problem Analysis* part and the *Software Design* part of system development. The *Problem Analysis* part must be (and will be) implementation-independent. In this paper, the *Software Design* part is geared towards SQL. We will also explain how the different aspects are coordinated.

To search for other UC-based approaches, we studied the solid literature review [3] and many of its cited papers. [3] constitutes a systematic literature review concentrating on use case specifications research. It thoroughly examined almost 120 papers on use case specifications, including their strengths and weaknesses. In it, we could not find a similar comprehensive and in-depth approach towards use case specifications with a concrete design follow-up towards SQL, not even in the industry white paper [4] of the Oracle corporation. Based on the papers [5–8], Tiwari et al. conclude in [3] that '*unavailability of formal representation of some natural language may result in confusion, difficulties and varied opinions in understanding the user requirements*'. There exist many papers about automatic translation to SQL regarding individual **queries** that are *well-formulated* in natural language [9]. However, our current paper is NOT limited to queries, NOT limited to individual interactions, and NOT about already well-formulated interactions.

Regarding the applicability of our approach: The feasibility study [10] works out in all detail a substantial part of Larman's large and known *Process Sale* example [11]. That technical report gives a good impression of the applicability and scalability of our approach in large, complex real-life situations. We also applied our approach to various other kinds of examples, such as *control systems*, where the emphasis is on the *processes* and less on the *data structures* [12]. And meanwhile we worked out (and taught our students) several 'common development patterns'. We successfully taught this approach already to a few hundred students, who applied to it various cases. Moreover, the approach is based on more than 40 years of development experience of the author.

We will illustrate the steps in our development approach with a carefully designed running example. Along the way, the running example will unfold step by step. We work out everything in detail because, as you know, the devil is in the details. And this especially holds when developing software.

The rest of the paper runs as follows: In Sect. 2 we give a general overview of the development path. Section 3 treats the *Problem Analysis* regarding the *Statics/Data-structures* and is implementation-independent. Section 4 subsequently treats the *Software Design* regarding the *Statics/Data-structures* and is geared towards SQL. Section 5 treats the *Problem Analysis* regarding the *Dynamics/Processes* and is implementation-independent. Section 6 treats the *Software Design* regarding the *Dynamics/Processes* and is geared towards SQL. The paper ends with an overview of its contributions (Sect. 7).

2 Overview of Our Development Path

We start with a general overview of our development approach. As we recall, explain, and illustrate in Sect. 3, for the *static* part of the system under development we can start with a *simple* and *small* domain model. The domain model can start simple because it might initially only contain concepts and their associations, (later) to be extended with the properties of the concepts and the multiplicities of the associations. The domain model can start small because it might initially contain only very few concepts and their associations, and extended later with more concepts and associations, following an *incremental*, *agile*, or *continuous* development.

To reach a full-fledged conceptual data model, each many-to-many association must be transformed into a few many-to-one associations, references must be made explicit, uniqueness properties must be added, and it must be indicated per property whether a value is required or optional. Last but not least, the possible values per property must be determined and there might be some remaining (integrity) constraints to be added as well.

Once we have such a detailed conceptual data model, we can prepare to transform it to an SQL-database. First, each reference to a concept is replaced by a uniqueness property of that referenced concept. After that, the resulting data model leads in a straightforward way to a default SQL-specification: First of all, a *database* is created. Then each concept translates to a *table* and each property of a concept translates to an *attribute* in that table, followed by 'NOT NULL' if a value is required for that property, else followed by 'NULL'. Each uniqueness condition translates to a *primary key* constraint or a *unique* constraint, each reference condition translates to a *foreign key* constraint, and other remaining integrity constraints translate to *check* constraints. This is shown and explained in detail in Sect. 4.

For the 'dynamic' part of the system under development we have to implement (very) many user wishes. As we explain and illustrate in Sect. 5, each time we will take an elementary User Wish (eUW) as a starting point, for example *Register a Student* or *Process a Sale*. Such a User Wish will be further developed by *stepwise clarification*, *stepwise refinement*, and *stepwise specification*: When we add the actor role and the reason for the User Wish then we get the familiar notion of a User Story [13–15]. A User Story is often formulated as '**As a** <actor role>, **I want to** <user wish> [**so that** <reason>]' where the reason-part is optional. A User Story (US) can be worked out into a Use Case, which consists of a Main Success Scenario (MSS) and zero or more Alternative Scenarios [16, 17]. A use case (UC) roughly corresponds to an *elementary business process* in business process modelling [11, 18]. Up to this point in the development, this all can be expressed by - and discussed with - the users in their own (natural) language.

To integrate the different scenarios of a Use Case into one structure, we use a *System Sequence Description* (SSD). An SSD is a kind of stylised Use Case which schematically depicts the interactions between the primary actor (user), the system (as a black box), and other actors (if any), including the messages between them. An SSD is usually drawn as a (UML-)diagram, see [11], but we introduce and prefer a *textual* SSD (tSSD) instead.

In Sect. 6 we explain and illustrate how tSSDs can be transformed to SQL using (stored) procedures in case of a Database Management System based on SQL [19, 20].

Now we give a bird's-eye view of our development approach and the order of steps we just sketched. We also indicate which 'arrow' (transformation) is treated in which section:

Topic	Problem Analysis	→ Software Design
Statics / Data structures (System has to **know**)	Domain Models* → Conceptual Data Model §3	→ Database Model §4
Dynamics / Processes (System has to **do**)	e UW → US → UC (= MSS + AS*) §5 §5	→ tSSD → SQL-Procedures §5 §6

*: zero or more

3   From Simple Domain Models to Conceptual Data Model

Regarding the question what the system under development must 'know' (i.e., which persistent data), an analyst often starts with developing a simple domain model. A Domain Model is a *visual* representation of the concepts, their properties, and their associations that might be relevant for the application to be developed (i.e., 'as we understood it until now'). The possible ingredients of a Domain Model are:

- concepts (a.k.a. conceptual classes),
- their relevant properties (a.k.a. their attributes), and
- their mutual associations (a.k.a. their relationships)

A Domain Model is usually drawn as a graph, consisting of nodes (for *concepts*, optionally with their *properties*) and lines (for *associations*). Although there are other popular ways to draw a domain model, e.g., using Entity-Relationship Diagrams [21], the ingredients could look as follows:

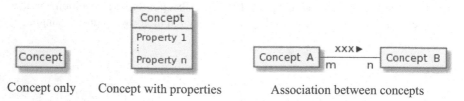

Concept only   Concept with properties   Association between concepts

where the phrase xxx (usually a verb phrase or preposition) indicates the association, the symbol ▶ indicates the reading direction, and m and n are multiplicities, usually '1', '0..1' (at most 1) or '*' (0 or more, a.k.a. 'many').

The ingredients of a Domain Model should be expressed in the terms as used in the application domain concerned. An early domain model represents a kind of minimum knowledge ('what we understood until now') and grows over time, sketching/making new versions. A series of simple, small domain models may help to structure the potentially unstructured information as provided by the users. The properties of the concepts and multiplicities of the associations need not be present in the Domain Model initially.

We will illustrate our development approach with a running example, which will be developed step by step.

Example 1: A simple domain model

Our running example concerns a university and is about *courses*, *students*, their *exams*, and their *grades*. Courses can have exams. Students can enrol for courses and for exams. Students can get graded on an exam. We at least need to know the *name* of each student and of each course, the *date* of each exam, and the *grade* after each grading.
   This leads to the simple domain model depicted on the right.

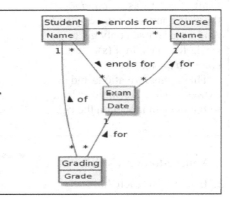

A many-to-many association (i.e., an association with a '*' on both sides) represents a 'hidden' concept, about which we need to know more. For instance, with respect to the m-to-m (many-to-many) association *Student enrols for Course* we must also know *which* students enrolled for *which* courses. We can transform any m-to-m association into two 'many-to-1' associations as follows, making the hidden concept explicit:

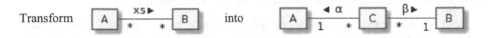

For instance, if A = 'Student', xs = 'enrols for', and B = 'Course'. then we get C = 'Enrolment', α = 'of', and β = 'for'.

Example 2: The domain model with the hidden concepts made explicit

Example 1 has two many-to-many associations. After the two transformations we have two new concepts, *Course Enrolment* and *Exam Enrolment*.

A student can only enrol for an exam if (s)he was *enrolled for* the corresponding course. And a student can only get a grade for an exam if (s)he was *enrolled for* that exam.

These transformations and extra 'business constraints' lead to the domain model on the right.

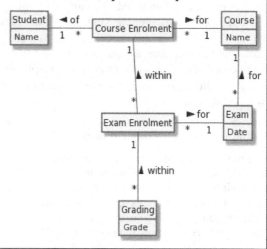

A many-to-one association ![A ►xs * 1 B] implicitly states that there is exactly one B related to each A.

Going to a Conceptual Data Model, that B must be indicated in A. ![A ^B ►xs * 1 B] We will indicate that as follows:

To emphasize the functional relationship, we replace the *line* by a ![A ^B ►xs → B]

many-to-one *arrow*. Then we can also leave out the multiplicities:

Next, per concept we must know and indicate by which (combinations of) properties each individual (a.k.a. 'entry') can be uniquely identified. We will indicate a uniqueness constraint by a '!' in front of the properties involved; i.e., within each concept the value (combination) of the property(s) preceded by '!' is unique. If there is another uniqueness constraint within the same concept, we will use '%' in front of those properties involved.

For each property we also have to know whether a value is <u>required</u> or <u>optional</u>. We will put properties for which a value is optional between the brackets '[' and ']'.

Example 3: The references, uniqueness properties, and optionality made explicit

Example 2 has 6 many-to-one associations to be transformed. This leads to the next model, next page on the left.

After further requirements analysis for our running example: A *student* is uniquely identified by his/her student number, a *course* by its name but also by its course code, an *exam* by the combination of the course and the exam date, a *course enrolment* by the combination of the student and the course, an *exam enrolment* by the combination of the underlying course enrolment and the exam, and a *grading* by the underlying exam enrolment. Moreover, students might have a phone number. This all leads to the second model below, on the right.

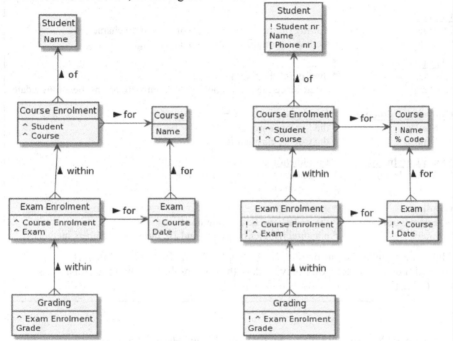

Further analysis is needed to find out for each property what its possible values are. Finally, there might be some other constraints besides the ones already treated (i.e., uniqueness, references, optionality, and allowed values).

Example 4: The possible values per property and remaining constraints

Per concept in Example 3, the elicited details of the possible values for its properties are summed up below. The possible values for a property that refers to a concept implicitly follow from the concept it refers to. Note that the property lists below include all the info contained in the last graph in Example 3.

Student	/*
! Student nr	/* a natural number of 6 digits and divisible by 11 (for simple checks)
Name	/* a string in the Latin alphabet
[Phone nr]	/* a string of at most 20 characters (being a digit, '+', '.', or ' ')

Course	/*
! Name	/* a string (in the Latin alphabet) of at most 50 characters
% Code	/* a combination of exactly 9 letters and digits

Exam	/*
! ^ Course	/* the Course the Exam is for
! Date	/* a date since the registration start (August 2010); maybe a future date

Course Enrolment	/* Enrolment of a Student for a Course
! ^ Student	/* the Student enrolled
! ^ Course	/* the Course enrolled for

Exam Enrolment	/* Enrolment for an Exam
! ^ Course Enrolment	/* the underlying Course Enrolment
! ^ Exam	/* the Exam enrolled for

Grading	/*
! ^ Exam Enrolment	/* the underlying Exam Enrolment
Grade	/* a natural number between 0 and 10, those two numbers included

There are no other constraints in this example. But if Course Enrolment (CE) and Exam Enrolment (EE) would have a date then we might have had the constraints that CE-date $\leq$ EE-date and EE-date < Exam date.

From Simple Domain Models to a Conceptual Data Model: Summary.

So, to come from a *domain model* to a full *conceptual data model*, we do as follows:

1. Replace the m-to-m associations in the domain model by many-to-1 associations
2. Extend the concepts with the references that follow from the associations in the (new) domain model
3. Add and indicate the properties following from the uniqueness discussions with the user organization
4. Indicate for which properties a value is optional, according to the user organization
5. Indicate the possible values for each property, after consulting the user organization
6. Add remaining constraints (if there are) after asking the user organization

The first two steps are more or less of a 'mechanical' nature. However, in the next steps (much) more requirements analysis is needed before you have a full conceptual data model, because a domain model is far from complete...

4   From Conceptual Data Model to SQL-Database

Once we have a detailed conceptual data model, it is pretty straightforward to transform it to an SQL-database. First of all, each reference to a concept is replaced by a uniqueness property of that referenced concept.

Example 5: References to a concept replaced by a suitable uniqueness property

In our running example, the concept *Course* has two uniqueness properties:
Name is unique and *Code* too. We will use Code since it is more fundamental/stable.

From top to bottom, we replace '^Student' in Course Enrolment by 'Student nr', '^Course' in Course Enrolment by 'Course code', '^Course' in Exam by 'Course code', the combination '^ Course Enrolment' and '^ Exam' in Exam Enrolment by 'Student nr', 'Course code', and 'Exam date', and finally '^ Exam Enrolment' in Grading by 'Student nr', 'Course code', and 'Exam date'. This leads to the data model on the right.

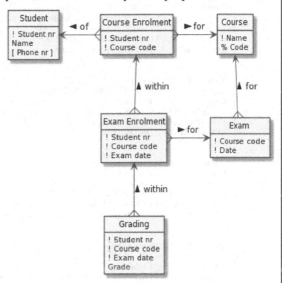

When each reference is replaced by a uniqueness property of the referenced concept, the resulting data model leads in a natural way to a default SQL-specification:

- First, a declaration CREATE DATABASE <database name> is introduced
- Each concept translates to a *table*
- Each property of a concept translates to an *attribute* in that table with the corresponding *data type* followed by 'NOT NULL' if a value is required for that property, else followed by 'NULL';
- the precise syntax of these data types might be implementation-dependent
- Each uniqueness condition translates to a *primary key* or a *unique* constraint
- Each reference condition translates to a *foreign key* constraint
- Each extra constraint translates to a *check* constraint
- Each constraint also must get a name in SQL
- Each space in a concept or property name has been replaced by '_' to make it 1 word

We illustrate all this in Example 6. Often, a Database Management System (DBMS) automatically creates default indexes on some well-chosen table attributes in order to boost the performance of retrievals.

Example 6: The resulting data specification in SQL

Applying the rules, the model as specified until now leads quite naturally to the default SQL-code below. Constraint C1 expresses that Student_nr must consist of 6 digits, C2 that it must divisible by 11, C3 that Phone_nr must not contain a character which is not a digit, '+', '.', or ' ', and C4 that Code must not contain a character which is not a letter or a digit.

CREATE DATABASE BMSD2021;

```
CREATE TABLE Student (
    Student_nr      INT           NOT NULL,      /* e.g. 123453           */
    Name            VARCHAR       NOT NULL,      /* e.g. John J. Smith    */
    Phone_nr        VARCHAR(20)   NULL,          /* e.g. +31.6.1234.5678  */
    CONSTRAINT C1 CHECK (100000 <= Student_nr AND Student_nr < 1000000),
    CONSTRAINT C2 CHECK (Student_nr % 11 = 0),
    CONSTRAINT C3 CHECK (Phone_nr NOT LIKE '%[!0-9+. ]%'),
    CONSTRAINT K1 PRIMARY KEY (Student_nr)
);


CREATE TABLE Course (
    Name            VARCHAR(50)   NOT NULL,      /* e.g. Requirements Analysis */
    Code            CHAR(9)       NOT NULL,      /* e.g. CS123BA02        */
    CONSTRAINT C4 CHECK (Code NOT LIKE '%[!a-z0-9]%'),
    CONSTRAINT K2 PRIMARY KEY (Code),
    CONSTRAINT K3 UNIQUE (Name)
);


CREATE TABLE Exam (
    Course_code     CHAR(9)       NOT NULL,      /* e.g. CS123BA02  */
    Date            DATE          NOT NULL,      /* e.g. 2020-10-10 */
    CONSTRAINT C5 CHECK ('2010-08-01' <= Date),
    CONSTRAINT K4 PRIMARY KEY (Course_code, Date),
    CONSTRAINT R1 FOREIGN KEY (Course_code) REFERENCES Course(Code)
);


CREATE TABLE Course_Enrolment (
    Student_nr      INT           NOT NULL,      /* e.g. 123453     */
    Course_code     CHAR(9)       NOT NULL,      /* e.g. CS123BA02  */
    CONSTRAINT K5 PRIMARY KEY (Student_nr, Course_code),
    CONSTRAINT R2 FOREIGN KEY (Student_nr) REFERENCES Student(Student_nr),
    CONSTRAINT R3 FOREIGN KEY (Course_code) REFERENCES Course(Code)
);


CREATE TABLE Exam_Enrolment (
    Student_nr      INT           NOT NULL,      /* e.g. 123453     */
    Course_code     CHAR(9)       NOT NULL,      /* e.g. CS123BA02  */
    Exam_date       DATE          NOT NULL,      /* e.g. 2020-10-10 */
    CONSTRAINT K6 PRIMARY KEY (Student_nr, Course_code, Exam_date),
    CONSTRAINT R4 FOREIGN KEY (Student_nr, Course_code)
      REFERENCES Course_Enrolment (Student_nr, Course_code),
    CONSTRAINT R5 FOREIGN KEY (Course_code, Exam_date)
      REFERENCES Exam(Course_code, Date)
);


CREATE TABLE Grading (
    Student_nr      INT           NOT NULL,      /* e.g. 123453     */
    Course_code     CHAR(9)       NOT NULL,      /* e.g. CS123BA02  */
    Exam_date       DATE          NOT NULL,      /* e.g. 2020-10-10 */
    Grade           TINYINT(3)    NOT NULL,      /* e.g. 7          */
    CONSTRAINT C6 CHECK (0 <= Grade AND Grade <= 10),

    CONSTRAINT K7 PRIMARY KEY (Student_nr, Course_code, Exam_date),
    CONSTRAINT R6 FOREIGN KEY (Student_nr, Course_code, Exam_date)
      REFERENCES Exam_Enrolment(Student_nr, Course_code, Exam_date)
);
```

Each of the two constraints C1 and C6 - each being a conjunction - could have been split into two constraints (which would lead to more refined error messaging).

5 From Elementary User Wish to SSD

Now we look at the 'dynamic' part of the system under development, i.e., the *processes* the system must support. Usually, (very) many user wishes have to be implemented. Informally, a User Wish (UW) is a 'wish', expressed in natural language, of a (future) user which the system should be able to fulfil. A UW often consists of an action verb and a noun (phrase). Examples of UWs in a university setting are *Register a Student, Enroll a Student for a Course, Update a Student Address, Enter a Grade*. Other examples are the following verb/noun-combinations:

Create/Retrieve/Update/Delete/Archive/Process/Handle **a**

Customer/Product/Order/Sale/Supplier/Employee/...

(Yes, indeed, the first 4 verbs are the well-known CRUD-operations.) We call such a UW without parameters an elementary user wish (eUW). Each time we will take an elementary User Wish as a starting point for development. Such a user wish will be developed by *stepwise clarification, stepwise refinement,* and *stepwise specification*. A parameterized user wish (pUW), another result of *stepwise refinement,* is an elementary user wish extended with its relevant parameters, e.g., the wish to '*Register a student with a given name, address, gender, and maybe phone number*' (because you must specify *what* to register of a student). However, the proper set of parameters might only become clear (grow and change) during development.

When we add the actor role and the reason to a User Wish then we arrive at the familiar notion of a User Story (US), often expressed as '**As a** <actor role>, **I want to** <user wish> [**so that** <reason>]' where the reason-part is optional [13]. A User Story can be worked out into a Use Case (UC), which consists of a Main Success Scenario (MSS) and zero or more Alternative Scenarios (AS); see [11, 16]. A Use Case roughly corresponds to an *elementary business process* in business process modelling [11].

We now summarize the refinement steps up to now: eUW → US → UC = MSS + AS*

Example 7: From User Wish via User Story to Use Case (= MSS + AS*)

We illustrate the refinement steps by working out the elementary User Wish *Enter a grade* into a User Story and then into a Use Case with a Main Success Scenario and four Alternative Scenarios in this case. Because data model and refinement steps should be in line with each other, we must keep the data model in mind. Note that those four ASs are in line with the Grading-part of the data model (see Example 4).

eUW1: **Enter a grade**

US1: As a <u>lecturer</u>, I want to <u>Enter a grade</u> so that <u>the grade is officially registered</u>

UC1: Enter a grade
Precondition: The user is authenticated as a <u>lecturer</u> and authorized for this UC.

MSS1:
1. The user asks the system to enter grade g for student s on exam e
2. The system tries to enter grade g for student s on exam e
3. The system informs the user about the result

Step 1 is the parameterized request, Step 2 the execution of the request, and Step 3 the result of the execution.
  We have the following Alternative Scenarios:

AS1.1: At Step 1: <u>As long as</u> the grade is not (syntactically) correct - i.e., not a natural number between 0 and 10 - the user is asked to adapt it

AS1.2: At Step 2: <u>If</u> the student is unknown*
          <u>then</u> the user is informed about that and 'nothing' happens

AS1.3: At Step 2: <u>If</u> the exam is unknown*
          <u>then</u> the user is informed about that and 'nothing' happens

AS1.4: At Step 2: <u>If</u> student is known and exam is known but <u>if</u> the student is not enrolled for the exam <u>then</u> the user is informed about it and 'nothing' happens

*: By 'unknown' we mean unknown to the system (not represented in the system)

Note that up to now, this all can be expressed by - and discussed with - the user in its own (natural) language!

To integrate the different scenarios of a Use Case into 1 structure, we use a *System Sequence Description* (SSD). An SSD is a kind of stylised Use Case which schematically depicts the interactions between the primary actor (user), the system (as a black box), and other actors (if any), including the messages between them. An SSD is usually drawn as a (UML-)diagram, see [11]. However, we introduce *textual* SSDs (tSSDs) instead.

Our textual SSDs are meant as more formal representations of use cases, and used as a follow-up of use cases towards SW design. They integrate the different scenarios of a Use Case into one structure and have a formal syntax [22] and declarative semantics [23].

UML-diagrams can also be positioned between (*textual*) use cases and the final computer programs (which are also *textual*), but the UML-diagrams themselves are *graphical*. According to UML (https://www.omg.org/spec/UML), the <u>semantics</u> of UML defines how the UML concepts are to be realized by computers. Its sections on semantics are in fact explanations only. So, at best UML has some kind of *operational semantics* - see [24] for instance - but no formal, declarative semantics. Operational semantics is already looking forward to implementations, e.g., looking at execution models, intermediate states, parallelization, etc. However, this should not be in the analysis part.

It is important to note that [25] contains rules to translate *textual* SSDs systematically to *natural language* (English) as well as to *graphical* SSDs (more or less UML-diagrams). This can help to verify the integration result with the customer! Examples 9 and 10 will show such translation results.

In [22] a grammar for textual SSDs is proposed. We recall a part of that grammar below. The terminals are written in bold. The nonterminal A stands for 'atomic instruction' (step), P for 'actor' (or 'participant'), M for 'message', S for 'instruction' (or SSD), C for 'condition', N for 'instruction name', and D for 'definition':

A ::= P ⟶ P: M   /* where 'X ⟶ Y: M' means: 'X sends M to Y'
P ::= **System** | **User** | ...
S ::= A | S ; S | **begin** S **end** | **if** C **then** S [**else** S] **end** | **while** C **do** S **end**
    | **repeat** S **until** C | **do** N
D ::= **define** N **as** S **end**

The construct '**do** N' is known as an *Include* or a *Call*. We note that the values for the nonterminals P, M, and N are application dependent ('domain specific'), apart from the values **System** and **User** for P. The values for P, M, and N will appear naturally during the development of the specific application. The terminal **System** represents the system under consideration.

For atomic instructions we can distinguish the following situations:

1. **Actor ⟶ System:** i   Elucidates the <u>input</u> messages the system can expect
2. **System ⟶ System:** y   Elucidates the <u>transitions</u> (or <u>checks</u>) the system should make
3. **System ⟶ Actor:** o   Elucidates the <u>output</u> messages the system should produce
4. **Actor ⟶ Actor2:** x   A step outside the system (might be helpful in understanding)

where Actor ≠ **System** and Actor2 ≠ **System** (but Actor and Actor2 might be the same). We call step (a) an *input* step, (b) an *internal* step, (c) an *output* step, (d) an *external* step.

A quite common interaction pattern is: A *request*, followed by an *action*, followed by a *result* (message). In the above terminology: An *input step*, followed by an *internal step*, followed by an *output step*.

The different scenarios of a Use Case can now be integrated into 1 structure by using a textual SSD, as explained in [22] and illustrated in the next example. The refinement steps until now can be summarized as follows:

$$eUW \rightarrow US \rightarrow UC = MSS + AS^* \rightarrow tSSD$$

Example 8: The resulting tSSD after integration

The <u>textual SSD</u> for <u>only the MSS</u> looks as follows:

1. User ➡ System: enter grade g for student s on exam e ;
2. System ➡ System: EnterGrade(g, s, e) ;
3. System ➡ User: Result

Now we must integrate the MSS and all the ASs for a <u>complete Use Case</u>.
We will do so by a <u>textual SSD</u>:

repeat
    User ➡ System: enter grade g for student s on exam e ;   /* Original user request
    System ➡ System: check whether g is correct ;   /* ⎤
    if g is not correct **then**   /* |AS1.1
        System ➡ User: "The grade is not correct. Please adapt it" **end** /* |
until g is correct ;   /* ⎦
System ➡ System: check whether s is known ;   /* ⎤AS1.2
if s is not known **then** System ➡ User: "Unknown student" **end** ; /* ⎦

System ➡ System: check whether e is known ;   /* ⎤AS1.3
if e is not known **then** System ➡ User: "Unknown exam" **end** ; /* ⎦
if s is known and e is known   /* ⎤
then System ➡ System: check whether s is enrolled for e ; /* |AS1.4
    if s is not enrolled for e   /* |
    then System ➡ User: "Student is not enrolled for the exam" /* |
    end   /* |
end ;   /* ⎦
if everything was okay   /* The system should keep track of that
then System ➡ System: EnterGrade(g, s, e) ; /* The execution of the request
    System ➡ User: "Done" /* The execution result in this case
end   /*

So, the complete Use Case starts with an <u>input</u> step followed by an <u>internal</u> check and maybe an <u>output</u> message. This will happen one or more times until the grade is (syntactically) correct. Then the system continues with several <u>internal</u> checks, each maybe followed by an <u>output</u> message. Finally, if everything was okay then the system does enter the grade and informs the user about it (via an <u>output</u> message).

We recall that [25] has rules to translate textual SSDs systematically to *natural language*.

Example 9: Translating the tSSD to natural language

The rules from [25] to translate tSSDs to *natural language* (English) will result in:

Repeat
  the User asks the System to enter grade g for student s on exam e.
  The System does check whether g is correct.   ⌉ 1
  If g is not correct **then** |
    the System sends "The grade is not correct. Please adapt it" **to the User end** |
until g is correct.   ⌋
The System does check whether s is known.   ⌉ 2
If s is not known **then the System sends** "Unknown student" **to the User end.** ⌋
The System does check whether e is known.   ⌉ 3
If e is not known **then the System sends** "Unknown exam" **to the User end.** ⌋
If s is known and e is known   ⌉ 4
then the System does check whether s is enrolled for e. |
    If s is not enrolled for e |
    then the System sends "Student is not enrolled for the exam" **to the User** |
    end |
end.   ⌋
If everything was okay   /* The system should keep track of that
then the System does EnterGrade(g, s, e).   /* The execution of the request
    The System sends "Done" **to the User** /* The execution result in this case
end

We recall that we also have rules to translate *textual* SSDs systematically to *graphical* SSDs.

Example 10: Translating the textual SSD to a graphical SSD

The rules from [25] to translate *textual* SSDs to *graphical* SSDs will result in:

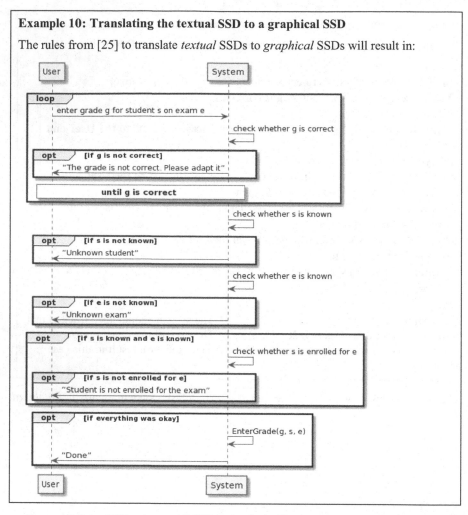

Summarizing tSSDs: A <u>textual SSD</u> schematically depicts the interactions between the <u>primary actor</u> (user), the <u>system</u> (as a black box), and <u>other actors</u> (if any), including the <u>messages</u> between them. A textual SSD integrates the different scenarios of a UC into one structure. A tSSD is written in a kind of 'structured natural language' and already exposes the final execution structure. Textual SSDs can be automatically translated back to *natural language* (such as English) as well as to *graphical* SSDs (more or less UML-diagrams), which is useful for verification purposes. Example 8 shows that a tSSD is already close to concrete programming, although it still is implementation-independent.

6   From Textual SSD to SQL-Procedures

To separate the *internal* representations in a system from the ways information is interchanged with an *external* actor, a system can (conceptually) be split into an 'interface' and a 'kernel'. The interface converts the input as received from an external actor into a proper call to the kernel (e.g., an OO-system or a relational DBMS) and it converts the output from the kernel into a proper message to the external actor. So, then the system is considered as a 'grey box' and no longer as a 'black box'. This is related to the MVC-pattern (Model-View-Controller) a well-known software design pattern. We schematize it below. We indicate the Controller-, Model-, and View-part too:

Step	Analysis	Design	MVC-part
Input step	User ➡ System: A	User ➡ Interface: A Interface ➡ Kernel: A′	*Controller part*
Internal step	System ➡ System: B	Kernel ➡ Kernel: B′	*Model part*
Output step	System ➡ User: C	Kernel ➡ Interface: C′ Interface ➡ User: C	*View part*

We graphically illustrate these steps (in combination) by indicating how the analysis-SSD below, a common analysis interaction pattern, transforms into the design-SSD next to it.

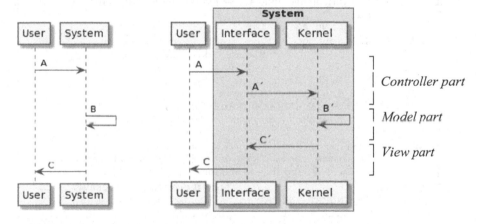

Here A is an input message from the user, B expresses what the system must do, and C is an output message to the user. In the second diagram, A′ is a call to the kernel, B′ specifies the execution by the kernel, and C′ is the output from the kernel. So, the interface converts A to A′ (*Controller*) and C′ to C (*View*). The interface can be seen as a 'front office' and the kernel as a 'back office'. The crux of the transformation is the specification of B′.

If the kernel is an SQL-DBMS then A′ is an SQL-call, B′ represents the SQL-execution, and C′ the SQL-output. Similarly if the kernel is an OO-system then B′ specifies an OO-execution (typically with *get*- and *set*-statements).

In order to make our SQL-design more resistant to all kinds of local SQL-dialects, we will use stored procedures in SQL. Then every SQL-call A′ can be a procedure call, i.e., the call of a (stored) procedure in SQL. An SQL-procedure might contain the typical SQL-statements SELECT, INSERT, UPDATE, and DELETE, but also control-of-flow language and calls to (other) procedures. A stored procedure will be compiled and gets an execution plan, which dramatically improves its performance.

In our next example we illustrate how a tSSD can be transformed into SQL.

Example 11: The resulting SQL-procedure needed for the textual SSD

The tSSD in Example 8 has only one <u>input</u> step, so we need only one procedure (though that procedure might be called repeatedly). The tSSD starts with an <u>input</u> step, followed by an <u>internal</u> check and maybe an <u>output</u> message. If the grade is not (syntactically) correct then the procedure is called again (until the grade is correct), and else the system continues with several <u>internal</u> checks, each maybe followed by an <u>output</u> message. Finally, if everything is okay then the system does enter the grade and informs the user about it via an <u>output</u> message.

Note that the resulting SQL-procedure below follows the structure of the tSSD. In the SQL-procedure, @output is declared as a return parameter. We recall that an exam is uniquely identified by the course and exam date.

```
CREATE PROCEDURE EnterGrade @g tinyint(3), @s int, @cc char(9),
                     @ed Date, @output varchar(50) OUTPUT AS
BEGIN              /* Invariant: @output = '' ⇔ Everything is okay until now */
   SELECT @output = ''
   IF NOT (0 <= @g AND @g <= 10)
      THEN SELECT @output = 'The grade is not correct.
                            Please adapt it. '
      ELSE
   IF @s NOT IN (SELECT Student_nr FROM Student)
      THEN SELECT @output = 'Unknown student. '
   IF (@cc, @ed) NOT IN (SELECT Course_code, Date FROM Exam)
      THEN SELECT @output = @output + 'Unknown exam. '
   IF @output = ''
      THEN IF (@s, @cc, @ed) NOT IN (SELECT Student_nr,
                  Course_code, Exam_date FROM Exam_Enrolment)
         THEN SELECT @output = 'Student not enrolled for exam.'
   IF @output = ''                      /* i.e., if everything was okay */
      THEN BEGIN  INSERT INTO Grading VALUES(@s, @cc, @ed, @g)
               SELECT @output = 'Done. '
            END
END
```

On hindsight we overlooked the scenario that if 'Everything was okay' (i.e., known student was indeed enrolled for known exam), the grade could have been in the system already. But thanks to the uniqueness constraint K7 (see Example 6), the kernel would have raised an error message (see position C′ in the diagram on the previous page). Generally speaking, all the constraints specified in the declaration of the database will guard the system's contents, even if some scenarios are overlooked in some use cases.

7 Contributions

First, the introduction of the notion of <u>elementary User Wish</u> allowed us to start development paths in an early phase of system development. The notion is concrete, simple to understand, and well-discussable with the user organization.

We recall that a Use Case consists of a Main Success Scenario plus zero or more Alternative Scenarios, all being texts. In the end, they must be integrated into one (computer) program, also being text. Then the question arises: What should come on the dots below to *integrate* all the scenarios and to have *aligned* development steps?

$$(UC =) MSS + AS* \text{ (texts)} \Rightarrow \ldots\ldots\ldots\ldots \Rightarrow \text{Program (text)}$$

We put <u>textual</u> SSDs in between (instead of, e.g., <u>graphical</u> SSDs such as a UML-diagrams).

Then we get:
$$(UC =) MSS + AS* \text{ (texts)} \Rightarrow tSSD \text{ (text)} \Rightarrow \text{Program (text)}$$

instead of:
$$(UC =) MSS + AS* \text{ (texts)} \qquad\qquad \text{Program (text)}$$
$$\Downarrow \qquad\qquad\qquad\qquad \Uparrow$$
$$\text{Several gSSDs } (\textit{diagrams})$$

So, to solve the *integration problem* and the *alignment challenge*, we use the notion of *textual* SSDs. They play a crucial role to obtain integration and alignment. Textual SSDs are theoretically sound: They have a <u>well-defined syntax</u> [25] as well as a <u>well-defined semantics</u> [23], as opposed to many other 'formalisms' (such as UML-diagrams). Textual SSDs can be automatically <u>translated to natural language</u> (e.g., English) and also to <u>well-formed graphical SSDs</u> [25], for instance for verification purposes. So, in that case we get the following feedback loops for verification:

$$\underline{\text{User:}} \ eUW \rightarrow US \rightarrow UC (= MSS + AS*) \rightarrow tSSD$$
$$ \Leftarrow \Leftarrow \textit{Text in Natural Language} \Leftarrow \Leftarrow $$
and

$$\underline{\text{User:}} \ eUW \rightarrow US \rightarrow UC (= MSS + AS*) \rightarrow tSSD$$
$$ \Leftarrow \Leftarrow \Leftarrow \textit{One graphical SSD} \Leftarrow \Leftarrow \Leftarrow $$

Because the grammar for tSSDs aligns with those for imperative and declarative programming languages, tSSDs form a suitable basis for <u>translations</u> to (computer) programs. Although implementations often use *imperative* (object-oriented) languages, we considered translations to SQL, a *declarative* database language. Authors such as Jacobson [17] and Cockburn [16] don't go all the way to concrete code, as we do. We made use of *(stored) SQL-procedures*, which are quite performant. It allowed us to treat a sequence of executions as one whole, which is very helpful.

Our approach concurrently takes into account the *static* part (i.e., the *data structures*) and the *dynamic* part (i.e., the *processes*) of the system to be developed.

By *stepwise clarification*, *stepwise refinement*, and *stepwise specification*, an aligned straightforward development path for processes resulted:

$$\underline{\text{User:}} \ eUW \rightarrow US \rightarrow UC = MSS + AS* \text{ (texts)} \rightarrow tSSD \text{ (text)} \rightarrow \text{SQL-procedures (text)}$$

As a consequence of the straightforward transformations and the alignment, our approach contributes to the (bi-directional) traceability of the generated artifacts as well [1, 2, 25]. The approach also brings semi-automatic software generation closer. Our contribution is not only in the individual steps, but also in their (new) *combination*, i.e., in the *choice/ selection* and the *alignment* of these steps.

References

1. Gotel, O.C.Z., Finkelstein, C.W.: An analysis of the requirements traceability problem. In: Requirements Engineering, pp. 94–101 (1994). http://discovery.ucl.ac.uk/749/1/2.2_rtprob.pdf
2. Cleland-Huang, J., et al.: Software and Systems Traceability. Springer, Heidelberg (2012). https://doi.org/10.1007/978-1-4471-2239-5
3. Tiwari, S., Gupta, A.: A systematic literature review of use case specifications research. Inf. Softw. Technol. **67**, 128–158 (2015). https://www.sciencedirect.com/science/article/abs/pii/S0950584915001081
4. Kettenis, J.: Getting started with use case modeling. White Paper, Oracle (2007). https://www.oracle.com/technetwork/developer-tools/jdev/gettingstartedwithusecasemodeling-133857.pdf
5. Fantechi, A., Gnesi, S., Lami, G., Maccari, A.: Applications of linguistic techniques for use case analysis. Require. Eng. **8**(3), 161–170 (2003)
6. Ilieva, M., Ormandjieva, O.: Automatic transition of natural language software requirements specification into formal presentation. In: [26], pp. 392–397 (2005). https://doi.org/10.1007/11428817_45
7. Savic, D., Antovic, I., Vlajic, S., Stanojevic, V., Milic, M.: Language for use case specification. In: Proceedings of the 34th IEEE Software Engineering Workshop, SEW, pp. 19–26 (2011)
8. Sinha, A., Paradkar, A., Kumanan, P., Boguraev, B.: A linguistic analysis engine for natural language use case description and its application to dependability analysis in industrial use cases. In: Proceedings of the IEEE/IFIP International Conference on Dependable Systems Networks, DSN 2009, pp. 327–336 (2009)
9. Kim, H., So, B.-H., Han, W.-S., Lee, H.: Natural language to SQL: where are we today? Proc. VLDB **13**(10), 1737–1750 (2020)
10. de Brock, E.O.: Converting a non-trivial Use Case into an SSD: an exercise. SOM Research Report 2018011, University of Groningen (2018)
11. Larman, C.: Applying UML and Patterns. Pearson Education, London (2005)
12. de Brock, E.O.: What to do when requirements are changing all the time? A control system example. In: Shishkov, B. (ed.): International Symposium on Business Modeling and Software Design (BMSD). LNBIP, pp. 317–329 (2021)
13. Lucassen, G., Dalpiaz, F., Werf, J.M.E.M.V.D., Brinkkemper, S.: The use and effectiveness of user stories in practice. In: Daneva, M., Pastor, O. (eds.) REFSQ 2016. LNCS, vol. 9619, pp. 205–222. Springer, Cham (2016). https://doi.org/10.1007/978-3-319-30282-9_14
14. Lucassen, G.G.: Understanding user stories. Ph.D. thesis, Utrecht University (2017). https://dspace.library.uu.nl/handle/1874/356784
15. Cohn, M.: User Stories Applied: For Agile Software Development. Addison (2004). https://www.pearson.com/us/higher-education/program/Cohn-User-Stories-Applied-For-Agile-Software-Development/PGM314163.html
16. Cockburn, A.: Writing Effective Use Cases. Addison Wesley (2001). https://www.infor.uva.es/~mlaguna/is1/materiales/BookDraft1.pdf

17. Jacobson, I., et al.: Use case 2.0: the guide to succeeding with use cases. Jacobson Int. (2011). https://www.ivarjacobson.com/publications/white-papers/use-case-ebook
18. Dumas, M., et al.: Fundamentals of Business Process Management. Springer, Heidelberg (2018). https://doi.org/10.1007/978-3-662-56509-4. https://www.springer.com/gp/book/978 3662565087
19. Ullman, J.D., et al.: Database Systems: The Complete Book. Pearson, London (2009)
20. Elmasri R., Navathe S.B.: Fundamentals of Database Systems. Pearson (2016). https://www.pearson.com.au/products/D-G-Elmasri-Navathe/D-G-Elmasri-Ramez-Navathe-Shamkant-B/Fundamentals-of-Database-Systems-Global-Edition/9781292097619?R=9781292097619
21. Chen, P.: The entity-relationship model - toward a unified view of data. ACM Trans. Database Syst. 1(1), 9–36 (1976)
22. de Brock, E.O.: From business modeling to software design. In: [28], pp. 103–122 (2020). https://doi.org/10.1007/978-3-030-52306-0_7
23. de Brock, E.O.: Declarative semantics of actions and instructions. In: [28], pp. 297–308 (2020). https://doi.org/10.1007/978-3-030-52306-0_20
24. Övergaard, G., Palmkvist, K.: A formal approach to use cases and their relationships. In: Bézivin, J., Muller, P.A. (eds.) The Unified Modeling Language. «UML»'98: Beyond the Notation. LNCS, vol. 1618, pp. 406–418. Springer, Berlin (1998).https://doi.org/10.1007/978-3-540-48480-6_31
25. de Brock, E.O.: On System Sequence Descriptions. In [27] (2020)
26. Montoyo, A., Munoz, R., Mtais, E. (eds.): Natural Language Processing and Information Systems. LNCS, vol. 3513, Springer, Heidelberg (2005)
27. Sabetzadeh, M., et al. (eds.): Joint Proceedings of REFSQ-2020 Workshops, Doctoral Symposium, Live Studies Track, and Poster Track. Pisa, Italy (2020)
28. Shishkov, B. (ed.): International Symposium on Business Modeling and Software Design (BMSD). Lecture Notes in Business Information Processing, vol. 391 (2020)

Towards Well-Founded and Richer Context-Awareness Conceptual Models

Boris Shishkov[1,2,3,4(✉)] and Marten van Sinderen[5]

[1] Faculty of Information Sciences, University of Library Studies and Information Technologies, Sofia, Bulgaria
[2] Faculty of Technology, Policy and Management, Delft University of Technology, Delft, The Netherlands
[3] Institute of Mathematics and Informatics, Bulgarian Academy of Sciences, Sofia, Bulgaria
[4] Institute IICREST, Sofia, Bulgaria
`b.b.shishkov@iicrest.org`
[5] Faculty of Electrical Engineering, Mathematics and Computer Science, University of Twente, Enschede, The Netherlands
`m.j.vansinderen@utwente.nl`

Abstract. We observe that context-aware systems currently developed in one domain or another are mostly technology-driven, and not so much user-centric. They are often not based on a thorough analysis of the effects they produce when interacting with their context, especially regarding the contribution of these effects to user needs. We argue that a conceptual framework is needed to support such analyses. In this paper we identify the concepts necessary to define important structural aspects of a context-aware system and its context, and to formulate generalizations about effects of the interaction of the context-aware system and its context related to user needs. Using this conceptual framework, we classify context-aware systems in terms of the kinds of context assumptions that we can make at design time, and we discuss several threats to validity of a context-aware system. We believe that the proposed conceptual framework can help to better assess the utility concerning a context-aware system design. We use various examples of context-aware applications to illustrate our ideas.

Keywords: Adaptive service delivery · Context-awareness · Conceptual modeling · Architectural structure · User needs · Utility analysis

1 Introduction

Context-awareness is receiving much attention in numerous application domains - from mobile health monitoring [12] to drone-driven monitoring in areas affected by disruptive events [13]. We argue that even though those applications are useful and well-reflected in corresponding R&D materials, scientific papers, and project documentation, they are often technology-driven and not driven by user needs. We argue that there is a lack of solid conceptual foundations that are rich enough to support top-down design of context-aware applications. In the current paper, we propose a conceptual framework that serves this purpose.

© Springer Nature Switzerland AG 2021
B. Shishkov (Ed.): BMSD 2021, LNBIP 422, pp. 118–132, 2021.
https://doi.org/10.1007/978-3-030-79976-2_7

Context-awareness essentially concerns adaptive service delivery [9, 16], for which three adaptation perspectives are possible, viz. serving (i) user needs; (ii) system needs; and (iii) public values. Although these perspectives are all equally important, for our conceptual framework, we currently only consider (i).

We claim that our conceptual framework helps to support user-centric design by making explicit which threats to utility exist and providing the concepts to discuss and resolve these threats at design time. Here, we consider a system to have utility (usefulness) if it provides services that satisfy the user needs. Although we cannot measure utility at design time, we can justify design choices with "satisfaction arguments": reason that those are the best among alternatives, using logical arguments that consider the user needs. As part of the framework, we also propose a classification of context situations in terms of how well context can be foreseen and defined at design time. In cases where context situations cannot be completely or properly defined, machine learning approaches can be used to detect (or predict) context situations related to user needs. This opens the possibility to extend the framework further to assess the suitability of machine learning methods [14, 15] with respect to their usefulness as it concerns context-aware systems. We plan this as future work.

The remaining of the current paper is structured as follows: Sect. 2 presents a historical perspective on technological developments that led to the context-aware systems of today and discusses the technological bias of many context-aware systems. In Sect. 3 we present our proposed conceptual framework. In Sect. 4, we partially exemplify our proposal. And in the end, in Sect. 5, we discuss the framework and its limitations as well as our plans for future work.

2 Background

In this section, we firstly mention some technological developments that led to context-aware systems and secondly we consider the technological bias of a number of such systems.

2.1 Historical Perspective

Back in the 1980s and 1990s, computers and information systems were quickly gaining popularity [16]; the behavior of such systems was initially fully user-input-driven, and any change of use/needs had to be explicitly indicated by the user [1]. In dynamic environments with corresponding changing user needs, this is considered a drawback. Automated adaptation of system behavior to context changes as well as seamless service provisioning only became possible in the new millennium, when three useful developments took place, namely: (i) Miniaturization of computers leading to mobile computing devices [2]; (ii) GPRS/wi-fi connectivity of these devices, allowing to receive support from more powerful computing systems in different situations – while walking, while visiting "another place", etc. [3]; (iii) Sensor technology embedded in the devices, enabling the measurement of physical variables and derivation of the user situation [4].

This led to the emergence of context-aware computing, in the first decade of the new millennium, assuming the possibility to adapt the delivery of ICT (Information and

Communication Technology) services to the situation of the user [5]. At the same time, we have witnessed developments in the area of autonomic computing [6], featuring the self-management of computing resources. Finally, value-sensitivity [7, 8, 18] has more recently been proposed, for the sake of using adaptation of service delivery for supporting particular relevant public values, such as privacy, accountability, and transparency.

We currently observe context-aware applications that are developed in various domains. Most of those applications are technology-driven (a "bottom-up" perspective), aiming to show new technology applications, without a thorough understanding of the effects produced by the corresponding context-aware services on the user and his/her environment and their contribution to context-dependent user goals (a "top-down" perspective).

2.2 The Technological Bias

Pioneering researchers in the area of context-awareness have definitely improved our understanding of the notion of **context** and made serious progress in the development of **context-aware applications** [1, 19, 28, 29]. We argue nevertheless that often: (i) there is a *bottom-up* approach to application development; (ii) the challenge of tackling situations, when context states cannot be foreseen at design time, is not explicitly considered. The same holds for many R&D context-awareness projects, such as CyberDesk [30], AWARENESS [12, 32], and SECAS [33]. In these works: **user-centricity** does not seem to play a major role in the design; the consideration of *user needs* is not an explicit part of the design cycle.

The useful survey of Alegre et al. [22] is mainly focused on the development of *context-aware applications* as well as on the consideration of *public values*. The same holds for the works of Alférez and Pelechano [23] – they consider the dynamic evolution of *context-aware* systems, the development itself, and the relation to *web services*. The latter holds also for the *service-orientation* perspective as proposed by Abeywickrama [24]. All these works take a primarily **technology-driven perspective** and are less concerned with the **user perspective**. The same holds for other works touching upon the *adaptive delivery of services*, always considered in a *bottom-up* perspective, featuring *decision-making* [25], *safety of stakeholders* [26], and *routing* [27].

Exceptions can also be mentioned. For example, in [20], the authors propose a modeling approach (based on Causal Loop Diagrams) for understanding the context in relation to *user needs/goals*, independent of any technology. Furthermore, in [31], the central role of *human users* is acknowledged and information modeling for the *context-aware* system is based on *knowledge descriptions* using *ontologies* and *rules* [21]. Nonetheless, a conceptual framework for understanding the nature of *context-awareness* and analyzing potential issues with *context-aware* systems from a *user perspective* is lacking.

3   Conceptual Framework

We need a *conceptual framework* specifically to be able to assess, *at design time*, the utility of a context-aware system in an intended *context*. With such an assessment the designers and other stakeholders can decide whether the proposed system is ready for transfer to practice, or whether another design cycle for further improvement should be entered. In this way it is possible to reduce the risk that the *context-aware* system, once implemented in its *context*, does not fulfil the expectations of the stakeholders, and especially of **end-users**. As stated before, the purpose of a *context-aware* system that is transferred to practice is not to be technologically innovative but to better serve the user needs.

3.1   Context-Awareness

As a problem theory for *context-aware* systems we postulate that *end-users* (*users*, for short) of *information systems* often have different needs for services provided by such systems, where different needs correspond to different context situations. *Context-aware* (information) systems are a "treatment" for this problem if they can provide **context-specific services to users in accordance to their context-dependent needs**. "Context" here is the *context* of the *context-aware* system, where the former is a given (i.e., not designed) and the latter is the object of design. A *context-aware* system that is transferred to practice would interact with its context. Two kinds of interactions can be distinguished: one for *collecting data on the context* and another one - for *delivering a service* that matches the *context*. The fact that the *service* is delivered to a *user* means that the user is part of the context. This makes perfect sense, as the *part-of* relation is an essential prerequisite for the system we want to design, viz. to make a connection between what the *context* is and what a *user* needs.

We frame the design problem with the diagram in Fig. 1. The diagram shows that a **user**, being *part of* a **context**, has *one or more* **user need**s (or sets of *user needs*), where each distinguished *user need* results from a corresponding unique **context situation**. A *context* can be conceived as a *temporal composition of one or more context situations*, where each *context situation* has a unique set of *properties* that collectively are relevant to a specific *user need*. A useful **context-aware system** is able to detect the *context situation* at hand and then offers one or more **situation-specific services** that satisfy the *needs* of the *user* being in, or experiencing, that situation.

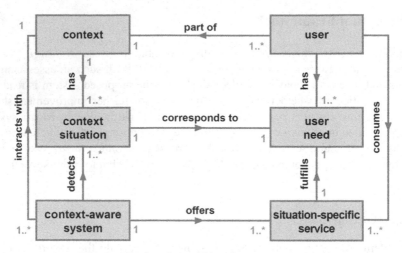

Fig. 1. Framing the problem of context-awareness

3.2 Context-Aware System

Many *architectures* of *context-aware systems* have been proposed in literature [5, 36, 37]. Figure 2 shows an <u>architectural structure</u> that identifies the main components and their relations. The main components are:

- **D**ata **A**cquisition & **P**reprocessing (DAP): Responsible for "measuring" the context using sensors, and for cleansing and aggregating the data from sensors, for the sake of obtaining a more reliable data set suitable for analysis.
- **S**ituation **D**etection (SD): Responsible for analyzing the data set, which consists of interpreting the data set as a context model (i.e. a sensor-data-based representation of the context) and deciding whether the represented context satisfies the properties of a context situation.
- **A**daptation to **S**ituation (AS): Responsible for creating or selecting the capabilities that are required to provide a service that is suitable for the context situation at hand.
- **S**ituation-specific service **O**ffering & **D**elivery (SOD): Responsible for offering the situation-specific service and delivering the service through interaction with the context. The service delivery can involve the use of actuators; this is to control a mechanism in the context and/or a user interface, for properly interacting with a user in the context.

What is referred above as the <u>data set</u> and the <u>context model</u>, respectively, are actually *a time series, representing the context evolution over (a period of) time.* The interactions between the mentioned components explain the behavior of a *context-aware* system: The **DAP** component collects *raw data* about the *context* and passes data useful for analysis to the **SD** component. It in turn analyzes the data and informs the **AS** component whenever a new *context situation* has been *detected*. The **AS** component then makes the *capability adaptation* necessary for a new *situation* and subsequently informs the **SOD** component that a *new service* must be provided. This component uses the adapted capability to offer and deliver the *new service* to the *context*.

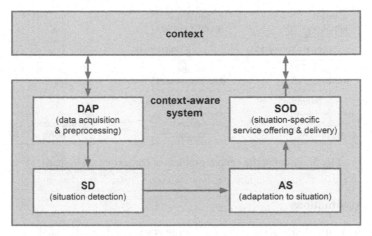

Fig. 2. Architectural structure of a context-aware system

3.3 Measuring the Context

In order to be able to better explain what the challenges are, featuring the design of **user-centric context-aware systems**, we introduce some additional concepts below (see also the diagram in Fig. 3):

We argued that a context situation has a unique set of *properties* that are collectively relevant to a specific user need. So, when "measuring" the *context*, one would actually be interested in these *properties*. For each property, one has to define one or more context indicators that can be measured. For example, the *context situation* with the *property* "hot" can be operationalized by the *indicator* "temperature". An *indicator* has one or more measurement methods. For example, *temperature* can be measured with a mechanical method (e.g. the expansion of an enclosed quantity of mercury) or with an electrical method (e.g., thermocouples). Indicator measurements, obtained with the selected measurement methods, are used to create a *context model* that focuses on the *properties* relevant to corresponding *user needs*. For *situation detection*, it is necessary to establish whether the *properties* of a *context situation* are satisfied. In the *context model* this is done by comparing *indicator* measurements with indicator norms. A *norm* is a required range of *values* of an *indicator*. For example, the *context situation* "hot" may have as *norm* for the *indicator* "temperature" the range [30 °C–45 °C]. If the *norms* of all *indicators* for all *properties* of a *context situation* are satisfied, a situation detection event for that *situation* can be generated, which then results in providing the situation-specific service.

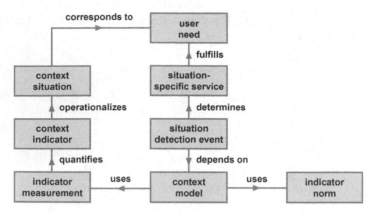

Fig. 3. Framing the design problem of context-aware systems

3.4 Context Situations

Regarding the **context situations**, the following cases can be distinguished:

- *Context situations* are defined, such that: (a-i) they can be recognized in the given *context* if they occur; (a-ii) different *context situations* cannot occur at the same time; and (a-iii) the *context* has an associated *context situation* at any time. In this case, if the *context situations* can be correctly *detected* by the *context-aware* system, there is always a situation-specific service that can be offered. As a special case, it is possible to define an "empty" *context situation* that has no corresponding *user need*, and therefore does not require any *service* offering.
- *Context situations* are defined, such that: (b-i) they can be recognized in the given *context* if they occur; (b-ii) different *context situations* cannot occur at the same time; but (b-iii) the *context* does not have an associated *context situation* at any time. This means that, even if the *context situations* can be correctly *detected* by the *context-aware* system, there may be times when the system is in an undefined state for which there is no designed behavior. To avoid this, it is possible to define a "fallback" behavior (and maybe *service* offering) that applies when no *context situation* can be *detected*.
- *Context situations* are defined, such that: (c-i) they can be recognized in the given *context* if they occur; (c-ii) the *context* has an associated *context situation* at any time; but (c-iii) different context situations can occur at the same time. This is undesirable, assuming that the *context-aware* system can only offer one *service*. Hence, either the *context situations* have to be redefined or the *context-aware* system must be able to prioritize context situations if they occur at the same time, only offering the *service* for the *situation* with the highest priority.
- *Context situations* are not (all) properly defined, such that it is not possible to recognize (some of) them in the given *context* if they occur. The reason could be that the *user needs* for different *situations* are not well understood and/or the properties to distinguish situations are not well understood or hard to define. In this case, *machine learning* could be used by the *context-aware* system to detect *context situations*, based

on *training sets* of *context models* labeled with *context situations* and/or *explicit user feedback*.

Figure 4 illustrates the first three mentioned cases (quadrant IV represents the combination of second and third mentioned ones).

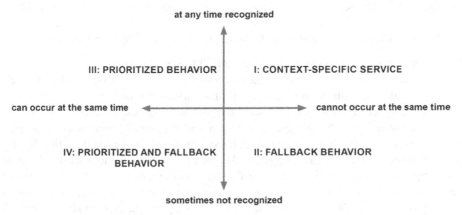

at any time recognized

III: PRIORITIZED BEHAVIOR   I: CONTEXT-SPECIFIC SERVICE

can occur at the same time ←——————————→ cannot occur at the same time

IV: PRIORITIZED AND FALLBACK   II: FALLBACK BEHAVIOR
BEHAVIOR

sometimes not recognized

Fig. 4. Context situations and context-aware system behavior

Designers of a *context-aware* system may consider the likelihood of *context situations* and decide that certain *situations* are so unlikely that it is not worthwhile defining separate situation-specific services for them. Such situations may be covered by fallback behavior, as discussed for the second mentioned case above.

3.5 Validity Threats

If we want to claim that a context-aware system is useful, it should be possible to ascertain that the system delivers services that fulfill the user needs in context situations that occur in the context. A number of complications are possible nevertheless, threatening the validity of this claim even if the technical system design is correct.

We illustrate these threats by means of a hypothetical context-aware application, which we call the *Wellbeing at Work Coach* (WWC). More examples are provided in Sect. 4. *The WWC application monitors the interaction of an end-user with his or her computer, providing advice to the user in a message on the screen*; it is indicated to the user whenever there is a high probability that (s)he is tired, loses focus, experiences stress, and becomes less productive. The advice is, for example, to stop working and take a break, do a physical exercise, socialize with a colleague, listen to relaxing music, read a fun book, and so on. Such an advice is triggered by observing the presence of the following conditions regarding the interaction of the user with his or her computer:

- *Typing accuracy* below threshold. Typing accuracy is measured as the number of backspace key presses per key press [34].

- *Active time* above threshold. Active time, i.e. the time during which the user is considered non-stop working, is measured as the time duration of a series of mouse or keyboard events in which the time gap between two consecutive events is less than 5 min [34].
- *Stressed mouse use* above threshold. Stressed mouse use is derived based on measurements of mouse movements. Mouse movement events are used to calculate two fundamental parameters of arm-hand dynamics that capture the effect of stress [35].

Now we identify the **threats** and discuss them using the WWC application:

the situation-specific service(s) do(es) not fulfill the user need(s)

There should be a one-to-one correspondence between services and user needs, and each service should contribute to the satisfaction of a corresponding need. WWC has only one service, which is notifying the user through a message on the screen. Assuming that: (a) the user has only one need (i.e., receiving support for well-being at work); (b) the situation for this need is clearly defined; and (c) the situation detection by the application is correct, there is still a possibility that the service would not fulfil the user need. The latter is the case if *the message formulates advice that is not appealing to the user* – for example, it is possible that *the user does not want to be interrupted* if (s)he is working against a deadline. This would indicate that there is at least another user need that has to be taken into account (and that the original user need has to be scoped down to: "receiving support for well-being at work unless there is a short-term deadline").

the relationship between user needs and context situations is unclear

There should be a one-to-one correspondence between user needs and context situations, and each user need should occur only in the corresponding situation. WWC has only one user need, and one corresponding context situation that is characterized by "*a high probability that the user is tired, loses focus, experiences stress, and becomes less productive*". Whether this is an exclusive situation in which the user need occurs depends on its definition in terms of properties. WWC defines the required properties using thresholds (norms) for typing accuracy, active time, and stressed mouse use. One could define additional properties to make the 'fit' between context situation and user need better or leave out properties if they do not contribute to the 'fit' and/or are too expensive to operationalize. Furthermore, one may expect that the situation depends on the specific program(s) the user is interacting with and therefore program-specific thresholds may be necessary. In any case, thresholds should be personalized. Obviously, there is also the complement of this context situation, for which no user need exists that is of concern to WWC.

context situations are not properly defined

According to Sect. 3.4, with regard to the delivery of situation-specific services, context situations should be defined such that: situations can be recognized in the given context if they occur; different situations cannot occur at the same time; the context has an associated situation at any time. Because WWC has only one context situation (besides the abovementioned complement, which we can ignore), we only discuss *recognizing the situation in the given context*. From the WWC description, we can derive that the context situation is defined by the properties: *typing accuracy is below a threshold, active time is above a threshold*, and *stressed mouse use is above a threshold*. Provided that these properties can be operationalized, the situation can be recognized in the context by comparing (processed) measurements of indicators with the thresholds (norms). Nevertheless, in more complex cases, it may be much more difficult to properly define the context situation in such a way.

the indicator(s) used for a property of a context situation do(es) not cover(s) all aspects of the property
WWC uses various indicators. *Typing accuracy* has as indicators the number of backspace key presses and the number of key presses. *Active time* has as indicator the time duration since the last keyboard/mouse event that was more than 5 min separated from its predecessor. And *stressed mouse use* has as indicator the time-stamped mouse movement events. Especially with respect to typing accuracy, one can wonder whether these indicators can be used for reliably and completely establishing typing accuracy. For example, if the user is correcting a document using a text editing program, the ratio of the number of backspace key presses and the total number of key presses would not correlate to typing accuracy. Also, the indicator for active time can be problematic, in the sense that the 5 min criterion for re-setting active time may prevent capturing actual active time (i.e., non-stop working) as experienced by the user. This criterion, representing an upper limit for the time the user has before (s)he interacts with the computer, in fact depends on the specific user task and the computer program being used. On the other hand, it is not trivial to come up with alternative indicators that are better in all circumstances.

the measurement method(s) used for an indicator do(es) not provide a reliable or proper value of the indicator
The WWC description mentions the indicators to be measured but does not cover the corresponding measurement methods. *Typing accuracy* and *active time* indicators could be measured by logging input behavior using the features available via the computer's OS API (e.g. Win32 API). The logging application may have limitations in terms of how often keyboard/mouse events are recorded, which may affect the accuracy of the indicator values. For measuring mouse movement events, a mouse motion recorder could be used that records raw-input events from the mouse. The mouse may have a limited spatial resolution, which may affect the accuracy of the measurements and ultimately the accuracy of the parameters of arm-hand dynamics.

4 Exemplification

In this section we illustrate our conceptual framework using simplified descriptions of context-aware applications.

4.1 Tele-Monitoring

A person needs to be health-monitored, such that help is provided if needed. The person is monitored from a distance, by capturing vital-sign-data through sensors.

Here, the DAP (see Sect. 3.2) uses sensors attached to the person's body, capturing vital signs, such as heart rate and blood pressure. On that basis, it is essential establishing whether the person is in a "normal" situation or in a situation assuming need for help. If, for instance, the monitored condition is epilepsy, then a combination of vital sign values would indicate a "high probability" of seizure occurrence. Hence, these are the two situations detected by the SD. On that basis, adaptations are done by the AS accordingly. For example, in the event of a "need help" situation, sensor readings would be sent in real time to a hospital, communication would be established with family or friends, and so on. These interactions constitute the delivery of the situation-specific services for the benefit of the monitored person.

Possible threats to utility here are as follows:

- Not always a "need help" situation would be captured and interpreted as precisely as to make a proper match to the actual user needs. For example, it is hard to determine whether the person would need immediate help from family/friends or is it better to wait for an ambulance that arrives with some delay.
- In case of no or poor network connectivity, fallback behavior is to be triggered but chances are small that such behavior would adequately match the user needs. For example: (i) If such a behavior would be about more and more attempts to get connected again, then a "need help" situation may be missed; (ii) If this behavior would be about just sending an ambulance, it may be that often ambulances are sent with no need for them.

4.2   Smart Lighting

A person usually needs proper illumination reflecting his or her individual preferences, in his or her living environment. Such persons are facilitated by a smart living environment, adjusting lighting accordingly in a room. The system can have a maximum number of registered users, each one identified by his or her weight.

The DAP uses a weight sensor to identify a person as a registered user when (s)he enters the room. When a person cannot be identified as a registered user (his or her weight is not close to any of the registered users), (s)he will be ignored by the system.

When a person is identified and in the room for the first time, the room lighting is turned on (if the outside illumination is below a threshold value), sticking to standard values. If the person would make any lighting adjustments, the room "memorizes" the corresponding values, associating them with the person and the time period. When the same person enters the room next time, the memorized values will be used for the lighting and any subsequent adjustments will replace (or be added to) the memorized values. Accordingly, each registered user has his or her own situation. The SD detects which situation applies, i.e. who is in the room, the AS makes adaptations according to standard or memorized values for the person, and the SOD delivers a situation-specific service for the benefit of the particular person.

Possible threats to utility here are as follows:

- If an identified person is alone in the room, being serviced by the system and another identified person enters the room, then the system is in an undefined state for which there is no designed behavior (whether to keep servicing the person who is already in or to stop servicing him/her and start servicing the person who has just entered).

- If some of the registered persons have weights that are close to each other, it might appear that context situations are not properly defined – imagine that these persons gain or lose weight; then they may be mixed up by the system.

4.3 Mission in the Sky

A drone is flying in the sky, fulfilling a mission for the benefit of border police officers who are navigating it from the ground.

Here, the DAP uses numerous sensors. Some sensors may establish that the weather is changing (for instance), other sensors may establish the flying altitude, still other sensors may "sense" objects in close proximity (if any), the fuel/battery reserves, and so on. The drone has many alternative behaviors superposed on the predefined mission behavior. They concern various situations that might occur. Each of them is characterized by a combination of conditions that can be captured by the sensors. For example: (i) One situation might be about change in the weather; (ii) Another situation might be about getting close to an object; (iii) Yet another situation might be about reaching the "point of no return" (after which the drone would not have sufficient fuel/battery resources to come back to the ground station). The SD identifies the situation based on the sensor readings from the DAP, and the AS does the adaptions necessary for this situation. For example: (a) Algorithms running in the drone's avionic engine, adjust altitude, speed, and so on, in response to changing weather conditions; (b) Cameras continue video-recording but with applying a blurring effect, when approaching human beings, such that their privacy is protected; (c) If the drone has reached the "point of no return", the person(s) navigating the drone may be asked either to "push" the drone to immediately fly back or to update its mission (meaning that the drone would not return to the "start point" but to another location). On that basis, situation-specific services are delivered: informing the border police officers that there are no persons (potential trespassers) along the border or transmitting videos (with faces of persons blurred) featuring (a group of) persons, indicating their location, or detecting damaged border facilities, and so on.

Possible threats to utility here are as follows:

- Obviously, in such a complex mission in the sky, different context situations can occur at the same time, for example: weather may deteriorate and at the same time trespassers may be detected. Hence, prioritization is needed – whether to keep on transmitting information featuring the trespassers but assume the risk of a drone crash or adjust the flying trajectory (to save the drone) but assume the risk of "losing focus" on the trespassers.
- Also, it is possible that a context situation is not properly defined, for example: an object hitting the drone may be caused by strong wind but also be an enemy bullet. Those are sharply different situations requiring different actions but the impossibility to define the context situation complicates things.

5   Conclusions

Current context-aware systems are mostly technology-driven. For this reason, they are often insufficiently capable of delivering services that correspond to the user needs at hand (specific to a context situation). Addressing this, we have proposed a conceptual framework that is claimed to be helpful in supporting the user-centric design of context-aware systems. Further, we have made explicit which threats to validity exist, providing the concepts to discuss and resolve them at design time. We have analyzed the so called "technological bias", together with related work and the developments over time featuring context-aware systems. This was a source of inspiration for us in our proposing a broader conceptual view and an architectural structure concerning context-aware systems – both reflected in the abovementioned conceptual framework.

The limitations of our work are two-fold: (i) We have not conducted a systematic literature review; (ii) We have only used simplified examples of context-aware systems to illustrate our conceptual framework.

Future work will focus on situations that are not foreseen and can also not be accounted for in the design. Here we need risk assessments [10] and change impact analysis [11]. We expect our previous work featuring Bayesian Modeling [15] to be useful in this regard. Further, we are interested in aligning our conceptual framework to systemics [17] and public values [8]. Finally, we would carry out real-life case studies and/or interviews with experts, for a stronger justification of our proposal.

References

1. Dey, A., Abowd, G., Salber, D.: A conceptual framework and a toolkit for supporting the rapid prototyping of context-aware applications. Hum.-Comput. Interact. **16**(2), 97–166 (2001)
2. Krejcar, O.: Benefits of building information system with wireless connected mobile device - PDPT framework. In: Proceedings of International Conference on Portable Information Devices, Orlando, FL, USA. IEEE (2007)
3. Calvagna, A., Morabito, G., Pappalardo, A.: WiFi mobility framework supporting GPRS roaming: design and implementation. In Proceedings of International Conference on Communications, Anchorage, AK, USA. IEEE (2003)
4. Kopják, J., Sebestyén, G.: Comparison of data collecting methods in wireless mesh sensor networks. In: IEEE 16th World Symposium on Applied Machine Intelligence and Informatics (SAMI), Kosice and Her-lany, Slovakia (2018)
5. Shishkov, B., van Sinderen, M.: From user context states to context-aware applications. In: Filipe, J., Cordeiro, J., Cardoso, J. (eds.) ICEIS 2007. LNBIP, vol. 12, pp. 225–239. Springer, Heidelberg (2008). https://doi.org/10.1007/978-3-540-88710-2_18
6. Zhao, Z., Gao, C., Duan, F.: A survey on autonomic computing research. In: Proceedings of Asia-Pacific Conference on Computational Intelligence and Industrial Applications (PACIIA), Wuhan, China. IEEE (2009)
7. Friedman, B., Hendry, D.G., Borning, A.: A survey of salue sensitive design methods. In: A Survey of Value Sensitive Design Methods, 1, Now Foundations and Trends (2009)
8. Van den Hoven, J.: Value sensitive design and responsible innovation. In: Owen, R., Bessant, J., Heintz, M. (eds.) Responsible Innovation: Managing the Responsible Emergence of Science and Innovation in Society. Wiley, Hoboken (2013)

9. Shishkov, B., Larsen, J.B., Warnier, M., Janssen, M.: Three categories of context-aware systems. In: Shishkov, B. (ed.) BMSD 2018. LNBIP, vol. 319, pp. 185–202. Springer, Cham (2018). https://doi.org/10.1007/978-3-319-94214-8_12

10. Hopkins, P.: Fundamentals of Risk Management - Understanding, Evaluating, and Implementing Effective Risk Management. IRM (2012)

11. Ali, H.O., Rozan, M.Z.A., Sharif, A.M.: Identifying challenges of change impact analysis for software projects. In: Proceedings of International Conference on Innovation Management and Technology Research, Malacca, Malaysia. IEEE (2012)

12. Wegdam, M.: AWARENESS: a project on context AWARE mobile NEtworks and ServiceS. In: Proceedings of 14th Mobile & Wireless Communications Summit. EURASIP (2005)

13. Shishkov, B., Hristozov, S., Verbraeck, A.: Improving resilience using drones for effective monitoring after disruptive events. In: Proceedings of 9th International Conference on Telecommunications and Remote Sensing (ICTRS 2020). Association for Computing Machinery, New York (2020)

14. Silvander, J.: On context frames and their implementations. In: Shishkov, B. (ed.) Business Modeling and Software Design. BMSD 2021. LNBIP, vol. 422. Springer, Cham (2021)

15. Shishkov, B.: Tuning the behavior of context-aware applications. In: Shishkov, B. (ed.) Business Modeling and Software Design BMSD 2019. LNBIP, vol 356, pp. 134–152. Springer, Cham (2019). https://doi.org/10.1007/978-3-030-24854-3_9

16. Shishkov, B.: Designing Enterprise Information Systems Merging Enterprise Modeling and Software Specification. Springer, Cham (2020). https://doi.org/10.1007/978-3-030-22441-7

17. Bunge, M.A.: Treatise on Basic Philosophy. A World of Systems, vol. 4. D. Reidel Publishing Company, Dordrecht (1979)

18. Shishkov, B., Mendling, J.: Business process variability and public values. In: Shishkov, B. (ed.) BMSD 2018. LNBIP, vol 319, pp. 401–411. Springer, Cham (2018). https://doi.org/10.1007/978-3-319-94214-8_31

19. Dey, A.K., Newberger, A.: Support for context-aware intelligibility and control. In: Proceedings of SIGCHI Conference on Human Factors in Computing Systems. ACM, USA (2009)

20. Bosems, S., van Sinderen, M.: Models in the design of context-aware well-being applications. In: Meersman, R., et al. (eds.) OTM 2014. LNCS, vol. 8842, pp. 37–42. Springer, Heidelberg (2014). https://doi.org/10.1007/978-3-662-45550-0_6

21. Cano, J., Delaval, G., Rutten, E.: Coordination of ECA rules by verification and control. In: Kühn, E., Pugliese, R. (eds.) COORDINATION 2014. LNCS, vol. 8459, pp. 33–48. Springer, Heidelberg (2014). https://doi.org/10.1007/978-3-662-43376-8_3

22. Alegre, U., Augusto, J.C., Clark, T.: Engineering context-aware systems and applications. J. Syst. Softw. **117**, 55–83 (2016)

23. Alférez, G.H., Pelechano, V.: Context-aware autonomous web services in software product lines. In: Proceedings of 15th International SPLC Conference. IEEE, CA, USA (2011)

24. Abeywickrama, D.B., Ramakrishnan, S.: Context-aware services engineering: models, transformations, and verification. ACM Trans. Internet Technol. J. **11**(3), Article 10 (2011)

25. Borissova, D., Cvetkova, P., Garvanov, I., Garvanova, M.: A framework of business intelligence system for decision making in efficiency management. In: Saeed, K., Dvorský, J. (eds.) CISIM 2020. LNCS, vol. 12133, pp. 111–121. Springer, Cham (2020). https://doi.org/10.1007/978-3-030-47679-3_10

26. Garvanova, M., Garvanov, I., Kashukeev, I.: Business processes and the safety of stakeholders: considering the electromagnetic pollution. In: Shishkov, B. (ed.) BMSD 2020. LNBIP, vol. 391, pp. 386–393. Springer, Cham (2020). https://doi.org/10.1007/978-3-030-52306-0_28

27. Dimitrova, Z., Dimitrov, V., Borissova, D., Garvanov, I., Garvanova, M.: Two-stage search-based approach for determination and sorting of mountain hiking routes using directed weighted multigraph. Cybern. Inf. Technol. **20**(6), 28–39 (2020). Print ISSN 1311-9702, Online ISSN 1314-4081. https://doi.org/10.2478/cait-2020-0058
28. Schilit, B., Adams, N., Want, R.: Context-aware computing applications. In: First Workshop on Mobile Computing Systems and Applications, pp. 85–90. IEEE (1994)
29. Harter, A., Hopper, A., Steggles, P., Ward, A., Webster, P.: The anatomy of a context-aware application. Wirel. Netw. **8**, 187–197 (2002)
30. Dey, A.K.: Context-aware computing: the CyberDesk project. In: AAAI Spring Symposium on Intelligent Environments, AAAI Technical Report SS-88-02, pp. 51–54 (1998)
31. Abecker, A., Bernardi, A., Hinkelmann, K., et al.: Context-aware, proactive delivery of task-specific information: the knowmore project. Inf. Syst. Front. **2**, 253–276 (2000)
32. van Sinderen, M., van Halteren, A., Wegdam, M., et al.: Supporting context-aware mobile applications: an infrastructure approach. IEEE Commun. Mag. **44**(9), 96–104 (2006)
33. Chaari, T., Laforest, F., Celentano, A.: Adaptation in context-aware pervasive information systems: the SECAS project. Int. J. Perv. Comput. Commun. **3**(4), 400–425 (2007)
34. Kegel, R.H.P., van Sinderen, M., Wieringa, R.J.: Towards more individualized interfaces: automating the assessment of computer literacy. In Proceedings of 7th International Workshop on Behavior Change Support Systems, BCSS@PERSUASIVE 2019, CEUR Workshop Proceedings, vol. 2340. CEUR-WS.org (2019)
35. Sun, D., Paredes, P., Canny, J.: MouStress: detecting stress from mouse motion. In: Proceedings of SIGCHI Conference on Human Factors in Computing Systems. Association for Computing Machinery, New York (2014)
36. Pawar, P., Van Beijnum, B., Hermens, H., Konstantas, D.: Analysis of context-aware network selection schemes for power savings. In Proceedings of Asia-Pacific Services Computing Conference, pp. 587–594. IEEE (2008)
37. Van Engelenburg, S.: Designing context-aware architectures for business-to-government information sharing. Ph.D. thesis. TU Delft Press (2019)

On Context Frames and Their Implementations

Johan Silvander[(✉)]

Software Engineering Research Lab Sweden, Blekinge Institute of Technology,
Karlskrona, Sweden
`Johan.Silvander@bth.se`

Abstract. When an actor is selecting an action in order to fulfill its intents, in a given context, the actor's knowledge and beliefs about the specific context will impact the possibility to achieve a desired outcome. The context is often affected by unobserved, or unmeasured, factors, which can impact the result of the desired outcome.

The context specific knowledge and beliefs an actor has about a domain, together with the possibilities to evaluate and learn which actions shall be taken, are packaged into a context frame. Our intention with this study is to evaluate an implementation of such a context frame. The context frame concept is meant to support actors to fulfill their intents in a given knowledge domain, by enforcing the needed, and available, actions which cause effects on the outcomes. We have built our implementation of the context frame on the OODA-loop, Pask's conversation theory, and structural causal models, by using a Bayesian approach, and probabilistic programming.

The research approach is based on evaluation research. We evaluated our implementation with the help of a proof of concept. During the proof of concept we used data sets containing decisions about treatment and survival analysis regarding cancer patients, information obtained during focus group interviews, and questionnaire data.

The proof of concept used to evaluate our implementation of a context frame was regarded as successful and the concept of context frames deemed as useful.

Our division of a context frame in three parts, supported by four different types of analysis functions, made it easier to create a solution which supports evaluation and learning.

Keywords: Bayesian approach · Structural causal models · Context frame

1 Introduction

A context frame captures the context specific knowledge and beliefs an actor has about a specific domain. The knowledge and beliefs are stated in a way which makes it possible to evaluate them, and learn from them. This makes it possible for a context frame to support evaluation and learning. The evaluation and learning aim to improve the knowledge of actors who are interacting with

© Springer Nature Switzerland AG 2021
B. Shishkov (Ed.): BMSD 2021, LNBIP 422, pp. 133–153, 2021.
https://doi.org/10.1007/978-3-030-79976-2_8

the context frame, and to improve a context frame's own knowledge about a domain. The evaluation and learning can be done by human actors or machine actors. Our main objective in this study is to evaluate our implementation of a context frame. The background to our concept of a context frame is described in [20,21].

We have based our implementation of a context frame on the ideas from Pask's conversation theory [13], an extended version of the OODA-loop [19], and structural causal models [14]. In our implementation of the context frame we have used a Bayesian approach, and probabilistic programming [4]. The Bayesian approach is supported by the Rethinking package [12].

Two key components in Pask's conversation theory [13] are language and domain. Actors interact on the same domain with the help of a common language. In order to construct, express, and validate a topic, two layers of procedures exist. The lower layer procedures operate upon the domain in order to bring about or explain topic relations. The top layer procedures operate on the lower level procedures in order to construct or reconstruct the topic relations.

Pask [13] stresses the fact that the different actors have obtained their specific domain information through several different interactions. This means each actor obtains its specific domain information in different situations. We define a context frame to contain information about a specific domain, which is available to a certain actor, or group of actors.

In recent work [19] the OODA-loop [16] was extended in order to make intents, knowledge and belief, and evaluation and learning, explicit in the OODA-loop. We use this work as a base for our construction of a context frame. Other contributions for introducing knowledge and beliefs into the OODA-loop exists in the literature. McCauley-Bell and Freeman [10] presents a methodology which proposes the analysis of evidence accrual by categorizing responses in the OODA-loop as a result of knowledge systems and belief systems. Consoli et al. [2], present how the relationship between the Belief-Desire-Intention framework and the OODA-loop can be enabled.

The structural causal model [14] provides a base for the functionality needed to implement a context frame. The idea of letting actors explicitly formulate their knowledge and beliefs in a certain domain, with the help of an acyclic graph, supports an important aspect of evaluation and learning, the understanding of the reasoning behind decisions taken.

In our implementation we have decided to support a split of a specific domain into fine grained context frames, and by composition support the whole domain. By using fine grained context frames, it is easier to add value to a process which supports the business of an actor. The possibility to take several decisions, based on the outcomes from different context frames, and use these as inputs to other context frames, makes it possible for an actor to evaluate, and plan, its decision making. As an example, the achievement of a specific outcome might be the intent of one actor, or it might be one step towards realizing the actor's, or another actor's, intent. This step wise approach is supported by the possibility to create compositions of context frames.

The remaining of the paper is structured as follows, the methodology is described in Sect. 2, and the results are presented in Sect. 3 and Sect. 4. The analysis, and discussion, of the results are presented in Sect. 5, and finally, in Sect. 6, the conclusion and future research are presented.

2   Methodology

In order to evaluate our implementation of a context frame we used evaluation research [17]. We choose to do the evaluation with medical practitioners since they are forced, by laws and regulations, to document their decisions. The evaluation was performed as a proof of concept.

The research data we used during the proof of concept consists of data sets regarding decisions about treatment (operation) and survival analysis of patients with stomach cancer, information obtained during focus group interviews [28], and questionnaire data which were obtained from a study done in 2020 [18].

The focus group interviews were approximately two hours in length and were based on semi-structured focus group interviews with the interview questions adapted to the findings during the previous focus group interviews or questionnaire analysis. The validation and correction of the captured material was conducted with the members of the focus group on the same day as the interview was held.

The questionnaires consist of several factors, and their measurement values, regarding fictive patients. The factors included age, C-reactive protein [25] (CRP), body mass index, and changes to the body mass index during the last six months. The practitioners decide the impact of each value, and if a treatment should be considered or not. After the questionnaires were answered, samples from the questionnaire were discussed among the practitioners.

In our proof of concept we used six factors from the data sets, two are outcomes (survival and decision of treatment) and four of them are factors that have effects on an outcome. Out of these four factors, three are immutable factors (age, risk and treatment) and one is a mutable factor (CRP). The survival, decision of treatment, and treatment, are binary factors. The age of the patient and a patient's CRP value are continuous factors. The risk factor is a value of a patient's health conditions, measured in an ordinal scale from zero to six.

3   The Design of a Context Frame

In this section we introduce our main reasoning behind our design and implementation of a context frame.

The first part of our context frame implementation supports an actor to describe its knowledge and beliefs with the help of a directed acyclic graph. This graph is a blueprint describing the interactions between the outcome factor, the factors which can be used to cause an effect on the outcome, and other factors relevant to the blueprint. With the help of obtained factor data, an actor can evaluate if a blueprint reflects the reality, and learn if a cause is strong enough to achieve a desired outcome. This part of the context frame we have named *knowledge and beliefs container*. The *knowledge and beliefs container* supports the observe, and the orient, steps in the OODA-loop. Resulting artifacts are models which are used by different types of analysis, supported by the *evaluation and learning container*.

In order to further support Pask's procedures in our implementation of a context frame, we added an *evaluation and learning container*, and a *data container*.

An *evaluation and learning container* supports the decide, and the act, steps in the OODA-loop. It can be used to estimate an outcome based on knowledge about the involved factors. Depending on the outcome factor, it is possible to support triage prioritization [22]. Another option is to use the *evaluation and learning container* to support actors with the possibility to evaluate if they can achieve the desired outcomes, and reach the desired intent with the help of changes to a factor value. The evaluation might be in the form of, "How can I impact a factor, in order to increase the probability to reach the desired outcome?". In order to gain new knowledge, it is important to be able to ask questions like, "Why did the chage to a factor value not increase the probability to reach the desired outcome?". The "How" will be supported by interventions [15], while the "Why" will be supported by counterfactuals [15]. The last option is to let actors state the desired outcome, together with data for all the factors which impact the outcome. This gives the possibility to indicate the difference between how an actor and a model perceive a domain.

The *data container* supports the addition of results from decisions taken when using the *evaluation and learning container*, and by adding knowledge from related communities. By using data in the *data container* to continuously evaluate or update the blueprint, and the models, we aim to support a continuous learning [9].

Since all models contain unknown information, which may require decision making under uncertainty [8], we decided to base a context frame on a Bayesian approach, and probabilistic programming [4]. This will give us the possibility to quantify the uncertainty of an outcome.

The *knowledge and beliefs container* is further described in Sect. 3.1, the *evaluation and learning container* in Sect. 3.3, and the *data container* in Sect. 3.4.

3.1   The Knowledge and Beliefs Container

The *knowledge and beliefs container* is used to make an actor's knowledge and beliefs about a certain domain explicit. This makes it possible for actors to learn about a domain. Another important aspect is the possibility for actors to improve the knowledge and beliefs. The possibility to analyze and discuss a blueprint is of major value in order to evaluate and learn, from knowledge and beliefs, in a specific domain.

An *knowledge and beliefs container* contains three different type of artifacts: blueprints, logic based on the blueprint, and models which are generated with the help of the logic. The translation of a blueprint into logic, which is used to create models, is further described in Sect. 3.2.

During a *knowledge and beliefs container*'s own evaluation and learning process, domain experts suggest factors to be added, or removed, from the blueprints. Likewise, how different factors interact with each other might changed as well. Even if a *knowledge and beliefs container* is domain specific, the tasks used to construct a *knowledge and beliefs container* follows the same process. The simplified process of constructing a *knowledge and beliefs container* is described below.

Actors use their knowledge, and beliefs, in order to create a blueprint of how an outcome factor is affected by different factors. The blueprint will contain information about factors which will be used to cause a change to the outcome factor.

We use a directed acyclic graph to describe the blueprint. With the help of tools like Dagitty [23], which supports d-separation [5] analysis, it is possible to decide which factors are needed in order to be able to apply causal effects on the outcome factor. If data is not obtainable for a needed factor, its data might be possible to obtain by using instrumental variables [15], or confirmatory factor analysis [7]. However, if data cannot be obtained for the needed factors, a new blueprint has to be designed, or we cannot solve the problem at hand.

The factors in a blueprint have different characteristics, and have different purpose in the blueprint. The relationship between the factors, and how the different factors impact each other, might be governed by an actor's mental model about a specific context.

For some factors, the impact a factor might have on the desired outcome, is not governed by a law, for example a physical law. Instead the impact is based on an actor's knowledge, and beliefs, about a factor's impact, in order to achieve its intents, and the desired outcome, for example how to increase the sales of a certain product.

Unobserved and unmeasured factors are unknown to the blueprint and can impact the desired outcomes [8]. A common concern is the possibility of one unknown factor affecting more than one known factor, or one unknown factor affecting the outcome factor and known factors. This might lead to scenarios were the logical models will introduce confounding factos. Our categorization of factors as known and unknown was further broken down with the inspiration of Johari window [26]. The result of the categorization is shown in Fig. 1.

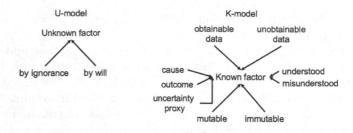

Fig. 1. A visualization of the factor definitions

Figure 1 shows two different types of characteristic models, the U-model and the K-model. The U-model shows the characteristics of unknown factors. The unknown factors were divided into two different characteristics, named "by ignorance" and "by will". Factors which are not known to exist by the actor are defined as unknown by ignorance. Factors unknown to the model can be left-out by will. Examples are factors which are left-out, since they do not bring valuable information into the model. Another reason to leave factors out of the model, is if different factors measure the same phenomenon, and are strongly correlated, which might affect the model in a negative way due to multicollinearity.

The K-model shows the different types of characteristics of known factors. A known factor can have multiple characteristics. Starting at the top in Fig. 1 and moving clockwise, we can see obtainable and unobtainable factors. Unobtainable factors can be factors for which its information cannot be measured or derived. However, with the help of confirmatory factor analysis [7], factors which are not directly obtainable, latent factors, can be derived and verified with the help of measured known factors. Another possibility is to use instrumental variables [15].

The known factors were further divided into two different types of characteristics, based on an actor's understanding of how a factor is affecting, or is affected by, the real-world. We named these two types of characteristics, understood factors, and misunderstood factors. These characteristics will be visible during the evaluation of the blueprint.

The characteristics of the different factors' values might vary. Some of the factor values can be changed to improve the possibility to reach the desired outcome. Other factor values cannot be changed, age is one example, or can be changed according to different lead times, one example is socioeconomic status, down to instant modification. Even if the value of a factor is possible to change, the modification of this factor value might only be possible to do to a certain extent during a specific timeframe, e.g. injecting a certain amount of a drug. Other constraints occur when factor values are not available to change at a specific point-in-time due to dependencies between decisions, or changes to a factor value are not reversible. There is an additional time aspect to the known factors. Some known factors can be found in historical records, while others are obtained during an investigation.

Another characteristic of a factor is the role of capturing the uncertainty an actor has. We named these type of factors uncertainty proxies. The outcome of a model is an outcome factor and we named the factors which are select to be used to affect the outcome, cause factors.

By translating the needed parts of the directed acyclic graph into a logical description we can use obtained factor data to verify the blueprint. The logical description of a blueprint is in the form of Bayesian equations, as described in Sect. 3.2. If the blueprint is falsified a new blueprint has to be created. If the blueprint is not falsified, its logical description can be used to build models.

The models can be used to verify if a causal factor has the desired causal effect on the outcome factor. Another use of the models is to measure if a causal factor as the desired relative effect on the outcome factor, compared with other factors. If the desired causal effects are not obtained, the blueprint might not be used as a base to produce models. It is important to stress two aspects of a blueprint. A blueprint which cannot fulfill the desired causal effects is a valid outcome. Secondly, a blueprint is only a limited view of a domain. There will always be unmeasured factors, either by ignorance, or by will, of the actor.

3.2   Logical Translation and Models

The translation of a blueprint into a logical form is performed with the help of an Bayesian approach. By using data which contain cases relevant to the blueprint, the Bayesian approach produces models which are used to validate the blueprint, and are the base for the functions described in Sect. 3.3. The current implementation supports factors which are continuous or categorical. This makes it possible to use linear regression or logistic regression as the base for the logical translation of a blueprint.

Below we describe the logical translations which are used to translate a blueprint into models. In the equations used to perform the translations, we use the following notation: α is the intercept, β is a coefficient, μ is the mean value, and σ is the standard deviation. When we are using multilevel models we use a set of parameters to capture the commonalities between the different populations. The $\overline{\alpha}$ is the intercept for the commonalities, σ_α is the standard deviation of the $\overline{\alpha}$, and $z\alpha$ is the standardized $\overline{\alpha}$.

In the equations below, we use variable names in the distributions which are used to find the value of a parameter. In the proof of concept we have used the values in Table 1.

Table 1. Parameter values used in the proof of concept.

Parameter	Value
α_value	1.5
β_value	1.5
σ_value	1
$z\alpha\_value$	1
$\bar{\alpha}\_value$	1.5
σ_α_value	1

When the outcome factor values are categorical and all other factors values are continuous, a model is built based on Eq. 1–4.

$$Outcome\_factor \sim Binomial(1, p) \tag{1}$$

$$logit(p) = \alpha + \beta_{factor^i} * factor^i_{value} + \dots + \beta_{factor^j} * factor^j_{value} \tag{2}$$

$$\alpha \sim Normal(0, \alpha\_value) \tag{3}$$

$$\beta_{factor^n} \sim Normal(0, \beta\_value) \tag{4}$$

When the outcome factor values are categorical and the other factors values are a mix of continuous and categorical values, a model is built based on Eq. 5–8 (cfv = categorical factor value).

$$Outcome\_factor \sim Binomial(1, p) \tag{5}$$

$$logit(p) = \beta[cfv] + \beta_{factor^i}[cfv] * factor^i_{value} + \dots + \beta_{factor^j}[cfv] * factor^j_{value} \tag{6}$$

$$\beta[cfv] \sim Normal(0, \beta\_value) \tag{7}$$

$$\beta_{factor^n}[cfv] \sim Normal(0, \beta\_value) \tag{8}$$

When the outcome factor values are continuous and all other factors values are continuous, a model is built based on Eq. 9–13.

$$Outcome\_factor \sim Normal(\mu, \sigma) \tag{9}$$

$$\mu = \alpha + \beta_{factor^i} * factor^i_{value} + \dots + \beta_{factor^j} * factor^j_{value} \tag{10}$$

$$\alpha \sim Normal(0, \alpha\_value) \tag{11}$$

$$\beta_{factor^n} \sim Normal(0, \beta\_value) \tag{12}$$

$$\sigma \sim Exp(\sigma\_value) \tag{13}$$

When the outcome factor values are continuous and the other factors values are a mix of continuous and categorical values, a model is built based on Eq. 14–18 (cfv = categorical factor value).

$$Outcome\_factor \sim Normal(\mu, \sigma) \tag{14}$$

$$\mu = \beta[cfv] + \beta_{factori}[cfv] * factor_{value}^i + ... + \beta_{factorj}[cfv] * factor_{value}^j \tag{15}$$

$$\beta[cfv] \sim Normal(0, \beta\_value) \tag{16}$$

$$\beta_{factorn}[cfv] \sim Normal(0, \beta\_value) \tag{17}$$

$$\sigma \sim Exp(\sigma\_value) \tag{18}$$

If a factor is influencing another factor, additional equations are needed to measure the influence. Depending on the value type of the outcome factor, the influenced factor, and the influencing factors, a combination of the equation models, described above, can be used.

Multilevel models [11] are used to preserve differences between different kind of populations, and at the same time capture the commonalities of these different populations. The use of multilevel models makes it possible to simulate new populations by using the captured commonalities. By adding Eq. 19–22 to the models descibed above, multilevel models can be constructed. In Eq. 19–22 the $\alpha[pid] = z\alpha[pid] * \sigma_\alpha + \overline{\alpha}$ (pid = population identifier). The $\overline{\alpha}$ can be used to simulate new populations.

$$logit(p) = z\alpha[pid] * \sigma_\alpha + \overline{\alpha} + ... \tag{19}$$

$$z\alpha[pid] \sim Normal(0, z\alpha \tag{20}$$

$$\overline{\alpha} \sim Normal(0, 1.5) \tag{21}$$

$$\sigma_\alpha \sim HalfNormal(0, \sigma_\alpha\_value) \tag{22}$$

The causal effects can be calculated with the help of the first four equation models. The factors in an equation model which is used to calculate a causal effect are the outcome factor, the cause factor, and factors which are needed to control for. The factors needed to control for are the members of an adjustment set which can be found by using Dagitty [23].

3.3 The Evaluation and Learning Container

The *evaluation and learning container* provides functions which use the models generated in the *knowledge and beliefs container*. The functions provide four different types of analysis: predictive analysis, prescriptive analysis [24], counterfactual analysis [15], and explorative analysis.

The predictive analysis uses the factor values for one context frame to predict its outcome factor value. The outcome factor value is presented as a distribution. If a chain of context frames is used to predict the final outcome factor value, the outcome factor value of the current context frame is input to the next context frame in the chain. This type of analysis is a passive form of achieving a desired intent.

The prescriptive analysis is an active form of achieving a desired intent. During a prescriptive analysis the desired outcome factor value is chosen. This value is used together with other factor values to obtain a distribution of the cause factor value needed to achieve the desired outcome. Since a cause factor might have different constraints, as discussed in Sect. 3.1, it might not be possible to achieve the desired outcome. If a chain of context frames is used to predict the final outcome factor value, the desired intent, the analysis is started with the last context frame in the chain. The current cause factor value is used as the outcome factor value to the previous context frame in the chain. This type of analysis can be based on triage prioritization [22].

The counterfactual analysis is based on structural causal models [14]. This type of analysis is used to answer questions like "Why did the cause factor value not increase the probability to reach the desired outcome?". The question can be answered with the question "What if I had changed the cause factor value to X?". The counterfactual analysis is done on an individual case level. By doing the counterfactual analysis on individual case level, it is possible for an actor to evaluate, and learn, from its decision regarding a specific individual case. However, a linear system is a prerequisite for doing counterfactual analysis on individual case level. If the system is not linear, we could use average causal effect [6]. However, an average causal effect does not have the same evaluating, and learning, benefits as a counterfactual analyze done on an individual case level. The counterfactual analysis can be combined with the other type of analysis.

The explorative analysis can be used for two different purposes. The first purpose is to show the difference between what an actor believes, and what the facts state. The second purpose is to find unrealistic results, created by the model. In both cases an actor provides all factor values, including the cause factor value, and the outcome factor value. The function returns the different distributions of each factor, needed to meet the outcome value when the other factor values are according to the actor's preferences.

All functions support the possibility to define a specific compatibility interval of the returned distributions. This can be used to analyze if the values within the desired probability ranges.

The analysis functions support Pask's procedures of explaining and reconstructing topic relations. As described in Sect. 3.4, the analysis functions provide data to the *data container*. This data is used to update the affected models. This feedback loop makes it possible for the analysis functions to support Pask's procedures of bring about and construct topic relations.

The possibility to use the functions in the *evaluation and learning container* to perform prediction of the outcome based on existing factor values, estimate the needed values of factors in order to obtain a desired outcome, perform counterfactual analysis [15], and perform knowledge and beliefs reasoning, makes it possible to create a workflow, based on the practitioners needs, and desires.

We have created a utility function named *The limit value function*. This function makes it easier to understand the impact of the different parameters used in a logical translation of a blueprint. The function obtains the value of one of the factors when the probability of an outcome factor is 0.5. We achieve this by keeping all other factors at their average value. This process can be repeated for all factors in a model.

3.4   The Data Container

The *data container* is responsible for managing the data from different sources. The foreseen sources are results obtained when using the different analysis provided by the *evaluation and learning container* and data external to the context frame.

The external data are originating from the actors working in the same domain as the context frame is designed to handle. This data can be seen as external knowledge to the context frame.

The analysis provided by the *evaluation and learning container* generates data which is logged. This log data can be seen as internal knowledge to the context frame.

The log data contains: the analysis type, the actor type, the outcome factor type, values of the affected cause factor, values of the outcome factor, and the actual values of the other factors. The values of a cause factor and the outcome factor is in the form of actual value, value suggested by the context frame, actor decided value, the used value. The type of an outcome factor is either an action or a result. Depending on the type of analysis, different type of log data are captured.

The log data described above, can be used to build different metrics. These metrics can be used to decide when a model or a blueprint should be updated. This will form a feedback loop, which is used to update the knowledge and beliefs of a context frame.

By using different labels for external knowledge data and internal knowledge data, it is possible to use multilevel models to provide analysis based on internal knowledge, external knowledge, or a combination of those. This can be seen as learning by doing, learning from sources, and a combination of both.

The decisions about which data shall be used as a population in multilevel models [11], or if the results of counterfactual analysis shall be used, are decisions taken when a model is constructed in the *knowledge and beliefs container*.

4   Evaluation of a Context Frame

In order to evaluate our implementation of a context frame we performed a proof of concept. The proof of concept is described in Sect. 4.1 and the role of an uncertainty proxy is discussed in Sect. 4.2.

4.1   The Proof of Concept

The proof of concept is based on the information described in Sect. 2. With this information we started to build two blueprints, according to our implementation of context frames. In Fig. 2 we can see the separation of the decision of being able to have a treatment, and actually having a treatment. Since not all patients, which can have a treatment, actually will get a treatment, we considered this separation of the blueprints as valid. This results in two different context frames, which supports the idea of fine grained, and composable, context frames.

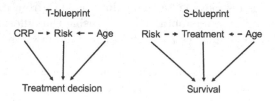

Fig. 2. A visualization of the models

Figure 2 describes four different blueprints. Two of the blueprints are built by using only the filled arrows, and the two other blueprints are built by using both the filled arrows and the dashed arrows. In the blueprints described with only filled arrows, none of the factors have any confounding factors [15]. This makes it possible to directly measure the direct effect of each factor on the outcome factor. In Fig. 2 the dashed arrows represent potential influences between the different factors. In this case we are interested in to measure these influences.

In this study, the risk factor is, to some extent, estimated, and the age factor is an uncertainty proxy. This makes the measurement of the causal effects of these factors interesting, in order to understand how actors' knowledge and beliefs, affect the outcomes.

In the blueprint named T-blueprint, the outcome factor is treatment decision, and the cause factor is the CRP factor. Our concern about the T-blueprint is about the risk factor. Since risk is based on data but might include knowledge, and beliefs, we investigated if age or CRP influence the value of risk. If there is a causal relationship the risk factor will act as a mediator [15].

In the blueprint named S-blueprint, the outcome factor is survival, and the cause factor is the treatment factor. Our concern about the S-blueprint is if risk or age can effect the treatment. If this is the case the treatment will have confounding factors [15].

We used Dagitty [23] to show which factors we need to control for if we want to measure the causal effect of the cause factor on the outcome factor. The factors we need to control for is called the adjustment set. The T-blueprint has empty adjustment sets for both its possible blueprints. The S-blueprint has a none empty adjustment set when influences are part of the blueprint. This adjustment set contains the age factor and the risk factor.

Our next step was to translate the T-blueprint into a logical representation which can be used to produce models. We started to create a model which is free from influences between the factors, and a causal effect model. According to the guidelines in Sect. 3.2, these models are built with Eq. 1–4. The results are presented in Table 2. In Table 2 we can see how the β_{CRP} has a lower negative value for the causal effect compared to its observed effect. A lower negative coefficient value means a higher cause factor value for when a treatment should not be recommended. This knowledge gives better possibilities to achieve a desired outcome.

Table 2. The model for decision of treatment.

Parameter	Compatibility interval (5.5%, 94.5%)
α	0.76 (0.09, 1.50)
β_{Age}	−1.24 (−2.15 −0.40)
β_{CRP}	−2.35 (−3.44, −1.39)
β_{Risk}	−1.80 (−2.67, −0.97)
causal effect	
α	0.56 (0.06, 1.08)
β_{CRP}	−1.40 (−2.14, −0.74)

We continued with a translation of the T-blueprint which contains influences on the risk factor. According to the guidelines in Sect. 3.2, this model is built with Eq. 1–4, in combination with Eq. 9–13. The focus is on the influences and these results are presented in Table 3.

Table 3. The model for decision of treatment with influences on the risk factor.

Parameter	Compatibility interval (5.5%, 94.5%)
α_{Risk}	0.00 (−0.19, 0.18)
$\beta_{Age->Risk}$	0.05 (−0.17, 0.28)
$\beta_{CRP->Risk}$	0.03 (−0.20, 0.26)

In Table 3, we can see how the influence on the risk factor can be neglected. Since the risk factor is not influenced by the CRP factor or the age factor, each factor is responsible for different knowledge and beliefs.

The next translation of the T-blueprint is a multilevel model where differences in sex are treated as different populations. According to the guidelines in Sect. 3.2, this model is built with Eq. 1–4, in combination with Eq. 19–22. The results are presented in Table 4.

Table 4. Multilevel model for decision of treatment.

Parameter	Compatibility interval (5.5%, 94.5%)
$\alpha[female]$	1.85 (0.74, 3.07)
$\alpha[male]$	−0.31 (−1.43, 0.76)
$\bar{\alpha}$	0.58 (−0.79, 1.92)
β_{Age}	−1.35 (−2.22, −0.48)
β_{CRP}	−2.41 (−3.47, −1.46)
β_{Risk}	−2.32 (−3.42, −1.37)

We use the *limit function* to calculate the limits for the different factors, regarding, when no treatment shall be given. The results are presented in Table 5. The *limit function* is described in Sect. 3.3.

Table 5. The limit value for a factor when no treatment shall be given.

Factor	Population	Standardized	Natural
Age			
	None multilevel	0.81	82.53
	Female multilevel	1.61	94.16
	Male multilevel	−0.29	66.50
	Common multilevel	0.52	78.29
CRP			
	None multilevel	0.36	40.77
	Female multilevel	0.82	56.07
	Male multilevel	-0.13	24.66
	Common multilevel	0.26	37.50
Risk			
	None multilevel	0.48	3.50
	Female multilevel	0.82	3.94
	Male multilevel	−0.11	2.76
	Common multilevel	0.27	3.24

Since all the β-values for the multilevel model (Table 4) are more negative compared to the none multilevel model (Table 2), the limit of not having a treatment will be reached with lower factor values in the multilevel model compared to the none multilevel model. This is shown in Table 5, when we compare the none multilevel factor values with the common multilevel factor values. This shows how the multilevel model is more restrictive with recommending a treatment, since it learns from both of the populations.

We continued with translating the S-blueprint into a logical representation which can be used to produce models. We started to create a model which is free from influences between the factors, and a causal effect model. According to the guidelines in Section 3.2, these models are built with Eq. 5–8. The results are presented in Table 6. In Table 6 we can see how the cause factor has a stronger positive effect on the outcome factor when a treatment is given, compared to when a treatment is not given. This shows how a treatment is beneficial for the possibility to survive. In the causal effect model we assume confounding factors, which is verified in Table 7.

Table 6. The model for survival.

Parameter	Compatibility interval (5.5%, 94.5%)
$\beta[not\ treated]$	0.53 (−0.39, 1.52)
$\beta[treated]$	1.39 (0.60, 2.33)
$\beta_{Age}[not\ treated]$	−0.37 (−1.31, 0.53)
$\beta_{Age}[treated]$	−1.60 (−3.11, −0.32)
$\beta_{Risk}[not\ treated]$	−1.26 (−2.17, −0.43)
$\beta_{Risk}[treated]$	−2.19 (−3.56, −1.04)
causal effect	
$\beta[not\ treated]$	0.53 (−0.39, 1.52)
$\beta[treated]$	1.39 (0.60, 2.33)

We continued with a translation of the S-blueprint which contains influences on the treated factor. According to the guidelines in Sect. 3.2, this model is built with Eq. 5–8, in combination with Eq. 14–18. The focus is on the influences and these results are presented in Table 7.

Table 7. The model for survival with influences on the treated factor.

Parameter	Compatibility interval (5.5%, 94.5%)
$\alpha_{Treated}$	0.65 (0.07, 1.22)
$\beta_{Age->Treated}[not\ treated]$	−1.18 (−2.09, −0.34)
$\beta_{Age->Treated}[treated]$	−0.42 (−1.26, 0.34)
$\beta_{Risk->Treated}[not\ treated]$	−0.88 (−1.70, −0.18)
$\beta_{Risk->Treated}[treated]$	−0.53 (−1.41, 0.30)

In Table 7, we can see how the influence on the treated factor cannot be neglected. The treated factor is influenced by the risk factor and the age factor, when no treatment is given. This will be discussed in Sect. 4.2.

The next translation of the S-blueprint is a multilevel model where differences in sex are treated as different populations. According to the guidelines in

Sect. 3.2, this model is built with Eq. 5–8, in combination with Eq. 19–22. The results are presented in Table 8.

Table 8. Multilevel model for survival.

Parameter	Compatibility interval (5.5%, 94.5%)
$\alpha[female]$	0.98 (−0.55, 2.55)
$\alpha[male]$	0.64 (−0.85, 2.09)
$\overline{\alpha}$	0.73 (−0.74, 2.15)
$\beta[not\ treated]$	−0.03 (−1.57, 1.48)
$\beta[treated]$	0.59 (−0.89, 2.14)
$\beta_{Age}[not\ treated]$	−0.47 (−1.44, 0.47)
$\beta_{Age}[treated]$	−1.72 (−3.25, −0.36)
$\beta_{Risk}[not\ treated]$	−1.40 (−2.37, −0.52)
$\beta_{Risk}[treated]$	−2.27 (−3.59, −1.06)

We use the *limit function* to calculate the limits for the different factors, regarding, when a person will not survive. The results are presented in Table 9. The *limit function* is described in Sect. 3.3.

Table 9. The limit value for a factor when a person will not survive.

Factor	Population	Treatment	Standardized	Natural
Age				
	None multilevel	No	1.12	87.00
	Female multilevel	No	2.01	100.04
	Male multilevel	No	1.29	89.54
	Common multilevel	No	1.47	92.18
	None multilevel	Yes	1.09	86.53
	Female multilevel	Yes	0.92	84.06
	Male multilevel	Yes	0.72	81.16
	Common multilevel	Yes	0.77	81.89
Risk				
	None multilevel	No	0.44	3.46
	Female multilevel	No	0.68	3.76
	Male multilevel	No	0.44	3.45
	Common multilevel	No	0.50	3.53
	None multilevel	Yes	0.72	3.81
	Female multilevel	Yes	0.70	3.78
	Male multilevel	Yes	0.54	3.59
	Common multilevel	Yes	0.58	3.64

When we compare Table 6 with Table 8 it is hard to draw a conclusion since both the α-values and the β-values are lowered when the multilevel model is used. If we compare the none multilevel factor values with the common multilevel factor values in Table 9, we can see how the multilevel model is more restrictive with estimating a survival if a patient is treated. However, the factors are relaxed when a treatment is not given. This will be discussed in Sect. 4.2.

In the proof of concept we utilized the possibility to compose the different context frames and their functions, into a process which suited the practitioners. We used fictive cases in order to validate our implementation of a context frame.

In order to find who benefits from a treatment, we started with the prescriptive analysis with respect to survival. If the patient was recommended to have a treatment we continued this type of analysis with respect to decision of treatment. At this stage, the result is a distribution of CRP values which indicates the feasibility of letting the patient have a treatment, based on the age and risk values. A defined compatibility interval was used to judge if the actual CRP value is acceptable in order to perform a treatment. If the CRP value is not acceptable in a real situation, a decision has to be made if it is possible to lower the patient's CRP value.

Counter factual analysis was done on treated and untreated, regarding survival. When the provided data sets were investigated, only one of the cases had benefited from having a different treatment.

In order to check the models, predictive analysis and explorative analysis were used on both survival and decision on treatment. The findings will be discussed in Sect. 4.2.

During the proof of concept, we used a utility function in order to make it easier to understand the impact of the factor parameters in a model. This function is described in Sect. 3.3.

4.2   The Uncertainty Proxy

In general, the creation and verification of the blueprints, gave evidence to the existing knowledge and beliefs. At the same time, the creation and verification of the blueprints raised concerns about the meaning of the age factor.

When we investigated the data from the questionnaire, and the information obtained during the focus group interviews, the age factor was playing the role of an uncertainty proxies. This became more evident when we compared the data from the questionnaire with the data in our data sets. The risk factor was absent in the questionnaire and the age factor dominated the decision if a treatment should be given or not.

In Table 2 we can see how the risk factor, to a great extent, capture the uncertainty, which was part of the age factor in the questionnaire data set. However, Table 2 shows how the age factor still impacts the decisions.

In the Tables 6–9 we can see how the age factor has no impact on survival, when no treatment was given. However, the age factor has an impact on the survival when a treatment is given.

We have not clarified if the age factor is used to hinder a patient from getting a treatment based on the estimated life time of a patient, or is the amount of uncertainty regarding a patient's possibility to survive a treatment. Both these options explain the lack of patients with an old age, who get a treatment. This can explain the results in the Tables 6–9. However, depending on the answer there might be changes to the blueprints.

5   Analysis and Discussion

The design of a context frame is described in Sect. 3. In this section we give a conceptual view of how a context frame supports evaluation and learning by using knowledge and beliefs from different actors. This is described in Sect. 5.1. The implementation used in the proof of concept is described in Sect. 5.2 and lessons learned are discussed in Sect. 5.3.

5.1   The Conceptual View of a Context Frame

We have decided to use fine grained context frames where each context frame is responsible for a specific task. By using composition of fine grained context frames, a graph of context frames can be created. This makes it possible to create a chain of decisions and outcomes, in order to reach a desired intent [1]. One way to use a context frame is to change cause factors in order to make it possible to perform a certain action. In this case a change factor can be seen as a state. Another way is to change cause factors in order to achieve a certain outcome. In this case a change factor can be seen as an action and the outcome as a desired change to a state.

A context frame is aimed to support actors based on its knowledge in a certain domain. At the same time, a context frame is able to learn from the actors it supports. These actors can be machine actors or human actors. This supports the idea of real-world evidence [3].

In order to be able to support other actors, a firm understanding of the domain is required. This can be achieved by using blueprints, created by subject matter experts, and validated with the help of data, in order to understand cause and effect in a specific domain. This is supported by using the work of Pearl [14], named structural causal models. A systematic literature review by Yao et al. [27] presents software supporting the use of structural causal models.

A context frame supports the creation of knowledge about a specific domain by supporting the following types of questions: "What will the outcome be, given the current state?", "How can a specific outcome be reached by changing the current state?", and"What changes to the state could have made the outcome different?". These questions are supported by predictive analysis, prescriptive analysis, and counterfactual analysis. The construction of the needed models are done with the help of an Bayesian approach which is supported by d-separation [5] analysis.

By logging the interactions during the different type of analysis, an understanding of how well the models perform can be obtained. This can be achieved by using the log data to build different metrics. These metrics are used to decide when models need to be updated. The same is true for blueprints. This forms a feedback loop which is used to support the update of the knowledge and beliefs, which makes it possible for a context frame to support continuous evaluation and learning.

5.2 The Proof of Concept Implementation

In the implementation of a context frame, used for the proof of concept, we base our support for blueprints on the work of Pearl [14]. We used Dagitty [23] and an Bayesian approach to validate the blueprints. A blueprint is translated to equations used by a Bayesian inference engine. This step is done manually in the proof of concept.

The models needed to support predictive analysis, prescriptive analysis, and counterfactual analysis, were built with equations used by a Bayesian inference engine. These equations supports logistic regression and linear regression, which can be in the form of multilevel models. The selection of needed factors in the equations was supported by the use of Dagitty [23]. The different analysis are supported and are based on the existence of one cause factor.

The logging of the interactions and its feedback loop are supported, but contains manual steps.

5.3 Lessons Learned

The process of creating the artifacts of a *knowledge and beliefs container* gave valuable insights to the problem at hand. Specifically the creation and verification of the blueprints, which gave evidence to the existing knowledge and beliefs.

The quantification of the causal effect to gain knowledge about a cause factor's influence on the outcome was useful. The limit value function was appreciated, since it made it easier to understand the effect of the parameters in a model.

The use of Dagitty [23] during the creation of the artifacts in a *knowledge and beliefs container* was appreciated.

The possibility to compose a workflow of functions and the functions themselves, was regarded as valuable in order to make useful analysis, and for the evaluation and learning.

The use of a Bayesian approach made it easier to understand the existing uncertainty in the presented results.

However, the need for a more rigid and efficient implementation of a context frame is needed.

6   Conclusion and Future Work

In this study we evaluated our implementation of a context frame with the help of a proof of concept. The proof of concept was regarded as successful and the concept of context frames deemed as useful.

The context frame architecture is based on structural causal models [14], an extended version of the OODA-loop [19], and Pask's conversation theory [13]. We have used a Bayesian approach, and probabilistic programming [4] for the realization of the context frame.

By dividing the implementation of a context frame in three parts and are offering four different type of analysis functions, we could adhere to the principles of Pask's conversation theory [13]. This makes it easier to create a solution which supports evaluation and learning.

The use of a blueprint creates an environment of evaluation and learning. At the same time, it makes it easier to make decisions based on knowledge, instead of beliefs. We believe the use of a blueprint makes it easier to quantify uncertainty proxies. This will be achieved by making an actors knowledge and beliefs, regarding an uncertainty proxy's impact, explicit.

In order to make our solution more efficient, from a usage perspective, we will continue to investigate in a framework which can be used to realize the needed processes. This involves an investigation of how we can use probabilistic programming [4] to its full extent.

We will investigate how we can use the concepts from the area of life long machine learning [9], in order for to fully support continuous learning,

Acknowledgement. To Anna for her patience, endurance, and thoughts, when forcing us to explain our ideas to her, and ourselves, in an understandable way.

References

1. Anthony, K.D.: Introduction to causal modeling, bayesian theory and major Bayesian modeling tools for the intelligence analyst. Eur. J. Oper. Res. 1–31 (2006)
2. Consoli, A., Tweedale, J., Jain, L.: Aligning cognitive models using AC3M. In: Proceedings - 1st International Conference on Emerging Trends in Engineering and Technology, ICETET 2008, pp. 882–886 (2008)
3. Crown, W.H.: Real-world evidence, causal inference, and machine learning. Value Health **22**(5), 587–592 (2019)
4. Davidson-Pilon, C.: Bayesian Methods for Hackers, 1st edn. Addison Wesley Data & Analytics Series (2016)
5. Hayduk, L.A., et al.: Pearl's d-separation: one more step into causal thinking. Struct. Equ. Model. **10**(2), 289–311 (2003)
6. Hernan, M.A., Robins, J.M.: Causal Inference: What if. CRC Press (2020)
7. Kline, R.B.: Principles and Practice of Structural Equation Modeling, 4th edn. The Guilford Press (2016)
8. Kochenderfer, M.: Decision Making Under Uncertainty. MIT Press (2015)
9. Liu, B.: Lifelong machine learning: a paradigm for continuous learning. Front. Comput. Sci. **11**(3), 359–361 (2017)

10. Mccauley-bell, P., Freeman, R.: Quantification of belief and knowledge systems in information warfare. In: Proceedings of the 5th IEEE international conference on Fuzzy Systems, vol. 3, pp. 1579–1585 (1996)
11. McElreath, R.: Statistical Rethinking. CRC Press (2016)
12. McElreath, R.: Rethinking package (2017). https://github.com/rmcelreath/rethinking. Accessed 09 Dec 2020
13. Pask, G.: Conversation Theory. Elsevier, The Netherlands (1976)
14. Pearl, J.: Causality, 2nd edn. Cambridge University Press (2009)
15. Pearl, J., Glymour, M., Jewell, N.P.: Causal Inference in Statistics, 1st edn. Wiley, Hoboken (2016)
16. Richards, C.: Boyd's OODA loop. In: Proceedings of Lean Software and Systems Conference **2011**, 127–136 (2011)
17. Robson, C.: Real World Research: A Resource for Users of Social Research Methods in Applied Settings, 3rd edn. Wiley, Chichester (2011)
18. Silvander, J.: Understanding human generated decision data. In: Shishkov, B. (ed.) BMSD 2020. Understanding Human Generated Decision Data, vol. 391, pp. 362–374. Springer, Cham (2020). https://doi.org/10.1007/978-3-030-52306-0_26
19. Silvander, J., Angelin, L.: Introducing intents to the OODA loop. In: Knowledge-Based and Intelligent Information & Engineering Systems, pp. 878–883 (2019). Procedia Computer Science
20. Silvander, J., Wilson, M., Wnuk, K., Svahnberg, M.: Supporting continuous changes to business intents. Int. J. Softw. Eng. Knowl. Eng. **27**(8), 1167–1198 (2017)
21. Silvander, J., Wnuk, K., Svahnberg, M.: Systematic literature review on intent-driven systems. IET Softw. **14**(4), 345–357 (2020)
22. Simmons, E.: Requirements triage: what can we learn from a "medical approach? IEEE Softw. **21**(4), 86–88 (2004)
23. Textor, J., van der Zander, B., Gilthorpe, M.S., Liśkiewicz, M., Ellison, G.T.: Robust causal inference using directed acyclic graphs: the R package 'dagitty'. Int. J. Epidemiol. **45**(6), 1887–1894 (2016)
24. Vaughan, D.: Analytic Skills for AI & Data Science. O'Reilly Media Inc (2020)
25. Wikipedia: C-reactive protein (2018). https://en.wikipedia.org/wiki/C-reactive_protein. Accessed 01 Apr 2021
26. Wikipedia: Johari window (2020). https://en.wikipedia.org/wiki/Johari_window. Accessed 30 Nov 2020
27. Yao, L., Chu, Z., Li, S., Li, Y., Gao, J., Zhang, A.: A survey on causal inference. arXiv **1**(1), 1–38 (2020)
28. Zrake, J., MacFadyen, A., McEnery, J.E., Racusin, J.L., Gehrels, N.: Numerical simulations of driven supersonic relativistic MHD turbulence. Ann. Rev. Sociol. **22**, 102–105 (2011)

Benefits and Challenges in Information Security Certification – A Systematic Literature Review

Mike Hulshof and Maya Daneva[✉]

University of Twente, 7522NH Enschede, The Netherlands
m.hulshof@student.utwente.nl, m.daneva@utwente.nl

Abstract. Information security certification (ISC) gets increasingly more complex. Although certain benefits, challenges and success factors have been recognized by both scholars and practitioners in the field, little has been done to consolidate the published knowledge. This systematic literature review attempts to consolidate what is currently known on the benefits of ISC, the issues and the challenges to certification, and the success factors that organizations consider while embarking on this process. Following the guidelines of Kitchenham et al., and Kuhrmann et al., we examined 42 papers that are relevant to our area of interest. We identified 12 benefits, 15 challenges, and 8 success factors. Our most important conclusion is that the current certification process is complex and suboptimal; it is expensive and it depends on the auditor's skills. Finally, we evaluated validity threats and derived some implications for practice and for research.

Keywords: Security accreditation · Security certification · Information security auditing practice · Systematic literature review

1 Introduction

Information security certification (ISC) is a process assuring compliance with established information security standards. This process is built on trust and operates based on two concepts: accreditation and certification. The first means officially recognizing someone as having a particular status or being qualified to perform a particular activity, whereas the second means providing someone with an official document attesting to a status or level of achievement. For a company, ISC is often seen as assurance by an independent third party that an organization is operating in compliance with certain security standards, whereas accreditation is the recognition of being qualified to grant ISC. The roles of the actors involved in the accreditation-certification process are explained in the work of Salminen [7] who modelled them as a hierarchic structure (see Fig. 1). In this figure, accreditation agencies are at the top. These are tasked with the responsibility of validating the competence of certification bodies based on accreditation regulations. The certification bodies can grant certifications based on their own audits or on audits performed by competent auditing agencies. These agencies (see the bottom of the hierarchy on Fig. 1) perform security audits through their information security auditors [7]. Security auditors examine and evaluate an organization's security management system by

© Springer Nature Switzerland AG 2021
B. Shishkov (Ed.): BMSD 2021, LNBIP 422, pp. 154–169, 2021.
https://doi.org/10.1007/978-3-030-79976-2_9

checking whether the organization complies with certain standard(s) based on generic audit controls to identify risks and catch any fraudulent practices. The standards are developed by organizations known as standardization bodies, which do so, based on drivers such as regulation, interoperability and trust. Although only accredited certification bodies have the authority to grant certifications, not every standard is accompanied by matching accreditation. It is still possible to perform audits and provide assurance despite the lack of accreditation, but the value of the assurance then depends on the reputation of the auditing agency.

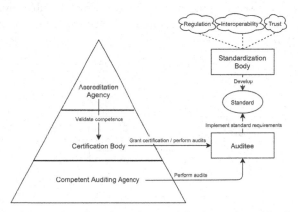

Fig. 1. The high level process model of security accreditation and certification as per Salminen [7]

Today, many companies are subjected to ISC. Therefore, they need to be informed on the benefits, challenges and good practices surrounding the acquisition of ISCs. The present paper responds to this need. Despite the fact that scholars in information security are concerned with the topic, to the best of our knowledge, little has been done to consolidate the published knowledge in the area of interest. To this end, in our paper we pose the following the following research questions (**RQ**):

- **RQ 1:** What are the benefits of ISC, according to scientific publications?
- **RQ 2:** What are the challenges of ISC that are reported in scientific publications?
- **RQ 3:** What are the success factors of information security audits (as part of information technology audits), according to published scientific articles?

RQ1 aims to get an understanding of the value of certification by reviewing the proclaimed benefits of ISC. RQ2 aims to address possible limitations or flat-out flaws associated with ISC. RQ3 aims to provide an overview of factors that contribute to the success of security auditing. We make the note that RQ3 includes in the scope of this work, the topic of IT auditing because (cyber)security is a component of the IT Audit profession. IT auditing in general is focused on determining how compliant an organisation is within the remit of its prescribed audit. IT auditors help with the ICS process by focusing on internal security controls and using their knowledge of the necessary security audit requirements.

In this paper, we answer RQ1, RQ2 and RQ3 by performing a systematic literature review that employed the methodological guidelines of Kitchenham [44] and of
Kuhrmann et al. [8]. In what follows, Sect. 2 presents our research process and its
execution. Section 3 reports our findings and Sect. 4 discusses them. Section 5 is on
limitations. Section 6 concludes with implications for research and for practice.

2   Research Method

The key steps in our research process are described in the subsections below. This
section covers the data collection process in detail (see Fig. 2) to ensure transparency
and reproducibility [8].

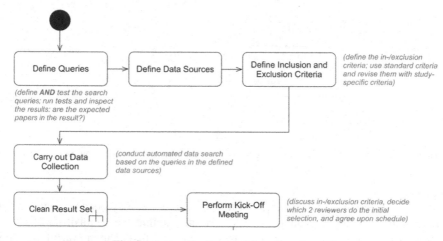

Fig. 2. Data collection workflow, based on [8].

To collect relevant publications, we used the Scopus online library, www.scopus.org.
Using the iterative process of Kuhrmann et al. [8], we constructed these search strings:

S1: ("Security certification" AND process AND (standard OR standards))
S2: ("Security certification" AND review)
S3: (("security certification")) AND (value OR benefit OR benefits OR efficacy)
S4: ("IT audit" OR "Information audit" AND review)

In what follows, we first explain our experimentation-based approach to forming the
above search string (Sect. 2.1). We then elaborate on the use of the so-called reference
studies which were instrumental to the evaluation of the appropriateness of this search
string for our purpose (Sect. 2.2). Next, we provide our list of inclusion and exclusion
criteria (Sect. 2.3). Finally, we report of the conduction of the review process, which
explains how we selected the 42 papers included in our study.

2.1 Finding Keywords and Forming Search Strings

Initial keywords derived from our research questions were used to construct search strings in an attempt to generate a list of reference studies. This was done through a trial-and-error approach [8] in Scopus. The trial-and-error approach entails running initial keywords or phrases through the database in order to iteratively narrow down the list of potential literature and provide candidate results for the detailed search later on [8]. The purpose of a trial-and-error approach is two-fold: first, it allows for testing (and revision where necessary) of the initial search queries and, second, it provides a list of reference publications, which can either be used for subsequent manual searches through a practice known as 'snowballing', or it can uncover key literature which can be used as a reference to assess whether the developed search queries are effective. This was done by checking whether the reference papers were included in the final search query results list. Absence of reference papers in this results list could indicate an overly narrowed-down search query and may pose a threat to the validity of the research. This was countered by constructing multiple search queries and combining the result sets, making sure to filter out duplicates.

The reference papers that result from the trial-and-error approach were then used to perform snowballing on. Snowballing is the practice of investigating the publications and manually extending the literature set by following the references [8]. A word cloud (Fig. 3) was generated based on the keyword list to help identify relevant and irrelevant search criteria. This also aided in the revision of the search queries until a sufficiently complete dataset was achieved.

2.2 Reference Studies

Four reference publications were identified. Through snowballing seven other papers were added to this list, resulting in 11 reference publications in total (see Appendix A: Reference publications). As already indicated, we generated a word cloud (see Fig. 3) from the list of keywords that the authors of these 11 papers used. This helped us identify relevant search terms and aided with the construction of the search queries.

The word cloud was used to analyse the appropriateness of the result set by checking whether the keywords match our expectations. It is clear that information security is the central theme, accompanied by terms such as 'audit', 'management' and 'certification'. Furthermore, 'assurance', 'compliance' and '27001' are also noteworthy, indicating a possible need for assurance in order to show demonstrable compliance. It appears that ISO 27001 could play a major role in this scenario.

What stood out is that the term 'standards' did not appear to occur in many papers, yet the word cloud did contain notable standards and frameworks such as the earlier mentioned 'ISO 27001', 'COBIT' and 'ITIL'. Nonetheless, this showed that the reference publications might not have had sufficient papers on the topic of the available information security standards. As such, the search queries were revised to include more publications in the field of security standards. Moreover, the reference publications appear to contain few publications on the topic of information security in the healthcare sector.

Overall, the word cloud (Fig. 3) did not indicate any unexpected or seemingly incorrect keywords and as such, showed the appropriateness of the initial searches with a

Fig. 3. Reference publications word cloud.

possible need for additional publications on information security standards and health care related certifications.

2.3 Inclusion and Exclusion Criteria

Once the dataset was established, the inclusion and exclusion criteria were specified. These criteria were used to clean up the dataset by eliminating results that were out of the research scope and narrowed the results to studies that were relevant for the proposed research questions.

We formulated the following inclusion criteria:

(I1) Title, keyword list and abstract of the paper state explicitly that it relates to ISC.
(I2) The paper presents certification-related contributions, e.g., benefits, value, drawbacks, success factors, auditing practices or industry developments.

Next, we used the following exclusion criteria:

(E1) The paper is not in English.
(E2) The paper is not in the information security or IT auditing domain.
(E3) The paper is a tutorial, workshop, or poster summary only.
(E4) The paper relates to security certification in its related work only.
(E5) The paper occurs multiple times in the result set.
(E6) The paper's full text is not available for download.
(E7) The paper is not peer-reviewed, e.g. master thesis.
(E8) The paper was published before 2005.

We note that 2005 was chosen because it is the publication year of the ISO 27001 standard. ISO 27001 and 27002 (which extends the former) are widely known international standards for information security management systems. They are among today's leading security standards (particularly in Europe). In the USA, the NIST cybersecurity framework that was published in 2014 is among the most popular. Therefore, standards prior to 2005, are unlikely to be relevant today.

2.4 Conducting the Review

Applying our search strings in Scopus brought 137 potentially relevant papers. Among those, we identified 13 duplicates which we removed from our set. The remaining 124 studies were subjected to our application of the inclusion and exclusion criteria. One author has read the abstracts of these studies and manually removed the papers that did not meet the inclusion criteria and did match at least one exclusion criterion. To assure internal validity of this process, the co-author read 30% of all 137 abstracts. Both authors reached agreement on those papers that met the inclusion criteria. After this step, we ended up with 42 papers which were read carefully by both authors. From each paper, we extracted the relevant pieces of information concerning (1) benefits, (2) challenges, and (3) success factors.

Our 42 papers included in this review were authored by researchers from 22 countries, with the majority coming from the United States (37%) and Europe (35%). More in detail, the following list displays the published research per European country: United Kingdom (3 papers), France (2), the Netherlands (2), Portugal (2), Switzerland (2), Denmark (1), Finland (1), Germany (1), Greece (1), and Norway (1).

We note that 72% of the papers were published by authors in universities, while 17% were published by practitioners from companies, and other 11% by co-authors from universities and companies. Below, we summarize the relevant findings of the 42 papers based on the RQs.

3   Results

3.1   Benefits of Information Security Certification (RQ1)

Table 1 summarizes the reported benefits of ISCs and security auditing as part of IT auditing. We categorized them in descending order based on the number of occurrences in the reviewed literature.

As shown in Table 1, the most reported benefits are risk management and increased security. Certification has been shown to aid with risk management by raising risk awareness [16] through improved security controls. In addition, certification also aids with the identification of security gaps [13, 14, 17] and forces employees to practice these security controls [4]. The ISO 27001 standard's strong link to risk management and management involvement assures that the security management system is based on the organization's needs [4, 7, 12]. Furthermore, the Cyber Essentials security scheme has been shown to either fully or partially mitigate the majority of security threats for SMEs [18]. The authors concluded that cloud-based services providers are encouraged to certify their

Table 1. Benefits of ISC and of security audit (as part of IT audit).

Benefits (# of occurrences)	Source
Risk management (11)	[1, 4, 7, 9–16]
Increased security (9)	[4, 7, 9, 11, 13–15, 17, 18]
Promotes organizational information management or IT governance (7)	[1, 4, 7, 14, 16, 21, 22]
Trust building (6)	[7, 9, 16, 17, 19, 20]
Compliance with standards (4)	[1, 4, 13, 16]
Involves and trains staff (3)	[7, 10, 16]
Provides feedback (3)	[7, 10, 14]
Cost reduction (2)	[9, 16]
Promotes communication (2)	[10, 14]
Ensures info validity and accuracy (2)	[4, 10]
Increased market value (1)	[11]
IT audit can complement financial statement audits (1)	[23]

protection (through frameworks such as ISO 27001) [15]. Moreover, the certification process provides a clear classification of nonconformities, which is useful for resolving the most significant security weaknesses [7]. Plus, frequent audits by independent competent auditing agencies ensures a regular review of security and the obligation to implement corrective actions ensures continuous security improvement in the certified environment [4, 7]. Finally, based on empirical research through the implementation of ISO 27001, Deane et al. [11] found that the certification generates value by reducing a firm's risk of damages in future attacks, instead of improving a firm's revenue generation.

Some authors (e.g. [9]) reported that the benefits of early adopters are different from late adopters, with early adopters being driven by loss aversion through future cost mitigation, which is obtained through minimizing risk exposure and increased security, as well as by building trust with important stakeholders. Late adopters on the other hand, experienced more economic benefits due to a shorter learning curve and fewer implementation challenges [9]. The notion that ISC generates trust is widely supported throughout the reviewed literature [7, 16, 17, 19, 20].

Regarding IT governance, Lateef et al. [10] conclude that the information security audit is an effective tool for improving organizational information management managing risk and improves the validity and accuracy of information. Similarly, Merhout and Havelka show that IT audits can contribute through cost reduction, as well as better organizational management by involving upper management in the decision-making process [16]. Arrifin et al. support the claim that the information audit provides strategic direction and guidelines to the management of information. The information audit also functions as a tool to identify the gap between information requirements and provision before information strategy and policy is developed [22]. IT audit frameworks are important for the alignment of organizational objectives [14]. They allow management to become risk aware and are useful in ensuring compliance with international IT governance standards [4, 13, 16].

To summarize, the primary benefits are risk assurance through better security, organizational information management and generating trust (see Table 1). IT audits can involve upper management and train the auditee's staff to promote better adherence and awareness. The remainder of the benefits with fewer occurrences mainly revolve around stimulating communication among the auditee's staff and involving upper management in the IT auditing process. Although research on tangible benefits is limited, there appears to be a potential for financial benefits, primarily in the form of future cost reduction. Lastly, it is not by any stretch of the imagination unreasonable to consider some degree of dependency among several benefits. Prominent benefits such as risk management and security are likely to be influenced by less cited benefits such as improved IT governance, better communication and continuous feedback.

3.2 Issues and Challenges (RQ2)

Table 2 summarizes the issues and challenges associated to ISCs and security auditing as part of IT auditing. Similar to the previous section, we categorized them in descending order based on the number of occurrences in the reviewed literature. The most commonly reported challenge is inadequate security assurance, which can have multiple causes. Emerging technologies and digital transformations have provided a number of issues and challenges for security auditing resulting in increased complexity of security audit practices. Rapid technological developments put IT audit controls (and information security controls) at continuous risk of becoming outdated [7] and has increased the need for qualified IT auditors [6]. Moreover, generic frameworks may be unable to effectively support IT audit practices [6], which is further exacerbated by the lack of uniformity across industries and regions [38]. Generic frameworks (such as COBIT) may not be appropriate for industry-specific security certifications [19] and could lead to an excessively large scope, whilst sacrificing depth and level of detail of the controls [21].

Our reviewed papers indicate that there is little practical guidance on information audit scope management and how to tailor it to individual circumstances and goals, which could provide the auditor with insufficient support [21]. No research has specified the common mandatory steps or stages that must be carried out by an organization when implementing information audits regardless of the adopted framework or methodology [22]. The lack of standardized methodology may make the selection of an appropriate audit framework an error-prone process [30]. As such, standardization and formalization of auditing policies and procedures are necessary [23].

Salminen [7] goes into detail on some of the more practical challenges associated with certification and provides insight into the role and challenges of individual IT auditors. She explains that the auditee often defines the scope of the certification. As a result, if the scope is limited and those limitations are not clearly communicated, certifications may provide a false sense of security in areas not included in the scope. Sometimes, the number of controls is large and the time for audits limited, resulting in an inability to properly review the requirements in the time allotted to the audit. Standards are complex,

Table 2. Issues and challenges of IT audits.

Issues/challenges (# of occurrences)	Source
Inadequate security assurance (13)	[3, 5, 7, 19, 24–32]
Significant financial investment (11)	[1, 5, 7, 13, 16, 19, 20, 22, 28, 29, 33]
IT auditing complexity (generic frameworks, multidimensional nature, scope management, system size, data volume) (9)	[1, 6, 19, 31, 33–37]
Lack of standardized methodology (high occurrence of errors in considering the necessary audit framework) (6)	[5, 21–23, 31, 34]
Dependence on IT auditor competence (6)	[5–7, 35, 38, 39]
Limited IT audit guidance (choosing correct methods) (4)	[7, 21, 31, 38]
Little empirical and practical validation (4)	[1, 5, 34, 40]
Nonconformity to requirements (3)	[7, 24, 25]
Lack of tangible benefits (3)	[5, 12, 16]
Emerging technologies (3)	[6, 41, 42]
Audits is imposed to upper management (3)	[5, 16, 20]
Failure to meet expectations (2)	[5, 25]
Time consuming (1)	[19]
Gaps b/n combined security certifications (1)	[7]
Reform requirements & regulations (1)	[6]

which can make it difficult to find auditors competent in the entire scope. When auditors are required to audit areas outside of their competence, significant security weaknesses may go unnoticed, or result in irrelevant findings [7].

Furthermore, competent auditing agencies compete with each other through price reduction, exposing organizations to two potential risks. Firstly, less time spent at the organization can result in a rushed audit that leaves unnoticed security flaws. Secondly, overly strict interpretations of controls may translate into nonconformities and higher auditing costs without significant additional risk. This overly strict interpretation could result in a narrower scope, potentially leaving out areas that would have benefitted from the audit [7]. The need for qualified IT auditors has increased as a result of the rapid technological developments and complexity of the IT auditing process [6].

Merhout and Havelka mention that IT audits are sometimes perceived as a necessary evil by the upper management of an organization, because the audits feel imposed rather than desired. According to the Sarbanes-Oxley Act of 2002 (SOX), large publicly traded organizations in the United States are required to certify their financial statements. Achieving this compliance requires frequent, detailed and expensive IT audits [16, 20]. Finally, any change within the scope of an already certified product will invalidate the certificate and require recertification. This may lead to situations in which organizations have to choose between fixing known issues in the system at the cost of additional audits or opt to delay the issue and maintain the certification [32]. IT audits are a significant financial investment due to the many regulations, frameworks, and the costs of ensuring control implementation [1, 5, 7, 13, 16, 19, 20, 22, 28, 29].

To summarize, according to the literature, the most documented challenges of ISC are the high costs combined with inadequate security assurance, which appears to be a multifactorial problem (see Table 2). Genericity of large frameworks, a lack of standardized methodology and limited IT audit guidance appear to result in higher audit complexity and a dependence on individual IT auditor competence. The role of the IT auditor seems complex but crucial in contributing to the success of the IT auditing process. The accumulation of these challenges might result in outdated standards or lingering security flaws that went unnoticed during the audit. Some of the current IT auditing practices, frameworks and methods may be sub-optimal in providing risk assurance and particularly upper management does not always recognize the benefits of security certification.

3.3 Success Factors (RQ3)

We found that only seven papers [5–7, 16, 23, 39, 42] in our set of 42 publications included in this review, treated success factors in security audit as part of IT audit. Table 3 summarizes the success factors that were identified from these seven papers. Although research on success factors of security auditing in particular, and IT auditing in general, is limited, we identified one framework from the literature that seemed the most comprehensive regarding IT audit quality, namely the framework of Merhout and Havelka's [16]. Because of its comprehensiveness, we decided to use it for the purpose of organizing our findings regarding RQ3, see Table 3.

In this table, the first column presents the eight IT audit success factors defined in Merhout and Havelka's framework [16]. The rightmost column of Table 3 indicates for each of the eight factors, those other papers in our set of selected literature that also treat this factor. For example, the first factor in Merhout and Havelka's framework is Process Audit [16]. This factor was also found in four other publications: [5, 7, 23, 39], as shown in the rightmost column of Table 3.

Furthermore, while Merhout and Havelka [16] differentiate between Client-Controlled Organizational Factors and Audit-Controlled Organizational Factors, Aditya et al. [5] and Chou [39] have assigned these under the collective category of Organizational Factors. Furthermore, Aditya et al. [6] state that the role of the IT audit varies between companies. They argue that companies should define the IT audit universe before engaging in IT audit practices. The IT audit universe defines the type of IT audit and they distinguish between four types: IT management, Technical infrastructure, Applications, External connections. Besides the well-documented success factors mentioned in Table 3, the following concrete guidelines were identified from the literature. Given the emergence of new technologies and continuous technological developments, auditing controls should have properly defined control objectives and include the possibility to use compensating controls [7]. In organizations where IT audits are performed in addition to financial audits, the financial and IT audits are complementary and financial

Table 3. Success Factors identified in this systematic literature review.

IT audit success factor in [16]	Examples	Source
Audit process	Well-documented auditing guidelines, existence of auditing methodology, scope definition, usage of automated tools and timely review of audit work	[5, 7, 23, 39]
Social IT auditor competence	Social & interpersonal skills, independence, communication skills, willingness and ability to change and motivation/enthusiasm	[5, 6, 39, 42]
Technical IT auditor competence	Understanding of risks and control weaknesses, project management and staff experience	[5, 6, 39]
Audit team	Communication, experience working together, cooperation and cohesiveness	[5, 6, 39]
Client-controlled organizational factors	Characteristics of or dependent on the auditee such as management support and adequacy of documentation on the auditee's side	[5, 6, 39]
IT audit–controlled organizational factors	Characteristics of the IT audit function within the organization such as relationship with clients, adequate time allocation for IT audit, leadership, understanding of business & IT organizational changes	[5, 6, 39]
Enterprise & organizational environment	Characteristics of the corporation and/or the unit being audited such as financial resources, corporate culture, audit reporting structure, value-added audit perceptions, audit frequency	[5, 6, 39]
Target process & system	Clearly defined project scope, system complexity, amount of manual versus automated processes and system/process documentation	[5, 39]

auditors and IT auditors should cooperate [23]. Information management quality should be measured and evaluated, by defining dimensions ahead of the audit and organizations should incorporate the use of modelling techniques [37].

Moreover, IT audits should be involved early on in major IT projects to identify security risks and prevent unnoticed risks and costs from accumulating [42]. IT audits should not be limited to just risk assurance, but should also include IT governance assurance and consulting [43]. Lastly, involving top management in the IT auditing process can prove useful, as well as making the effectiveness of the IT implementation measurable through the construction of key performance indicators (KPIs) [6].

4 Discussion

We now discuss our findings and aim to put these into practical and theoretical perspectives. Regarding RQ1 (benefits) and RQ2 (challenges), at a first glance, the most prominent benefits and challenges of ISC are seemingly contradicting. The proclaimed security and risk management benefits are contrasted by publications showing inadequate security and risk assurance. These findings do not detract from the value of the results, but rather show that current IT auditing practices leave room for improvement. In fact, our findings indicate that the quality of ISC is a multi-faceted concept, and also highlight the difficulty of the security auditing as part of IT auditing process. Information security is complex by nature, which makes it difficult to describe well in a clear and unambiguous framework. In turn, this leads to difficulty for both the auditor and auditee in performing good IT audits and finding appropriate auditing frameworks. Furthermore, based on the commonly reported challenges from the reviewed literature (see Sect. 3.3), it appears that the inadequate security assurance can be explained by generic large frameworks, a lack of standardized methodology and limited IT audit guidance. This shifts a significant portion of the responsibility to the IT auditors, resulting in individual auditor competence to be a critical factor in contributing to the success of IT audits [5, 7, 35, 38, 39].

Regarding RQ3 (success factors), our review found that there is no one-size-fits-all certification approach as it relies on the individual auditor's professional judgement and scoping. It seems that security audits/IT audits are performed on a case-by-case basis and many real-world problems are too complex to judge based on generic controls. Auditors utilize their knowledge and experience to strike a balance between compliance for the sake of compliance and inadequate risk assessment. Because of this major shift in responsibility to the IT auditors (mentioned in the previous paragraph), we believe that the topic of individual auditor competence warrants additional discussion by delving into publications that discuss the topic of IT auditing and auditor competence in more depth.

Salminen's research [7] on the success factors and pitfalls of security certifications provides valuable insight into the complexity of IT auditing. This author mentions that it is often difficult in practice to review the entire set of requirements in the limited amount of time available for the audit. In some cases, the auditing framework even predetermines the timeframe. Moreover, although auditors tend to have deep knowledge in specific areas, the large scope of the standard may be too complex [7].

5 Limitations

This review has some limitations. Our research process followed Kuhrmann's systematic approach for data collection [8]. The inclusion criteria narrowed-down the scope of this review to the field of ISC and IT auditing. The exclusion criteria ensured that irrelevant publications are eliminated. Given the rapid developments within the IT auditing industry, the cut-off point of 15 years might risk the inclusion of potentially outdated literature. Luckily, the vast majority of the literature was published within the last 10 years.

Next, it is worthwhile noting that no author of this paper has any prior published work in the field of ISC or on the topic of IT auditing. Therefore, we believe that no subjective bias is passed into this review due to possible researcher's knowledge of authors of included papers.

Lastly, the IT auditing field is still in development and there is little mapping of the research. The academic literature is predominantly theoretical as little practical testing has been done up until this point.

6   Conclusions and Implications

This systematic literature review identified the benefits, the challenges and the success factors in ISC, considered as part of IT auditing. Using 42 selected papers, we found: (1) the most pronounced benefits appear to be effective reduction of risks due to increased security measures, trust establishment, and promotion of organizational security management and governance; (2) the most pronounced challenges appear to be inadequate security assurance due to genericity of frameworks, increasing complexity of the IT security audit landscape, significant financial costs associated to certification, dependence on individual auditor competence; (3) the most comprehensive success factors come from Merhout and Havelka's [16] IT audit success factor model, which defined the following eight factors: Audit process, Social IT auditor competence, Technical IT auditor competence, Client-controlled organizational factors, IT audit-controlled organizational factors, Enterprise & organizational environment, Target process & system.

This work has some implications for researchers and practitioners. First, based on our findings, we think that two open questions are worthwhile investigating in the future: (1) How to improve the IT auditing process? and (2) How to reduce the dependence on individual IT auditor competence? Finding answers to these questions is important because of the continuous technological developments within the IT auditing field in general and in the security auditing field in particular. Existing information security standards are getting more complex and new frameworks are continuously emerging, all while the need for ISC is increasing. Therefore, relying on a certification process whose success is less contingent on the security auditor's skills, qualifications and experience, seems a logical way to go.

Second, this paper has some implications for practitioners. The practical takeaway from this research is that current IT auditing practices are sub-optimal. Practitioners interested in establishing security certification processes, should carefully consider the wide range of existing ISCs and the degree to which one certification complements or substitutes another one, as well as the potential sector-specific limitations or requirements associated with them. It may also be wise for compliance officers to incorporate upper management into the IT auditing process. Finally, as shown in this literature review, the value of the ISC highly depends on the individual IT auditor competence. As such, when practitioners are considering the services of potential IT auditing firms, it is advisable to incorporate the complexity of the IT audit in the selection process. In order to reap the benefits of ISC, more complex IT audits may warrant more competent (and potentially more expensive) IT auditing partners.

Appendix

A Reference Publications

Reference publication	Snowball result
J. K. Deane et al., The effect of information security certification announcements on the market value of the firm. [11]	
J. M. Such et al., Basic Cyber Hygiene: Does It Work? [15]	- European Union Agency for Network and Information Security, Review of cyber hygiene practices [20] - J. M. Vidler et al., Cyber Security Controls Effectiveness: A Qualitative Assessment of Cyber Essentials [18]
R. B. Frost et al., Revisiting the information audit: A systematic literature review and synthesis [37]	
B. R. Aditya et al., Toward Modern IT Audit-Current Issues and Literature Review [5]	- P. Lovaas et al., IT Audit Challenges for Small and Medium-Sized Financial Institutions [33] - M. Majdalawieh et al., Paradigm shift in information systems auditing [2] - T. Rosário et al., Formalization of the IT Audit Management Process [1] - B. R. Aditya et al., The Role of IT Audit in the Era of Digital Transformation [6] - G. Felley and R. Dornberger, How to Efficiently Conduct an IT Audit [3]

References

1. Rosário, T., et al.: Formalization of the IT audit management process. EDOCW **1–10**, 2012 (2012)
2. Majdalawieh, M., et al.: Paradigm shift in information systems auditing. Eletronic Libr. **34**(1), 1–5 (2017)
3. Felley, G., Dornberger, R.: How to efficiently conduct an IT audit - In the perspective of research, consulting and teaching. In: IMSCI 2016 - 10th International Multi-Conference on Society, Cybernetics and Informatics, Proceedings, pp. 29–33 (2016)
4. Ali, S., et al.: Application integration and audit control in organisational merger: case of Oman. J. Theor. Appl. Inf. Technol. **79**(3), 514–527 (2015)
5. Aditya, B.R., et al.: Toward Modern IT audit- current issues and literature review. ICST **1**(1–6), 2018 (2018)

6. Aditya, B.R., et al.: The role of IT audit in the era of digital transformation. IOP Conf. Ser. Mater. Sci. Eng. **407**(1) (2018)
7. Salminen, H.: Success factors and pitfalls in security certifications. In: European Conference on Information Warfare and Security, ECCWS, pp. 811–818 (2019)
8. Kuhrmann, M., Fernández, D.M., Daneva, M.: On the pragmatic design of literature studies in software engineering: an experience-based guideline. Empir. Softw. Eng. **22**(6), 2852–2891 (2017). https://doi.org/10.1007/s10664-016-9492-y
9. Ni, J., et al.: Why be first if it doesn't pay? The case of early adopters of C-TPAT supply chain security certification. Int. J. Oper. Prod. Manag. **36**(10), 1161–1181 (2016)
10. Lateef, A., et al.: Information audit as an important tool in organizational management: a review of literature. Bus. Inf. Rev. **36**(1) (2019)
11. Deane, J.K., Goldberg, D.M., Rakes, T.R., Rees, L.P.: The effect of information security certification announcements on the market value of the firm. Inf. Technol. Manage. **20**(3), 107–121 (2019). https://doi.org/10.1007/s10799-018-00297-3
12. Axelsen, M., et al.: Explaining the information systems auditor role in the public sector financial audit. Int. J. Account. Inf. Syst. **24**, 15–31 (2017)
13. Doomun, M.R.: Multi-level information system security in outsourcing domain. Bus. Process Manag. J. **14**(6), 849–857 (2008)
14. Kilzer, R.: Information audit: keys for understanding the academic library. Tech. Serv. Q. **29**(3), 200–206 (2012)
15. Such, J.M., et al.: Basic cyber hygiene: does it work? Computer **52**(4), 21–31 (2019)
16. Merhout, J.W., et al.: Information technology auditing: a value-added IT governance partnership between IT management and audit. Commun. Assoc. Inf. Syst. **23**, 463–482 (2008)
17. Lotz, V., et al.: Towards security certification schemas for the internet of services. In: NTMS 2012 Conference and Workshops (2012)
18. Vidler, J.M., et al.: Cyber security control effectiveness: a qualitative assessment of cyber essentials. Secur. Lancaster 1–28 (2015)
19. Di Cerbo, F., Bezzi, M., Kaluvuri, S.P., Sabetta, A., Trabelsi, S., Lotz, V.: Towards a trustworthy service marketplace for the future internet. In: Álvarez, F., et al. (eds.) FIA 2012. LNCS, vol. 7281, pp. 105–116. Springer, Heidelberg (2012). https://doi.org/10.1007/978-3-642-30241-1_10
20. European Union Agency for Network and Information Security, "Review of Cyber Hygiene Practices," ENISA Website, no. December, p. 25 (2016)
21. Buchanan, S., et al.: The information audit: theory versus practice. Int. J. Inf. Manage. **28**(3), 150–160 (2008)
22. Ariffin, I., et al.: Information audit in electricity utilities: roles, methodologies, issues and challenges. In: ICCOINS 2014 (2014)
23. Kanellou, A., et al.: Auditing in enterprise system environment: a synthesis. J. Enterprise Inf. Manag. **24**(6), 494–519 (2011)
24. Rahaman, S., et al.: Security certification in payment card industry: testbeds, measurements, and recommendations. In: ACM CCCS, 2019, pp. 481–498 (2019)
25. Lope Abdul Rahman, A.A., et al.: Measuring sustainability for an effective Information System audit from public organization perspective. In: RCIS 2015 (2015)
26. Di Giulio, C., et al.: Cloud security certifications: a comparison to improve cloud service provider security. In: ACM CPS (2017)
27. Di Giulio, C., et al.: Cloud standards in comparison: are new security frameworks improving cloud security?. In: CLOUD 2017, vol. 2017-June, pp. 50–57 (2017)
28. Brosgol, B.M.: Safety and security: certification issues and technologies. CrossTalk **21**(10), 9–14 (2008)

29. Schierholz, R., et al.: Security certification - a critical review. In: ISA Automation Week 2010: Technology and Solutions Event, pp. 156–178 (2010)
30. Smith, B., et al.: Challenges for protecting the privacy of health information: required certification can leave common vulnerabilities undetected. In: CCCS 2010, pp. 1–12 (2010)
31. Taubenberger, S., et al.: Problem analysis of traditional IT-security risk assessment methods - an experience report from the insurance and auditing domain. In: IFIP AICT 2011, vol. 354, pp. 259–270 (2011)
32. Schierholz, R., et al.: Security Certification-A critical review (2010)
33. Lovaas, P., et al.: IT audit challenges for small and medium- sized financial institutions. In: Annual Symposium Information Assurance & Secure Knowledge Management, pp. 16–22 (2012)
34. Bukhsh, F.A., et al.: Information audit for knowledge discovery: a systematic literature review. In: CEUR Workshop Proceedings, vol. 2383 (2019)
35. Yeghaneh, Y.H., et al.: Factors affecting information technology audit quality. J. Invest. Manag. 4(5), 196 (2015)
36. Rosário, T., Pereira, R., da Silva, M.M.: IT audit management architecture and process model. In: Abramowicz, W. (ed.) BIS 2013. LNBIP, vol. 157, pp. 187–198. Springer, Heidelberg (2013). https://doi.org/10.1007/978-3-642-38366-3_16
37. Frost, R.B., et al.: Revisiting the information audit: a systematic literature review and synthesis. Int. J. Inf. Manage. 37(1), 1380–1390 (2017)
38. Islam, M.S., et al.: Factors associated with security/cybersecurity audit by internal audit function: an international study. Manag. Audit. J. 33(4), 377–409 (2018)
39. Chou, D.C.: Cloud computing risk and audit issues. Comput. Stand. Interfaces 42, 137–142 (2015)
40. Hallgren, E.W.: How to use an innovation audit as a learning tool: a case study of enhancing high-involvement innovation. Creat. Innov. Manag. 18(1), 48–58 (2009)
41. Dzuranin, A.C., et al.: The current state and future direction of IT audit: challenges and opportunities. J. Inf. Syst. 30(1), 7–20 (2016)
42. Brand, D.: A global look at IT audit best practices. EDPACS 54(2) (2016)
43. Zororo, T.: IT Governance assurance and consulting: a compelling need for today's IT auditors. EDPACS 49(6) (2014)
44. Kitchenham et al.: Evidence-Based Software Engineering and Systematic Reviews. Chapman and Hall/CRC (2015)

Privacy as a Service (PraaS): A Conceptual Model of GDPR to Construct Privacy Services

Ella Roubtsova$^{(\boxtimes)}$ ⓘ and Rachelle Bosua ⓘ

Open University, Valkenburgerweg 177, 6419 AT Heerlen, The Netherlands
{ella.roubtsova,rachelle.bosua}@ou.nl

Abstract. The General Data Protection Regulation (GDPR) requires transparency about the use of personal data. However, what does the transparency mean for an individual? This transparency is an ability of an individual to uniformly fulfill actions stated in the GDPR from checking his/her data usage to erasing data. An individual assumes that these actions are supported by services. Such a uniform aspect "Privacy as a Service" is proposed in this paper. The contribution of this work is a conceptual model of the GDPR for designing privacy services. This model has been built by a content coding of key Articles from the GDPR, followed by incremental conceptual modelling and, finally, adopting the business-generic pattern of a contract. With executable protocol models of two privacy services identified from the GDPR we illustrate how to use our conceptual model. This work contributes to a uniform understanding of privacy by design as "Privacy as a Service". We discuss the semantic and organizational value of the proposed model.

Keywords: Business process modelling · Privacy aspect · Privacy as a Service (PraaS) · Conceptual model · Executable protocol model · General Data Protection Regulation (GDPR)

1 Introduction

The General Data Protection Regulation [5] aims to regulate the collection, recording and storage of EU citizens' personal data in the European Economic Area (EEA) and the transfer of personal data outside this area. At the same time, the GDPR aims to increase data subjects' (EU citizens') awareness of privacy and support their rights to control the lawful collection, processing and management of their personal data [26]. Since the implementation of the GDPR in May 2018, EU organizations have operationalised the GDPR in one or more forms. Examples include the appointment of Data Protection Officers, updated privacy policies and statements on websites, and formal letters or statements from employers of insurance and utility companies or governmental organizations, describing their commitment to protect an EU citizens' personal data.

© Springer Nature Switzerland AG 2021
B. Shishkov (Ed.): BMSD 2021, LNBIP 422, pp. 170–189, 2021.
https://doi.org/10.1007/978-3-030-79976-2_10

The GDPR requires transparency about the use of personal data. An individual interprets the transparency as an ability to **uniformly** fulfill actions stated in the GDPR from checking his/her the data usage to erasing data. An individual assumes that these actions are supported by services. Some companies, like tax departments and pension funds are not allowed to provide some services, for example, the services of asking for consent of the data subject to use the data or of erasing the data after a request of the data subject. In this case, an individual should be informed about the legal reasons of not providing services. The increasing awareness of individuals about privacy rights as touted by the GDPR and the increasing control of GDPR compliance makes it relevant to model the requirements of GDPR as privacy services and direct organizations to be transparent in terms of a unified set of provided services and the reasons of implementing or not implementing them.

Therefore, we introduce the concept Privacy as a Service (PraaS), having in mind the design of uniform privacy services, and formulate the following main research question: *What conceptual model, derived from the GDPR, can allow for the construction of privacy services that support GDPR conformance checks and the execution of privacy rights of data subjects?* This main research question is refined to the sub-questions:

- *What are the abstractions (objects, events, use cases) that allow organizations to construct privacy services?*
- *How can the conceptual model with the identified abstractions be used to increase data subjects' awareness of their privacy rights?*
- *How may service providers use the identified abstractions to demonstrate GDPR compliance?*

The research aim of this paper is to propose a conceptual model for privacy services using GDPR concepts and relations. The aim is also to demonstrate the application of the conceptual model with executable protocols of privacy services.

We use a sequential multi-method research approach to achieve this aim. Section 2 presents a review of the literature related to GDPR compliance both before and after the GDPR launch. The literature review has been conducted to identify the requirements for GDPR compliance and the existing conceptual models of GDPR. We have found that there are two goals caused by the GDPR for businesses: (1) allow businesses to demonstrate GDPR compliance to controlling institutions, and (2) allow individuals to explore and exercise their privacy rights. For both goals, the GDPR indirectly defines new services that should be provided by businesses to controlling institutions and individuals. Section 3 and Appendix A present the context coding of the GDPR to identify the concepts and relations allowing to construct services. Section 4 presents our conceptual model built from the GDPR. Section 5 and Appendix B describe the protocol model of privacy services developed to illustrate the application of our conceptual model. We show the executable protocol model that can be used for exploring privacy rights by individuals and for demonstrating GDPR compliance of business processes. Section 6 discusses the specific characteristics and the semantic and organizational value of our conceptual model. Section 7 concludes the paper and proposes future work.

2   Related Work: Conceptual Models of Privacy Laws Before and After GDPR

In order to deepen our research problem, we first conducted a literature review covering privacy-related concepts before and after the launch of the GDPR (from 2005 to 2020). The key goals of our search were to identify conceptual models of privacy regulations representing the duties of enterprises and the rights of individuals, and attempts to identify privacy services from such models. A small set of 13 papers was identified which confirmed that there were scant papers that modelled privacy services for the GDPR conceptually.

Our analysis of the literature found that conceptual models and taxonomies of privacy laws before the GDPR aimed to defend the rights of individuals. These taxonomies introduced the terminology for all following regulations. Based on a legal perspective of privacy prior to 2005, Solove [21] has developed a taxonomy that attempts to clarify how the legal system can be better understood in terms of the data that flows from a **data subject** to a **data holder**. Data subjects are individuals. Data holders include other people, businesses, and the government who collect and then process this data through storage, combining, manipulating, searching and using this data. This taxonomy presents the **violation of an individual's privacy as a list of harmful activities** and corresponding problems that may arise when personal data/information flow from the **data source** (the data subject whose data is being collected), to data holders (those who collect, process and disseminate personal data/information). Once collected and processed, data is disseminated (i.e. transferred or released).

In order to exclude harmful activities Cavoukian [4] and Schaar [20] introduced the "Privacy by Design" (PbD) idea stating that "privacy must be embedded into every standard, protocol and process that touches our lives". However, "Privacy by Design" does not define the details of design, it is just a declaration and this was criticized by practitioners. Koops and Leenes [9]) conclude that "Privacy by Design should not be interpreted as a general requirement for system developers to embed as many data protection requirements as possible in the design of the system."

Starting to define the PbD in detail, Guarda, Ranise, and Siswantoro [6] proposed a declarative framework that supports Information System specification, purpose-aware access control policies and legal requirements derived from the GDPR. The authors developed a methodology and accompanying technique that integrate legal compliance and security checks at the start of the design process of any Information System, allowing for formalization of (parts of) the regulation, to permit the application of automated techniques for security analysis and compliance checking. The authors provide detailed results to systems designers why a security analysis compliance check fails.

There are also attempts to automate legal compliance checking. Bartolini, Calabro and Marchetti [1] propose their "legal model of the GDPR to enrich a business process with annotations that express data protection requirements". This legal ontology GDPR model labelled PrOnto is an acronym for Privacy Ontology [14]. This model automates legal compliance checking for e-Government services taking into consideration the rights of individuals. The authors argue that the semantic web and legal reasoning techniques can support the application of Privacy by Design (PbD) principles for the day-to-day operations of firms, not-for-profit organizations and public administrators. PrOnto's legal knowledge model includes privacy agents, data types, types of processing operations, rights and obligations to support legal reasoning and compliance checking using LegalRuleML. "PrOnto consists of different modules: (i) documents and data, (ii) actors and roles, (iii) processing and workflow, (iv) legal rules and a deontic formula (formal expression of a duty or an obligation), (v) purposes and legal bases". The authors use the Reified Input/Output (RIO) logic [17] for constraints to present rules from the GDPR.

As a result of scientific discussions and attempts to automate legal compliance, the GDPR demands to guarantee "data protection by design" (GDPR, Article 25.1) and rights of individuals to know about their data and actively restrict the use of their data, erase their data, etc. These GDPR statements define two goals of conceptual models to support these: (1) the demonstration of compliance of companies to privacy law and (2) the execution of the rights of individuals. This has been discussed by the European Commission [7].

Tom, Sing and Matulevičius [25] propose a conceptual model of the GDPR that consists of two parts. Part 1 "GDPR entities and their associations" attempts to model a data structure in an organization that is needed to comply with the GDPR. Part 2 presents "GDPR rights and their associations to entities". This model relates concepts such as Right, Portability, Rectification, and Erasure from the position of the individual. The authors claim that "the model is a tool to aid development of organizational privacy policy." The authors present two policy examples, however, they doubt that the concepts are sufficient to prove compliance to GDPR. They illustrate this doubt with an example where policy related to "ease of data removal" is subjective. The potential application of the model is seen "in the development of GDPR-compliant extensions to modeling languages" and organizational privacy policies. The authors themselves state: "We presented a preliminary version of a GDPR model. This representation is intended to provide a simpler, visual overview to aid process implementers in understanding the associations between different entities in the GDPR. ... An approach to use this model as a tool to develop organizational privacy policy was also described along with an illustration on compliance rule extraction". Bonatti et al. [3] also understand the compliance to GDPR as compliance to privacy policies. The policies need to be formulated and formalized for automated checking. Therefore, they introduce a policy language SPECIAL, and present an algorithm for compliance checking. Their article presents an example associated with a data usage policy.

Romansky and Kirilov [18] present a preliminary design of an app's architecture with a formal description of the main procedures of privacy requests. The authors model a privacy request service with registration, identification, authentication, request analysis, request processing and the use of stochastic modelling using Markovian chains for verification of the input-output connections. Blanco-Lainé, et al. [2] have identified some business services related to the GDPR and modelled the following services in ArchiMate [24]: (1) Data Processing and Maintenance; (2) Consent Management; (3) Data Retention Management; (4) Data Security Management, and (5) Mapping GDPR types for personal data and related processing operations on real data and processing operations. The authors present an ArchiMate orchestration model of these services. Although the idea of services related to the GDPR is realistic, the ArchiMate models of services related to the GDPR cannot present the conceptual abstractions needed for realization of services, just because ArchiMate is not aimed for that.

3   Content Coding of the GDPR Articles in the Search of a Conceptual Model for Privacy Services

The first research method in our search of a conceptual model was a content coding of the GDPR Articles (Articles 12–23, 26 and 28 of the GDPR [5] followed by incremental conceptual modelling addressing our goal to identify abstractions and a conceptual model for design of privacy services.

Content coding selects concepts (nouns) and their relations (verbs) from the GDPR articles. Both authors first coded the GDPR rules for these articles separately, then compared individual coding to compile a collective coding scheme. The results of the coding are presented in Appendix A. As the goal of our conceptual model is to select in the GDPR the concepts and relations and construct from them the abstractions enabling the design of privacy services, our choices of concepts and relations has been driven by the definition of a service [16], namely:

– An instance of a service is a sequence of states and messages that ends with one of the specified result-states. Therefore, we select the concepts that allow to define states of a service.
– A service is provided and consumed at the same time. Therefore, we recognise the concepts of a provider (controller, supervisory authority) and a consumer (data subject, recipient) within the model during our GDPR coding.
– The provider and the consumer instances of a services communicate by message passing. This means that we select relations presenting messages (collects data, updates, constructers etc.).
– The valuable result of a service for a consumer may be a document or an information structure answering a consumer request. We create this information structure from the concepts.

The context coding provides sets of concepts and relations, but it does not help to build abstractions. Our conceptual model has been constructed using iterative experiments with different abstractions and attempts to use them in executable protocol models of privacy services identified from the GDPR.

4   The GDPR Based Conceptual Model for Privacy Services

After experimenting with different abstractions, we come to the conceptual model shown in Fig. 1.

In this model, the concept *Data Subject* presents a key consumer of a privacy service. The GDPR does not define concepts "data holder" nor "provider". According to the GDPR, the responsible concept for data is a *Controller*. A *Controller* creates an instance of *Information* (Art 14) for each *Data Subject* and his data. The GDPR does not define the nature of a *Controller*. It could be a business role, but it would be difficult to manage all the controls that need to be done for each data subject. We assume that this is a program, i.e. a service provider.

Many concepts defined in Art. 12–18 we see as attributes of the concept *Information*, i.e. metadata about actual data of a *Data Subject*. These attributes are used at different moments of the life cycle of data: data collection, usage and executing the rights of the *Data Subject*. These concepts being the attributes of the concept *Information* are the following (Fig. 1):

1. *Data Subject,*
2. *Controller,*
3. *Data Type,*
4. *Source from which data originate,*
5. *Recipient of data,*
6. *International Recipient of data,*
7. *Purpose,*
8. *Begin (or start) of the Period of storage,*
9. *End of the Period of storage,*
10. *Automated decision,*
11. *Right to Access,*
12. *Right to Restrict,*
13. *Right to Erase,*
14. *Right to Make Portable,*
15. *Right to Complain*, and
16. *Consent Status.*

Explaining these attributes, let us remind that *Data Subject* and *Controller* are two sides of a privacy service.

The *Data Type* is clarified by TermsFeed [23] issued by the European Commission. It gives some examples of *Data Type* instances: Name and Surname, Home address, Email address, Identification card number, Location data, IP address, Cookie ID, Advertising identifier on a mobile phone, Data held by a doctor or hospital including symbols that uniquely identify a person.

The *Source from which data originate* may be the *Data Subject*, the Internet, or an official registry.

Concepts *Recipient of data,* and *International Recipient of data* present organizations that receive the data permitted in the *Information*.

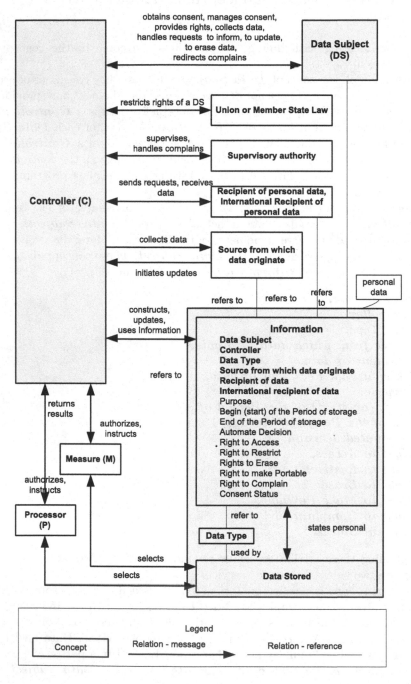

Fig. 1. The GDPR - based Conceptual model for privacy services

Concepts *Begin (or start) of the Period of storage* and *End of the Period of storage* define the period of data storage.

The *Purpose* is considered for now as a textual expression. The examples of *Purpose* are Marketing, Taxation, etc. The GDPR does not state the lawful purposes.

We have included the concepts representing rights from *Automated decision,...* to *Right to Complain* into the *Information* concept. The rights are given to any *Data Subject* by default, but the GDPR defines the role *Union or Member State Law* that may restrict these rights.

Art. 7 presents the concept *Consent* given by a *Data Subject* about the use of his/her data to a *Controller*. A *Consent* means acceptance of all values of attributes in the concept *Information*. Therefore, we added the concept *Consent Status* as an attribute of the concept *Information*.

The GDPR defines relations of concepts that may become potential privacy services. We present each of these relations as an arrow between the corresponding concepts. The arrow is labelled with the name of the relation. Figure 1 shows that

- *Controller* *obtains consent, manages consent* of *Data Subject (DS)*, *provides* DS's *rights, collects data* from DS, *handles* DS's *requests to inform, to update, to erase data* and *redirects* his *complains*.
- *Union or Member State Law* *restricts the rights* of a *Data Subject* and influences the services provided to a *Data Subject*;
- *Supervisory authority* *supervises* the quality of communication and *handles complains* of a *Data Subject*;
- *Recipient of Personal Data* and *International Recipient of Personal Data* *receive the data* permitted in the *Information* instance corresponding to this data.
- *Source from which data originate* is used by *Controller* for *collecting* data and may *initiate* the data *updates*.

The GDPR also defines the concepts *Processor* and *Measure*. E.g. "In a controller-processor relationship, the latter is only allowed to process personal data based on the documented instructions from the controller". This means that instances of the concept *Processor* are *authorised* and *instructed* by the *Controller*. Instances of the concept *Measure* are used to control the quality of services, for example, "information requests and supervisory requests" (Art. 61), "intended to produce legal effects" (Art. 66). It is not directly stated in the GDPR, but both concepts need a relation to *Data Stored* to *select* data values for processing them.

In addition, we have found that Article 4(1) of the GDPR defines that "personal data means any information relating to an identified or identifiable natural person ('data subject'); an identifiable natural person is one who can be identified, directly or indirectly, in particular by reference to an identifier". However, this definition does not define who is responsible for the analysis on whether a data set of a particular type makes a person identifiable. This analyses may depend both on the business domain and on the open information [22]. The GDPR leaves this analysis out of its scope. According to GDPR, a *Data Type* or a *Data Stored* is considered as *personal data* if it has a related *Information* instance defined by a *Controller*.

5 Illustration of the Usage of Our Conceptual Model for Privacy Services

In order to illustrate the usage of our conceptual model based on the GDPR analysis and coding, we have built an executable protocol model of the services "Obtaining Consent" and "Erasing Data". The models of services corresponding to other rights of a *Data Subject* can be built by analogy. The conceptual model is considered useful if the concepts and relations of the conceptual model are sufficient for the protocol of the chosen privacy services.

5.1 Goals and Requirements of the Services: "Obtaining Consent" and "Erasing Data"

The goals of the services "Obtaining Consent" and "Erasing Data" are refined to requirements via milestones and alternatives [19]:

1. A *Consent* is an agreement of a *Data Subject* to give the permission to a *Controller* of using his data.
2. A *Controller* creates a new *Information* instance about the collected data (*Data Stored*).
3. The *Controller* requests a *Data Subject* to sign the *Information* instance (in this context a consent form);
4. The *Data Subject* has two exclusive alternatives:
   (a) To withdraw his *Consent* (*No Thanks*);
   (b) To give his *Consent* (*Sign*).
5. If the *Information* instance is signed as a contract, the data corresponding to this *Information* can be stored by the *Controller*.
6. A *Data Subject* who has the *RightToErase* in the *Information* about data of this *Data Subject*, can *erase* data.
7. Erasing data means that each *Data Stored* is replaced with a stub "XXX". Erasing data also means the transition of the *Consent Status* of the corresponding *Information* into the state "*rejected*".

5.2 Protocol Model for Privacy Services: "Obtaining Consent" and "Erasing Data"

We use the Protocol Modelling method [10,11] for executable modelling of services. This method suggests the modelling of each concept as a protocol machine with associated attributes, recognized events from the environment and the life cycle transitions.

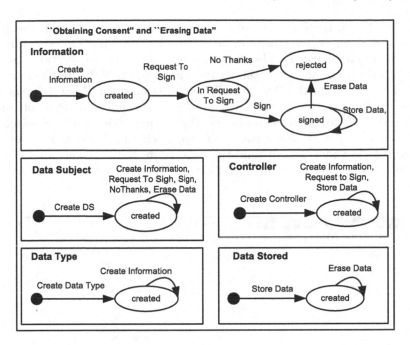

Fig. 2. Graphical presentation of a Protocol Model of the services: "Obtaining Consent" and "Erasing Data"

The uniqueness of Protocol Modelling, making it very efficient for executable modelling for business, is in its composition operator, the CSP parallel composition with data [10]. It synchronises behaviour of instances of different protocol machines. This operator replaces many intermediate communication operations (like multiplication replaces many summations in mathematics). The CSP parallel composition means that an event can fire only if all the protocol machine instances that recognize it, are in the state to accept it. Such synchronization of protocol machines causes the right level of abstraction of protocol models to focus on sequences of events of the communication between business concepts and environment [15]. The events are modelled as structures carrying data. The data of accepted events are used for updating attributes of protocol machines. The operator is implemented in the ModelScope tool [12].

The textual protocol model of services "Obtaining Consent" and "Erasing Data" is shown in Appendix B. Figure 2 shows only a graphical presentation of protocol machines, events and states without data. As the reader can see in Fig. 2, the underlying protocol machines of this model are *Data Subject*, *Controller*, *Data Type* and *Data Stored*. The protocol model *Information* presents the life cycle of privacy services.

Figure 3 shows a state of model execution in the ModelScope tool. Suppose a retailer Etos collects addresses of its clients for marketing. Let us introduce an instance of *Data Subject* "AB", a *Controller* "EtosIT", and a *Data Type*

"Address". When the instances of the concepts have been defined, the *Controller* may submit event *Create Information* (Fig. 2). Figure 3 shows this step of execution in ModelScope. The purpose, the source of data collection, the time period of data usage and the rights of the data subject "AB" are filled in.

After that, the *Controller* "EtosIT" submits an event *RequestToSign* with the consent form to the model. The consent form includes the elements of the corresponding *Information* about its *Data Type*. The *Data Subject* can *Sign* it or submit *No Thanks*. If the event *Sign* has been submitted, the *Consent Status* gets the value "signed" and the event *Store Data* becomes enabled. The *Controller* stores *Data Name* "Address-AB-stored" with a *Data Value*, say, "AB street, 202".

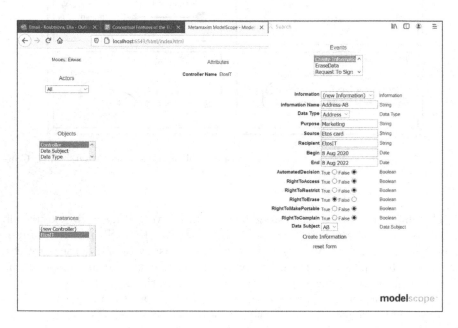

Fig. 3. A screen of a Protocol model execution: an instance of event Create Information

The "Erasing Data" service is one of the services supporting rights of a *Data Subject*. The right is stated in his/her *Information* instance: *RightToErase = true*. By erasing we mean the updating of the data values with stubs "XXX", and changing the *Consent Status* to "*rejected*". Figure 4 shows the result of the service of erasing data.

The protocol model clarifies the GDPR notion of *personal data*. In correspondence with the GDPR, an instance of data can be stored (OBJECT Data Stored) and handled as *personal data* only if there is a related contract being an instance of *Information* with all included attribute values. For the authors of this work, the semantics of *personal data* defined in the GDPR has become clear only after executable modelling. The protocol model is presented in Appendix B and can be downloaded from [15].

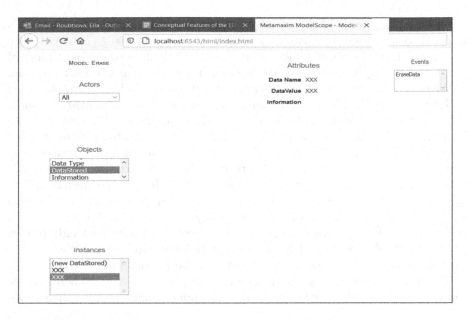

Fig. 4. A screen of a Protocol model execution: after acceptance of an instance of event Erase Data

6 Discussion of the Proposed Conceptual Model for Privacy Services

Let us return to the main research question: What conceptual model, derived from the GDPR, can allow for the construction of privacy services that support GDPR conformance checks and the execution of privacy rights of data subjects?

After experimenting with different abstractions, we come to the conclusion that a conceptual model that refines the business-generic pattern of a contract is the best to allow for the construction of privacy services that support GDPR conformance checks and the execution of privacy rights of data subjects. Indeed, the business-generic pattern of a contract is a composition of parties, subject matter and consideration [8]. All these elements are needed for a privacy service. In our conceptual model, the main parties are *Controller*, *Data Subject*, while the subject matter is presented by the concept *Data Type* and the consideration is combined in the concept *Information*. On the basis of an *Information* instance, a consent contract can be made and give rise to services for the *Data Subject* and for other related parties such as *Supervisory authority*, *Recipient of Personal Data*, *International recipient of Personal Data*, and *Union or Member State Law* (Fig. 1).

As an example of application of the business-generic pattern of a contract, our conceptual model for privacy services contributes to the theory of business-generic patterns extending the area of application of the business-generic pattern of a contract.

On the other hand, our conceptual model is a practical contribution. It is designed with the focus on creating privacy services and made compact, to be used in practice. It respects Miller's law [13], i.e. it is close to the psychological limit for an average human to recognize the number of concepts 7–9 in the model.

We have compared our conceptual model with the conceptual model proposed by Tom et al. [25]. The comparison shows that we have identified the same sets of concepts. Appendix A shows our coding of the GDPR. However, the difference in the goals of our models, results in different abstractions relating the concepts in the models. Tom et al.'s model [25] is "a tool to aid development of organizational privacy policy". A privacy policy is a textual rule that needs to be formulated in concepts and relations of GDPR and the business. This explains the extensive inclusion of all concepts and relations that may be used as templates for formulation of a privacy policy. For example, "Purpose is given for Consent", "Erasure erases Personal Data", etc. On the other hand, Tom et al.'s model [25] does not identify the concept *Information* (Art. 12) as privacy policies do not need any contract and any metadata about personal data.

The goal of our model is the development of privacy services. Therefore, we identify the abstraction *Information* as metadata about collected *personal data*:

1. We interpret a data subject's privacy rights as boolean attributes for the concept *Information* that switch the services available for data subjects to "on"/"off". For example, if an instance of **Information** and a *Data Subject* with the *Right to Access* is "true", then the *Data Subject* should have a service allowing access to his/her *Information* instance and to the data named in it.
2. Other attributes of the concept *Information* are used by the *Data Subject* to give or deny the consent related to the usage of data.

Our conceptual model for privacy services is business process independent and can be used by businesses that are changing their Information Systems to conform to the GDPR. An organization should define *personal data* as a relation between each *Data Stored* and the *Information* for it. The organization implements a *Controller* that provides privacy services. Using the names of concepts and relations from the GDPR will help to standardize the privacy-related elements of Information Systems.

The executable protocol model of privacy services, built on the basis of our conceptual model, allows to play scenarios and shows how the proposed abstractions can be used to increase data subjects' awareness of their privacy rights and to give service providers an ability to demonstrate GDPR compliance. The protocol model has transformed the relations of concepts into event sequences, so that the roles of a data subject and a controller can be played and the execution of rights of a data subject and the compliance to each GDPR statement can be demonstrated with examples.

7 Conclusion

Rising awareness about any law is useful for society. A uniform way of understanding the privacy aspects as privacy services will direct the thoughts of businesses to the selection of a set of data that should be handled as personal data. After the choice the handling of such a set of data is systematically organized as services. The understanding Privacy as a Service (PraaS) indicates the need of standardisation of GDPR implementation in organizations, so that the individuals can take control on their personal data and the supervisory authorities can easily check GDPR compliance.

The contribution of this work is a conceptual model of the GDPR adopting the business-generic pattern of a contract [8]. Another contribution is the executable way of exploration of privacy services derived from our conceptual model. Our conceptual model contributes to a uniform understanding of privacy rights and privacy services that need to support them. The semantic value of our model is in its ability to clarify the notion "personal data" in the GDPR. The model shows that the GDPR does not focus on analyzing whether data enables identification of a particular person. The GDPR defines "personal data" legally: if there is a contract, i.e. an "Information" instance for a data type, each (stored) data of this data type is considered as "personal data". The organizations can see the proposed conceptual model as a framework for developersof business processes and Information Systems that need to conform to the GDPR. The privacy services can be seen as aspects of business processes [11].

The conceptual model (Fig. 1) identifies many potential services that can be modelled. Among them are:

1. Services for Data Subjects and Controllers: Obtaining Consent, Consent Management, Accessing Information and Data Values, Initiating Data Updates, Restringing usage of Data Types, Erasing Data Values and Information, Making Data Portable, and Complaining.
2. Services for Supervisory Authorities and Recipients: Receiving Data According to Given Information, Control Measures of Communication Quality, Handling Complaints of Data Subjects, Access of a Supervisory Authority to Information and Data Storage.
3. Services for the Union or Member State Law: Enforcing the Restrictions from the Union or Member State Law.

As future work, new insights can be gained by conducting a study on composition of privacy services identified in this work with business processes existing in organizations.

A   Appendix. Coding of the GDPR articles

GDPR ARTICLE (paragraph)	Citation	Concepts	Relations
Article 12 Transparency of information [1], p. 1, 2, 3	1. "The controller shall take appropriate measures to provide any information referred to in Art. 13, 14, 15–22 and 34 ...relating to processing to the data subject . . . in writing, or by or by other means, including, where appropriate, by electronic means." "When requested by the data subject, the information may be provided orally, provided that the identity of the data subject is proven by other means." 2. "the controller shall not refuse to act on the request of the data subject for exercising his or her rights " 3" The controller shall provide information on action taken on a request... to the data subject without undue delay and in any event within one month of receipt of the request. "	Controller (C), Data Subject (DS), Request (R), Information provided to DS about data processing	C takes measures and provides DS written, electronic or oral information about data processing. DS can request C about information about data processing C answers any request initiated by DS within one month on request. Aspect: Timeliness of a response to a request of a DS
Article 12, p. 3	3. "That period may be extended by two further months where necessary, taking into account the complexity and number of the requests. The controller shall inform the data subject of any such extension within one month of receipt of the request, together with the reasons for the delay."	Controller (C), Data Subject (DS)	C informs DS about additional extension of reactions with one month and the reasons. Aspect: Timeliness of a response to a request of a DS
Article 12, p. 4.	4. " the controller shall inform the data subject without delay and at the latest within one month of receipt of the request of the reasons for not taking action and on the possibility of lodging a complain with a supervisory authority and seeking a judicial remedy."	C, DS, Supervisory Authority (SA)	C informs DS about not taking action and on the possibility to complain with a SA
Article 12, p.5	5. "Information ...shall be provided free of charge". " Where requests from a data subject are manifestly unfounded or excessive, in particular because of their repetitive character, the controller may either: charge a reasonable fee taking into account the administrative costs of providing the information or communication or taking the action requested; or refuse to act on the request." "The controller shall bear the burden of demonstrating the manifestly unfounded or excessive character of the request."	C, DS	Aspect: Costs of Repeated requests: C Charges DS; C sends a refuse to act with explanation to DS
Article 12, p.6	6. "the controller may request the provision of additional information necessary to confirm the identity of the data subject."	C, DS	C asks DS to provide identity information DS provides identity information to C

GDPR ARTICLE (paragraph)	Citation	Concepts	Relations
Article 14.	"Where personal data have not been obtained from the data subject, the controller shall provide the data subject with" the elements of the given list similar to Article 13 p. 1, 2. The new elements are source from which the personal data originate" and "existence of automated decision- making including profiling".	Personal Data, Source from which the personal data originate, Information Collection	C informs DS about all attributes of Information collection when the data of DS have been obtained from another source
Article 13 p. 1, 2	1."Where personal data relating to a data subject are collected from the data subject, the controller shall,.. provide the data subject with all of the following information: -the identity and the contact details of the controller and, where applicable, of the controller's representative; -the contact details of the data protection officer, where applicable, -the purposes of the processing for which the personal data are intended as well as the legal basis for the processing;... -the recipients or categories of recipients of the personal data, if any -where applicable, the fact that the controller intends to transfer personal data to a third country or international organisation ..." 2.-" the period for which the personal data will be stored, or if that is not possible, the criteria used to determine that period; -the existence of the right to request from the controller access to and rectification or erasure of personal data or restriction of processing concerning the data subject or to object to processing as well as the right to data portability;" -"...the existence of the right to withdraw consent at any time, without affecting the lawfulness of processing based on consent before its withdrawal; -the right to lodge a complaint with a supervisory authority; whether the provision of personal data is a statutory or contractual requirement, or a requirement necessary to enter into a contract, as well as whether the data subject is obliged to provide the personal data and of the possible consequences of failure to provide such data;..."	Personal Data, Information Collection, Recipient of personal data, Supervisory Authority	Information Collection contains the following attributes: -DS; -contacts of the Controller, protection officer; -purpose of personal data processing; -recipients of personal Data; -International recipients; -period of data storage, -existence of DS rights to 1. access, 2. restrict, 3. erase, 4. make portable, 5. complain to a supervisory authority
Article 15–22	Rights of DS Access, Rectify, Erase, Restrict, Be notified, Make personal data portable, Object, complain, Give permission for automated decision making and profiling	DS	Rights may demand potential services
Article 23	"Union or Member State law to which the data controller or processor is subject may restrict by way of a legislative measure the scope of the obligations and rights ..., when such a restriction respects the essence of the fundamental rights and freedoms and is a necessary and proportionate measure in a democratic society to safeguard: national security; defence; public security"	Union or Member State law	Aspect: Restriction of rights and access to services

GDPR ARTICLE (paragraph)	Citation	Concepts	Relations
Art. 26	"In a controller-processor relationship, the latter is only allowed to process personal data based on the documented instructions from the controller."	C, Processor (P)	C instructs P
Art. 28	Processing by a processor shall be governed by a contract or other legal act under Union or Member State law, that is binding on the processor with regard to the controller and that sets out the subject-matter and duration of the processing, the nature and purpose of the processing	C, Processor (P)	C and P are bound by a contract or an act

B   Appendix. Protocol Model of the Services Obtain Consent and Erase Data

```
MODEL Erase
OBJECT Data Subject
    NAME Data Subject Name
    ATTRIBUTES Data Subject Name: String,
    STATES created, asked, agreed, disagreed
        TRANSITIONS @new*Create DS=created,
                    created*Create Information=created,
                    created* Request To Sign=created,
                    created*Sign=created,
                    created*NoThanks=created,
                    created*EraseData=created,
 OBJECT  Controller
    NAME Controller Name
    ATTRIBUTES Controller Name: String,
    STATES created,inProject, inRequest,
        TRANSITIONS @new*Create Controller=created,
                    created*Create Information=created,
                    created* Request To Sign=created,
                    created*StoreData=created,
                    created*EraseData=created,
OBJECT Data Type
    NAME Data Type Name
    ATTRIBUTES Data Type Name: String,
    STATES created,
        TRANSITIONS @new*Create Data Type=created,
                created*Create Information= created,
OBJECT Information
    NAME Information Name
    INCLUDES DuplicateCheck
    ATTRIBUTES
        Information Name: String,Data Type:Data Type,
        Purpose:String,Source: String,Recipient:String,
        Begin:Date, End:Date,AutomatedDecision:Boolean,
        RightToAccess:Boolean,RightToRestrict:Boolean,
        RightToErase:Boolean,RightToMakePortable:Boolean,
        RightToComplain:Boolean,Data Subject:Data Subject,
        Controller:Controller,!ConsentStatus: String,
    STATES created, inRequestToSign, signed,  rejected
        TRANSITIONS @new*Create Information =created,
                created*Request To Sign=inRequestToSign,
                inRequestToSign*NoThanks=rejected,
                inRequestToSign*Sign=signed,
                signed*StoreData=signed,
                signed*EraseData=rejected,
OBJECT DataStored
    NAME Data Name
    ATTRIBUTES Data Name: String, DataValue: String,Information:Information,
```

```
         STATES created,
             TRANSITIONS @new*StoreData=created,
                     created*!EraseData= created,
BEHAVIOUR !DuplicateCheck
     STATES unique, duplicate
              TRANSITIONS @any*Create Information=unique,
EVENT Create DS
     ATTRIBUTES Data Subject: Data Subject, Data Subject Name: String,
EVENT Create Controller
     ATTRIBUTES Controller:Controller,Controller Name:String,
EVENT Create Information
     ATTRIBUTES
           Information: Information, Information Name: String, Data Type:Data Type,
           Purpose:String, Source: String, Recipient:String, Begin:Date, End:Date,
           AutomatedDecision:Boolean, RightToAccess:Boolean, RightToRestrict:Boolean,
           RightToErase:Boolean, RightToMakePortable:Boolean, RightToComplain:Boolean,
           Data Subject:Data Subject,Controller:Controller,
EVENT  Create Data Type
     ATTRIBUTES Data Type: Data Type,Data Type Name:String,
EVENT  Sign
      ATTRIBUTES Data Subject: Data Subject,Information:Information,
EVENT  NoThanks
     ATTRIBUTES Data Subject: Data Subject,Information:Information,
EVENT  Request To Sign
     ATTRIBUTES Information:Information, Data Subject: Data Subject,Controller: Controller,
EVENT StoreData
     ATTRIBUTES Data Name: String, DataValue:String, DataStored:DataStored,
                Controller:Controller, Information:Information,
EVENT EraseData
   ATTRIBUTES  DataStored:DataStored, Data Subject:Data Subject,
                Controller:Controller, Information:Information,
----------------------------------------------------------------
#Callbacks to the model
package Erase;
import com.metamaxim.modelscope.callbacks.*;
import com.metamaxim.modelscope.callbacks.Behaviour;

public class ConsentControl extends Behaviour {
public String getState() {
Instance myInformation= this.getInstance("Information");
Instance[] signedIs = this.selectInState("Information", "signed");
for (int i = 0; i < signedIs.length; i++)
        if (signedIs[i].getInstance("Information").equals(myInformation) )
 return "Signed";
              return "NotSigned";
     }}
public class DuplicateCheck extends Behaviour {
public String getState() {
 Instance myDS=getInstance("Data Subject");
 Instance myDT=getInstance("Data Type");
  Instance[] existingCF = this.selectInState("Information", "@any");
for (int i = 0; i < existingCF.length; i++)
        if (existingCF[i].getInstance("Data Subject").equals(myDS) &&
          existingCF[i].getInstance("Data Type").equals(myDT) &&
             !existingCF[i].equals(this)) return "duplicate";
     return "unique";
     }}
public class DataStored extends Behaviour{
public void processEraseData (Event event, String subscript) {
    this.setString("DataValue", "XXX");
    this.setString("Data Name","XXX");
    this.setNull("Information");
    }}
public class  Information extends Behaviour {
public String getConsentStatus() {
    return this.getState("Information");
    } }
----------------------------------------------------------------
```

References

1. Bartolini, C., Calabró, A., Marchetti, E.: Enhancing business process modelling with data protection compliance: an ontology-based proposal. In: ICISSP, pp. 421–428 (2019)
2. Blanco-Lainé, G., Sottet, J.-S., Dupuy-Chessa, S.: Using an enterprise architecture model for GDPR compliance principles. In: Gordijn, J., Guédria, W., Proper, H.A. (eds.) PoEM 2019. LNBIP, vol. 369, pp. 199–214. Springer, Cham (2019). https://doi.org/10.1007/978-3-030-35151-9_13
3. Bonatti, P.A., Kirrane, S., Petrova, I.M., Sauro, L.: Machine Understandable Policies and GDPR Compliance Checking. arXiv preprint arXiv:2001.08930 (2020)
4. Cavoukian, A., et al.: Privacy by design: The 7 foundational principles. Information and privacy commissioner of Ontario, Canada 5 (2009)
5. GDPR: General Data Protection Regulation. https://gdpr-info.eu
6. Guarda, P., Ranise, S., Siswantoro, H.: Security analysis and legal compliance checking for the design of privacy-friendly information systems. In: Proceedings of the 22nd ACM on Symposium on Access Control Models and Technologies, pp. 247–254 (2017)
7. Information Commissioner's Office (ICO): Privacy by Design (PbD). https://ec.europa.eu/eip/ageing/standards/ict-and-communication/data/pbd-privacy-design_en (2020)
8. Kilov, H.: Business modelling: understandable patterns, practices, and tools. In: Roubtsova, E., McNeile, A., Kindler, E., Gerth, C. (eds.) Behavior Modeling – Foundations and Applications. LNCS, vol. 6368, pp. 3–27. Springer, Cham (2015). https://doi.org/10.1007/978-3-319-21912-7_1
9. Koops, B.J., Leenes, R.: Privacy regulation cannot be hardcoded. a critical comment on the 'privacy by design' provision in data-protection law. Int. Rev. Law Comput. Technol. 28(2), 159–171 (2014)
10. McNeile, A., Roubtsova, E.: CSP parallel composition of aspect models. In: Proceedings of the 2008 AOSD Workshop on Aspect-Oriented Modeling, pp. 13–18 (2008)
11. McNeile, A., Roubtsova, E.: Aspect-oriented development using protocol modeling. In: Katz, S., Mezini, M., Kienzle, J. (eds.) Transactions on Aspect-Oriented Software Development VII. LNCS, vol. 6210, pp. 115–150. Springer, Heidelberg (2010). https://doi.org/10.1007/978-3-642-16086-8_4
12. McNeile, A., Simons, N.: http://www.metamaxim.com/
13. Miller, G.A.: The magical number seven, plus or minus two: some limits on our capacity for processing information. Psychol. Rev. 63(2), 81 (1956)
14. Palmirani, M., Martoni, M., Rossi, A., Bartolini, C., Robaldo, L.: PrOnto: privacy ontology for legal reasoning. In: Kő, A., Francesconi, E. (eds.) EGOVIS 2018. LNCS, vol. 11032, pp. 139–152. Springer, Cham (2018). https://doi.org/10.1007/978-3-319-98349-3_11
15. Protocol Modelling: Models. https://newprotocolmodelling.weebly.com/models.html (2020)
16. Reisig, W., Bretschneider, J., Fahland, D., Lohmann, N., Massuthe, P., Stahl, C.: Services as a paradigm of computation. In: Formal Methods and Hybrid Real-time Systems, pp. 521–538. Springer (2007)
17. Robaldo, L., Sun, X.: Reified input/output logic: combining input/output logic and reification to represent norms coming from existing legislation. J. Logic Comput. 27(8), 2471–2503 (2017)

18. Romansky, R., Kirilov, K.: Architectural design and modelling of a web based application for GDPR clarification. In: AIP Conference Proceedings, vol. 2048, p. 060006. AIP Publishing LLC (2018)
19. Roubtsova, E.: Goal modeling for interaction. Interactive Modeling and Simulation in Business System Design. SFMA, pp. 47–60. Springer, Cham (2016). https://doi.org/10.1007/978-3-319-15102-1_3
20. Schaar, P.: Privacy by design. Identity Inf. Soc. **3**(2), 267–274 (2010)
21. Solove, D.J.: A taxonomy of privacy. U. Pa. L. Rev. **154**, 477 (2005)
22. Sweeney, L.: k-anonymity: a model for protecting privacy. Int. J. Uncertainty Fuzziness Knowl.-Based Syst. **10**(05), 557–570 (2002)
23. TermsFeed: What Activities Count as Processing Under the GDPR? https://www.termsfeed.com/blog/gdpr-processing-activities/ (2020)
24. The Open Group: ArchiMate 3.1 Specification (2012–2019)
25. Tom, J., Sing, E., Matulevičius, R.: Conceptual representation of the GDPR: model and application directions. In: Zdravkovic, J., Grabis, J., Nurcan, S., Stirna, J. (eds.) BIR 2018. LNBIP, vol. 330, pp. 18–28. Springer, Cham (2018). https://doi.org/10.1007/978-3-319-99951-7_2
26. Voigt, P., von dem Bussche, A.: The EU General Data Protection Regulation (GDPR). A Practical Guide. Springer, Cham (2017). https://doi.org/10.1007/978-3-319-57959-7

Privacy Enabled Software Architecture

Emilia Stefanova and Aleksandar Dimov[✉]

Faculty of Mathematics and Informatics, Sofia University "St. Kliment Ohridski", J. Bouchier Blvd., 1164 Sofia, Bulgaria
emilia.l.stefanova@gmail.com, aldi@fmi.uni-sofia.bg

Abstract. Establishment of privacy legislation regulations like the General Data Protection Regulation (GDPR) makes privacy to become one of the very important quality requirements towards software systems. Software companies need to develop strict strategies to comply with such regulations. However, currently privacy is frequently studied together with security, nevertheless these two characteristics may have different scenarios and hence – different approaches towards satisfying them. This paper studies privacy requirements of service-based software systems with respect to privacy regulations (specifically – GDPR) and methods at architectural level to meet them. Based on this, we present an architectural approach to ensure privacy, especially in the case, when the software have not been developed with privacy in mind, as such regulations did not exist. Main aspect of this approach are some additional components to system architecture, which may also be developed as services. Our approach may be easily applied to already implemented legacy software systems. Its application is straightforward as very small changes in system implementation should be done. A short illustrative case study is also included at the end of the paper.

Keywords: Privacy · Software architecture · GDPR

1 Introduction

With the advancement of cloud systems and cloud-based data collection and storage, privacy has become one of the most important issues in the modern digital world. From individuals to large companies, all stakeholders have very high and demanding requirements towards software intensive systems to ensure privacy of their data. Even before the internet era in computer systems, privacy was considered one of the main human rights. Nowadays, information systems are spreading in almost every domain and collect and process large variety of data like health condition information, bank credentials, living addresses, phone numbers, etc.

In such conditions software intensive systems should ensure privacy in order to receive user trust and thus – to be successful. Another issue, besides the ethical considerations is that recent regulations in this area may put big fines on companies that develop software without taking respect to privacy of their users. For example, one such regulation within European Union is the General Data Protection Regulation (GDPR) [24]

© Springer Nature Switzerland AG 2021
B. Shishkov (Ed.): BMSD 2021, LNBIP 422, pp. 190–206, 2021.
https://doi.org/10.1007/978-3-030-79976-2_11

and there exist many other similar legislations all over the world. Currently, most software systems are designed and developed according to the principles of service-oriented architecture and are usually deployed in cloud. All companies that develop or use such systems have the duty to conform to privacy constrains posed by these regulations. One of the main concerns in this situation is that such companies should make similar or even the same design and implementation efforts to make services in compliance with official privacy regulations. A common approach towards the development of privacy enabled software systems would help to minimize these efforts, while satisfying privacy requirements at the same time.

The goal of this paper is to address the aforesaid issue by defining an architectural approach aimed towards enabling data privacy in service-based software applications. For this purpose, first part of this research was to study the area and identify existing efforts at architectural level to software privacy. As our approach is targeted towards service-oriented cloud-based software systems, the necessary components (i.e., services) that help to satisfy privacy requirements should also be defined. The approach should be suitable both for stand-alone services and applications and for larger sets of services developed within a large enterprise. Another benefit would be that not only future-developed software systems by a given company may take advantage of privacy solutions, but it may be also easily applied to legacy systems and services. In order to focus the research, we have oriented the approach towards GDPR compliance.

The rest of the paper is structured as follows: Sect. 2 defines the context of this research and makes an overview to the related work; Sect. 3 presents the privacy requirements that should be part of a privacy enabled software architecture; Sect. 4 provides some information about currently known approaches at architectural level to provide privacy; Sect. 5 presents the architectural approach for ensuring privacy of service-oriented software systems; Sect. 6 shows a case study that validates our approach and finally, Sect. 7 makes the conclusion remarks and states the directions for future research in the area.

2 Related Work

Privacy is considered part of the so-called quality (or also non-functional) requirements towards software systems. Functional requirements define the purpose of the system and what it should do, while non-functional requirements put some additional conditions (in form of constraints or specifications) on how the system should perform or deliver its functionality. It is recognized that software architecture and design are the means to fulfil and cope with quality requirements [2]. Being purely a matter of design, it may be relatively easy to ensure certain levels of privacy, when the requirements are known in advance. However, if dealing with legacy systems, satisfaction of privacy becomes quite challenging.

One major portion of research works that are directly related to ours, concern the notion of privacy-by-design. Further, a big domain for privacy research work is Internet-of-Things (IoT) with many applications. One such framework in the form of guidelines and a method to apply them is proposed in [14] to help software engineers design for privacy into IoT applications.

A review particularly aimed at the healthcare sector summarizes privacy-by-design approaches into healthcare sector [16]. Several privacy-by-design frameworks are listed there and their main characteristics together with advantages and drawbacks are discussed.

Concept of privacy-by-design is further elaborated by a more recent work [21] that aims to analyze how design may be used to ensure privacy from the viewpoint of Human-computer interaction. A mapping of design approaches to privacy a is provided which is further classified according to actors, involved in privacy by design research.

A similar to our approach in the domain of blockchain [18], utilizes the so-called Holochain to overcome limitations that blockchain technology pose over privacy. The Holochain is a platform that supports execution of distributed, server-less apps running on devices with localized data storage and management. Each such device in the Holochain supports its own blockchain in order to increase privacy. Another research, in the same direction presents a privacy-enabled solution for personal data sharing and tracking that shows how to provide blockchain with GDPR-compatible privacy mechanisms [13].

A specific subdomain of closely related privacy works, concerns development of particular privacy-aware-architectures. Very popular research topic in this respect is about avoiding privacy problems with applications that support live video analytics [10, 19, 20]. One such architecture, that deals with ensuring privacy into systems for identification of people, based on video surveillance devices is given in [10]. For this purpose, a pipeline is proposed which runs a neural-network algorithm capable to find specific people, based on images of crowd without knowing or revealing their real identity. An approach in the same area [19, 20] presents a privacy aware IoT service for live video analytics. However, the method taken there, relies not on some specific architecture, but on algorithm that blurs peoples' faces in video-streams, such that their privacy is protected. Further a policy mechanism is used in order to make exceptions to this, so that identification becomes actually possible.

There also exist some works, developed before GDPR, aimed at dealing with privacy at architectural level. For example, in cloud architectures used in smart grids [17], a proposal is made for an architecture that applies the following architectural tactics: (1) sensitive data storage in encrypted form; (2) access control policy that maintains different levels of access and ensures that the data is used only for agreed purposes, (3) archival of data that is no longer relevant but should be stored for a long time due to legislations; (4) audit log for all access attempts and actions on sensitive data and etc.

Another research proposes an architecture that provides confidentiality, of user location [7]. Methods proposed there include automatic deletion of old data, access control mechanism, automatic logging of actions on sensitive data, addition of privacy tags and data disclosure mechanisms. An architecture for large computing systems also provides a model of access, use of encryption, application of the principle for minimalistic collection of information, and limitation of the purposes for which the information can be used [4].

In [5] privacy is examined together with security and an overview of most widespread methods for data security and privacy protection in cloud systems is made. A few solutions based on such methods are briefly discussed. Further, research presented in [11], debates main known techniques for IoT smart homes. Among such methods, some issues regarding privacy and security of systems operating in smart homes are discussed. Most of these issues concern threats to both security and privacy. None of these works focus specifically on eventual software architectural approaches that will help to deal with privacy.

An interesting survey on privacy design strategies is proposed in [6]. It identifies eight design strategies and analyses their ability to provide for different privacy principles. Also, the author makes a reference to published design patterns that are capable to implement the presented design strategies. This research is very closely related to ours, although more general. The architectural approach presented in this paper, complements it by proposing a particular architecture that enables privacy compliance with GDPR in service-oriented cloud-based software systems.

Confab [7] is a toolkit aimed to provide means for ensuring privacy into ubiquitous software applications. It should facilitate implementation of interaction patterns for such applications. The solution presented in that work neither solves specific privacy challenges with respect to legislation regulations in the area, nor targets specifics of modern cloud-based software systems.

A survey of the so-called privacy policy languages is provided in [8]. Such languages aim to express privacy requirements in terms of privacy policies and specific controls that enable them.

In terms of research work, privacy is also often studied together with security when making a deeper research particularly into methods for ensuring privacy of software systems at architectural level. With respect to security, issues like how users should protect their data from the reach of other users or how to prevent hacking of data, become more important. However, as most of the contemporary software systems are considered also as data intensive systems, a higher attention to privacy should be raised and it should be distinguished from security. In this way, users may be interested in voluntarily providing their data for a specific purpose (like online shopping, event registration, etc.), while getting some confidence that they will be in full control of how this data will be further used. It should be noted that privacy and security have many common properties and cannot be studied completely separately. Nevertheless, privacy has not received enough attention and only in recent years a number of research works aimed at this quality characteristic appeared. In this paper we add to already existing research in two main directions: (1) our approach is aimed at general purpose data-intensive service-oriented software systems; (2) it is applicable both as an architectural style for newly developed software and also as architectural approach for legacy applications.

In the next section we continue with more information about requirements of privacy enabled software systems.

3 Analysis of the Requirements

At the European level, the first document that deal with privacy is directive 95/46/EO of the European Parliament from 1995 [23], which has been further elaborated by GDPR at 2018 [24]. The functional requirements for ensuring privacy of software systems are derived by these European regulations and are as follows (Fig. 1):

- **R1. Giving a consent** – each system user should be able to give consent for his data to be collected. User data can only be collected after consent has been obtained. User must be informed of what data will be collected and for what purpose it will be used. Consent must be given explicitly. System itself, must provide means to prove that user has given consent and also – to verify the moment at which the consent has been given. If personal data collected by the system has changed or the purposes of its processing has been changed, users must be prompted for a new consent, according to the conditions changed. Until that, personal data and processing against changes should not be performed. In case when data collected is about a child, the system must require the consent of the parents (guardians) and to require their declarations about parental rights.
- **R2. Consent withdrawal** – each user must have the right to withdraw already given consent and from that moment, the system should stop gathering and processing data about that specific user.
- **R3. Data access** – each user should have access to information about exactly what data the system collects and process about them. Complete copy of the data collected must be provided to the user upon request.

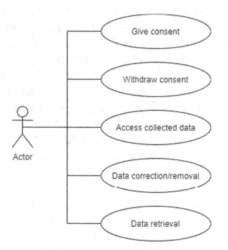

Fig. 1. Main privacy requirements for software systems

- **R4. Data correction and removal** – each user must be able to edit or completely erase data collected about them. Moreover, in such case, if some or all of the data is transferred to third systems, a request should be sent for correction/removal of data in all third-party products.
- **R5. Data retrieval** – the system should guarantee that the correct user receives this data and information.

With respect to these requirements, some of the typical problems that arise within software development companies are in the case when they provide many different services as cloud solutions and these services also store and process users' personal data. Some of them are also legacy and it would take a lot of effort to refactor their code to make them compliant with the privacy requirements. As said in the introduction, these requirements are also legislation constraints and the company is obliged to comply with them. Additionally, to make services compliant, high level of security must be achieved for storage and processing of personal data and all these must be met by each of the provided services. The best possible scenario is when this could be achieved with minimal changes to already existing services and to further reduce development costs and doing the same work multiple times should be avoided. In the next section, we describe our architectural approach, which will facilitate implementation of compliance with privacy regulations.

4 Privacy Architectural Approaches

Software architecture is widely recognized as an important aspect of software intensive systems. Bass [2], defines architecture as "the structure or structures of the system, which comprise software components, the externally visible properties of those components and the relationships among them". Architecture is supposed to serve many goals and is used in many software development related activities, and in all phases of software development cycle. The particular software architecture of a given system is highly dependent on quality requirements as for instance privacy. There exist quite a few methods in software architectural community, aimed at satisfaction of different quality requirements of software systems, like how one could achieve modifiability [1] or availability [15]. In the context of privacy, some known architectural tactics are as follows: (1) Separation of roles; (2) Audit Logging; (3) Access Control (4) Data Revelation; (5) Data Retention; (6) Data encryption; (7) Multifactor authentication. Next few paragraphs provide a brief description of these tactics.

Separation of roles is a main technique used to moderate access of users to different resources. Roles may be used to force users to have access to only specific system functionalities or to audit user activities. Main principles of separation of roles are the following:

- Separation of roles and authorizations [3] – these are specific proposals on how roles can be distributed in a software system, which role gives access to which parts of the system and how to track the actions of the role into the software system.
- Observation – Typical set of observations that can result from role separation can look like this, for example: end users can be observed by application administrators, application administrators can be observed by system administrators, and finally – system and hardware administrators should not be able to view personal data. Each of them may receive appropriate warnings when the action of a user in another role is potential abuse [3].
- Principle of least privileges – each module or service within the system should have access only to specific information and resources necessary to perform its duties. In

addition, each role should initially have minimal privileges and more should added only if necessary [9, 22].

Audit logging is important for internal verification purposes, to ensure accountability, to address public privacy issues, to ensure that data is not misused either intentionally or by accident, and to protect the company against legal charges. Auditing is used as a tactic to ensure confidentiality in a wide variety of domains [7, 17]. There are developments that offer a specific software architecture for logging and auditing [12], together with some commercial services (AWS CloudTrail). With respect to privacy, the audit strategy should consider that it is needed to track an iteration of sensitive data. It is necessary to anticipate the different scenarios for iteration with this data and to determine which parts of the system offer an appropriate view of these actions. The most appropriate and often used way to implement audit logging in software architecture is by introducing an additional system or component to deal with it and it is also important that log processing should have lower priority than the main functionality [3, 12].

Access control is key mainly for ensuring security of data, however with respect to the requirements defined in the previous section, it also should influence privacy. Some of the most common access control methods are:

- Role-based access – this is complementary to separation of roles and is based on the characteristics and the role (and hence authorization privileges) of the individual user.
- Time-based access – means to provide users with access to data for a predetermined time, at the end of which the system automatically revokes all privileges. This encourages sharing of data when it is needed and at the same time guarantees that access privileges will be revoked once they are no longer needed, without the need for further action by the data controller.
- Rule-based access control – this is when access rights are based on user-defined rules.
- Others – Access based on functionality; access based on previous actions; identity-based access; rule-based access; organization-defined access.

Data Revelation – while access control defines who has the right to access sensitive information, data revelation strategies determine who needs to access that information. The aim is to minimize disclosure of information in such a way as not to significantly limit the ability of authorized users to use data properly. To achieve this, for example, data can be disclosed selectively, in proportion to the needs of the specific scenario. This strategy is very suitable for different kinds of analytics, when only specific part of the sensitive data is needed and there is no need to even know to which person it refers. Another way to achieve revelation is to employ targeted data disclosure. It is applicable in information systems that provide mechanisms for indexing and search. It relies on certain predicates and is easily applied to both SQL and noSQL databases that are designed to support data retrieval. Their interfaces that provide search functionality may be parameterized by adding additional predicates to minimize the scope of the returned information, as well as to define the range and type of acceptable set of results.

Data removal – a good privacy strategy for user data should inevitably include appropriate strategy to remove all sensitive data when it is not needed anymore. All strategies for removal of sensitive data should comply first with existing state laws (even prior to privacy regulations). For example, there may exist data that should be kept over a certain amount of time regardless of user's will to delete it (like information about social insurance or state taxes). In this regard, data removal techniques for ensuring privacy are divided into two broad categories: data hiding and physical deletion. Data hiding architectural techniques may include:

- Partial deletion – only some parts and fields of the sensitive information, usually defined by law, are deleted.
- Anonymization – deletes only the information that associates sensitive data with its owner.
- Access control – adjusting access rights of different users, in order to place sensitive data completely out of the reach of users.
- Data Leasing – Data is accessible after explicit request by users and administrators should approve this request. Such approval may be time dependent with expiration setting when it will again become restricted and inaccessible to users.
- Backup – may be used to remove access and move data to a more secure and restrictive storage environment. Advantage of this approach is that it is possible to reproduce data if required (e.g., in court proceedings), while keeping it out of the reach of system users who do not have a real need to access it.

On the other hand, data deletion architectural approaches tactics include:

- Conditional deletion – This approach is very similar to data hiding approaches, as it suggests that end-users should be denied access to data entries, but the latter could eventually be retrieved by server application administrators. If space is needed data may be rewritten and this way, space allocated by it to be freed up. Such approach is appropriate for lighter privacy policies.
- Delete by encryption – This approach removes the key that encrypted the data.
- Complete Delete – Instantly overwrite all bits containing sensitive entries, both in memory and in storage. Used for stricter regulations.
- Hardware Destruction – The most complete and irreversible method of data removal. When techniques for repeatable rewriting of data is not sufficient for its removal, most severe methods include destruction of hardware.

Data encryption and **multifactor authentication** are tactics used to generally provide security, although they are also widely applicable for privacy as well. Encryption of network traffic solves a common problem by ensuring that data cannot be obtained by interception and sniffing over the network; encryption of data also could be used to protect it in many cases.

5 Data Privacy-Enabled Architecture

This section describes the main components of the data privacy architecture that we propose. These components are service-oriented and are designed to be capable for deployment and integration with cloud-based applications. This architecture should comply with the requirements set out in Sect. 3. The essence of the proposed approach is in the introduction of the following infrastructure services:

- Data Governance Service (DGS) – its main role will be to be an intermediate layer between customer services and the database and to prevent unauthorized access. It should ensure correct handling of personal data by customer services. This way, only authorized users will have access to personal data. The service is also responsible for storing data in a more secure way (for example, encrypting and replicating personal data), as well as ensuring traceability of actions performed on sensitive data by maintaining a transaction log. Another important role of this service is that it will provide access to the data of the Personal Data Access Service. As again, it will only guarantee authorized access. A key aspect in the implementation of the service is the existence of a separate instance to serve the needs of its corresponding customer service. In this way, customer service needs for fast data access can be covered and potential performance issues can be eliminated.
- User Personal Data Access Service – it will serve as a portal through which customers can access, delete, and change their personal data collected, and processed by all solutions offered by the company. It will provide a GUI to help end users to view, modify, delete and retrieve personal data collected about them from all other operational services of the company. Its main functionalities are to extract user data (collected by various other services), to aggregate and present data in an understandable form.
- Client Services – These are the legacy services that the company provides to its end users. They need modifications in order to comply with the requirements defined in the General Data Protection Regulation. These services will consume the functionality provided by DGS.
- Database Service – it provides the functionality needed for all other services to connect to the database. Practice shows that we should follow the assumption that large companies operating in cloud environment invest in development of a core of basic services, implementing common functionalities needed by others to perform their work. In the current template, we rely on the fact that we have such a service available.
- Authentication Service – This service is part of the company's existing core of general services. They are integrated and widely used by all other customer services. The role of the Authentication Service is to provide an opportunity to verify the identity of the end users of the company's software. It also implements the functionality that satisfies the requirement for giving consent by system users.

Current solution expands the already existing functionalities of the Authentication Service by introduction of an additional module (Data Processing Consent Module), which has the duty to satisfy the requirement that collection and processing of personal data of end users should be made only after their consent.

The modular diagram shown on Fig. 2 shows the main types of services that are present in the proposed architecture, their constituent components, and high-level interactions. The left part of the picture presents the client services, for the sake of example, three services are shown here, denoted with *Client Service A*, *B* and *C*. The goal is that they achieve compliance with privacy regulations and at the same time, usage of these

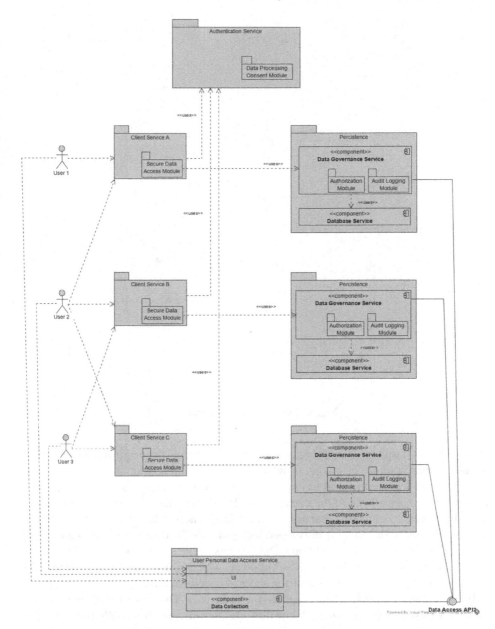

Fig. 2. Privacy enabled architecture – general view

services by end users (denoted by *User 1, 2,* and *3* on the picture) should remain unaffected. Each client service also has a corresponding instance of a persistence module – it is abstraction of the data storage for each particular service. Our proposed solution introduces an additional infrastructure component, called *Data Governance Service (DGS)*. It will become the only point where client services have access to the data they

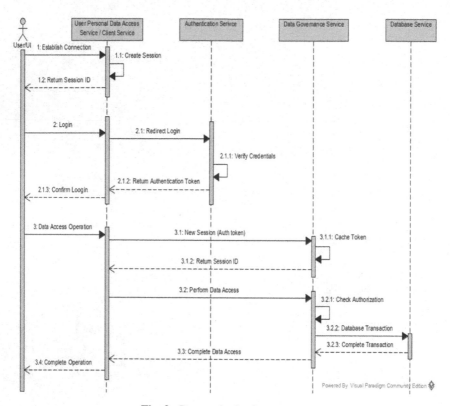

Fig. 3. Data authorization process

store. For this purpose, it should have the same interface as the original data service. It should support a query language, to which extensions and restrictions can be defined. This way, we achieve the goal to impose on client services restrictions to use personal data which is only related to the current user. Then, actual data storage is implemented as an instance of a standard database service, which is accessible only via the DGS. For access to personal data a UI is developed and a module for data collection and they are encapsulated within the User Personal Data Access Service (also shown on Fig. 2). The essence here is the Data Collection sub-module, which is used as a proxy to the DGS by all client services. Upon request for access to personal data by a given end user it collects and aggregates all data associated with the user. The sequence diagram shown on Fig. 3 illustrates the control and data flow used to achieve correct authorization when accessing data.

According to the privacy requirements, outlined in Sect. 3, they are fulfilled as follows:

- R1 and R2 are fulfilled by the Authentication Service and the Data Processing Consent Module, which is part of it.
- R3 and R4 are fulfilled both by User Personal Data Access Service and Data Governance Service

- R5 is fulfilled by the Data Governance Service

Next section will provide a short case study to illustrate and justify application of the approach.

6   Case Study

In order to illustrate the described approach, we have developed a test client service, called Delivery Service. It has the functionality to create a user account together with the set of information about them, to modify this information, as well as possibility to delete a user. Once logged in, the user can place orders for goods and services, which will be delivered to them. For each order there is additional information including, but not limited to: order description, status, and the delivery address. Users can check order details by the order id. There is also functionality for managing of the orders, which is available for administrators.

In this case, the delivery service should represent a legacy software product, which has been developed without taking into consideration privacy requirements but at some point of time has to comply with them due to introduction of legislation regulations (i.e., GDPR). Being a legacy application, the Delivery services shares a common repository for both user data and orders-specific information. This way, for the purposes of the case study, there exists a feature in the Delivery Service implementation, that can however be regarded as a privacy design fault – users may normally request order details by order ID for various purposes, like statistics about the most popular goods, relations between different goods, based on popularity and so on. This way, when the current user requests order details, they may also get access to orders placed by other users. Order details contain data that at some circumstances may be considered sensitive, like address, phone number and contents may be associated with specific customer which is of course undesired from privacy point of view. The class diagram on Fig. 4 illustrates this implementation of the original delivery service (before application of the privacy architectural approach, proposed here).

First step of application of the privacy architectural approach, is to develop the additional services as described in Sect. 5 – the Data Governance Service (DGS) and user Personal Data Access Service (PDAS). The class diagram of the delivery service after application of the approach is shown on Fig. 5. To achieve easy integration between delivery service and DGS, one integration point between the two services should be implemented. In addition, this integration point is on the lowest level in the client service, which is important, as no changes in the business logic are needed. In fact, DGS serves as a proxy between the client service and the database. In this way, additional logic can be added to DGS, in order to implement additional requirements forced by particular privacy regulations. For instance, with respect to GDPR, DGS developed here introduces an additional check – for all CRUD operations with users' personal data, there is a verification if the currently logged in user, who wants to perform an operation over the data, is the real owner of this data. Now, DGS will perform a check if the currently logged in user is the owner of the personal data and if not may filter data, marked as sensitive.

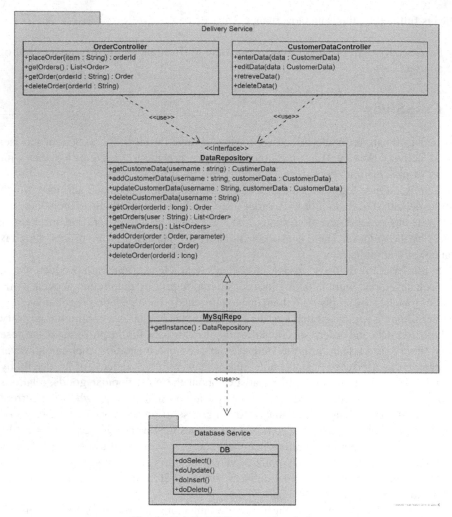

Fig. 4. Original delivery service design

The other service created as a part of the proposed approach is the User Personal Data Access Service (not shown of Fig. 5). It provides to the end users functionality for access, correction, removal, and retrieval of the collected personal data of them. According to the proposed architectural approach, the User Personal Data Access Service takes all the information it needs from the Data Governance Service. This means that no integration is needed between the client service and the User Personal Data Access Service.

For simplicity and ease of demonstration, the case study shows only low architectural level of application of the privacy approach. However, it is not implementation specific and may be applied also to more abstract system components and entities. The only modification to the existing system and its services is changes in the API of the original service (the delivery service in this case) and providing some information into

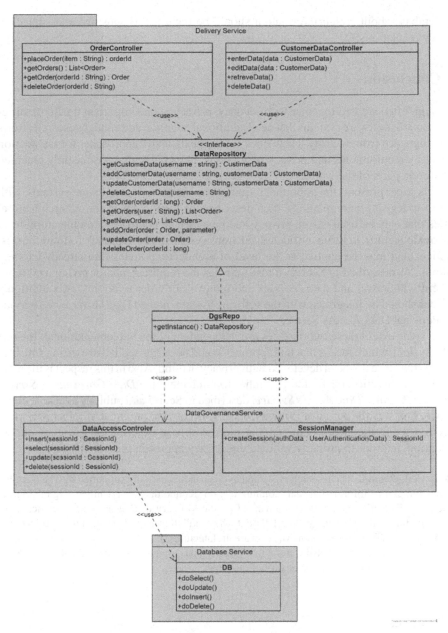

Fig. 5. Delivery service after application of the privacy approach

the database about which information should be regarded as sensitive and subject to privacy regulations.

7 Conclusion

Although often studied together with security, privacy is one important quality requirement towards software systems that need additional attention and enough research efforts to distinguish it from security. There does not exist exhaustive approaches for satisfaction of privacy requirements and privacy regulations, like GDPR that has recently emerged in different parts of the world.

This paper presents the important requirements for privacy in software systems, with respect to legislation regulations, then describes the most popular current architectural tactics that may be used ensure privacy and proposes an approach at architectural level to provide privacy in service-oriented software systems. The approach follows the best practices and may be applied at the level of architectural styles into already existing systems. As described in Sect. 5, it also satisfies the requirements for giving a consent, consent withdrawal and data accesses and removal. In order to do this, two additional services should be integrated with the software system, named Data Governance Service and Personal Data Access Service.

To some extent these two services are independent of the implementation of the rest of the system, which means that this approach could be easily applied to existing software systems that have not been developed with privacy in mind. Also in this respect is the most appropriate direction for future research – to implement the *Data Governance Service* and *User Personal Data Access Service*, described in Sect. 5 as a publicly available cloud service. This way the notion of *Privacy as a Service* could be provided. Another important direction for further work is to conduct more real-case experiments and comparative evaluation, in order to properly validate the privacy approach presented here[1].

Acknowledgements. The research presented in this paper is partially supported by The National Science Program "Information and Communication Technologies for Unified Digital Market in Science, Education and Security" financed by the Ministry of Education and Science, Bulgaria and the Sofia University "St. Kliment Ohridski" Research Science Fund project No. 80-10-74/25.03.2021 ("Data intensive software architectures").

Authors of the paper are also grateful to the anonymous reviewers for their valuable comments and remarks, which increased the quality of the paper.

References

1. Bachmann, F., Bass, L., Nord, R.: Modifiability tactics. Technical Report. Carnegie-Mellon University Pittsburgh. Software Engineering Institute (2007)
2. Bass, L., Clements, P., Kazman, R.: Software Architecture in Practice, 3rd edn. Addison-Wesley Professional (2013)

---

[1] All web sources in the References section were last visited in April 2021.

3. Bowman, C., Gesher, A., Grant, J. K., Slate, D., Lerner, E.: The Architecture of Privacy: On Engineering Technologies that Can Deliver Trustworthy Safeguards. "O'Reilly Media, Inc." (2015)
4. Cardoso, R., Issarny, V.: Architecting pervasive computing systems for privacy: a survey. In: Sixth Working IEEE/IFIP Conference on Software Architecture: WICSA 2007, 2007, Mumbai, Maharashtra, India, pp. 26 (2007)
5. Chen, D., Zhao, H.: Data security and privacy protection issues in cloud computing. In 2012 International Conference on Computer Science and Electronics Engineering, vol. 1, pp. 647–651. IEEE (2012)
6. Hoepman, J.H.: Privacy design strategies. In: IFIP International Information Security Conference, pp. 446–459. Springer, Heidelberg, June 2014. https://doi.org/10.1007/978-3-642-55415-5_38
7. Hong, J.I., Landay, J.A.: An architecture for privacy-sensitive ubiquitous computing. In: Proceedings of the 2nd International Conference on Mobile Systems, Applications, and Services, pp. 177–189 (2004)
8. Kumaraguru, P., Cranor, L., Lobo, J., Calo, S.: A survey of privacy policy languages. In: Workshop on Usable IT Security Management (USM 07): Proceedings of the 3rd Symposium on Usable Privacy and Security. ACM (2007)
9. Lord, N.: What is the Principle of Least Privilege (POLP)? A Best Practice for Information Security and Compliance (2020). https://digitalguardian.com/blog/what-principle-least-privil ege-polp-best-practice-information-security-and-compliance
10. Miraftabzadeh, S.A., Rad, P., Choo, K.K.R., Jamshidi, M.: A privacy-aware architecture at the edge for autonomous real-time identity reidentification in crowds. IEEE Internet Things J. 5(4), 2936–2946 (2017)
11. Mocrii, D., Chen, Y., Musilek, P.: IoT-based smart homes: a review of system architecture, software, communications, privacy and security. Internet Things 1, 81–98 (2018)
12. Noeparast, E., Ravanmehr, R.: A Novel Event-Oriented architecture for logging and auditing in distributed systems. Adv. Netw. Commun. 1, 36–44 (2012)
13. Onik, M.M.H., Kim, C.S., Lee, N.Y., Yang, J.: Privacy-aware blockchain for personal data sharing and tracking. Open Comput. Sci. 9(1), 80–91 (2019)
14. Perera, C., Barhamgi, M., Bandara, A.K., Ajmal, M., Price, B., Nuseibeh, B.: Designing privacy-aware internet of things applications. Inf. Sci. 512, 238–257 (2020)
15. Scott, J., Kazman, R.: Realizing and refining architectural tactics: Availability. Carnegie-Mellon Univ. Pittsburgh Pa Software Engineering Inst. (2009)
16. Semantha, F., Azam, S., Yeo, K., Shanmugam, B.: A Systematic literature review on privacy by design in the healthcare sector. Electronics 9(3), 452 (2020). https://doi.org/10.3390/ele ctronics9030452
17. Simmhan, Y., et al.: An analysis of security and privacy issues in smart grid software architectures on clouds. In IEEE 4th International Conference on Cloud Computing, pp. 582–589 (2011)
18. Wahlstrom, K., Ul-haq, A., Burmeister, O.: Privacy by design: a holochain exploration. Australas. J. Inf. Syst. 24 (2020). https://doi.org/10.3127/ajis.v24i0.2801
19. Wang, J., Amos, B., Das, A., Pillai, P., Sadeh, N., Satyanarayanan, M.: A scalable and privacy-aware IoT service for live video analytics. In: Proceedings of the 8th ACM on Multimedia Systems Conference, pp. 38–49, June 2017
20. Wang, J., Amos, B., Das, A., Pillai, P., Sadeh, N., Satyanarayanan, M.: Enabling live video analytics with a scalable and privacy-aware framework. ACM Trans. Multimed. Comput. Commun. Appl. (TOMM) 14(3s), 1–24 (2018)
21. Wong, R.Y., Mulligan, D.K.: Bringing design to the privacy table: Broadening "design" in "privacy by design" through the lens of HCI. In: Proceedings of the 2019 CHI Conference on Human Factors in Computing Systems, pp. 1–17 (2019)

22. Principle of least privilege (POLP). Definition. https://searchsecurity.techtarget.com/defini tion/principle-of-least-privilege-POLP
23. Directive 95/46/EC of the European Parliament and of the Council of 24 October 1995. OJ CL 281, 0031–0050 (1995)
24. Regulation (EU) 2016/679 of the European Parliament and of the Council of 27 April 2016. https://eur-lex.europa.eu/eli/reg/2016/679/oj

Modeling the Handling of Knowledge for Industry 4.0

Norbert Gronau(✉) [iD]

University of Potsdam, 14482 Potsdam, Germany
norbert.gronau@wi.uni-potsdam.de

Abstract. Industry 4.0, i.e. the connection of cyber-physical systems via the Internet in production and logistics, leads to considerable changes in the socio-technical system of the factory. The effects range from a considerable need for further training, which is exacerbated by the current shortage of skilled workers, to an opening of the previously inaccessible boundaries of the factory to third-party access, an increasing merging of office IT and manufacturing IT, and a new understanding of what machines can do with their data. This results in new requirements for the modeling, analysis and design of information processing and performance mapping business processes.

In the past, procedures were developed under the name of "process-oriented knowledge management" with which the exchange and use of knowledge in business processes could be represented, analyzed and improved. However, these approaches were limited to the office environment. A method that makes it possible to document, analyze and jointly optimize the new possibilities of knowledge processing by using artificial intelligence and machine learning in production and logistics in the same way and in a manner compatible with the approach in the office environment does not exist so far. The extension of the modeling language KMDL, which is described in this paper, will contribute to close this research gap.

This paper describes first approaches for an analysis and design method for a knowledge management integrating man and machine in the age of Industry 4.0.

Keywords: 4th industrial revolution · Knowledge management · Business process management

1 New Requirements by Industry 4.0

Industry 4.0 and the merging of the real and virtual world have already become part of our everyday life [1]. On the one hand, the networking of individual objects with the Internet, such as alarm systems, heat regulators or smartphones, makes it possible to communicate with these objects. On the other hand, these objects perform various tasks independently. To this end, companies have implemented further technical developments and comprehensive networking that allow the integration of embedded systems with web-based services into production processes [2, 3]. In this way, the technical entities in the factories can (mutually) regulate and control themselves independently, make decisions, forward information and incorporate current changes in the environment.

© Springer Nature Switzerland AG 2021
B. Shishkov (Ed.): BMSD 2021, LNBIP 422, pp. 207–223, 2021.
https://doi.org/10.1007/978-3-030-79976-2_12

In an Industry 4.0 environment, digitized work processes require employees to have the competence to adequately deal with fluid situations on the basis of their own knowledge and the ability to place this in situation-specific contexts [4]. To achieve this, the development of a comprehensive understanding of processes [5] in relation to digitized working environments is essential. Adult learners also benefit from building on existing knowledge [6] and from learning units close to the real work process [7].

Another effect of digitization in the industry is disspecialization [8]. The availability of electronic task assistants and assistance systems means that tasks that used to require highly trained specialists can now be performed by largely laypersons. For example, machines that have self-regulating capabilities such as SPC (Statistical Process Control) can also be operated by semi-skilled employees. This disspecialization leads to a loss of jobs for exactly those tasks that were previously performed by humans and can now be performed by machines. At the same time, however, there is a considerable additional demand for new specialists for tasks that cannot be performed by automated or computerized systems.

This de-specialization of existing tasks therefore leads to an increased demand for new specialists, as can be seen in some metropolitan areas, where IT specialists are sometimes paid higher annual salaries than experienced university professors.

Against this background, business processes must be designed in such a way that they take into account both the communication aspects, such as machine-to-machine communication [9] and human-machine interaction [3], and the individual customer and supplier requirements. In addition to the development of technologies and the conversion of production, existing obstacles to the ability to change must be recognized in the organizational area and ways must be sought to overcome them [10]. The qualification of management and workers plays an important role in this context, as the degree of automation in production processes is increasing [11]. Only well-trained specialists can make the necessary quick and qualified decisions in the event of tool or process malfunctions [12].

1.1 A Stronger Demand for Qualification

The design of complex value chains with rapid technology changes, shortening production cycles and a multitude of interfaces between the participating companies and employees (in the following the male form is mostly used) requires competent specialists who are involved in a structured and creative way. Only they can contribute to the optimization of internal and cross-company structures in a targeted and solution-oriented manner due to their extensive process and technical knowledge. This requires the participatory co-design of working conditions and processes along the entire value chain, taking into account the perspectives of management and executives on the one hand and employees and works council on the other [13].

The acquired understanding of processes also enables employees to share their individual experiences in different work processes and thus generate socially acceptable innovations in the workplace. At the same time, they should be given the opportunity to learn, to develop their personal competence profile while working, to acquire qualifications in related occupational fields or to acquire social and methodological skills. Only in this way can the changes induced by Industry 4.0 can be successfully countered by new qualifications among employees.

The understanding of comprehensive competence management is oriented along the entire value chain, with a focus on activation and integration of all intra- and inter-individual as well as company-specific competences. This requires a suitable recording, analysis and design approach.

1.2 Considering Knowledge of Machines

To date, the set of criteria proposed by Davenport has been used to define tacit knowledge, consisting of information of professional insight, values, experience and context [14, 15]. Conventional concepts for distinguishing tacit and explicit knowledge [16] or the handling of knowledge, such as the SECI model [17], locate tacit knowledge exclusively in human knowledge carriers. This is no longer appropriate due to the penetration of organizations and their service creation processes with cyber-physical systems [18, 19] as self-organizing and decision-making technical entities. Decision-making powers now also lie with technical actors. Digitalization, virtualization and the Internet of Things are forcing major changes in the roles of employees and technical actors. Machines and systems as well as products take in data of their environment by means of sensors, process them and intervene in their environment with the help of actuators. Data is passed on to information systems - which in turn receive, process and send it; analogous to the reception, processing and sending of information by humans. "Processing" includes both the use of information according to predefined rules and a given space of alternative solution paths and possibilities (inference) and the (creative) development of facts and solutions across given structures with an undetermined result (intelligence; [20]). Knowledge as "purpose-oriented networking of information" [21] enables actors to act and make decisions. It prepares them and is an essential building block for developing competencies. This networked information consists of data with appropriate semantics and data in a predefined syntax. With currently available technology, both human and technical actors are able to process signs, data, information and also knowledge in a purposeful way.

Technical actors are considered to be all units in production or logistics processes that can be regarded as cyber-physical systems because they have great capabilities for processing information and are networked with each other.

Accordingly, it is obvious to understand and treat technical entities as potential knowledge carriers. In the age of increasingly frequent cyber-physical systems that permeate value-added processes, some of the criteria for personal knowledge established in conventional concepts can now also be attributed to machines. These are the aspects of professional insight into the respective special domain and the experience that a machine can definitely exhibit, for example by using a case-based reasoning tool.

1.3 Operationalize Knowledge

In most modeling approaches for knowledge-intensive business processes, the representation of knowledge has been purely qualitative until now. Sultanow et al. [22], for example, evaluated 13 different approaches to modeling business processes, including from a knowledge-oriented perspective. Most of the approaches examined only mastered the mapping of knowledge, for example by showing knowledge maps or topic maps. Although semantic aggregation was often possible (e.g. Java → programming language), a more precise quantitative modeling of knowledge, e.g. for its inclusion in simulation models, was not possible.

For example, in the Knowledge Modeling and Description Language (KMDL) up to version 2, only the specification of a single knowledge level was possible as an attribute of a knowledge object. This was regarded as unsatisfactory, since knowledge is often explained in a constructivist way and should therefore be assessed with several independent evaluation standards.

2 Modeling of Knowledge-Intensive Processes with KMDL

One of the modeling techniques that expressed knowledge of people as separate objects in business processes was the Knowledge Modeling and Description Language (KMDL). Its development began more than 10 years ago. With version 2.1, very comprehensive practical experience in various knowledge-intensive processes in the areas of software development, product development, innovation management, quality management and many others is available.

The Knowledge Modeling and Description Language (KMDL) method was developed for modeling, analyzing and evaluating knowledge-intensive business processes or knowledge-intensive parts of business processes.

The KMDL is a semiformal modeling language based on a clearly defined set of symbols and a predefined syntax. KMDL in version 2 has been described in detail e.g. in [23] KMDL is used for the analysis, modeling and evaluation of knowledge-based business processes by taking into account not only the process and information aspects but also personal knowledge, requirements for knowledge-intensive tasks and the conversion mechanisms (called conversions) between knowledge types.

Conversions are the focus of the KMDL concept. Based on the assumption that person-bound knowledge evades direct capture, KMDL starts where person-bound knowledge changes its form or is gained. KMDL provides descriptive mechanisms to make clear, for example, the internalization of knowledge by reading a text, the interpretive extraction by expert analysis of a physical object or the externalization by writing a text from memory. Socialization, perhaps the most significant conversion, also describes the direct exchange of knowledge between people through communication, observation or imitation. Only when these conversions are taken into account is it possible to include personal knowledge in the design of business processes.

While previous modeling methods focused mainly on the data and control flow in business processes, only KMDL enables the capture, generation and distribution of knowledge along business processes. This aspect designs an extended analysis of business processes with regard to the processing of knowledge and thus offers starting points for the improvement of knowledge work in the company [24].

KMDL was developed because other concepts for modeling and analysis of business processes did not sufficiently meet the requirements of a knowledge management orientation on business processes [22]. In most cases they do not have the possibility to represent person-bound knowledge, to represent requirements for the successful transformation between different types of knowledge and to link machine knowledge with person-bound tacit knowledge.

2.1 Knowledge in KMDL 2

The consideration of tacit and explicit knowledge in the KMDL aims at describing the different articulability of knowledge [16].

Tacit Knowledge
Tacit knowledge is often unconscious for humans and lies hidden [25]. It consists of complex elements such as experiences and expresses itself through intuitive processes. The unconscious application of tacit knowledge leads to the fact that it can only be formally articulated or transferred to a limited extent Faber [26]. Tacit knowledge is thus strongly dependent on the individual.

Explicit Knowledge
Explicit knowledge is that part of knowledge that is formulated in a formal and systematic language and can be easily transferred and exchanged [21]. Explicit knowledge is thus reproducible, since it can be made accessible to the organizational knowledge base [27]. It is independent of persons and is often described as "disembodied knowledge" [28]. In the understanding of KMDL, explicit knowledge is equated with information [24].

2.2 The Further Development to KMDL 3

The experiences made with KMDL 2 show that an extension and adaptation of the modeling is necessary to meet the current requirements. Table 1 shows an overview of the changes from KMDL 2 to KMDL 3.

In order to avoid disturbing the reading flow by discussing the differences between KMDL 2 and 3, the following is an overview of the state of KMDL 3. Changes to the previous version are explained at appropriate points.

Essentially, the changes are related to improving the mapping of the handling of physical objects that could not be displayed before. In order to distinguish more clearly than before between the handling of person-bound knowledge and the machine aggregation of information, the information object has been moved to the process perspective. This created equivalence to the other process modeling methods. As a consequence, the conversion type "combination" in the knowledge perspective had to be dropped. In order to be able to represent the gain of person-bound knowledge from the observation of physical objects, the conversion type "interpretive extraction" was newly introduced.

Embedded Knowledge
In KMDL 3.0 embedded knowledge is added. Embedded knowledge or embodied knowledge is the personal knowledge that manifests itself in man-made objects. The conversion from tacit to embedded knowledge is called engineering.

Embodied knowledge is understood to be those attributes inherent in physical objects that can be extracted from the object through expert observation and transformed into tacit knowledge. This conversion is called interpretive extraction.

Table 1. Changes from KMDL 2 to KMDL 3

Heading level	KMDL 2	KMDL 3
Objects of the process perspective		
Task	✓	✓
Operators	✓	✓
Process interface	✓	✓
Information system	✓	✓
Role	✓	✓
Physical object	✗	✓
Information object	✗	✓
Machine	✗	✓
Objects of the knowledge perspective		
Activity	✓	✓
Knowledge object	✓	✓
Requirement	✓	✓
Person, Team	✓	✓
Information object	✓	✗
Method, Function	✓	✗
Machine knowledge	✗	✓
Conversions of the knowledge perspective		
Internalization	✓	✓
Externalization	✓	✓
Socialization	✓	✓
Combination	✓	✗
Interpretive Extraction	✗	✓

✓ = included ✗ = not included

Physical objects should be considered when modeling knowledge-intensive activities if they contain or generate embodied knowledge. The assessment criterion is the purpose of the modeling. Figure 1 shows an overview of the conversion types extended in KMDL 3.0.

In KMDL, two perspectives are basically taken, the process perspective and the knowledge perspective. While the process perspective considers the business process flow as well as concepts for mapping organizational relationships, the knowledge perspective focuses on concepts for capturing the handling of personal knowledge. In addition to the different perspective, the level of abstraction is also varied between these two perspectives. The process perspective considers knowledge-intensive business processes on a more aggregated level than the knowledge perspective, which depicts in detail the

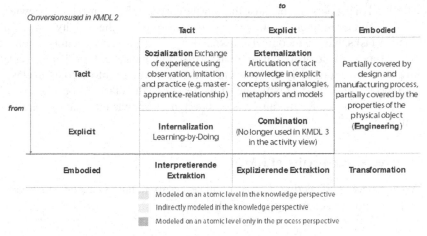

Fig. 1. Different types of knowledge conversion

knowledge flows and transformations necessary for task fulfillment and thus makes them accessible for investigation.

The two perspectives include several views, which can be used to take a closer look at individual aspects by hiding individual modeling objects (Fig. 2).

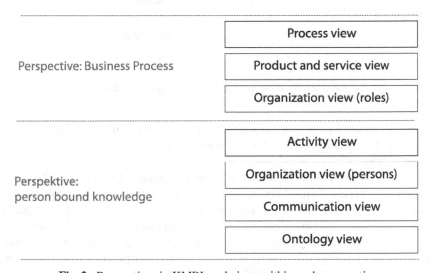

Fig. 2. Perspectives in KMDL and views within each perspective

The process view itself describes the flow of a business process. The service creation view describes the process of creating physical products within the organization under consideration. The role-based organization view describes the hierarchical structure of the organization, i.e. the super- and subordination as well as the functional structure of the organizational units. The knowledge perspective also includes an organization view, but now on the level of the persons, because they are the carriers of person-related knowledge, not the roles. The assignment to the process is performed by the activity view, which further details tasks that are recognized as knowledge-intensive. A communication view addresses the special role of socialization as an essential means of knowledge exchange between persons. It is precisely this conversion that is not taken into account in classical business process modeling. This is one of the reasons why classical business process modeling is not suitable for the analysis and design of knowledge management in the organization.

2.3   The Process Perspective of KMDL

The KMDL process perspective consists of all necessary notation elements to model the operations of a power generating process (Fig. 3).

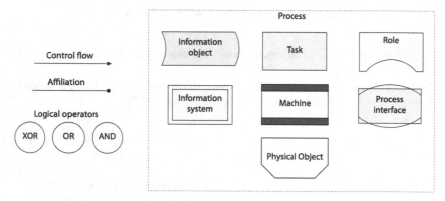

Fig. 3.   Symbols for the process perspective [29]

A process serves as container or frame for a finite number of objects of the KMDL process view. Nouns are used to label a process, for example software development or project financing.

A task stands for a set of activities that are not considered further at the process level. Tasks can repeat themselves in the process and serve to structure processes. A task represents a closed fact in the process. To open up the knowledge perspective, knowledge-intensive tasks are identified in the process and then modeled in more detail by activities. For the labeling of tasks the default object-compound is valid. The verb is always in the present tense, for example, testing software or procuring raw materials.

Each task at process level is assigned at least one role that is responsible for processing the task. The assignment of a role to one or more persons is done in the knowledge perspective. Roles are designated person-neutral. No names are given, only the roles of the persons are described in which they are involved in the task in the process. Groups of people with the department as role can also be represented, for example developers or production.

An information system represents information or communication technology that is used in the process. Information systems can create or process information objects by algorithms such as sorting, combining or the calculation of mathematical functions.

Process interfaces are used to combine individual processes into process chains. Furthermore, process interfaces offer the possibility of a cross-process evaluation and improvement of the modeled knowledge conversions.

Conjunction operators are used to represent the following possible facts of tasks:

- Decision: Exclusive Or (XOR), if only one of the specified options should be possible,
- Option: Logical OR, if several options are possible,
- Shortcut: Logical AND, if tasks should be executed in parallel

The control flow connects tasks with each other or with link operators and specifies the order in which the tasks are executed.

Information is modeled as an information object. Information can exist as text, drawing or diagram on paper as well as in electronic form, in documents, audio files, bitmaps or video formats. Information exists independently of persons and can contain explicable knowledge of persons. Examples for information objects can be a recipe or a SOP (Standard Operating Procedure).

Physical objects are modeled if they are necessary for the purpose of modeling. They can contain embedded knowledge. It is not only important for the process perspective to model these objects. For example, in the knowledge perspective the knowledge gain can be shown when an expert examines a physical object. It is assumed that physical objects contain knowledge that can be gained by suitable investigation methods. It can also be shown which knowledge is necessary to create or produce a physical object.

In the age of cyber-physical production systems, machines can also serve as information carriers. Due to the data processing function of machines, it has turned out to be reasonable to model them with a separate symbol, since they also have a physical representation, unlike information systems.

2.4 The Knowledge Perspective of KMDL

The KMDL knowledge perspective provides various notation elements to model the handling of knowledge within a task. The objects of the knowledge perspective are shown in Fig. 4.

The task specifies the relation between knowledge conversions in the knowledge perspective and the process perspective. A task in the activity perspective is a reference to a task from the process perspective. The names of the task are taken from the process model.

Knowledge objects are artifacts that represent the knowledge of a person or a team. The knowledge object comprises the representation of the competencies, experiences, skills and attitudes of the person or team. Knowledge objects can be input or output objects of conversions. If a knowledge object is an input object of a conversion, its content contributes to the conversion, if it is an output object of the conversion, it is a result of the conversion. Knowledge objects are modeled to a person or a team. Each knowledge object modeled in this way indicates that this person possesses this knowledge.

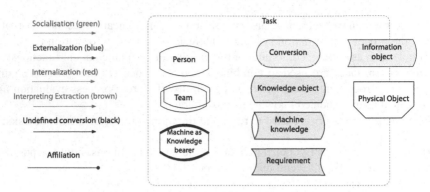

Fig. 4. Objects of the Knowledge Perspective of KMDL

The object machine knowledge has been added to KMDL 3 in order to be able to evaluate the strongly grown possibilities of technical entities, data and to recognize correlations and thus e.g. to gain experience to be able to express it in KMDL as well. If today the generation, processing and use of knowledge, e.g. in the production area, is investigated, the ability of machines and other technical entities to acquire and transfer knowledge must be given equal importance to the knowledge of employees. If, for example, technical entities have the ability of machine learning [30, 31] then this should be as representable and analyzed as the knowledge of a person. Therefore, in KMDL 3, emphasis was placed on making the knowledge of machines as operationalized and assessable as the knowledge of humans.

Conversions describe the generation, application and distribution of knowledge and the generation, distribution and preservation of information. They have input and output objects, which are represented by information or knowledge objects. The conversion type and the conversion category are uniquely determined by the input and output objects of a conversion. The edges of a conversion between the input and output objects are assigned a conversion name or are undefined. The frequency of a conversion can be specified as attribute. Conversions are always connected to each other via knowledge and information objects as input or output objects. A direct link between two conversions is logically wrong, since the meaning of conversion as a descriptor of knowledge conversion is lost.

Activities describe knowledge-intensive tasks. From the task "Create recipe" the following activities can be derived, for example, in which personal or machine knowledge is used to complete the task: Order raw materials, check raw materials, create test product.

The knowledge-based requirements that are placed on a conversion in order to be able to carry it out successfully are captured by the "Requirement" object. Requirements can be covered by the knowledge of persons or teams. A requirement can be differentiated into technical, methodical, social and action-oriented aspects.

The object Person represents a real existing person or in case of a target model an ideal person in an organization, who performs tasks in a business process and thereby takes on one or more roles. Persons are knowledge carriers. Persons are modeled as knowledge carriers with the edge "belonging" to the knowledge object.

A team represents a group of people working together on a knowledge-intensive task. Teams are also knowledge carriers. The knowledge modeled on a team (in the form of knowledge objects) represents the collective knowledge of the team. The collective knowledge of a team consists of the entire knowledge of all individuals of the team and additionally of the knowledge that exists through the group, such as rules of conduct or approaches to problem solving. The team element is used if the criteria can be modeled well and if the group dynamics in the team should not be modeled. In the latter case, the members of the team would have to be considered. If a person has a special influence in the group, this person is modeled separately. The characteristics of the knowledge objects are evaluated by the modelers for the entire group.

The conversion types describe the type of knowledge conversion.

- Socialization
- Externalization
- Internalization
- Interpretive Extraction
- Undefined

Unlike in KMDL 2, combinations are no longer regarded as conversions of the knowledge perspective. From KMDL 3.0 on, the combination of information is a process that is represented in the process perspective. This makes it easier to explain in the knowledge perspective which knowledge is necessary to successfully extract output information from input information.

3   Use for Industry 4.0

KMDL in version 3 brings numerous new possibilities to meet the requirements of the 4th industrial revolution [29].

- Derivation of qualification requirements
- Machines can have knowledge
- Operationalization of knowledge

These new possibilities, which were defined by the research group knowledge, learning, further training of the University of Potsdam and the Weizenbaum Institute for the Networked Society in conceptional work for many years, are briefly described in the following.

3.1   Derivation of Qualification Needs

Using a KMDL model of the activity view, for example, the individual training needs of a person filling a role can be identified (Fig. 5).

Through the improved operationalization of knowledge, the scope of the necessary qualification measures can be estimated. This makes it possible to combine the personal profiles of employees with necessary - and then successfully completed - personnel development measures.

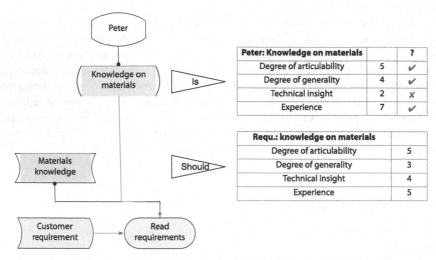

Fig. 5. Recognition of individual training needs

The section in Fig. 5 shows that material knowledge is required to interpret the customer's requirement (this is available as information) (the orange-colored requirement). In order to be able to determine the need for further training, an operationalization of the knowledge objects is necessary, the concept of which is described in the following section.

3.2 Operationalization of Knowledge

In order to operationalize knowledge, five assessment criteria for knowledge were defined [29], the degree of articulation or interpretation, the degree of generality, the degree of professional insight and the degree of experience of the bearers of this knowledge.

Articulation and Interpretation
Several approaches from the literature were used to describe articulation. Neuweg [32] differentiates four gradations tacitly, non-verbalizable, non-formalizable, experience-bound. Nonaka [33] merely spans a range from tacit to explicit and vice versa. Cowan et al. [34] differentiates only three levels: articulated, unarticulated and inarticulable. The level "unarticulated" is further differentiated, whether a cataloguing is possible (e.g. by a codebook) or not (e.g. if no codebook exists).

The degree of articulation is the ability, expressed in numbers, to express facts about a knowledge object in words, sentences and statements. The expression dimension represents the degree of articulation as a continuum and lies between the polar expressions tacit (0) and explicit (10).

The degree of articulation increases when the own mental model becomes a knowledge object of the environment and becomes more transparent to oneself. A person's degree of articulation varies depending on the knowledge object. It is assumed that the degree of articulation cannot decrease through conversion.

An articulation only takes place if the knowledge object of a knowledge carrier enters a conversion as input. Therefore, there must be an equivalent to the degree of articulation for receiving knowledge for internalization. This equivalent is the degree of interpretation. The degree of articulation and the degree of interpretation of a knowledge carrier for a knowledge object are independent of each other - someone who can explain well does not have to be very good at receiving new knowledge and vice versa.

The degree of interpretation is defined as the ability, expressed in numbers, to absorb, index and interpret articulated facts, so that the knowledge object can at best be completely internalized.

It is assumed that the degree of interpretation cannot easily be higher than the degree of articulation. An exception would be, if in combination with other characteristics of the knowledge object, e.g. the professional insight, a better interpretation is made possible.

Degree of Generality
The generality of a knowledge object is its specificity expressed in numbers. This form dimension represents the generality of knowledge as a continuum and lies between the polar expressions particular (0) and general (10). A high degree of universality means better transferability to persons with other backgrounds. A low degree of generality indicates highly specific/adhesive knowledge that is more difficult to transfer to people with other backgrounds. For people with the same background the transfer is more effective or easier. A comprehensive study of the conditions of knowledge transfer and the influence of stickiness can be found in [35].

Degree of Professional Insight
The degree of professional insight describes the intellectual penetration of matter into a knowledge object by a knowledge carrier. It lies between the polar forms ignorant (0) and in possession of all knowledge available for this knowledge object (10). The degree of professional insight increases when new things are intellectually perceived, their relevance is grasped and they are integrated into existing knowledge.

It is assumed that the degree of professional insight cannot be reduced by knowledge conversion. However, if someone has not dealt with the matter for a long time, the degree of his professional insight may decrease. An S-curve-shaped course is assumed here (logistic function).

Experience
Experience is defined as subjective knowledge relevant to the work environment that has been acquired over time by a knowledge carrier [36]. Experience arises from the practical involvement with an object and lies between the polar forms inexperienced (0) and highly experienced (10). The intensity and duration of the practical involvement is evaluated.

The degree of experience increases with the duration and intensity of the practical examination.

Analogous to the professional insight, it is assumed that the level of experience decreases if the duration and intensity of the practical examination is reduced.

Tables are available for all quantification criteria to help the modeler to make an assessment [29].

3.3 Personal Knowledge and Machine Knowledge

Modern machines used in the manufacturing sector certainly have some abilities to evaluate the data they generate, which makes it seem reasonable to call this knowledge. For this purpose, an object has been added to KMDL 3 that provides the knowledge of a machine with the same operationalization possibilities as the knowledge of a human being. This way, the interrelations between machine knowledge and person-related knowledge can be analyzed and incorporated into concepts of operational knowledge management.

In the previous section, the criteria degree of articulation or interpretation, degree of generality, professional insight and experience were differentiated and their characteristics operationalized by a ten-level scale. In view of the increasing spread of cyber-physical systems with their large data storage and comprehensive analytical and prognostic processing capabilities, these classification characteristics can also be applied to machine knowledge that can be retrieved by machines:

In this case, the degree of articulation describes the explanatory capacity of the cyber-physical system to explain its decision proposals. This explanatory power can be very low for certain AI techniques such as neural networks, for example, and very high for others (e.g., rule-based systems).

Likewise, the degree of interpretation can indicate how extensively the analytical and prognostic abilities available in the machine knowledge carrier are developed.

The degree of generality also allows an estimation of the range of the knowledge domain represented in machine knowledge.

Likewise, at least the first stages of technical insight can also be applied to machine knowledge. However, classifications higher than 6 seem unlikely at present.

Finally, in the case of machine knowledge, experience can be estimated at least on the basis of the period for which evaluable data is available. This makes it possible in KMDL to consider person-related and machine knowledge within conversions in the same way and to assess their effect quantitatively.

In case a distinction is to be made in graphical modeling between person-bound and machine knowledge, knowledge carrier and knowledge object can be represented with different symbols (Fig. 6).

4 Summary and Outlook

Industry 4.0 and the upheavals of the digital transformation are placing considerable new demands on knowledge management and on the qualification of employees in cyber-physical production systems and beyond.

With KMDL 3.0 a modeling language is available, with the help of which the requirements of industry 4.0 for a complete representation of the generation, use and transfer of personal and machine knowledge can be fulfilled. For example, required qualification characteristics can be recorded and quantitatively evaluated. This is an essential prerequisite for creating qualification plans for individual persons.

However, there are still a lot of questions that need to be answered in future versions of KMDL, e.g.:

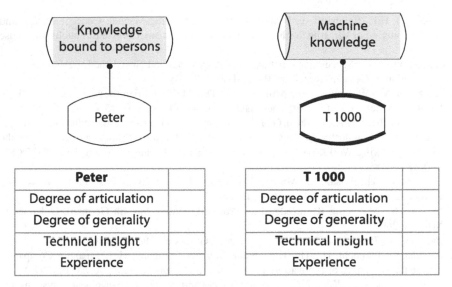

Fig. 6. Equal treatment of human and machine knowledge

- The aggregation of knowledge from several people, whether in a commnity of practice or in meeting the conversion requirement, will need to be considered in more detail. What could be appropriate rules for aggregation?
- Can the quantitative effects be substantiated by experimental investigations?
- What practical effect do the additional conversions with physical objects have on the knowledge objects?

References

1. Dorst, W.: Factory and Production Processes in Industry 4.0 in 2020 Information Management and Consulting, pp. 34–37 (2012)
2. Geisberger, E., Broy, M.: agendaCPS: Integrated Research Agenda Cyber-Physical Systems. German Academy of Science and Engineering, Munich: acatech (2012)
3. Gronau, N.: Encyclopaedia of Business Informatics - Industry 4.0 (in German) (2014). https://www.enzyklopaedie-der-wirtschaftsinformatik.de/wi-enzyklopaedie/lexikon/inform ationssysteme/Sektorspezifische-Anwendungssysteme/cyber-physische-systeme/industrie-4.0/ [June 4, 2020].
4. Teichmann, M., et al.: Mobile IIoT technologies in hybrid learning factories (in German). Industry 4.0 Manage. **34**(3), 21–24 (2018). https://doi.org/10.30844/IM18-3_21-24
5. Spötl, G.; Gorldt, C.; Windelband, L.; Grantz, T.; Richter, T.: Industry 4.0 - Effects on education and training in the M+E industry (in German), Munich (2016)
6. Arnold, R.: Assisted Learning. A Workbook. Landau (2010)
7. Dehnbostel, P.: In-Company Training. Competence-Based Training and Further Education in Companies. Baltmannsweiler (2010)
8. Gronau, N.: Effects of digitization on ERP systems. ERP Manage. **14**(1), 22–24 (2018)
9. Baum, G., et al.: Industry 4.0: Mastering Industrial Complexity with SysLM. Springer – Vieweg (2013)

10. Wiendahl, H.P., Reichardt, J., Nyhuis, P.: Factory Planning Manual: Concept, Design and Implementation of Versatile Production Facilities (in German). Carl Hanser publishing house (2014)

11. Bettenhausen, K.: Success Factors Industry 4.0: Qualification, Speed and Infrastructure. VDI Association of German Engineers, Baden-Baden (2014)

12. Hergesell, M.: With apps at the Milkrun: WITTENSTEIN bastian (be)lebt Industrie 4.0, (in German) Wittenstein AG - Customer magazine move, October, no. 13, pp. 12–17 (2014)

13. Norbert, G., Ullrich, A., Vladova, G.: Process-related and visionary further education concepts in the context of industry 4.0 (in German). In: Meier, H. (ed.) Teaching and Learning for the Modern Working World, pp. 125–143. Gito-Verlag (2015).https://doi.org/10.1007/978-88-470-5720-3_8

14. Davenport, T.H., Prusak, L.: Working Knowledge: How Organizations Manage What They Know. Harvard Business School Press, Boston (1998)

15. Gronau, N.: Managing Knowledge in a Process-Oriented Way (in German). Oldenbourg, Munich (2009)

16. Polanyi, M.: The Tacit Dimension. Peter Smith, Glocester, Mass (1966)

17. Nonaka, I., Takeuchi, H.: The Knowledge Creating Company: How Japanese Companies Create the Dynamics of Innovation, p. 284. Oxford University Press, New York (1995)

18. Lee, J., Bagheri, B., Kao, H.A.: Recent advances and trends of cyber-physical systems and big data analytics in industrial informatics. In: International Proceeding of International Conference on Industrial Informatics (INDIN), pp. 1–6 (2014)

19. Gronau, N.: The influence of cyber-physical systems on the design of production systems (in German. Ind. Manage. **31**(3), 16–20 (2015b)

20. Turing, A.M.: Computing machinery and intelligence. Mind **59** 433–460 (1950)

21. Rehäuser, J., Krcmar, H.: Knowledge management in the company (in German). In: Schreyögg, G., Conrad, P. (eds.) Management Research 6: Knowledge Management, pp. 1–40. De Gruyter, Berlin (1996)

22. Sultanow, E., Zhou, X., Gronau, N., Cox, S.: Modeling of processes, systems and knowledge: a multi-dimensional comparison of 13 chosen methods. Int. Rev. Comput. Softw. **7**(6), 3309–3319 (2012)

23. Gronau, N.: Handbook Process-Oriented Knowledge Management: Methods and Practice (in German). Gito, Berlin (2014)

24. Gronau, N., Fröming, J.: KMDL-a semiformal description language for modeling knowledge conversions (in German). Inf. Syst. **48**(5), 349–360 (2006)

25. Renzl, B.: Central aspects of the concept of knowledge - core elements of the organization of knowledge (in German). In: Wyssusek, B. (eds.) Knowledge Management Complex. Perspectives and Social Practice, pp. 27–43. Erich Schmidt Verlag, Berlin (2004)

26. Faber, P.: Development of an Integrative Reference Model for Knowledge Management in Companies. Frankfurt am Main, Lang (2007)

27. Hasler Roumois, U.: Study Book Knowledge Management. Fundamentals of Knowledge Work in Economic, Non-Profit and Public Organizations (in German). Orell Füssli Publishing House, Zurich (2010)

28. Blackler, F.: Knowledge, knowledge work and organizations: an overview and interpretation. Organ. Stud. **16**(6), 1021–1046 (1995)

29. Gronau: Knowledge Modeling and Description Language 3.0 An introduction (in German). Gito Publishing House, Berlin (2020)

30. Windt, K., Knollmann, M., Meyer, M.: Application of data mining methods for knowledge generation in logistics - critical reflection of the analytical ability to improve on-time delivery performance. In: Spath, D. (eds.) Knowledge Work - Between Strict Processes and Creative Leeway (in German), pp. 223–249. Gito, Berlin (2011)

31. Freitag, M., Kück, M., Ait Alla, A., Lütjen, M.: Potentials of Data Science in Production and Logistics. Part 1 - An Introduction to Current Approaches of Data Science, Industry Management 5/2015, pp. 22–26 (2015)
32. Neuweg, G.H.: Implicit knowledge as the object of research (in German). In: Rauner, F. (eds.) Handbook of Vocational Training Research, pp. 581–588. Bertelsmann, Bielefeld (2005)
33. Nonaka, I., Von Krogh, G.: Perspective-tacit knowledge and knowledge conversion: Controversy and advancement in organizational knowledge creation theory. Organ. Sci. **20**(3), 635–652 (2009). Polanyi M (1966) The tacit dimension. Garden City, Doubleday, 1966 (2009)
34. Cowan, R., David, P.A., Foray, D.: The explicit economics of knowledge codification and tacitness. Ind. Corp. Chang. **9**(2), 211–253 (2000)
35. Gronau, N., Grum, M.: Knowledge Transfer Speed Optimizations in Product Development Contexts. Gito-Verlag, Berlin (2019)
36. Quinones, M.A., Ford, J.K., Teachout, M.S.: The relationship between work experience and job performance: a conceptual and meta-analytic review. Pers. Psychol. **48**, 887–910 (1995). https://doi.org/10.1111/j.1744-6570.1995.tb01785.x

Quantification of Knowledge Transfers

The Design of an Experiment Setting for the Examination of Knowledge Transfers

Marcus Grum[(✉)] and Norbert Gronau

University of Potsdam, 14482 Potsdam, Germany
mgrum@lswi.de

Abstract. Faced with the triad of time-cost-quality, the realization of knowledge-intensive tasks at economic conditions is not trivial. Since the number of knowledge-intensive processes is increasing more and more nowadays, the efficient design of knowledge transfers at business processes as well as the target-oriented improvement of them is essential, so that process outcomes satisfy high quality criteria and economic requirements. This particularly challenges knowledge management, aiming for the assignment of ideal manifestations of influence factors on knowledge transfers to a certain task. Faced with first attempts of knowledge transfer-based process improvements [1], this paper continues research about the quantitative examination of knowledge transfers and presents a ready-to-go experiment design that is able to examine quality of knowledge transfers empirically and is suitable to examine knowledge transfers on a quantitative level. Its use is proven by the example of four influence factors, which namely are stickiness, complexity, competence and time pressure.

Keywords: Knowledge management · Knowledge transfer · Conversion · Empirical examination · Experiment

1 Introduction

Process management traditionally improves business processes by either small modifications at a company's actual process models [2] or by the effortful reengineering of those processes [3]. Recent research about the process-oriented knowledge management contributes here because of novel forms of process improvement approaches: knowledge is controlled at knowledge-intensive tasks to systematically improve business processes [1]. This research aims to expand the knowledge about knowledge transfers by experiments, so that relevant influence factors on knowledge transfers can be identified in a first step. Based on these factors, the target-oriented modification of knowledge transfers is enabled further, so that business processes are improved by more efficient knowledge transfers.

The importance of knowledge for the realization of competitive advantages of organizations is well accepted [4]. Although first insights about influence factors

© Springer Nature Switzerland AG 2021
B. Shishkov (Ed.): BMSD 2021, LNBIP 422, pp. 224–242, 2021.
https://doi.org/10.1007/978-3-030-79976-2_13

on knowledge transfers are present, these mostly refer to qualitative research, such as [5–7]. First quantitative results can be found at simulations [8], experiments [9] and field studies [10]. By now, these focus only on factors influencing the time consumption of knowledge transfers. Although various target dimensions are suitable to measure the effect of knowledge transfers in addition, here one can find costs required [11] and quality of knowledge transfer outcomes, the following focuses on quality aspects and intends to discuss how to empirically research knowledge transfers. So, the following research will address the examination of knowledge transfers and focuses on the following research question:

"How can quantitative effects of influence factors on knowledge transfers be examined by an experiment?"

This paper rather outlines the design of an experiment than presenting a ready-to-go experiment implementation. The core conceptual question structuring the research process and focused here refers to the identification of requirements for its implementation and the demonstration of the design's usefulness to examine example influence factors.

In accordance with MacKenzie et al., the following assumes an experiment to be useful in regard with the research question, if it describes the measurement of the construct of knowledge transfers and supports validation procedures [12]. So, for instance, the evaluation of the influence factor significance, direction and proportion on concrete constructs of knowledge transfers to be examined shall be enabled through their experimental manipulation. Hence, the design needs to characterize the process of data gathering in an experiment setting, that is suitable to examine the quantitative influence of factors on knowledge transfers with the aid of statistical methods. For this reason, the research presented provides a modeling attempt specifying the experiment process and relevant knowledge transfers.

The research approach is intended to be design-oriented in accordance with the Design-Science-Research Methodology (DSRM) [13]. Thus, the second section provides the foundation of knowledge transfers, from which requirements are derived that need to be reflected by the experiment. The third section justifies the concrete requirements for the experiment. The design artifact is presented in the fourth section. Its usefulness will be demonstrated with the aid of four example factors in section five. It issues how to examine quantitative effects on knowledge transfers and clarifies how to manipulate the construct to be examined in experiments. In section six, it will be evaluated inhowfar the experiment design is suitable to examine knowledge transfers on a quantitative level. The insights are concluded in the last section.

2   Theoretical Foundation

The theoretical foundation mainly refers to the characterization of knowledge, knowledge transfers as well as the modeling of knowledge transfers. Each is issued in the following.

Knowledge. Knowledge is present at explicit and tacit forms of knowledge [14] as well as embedded knowledge [15]. While the first refers to a well documentable form of knowledge, that can be handed among any kind of process participant easily (e.g. a book), the second form of knowledge is hard to document as it is knowledge-bearer-bound (e.g. experience), and the third form of knowledge refers to their physical manifestation (e.g. produced circuit bords).

Origin \ Target	Tacit Knowledge	Explicit Knowledge	Embodied Knowledge
Tacit Knowledge	Socialization	Externalization	Engineering
Explicit Knowledge	Internalization	Combination	Decodification
Embodied Knowledge	Extraction	Codification	Transformation

Legend:

☐   Forms of Knowledge

▩   Knowledge-based activities (examined in experiment, described in activity view)

▨   Knowledge-based tasks (specified in activity view, described in process view)

Fig. 1. The different compartments of knowledge transfers.

Knowledge Transfers. Knowledge transfers are considered as the process of the identification of knowledge, its transmission from knowledge carrier to knowledge receiver and its application by the knowledge receiver [9]. Particularly, the application is essential, so that the result or manifestation of knowledge transferred can be observed. In terms of knowledge forms, nine kinds of knowledge form interrelations (the so called *conversions*) can be found in knowledge transfers. While Fig. 1 presents them as an overview, the following characterizes them in detail.

1. **Internalization:** An explicit knowledge carrier (origin) is perceived by a knowledge carrier (target), so that the target integrates perceived knowledge with its individual knowledge base [14]. An example refers to a person studying a book about process modeling. As knowledge about process modeling is enriched e.g. by mental models and personal experiences, new knowledge is constructed at the target carrier.
2. **Extraction:** Embodied knowledge (origin) is perceived by a knowledge carrier (target), so that the target recognizes knowledge by interpretation and integrates it with its individual knowledge base [15]. For instance, the modeling notation is recognized by studying process model examples. If a person recognizes the notation rule set, person-bound tacit knowledge is created.
3. **Socialization:** Knowledge carrier-bound tacit knowledge is transferred among knowledge carriers through interactive data and information exchange

[14]. For example, two persons are speaking about how to create process models. Here, each person functions as both origin and target. Because of their interaction, knowledge is integrated with their individual knowledge bases.

4. **Externalization:** Knowledge carrier-bound tacit knowledge (origin) is explicated so that the knowledge carrier-unbound explicit form of knowledge is created (target) that can be transmitted easily [14]. When a person writes a book, its tacit knowledge is made explicit so that the book can be easily passed among people.

5. **Engineering:** Knowledge carrier-bound tacit knowledge is applied in a task to embody knowledge at a physical object [15]. For instance a person constructs process models. Here, tacit knowledge about the act of process modeling and about the modeling language notation are applied to the process model.

6. **Codification:** Embodied knowledge (origin) is perceived by a knowledge carrier and transferred to an explicit form of knowledge (target) [16]. If a person recognizes the notation rule set on the basis of process models (extraction) and the rule set is written down to a book (externalization), the description holds the codified knowledge about the notation rule set.

7. **Combination:** Explicit knowledge (origin) is perceived by a knowledge carrier and conversed to new explicit knowledge (target) [14]. For instance, an evaluation of a process model shall be realized on the basis of a notation rule set. Here, explicit knowledge forms of the process model and notation rule set are combined into the explicit form of a failure report.

8. **Decodification:** Explicit knowledge (origin) is perceived by a knowledge carrier and transferred by engineering activities into an object embodying knowledge (target) [16]. If a person studies the rule set of a modeling notation (internalization) and comes up with a process model example (engineering), the model constructed holds the decodified knowledge about the notation rule set.

9. **Transformation:** Embodied knowledge (origin) is modified by a knowledge carrier so that a new object manifests embodying knowledge (target) [17]. For instance, a process model is transformed from one modeling notation to another. If both modeling languages satisfy the same notation rule set, both of its process model examples would lead to the same rule set description (codification result).

This research will focus on the examination of knowledge-based activities, which have been highlighted in green at Fig. 1. Since the kind of knowledge-based tasks (highlighted in yellow) are considered as a kind of composition of knowledge-based activities and therefore show numerous kinds of conversions simultaneously, these are not suited for the individual examination of knowledge conversions in a laboratory study or rather experiments. A field study that focuses on more complex tasks than an experiment can encompass is more suitable for their investigation.

Modeling Knowledge Transfers. In order to specify the experimentation of knowledge transfers, particularly the process-oriented knowledge management has been proven to function efficiently, because of the objectification of knowledge, which means its provision as impartial form as modeling object. By this, the dynamic of knowledge can be specified over the course of time and visually represented by process models. So, knowledge changes can be identified during the knowledge transfer and by whom they occur. This regards the behavioral perspective of knowledge [18]. Further, conditions of knowledge transfers can be addressed that need to be reflected by the experiment tool [10].

Hence, beside the dealing with different forms of knowledge and their conversion through activities, at this research, the sequential description of a knowledge-intensive process (process perspective) will be separated from the process of knowledge creation, transfer and application (knowledge perspective). So, the knowledge transfer can be specified individually. As it will be embedded in the experiment process, the dynamic of the transfer can be captured and visually represented. It becomes controllable and an object to modifications [19]. Following comparable experiments on knowledge transfers [9], knowledge transfers will be specified with the KMDL [20].

3   Objectives of a Solution

Following the DSRM [13], requirements are defined before the design of artifacts is carried out. These have served as the design maxims for the experiment design. Further, they have functioned as quality gates for artifacts presented here and they can stand as quality gates for subsequent research, which supports comparability.

In accordance with the process of deriving requirements [21], requirements have been elicited from the theoretical foundation provided at Sect. 2 and represented in a written form. These were then discussed and supplemented with experts from the fields of business process management, product development and knowledge engineering, and illustrated in a workshop session with examples from business context. Based on expert consensus on key requirements, the following collection of requirements was validated.

1. The experiments need to address relevant forms of knowledge transfers. Here, one can find conversions presented at Fig. 1. Since the socialization is based on the interaction of at least two test persons, the experiment needs to differentiate single and team experiments.
2. The different kinds of conversions need to be observed individually, so that effects of interrelating activities can be controlled.
3. The experiment needs to observe novel knowledge, so that no pre-experience about the knowledge to be transferred is available.
4. The experiment has to differentiate between the creation of explicit knowledge, such as a written description of a process modeling language, and further forms of knowledge. Here, one can find tacit knowledge, such as person-bound knowledge about a process modeling notation, and embodied knowledge, such as example models corresponding to a process modeling notation.

5. Since the creation of tacit knowledge cannot be observed directly because of its non-transparency, the experiment has to provide a test to infer what is not visible because of the tacit nature of knowledge.
6. Even if different kinds of tasks are presented in the experiment in order to observe the required kinds of knowledge transfers, artifact quality needs to be measured by the same type of measurement instrument.
7. The experiment must perfectly control the kind of subjects that is faced with a certain kind of knowledge at a specific moment.

4   Design

Following the DSRM [13], the design phase produces a blueprint for solving the research problem in the form of artifacts, the use of which is demonstrated in section five. As was identified in section two, this artifact refers to the experiment design. It is presented in form of process models of the KMDL because it can capture the complex behavior of experiments examining knowledge transfers. Individual knowledge transfers are specified with the aid of the *activity views* first (knowledge perspective). Then, the experiment behavior is concretized by *process views* presenting the sequential order of knowledge-intensive tasks (process perspective). Finally, these models are interlinked by one experiment process that supports the experiment controlling.

4.1   Activity Views on the Experiment

The knowledge perspective on the experiment can be found at Fig. 3 and Fig. 4 of Appendix A. Here, one can see that five different kinds of activity views have been specified to examine conversions in accordance with Fig. 1 individually. Since relevant conversions to be examined have been highlighted by individual colors (directed arcs having arrowheads) and conversions used for controlling the experiment (directed arcs having arrowheads, no color and dashed lines) have been separated, the knowledge transfer situations on which the focus is placed can be identified. Variations in the experiment realization have been indicated by directed arcs having arrowheads and doubled lines - these will be issued at the demonstration Sect. 5. Modeling objects used throughout the models are explained in the following:

1. **Instruction:** It is clarified that relevant knowledge about a novel process modeling notation is provided by the given material, which either refers to an explanatory video (internalization, externalization, engineering, socialization focus) or example process model (extraction focus).
2. **Explanatory Video:** For the *Task 1/2* required knowledge about a novel process modeling notation is presented by audio and image material.
3. **Explanatory Model:** For the *Task 1/2* required knowledge about a novel process modeling notation is presented by an example process model embodying knowledge.

4. **Task 1:** The first kind of tasks refers to the construction of a process model on the basis of a case study given using the process modeling notation presented before. It so provides an engineering focus. It is considered as control task (in the case of internalization, socialization and extraction) in order to infer the quality of the tacit knowledge because this knowledge form cannot be examined directly.

5. **Task 2:** The second kind of tasks refers to the description of the process modeling notation presented before by writing. It so provides an externalization focus.

6. **Task Solution 1:** The first kind of task solutions refers to the process model constructed by the test persons called *Test Person R.*

7. **Task Solution 2:** The second kind of task solutions refers to the description of the process modeling notation written down by the test persons called *Test Person R.*

8. **Sample Solution 1:** The first kind of sample solution refers to a sample process model. It perfectly satisfies the quality criteria demanded.

9. **Sample Solution 2:** The second kind of sample solution refers to a sample description. It perfectly satisfies the quality criteria demanded.

10. **Survey Grid 1:** A collection of questions about the knowledge transfers experienced allows the assessment of the tacit knowledge because it cannot be examined directly.

11. **Survey Grid 2:** A collection of questions about the solutions constructed allows the assessment of the embodied knowledge called *Task Solution 1* and explicit knowledge called *Task Solution 2* because it addresses the same quality criteria.

12. **Knowledge Understanding:** On the basis of the *Survey Grid 1* conducted by the test persons, the quality of the tacit knowledge shall be inferred because this knowledge form cannot be examined directly.

13. **Experience:** Individual knowledge carrier-bound impressions about the knowledge transfer emerge on the basis of the conversion being part of the knowledge transfer examined.

14. **Modeling Notation:** Individual knowledge carrier-bound tacit knowledge about the process modeling notation emerges when test persons study the *Explanatory Video* or *Explanatory Model* presented.

15. **Quality Evaluation of Artifact 1:** On the basis of the *Survey Grid 2* conducted by scientists, the quality of the process model can be assessed on the basis of the by comparison of *Task Solution 1* and *Sample Solution 1.*

16. **Quality Evaluation of Artifact 2:** On the basis of the *Survey Grid 2* conducted by scientists, the quality of the notation description can be assessed on the basis of the by comparison of *Task Solution 2* and *Sample Solution 2.*

4.2   Process Views on the Experiment

The process perspective on the experiment can be found at Fig. 5 and Fig. 6 of Appendix B. Here, one can see that five different kinds of process views have been specified to describe the conversion-specific sequence of experiment tasks by control flows (directed arcs having arrowheads) and resource allocation by memberships (directed arcs with circular heads). While ingoing objects have been presented at the left of each task's vertical center and outgoing objects have been presented at the corresponding right, modeling objects used throughout the models are explained in the following:

1. **Tasks:** Each green rectangle represents one period of time in the experiment. As long as a test person is part of that period, it is faced by a task-specific experiment screen presenting instructions,, experiment tasks, explanatory material or demanding for realizing a process model by a modeling software, etc.

2. **Time Measured Tasks:** Green rectangles having a bold border indicate tasks at which the time measurement is essential for quantifying the knowledge transfer examined. Time is measured automatically by an IT system called *Experiment Tool*. The corresponding activities can be identified by the activity view's system borders having the same labels.

3. **System Borders:** Rectangles having dashed borders indicate the separation of physical or virtual spaces. For instance, the team experiment consists of two virtual spaces that bring *Test Person R* and *Test Person S* together at the task called *Perform Task of Socialization*.

4. **Experiment Tool:** Since the single experiment (internalization, externalization, extraction and engineering focus) can be realized by one person, only one instance of the experiment tool can be used to guide the test person through the experiment and survey relevant items. At the socialization experiment, two experiment tool instances need to be synchronized so that both test persons can meet in one virtual space to communicate about the process modeling notation presented.

5. **Knowledge Recipient:** The *Test Person R* takes the role of the *Knowledge Recipient*. It gets knowledge about the process modeling notation presented either by video (internalization, externalization, engineering), by interaction with *Test Person S* (socialization) or by an exemplary process model (extraction). Then, the *Knowledge Recipient* will use the knowledge presented to solve a certain task.

6. **Knowledge Source:** The *Test Person S* takes the role of the *Knowledge Source*. It is only present at the team experiment (socialization) to present knowledge about a process modeling notation to *Test Person R*.

7. **Scientist:** Experiment organizers are responsible for the team assignment (socialization) as well as the evaluation of task solutions of test persons. As Fig. 2 shows, the team assignment can be realized before the experiment day and the evaluation can be realized after test persons have completed the experiment.

Bringing the different kinds of conversion-specific process views of Fig. 5 and Fig. 6 together, Fig. 2 interlinks these detailed models and presents one experiment process. The direct association can be identified by the same label of tasks at Fig. 2 and system borders at Fig. 5 and Fig. 6. So, the controlling of the joint experiment realization can be issued effectively as follows:

- **Randomization:** Before the experiment starts, the experiment-specific configuration is diced out. So, the level of *stickiness, complexity, time pressure* and *kind of conversion* are characterized.
- **Preparation:** Before the concrete experiment is conducted, the competence is surveyed. In the case of team experiments, this will be realized before the day of experiments, so that socialization teams can be built that consider the test person's competences. In the case of single experiments, the competence can be surveyed right before the experiment conductance.
- **Genotypical Treatments:** The task *Characterize Transfer* will be realized right when the corresponding knowledge transfer has been finalized by design decision (compare with Fig. 5 and Fig. 6). This is because stickiness has been defined genotypically as something that exists inside of a person that causes a distinctive pattern of behavior over time and across situations [12]. Hence, the transfer characterization will be carried out by the test persons themselves as the best source of information, so that the situation is avoided in which the incorporation of experience 'pollutes' the understanding of tacit knowledge that has been transferred.
- **Follow-Up:** The evaluation will be conducted either right when the corresponding experiment has been conducted or all experiments have been realized. This is because knowledge quality has been defined phenotypically as the tendency to exhibit a particular distinctive pattern of behavior over time and across situations that cause the creation of a certain artifact quality. Hence, the quality assessment will be carried out by experts who know the artifact domain well and are good sources of information about the extent to which the test person exhibits the distinctive pattern of behavior [12].
- **Extension:** The number of conversion-specific experiment instances can be expanded as desired. So, for example, dynamic effects can be focused in a sequence of experiment conductances. Further, later experiment instances can increase in complexity, so that test persons are challenged more and more similar to an education. In addition, the forgetting of test persons can be examined by a greater number of experiment instances.
- **Investigation:** The statistical analysis can be carried out right when all evaluations have been finalized. As conversion-specific process views are interlinked by one experiment process, knowledge transfers can be investigated at a common level.

Randomization:
Dice out the level of stickiness, complexity, time pressure and kind of conversion, etc.
Competence can be assigned manually on the basis of survey.

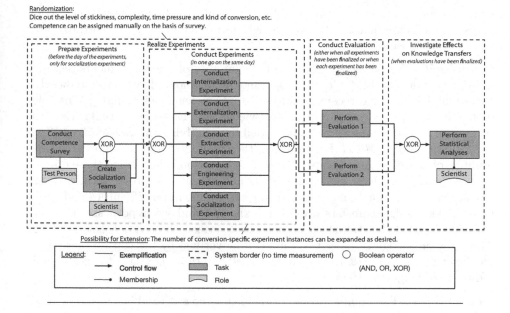

Fig. 2. The process of the experiment.

5 Demonstration

As demanded by the design-oriented research [13], the demonstration applies designed artifacts and demonstrates their use for the examination of four example influence factors. The four factors have been chosen by following experiments of Gronau and Grum [9]. The following assumes that experiments present a new modeling notation, so that test persons need to build relevant knowledge from the ground up for the experiment.

Stickiness. The attribute of knowledge tending to remain at the outgoing perception border of a knowledge carrier or to remain at the incoming perception border of a knowledge receiver and thus retard the transfer of knowledge is defined as stickiness of knowledge [9]. Faced by activity views of Appendix A, the stickiness can be varied by modifying the *Explanatory Video* or the *Explanatory Model*. For example, the stickiness can be increased if modeling shape labels are not presented. Since it is more difficult to understand the presented knowledge when faced with blank modeling shape labels, more difficulties and problems in knowledge transfers are to be expected [6,7] and we hypothesize that the quality of knowledge transfer outcomes will worsen. Inhowfar this indeed has lead to a knowledge transfer variation can be verified by the task called

Characterize Transfer. It conveys information about the individual knowledge carrier-bound experience of the knowledge transfers and so can be used to verify the level of stickiness.

Complexity. The reversed relation of the number of mental elements required to represent a clearly distinguishable amount of knowledge by the knowledge carrier and knowledge receiver relative to interdependencies among those elements is defined as complexity of knowledge [9]. Faced by activity views of Appendix A, the complexity can be varied by modifying the *Explanatory Video* or the *Explanatory Model*. For example, the complexity can be increased, if the number of modeling objects and syntactic association rules among these objects is increased. Since it is more difficult to understand the presented knowledge when faced with more complex modeling notations, more difficulties and problems in knowledge transfers are to be expected and we hypothesize that the quality of knowledge transfer outcomes will worsen. Inhowfar this indeed has lead to a knowledge transfer variation can be verified by the control task called *Perform Evaluation 1/2*. It assesses the *Task Solutions 1/2* as outcomes of individual knowledge transfers.

Competence. The competences are defined as cognitive abilities and skills of individuals which are available or learnt in order to solve certain problems, along with their connected motivational, volitional and social willingness and abilities to create and implement problem solutions in variable situations responsibly [9]. Faced by activity views of Appendix A, the competences can be varied by modifying the *Test Person R* and *Test Person S*. These are assigned into teams before the experiment is conducted (Fig. 2). For example, the competence can be increased, if another test person is selected that has a higher competence. Since it is more easy to understand the presented knowledge when faced with a modeling notation, less difficulties and problems in knowledge transfers are to be expected and we hypothesize that the quality of knowledge transfer outcomes will improve. Inhowfar this indeed has lead to a knowledge transfer variation can be verified by the control task called *Perform Evaluation 1/2*. It assesses the *Task Solutions 1/2* as outcomes of individual knowledge transfers.

Time Pressure. The presence of time in order to solve certain problems by the creation and implementation problem solutions in variable situations is defined as time pressure [22]. Faced by activity views of Appendix A, the time pressure can be varied by modifying the time provided in order to realize the conversions in the experiment. For example, the time pressure can be increased, if the time provided is reduced. Since it is more difficult to understand the presented knowledge when being faced with the task to understand a modeling notation (internalization, extraction, socialization), to describe the modeling notation (externalization) or to construct a process model by a modeling notation (engineering), more difficulties and problems in knowledge transfers are to be expected and we hypothesize that the quality of knowledge transfer outcomes will worsen. Inhowfar this indeed has lead to a knowledge transfer variation can be verified by the control task called *Perform Evaluation 1/2*. It assesses the *Task Solutions 1/2* as outcomes of individual knowledge transfers.

6 Evaluation

In order to satisfy design-science-oriented research approaches [13], the following evaluates inhowfar requirements of Sect. 3 have been fulfilled. Since this is based on the requirements presented, the following considers the same requirement numbering.

1. The first requirement has been fulfilled, as all forms of knowledge have been reflected by the experiment. While the extraction, internalization, externalization and engineering can be realized by a one person efficiently, the socialization needs to be realized in a more expensive two person experiment.
2. The second requirement has been fulfilled, as relevant conversions (highlighted in green in Fig. 1) have been reflected by the experiment. Since each conversion-specific activity has been considered by separate control flows in the experiment process (Fig. 2), the effects of interrelating activities can be controlled throughout the experiment.
3. The third requirement has been fulfilled, as a novel process modeling notation is designed and presented by the experiment as *Explanatory Video* or *Explanatory Model*. Since the test persons do not know the modeling language before the experiment, knowledge to be transferred can be controlled efficiently.
4. The fourth requirement has been fulfilled, as two different kinds of tasks are considered by the experiment. Explicit knowledge is constructed when performing *Task 2*. The knowledge constructed here is called *Task Solution 2*. When performing *Task 1*, embodied knowledge is constructed, which is called *Task Solution 1*. With the aid of this knowledge transfer outcome, the presence of tacit knowledge is inferred because it cannot be observed directly.
5. The fifth requirement has been fulfilled, as *Task 1* functions as control task to infer about the characterization of knowledge about the modeling notation presented. Although a description of the modeling notation presented would be suitable to do this inferring, too, this resembles *Task Solution 2*, the embodied knowledge form has been chosen because the analysis of process models can be realized more efficiently than a text analysis.
6. The sixth requirement has been fulfilled, as the quality of different kinds of artifacts (process models as *Task Solution 1* and descriptions as *Task Solution 2*) is measured by the same type of instrument. Here, a task-specific

quality grid called *Survey Grid 2* shall be used that addresses the same quality criteria, which are in regard with *Sample Solution 1* in the first case and in regard with *Sample Solution 2* in the second case.

7. The seventh requirement has been fulfilled, as process views have been used for specifying the experiment behavior. Here, it becomes clear at which time and under what conditions a test person is asked to realize a certain activity. The specific form of a conversion and the characterization of the knowledge transfer is specified by the associated activity view. Here, it becomes clear which test person is faced with a certain kind of knowledge.

7   Conclusion

In accordance with the DSRM [13], design-science oriented research demands for being communicated. Thus, the following concludes the paper by outlining insights achieved and justifying its contribution to the state-of-the-art.

Summary. This paper has presented a design for an experiment that examines the quantitative effects of influence factors on knowledge transfers. While the different kinds of conversions have been specified by conversion-specific activity views (Appendix A), the knowledge transfers have been specified by process views (Appendix B). The conversion-specific activities were separated by non-overlapping knowledge-intensive tasks. Since these were integrated in one experiment process (Fig. 2), the experiment behavior has been specified and the experiment controlling has been enabled. This is required to examine relevant knowledge transfers. The meaning of all the modeling objects being part of these process models have been explained in detail. The experiment design usefulness has been demonstrated by the simulated modification of four example factors, which is required for the examination of statistic effects by experiments [12]. Further, it has been confirmed that requirements specified in advance have been satisfied, which is required by the design-oriented experiment creation [13].

Critical appraisal. The research question (*"How can quantitative effects of influence factors on knowledge transfers be examined by an experiment?"*) can be answered with regard to the experiment design presented. This refers to the design of activity views specifying relevant knowledge transfers, the design of process views characterizing the experiment behavior, as well as the specification of the meaning of all the modeling objects being part of those views. It has been shown that relevant knowledge transfers can be observed by the experiment design presented because of the following two reasons. First, the demonstration has shown that the experiment was able to capture the modification of influence factors selected. Second, the experiment design enables the observation of the effect of those modifications at conversion-specific outcomes. The experiment design was validated, because the evaluation clarified how the requirements for observing relevant quantitative effects are met.

Limitations. The results and insights presented here are limited in regard with the following points. First, the demonstration refers to four example factors, which have not been realized in the experiment setting presented, yet. The number of influence factors being examined by this design is limited by four factors. Next experiment configurations can extend the number of factors to be examined, because this will lead to further insights. Second, the experiment designed has been demonstrated in proof-of-concept context only. It still needs to be verified in a practical investigation. Third, the concrete implementation of the task layouts of *Task 1* and *Task 2*, the concrete modeling notation presented at the *Explanatory Video* and *Explanatory Model* as well as the grids for conducting information about knowledge and quality (*Survey Grid 1* and *Survey Grid 2*) have not been presented, here. Their concrete implementation needs to be worked out in order to operationalize knowledge transfers further and realize the concrete experiment design.

Outlook. The article presented has aimed to present a design for experiments examining the quantitative effects of influence factors on knowledge transfers. The design shall be suitable to guide numerous different kinds of experiments. Next research attempts will focus on the concretization of modeling objects presented, so that one further concrete experiment can be carried out. Thereafter, data gathered will be analyzed and concrete kinds of business process improvements can be derived. Finally, these need to be integrated or rather harmonized with insights of experiments of Gronau and Grum [9].

Acknowledgments. The authors wish to thank C. Thim, M. Klippert and A. Albers for the valuable feedback on process models. The scientific project is sponsored by the German Research Foundation DFG (ID GR 1846/19-3).

Appendices

A   Activity Views of the Experiment

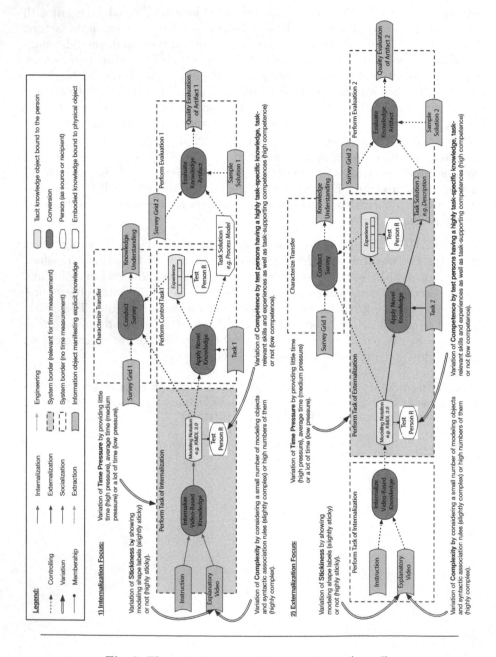

Fig. 3. The activity views of the experiment (part I).

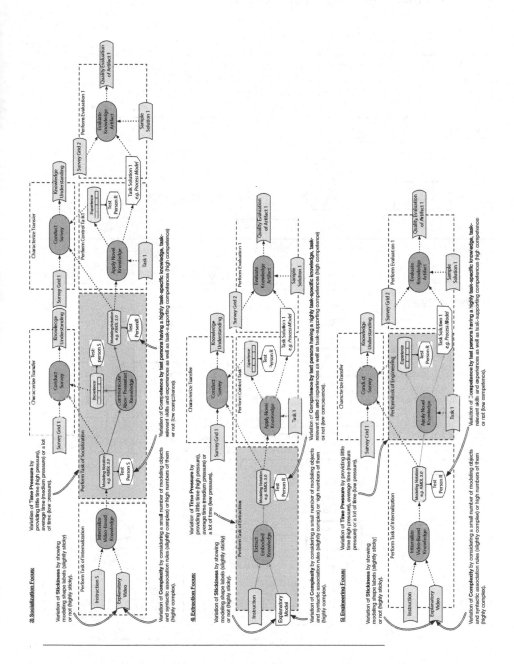

Fig. 4. The activity views of the experiment (part II).

B   Process Views of the Experiment

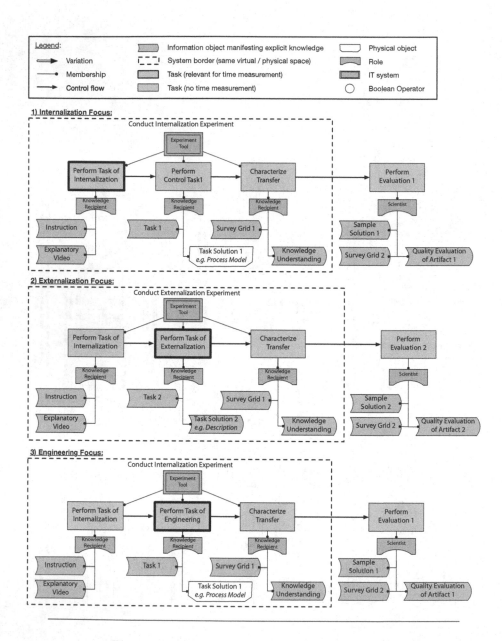

Fig. 5. The process views of the experiment (part I).

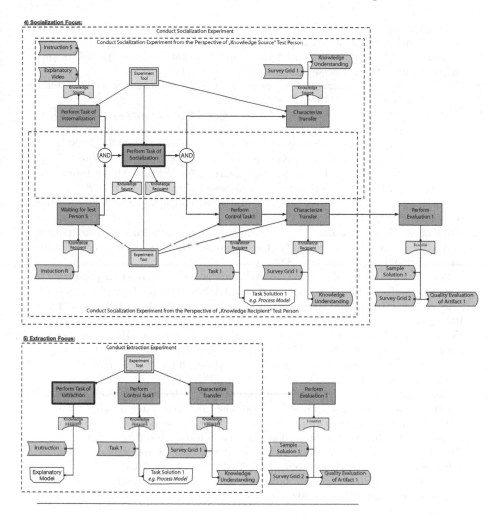

Fig. 6. The process views of the experiment (part II).

References

1. Grum, M., Rapp, S., Gronau, N., Albers, A.: Accelerating knowledge - the speed optimization of knowledge transfers. In: Proceedings of the Nineth BMSD (2019)
2. Masaaki, I.:"Kaizen: The key to Japan's Competitive Success", New York, ltd: McGraw-Hill, New York (1986)
3. Davenport, T.: Process Innovation: Reengineering Work Through Information Technology. Harvard Business Review Press, Boston (1993)
4. Eisenhardt, K.M., Santos, F.M.: Knowledge-based view: a new theory of strategy. Handb. Strategy Manag. **1**(1), 139–164 (2002)
5. Arrow, K.J.: Classificatory notes on the production and transmission of technological knowledge. Am. Econ. Rev. **59**(2), 29–35 (1969)

6. Szulanski, G.: Exploring internal stickiness: impediments to the transfer of best practice within the firm. Strateg. Manag. J. **17**(S2), 27–43 (1996)
7. Szulanski, G.: The process of knowledge transfer: a diachronic analysis of stickiness. Organ. Behav. Hum. Decis. Process. **82**(1), 9–27 (2000)
8. Fröming, J.: Ein konzept zur simulation wissensintensiver aktivitäten in geschäftsprozessen, GITO mbH Verlag, (2009)
9. Gronau, N., Grum, M.: Knowledge Transfer Speed Optimizations in Product Development Contexts, ch. Towards a prediction of time consumption during knowledge transfer, pp. 25–69. Empirical Studies of Business Informatics, GITO (2019)
10. Albers, A., Rapp, A., Grum, M: Knowledge Transfer Speed Optimizations in Product Development Contexts, ch. Knowledge Transfer Velocity Model Implementation, pp. 93–104. Empirical Studies of Business Informatics, GITO (2019)
11. Drucker, P.: Post-Capitalist Society. Butterworth-Heinemann, Oxford, United Kingdom (1994)
12. MacKenzie, S.B., Podsakoff, P.M., Podsakoff, N.P.: Construct measurement and validation procedures in MIS and behavioral research: Integrating new and existing techniques. MIS Q. **35**(2), 293–334 (2011)
13. Peffers, K., et al.: The design science research process: a model for producing and presenting information systems reseach. In: 1st International Conference on Design Science in Information Systems and Technology (DESRIST), vol. 24, no. 8, pp. 83–106 (2006)
14. Nonaka, I., Takeuchi, H.: The Knowledge-Creating Company: How Japanese Companies Create the Dynamics of Innovation. Oxford University Press, Oxford (1995)
15. Gronau, N.: Knowledge Modeling and Description Language 3.0 - Eine Einführung. Empirical Studies of Business Informatics, GITO (2020)
16. Kruse, R., Borgelt, C., Braune, C., Klawonn, F., Moewes, C., Steinbrecher, M.: Computational Intelligence: Eine methodische Einführung in Künstliche Neuronale Netze, Evolutionäre Algorithmen, 2nd edn. Fuzzy-Systeme und Bayes-Netze. Computational Intelligence, Springer Fachmedien Wiesbaden (2015)
17. Gronau, N., Grum, M., Bender, B.: Determining the optimal level of autonomy in cyber-physical production systems, pp. 1293–1299 (July 2016)
18. Grum, M., Gronau, N.: Process modeling within the augmented reality - the bidirectional interplay of two worlds. In: Proceedings of the Eighth BMSD, pp. 206–214 (2018)
19. Grum, M., Gronau, N.: A visionary way to novel process optimizations. In: Shishkov, B. (ed.) BMSD 2017. LNBIP, vol. 309, pp. 1–24. Springer, Cham (2018). https://doi.org/10.1007/978-3-319-78428-1_1
20. Gronau, N., Müller, C., Korf, R.: KMDL - capturing, analysing and improving knowledge-intensive business processes. J. Univ. Comput. Sci. **11**, 452–472 (2005)
21. Paul, J.C., Swatman, P.A.: The process of deriving requirements: learning from practice. In: Proceedings of the ninth Annual Australasian Conference on Information Systems, pp. 51–63 (1998)
22. Albers, A., et al.: Influencing factors and methods for knowledge transfer situations in product generation engineering based on the seci model [in press]. In: NordDesign, Linköping, Sweden, 14–17 August 2018 (2018)

Digital Transformation of Business Process Governance

Mathias Kirchmer[(✉)]

BPM-D, University of Pennsylvania, Philadelphia, USA
Mathias.Kirchmer@bpm-d.com

Abstract. Many organizations have started digital transformation initiatives. New digital tools are available with increasing regularity – and many of them have a major impact on business processes. However, only a small number of organizations have their business processes sufficiently under control to realize the full business potential of new digital technologies. Appropriate business process management (BPM) capabilities, have a significant impact on the value achieved through digitalization. This is especially true for establishing appropriate business process governance. Process governance keeps processes on track. It identifies necessary adjustments of the process, defines the required actions, and ensures their execution. This has a significant impact on the realization and sustainment of the targeted digitalization benefits as well as the ongoing performance of the processes. However, digital operational processes have new requirements for process governance. And digital process management tools provide new opportunities for effective governance. Therefore, process governance must go through a digital transformation itself, leveraging appropriate tools such as process mining or dynamic process modelling and simulation tools. Result is digital process governance, an important foundation of successful digital transformation.

Keywords: BPM · Business process management · Digitalization · Digital process governance · Digital transformation · Governance · Prioritization · Process governance · Process mining · Process of process management · Process repository · Repository governance

1 The Impact of Digital Transformation on Process Governance

Most organizations have started or at least planned digital transformation initiatives [1]. New digital tools are available with increasing regularity – and many of them have the potential for a major impact on business processes. Hyper-Automation has become a reality which changes the way business processes are organized and executed [2]. However, only a small number of organizations have their business processes sufficiently under control to realize the full potential of new digital technologies and the related transformation [3, 4]. Appropriate business process management (BPM) capabilities, delivered through the process of process management, have a significant impact on the value achieved through digitalization initiatives [5]. This is especially true for establishing appropriate business process governance. Process governance drives the realization

© Springer Nature Switzerland AG 2021
B. Shishkov (Ed.): BMSD 2021, LNBIP 422, pp. 243–261, 2021.
https://doi.org/10.1007/978-3-030-79976-2_14

of the targeted digitalization benefits as well as the ongoing improvement and change of digital processes [6–9]. Process governance identifies necessary adjustments of the process, defines the required actions, and ensures their execution. It enables the desired level of process performance. In a digital environment where an increasing number of applications is housed in the cloud, processes, hence the way how to use the digital tools, have become a key asset of an organization [10, 11]. To manage those assets successfully, governing digital processes properly is crucial.

Digital processes require a new governance approach to realize their potential. Speed, flexibility, and effectiveness must be combined. The new process governance leverages the opportunities of digitalization systematically to deliver the targeted value.

The tools and technologies supporting a digital business process deliver data about a process that has not or not fast enough been available with traditional business processes. This includes data about the performance of a process as well as about its compliance with the process design and related compliance requirements. Process governance in a digital environment can use this data to increase its effectiveness. This enables the necessary speed and flexibility in adjusting digital processes and frees up time to deal with people-related topics that cannot be automated. The resulting agility is a main benefit of digital transformations.

The ongoing adjustment and re-configuration of digital technologies can more and more often be done by the involved business departments, without using the information technology (IT) organization. Process supported through robotic process automation (RPA), for example, are most effective if at least routine adjustments of the used bots are done by the business users [12, 13]. Management oversees bots and humans. Therefore, digital processes require a hybrid workforce management, addressing people and technologies. Process governance needs to reflect this new business reality to simplify compliance and performance management.

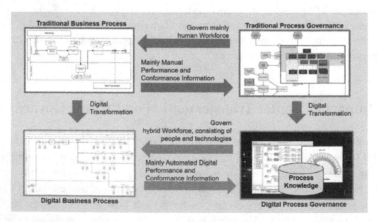

Fig. 1. Impact of digital transformation on process governance

Business process governance must go through a digital transformation itself, leveraging appropriate tools, such as process mining or dynamic process modelling and simulation, to meet those needs of a digital environment. The result is digital process governance, leveraging the opportunities operational digital processes provide by applying appropriate digital tools themselves. Digital process governance is value-driven, tool-enabled, and people-centric. The impact of digital transformation on process governance is visualized in Fig. 1.

This article identifies key digitalization opportunities for process governance. Then it examines how digital process governance can be achieved. After presenting first practice experience the articles concludes with a short outlook.

2 Opportunities for Digital Transformation of Process Governance

A digital business environment provides opportunities to move process governance to the next level enabling improved performance of operational business processes. After defining process governance in general and identifying its key components, specific digitalization opportunities for process governance will be identified. This provides the basis for the definition of digital process governance and its components.

2.1 Definition of Process Governance

Process governance is the organizational framework to establish and maintain end-to-end process performance in an organization. It exists in parallel to the structural, often function-oriented, organization with its reporting lines. Process governance manages the alignment of different activities with the requirements of internal and external clients.

Governance in general relates to processes and decisions that seek to verify performance, define actions, and grant power [14]. This definition can be transferred to business process governance: Process Governance relates to processes and decisions that seek to verify performance, define actions, and grant power related to the management of operational processes through the "process of process management" [7, 8, 10]. Process governance does not replace the existing organization structure. It adds an additional market and customer-focused view to ensure appropriate business process performance [15] and with that the realization of the overall goals of a company. Business trends, corporate strategies, legal requirements, and other aspects, like the use of specific supporting technologies, influence the design of a process governance approach.

The application of process governance must be defined in the context of a specific organization. It is delivered through a combination of different mechanisms [16]:

- Structural: Business process related roles and responsibilities are defined, for example the role of a process owner
- Procedural: Governance processes are defined, for example how to measure the end-to-end performance of a process and define improvement initiatives
- Relational: Informal relationships between people enable process governance, for example the long tenure and reputation of one department head can be used to align an end-to-end process across several departments.

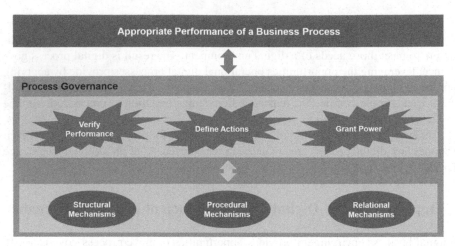

Fig. 2. Definition of process governance

The definition of process governance is visualized in Fig. 2.

Process governance addresses the entire lifecycle of a business process: design, implementation, execution, and control. Its key focus is on the running process, hence the execution control phase and delivering the required direction for the design and implementation of new and enhanced processes.

All process components, as described in the ARIS architecture, are relevant for the governance approach: organization, functions, data, deliverables, and control flow, as well as the technology support of process execution [17]. This leads to a close relation between process governance and other governance approaches, such as IT governance or data governance. The alignment with those related governance organizations needs to be reflected in the process governance approach.

2.2 Key Components of Process Governance

This definition of process governance is operationalized to establish it in an organization. It is realized through six key components [10]:

- A high-level identification of the company's main, cross-functional processes.
- Clarity on the goals to frame the definition of key performance indicators (KPI) of these business processes.
- Accountability and ownership for the management of business processes, combined with the appropriate empowerment, control and guidelines.
- Management of the knowledge about processes to achieve the necessary transparency enabling fast well-informed decisions and related actions.
- Aligned recognition and reward systems.
- A set of priorities to focus on what matters most for an organization.

In order to govern business processes, those processes need to be identified, from the external event that starts them until the result of value they deliver. The goals of those processes are to be defined clearly as basis to measure and verify the process performance. Key performance indicators (KPI) operationalize those goals by defining how to measure success. Accountabilities and ownership, combined with appropriate empowerment and direction, must be defined to enable necessary performance improvements. This is the core structural component of a process governance approach which reflects the people-centricity. It also includes the definition of the relation to other governance bodies, such as data governance. To enable fast decisions and the definition of required actions, the right degree of transparency over the business process and its behavior is required. This is achieved though the appropriate management of knowledge about the business process and the way it is executed. Recognition and reward systems must be aligned with the defined ownership roles and accountabilities to provide the right motivation of the involved people. This can include, for example, bonus payments for the achievement of specific process performance goals, measured through the defined KPIs. A company only competes through 15–20% of its business processes [9]. These high impact processes must be in the focus of process management and improvement initiatives. Also, various initiatives related to those processes are of different importance for the overall process goals. Hence, appropriate priorities for the use of resources must be set and applied as part of the process governance.

The key components of process governance are summarized in Fig. 3. The graphic illustrates the central role of ownership and accountabilities for effective process governance. Hence, it stresses the people centricity. Priorities and process goals reflect the value-driven approach.

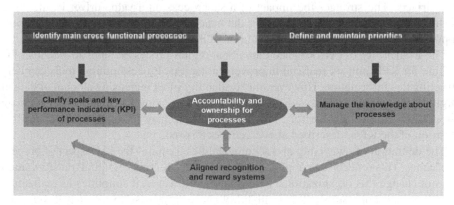

Fig. 3. Key components of process governance

2.3 Enhancement Opportunities for Process Governance Through Digitalization

The possible improvement of process governance through digitalization is examined using the six key components of process governance as a basis. These governance components are impacted in two ways through the effects of a digital transformation:

- Faster and more comprehensive information about the operational process through the underlying digital technologies and the data they produce.
- Use of digital tools to support process governance processes themselves, especially process and project prioritization, modelling and repository, process mining and intelligence tools.

Hence, all process governance components are examined regarding improvement opportunities through those digitalization effects. Goal of this improvement is to improve effectiveness and efficiency of process governance. This leads to more agile and reliable ongoing adjustments of processes.

The identification of the key business processes is not really impacted though the digitalization. However, leveraging process reference models in a dynamic digital format, leveraging a repository tool, can simplify this activity [10, 18]. The reference models can be used as guideline to identify the company specific core processes and describe those on a high level as basis for the process governance. Having the company specific process models available in a digital formal also enables the ongoing adjustment of the process scope. Process mining tools may also help identifying processes if they are already sufficiently automated. Results are cost and time savings as well as more reliable results.

The goals of processes and related KPIs are defined based on the overall business strategy of the organization. Digital process and project prioritization tools can help to break down strategic imperatives into value-drivers and to assess the impact of sub-processes on those value-drivers. Process KPIs describe the relation of sub-process to value-drivers. The stronger the impact of a subprocess on a value-driver is, the more important is it to define a KPI enabling the management of this impact. Digital tools support the definition of the most relevant of KPIs in and efficient way.

The availability of performance data about digital processes helps to establish the baseline for KPIs and set realistic improvement targets. Process mining tools can help extracting this information. However, the availability of an increasing amount of data in a digital environment increases the risk of defining too many KPIs and with that create unnecessary administrative effort. Process governance may lose focus. The controlled definition of the KPIs, described above, reduces this risk.

The definition of ownership and accountabilities, remains the key aspect of process governance. This reflects the people-centricity of the governance. Digital transformation does not change this organizational activity itself. However, it simplifies its realization and day-to-day application. The availability and easy access to relevant governance information allows to streamline the structure of the governance organization. This is the same effect information technology has on the organizational structure of a company where middle management positions can be cut out since their role to aggregate data is no longer required [19]. Having comprehensive and accurate information about the process, delivered through process repositories and mining tools, speeds up decision making and increases the acceptance of those decisions as well as the resulting actions. Digitalization of process governance makes therefore ownership and accountabilities more effective and allows to broaden the scope as required to meet performance goals. The collaboration between different people involved in process governance can be supported through digital collaboration and workflow tools which increases those effects even further.

Basis for all process governance activities is the availability and management of the required knowledge about the process. This governance component can be significantly improved in a digital environment. The availability of performance and conformance information though process mining applications used by the governance organization allows fast-well informed decisions and focused actions [20, 21]. Structural information about the process, captured in process modelling and repository tools [10, 22, 31], is important to create a baseline and manage the process conformance, for example, compliance requirements or consistency the actual process execution with the process design. The use of process reference models as design templates across business units simplifies the governance of process standardization and makes it more effective.

Recognition and reward systems reflect the achievement of end-to-end performance goals of a business process. This is in general independent of the digital process transformation. However, the simpler and more reliable measurement of KPIs through tools like process mining improves this governance component. The simple access to information about process priorities and process models further supports this governance activity.

Using the right priorities when defining process governance actions and related improvement initiatives is also independent of the degree to digitalization of a process. High impact low maturity processes are the best targets for optimization and innovation initiatives since they are most important for the realization of the strategy of an organization [9]. Process governance priorities need to reflect this and evaluate initiatives based on their effect on those high impact processes. Digital tools supporting a process and project impact assessment as well as the resulting prioritization enhance this governance component [18]. Process mining tools deliver the required information about actual processes to confirm or adjust those priorities.

The main enhancement opportunities for process governance through digital transformation are summarized in Fig. 4.

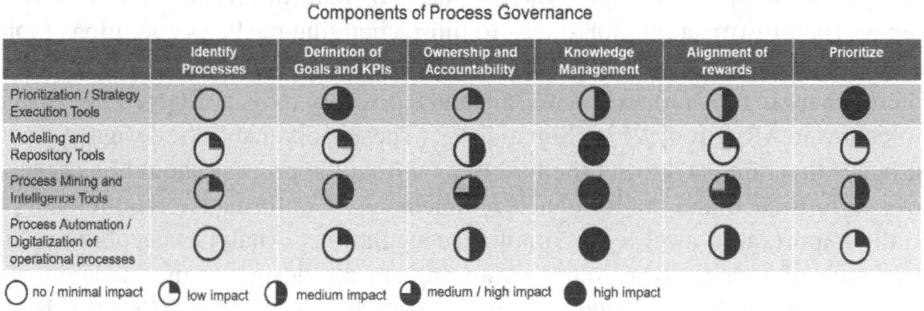

Fig. 4. Main enhancement opportunities of process governance through digitalization

3 Digital Process Governance

The realization of the improvement opportunities of process governance results in digital process governance. The use of digital enablers is examined further. This is the basis for a discussion of the impact on the governance organization and its processes.

3.1 Digital Enablers for Process Governance

In order to realize the improvement opportunities of process governance through digitalization a combination of key process management tools is required:

- Prioritization tool to target best value for the organization.
- Process modelling and repository tool to manage knowledge about the process type and its design.
- Process mining tool to provide conformance and performance information about process instances.

These tools must be appropriately integrated with the digital technologies supporting the execution of the operational business processes. This allows the efficient collection of the required data. The right integration among each other further supports the digital process governance by re-using information. General digital tools, like a workflow system, are added to further enhance governance processes.

Examples for digital prioritization tools are the BPM-D Application [23] or i-Nexus [24]. Those tools help identifying high impact low maturity processes and the definition of related improvement projects delivering best value for the organization [18, 25]. To enable this process and project prioritization, the process hierarchy, defined in a process repository is re-used. The technical integration between the prioritization and modelling tool is less important since it is a small volume of data that is transferred in a low frequency. The prioritization tool allows to move changing business conditions rapidly into adjusted priorities, supporting an agile governance approach.

There are numerous process modelling and repository tools available [10]. Specific examples are the ARIS Tool [26] or Signavio [27] These tools enable the design of process types; hence they are used to set the baseline for how the process should be organized to meet performance and conformance requirements. Conformance requirements are especially important to meet legal compliance regulations. Analytics capabilities, such as simulation of process types, support an appropriate design or modification of an existing process definition. Process modeling methods, such as BPMN [28], help to make the use and impact of digital technologies transparent. While most of the use cases of such modelling tools are during the design and implementation of digital processes, the tools and their content also support the ongoing process governance [29]. The tools provide the structured digital models of the target process. This allows to govern actual process instances towards those targets.

The governance of process standardization is supported through reference models that show where a process can be modified to reflect, for example, product or geography specifics and where it must follow the company-wide standard [22]. Process repository tools enable the efficient use and roll-out of such reference models.

The process models in the repository can be integrated with even more detailed standard operating procedures (SOP) so that those can be easily accessed and maintained in the end-to-end process context. This helps to meet compliance requirements.

The integration of process modelling and repository tools with the applications supporting the operational processes drives the configuration of those applications according to business requirements [10]. This simplifies the governance of business-driven process changes. Practice has shown, however, that this does in general not mean that the operational systems are adjusted automatically. Hence, the models are in most cases used as guideline for configuration adjustments. An integration of process modelling tools with process mining tools, helps to compare the process design with actually executed process instances to govern the process conformance.

Process models also identify digital technologies that can be modified directly through the business units. If adjustments are required to meet process performance goals, this enables the definition of governance actions suited for a hybrid workforce.

Process modelling and repository tools require a governance approach for themselves. This is necessary to keep the models up to date and usable by the process governance organization [9, 10]. Repository governance defines, for example, who can see or modify models or when an update is necessary.

Performance and conformance related data is extracted from the system logs of the applications supporting the digital processes using process mining tools [21], if required complemented through task mining tools. Examples for such process mining tools are Celonis [30], Disco [31], ARIS Process Mining [32], and Signavio Process Intelligence [33]. ARIS and Signavio offer an entire process management suite, including the process modelling and repository tool as well as execution software. This simplifies the required integration. Process mining tools use event information from system logs of applications to calculate performance information, for example the cycle time of a process and of different process components. This information is key to govern a process towards the desired performance level. Aligning the extracted events, with the appropriate steps of the defined process design, shows where specific process instances, is handled according to the design and where the actual process execution deviates from it. This allows corrective actions or the adjustment of the process design.

The analysis of as-is processes at the beginning of digitalization projects is often seen as the main usage scenario for process mining tools [34]. However, numerous organizations still have many processes with lots of manually executed steps or they use different systems which do not deliver consistent events across different sub-processes. This lack of appropriate data limits the use of process mining. This is different for the governance of digital processes. The technology support is more consistent, and the degree of automation is higher. Hence, the use of process mining tools to govern those processes is more effective and simplifies governance processes significantly [35].

The use of process mining is especially well suited in environments where an operational process is supported through an automation platform that integrates different applications and other digital services. Such a platform provides consistent information in the various logs and a simple access to the relevant data. No-code or low-code platforms, such as Unqork [36] or Appian [37], allow a customized support of a specific

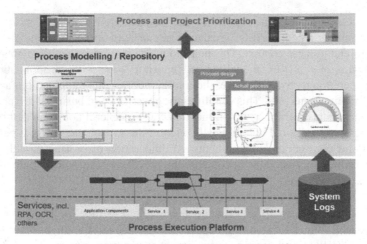

Fig. 5. Main enhancement opportunities of process governance through digitalization

operational process and agile adjustments. Especially the use of no-code approach, as provided by Unqork, simplify the execution of governance actions.

An architecture of tools to support digital process governance is shown in Fig. 5. This tool architecture can be leveraged to support the larger BPM-Discipline [6]. However, in this article we focus on the aspects as they relate to process governance.

3.2 Simplified Organization for Process Governance

Structural mechanisms, especially a formalized process governance organization, is the core component of an effective process governance. It makes people-centric governance sustainable and scalable. It helps to create the right balance of power between the process management and functional management, based on the official organizational structure of a company. The timely availability of reliable information about processes and their performance allows the process governance organization to act effectively across organizational boundaries. The interaction between members of the governance organization and the functional leadership is simplified through a digital data-driven process management approach. People can discuss facts, not anecdotes. The described digital tools are the foundation for this effective people-centric governance.

The roles forming the process governance organization are summarized in Fig. 6 [38]. Extended roles are part of the operational business units where they apply the principles of process management. The core team, often organized as BPM center of excellence (CoE), supports the extended roles through deep process management know and skills. In a specific company context, it is defined for each role if it is centralized or decentralized, project-based or permanent, in-house, or out-sourced.

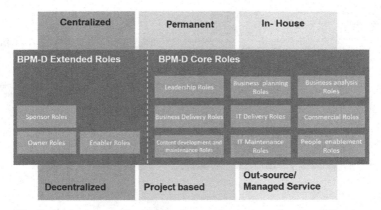

Fig. 6. Main groups of roles forming a process governance organization

Ownership roles and the definition of supporting roles with their accountabilities is a key component of process governance [9, 10]. A key role is the process owner, managing an operational process on a daily basis. Main accountabilities include:

- Define and manage process-oriented KPIs.
- Ensure the compliance with company standards and process design.
- Initiate process improvements based on external events or performance issues.
- Review proposed changes to the process and governance structure.
- Review integration issues between the various processes.
- Promote the business process management vision and strategy.
- Initiate process related training.
- Function as a point of escalation, when required.
- Collaborate with functional leaders and other governance organizations.

The process owners are often complemented through process stewards who represent the process view in different functional areas. This is especially important in larger organizations. Process sponsors are responsible to set overall directions and resolve conflicts, for example between process and functional leaders.

These extended governance roles are supported through a BPM core team, in most cases a BPM CoE. This BPM CoE includes roles like business process analysts and architects, various project delivery roles as well as roles required to maintain the process management infrastructure. An emerging leadership role is the chief process officer (CPO) who owns the process of process management [39]. The CPO provides the link of the process organization to the top-management and oversees its roll-out.

The different governance roles are collaborating which resulting in governance bodies, such as oversight teams or working groups. Figure 7 shows a typical example for such a process governance organization, reflecting its people-centricity [38].

In a digital governance approach the process owner role becomes even more effective. Performance and conformance information can be obtained faster and easier. Larger organizations often define a hierarchy of process owners, for example, global regional or local process owners. In those cases, the digital governance approach can reduce

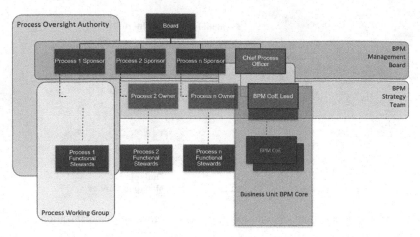

Fig. 7. Reference structure for a process governance organization

those hierarchy levels. The global process owner can manage target processes designs based on the models in the repository as well as receive the required information about regional and local processes through a process mining tool. Hence, the collaboration with process stewards in the different functions can be sufficient to ensure appropriate governance. This must, however, be decided in the context of a specific organization. Digital process governance reduces administrative governance work. This frees up time for people-related activities and reduces the overall cost. Process owners can concentrate on using information to set appropriate action.

The effort for ongoing support of digital tools, to be delivered through the BPM CoE, increases through a digital process governance approach. While tools for modelling, mining or related activities are also required for process improvement activities, now they become part of the "business as usual". The ongoing more intense use of those tools and their content increases the needs for maintenance, tool governance and support service levels.

The enterprise-wide roll-out of the tools becomes more important which requires appropriate enablement activities, especially training. In larger organizations an eLearning approach may be required to support a rapid roll out of governance tools and techniques.

The CPO manages the progress of the process of process management, hence of the BPM-Discipline. While people related activities still stay in the center of CPO activities, the definition of appropriate tool strategies and their role-out becomes more important.

3.3 Improved Processes for Process Governance

Process governance is delivered through appropriate governance processes [6, 7]. Digital process governance improves those processes leveraging suitable digital tools. Those governance processes are defined in the context of a specific organization.

The digital transformation of governance processes requires a more formal process definition to facilitate the appropriate value-driven use of the digital tools An overall governance approach is defined first and then detailed in process models explaining the tool support in the different activities. The seamless collaboration between process ownership roles and the supporting BPM CoE is especially important to achieve and maintain the desired governance level. Examples for typical governance processes are:

- Ongoing performance management.
- Managing process standardization and compliance.
- Launch of improvement and transformation initiatives.
- Acceptance and roll-out of process improvements.
- Collaboration between governance bodies.

An example of an overall governance approach of a health research organization is shown in Fig. 8. Here the process owners manage key digital governance components, such as process modelling, analytics, and automation. The BPM CoE supports this.

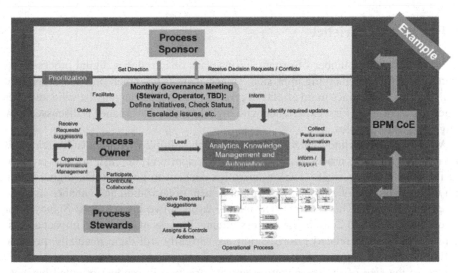

Fig. 8. Example of an overall process governance model leveraging digital tools

Figure 9 shows an example of a detailed governance process in BPMN format. This is an excerpt of the process for ongoing performance management. It shows how the process mining tool Celonis is used to determine performance levels and identify potential issues while the modelling tool Signavio is used to analyze potential issues and define necessary actions. The careful definition an ongoing management of those governance processes are the foundation for an effective governance.

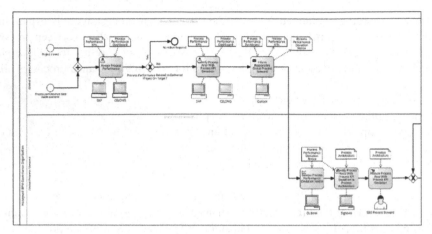

Fig. 9. Example of an overall process governance model leveraging digital tools

4 Practice Experience

While an increasing number of organizations plans or introduces digital process governance, it is till san emerging approach. Hence, there is not much practice experience available, especially since main effects of process governance can only be validated over longer period of time. First experience with digital process governance is discussed now using two case examples.

A major global technology company has launch multiple digital transformation initiatives, including the processes procure-to-pay, opportunity-to-cash, idea-to-product, and integrated supply chain. The organization decided to combine the digitalization with the introduction of a new process management organization and enhance its basic process governance. This is supported mainly through two digital tools: Signavio for process modelling and Celonis for process mining. Process maturity and impact assessments as well as the related prioritization are currently still done manually, possible digital tools are under evaluation.

Due to the size of the organization and its structure in product-oriented business units, the ownership for processes is defined on two levels: global process owners (Level 1) and business unit process owners (Level 2). Level 1 process owners govern global process standards for all business units as well as centralized corporate processes to ensure consistent use of best practices, documented in company specific reference models using Signavio. This includes the identification of areas where busienss units can deviate from the standard. Twice a year they assess the adherence to the standards and provide recommendations for improvements or suggestions. If necessary, they trigger adjustments of the design. In monthly meetings which include functional leadership, the process owners exchange experience and decide on actions relevant for several processes, such as the roll-out of efficiency tools like RPA.

The business unit specific performance management is provided through Level 2 owners. They receive performance information through Celonis process mining as well as traditional monitoring tools. Process models are used to manage the value realization and evaluate the maturity level of the existing processes. Depending on the complexity of the process, the Level 2 owners are supported through process stewards. Process owners are organizationally part of the business units.

A newly founded BPM CoE supports the governance organization and ensures the appropriate service levels for the tools und supports improvement and transformation projects, requested by the business units through the process owners. Further, decentralized BPM CoEs, are planned for the different business units. The corporate CoE provides then the necessary standards and guidelines, whereas the decentral units focus on the execution of improvement and transformation projects, applying those guidelines.

The mining tool is mainly used to get process performance information. Conformance information is collected through regular process audits, hence, in a traditional way. The supporting software landscape is still very heterogeneous so that a broader use of the mining software has been considered as too complex so far. The modelling and repository tool houses the reference models for processes, describing best practices in form of company-wide process reference models. Business units adopt those as required, based on guidelines provided by Level 1 process owners. The process variants are also stored in the repository. This enables the collaboration of the community around a process to identify improvement opportunities, guided by the Level 2 process owners.

Figure 10 describes the governance approach, well linked to the strategic objectives of the organization. Resulting governance processes are described in BPMN and included the BPM Playbook, outlining the entire BPM-Discipline of the organization. Significant process improvements, including cost reductions and increased service quality, have been sustained through this governance approach.

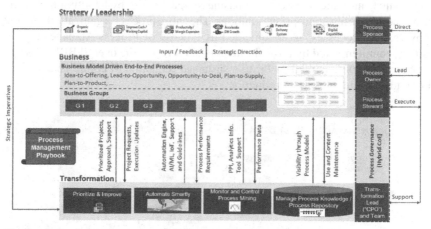

Fig. 10. Example of a process governance model leveraging digital tools in a technology company

A leading biologics company decided on an incremental digitalization of their mainly manual processes. While doing this, they build a basic process management discipline, including process governance. They leverage the BPM-D Application for prioritization activities, Signavio as modelling tool, and some self-developed analytics tools to support the collection of KPIs. The integration of process models with the digitally available standard operating procedures is currently evaluated. For four core processes the owners are defined and for complex sub-processes additional sub-process owners. A newly founded BPM CoE owns the tools and provides the necessary information in form of priorities, process models and KPIs to the owners who use the information to support decision making and define follow up actions. Here the Signavio's collaboration environment, the Collaboration Hub, plays a key role.

The strategic value-drivers, process hierarchy, and the process impact assessment matrix are stored and updated in the prioritization tool. This information is used to prioritize improvement initiatives since the demand from business is higher than available resource capacities. All process models are stored in the process repository, helping process owners to manage their processes towards the defined standards. This is supported by reports generated through the repository, referred to as Process Playbooks. They transfer the process models into a tabular description of each step, the input and output data as well as the accountabilities. This allows to give clear instructions to the people involved in the process without teaching the formal modelling methods. Process mining is currently not applied since the degree of system support of the operational processes is still too low to deliver sufficient data. Mining initiatives are planned for a second step. Related Signavio capabilities are currently tested. The process hierarchy in the modelling and repository tool are currently redundantly kept in the prioritization too, so that they need to be aligned manually. So far, this has not been an issue due to the low number of changes in the first three levels of the process hierarchy.

The overall governance approach is shown in Fig. 11. In this specific environment it has been important to define clearly how the process management and governance approach aligns and interacts with the business organization by handling improvement requests and delivering appropriate solutions. The entire process organizations, including the governance processes, is documented as Process of Process Management in the repository, complemented by a BPM Playbook, describing the overall BPM-Discipline. The governance approach led so far to a sustained reduction of compliance issues and with that to cost and cycle time reduction.

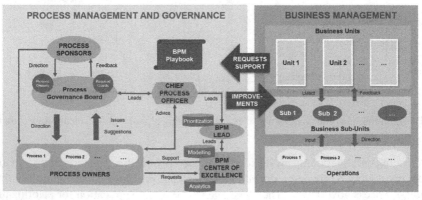

Fig. 11. Example of a process governance model leveraging digital tools in a biologics company

In both cases the process governance relies on the use of digital tools. They provide the transparency required to govern the processes while minimizing the effort required for this. However, both organization in an early stage of their digital process governance. It will be step by step improved and rolled out into the organizations.

5 Future Developments in Digitalization of Process Governance

Process governance has become a main topic for many organizations. The interest in this field has increased due to digitalization initiatives. In order to benefit from new technologies, such as process automation or the digital integration of devices, companies need to govern their processes appropriately, so that the full potential of the digital transformation is realized, and the expected value is delivered. A highly flexible no-code platform, for example, only leads to real business agility if it is clearly defined who decides on adjustments and how to execute them rapidly. Process governance addresses those topics.

Key challenge of process governance is still the definition of appropriate responsibilities and accountabilities. The availability of timely accurate information about business processes, simplifies this task. It is easier to justify decisions and set appropriate actions if you have the required information at your fingertips. The digital transformation of process governance enhances all key governance components, it increases effectiveness of governance and makes it more cost and time efficient. Therefore, digital transformation of process governance is becoming an important component of digitalization initiatives in general. Result is digital process governance.

Digital process governance is still in an emerging state. Research and development activities are required to move it to the next level. Here some examples:

- The development of a reference model for digital process governance, especially the governance processes, can jump start and accelerate its use [6, 13].
- More seamless integration of process modelling and mining tools as well as process automation systems would streamline governance processes further.
- Using artificial intelligence (AI) methods in conjunction with process mining [27] could result in interesting predictive information, increasing the impact of governance.
- A more systematic definition of the integration of process governance with other governance approaches, especially data governance, would enhance the effectiveness of the process governance. This could mean an extension of the digitalization to other governance areas.
- The organizational aspects should be examined further to identify new or revised governance roles and structures due to digitalization.
- The inter-enterprise process governance approach must be refined and enhanced to become sustainable and scalable.

Establishing digital process governance improves the overall performance of the BPM-Discipline and its role in strategy execution. This leads to an improved process lifecycle management and with that the systematic transfer of strategy into technology and people-based execution, at pace with certainty [6].

References

1. Fahland, D., Ghidini, C., Becker, J., Dumas, M. (eds.): BPM 2020. LNCS, vol. 12168. Springer, Cham (2020). https://doi.org/10.1007/978-3-030-58666-9
2. Stoudt-Hansen, S., et al.: Predicts 2020: Barriers Fall as Technology Adoption Grows. A Gartner Trend Insight Report, Boston (2019)
3. Kirchmer, M.: Value-driven Digital Transformation: Performance through Process. In: IM+io, Best & Next Practices aus Digitalisierung | Management | Wissenschaft, Heft 2, Juni 2019
4. Cantara, M.: 'Start up your business process competency center'. In: Documentation of The Gartner Business Process Management Summit, National Harbour (2015)
5. Antonucci, Y., Fortune, A., Kirchmer, M.: An examination of associations between business process management capabilities and the benefits of digitalization: all capabilities are not equal. In: Business Process Management Journal, Vol. ahead-of-print No. ahead-of-print (2020). https://doi.org/10.1108/BPMJ-02-2020-0079
6. Kirchmer, M.: The process of process management – mastering the new normal in a digital world. In: BMSD Proceedings, July 2015
7. Rosemann, M.: The service portfolio of a bpm center of excellence. In: vom Brocke, J., Rosemann, M. (eds.) Handbook on Business Process Management 2. IHIS, pp. 381–398. Springer, Heidelberg (2015). https://doi.org/10.1007/978-3-642-45103-4_16
8. Hove, M., Storms, B.J.: Business process management governance. In: Rosing, M.V., Scheer, A.-W., Scheer, H.V. (eds.): The Complete Business Process Handbook – Body of Knowledge from Process Model to BPM. vol. 1, Elsevir, Waltham, MA, pp. 599–611 (2015)
9. Franz, M., Kirchmer, M.: Value-Driven Business Process Management: The Value-Switch for Lasting Competitive Advantage. 1st edition, New York (2012)
10. Kirchmer, M.: High Performance through Business Process Management –Strategy Execution in a Digital World. 3rd edition, Springer, New York, Berlin (2017)
11. Abolhassan, F.: The Drivers of Digital Transformation – Why there's no way around the Cloud. 1st edition, Springer, Berlin (2016)
12. Smeets, Erhard, Kaussler: Robotic Process Automation (RPA) in der Finanzwirtschaft – Technologie, Implementierung, Erfolgsfaktoren fuer Entscheider und Anwender. 1st edition, Springer Fachmedien Wiesbaden, Wiesbaden (2019)
13. Kirchmer, M., Franz, P.: Value-driven robotic process automation (RPA) – a process-led approach for fast results at minimal risk. In: Proceedings of the 9th International Symposium on Business Modelling and Software Design, Lisbon, 1–3 July 2019
14. Wikipedia: Governance. In: https://en.wikipedia.org/wiki/Governance (2021)
15. Spanyi, A.: The governance of business process management. In: vom Brocke, J., Rosemann, M. (eds.) Handbook on Business Process Management 2. IHIS, pp. 333–349. Springer, Heidelberg (2015). https://doi.org/10.1007/978-3-642-45103-4_14
16. Janssen, M.: Architectural governance and organizational performance. In: Keynote Presentation at the 5th International Symposium on Business Modelling and Software Design, Milan, 6–8 July 2015
17. Scheer, A.-W.: ARIS – Business Process Frameworks, 2nd edition. Springer, Berlin (1998)
18. Kirchmer, M., Franz, P.: Value-driven Process and Project Prioritization – Basis for Focused Digital Transformation and Business Continuity Planning. BPM-D Publications, Philadelphia, London (2020)
19. Hammer, M., Champy, J.: Reengineering the Corporation – A Manifesto for Business Revolution, 4th edn. Harper Business, New York (1993)
20. Scheer, A.-W.: Unternehmung 4.0 – Von disruptiven Geschaeftsmodell zur Automatisierung von Geschaeftsprozessen. 1st edition, AWSi Publishing, Saarbrucken, Germany (2018)

21. Van der Aalst, J.: Process Mining – Data Science in Action. 2nd edition, Springer, Berlin (2016)
22. Kirchmer, M., Franz, P.: Process reference models: accelerator for digital transformation. In: Shishkov, B. (ed.) BMSD 2020. LNBIP, vol. 391, pp. 20–37. Springer, Cham (2020). https://doi.org/10.1007/978-3-030-52306-0_2
23. BPM-D (ed.): Digital Transformation Management (2021). In: https://bpm-d.com/application/
24. i-Nexus (ed.): Take Control of your Business Performance (2021). In: https://i-nexus.com/
25. Kirchmer, M., Franz, P., Gusain, R.: Digitalization of the Process of Process management – The BPM-D Application. In: Proceedings of the Seventh International Symposium on Business Modelling and Software Design, Barcelona, 03–05 July 2017
26. Software AG (ed.): Business Design and Strategy (2021). In: https://www.softwareag.com/en_corporate/platform/aris/business-process-improvement.html
27. Signavio (ed.): Signavio Process Manager (2021). In: https://www.signavio.com/products/process-manager/
28. Fisher, L.: BPMN 2.0 Handbook – Methods, Concepts, Case Studies and Standards in Business Process Modelling Notation (BPMN). Lighthouse Point (2012)
29. Kirchmer, M.: Enterprise Architecture enabling Process Governance for Agility, Compliance and more. In: CIO Review, Enterprise Architecture Special, 5 April 2018
30. Celonis (ed.): The #1 Process Mining Product (2021). In: https://www.celonis.com/process-mining-core/
31. Fluxicon (ed.): Disco – Process Mining has arrived (2021). In: https://fluxicon.com/
32. Software AG (ed.): Process Mining (2021). In: https://www.softwareag.com/en_corporate/platform/aris/process-mining.html
33. Signavio (ed.): Signavio Process Intelligence (2021). In: https://www.signavio.com/products/process-intelligence/
34. Reinkemeyer, L.: Process Mining in Action – Principles, Use Cases and Outlook. 1st edition, Springer, Berlin (2020)
35. Reinkemeyer, L.: Business View: Towards a Digital enabled Organization. In: Reinkemeyer, L. (ed.): Process Mining in Action – Principles, Use Cases and Outlook. 1st edition, Springer, Berlin (2020)
36. Unqork (ed.): Unqork Insurance Software (2021). In: https://www.unqork.com/solutions/insurance
37. Appian (ed.): Low-code Automation made Fast and Simple (2021). I https://www.appian.com/
38. Kirchmer, M., Franz, P.: BPM Governance and Organization – The Agility Network. BPM-D Training Documentation, Philadelphia, London (2020)
39. Kirchmer, M., Franz, P.: Chief Process Officer – The Value Scout. BPM-D Publications, Philadelphia, London (2014)

Short Papers

Revisiting Human Relativism – Guidelines for Precision in Information Systems Modelling

José Cordeiro[1,2](✉)

[1] INCITE – Centre for Innovation in Science and Technology, IPS, Setúbal, Portugal
jose.cordeiro@estsetubal.ips.pt
[2] Setúbal School of Technology, Polytechnic Institute of Setúbal,
Campus do IPS, Setúbal, Portugal

Abstract. Human Relativism (HR) was presented a decade ago as a new philosophical stance for thinking and modelling Information Systems. The Normative Approach for Modelling Information Systems (NOMIS) adopted HR by using a human-observable-action centred perspective of information systems. By using HR, NOMIS claims to have reduced unpredictability, attributed to *human behaviour*, and increased precision, required by formal methods. Still, there are other approaches, some of them using formal methods, supported by different ontologies, such as the well-known Bunge–Wand–Weber ontology, that lack the necessary precision. In this paper, we explore different ontologies, their relationship to language and why they fail to deliver *precision*. *Precision*, a concept introduced in HR, as a basis for engineering, is analysed, and the way to achieve it is proposed through suggesting guidelines for further discussion and research.

Keywords: Ontology · Human relativism · Enterprise ontology · BWW ontology · Semiotics · Information systems · Information systems modelling · Precision in information systems modelling

1 Introduction

An information system, particularly a computer system, can be seen as a digital support of organizational reality as it collects, retrieves, processes, stores, and distributes information. Information, stored in bytes, is just data waiting for some individual to interpret it and give it meaning. Often, this data takes the form of words and numbers, that are processed by programs and stored in databases. Interpretation of this data is a source of imprecision and ambiguity given its dependency on the human element. Moreover, words and numbers are also embodied in database schemas, interfaces, and programming source code. If there is interpretation involved, how can we assure the necessary *precision* when developing and using computerized information systems?

In this position paper, we analyse a few theories expressing different world views to clarify how reality is mapped to our information systems and how language and interpretation should be understood from the point of view of semiotics. Human Relativism is revisited, as a partial solution to the *precision* problem.

© Springer Nature Switzerland AG 2021
B. Shishkov (Ed.): BMSD 2021, LNBIP 422, pp. 265–274, 2021.
https://doi.org/10.1007/978-3-030-79976-2_15

This paper is organized as follows: in Sect. 2, we present a brief overview of Human Relativism, and the world views provided by Enterprise ontology, BWW ontology and typical formal ontologies in Information Systems. In Sect. 3, we analyse the dependency of ontology on language by using the semiotic notion of a sign and the specific views of it from Enterprise ontology and Human Relativism. Based on concepts presented in previous sections, in Sect. 4 we introduce and discuss the notion of *precision* proposed in HR and we point some future research directions to achieve it within Information Systems. Section 5, concludes this paper.

2   Ontology and ontology (ies)

In philosophy, Ontology is a branch of metaphysics that deals with the nature of being. It seeks to answer questions such as the nature and structure of reality, what entities or things exist, how they are grouped in categories, what properties they have or how they relate to each other. In information systems, ontology or ontologies, with a lowercase first letter and as a countable noun, are formal explicit specifications of the terms or concepts and the relationships between them in a specific domain. Both, Ontology and ontologies provide a world view that is expressed by language. In this section, we look into a few different world views, as a basis for our discussion.

2.1 Human Relativism

Human Relativism (HR) [1, 2] is a philosophical stance that recognises *reality* as having a human-related perspective without adopting a subjectivist approach. This ontological stance is rooted in the concept of *information* where *information* is seen as dependent on individuals and their perceptions, interpretations, knowledge, experience or judgment. Therefore, HR proposes an *objective reality* as *human-related* and introduces the concept of *observability* to deal with factors of unpredictability and inaccuracy introduced by the human element. In order to understand the concept of *observability* is necessary to distinguish between *perception*, the process of acknowledging the external reality through our senses, and *interpretation*, the meaning making process. Only *information* goes through the *interpretation* process, all other elements of human reality are just perceived. This restricts what is perceived by humans and, consequently, what is understood as *observable*. *Observable things* can be viewed as material or physical individual things from the objectivist point of view.

From this perspective, HR makes the following assumption:

"Anything that is observable will be more consensual, precise and, therefore more appropriate to be used by scientific methods" [1].

In practice, *observability* intends to remove ambiguities from *human reality* and to achieve the necessary precision needed to apply and use scientific methods.

These simple ideas proposed by HR are, in fact, aligned with social constructivism and objectivism making a proper connection between them.

2.2 Enterprise Ontology

Enterprise ontology (EO), proposed by Jan Dietz [3], provides the foundations for designing and engineering of enterprises seen as social information systems. It is based on the Language Action Perspective [see 4] that acknowledges language as the primary dimension of human cooperative activity. Indeed, organisations seen at an *essential level*, from where we subtract all material and technical things, are just a group of communicating people. At this level, work is produced as a result of language acts; Thus, this production work is the result of people intentions, commitments, obligations and responsibility.

EO is supported by a *well-founded* ontology that defines objectively and formally its world view. It is based on *states of the world* and *state transitions*. The *state of the world* is simply defined as a set of objects that exist during the duration of the state. A *state transition* is an *event* corresponding to a state change. For better understanding what a state of the world is, EO makes a distinction between two kinds of objects: *statum* and *factum* objects. A *statum* is a constant object, something that is the case, has always been the case and always be the case. An example from Dietz [3] is the author of a particular book. In this case, is understood as being the author whenever, although before the book was written this was not known. A *factum* is the result or effect of an act that is brought to existence by an event. An example from the same source is "book title T has been published". A *statum* is subjected to existence laws and a *factum* is subject to occurrence laws.

Using above notions EO precisely defines the ontological model of a world as:

"The ontological model of a world consists of the specification of its state space and its transition space" [3, pp. 42].

The state space is specified by a state base, the set of status types existing during a state, and the existence laws. The transition space is specified by a transition base, the set of factum types that may occur, and the occurrence laws.

The world ontology defined in EO and applicable to any system (or organisation) is specified by a formal language called World Ontology Specification Language (WOSL) [5], based on ORM [6], a language used to represent database conceptual schemas. WOSL was created specifically for EO and its scope is also limited to EO.

2.3 The BWW Ontology

Wand & Weber [7] made an interesting proposal to use ontology as a basis for the representation of real systems within information systems analysis and design. Their claim is that a good representation of the real system should contain a representation of the meaning of reality. So, they adapted the ontology formalized by Bunge [8, 9] that is currently known as the Bunge-Wand-Weber (BWW) ontology. Although this adaptation is partial or reductionist it became popular in the conceptual modelling field. Some of the constructs used are *thing,* that have *properties* as understood in philosophy. A *composite thing* is a set of things. *Conceivable States* that a *thing* may assume or *Stable States* that a *thing* is, unless forced to change. *System* and *Subsystem* as set and sub-sets of *things* among some other concepts. A simple object-oriented modelling of the BWW Ontology that can help understanding the concepts used can be found in [10].

2.4 Formal Ontologies in Information Systems

In Computer Science, ontology or ontologies are understood as "*a formal, explicit spec-ification of a shared conceptualization*" [11]. In [12], there is an emphasis in the terms "conceptualization", "formal, explicit specification" and, "shared". Conceptualization is described as an "abstract, simplified view of the world that we wish to represent for some purpose". A conceptualization involves concepts and relationships between them within a particular domain of discourse. These domains are composed by sets of things. As an example from [12], a domain can be a group of people from a particular orga-nization whereas *person, manager, researcher, cooperates-with* and *reports-to* are seen as relationships within that domain. A conceptualization is shared since it expresses a shared and consensual view instead of an individual view. Usually, conceptualiza-tions are formally defined using a first-order logic language which makes them machine readable.

3 Ontology and Language

In the previous chapter, different world views are presented that describe the nature and structure of reality in distinct ways. All of them share a common way of describing this *reality*: they use human *language* for that purpose. This biased view is always dependent on human understanding, human knowledge, human interpretation. Information systems, in general, and computer systems, in particular, also use language for *processing, storing* and *distributing* information. Textual data is present in databases, program source code, interfaces that is communicated in different ways to the computer user. Thus, making these texts dependent on the human element. In this section, we analyse this dependency by looking at semiotics, and other related views that explore the concept of meaning and its use in language.

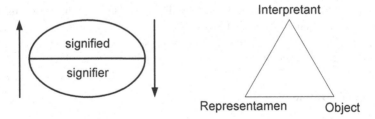

Fig. 1. The Saussurean and the peircean models of the sign

3.1 Semiotics

Semiotics is described as being 'the study of signs', which is concerned with their creation/production, representation and interpretation. The 'study of signs' could be replaced by the 'study of meaning and its role in human life', how it is created, rep-resented, communicated or interpreted through signs, giving a clearer description of semiotics.

There is no consensual model or a universal definition of a sign. Even so, two most known and dominant models of what constitutes a sign are those of Ferdinand de Saussure [13] and Charles Sanders Pierce [14], both presented in Fig. 1.

According to De Saussure the sign is composed by

- a '*signifier*' – the *form* which the sign takes and
- a '*signified*' – the *concept* it represents.

Those two indivisible parts are the '*whole*' that constitutes the sign. The signified relates to the *meaning* and the signifier relates to *something that means*. Saussure saw linguistics as a branch of semiotics, or *semiology* as he called it.

On the other hand, Peirce conception of a sign involves three parts:

- the *Representamen* - the *form* which the sign takes,
- an *Interpretant* – the *sense* made of the sign and
- an *Object* – to which the sign refers or alludes.

His definition of a sign is *ibid*: 'A sign . . . is something which stands to somebody for something in some respect or capacity.' [14]. Relating these two models and, according to [15], the *Representamen* can be seen as similar in meaning to the *signifier* and the *Interpretant* as similar in meaning to the *signified*. However, it should be noted that the *Interpretant* in the Peircian model is itself a sign of its own. The *Object* doesn't feature directly in the Saussurean model. Many other definitions of signs from different semioticians follow the triadic model proposed by Peirce, but offering different names to the three vertices [see 16].

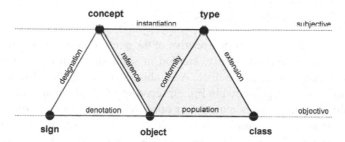

Fig. 2. The semiotic triangle and the ontological parallelogram (adapted from [3])

3.2 Enterprise Ontology and Semiotics

EO, as mentioned before, is supported by a well founded ontology that defines objectively and formally its world view. The basis of this ontology are the concepts presented in Fig. 2. as nodes or vertices of a triangle (the non shaded area) and a parallelogram (the shaded area). The first figure, the triangle, corresponds to the semiotic triangle of the Peirce's sign model. In this case, the *sign* is the objective representation of an individual

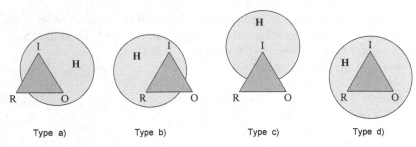

Fig. 3. Human/material views of the peircian sign [17].

object (the *Representamen*) and the *object* is an observable individual thing (the *Object*) that is linked to a particular *concept*, the thought or mental picture of the *object* (the *Interpretant*). Although observable, an object may be *abstract* such as the number four. Both the *sign* and the *object* are seen as objective, whereas the *concept* is subjective. While concepts and signs may be composite structures they are always individual things or *Particulars*. These notions of *concept* and *object* came from Bunge's ontology [8, 9]. In the parallelogram, two other notions are added, namely *type* and *class*. A *type* is a generic concept or a *Universal* resulting from the conceptual classification usually defined by humans. A *class* is just a collection of objects. All these notions are related in the *parallelogram*: a *concept* is an *instantiation* of a *type* and *refers* to a single *object*. A *type* defines by *extension* the *class* that contains the *objects* of that *type* or, on the other hand, the *objects* that *conform* to that *type*.

The parallelogram, named *the ontological parallelogram*, furnishes the basis of a new formal world ontology used in EO, the WSOL described in Sect. 2.2.

3.3 Human Relativism and Semiotics

Human Relativism gives another perspective of the semiotic sign by relating signs and the human element. Sign materiality, studied in semiotics, can be seen through the *observability* concept mentioned before. A combined Human/Material view of the sign is presented in [17] and reproduced in Fig. 3, according to the human relativistic stance. This view allows us to separate material or objective things, that are *observable*, from mental concepts inside the human element. The circle in these figures represent the human element (the **H** label) and outside the circle are the observable things subtracted from interpretation or meaning. Type a) refer to an *observable representation* such as a written or spoken word or any other physical entity as, for example, the word "tree". Type b) does not have an observable representation but an observable object. This is the case of the "tree" concept generated by observing a real tree. The object turns to be a representation of a general "tree" concept. It could be also a mind representation of a real object that is not currently observed. Both cases are not seen as useful as the considered representation is not observable. Type c) shows both the object and its representation as observable. This is the case of great part of physical or material things, understood as representations or not, that can exist as observable without attached meaning. Type d) is a pure mental sign only useful when it is turned to an observable representation.

4 Precision and Its Role in Information Systems

Ontology and ontologies presented in Sect. 2 can be used to represent reality but reality representation is mostly expressed by language where observability and interpretation play a central role. In this chapter, we present and discuss the concept of *precision* and its role in language. There is a need for *higher precision* in Information Systems that is discussed together with some guidelines to achieve it.

4.1 Precision and Human Relativism

HR defines *precision* as the understanding of an element without ambiguity. In information systems (IS), this element often take the form of a word or words used to describe and to model those IS. Also, data – referred as *information* – that is collected, stored, processed and retrieved in IS uses words as their elements.

Precision should be understood as a continuous from *low precision* to *high precision*. Ideally, an element or term understood the same way by all the people would have the highest degree of precision.

The *observability* concept of HR is a way to achieve precision. Everything that is *observable* is *precise* but the opposite is not true. In fact, mathematical concepts, such as numbers, are understood as precise but not directly observable. We only have access to mathematical representations in form of symbols that do not have meaning unless there is interpretation by an individual. In order to model, to engineer and to deliver correct computerized information systems we need *precision* as it is required and used by other traditional engineering disciplines such as mechanics or electronics. Our computerized information systems rely on language, written language appears in interfaces, programming languages, database schemas among other places. Those embodied languages are always ultimately connected to people that extracts meaning from them. Before meaning is extracted, computers just store and process data in form of words, numbers, sounds, images or video, that are observable representations, according to HR. The problem of meaning is that it is extracted from human interpretation of those representations. Interpretation is a form of human behaviour that should be seen as introducing unpredictability. For example, we can store in a database the details of a book such as the author, the price, the dimensions, if it is big or small and a picture of it. What links these details to reality? In fact the physical/material book may have observable (printed) representations of the author or the price. In this case, these observable details can be extracted automatically using engineered tools and processes. A vision system with automatic optical character recognition could be used. However, neither price or author are physical properties of the book and may be unprecise. On the other hand, dimensions can be extracted by measuring the book, this will result in precise information. Physical measurement is another way to achieve precision. Regarding the big/small property of the book. This is imprecise, relative to human qualitative interpretation unless there is a rule to determine it.

HR states that "to have a high degree of precision means to have a reduced level of ambiguity and different meanings in some term or element making it generally accepted, recognised and shared". This does not mean to make everyone agree on it based on negotiation as in the case of constructivism. The solution goes by adopting a kind of operational meaning or human observable independence that makes it clear and precise. Human observable independence is achieved if everyone is able to interpret in the apparently same way. It may be necessary to have previous knowledge to reach this shared and accepted interpretation. One way of achieving precision already invented by humans is the use of physical measurement. It is simple to say, to be precise, if a specific string has or has not one meter of length, spite some possible minor measure inaccuracies. Some people could argue about this but without relevance for scientific purposes where a measuring instrument would reveal a sufficiently *precise* measurement value that would be used without ambiguities.

If we could measure the precision degree of each term used in IS we would be able to assign each one a different value. Surely the elements analysed and used by science, the physical things less correlated with human interpretation would achieve the higher degree of precision. Concepts, in general, are difficult to be precise; they are the result of human creation and therefore very much human dependent. Consequently, they have to be treated with special attention in order to make them or to select them as precise as possible.

So, an important Human Relativistic Hypothesis is:

> By adopting observable elements or high precision elements under a human relativistic view it is possible to derive a scientific and theoretical well founded approach to IS [1].

4.2 Analysing Ontologies

All the ontologies analysed in Sect. 2 seek to add precision to information systems by adopting a formal view. Still, they base *precision* on concepts and relations, most of the time not observable. Moreover, they use language, a source of imprecisions, as their modelling constructs. Practice of defining ontologies show us how ambiguity makes difficult to create *shared* formal definitions. Still, all these formal approaches claim to remove ambiguity by analysing the graph of concepts and relations created. A practical example of this is the promise of a *semantic web* [18]. However, formal ontologies and the semantic web are used in a small part of developed information systems.

4.3 Precision in NOMIS

Human Relativism uses the *observability* concept to assure a sufficient degree of precision in information systems. The Normative Approach for Modelling Information Systems (NOMIS) described in [2] adopted HR by using a human-observable-action centred perspective of information systems. Human *observable* actions are less prone to ambiguity because they are observable making easy to obtain a shared understanding as will be the case for any other physical element. Another distinctive solution proposed by NOMIS is the way it models "information". It defines a proper view for *information items* where there is a distinction between observable or material information and not-observable information. In the example of a book mentioned before, dimension and physical properties of a book are acknowledge as regular or *observable* properties and the price is an *informational* property. Also, a flexible database schema is proposed for dealing with change and imprecision. In this schema, table names, fields are identified univocally by using a global unique identifier. For example, a specific team modelled as a group of people can change the name, their members and be the same team as it is identified univocally. Also, the structure of an element can have different forms. For instance, an "address" can be described in detail so it can be reached in a big city or have a simpler description for a country site location. This *description* is stored with different fields in a database, not obeying to a static schema.

4.4 Towards Precision in Information Systems

Achieving precision and removing ambiguity is an aim if we want to have a formal development of computer systems and a real engineering discipline of software engineering. Observable elements allows us to remove ambiguities but are not unique for achieving precision. HR proposes also the use of measuring instruments to extract quantitative information as a source for high precision. Still, we propose other ways to achieve precision. Starting with language, we may analyse each term and assign different degrees of precision to each one. A term used to identify an observable individual item is usually highly precise. The observable element can be used for disambiguation purposes. Terms used to conceptualize sets of observable individual items have a second order in a ranking of precision. As an example, we can have a particular tree identified by a unique name, and the concept of *tree* taken for a set of trees, although less precise has also a high degree of precision. If a term is used to characterize a particular property of an observable element, we have to understand if the property is itself observable and, therefore with high precision or just informational. This is the case of the dimensions of a book or its price, respectively.

Besides terms, there is a need to formalize relations between terms. Ontological dependency can be used as a formal relation. Formal ontologies, define these relations as propositions using first-order logics. However, these relations specified with language may introduce some ambiguity. Also relations require precision. Typical compositional relations as part-whole relationships of observable elements are on the top of precision level. Hierarchical relationships, on the other hand, may introduce imprecision in the way branches are derived. For example, a motor inside a car is more precise that an ostrich as a bird as an animal. In this last case, we may understand a bird as a flying animal which is not the case of an ostrich. Other types of relations require further analysis.

In summary, we propose further research in precision by analysing language, its words and phrases, as atoms and molecules of a new physics under the observable view introduced by human relativism.

5 Conclusions

In this position paper, we discussed the notion of *precision* assumed as required for a proper *engineering* of information systems. The ambiguity issues raised by the use of language were analysed in the perspective of semiotics as understood by different theories. Also, the need of understanding reality in order to properly model and develop computer systems is described and emphasized. Different guidelines and examples are suggested to achieve precision in information systems.

References

1. Cordeiro, J., Filipe, J., Liu, K.: Towards a human oriented approach to information systems development. In: Proceedings of the 3rd International Workshop on Enterprise Systems and Technology (2009)
2. Cordeiro, J.: Normative Approach to Information Systems Modelling. PhD Thesis. The University of Reading, UK (2011)
3. Dietz, J.: Enterprise Ontology, Theory and Methodology. Springer-Verlag, Berlin, Heidelberg (2006)
4. Winograd, T., Flores, F.: Understanding Computers and Cognition. Ablex Publishing Corporation, Norwood, NJ, USA (1986)
5. Dietz, J.L.G.: A world ontology specification language. In: Meersman, R., Tari, Z., Herrero, P. (eds) On the Move to Meaningful Internet Systems 2005: OTM 2005 Workshops. OTM 2005. Lecture Notes in Computer Science, vol. 3762, pp. 688–699. Springer, Heidelberg (2005). https://doi.org/10.1007/11575863_88
6. Halpin, T.: Information Modeling and Relational Databases. Morgan Kaufmann, San Francisco (2001)
7. Wand, Y., Weber, R.: On the ontological expressiveness of information systems analysis and design grammars. Inf. Syst. J. 3(4), 217–237 (1993)
8. Bunge, M.: Treatise on Basic Philosophy, vol. 3. Ontology I: The Furniture of the World. D. Reidel Publishing Company, Dordrecht, The Netherlands (1977)
9. Bunge, M.: Treatise on Basic Philosophy, vol. 4. Ontology II: A World of Systems. D. Reidel Publishing Company, Dordrecht, The Netherlands (1979)
10. Rosemann, M., Green, P.: Developing a meta model for the bunge–wand–weber ontological constructs. Inf. Syst. 27(2), 75–91 (2002)
11. Studer, R., Benjamins, V.R., Fensel, D.: Knowledge engineering: principles and methods. Data Knowl. Eng. 25(1–2), 161–197 (1998)
12. Guarino, N., Oberle, D., Staab, S.: What is an ontology? In: Staab, S., Studer, R. (eds) Handbook on Ontologies. International Handbooks on Information Systems, pp. 1–17. Springer, Berlin, Heidelberg (2009). https://doi.org/10.1007/978-3-540-92673-3_0
13. de Saussure, F.: Course in General Linguistics. Roy Harris (translator). Duckworth, London (1983). [1916]
14. Peirce, C.S.: Collected Writings, vol. 8. In: Hartshorne, C., Weiss, P., Burks, A. (eds). Harvard University Press, Cambridge, MA (1931–58)
15. Silverman, E.: The Subject of Semiotics. Oxford University Press, New York (1983)
16. Eco, U.: Segno. ISEDI, Instituto Editoriale Internazionale, Milao, Italia (1973)
17. Cordeiro, J., Filipe, J.: The semiotic pentagram framework--a perspective on the use of semiotics within organisational semiotics. In: Proceedings of the 7th International Workshop on Organisational Semiotics (2004)
18. Antoniou, G., Van Harmelen, F.: A Semantic Web Primer. MIT press, Cambridge (2004)

Digital Transformation: Current Challenges and Future Perspectives

Ivan I. Ivanov[✉]

Empire State College of the State University of New York, Selden, NY 11784, USA
ivan.ivanov@esc.edu

Abstract. We observe increasing needs for remote collaboration, inspired by corresponding technical and technological possibilities. This was further justified during the COVID-19 pandemic when most businesses went on-line. Many positive effects of the Digital Transformation were seen in this period, but also a number of new challenges popped up. This paper is based on previous research featuring Digital Transformation and it is extended towards explicitly considering particular challenges that pose societal relevance. There are three main contributions of this paper. First, a modified model is created and presented as evolution of the enhanced socio-technical system to better describe the prospects and challenges associated with platform technologies and digital driven transformations. The second contribution is a systematic review of recent publications on digital driven transformations, and five key points and four crucial steps are suggested to be intended with digital transformations. Third, three examples are considered to support the author's claims. Those examples have to do with domains of high relevance, namely: (i) Education; (ii) Health Care; (iii) Finance-banking.

Keywords: Digital transformation · Digital platform · Telehealth · Extended socio-technical system model · SMACIT

1 Introduction

We observe increasing needs for remote working and e-collaborations, inspired by corresponding technical and technological possibilities. This was further justified during the COVID-19 pandemic when most businesses were forced to transform their fully on-site work to a blend of fully remote or hybrid operations. Many positive effects of the digital transformation were seen in this period, but also a number of new challenges popped up. Digital technologies have been challenging the traditional boundaries of firms and global corporations as rapidly evolving digital platforms have enabled clusters of businesses to form and flourish in any geographic areas.

This paper is based on previous research featuring enhance socio-technical system model and digital transformations, and it is extend towards explicitly considering particular challenges that pose societal relevance. As it will be discussed later in this paper, there are three main contributions of this paper. First, a modified model is created and presented as evolution of the enhanced socio-technical system to better describe the

© Springer Nature Switzerland AG 2021
B. Shishkov (Ed.): BMSD 2021, LNBIP 422, pp. 275–285, 2021.
https://doi.org/10.1007/978-3-030-79976-2_16

prospects and challenges associated with platform technologies and digital driven transformations. The second contribution is a systematic review of recent publications on digital transformations to present a comprehensive picture of existing and the adopted processes. In addition, five key points and four crucial steps are suggested to be intended with digital transformation. Third, three examples are considered to support the author's claims. Those examples concern domains of high relevance, namely: (i) Education; (ii) Health Care; (iii) Finance - banking.

The remaining of the current paper is structured as follows: Sect. 2 presents background information. Section 3 presents the claims and recommendations. In Sect. 4, three cases partially exemplify them. And in the end, Sect. 5 concludes the paper.

2 Background

To explore the complexity of the problems inside organizations, and to avoid unrealistic expectations when aligning technologies and processes to the business strategy, a formal methodology of examining and evaluating technology capabilities in the organizational context should be applied. According McKeen, Smith and Singh [1], "capability is the ability to marshal resources to affect a predetermined outcome." The core digital technology capabilities are discussed later in the paper and they are critical to meet the enduring challenges of digital driven business strategy, designing and delivering digital services.

The contemporary Information Systems approaches incorporate multidisciplinary theories and perspectives with no dominance of a single discipline or model. Gabriele Picolli in his Information Systems for Managers text features IT as a critical component of a formal, sociotechnical information system designed to collect, process, store, and distribute information [2]. Kenneth and Jane Laudon in Managing Information Systems define Information Systems as Sociotechnical Systems incorporating two approaches: Technical and Behavioral, with several major disciplines that contribute knowledge and competency in the study of Information systems [3].

The notion of above definitions is based on the Sociotechnical theory work developed by Tavistock Institute in London in late fifties of the last century. The IS Sociotechnical approach not only visualizes the concept, but reveals the impact of new technologies and processes –the technical subsystem- on the entire organization system, and the dependencies and interactions between all other facets and components of the sociotechnical system. According to Picolli any organization Information System can be represented as a Sociotechnical system which comprises four primary components that must be balanced and work together to deliver the information processing and functionalities required by the organization to fulfill its information needs. The IS Sociotechnical model validates the most important components, and at the same time illustrates primary driving forces, within organizations: structure, people, process, and technology. The first two – people and structure – shape the social subsystem, and represent the human element of the IS. The latter two – process and technology – contour the technical subsystem of the IS and they relate to a wide range of technical resources and services intertwined with a series of steps to complete required business activities [4].

The sociotechnical system approach is instrumental in helping policy and decision makers to strategize and manage organizational change particularly when introducing and implementing new technologies. This approach not only validates the four critical components of the system's interdependency, but proves that none of them works in isolation. They all interact, are mutually dependent, and consequently are subject to "systemic effects" - defined as any change in one component affecting all other components of the system. The process of changes and reciprocal adjustment of both technical and social subsystems should continue to interplay and growing closer until a mutually satisfying results are reached. However, the model in reality could not be with equal subsystems' changes. It should grow from micro to macro level to reflect crucial influences of the external environment, including regulatory requirements, social and customers' expectations, business trends, competitive pressures, and to some extend - interoperability of the platforms and systems within associated institutions.

To understand the prospects and challenges associated with the digital driven business strategy and operational transformations, a modified model of the socio-technical system is created and presented at Fig. 1. The figure depicts at macro level how digital technologies and utility type computing platforms act as drivers for supporting digital business strategies and advancing with the customers. While it simplifies the relations of the internal organization socio-technical model with the external world, the enhanced socio-technical model indicates the interactions of the four organization's forces: structure, people, technology and processes with the platform technologies such as SMACIT and further with the crowds.

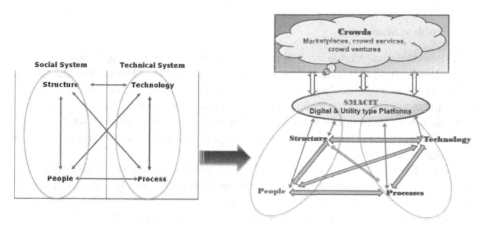

Fig. 1. The evolution of the Socio-Technical System

While in-house technologies and infrastructure are important to handling the internal systems and external integration, the critical differentiation and advantage in creation and revenue growth can be achieved by adopting new technological reality that increasingly revolves around digital platforms. The core technologies of these platforms are not only enablers of efficiency, but has led to what Gartner called the Nexus of Forces. The immediate effects can lead to competitive intelligence, holistic innovation, process and capacity optimization. The outcomes would include new business designs by blurring the physical and digital worlds and becoming an active performer of a dynamic ecosystem of values. This ecosystem connects digital resources inside and outside the company to create new services and value to customers targeting and making the most of the digital platforms and the crowds [5]. Important consideration here is the fact that Social and Technical subsystems will be spreaded beyond organization's realm and will blend with the digital platform of the utility provider(s) and such mixtures even with an existing SLA could be problematic in critical or political intense times.

From customers' experience the value they would gain through the new channels and platforms should come first from disproportionate market shares versus direct and indirect alternatives. A growing number of new and existing companies are shaping their business operations to create or gain value using crowds. New crowd business models such as marketplace, crowd platform and processes, content & product markets, crowd ventures, crowd services are emerged differentiating themselves how resources are brought together to create monetizable value [6]. The extended value for the businesses will be the interactive communications and immediate feedback from the customers and their demand and expectations about the provided products or services.

3   Claims and Recommendations

In this section, we make several claims featuring a problem statement and we give a list of recommendations featuring a solution direction.

3.1   Problem Statement

In the current digital economy, rapid pace of change in technology capabilities and customer desires entail that business strategy must be fluid and the business design should enable a company to quickly pivot in response to new competitive threats and opportunities. In companies that are designed for digital operations people, processes, data, and technology are synchronized to identify and deliver innovative customer solutions, and redefine strategy, thus digital design, not strategy, is what separates winners from losers in the digital economy.

In the digital driven transformations, digital technologies unquestionably needs to serve as a platform for the business operations. The author of Driving Digital, Issac Sacolick defined precisely "Digital Transformation is not just about technology and its implementation. It's about looking at the business strategy through the lens of technical capabilities and how that changes how you are operating and generating revenues [7]. The globally recognized digital expert David L. Rogers argues that digital transformation is not about updating your technology, but about upgrading your strategic thinking. In his book: The Digital Transformation Playbook, Rogers shows why traditional businesses need to rethink their underlying assumptions in five domains of strategy—customers, competition, data, innovation, and value. He reveals how to harness customer networks, platforms, big data, rapid experimentation, and disruptive business models—and how to integrate these into your existing business and organization [8]. While many authors offer advice for digital start-ups, Rogers distills the lessons of today's greatest digital innovators and makes them usable how legacy businesses can transform to thrive in the digital age. The author emphisizes that digital transformation is about a strategy aiming developing organizational agility to successfully keep up with fast-paced evolution of digital age.

In the Design for Digital: How to Architect Your Business for Sustained Success (Management on the Cutting Edge) Ross, Beath and Mocker encapsulate that "Digital technologies are game changing because they deliver three capabilities: ubiquitous data, unlimited connectivity, and massive processing power ... [for] develop[ing] new offerings to help solve customer problems." The authors distinguish between 'digitization of a company" versus "new digital offerings," and speak about how businesses need to give much attention to the five building blocks of digital transformation success: shared customer insights, operational backbone, digital platform, accountability framework, and external developer platform [9]. They stress that "the digital journey is long, people take time to embrace, and adapt to new ways of working," and in addition the efforts involve "... more fundamental organizational change than simply adopting Agile methodologies."

In Driving Digital Strategy, Harvard Business School professor Sunil Gupta provides an actionable framework for fundamentally change the core of any business and ensure that the digital strategy touches all aspects of the organization: the business model, the value chain, the customer relationships, and the company culture. The challenge is straddling the technology and operations side along with the change management implications. Often these pivot points are areas of huge resistance. Often mature companies are riddled with complacency and refusing to acknowledge failing business models. The speed at which business models are reinvented now requires that companies implement digital strategies and change their mindset to act quickly or get disrupted in the current marketplace. The speed of this shift is staggering and understanding this dynamic in the context of the way the current business environment works is crucial. Sunil has effectively simplified the process and outlined a roadmap that works as a sort of framework to assist in this process: (a) Reimagining your business (Scope, Business Model, Platform); (b) Reevaluating your value chain (R&D, Operations, Omnichannel); (c) Reconnecting with customers (Acquiring, Engaging, Measuring); (d) Rebuilding your organization (Transition, Organization Design, Skills/Talent) [10]. The provided simple and comprehensive framework for reinventing business operations is comprehensive, actionable, insightful and immediately applicable irrespective of industry or organization.

We could summarize the appeal and needs of digital transformation from the above readings and beyond observations to following key points:

- The combination of disruptive technologies: SMACIT and artificial intelligence are dramatically changing the way businesses compete.
- The smooth rate of change implied by Moore's law doesn't capture today's upheaval, in reality, since 2000, 52% of the Fortune 500 companies have been acquired or gone out of business.
- To survive, most companies will have to make revolutionary digital transformation changes toward key corporate processes.
- Large companies can turn their existing data into a competitive advantage to deter new entrants and stimulate digital transformation.
- Thanks to digital transformation, the productivity improvements can be enormous. According Thomas Siebel, author of Digital Transformation: Survive and Trive in an

Era of Mass Extinction, John Deere estimates it will save over $100 million per year using AI to optimize its inventory, 3M hopes to save over $500 million per year from its AI applications, and the U.S. Air Force has significantly increased mission-capable readiness by applying AI to predict the need for unscheduled aircraft maintenance [11].

3.2 Recommendations

Ultimately, digital transformation is a product of strategy, technology, culture and leadership and it is a journey that iterates towards organization's digital future. For new and existing businesses it requires automating operations, generating revenue by leveraging digital capabilities, enabling new product offerings, providing new convenience and value to customers [12].

We consider, a company first needs to have a vision for what they want to do (business strategy), and then to think over how technology can help to create a platform to accomplish the vision, and later to execute digital transformation for achieving progress and profit. The following key steps should be aimed with the digital transformation:

- Improving the effectiveness of your employees - retaining and recruiting talents, providing flexible and stimulating work environment
- Streamlining key processes – focusing on platform technologies
- Increasing customer satisfaction – harnessing customer networks
- Focusing on value proposition evolution and how to reduce risk in emerging critical situations

4   Examples

In this section we illustrate our claims/recommendations using simplified descriptions featuring Digital Transformation. We will illustrating with three examples from three different industries –education, healthcare and banking- how different companies, are bringing together specific requirements to their digital driven strategies' to achieve a sustainable success even in a critical period such as COVID-19 pandemic lockdowns.

4.1   The Education Perspective

The first case is about a comprehensive state college in the USA with 30+ offices spread across the state and serving annually 20K+ undergraduate and graduate students. The college is a recognized leader in the USA for delivering hybrid modes of educational services -online and individualized courses, virtual and onsite residencies and study groups, individualized academic planning and mentoring- for primarily working adults returning to school. The college community – faculty, professionals, support personal and the administration- is well trained and savvy with large variety of online college systems and IT applications. Most of the educational systems and applications including the online Learning Management Systems (LMS) are web-based and accessible remotely; however some administrative and financial systems are available only through the college intranet – from the office computers or Citrix server access. The e-collaborative tools such as Skype for Business, Zoom and GoToMeeting were widely utilized prior COVID pandemic for academic, administrative and teaching events.

In order to support its educational services and to remain on leading position during the critical COVID-19 lockdowns since March 2020, the college has implemented swiftly massive digital transformations to all educational related systems to have web-based interface and remote access. The college IT has unified the MS Team as a tool for virtual meetings and teaching remotely individualized courses. The administration and the IT professionals supported all faculties to obtain new fully managed laptops or to take home their office computers, and to transfer and use the college phone numbers with the Voice over IP Mitel systems from their homes. Special attention has been taken for improving accessibilities to students' online support systems, apps and services. In addition to 1 Stop Student Services, several online tools for success such as: help writing with sources, creating thesis and building arguments, help with graphics and extended library support including library workshops and research skills tutorials. Variety of free tutoring services have been made available onsite, online and by phone with learning coaches assisting with writing assignments, study skills, time management and tutoring in math, statistics, and accounting.

The above listed quick transformations allow the college successfully to provide the educational and administrative services remotely and to complete smoothly the academic 2019/2020 year and to run the entire 2020/2021 AY at a distance. While the faculty and some professionals expressed concerns of extended workdays and blurring the workhours beyond weekdays, the students' satisfaction and course & degree completions were in the similar level compering to pre-COVID academic years. The college succeeded to keep the student retention and enrolment in the same range of previous academic years while most of the regional colleges experienced average drop of 17% in their students in the last two academic years.

4.2 The Healthcare Perspective

The second example is about a large healthcare system (80K+ employees) with hospitals, clinics and private doctors' practices in several states and centralized administrative scheduling and billing systems. A year prior the COVID-19 lockdowns, the central administrative and billing offices experimented some digital transformations to allow most of the professionals to work remotely in case of some natural disaster periods: heavy snow storms, hurricanes, blackouts, etc. They started the experiment with allowing initially working remotely on Fridays. Later, since September 2019 – they experimented half of them to work remotely on even days, the other half to be in the offices and they rotated on the odd days. They kept track of the workhours with an online registration and time-scheduling sign-in system. After three months the entire experiment has been reported as very successful and overall results demonstrated increased first productivity.

When the first COVID-19 lockdown started on March 9, 2020 all professionals and administration from the central billing offices started to work from home – they have company's managed laptops and docking stations set up for remote communications with additional smart phone Authenticator app embedded verification for login in the company VPN. In the next few weeks there were rapid transformations in the web-based testing and production systems, including the e-collaborative tool and the MS Team has been adopted for all everyday meetings and coordinating projects' discussions. The contracting teams and other internal end-users from patient registration/ scheduling and billing also use the same tool and applications.

Additionally doctors' practices although continuing to work primarily in the office started adopting Telehealth – online non-emergency doctor's visits for consultations, preparation for hospital admission, mental health, etc. Those virtual visits are mainly performed on mobile devices and were fully managed by the corporate IT and doctors' offices. Prior COVID-19 lockdowns, Telehealth practices have not been approved by the Healthcare insurance companies in the USA, but the COVID-19 pandemic changed this and now even the government healthcare plans accept and pay for these services, as furthermore they are less expensive than the in office visits.

As a result of these promptly digital transformations, some of them initiated and adopted in the pre-pandemic period, the central billing business analysts and IT professionals were able precisely to accomplish their job duties and to achieve remarkable performance and productivity and customer satisfaction. Working remotely, for many of those professionals provides greater flexibility with some family obligations especially with kids and senior family members in this critical situation, and most of them added voluntary more workhours to express their thankfulness.

4.3 The Finance-Banking Perspective

The last case exemplifies how a large US bank leading in online services, started timely some digital transformations prior the COVID-19 pandemic and this experience and expertise was a solid foundation for rapid digital transformations in the last moment before the full lockdown in early March, 2020. In late 2019, the Bank was running several software development projects for updating and transforming existing online banking systems and applications with several teams in their offices in major cities in the USA. To attract new and keep their talents, the Bank provided some flexibility for working one or two days a week from home not only for their employees but also for the contractors and the results were very positive as increasing productivity and running all activities on time and advance the scheduled due dates. To capitalize and save budget for expensive office space in downtown major cities, the Bank introduced flex-office space for majority of the developers and in late February run a stress-test for all systems and applications by asking all employees to work intensively two days from home to test how the systems could handle the load and to evaluate different security risks. The outcomes were positive and encouraging and the Bank was ready to run all development projects remotely since March 9, 2020 when the first COVID-19 lockdown was enforced.

Working with fully managed laptops remotely within only the US territory, a year and a half later the development teams successfully completed all projects on time or some of them few weeks earlier. All security setting and profiling was precisely controlled and periodically audit distantly from the dedicated IT professionals and the access to development tools, testing and production environments was strictly enforced based on the security profiles of the developers. The overall productivity and efficiency of all development and testing teams were beyond expectations, the employees and contractors were fully satisfied of the flexible distantly work, and the Bank consider to continue the recent remote working mode for longer period and reduce substantially the costly city offices.

5 Discussion and Conclusion

After analyzing the three cases and matching up them with the five key points and the four critical steps suggested to be anticipated within digital transformation process, the following important insights can be identified:

- The organizations with well scaled digital platforms as IT infrastructure, systems and applications are prepared to react quickly and align successfully their operations in critical situations and continue successfully their business operations.
- Normally in such organizations their professionals are IT savvy, well trained and flexible to adapt new technologies, tools and systems. According to McKensey survey from November 2020, after the pandemic hit, it took businesses and average of 10.5 days to increase remote working and/or collaboration vs. the 454 days the changes were expected to take if there were no pandemic. In the suggested cases the three organizations were even faster because of their readiness as infrastructure, web and cloud based systems and employees training.
- The leadership in the three cases were fully in compliance with the recent Gartner findings regarding accelerated digital business transformations in the wake of COVID-19 pandemic – Fig. 2. These cases concur the recent IDC conclusion related to digital and workforce transformations: *"Enterprises leading in digital transformation are significantly less vulnerable to the epidemic, while enterprises leading in work resources transformation have better ability of long-distance coordination and higher overall work efficiency."*

There are many considerations and challenging implications forced by the accelerated digital transformations because COVID-19 pandemic related Work from Home (WFH) experiment. From the provided cases the facts confirm there is no best model that can fit to all, however the companies with initially started digital transformations are in a better position and were ready to speed up digital transformation, to increase productivity (all three cases in education, healthcare and finance-banking), and advance in customer satisfaction (the education and healthcare cases). In addition, according to latest Fortune-Adobe CIO survey from April 2021, "it's another big year for tech investment ..." mostly focused on cybersecurity and privacy. All these challenges require yet more efforts and analyses on how to select the set of technologies and to boost the strategic business objectives to excel with digital transformations. The concept of modified socio-technical model, the summarized key point of digital transformation and the suggested recommendations, along with the three cases, should be helpful and provide a positive experience when dealing digital transformations.

Further work is planned in two directions: exploring some negative effects of digital transformations such as holding back innovation and offshoring white-collar jobs as unintended consequence of the pandemic and WFH experimentation; and the business point of view of the effects of digital transformations on organizations' strategy and the raise of the hybrid remote-work model post-pandemic.

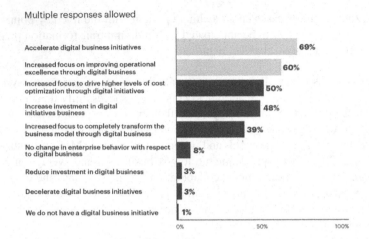

Seven in 10 boards of directors have accelerated digital business initiatives in the wake of COVID-19 disruption

Impact of COVID-19 disruptions on organizations' digital business initiatives

gartner.com/SmarterWithGartner

Fig. 2. Accelerated Digital Transformations because of COVID-19 disruption [13]

References

1. McKeen, J., Smith, H., Singh, S.: A framework for enhancing IT capabilities communications of the association for information systems, **15**, Article 36 (2005)
2. Picolli, G.: Information Systems for Managers: Text and Cases. Wiley, Hoboken (2012)
3. Laudon, K., Laudon, J.: Management Information Systems: Managing the Digital Firm. Pearson Education, Upper Saddle River (2016)
4. Ivanov, I.: Exploring business - IT nexus: make the most of IT-enabled capabilities. In: Shishkov, B. (ed.) BMSD 2015. LNBIP, vol. 257, pp. 152–170. Springer, Cham (2015). https://doi.org/10.1007/978-3-319-40512-4_9
5. Bartlam, M., Day A.: Digital Transformation in Financial Services, DLA Piper Global (2019). https://www.dlapiper.com/fsdigitaltransformation/
6. Dawson, R., Bynghall, S.: Getting results from crowds. Advanced Human Technologies Incl. (2012)
7. Sacolick, I.: Driving Digital – The Leader's Guide to Business Transformation through Technology, Amacom, American Management Association, New York (2018)
8. Rogers, D.: Digital Transformation Playbook: Rethink Your Business for the Digital Age. Columbia Business School Publishing, New York (2016)
9. Ross, J., Beath, C., Mocker, M.: Designed for Digital: How to Architect Your Business For Sustained Success. The MIT Press, Cambridge (2019)
10. Gupta, S.: Driving Digital Strategy: A Guide to Reimaging Your Business. Harvard Business Review Press, Brighton (2018)
11. Siebel, T.: Digital Transformation: Survive and Thrive in an Era of Mass Extinction. Rosetta Books, New York (2019)

12. Ivanov, I.: Chasing the crowd: digital transformations and the digital driven system design paradigm. In: Shishkov, B. (ed.) BMSD 2019. LNBIP, vol. 356, pp. 64–80. Springer, Cham (2019). https://doi.org/10.1007/978-3-030-24854-3_5
13. Goasduff, L.: COVID-19 Accelerates digital strategy initiatives, smarter with gartner. https://www.gartner.com/smarterwithgartner/covid-19-accelerates-digital-strategy-initiatives/

Conceptual Model of the Ecosystem Value Balance

Krista Sorri[1]([✉]) [iD], Katariina Yrjönkoski[2] [iD], and Linnea Harala[3] [iD]

[1] Unit of Information and Knowledge Management, Tampere University, Pohjoisranta 11, 28100 Pori, Finland
krista.sorri@tuni.fi
[2] Innovation Services and Partnerships, Tampere University, Korkeakoulunkatu 7, 33720 Tampere, Finland
[3] Unit of Industrial Engineering and Management, Tampere University, Korkeakoulunkatu 7, 33720 Tampere, Finland

Abstract. Despite the growing interest in ecosystems, research on ecosystem-level value distribution is still scant. Value creation and different value dimensions have a relatively wide knowledge base in the context of dyadic relationships and networks. However, the existing ecosystem literature does not recognize these dimensions at the ecosystem level. This article proposes an initial framework for assessing the value, particularly at the ecosystem level. Furthermore, the majority of the existing literature focuses merely on financial and functional values. This framework denotes also social, emotional, and epistemic dimensions of value. The framework is built as a constructive process. This study presents a theoretically founded iterative design phase followed by the first empirical test with one case ecosystem. The findings indicate the value balance exists in a case ecosystem, which is in a stable and established state. The article also proposes the next steps to develop the framework further. These include e.g. testing the framework with ecosystems, which are in more volatile phases (i.e. pioneering or renewal phase) and developing a measurement regime for evaluating the importance of each different value dimension.

Keywords: Ecosystem · Value · Value co-creation · Value balance

1 Introduction

Ecosystems, like any other complex systems, are difficult to design as they are open to the effects of their environments, and hence their behavior is difficult to understand and predict [1, 2]. The flows of resources, nor the value proposition, do not necessarily follow the intended design of the system when companies and people are interconnected and the business models of the companies may overlap [3]. Thus far, ecosystems do not have the tools to evaluate the quality of their value proposition nor the value balance on the ecosystem level.

For an ecosystem to be viable its' actors need to find the value sharing equitable and the effort they invest in value co-creation to be in balance with the value they can

© Springer Nature Switzerland AG 2021
B. Shishkov (Ed.): BMSD 2021, LNBIP 422, pp. 286–295, 2021.
https://doi.org/10.1007/978-3-030-79976-2_17

capture in the ecosystem [4]. Value co-creation refers to a principle where the customer participates in the value creation process together with the supplier [5, 6]. The co-created value should be sustainable and unique, and the co-creators should trust each other [7]. Innovating new business models based on co-created value propositions is an ecosystem-wide challenge requiring an understanding of the real-time and future needs of the actors [8].

Mutually shared value propositions have been found to be pivotal to the attractiveness of an ecosystem [9]. These value propositions are also the core elements of a success-ful business model [10], hence essential for the success of the ecosystem. However, frameworks for evaluating multilateral ecosystem-level value propositions require more scientific attention. For example, an ecosystem business model design tool, for describ-ing the distribution of financial value has been introduced [11]. The model, however, omits the other value dimensions. Also, there is a framework for the IoT ecosystems, where one of the categories used is 'benefits' [12]. The deficiency in this model is, it assumes value creation to be a one-way process. Consequently, it omits the ecosystems' fundamental principle of co-creation and mutual value sharing.

This study addresses the insufficient body of knowledge of evaluating the ecosystem level value proposition by proposing an initial framework for assessing an ecosystem level value balance. The framework is built through a constructive process, including the first empirical test with a case ecosystem.

The article begins by summarizing the theoretical background, followed by the description of the research method. Next, it presents the proposed framework and the case example. It concludes with a discussion chapter and the proposals for future research.

2 Theoretical Background

Designing the framework requires an understanding of ecosystems, the importance of value within the ecosystems, and the different dimensions of value. This section summarizes the theories of these concepts.

2.1 Ecosystem

This study follows the ecosystem definition where "ecosystems are groups of firms that must deal with either unique or super-modular complementarities that are non-generic, requiring the creation of a specific structure of relationships and alignment to create value" [13]. Ecosystem as a concept was first introduced by Moore when he coined a metaphor from ecology in the business context in the mid-1990s [14]. As in ecology, also in business, the actors of the ecosystem share their faith and their success relies on co-evolution and winning their rivals together [14]. Ecosystems consist of loosely interconnected [15], a multilateral and mutually consistent set of actors [16]. Ecosystems can either emerge non-predictively or be decisively designed, but in both situations, the core of the ecosystem is a value proposition [4].

The core of an ecosystem is the final value proposition, which can be co-created when all required complementary components are in place [17, 18]. During the past few years, scholars have been increasingly interested in value co-creation. However, this does not guarantee higher appropriation by the ecosystem actors [19]. Value is defined by the customer [8], i.e. the actors of the ecosystem the value is offered to.

2.2 Value

Value is the benefit one gains, compared to the sacrifice one needs to invest in the process [18]. Value is the desirability of a thing, often in respect of some property such as usefulness or exchangeability; worth, merit, or importance [20]. Valuation as such is a continuous process, not a single activity [21]. The values and preferences, along with financial resources and needs of the customer, perpetually affect their perception of the value [22], thus, it is essential to understand the customers' expectations – and in ecosystems, the understanding needs to be multilaterally on the ecosystem level. As 'being valuable' is a subjective and relative view measuring it scientifically accurately is difficult – if not impossible [17].

The current literature on value has focused on financial value, considering e.g. price as a primary driver of customer value (see e.g. [23]). Seems that thus far scholars have paid less attention to other value dimensions, like social and emotional value, particularly in multilateral ecosystem contexts. This omits e.g. the provably successful databased platform business models e.g. Google is using, where the users capture emotional, social, and epistemic value, the platform financial value, and the enterprise using the users' data captures epistemic, and potentially, financial value. Without one side, the others could not capture value.

There are five *value dimensions*: conditional, emotional, epistemic, functional, and social value [24]. The conditional value describes the alternative, which often depends on the situation. Typical conditional values are offered e.g. with seasonal products or services related to a certain situation like fairs. The emotional value actualizes when the customer experiences positive feelings like charity may cause. The epistemic value is based on the feeling of novelty or learning something new. Epistemic value includes all data, information, and knowledge-related aspects. For example, collaborative filtering offers an epistemic value. The functional value is a customers' valuation of the charac-teristics of the goods – including services. These perceptions include e.g. usability and availability of the service or quality of the good. Social value is addressed when the customer values to be identified into a group (or avert that). Being a part of a fan club is an example of social value. Financial value was added in 2005 to the dimensions [22]. It is impossible to explicitly list everything included in a certain value dimension but Table 1 includes examples [25–27] to clarify the diversity.

Some values may have more than one dimension. For example, co-design has social (interaction) and epistemic (new product or service) aspects.

In ecosystems, all its actors should participate in the co-creation of the value aiming to maximize the value for the ecosystem as a whole [4]. Compared to networked firms the target also is to share the value with all actors, not just maximize the value capture for the leader firm [4]. The actors are interdependent, which enables more value to the customer than none of the actors could offer alone [28].

Table 1. Examples of types of value per value dimension

Value dimension	Examples
Emotional	Motivation, risk reduction, sensory appeal, loyalty, wellness, nostalgia, aesthetics, fun/entertainment, self-actualization, badge value, cultural fit (e.g. ethics), stability, responsiveness, achievement, attention, fame, trust
Epistemic	Data, information, knowledge, novelty, learning, insight, innovativeness, transparency, interesting, collaborative filtering
Financial	Make money, reduce cost, increase brand value, gain investors
Functional	Time savings, simplicity, usability, convenience (reduce effort, avoid the hassle), quality, integration, security (e.g. data security), accessibility, customization, scalability, meeting specifications, flexibility, availability, durability
Social	Reference, interaction, sense of belonging, group identification, engagement, status, network expansion, reputation, social responsibility

3   Research Method

The research topic has both high practical relevance and theoretical interest. Therefore, this study was conducted as constructive research, which is one of the design-oriented research frameworks available and applicable particularly in the context of management science [29]. The seven-step procedure [30] was conducted as follows:

1) Finding a relevant problem:
   An ecosystem-level understanding of value distribution is insufficient. A tool for assessing the viability and sustainability of ecosystems is required.
2) Selecting the target organization
   An ecosystem led by Palpa (Suomen palautuspakkaus Oy) was selected, as it has sustained its viability. Therefore, it was able to demonstrate value co-creation and sharing on the ecosystem level.
3) Obtaining deep understanding
   A theoretical understanding of ecosystems and value was acquired by conducting a literature review. The review was based on a Scopus literature search (ecosystem AND "value proposition"), which gave 199 articles between 1987 and January 2021. A full-text review was conducted from the most recent ones backward in six-month sets. This was done to complete the review when new descriptions of the value propositions cease to emerge. In total, 57 articles were reviewed. The descriptions were classified into the dimensions identified from theories. There were no descriptions related to conditional value in the ecosystem context, hence it was not included in the framework.
4) Develop a construction
   The construction was developed in five iterations, based on three main constructs identified in prior literature: 1) values captured, 2) potential value, and 3) sacrifices needed in value creation. In addition, the construction was required to describe the value distribution across the ecosystem.

5) Implement and test the solution

The framework was tested with the packaging recycling ecosystem lead by Palpa Oy. The value propositions and sacrifices were collected through interviews [31] and publicly available information. The testing is described in more detail in Sect. 4.1.

Steps 6) Pondering the scope of applicability, and 7) theoretical contribution are elaborated in the Discussion and conclusions chapter.

4   Proposed Framework

The purpose of the framework is to elaborate on what kinds of value actors expect to have, what the other actors can offer, and are all expectations equitably met.

The framework demonstrates, have all actors been (and can they even be) satisfied with their value capture in the ecosystem. If an actor is making major investments in the value creation but receives only minute value, it is inclined to search for a more satisfactory ecosystem to join. On the other hand, if an actor captures value without a reasonable effort to value creation, it can be considered to be a "free-rider" and the ecosystem would not suffer from excluding it. The value potential is important information for the whole ecosystem [8] but especially for the ecosystem leader, as it helps to identify potential new actors to the ecosystem and, thus, improving the vitality and resilience of the ecosystem. An overview of the framework is presented in Fig. 1.

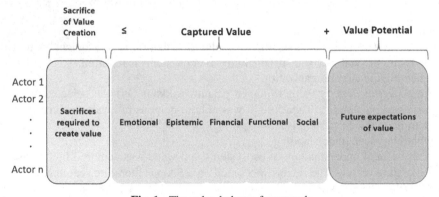

Fig. 1. The value balance framework

Each actor describes what they are investing in value creation, what value they capture, and what kind of value potential they see. The dimensions of value are included in the framework to emphasize the diversity of value.

Particularly, in the pioneering phase, mapping the value potential helps the ecosystem to find a viable value proposition. If the actors are listing plenty of new potential during the authority phase, the ecosystem leader can assume the ecosystem is approaching the final (i.e. renewal or death) phase.

4.1 Case Example

The proposed framework was applied to the ecosystem formed for the beverage package recycling in Finland to evaluate the balance of value creation and capture within this established circular economy ecosystem. The ecosystem consists of a wide variety of actors and organizations from multiple industries. The central actor for the ecosystem, Suomen Palautuspakkaus Oy (Palpa), was established in 1996, which can be seen as the beginning of the pioneering phase of the ecosystem.

It administrates and coordinates the operations within the recycling ecosystem and facilitates the collaboration between different actors. It is a non-profit company owned by the major brewery and retail companies. The ecosystem has reached one of the highest return rates (92% in 2016) in the world [32].

The value balance framework of the case ecosystem considering the different value dimensions is presented in Table 2. The table categorizes, by value dimensions, the benefits each actor of the ecosystem gains from participating in the ecosystem's activities.

As described in Table 2, all actors of the ecosystem participate in value creation and all of them also can capture value. Nearly all value expectations are met, which means the ecosystem is well in balance, as it should be as it was expected to be in the authority phase. This is also supported by the fact that the only retail chain outside the Palpa ecosystem had to join it (cans and glass bottles) due to customer pressure after few years of trying to manage its separate system. The comprehensiveness, high return rates, and efficient operations of the recycling system further validate our findings, which imply that the value balance of the studied ecosystem is adequate to enable long-term success for the ecosystem's operations. The value dimensions emphasize the social and emotional values, which are likely to stem from the ecosystem's circular economy-focused mission.

The financial value is often seen as increased revenue or increased efficiency. Palpas' case demonstrates that tax redemption can also be seen as an attractive value proposition, thus government can have a significant role in value creation.

The only new expectation, and identified potential to add value, comes from the consumers. They have proposed to develop the return system in a way, which enables giving the deposits to charity. The ecosystem has reacted to the demand. It has piloted with one nationwide charity community a donation raffle application included in the return vending machines. Also, in some retail stores, the consumers can donate the deposit receipt to a local association e.g. sports association or Scouts.

As expected, co-design was included in multiple value dimensions, hence it is likely to have more emphasis when evaluating the level of satisfaction of acting in an ecosystem.

Table 2. The value balance of the Finnish beverage package recycling system

Actor	Sacrifices in value creation	Captured value					Value potential
		Emotional	Epistemic	Financial	Functional	Social	
Palpa	Administration, deposit management, standardization, facilitation of collaboration	Achievement	Laws and regulations	The ecosystem finances the operation	Return container management, collecting and returning, developing and manufacturing the machines, logistics service, consumers returning the packages	Environmental impact, co-design	
Government	Beverage packaging tax					Environmental impact, employment impact	
Breweries	Recycling fees and return package management	Badge value, cultural fit, trust	Standardization	Beverage packaging tax exemption, cost reduction	Package returning and collecting	Environmental impact, brand	
Retailers	RVM investments, management of the return location and its customer experience, co-creation of RVMs	Cultural fit, trust		Potentially more revenue enabled by well-managed return locations	RVM maintenance	Reputation, social responsibility	
RVM manufacturers	Product development, manufacturing costs		Standardization Co-design	Revenue	Co-design	Co-design, reference, reputation, environmental impact	
Logistic provider	Logistic costs	Cultural fit	Standardization	Revenue			
Material processor	Process costs			Revenue	Raw material	Environmental impact	
Consumer	The effort of returning the deposit packages	Feeling of righteousness, cultural fit		Deposit	Convenience, availability	Environmental impact	Possibility to charity

5   Discussion and Conclusions

The framework strives to offer a clear picture of what kind of value is created and captured in the ecosystem. The case was assumed to be in the authority phase. This is supported by the balanced distribution of value. All actors participate in value creation and also capture value. These findings seem to confirm the original assumption. However, as the findings are based on a single real-world case, the results are mainly explorative. More real-world studies are needed to refine and validate the framework.

We identified four subjects for future research:

(1) *Delineating a measurement regime*
The initial framework does not yet demonstrate, how valuable each of the value propositions is. When discussing, how valuable something is, there are no clear nor right answers as "beauty is in the eye of the beholder". Nonetheless, more research is required to delineate a measurement regime for the value balance framework to be accurate.

(2) *Addressing the ecosystem value balance in different ecosystem life cycle phases*
The value proposition is more critical particularly on business ecosystems that are in pioneer and renewal phases in their life cycle [14]. In these life cycle phases, not only the current value but especially the potential value may have importance in attracting ecosystem actors. Hence, ecosystems in these life cycle phases would particularly benefit from a better understanding of the total value balance, and the distribution of current needs and expectations of ecosystems' potential. Future research should evaluate, how the value potential is addressed in less stable phases of the ecosystems.

(3) *Addressing the ecosystem value balance in more diverse ecosystem cases*
The importance of value dimensions is likely to vary in different ecosystems. The significance of different dimensions may be related e.g. to the ecosystem's mission and structure. Testing the proposed framework with more diverse cases is required in developing the model further.

(4) *Addressing the value balance change over time*
As valuation is a continuous process the balance is likely to change over time. Especially, when the ecosystem develops towards fulfilling the expected potential and new potential emerges. A longitudinal study is required.

These aspects will be addressed as a part of finalizing the constructive process initiated during this study.

In an optimal situation when the framework is finalized, it should provide also a practical one. For it to be used by the practitioners as an ecosystem design tool without a researchers' support a questionnaire, workshop concept, or other kinds of means to facilitate the application, needs to be designed.

References

1. Skyttner, L.: General Systems Theory: Problems, Perspectives, Practice, 2nd edn. World Scientific Publishing Company, Singapore (2006)

2. Tsujimoto, M., Kajikawa, Y., Tomita, J., Matsumoto, Y.: A review of the ecosystem concept—Towards coherent ecosystem design. Technol. Forecast. Soc. Change **136**, 49–58 (2018). https://doi.org/10.1016/j.techfore.2017.06.032

3. Langley, D.J., van Doorn, J., Ng, I.C.L., et al.: The internet of everything: smart things and their impact on business models. J. Bus. Res. **122**, 853–863 (2021). https://doi.org/10.1016/j.jbusres.2019.12.035

4. Li, J., Chen, L., Yi, J., et al.: Ecosystem-specific advantages in international digital commerce. J. Int. Bus. Stud. **9**, 1448–1463 (2019). https://doi.org/10.1057/s41267-019-00263-3

5. Lusch, R.F., Vargo, S.L.: Service-dominant logic: reactions, reflections and refinements. Mark Theory **6**, 281–288 (2006). https://doi.org/10.1177/1470593106066781

6. Vargo, S.L., Maglio, P.P., Akaka, M.A.: On value and value co-creation: a service systems and service logic perspective. Eur. Manag. J. **26**, 145–152 (2008). https://doi.org/10.1016/j.emj.2008.04.003

7. See-To, E.W.K., Ho, K.K.W.: Value co-creation and purchase intention in social network sites: the role of electronic word-of-mouth and trust - a theoretical analysis. Comput. Human Behav. **31**, 182–189 (2014). https://doi.org/10.1016/j.chb.2013.10.013

8. Matthyssens, P.: Reconceptualizing value innovation for Industry 4.0 and the Industrial Internet of Things. J. Bus. Ind. Mark. **34**, 1203–1209 (2019)

9. Schlecht, L., Schneider, S.: The joint value proposition of business ecosystems: a consumer's perspective. In: ISPIM Conference Proceedings, pp. 1–8 (2019)

10. Gassmann, O., Frankenberger, K., Csik, M.: The Business Model Navigator: 55 Models That Will Revolutionise Your Business, 1st edn. Pearson Education Limited, London (2014)

11. Bahari, N., Maniak, R., Fernandez, V.: Ecosystem business model design. In: XXIVe Conférence Internationale de Management Stratégique (2015)

12. Chan, H.C.Y.: Internet of things business models. J. Serv. Sci. Manag. **08**, 552–568 (2015). https://doi.org/10.4236/jssm.2015.84056

13. Jacobides, M.G., Cennamo, C., Gawer, A.: Towards a theory of ecosystems. Strateg. Manag. J. **39**, 2255–2276 (2018). https://doi.org/10.1002/smj.2904

14. Moore, J.F.: The Death of Competition: Leadership and Strategy in the Age of Business Ecosystems. Wiley, Hoboken (1996)

15. Iansiti, M., Levien, R.: Strategy as ecology. Harv. Bus. Rev. **82**, 68–78 (2004). https://doi.org/10.1108/eb025570

16. Adner, R.: Ecosystem as structure: an actionable construct for strategy. J. Manag. **43**, 39–58 (2017). https://doi.org/10.1177/0149206316678451

17. Den Ouden, E.: Innovation Design: Creating Value for People, Organizations and Society. Springer, London (2012). https://doi.org/10.1007/978-1-4471-2268-5

18. Polizzotto, L., Molella, A.: THE value balance. IEEE Eng. Manag. Rev. **47**, 24–31 (2019). https://doi.org/10.1109/EMR.2019.2948347

19. Hannah, D.P., Eisenhardt, K.M.: How firms navigate cooperation and competition in nascent ecosystems. Strateg. Manag. J. **39**(12), 3163–3192 (2018). https://doi.org/10.1002/smj.2750

20. Collins: Value—Definition of value by collins english dictionary. In: Collins English Dict (2021). https://www.collinsdictionary.com/dictionary/english/value. Accessed 20 Apr 2021

21. Stark, D.: The Sense of Dissonance. Princeton University Press, Princeton (2009)

22. Pura, M.: Linking perceived value and loyalty in location-based mobile services. Manag. Serv. Qual. **15**, 509–538 (2005). https://doi.org/10.1108/09604520510634005

23. Keränen, J.: Towards a broader value discourse: understanding sustainable and public value potential. J. Creat. Value **3**, 193–199 (2017). https://doi.org/10.1177/2394964317725449

24. Sheth, J.N., Newman, B.I., Gross, B.L.: Why we buy what we buy: a theory of consumption values. J. Bus.. Res. **22**, 159–170 (1991). https://doi.org/10.1016/0148-2963(91)90050-8

25. Almquist, E., Senior, J., Bloch, N.: The elements of value. Harv. Bus. Rev. **94**, 46–92 (2016)

26. Almquist, E., Cleghorn, J., Sherer, L.: The B2B elements of value. Harv. Bus. Rev. **96**, 72–81 (2018)
27. Parker, G., Van Alstyne, M., Choudary, S.P.: Platform Revolution: How Networked Markets are Transforming the Economy and How to Make them Work for You, 1st edn. W. W. Norton & Company Inc., New York (2016)
28. Adner, R.: Match your innovation strategy to your innovation ecosystem. Harv Bus Rev **84**, 98–107 (2006)
29. Piirainen, K.A., Gonzalez, R.A.: Constructive Synergy in design science research: a comparative analysis of design science research and the constructive research approach. Finnish J. Bus. Econ. **3**, 206–234 (2014)
30. Lukka, K.: The constructive research approach. In: Ojala, L., Hilmola, O.-P. (eds.) Case Study Research in Logistics. Turku School of Economics and Business Administration, Turku, pp. 83–101 (2003)
31. Harala, L.: Coopetition and Alignment in Circular Economy Ecosystems : Beverage Package Recycling System and Circular Economy Service Platform. Tampere University (2021)
32. Millette, S.: Deposit Systems for One-way Beverage Containers: Global Overview (2018)

Enterprise Architecture and Agility:
A Systematic Mapping Study

Hong Guo[1,2(✉)] ⓘD, Darja Smite[2,3] ⓘD, Jingyue Li[2] ⓘD, and Shang Gao[4] ⓘD

[1] Anhui University, No. 111 Jiulong Road, Hefei, China
[2] Norwegian University of Science and Technology, Trondheim, Norway
{hong.guo,darja.smite,jingyue.li}@ntnu.no
[3] Blekinge Institute of Technology, Karlskrona, Sweden
darja.smite@bth.se
[4] Örebro University, Örebro, Sweden
shang.gao@oru.se

Abstract. This article presents a systematic mapping study of published scientific papers on Enterprise Architecture (EA) and agility. More specifically, we reviewed studies on applying agile practices to EA and applying EA to the organization's agility. A categorical structure is proposed for classifying the research results based on the extracted topics discussed. The categories include agile traits (i.e., principles and practices), EA practices, and organizational contexts. By mapping the published works and analyzing them, the article also highlights some trends and indicates some obstacles and needs for future research and practice.

Keywords: Enterprise architecture · EA · Agility · Systematic mapping study

1 Introduction

In the field of Enterprise Architecture (EA), there is an ongoing discussion about the relationship between EA and Agility. On the one hand, EA was considered as an effective tool to bring agility to organizations [1, 2], and organizations are increasingly relying on the agility to "cope with rapid, relentless, and uncertain changes and thrive in a competitive environment of continually and unpredictably changing opportunities" [3]. On the other hand, researchers advocated that EA by itself should be agile [4, 5], as traditional frameworks-based EA is often "too rigid, and full-scale use requires quite a lot resources" [6] and "in some cases benefits of EA are unclear" [6].

Despite that some existing studies have also paid attention to these two perspectives [7, 8], there is no integrated and widely agreed understanding about how EA could be agile, and how EA could contribute to organizations' agility. This motivated present research. In this article, we use the definition of EA as "the fundamental organization of a system, embodied in its components, their relationships to each other and the environment, and the principles governing its design and evolution" [8] where an enterprise is viewed as a "system" [8]. We refer to an extended view of EA in this article. While a narrow view of EA is "specifically concerned with the level of an entire organization

© Springer Nature Switzerland AG 2021
B. Shishkov (Ed.): BMSD 2021, LNBIP 422, pp. 296–305, 2021.
https://doi.org/10.1007/978-3-030-79976-2_18

where business aspects are included," an extended view of EA also includes various architectural domains that EA (a narrow view) depends on such as Information Systems (IS) architecture and Information Technology (IT) architecture [9]. The main Research Questions (RQs) are:

RQ1: What has been studied to make EA agile?
RQ2: What has been studied to leverage EA to help organizations be agile?

2 Systematic Mapping Study Design

We used a **systematic mapping** method [10, 11] for the present study to provide a categorical structure and classify published scientific papers and results that have been published and indexed until December 2020. There are very few review studies relevant to the research questions [12–14], which are not systematic reviews and did not provide a full literature list. The most relevant study (i.e., [12]) is eight years ago and only covers agile EA management.

2.1 Searching and Screening

We searched one primary scientific database: SCOPUS, which claims to be the largest database of abstracts and citations [15]. Our keywords included "enterprise architecture" and "agile" or "agility." The overall searching string was as follows:

```
( TITLE-ABS-KEY ( agile OR agility ) AND TITLE-ABS-KEY ( "enterprise architecture" ) )
AND ( LIMIT-TO ( SRCTYPE,"p" ) OR LIMIT-TO ( SRCTYPE,"j" ) ) AND ( LIMIT-TO (
LANGUAGE,"English" ) ) AND ( EXCLUDE ( DOCTYPE,"cr" ) )
```

The screening process for inclusion was performed in several rounds. *First*, we excluded studies that are not published in peer-reviewed conferences or journals and not written in English. *Second*, based on abstracts, we filtered out all publications that were not related to the research questions. *Third*, based on the full text, we excluded those with no full text or did not contain comprehensive descriptions and clear propositions about the relations and implementations of the relations. Finally, we had **53** papers as primary studies to analyze.

2.2 Categorizing Scheme

To extract data, map existing studies, and answer the research questions, we performed a concept-centric review focusing on categories relevant to the research subjects. We considered the following categories [10] to classify included studies: Agile traits, EA practices, Organizational context.

With regard to the categorization of **the agile traits,** we first surveyed the existing conceptual and literature-review publications on agile (not included in the reviewed papers). However, we discovered that there was not a commonly agreed classification of agile traits. The most relevant framework might be [16]. But it was used to evaluate the degree of agility of software development methods, and thus too concrete and qualitative for our classification purpose for the agility of EA and organizations. We further examined two notable frameworks, which were mostly referred to: Dynamic System Development Method (DSDM) [17] and Manifesto for Agile Software Development (ASD) [18]. While the latter is generally recognized as the starting point for rising interest in agile methods, the former covers the entire project lifecycle (not only software development) and is thought to have helped formulate the Manifesto. Both theories define agile traits at two levels of abstraction.

To map the mentioning of agile traits in the EA studies, we used a *two-level framework* similar to the Manifesto and the DSDM. The first level summarizes higher-level, more abstract requirements and goals, referred to as *agile principles* as shown in Table 1 (with a prefix of "APri-"). In the second level, we enumerate more concrete *agile practices* (with a prefix of "APra-", as shown in Table 1) which in some way help fulfill the principles. As the two frameworks have different naming for similar practices, we combined those with similar meanings. As a result, we extracted 19 agile practices.

Table 1. Agile traits (principles and practices)

Principles	Practices
APri-1: Deliver *pragmatic* value (valuable and evaluable)	APra-1: Deliver valuable (products) APra-2: Deliver working (products) APra-3: Deliver early APra-4: Deliver frequently APra-5: User feedback
APri-2: Be lean (*reduce waste and cost* without compromising on *quality*)	APra-6: Never compromise quality APra-7: Simplicity APra-8: Reuse (building blocks) APra-9: Align projects to business goals APra-10: Develop iteratively APra-11: Build incrementally from firm foundations APra-12: Regularly reflects and adjusts APra-13: Demonstrate control APra-14: Maintain a constant pace indefinitely APra-15: Sustainable development
APri-3: Respond to *changes* (iteration and autonomy)	APra-16: Build projects around motivated individuals APra-17: Communicate continuously and clearly APra-18: Collaborate APra-19: Self-organizing teams

In order to categorize **EA practices**, we used the framework proposed in [9] where three main categories of EA research were defined. *EA Understanding* refers to architectural content, including key concepts like architectural building blocks, ther interdependencies, views and viewpoints, and reference architectures. *EA Modelling* refers to activities related to architectural models such as EA modelling languages, modeling tools, and modelling deliverables. *EA Management* refers to how EA is applied and managed including key concepts like development and implementation of architectures, their lifecycles and EA governance.

2.3 Data Analysis

The analysis of the included 53 studies started by mapping them to three groups according to their research focus, as shown in Table 2. For the group of "Agile EA" (left part of Table 2), the studies are focusing on how to make EA agile (RQ1). For the group of "EA for Agility" (right part of Table 2), the studies are focusing on how to leverage EA to make an organization agile (RQ2). For the group of "Agile EA for Agility," the studies covered both efforts. As a result, 16, 15, and 22 studies are included in these groups.

Table 2. Categorization of the studies by their focus on agility.

Agile EA (16)	Agile EA for agility (15)	EA for agility (22)
[6, 19–33]	[7, 34–47]	[2, 48–68]

3 Mapping Study Results

To demonstrate the timeliness of the 53 papers included in our study, we show the distribution of the papers by year of publication (see Fig. 1). Evidently, the majority of the articles are published in the recent six years.

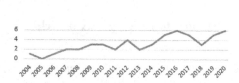 

Fig. 1. The distribution of included papers by the year of publication.

Fig. 2. (Agile EA) Mapping to agile principles.

3.1 Agile EA (RQ1: What has been Studied to Make EA Agile?)

For RQ1, we analyzed which *agile* traits (*i.e., principles and practices*) and which *EA practices* have been linked to making EA agile. As Fig. 2 shows, the most referred agile principle which is claimed to make EA agile is "Responding to changes," which was also recognized as the main trait of organizational agility [69]. The changes might arise from different channels such as development needs [20], requirements [28, 70], market demands [30], and circumstances [22]. In Fig. 3, we report the coverage of the agile practices among the included papers. Evidently, Alignment to business goals is the top category, which might need to be "end to end" [29] or bridging the gap between strategy and implementation [23]. The second most popular category is "Iterative development".

In Fig. 4, we see that more papers about EA understanding and management have been found than those about EA modeling. This indicates that issues relevant for EA are more social and organizational than technical.

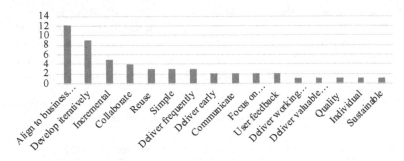

Fig. 3. (Agile EA) Mapping to agile practices.

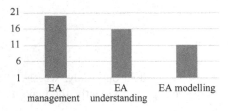

Fig. 4. (Agile EA) Mapping to EA practices.

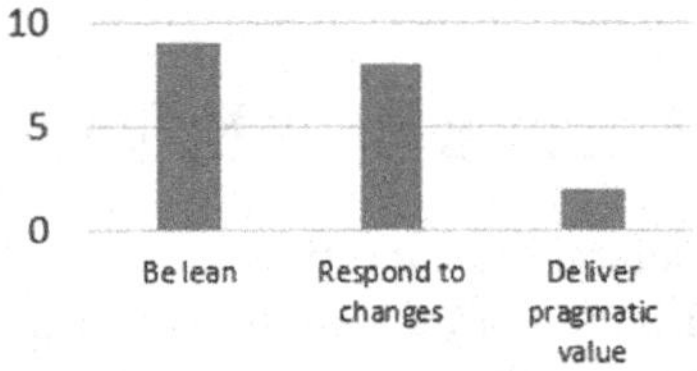

Fig. 5. (EA for Agility) Mapping to agile principles.

3.2 EA for Agility (RQ2: What has been Studied to Leverage EA to Help Organizations be Agile?)

For RQ2, we investigated "According to which *agile traits (principles and practices)*, have EA application contributed to making an organization agile?", "Which *EA practices* have been applied for this contribution?" and "What *organizational contexts* are relevant to the EA application?".

Regarding the agility traits employed by EA to contribute to organizational agility, most studies point out that EA helps organizations be lean and respond to change (See Fig. 5). A more detailed mapping (See Fig. 6) shows that most studies recognized that alignment is far the most important use of EA for improving organizational agility, often referred to as "business-IT alignment" [55]. But actually, alignment can be used to indicate more general relations between higher-level and lower-level components. While higher-level components can include strategies [49, 50, 59, 71], goals [52], or business [52, 62], lower-level components include executions [71], projects [50], (information) systems [59, 62] or IT [49, 52]. As described in [64], EA provides "the insight and overview necessary to guide the lower level agility in the right overall direction."

Similar to the papers in the Agile EA category, Fig. 7 shows that there are more studies discussing EA management and understanding than EA modeling. However, modeling aspects such as formal models [61] and how to model an enterprise ontology [60] were also thought of as important and raised.

As shown in Fig. 8, a number of studies addressed how to make EA work in an agile environment [7, 45, 52, 53], e.g., by using Scrum [54], large-scale agile development environment [40, 50, 51] and geographically distributed agile development [34]. In addition, several studies also discussed how EA could work with different architecture styles like SOA [23, 62, 63, 65, 66] and microservice[38, 39] to contribute to agility together.

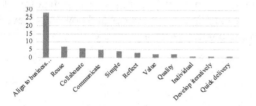

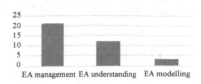

Fig. 6. (EA for Agility) Mapping to agile practices.   **Fig. 7.** (EA for Agility) Mapping to EA practices.

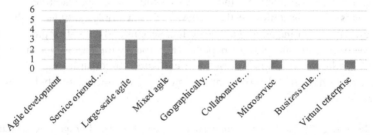

Fig. 8. (EA for Agility) Mapping to organizational contexts.

4 Discussion

According to the results, we see that over the past fifteen years, academia has continuously paid attention to the relation between EA and agility. We found the division between the questions of making EA agile and agility arising from the use of EA quite balanced in terms of contributions (16, 22, and 15 papers in each category).

What is most intriguing in our findings is the focus of the papers. The importance of both "Responding to change" and "Being lean" scored high when talking about *how to make EA agile* and *leveraging EA to achieve organizational agility*. This means that while EA helps organizations to respond to change (discussed in 8 papers) and being lean (discussed in 9 papers), it is important to improve EA processes themselves to better react to changes (discussed in 14 papers) and be leaner (discussed in 12 papers). The latter does confirm the heavy-weight reputation of EA processes.

A more detailed analysis shows that the majority of reviewed studies regarded alignment as the most significant value of EA in helping organizations become agile. We also see some recent **trends** indicating EA is required to be applied in an existing agile environment (small or large scale or mixed) and co-work with architectural styles like SOA and microservice. Another interesting finding is that EA practices relevant to management and understanding (social and organizational aspects) have drawn more attention than modeling (technical aspects). Finally, we identified several research **gaps**. According to the agile spirit, users' feedback is crucial as it is the key to receiving changes and knowing what value should be delivered. But few studies have addressed relevant traits such as "deliver pragmatic value," "deliver working (products)," "deliver early," and "deliver frequently" when considering how to make EA agile. Besides, alignment is commonly agreed to as the most important benefit EA brings to organizations to improve agility. But few studies clarified what alignment includes and how to achieve a cost-efficient alignment without compromising the necessary quality.

5 Conclusion

The goal of the present research is to review the directions and tendencies of existing studies on applying agile practices to EA and the role of EA in organizational agility. By performing a systematic mapping and analyzing the results, we identified some trends as well as gaps. One limitation of the review is that we only included highly relevant papers. We did not examine other *databases* than Scopus and did not employ *snowballing* to exhaustively include all relevant papers. Therefore, we plan to do a more inclusive review and synthesize relevant information extracted to construct more concrete and prescriptive guidelines to help companies achieve organizational agility by leveraging a more agile EA.

Acknowledgments. This research is financially supported by The European Research Consortium for Informatics and Mathematics (ERCIM) (https://www.ercim.eu/). This work has been partially supported by NFR 295920 IDUN.

References

1. Foorthuis, R., van Steenbergen, M., Brinkkemper, S., Bruls, W.A.G.: A theory building study of enterprise architecture practices and benefits. Inf. Syst. Front. **18**(3), 541–564 (2015). https://doi.org/10.1007/s10796-014-9542-1
2. Hazen, B.T., et al.: Enterprise architecture: a competence-based approach to achieving agility and firm performance. Int. J. Prod. Econ. **193**, 566–577 (2017)
3. Lu, Y., Ramamurthy, K.: Understanding the link between information technology capability and organizational agility: an empirical examination. MIS Q. 931–954 (2011)
4. Guo, H., Li, J., Gao, S.: Understanding challenges of applying enterprise architecture in public sectors: a technology acceptance perspective. In: 23rd EDOCW Workshop. IEEE (2019)

5. Guo, H., et al.: Agile enterprise architecture by leveraging use cases. In: Proceedings of the 16th MDI4SE Conference. SciTePress (2021)
6. Hosiaisluoma, E., et al.: Lean enterprise architecture method for value chain based development in public sector. In: 18th ECDG Conference (2018)
7. Hanschke, S., Ernsting, J., Kuchen, H.: Integrating agile software development and enterprise architecture management. In: 48th HICSS Conference. IEEE (2015)
8. ISO/IEC/IEEE: ISO / IEC / IEEE 42020:2019 (2019)
9. Gampfer, F., et al.: Past, current and future trends in enterprise architecture—A view beyond the horizon. Comput. Ind. **100**, 70–84 (2018)
10. Petersen, K., et al.: Systematic mapping studies in software engineering. In: 12th International Conference on Evaluation and Assessment in Software Engineering (EASE), vol. 12 (2008)
11. Petersen, K., Vakkalanka, S., Kuzniarz, L.: Guidelines for conducting systematic mapping studies in software engineering: an update. Inf. Softw. Technol. **64**, 1–18 (2015)
12. Hauder, M., et al.: Agile enterprise architecture management: an analysis on the application of agile principles. In: The 4th International Symposium on Business Modeling and Software Design (2014)
13. Canat, M., et al.: Enterprise architecture and agile development: friends or foes? In: 22nd EDOC Workshop. IEEE (2018)
14. Kaddoumi, T., Watfa, M.: A proposed agile enterprise architecture framework. In: Sixth International Conference on Innovative Computing Technology (INTECH). IEEE (2016)
15. Kitchenham, B., Charters, S.: Guidelines for performing systematic literature reviews in software engineering. Citeseer (2007)
16. Qumer, A., Henderson-Sellers, B.: An evaluation of the degree of agility in six agile methods and its applicability for method engineering. Inf. Softw. Technol. **50**(4), 280–295 (2008)
17. Stapleton, J.: DSDM, Dynamic Systems Development Method: The Method in Practice. Cambridge University Press, Cambridge (1997)
18. Beck, K., et al.: Manifesto for agile software development (2001)
19. Wissal, D., Karim, D., Laila, K.: Adaptive enterprise architecture: initiatives and criteria. In: 7th CoDIT Conference. IEEE (2020)
20. Daoudi, W., Doumi, K., Kjiri, L.: An approach for adaptive enterprise architecture. In: ICEIS, no. 2 (2020)
21. Polovina, S., von Rosing, M., Etzel, G.: Leading the practice in layered enterprise architecture. In: CEUR Workshop Proceedings. ceur-ws.org (2020)
22. Utz, W.: Design of a domain-specific metamodel for industrial business process management. In: 8th IIAI-AAI Congress. IEEE (2019)
23. Ni, F., Li, R.: Hierarchical iterative modeling approach for agile SOA. In: 2nd ITNEC Conference. IEEE (2017)
24. Noran, O., Turner, P., Bernus, P.: Towards a lightweight enterprise architecture approach for building transformational preparedness (2018)
25. Premchand, A., Sandhya, M., Sankar, S.: Roadmap for simplification of enterprise architecture at financial institutions. In: 2016 International Conference on Computation of Power, Energy Information and Communication (ICCPEIC). IEEE (2016)
26. Gill, A.Q.: Agile enterprise architecture modelling: evaluating the applicability and integration of six modelling standards. Inf. Softw. Technol. **67**, 196–206 (2015)
27. Jugel, D., Kehrer, S., Schweda, C.M., Zimmermann, A.: A Decision-Making Case for Collaborative Enterprise Architecture Engineering. Gesellschaft für Informatik eV (2015)
28. Ramos, H., Vasconcelos, A.: Extreme Enterprise Architecture Planning (XEAP) (2014)
29. Motta, G., Sacco, D., Barroero, T.: General enterprise framework (GEF). In: Proceedings of 2012 IEEE International Conference on Service Operations and Logistics, and Informatics. IEEE (2012)

30. Kim, H., Oussena, S.: A case study on modeling of complex event processing in enterprise architecture (2012)
31. Buckl, S., et al.: Towards an agile design of the enterprise architecture management function. In: 2011 IEEE 15th International Enterprise Distributed Object Computing Conference Workshops, pp. 322–329. IEEE (2011)
32. Song, H., Song, Y.-T.: Enterprise architecture institutionalization and assessment. In: 9th International Conference on Computer and Information Science. IEEE (2010)
33. Najafi, E., Baraani, A.: CEA framework: a service oriented enterprise architecture framework (SOEAF). J. Theor. Appl. Inf. Technol. **40**(2), 162–171 (2012)
34. Alzoubi, Y.I., Gill, A.Q.: An empirical investigation of geographically distributed agile development: the agile enterprise architecture is a communication enabler. IEEE Access **8**, 80269–80289 (2020)
35. Duijs, R., Ravesteyn, P.: Adaptation of enterprise architecture efforts to an agile environment (2018)
36. Drews, P., et al.: Bimodal enterprise architecture management: the emergence of a new EAM function for a BizDevOps-based fast IT. In: 21st EDOCW Workshop. IEEE (2017)
37. Hinkelmann, K., et al.: A new paradigm for the continuous alignment of business and IT: combining enterprise architecture modelling and enterprise ontology. Comput. Ind. **79**, 77–86 (2016)
38. Bogner, J., Zimmermann, A.: Towards integrating microservices with adaptable enterprise architecture. In: 20th EDOCW Workshop. IEEE (2016)
39. Zimmermann, A., et al.: Digital enterprise architecture with micro-granular systems and services (2016)
40. Gill, A.Q.: Adaptive enterprise architecture drivenagiledevelopment. In: International Conference on Information Systems Development, ISD 2015 (2015)
41. Zimmermann, A., et al.: Collaborative decision support for adaptive digital enterprise architecture (2015)
42. Carvalho, J.A., Sousa, R.D.: Enterprise architecture as enabler of organizational agility: a municipality case study. Association for Information Systems (2014)
43. Fallmyr, T., Bygstad, B.: Enterprise architecture practice and organizational agility: an exploratory study. In: 2014 47th Hawaii International Conference on System Sciences. IEEE (2014)
44. Castellanos, C., Correal, D.: A framework for alignment of data and processes architectures applied in a government institution. J. Data Semant. **2**(2–3), 61–74 (2013). https://doi.org/10.1007/s13740-013-0021-5
45. Steinhorst, M.: iARIS-supporting enterprise transformation using an iterative ISD method (2013)
46. Sidorova, A., Kappelman, L.: Realizing the benefits of enterprise architecture: An actor-network theory perspective. In: Hammami, O., Krob, D., Voirin, J.L. (eds.) Complex Systems Design & Management, pp. 317–333. Springer, Heidelberg (2012). https://doi.org/10.1007/978-3-642-25203-7_23
47. Comm, C.L., Mathaisel, D.F.: A lean enterprise architecture for business process re-engineering and re-marketing. In: ICEIS, no. 3 (2010)
48. Pattij, M., van de Wetering, R., Kusters, R.: From enterprise architecture management to organizational agility: the mediating role of IT capabilities. In: Bled eConference (2019)
49. Pattij, M., Van de Wetering, R., Kusters, R.J.: Improving agility through enterprise architecture management: the mediating role of aligning business and IT (2020)
50. Uludag, Ö., et al.: What to expect from enterprise architects in large-scale agile development? A multiple-case study (2019)
51. Uludag, Ö., Nägele, S., Hauder, M.: Establishing architecture guidelines in large-scale agile development through institutional pressures: a single-case study (2019)

52. Noreika, K.: Business capabilities utilization enhancement using archimate for EAS projects delivery in an agile environment (2020)
53. Noreika, K., Gudas, S.: Aligning agile software development with enterprise architecture framework. In: IVUS (2019)
54. Werewka, J., Spiechowicz, A.: Enterprise architecture approach to SCRUM processes, sprint retrospective example. In: FedCSIS Conference. IEEE (2017)
55. Wagner, H.-T., Meshtaf, J.: Individual IT roles in business–IT alignment and IT governance. In: 49th HICSS Conference. IEEE (2016)
56. Asadi Someh, I., et al.: The role of synergy in using enterprise architecture for business transformation (2016)
57. Aghaei, M., Bayat, R.A.N.G.K.: An examination of effects the business intelligence on strategic decisions. Iioab J. **7**, 13–22 (2016)
58. Guetat, S.B.A., Dakhli, S.B.D.: The four spaces model: a framework for services governance in urbanized information systems. Procedia Comput. Sci. **100**, 1208–1219 (2016)
59. Malta, P.M., Sousa, R.D.: The organizational competences model: a contribution for business-IT alignment (2011)
60. Hinkelmann, K., Merelli, E., Thönssen, B.: The role of content and context in enterprise repositories. Framework **18**, 10 (2010)
61. Goel, A., Schmidt, H., Gilbert, D.: Towards formalizing virtual enterprise architecture. In: 2009 13th Enterprise Distributed Object Computing Conference Workshops. IEEE (2009)
62. Schelp, J., Aier, S.: SOA and EA-sustainable contributions for increasing corporate agility. In: 2009 42nd Hawaii International Conference on System Sciences. IEEE (2009)
63. Erol, O., Sauser, B., Boardman, J.: Creating enterprise flexibility through service oriented architecture. Glob. J. Flex. Syst. Manag. **10**(1), 11–16 (2009). https://doi.org/10.1007/BF0 3396551
64. Van Roosmalen, M.W., Hoppenbrouwers, S.J.B.A.: Supporting corporate governance with enterprise architecture and business rule management: a synthesis of stability and agility. In: Proc. Int. Workshop on Regulations Modelling and Deployment, pp. 13–24. Springer Montpellier, France (2008)
65. Roach, T., Low, G., D'Ambra, J.: CAPSICUM a conceptual model for service oriented architecture. In: 2008 IEEE Congress on Services-Part I. IEEE (2008)
66. Schelp, J., Winter, R.: Towards a methodology for service construction. In: 2007 40th Annual Hawaii International Conference on System Sciences (HICSS 2007). IEEE (2007)
67. Chae, H., Choi, Y., Kim, K.: Component-based modeling of enterprise architectures for collaborative manufacturing. Int. J. Adv. Manuf. Technol. **34**(5–6), 605–616 (2007). https://doi.org/10.1007/s00170-006-0620-5
68. Hoogervorst, J.: Enterprise architecture: Enabling integration, agility and change. Int. J. Coop. Inf. Syst. **13**(03), 213–233 (2004)
69. Gren, L., Lenberg, P.: Agility is responsiveness to change: an essential definition. In: Proceedings of the Evaluation and Assessment in Software Engineering, pp. 348–353 (2020)
70. Ramos, H., Vasconcelos, A.: eXtreme enterprise architecture planning. In: Proceedings of the 29th Annual ACM Symposium on Applied Computing (2014)
71. Uludag, Ö., Matthes, F.: Investigating the role of enterprise architects in supporting large-scale agile transformations: a multiple-case study (2020)

View and Viewpoint Reconstruction for Assisting the Preparation of Participatory Modeling Sessions

David Naranjo[✉] and Mario Sánchez

Department of Systems and Computing Engineering,
Universidad de los Andes, Bogotá, Colombia
{da-naran,mar-san1}@uniandes.edu.co

Abstract. Due to the inherent complexity of Enterprise Models, it is common to employ multiple views for model exploration. Currently, this exploration remains a daunting task in collaborative modeling sessions, due to ineffective mechanisms for organizing views and presenting the relevant ones to each stakeholder. To address these issues, we propose an approach that reconstructs view-related information from the structure of the Enterprise Model and tool metadata. Then, we perform a viewpoint analysis, in order to identify the most appropriate view for each participant of the modeling session.

Keywords: Enterprise models · Architectural views and viewpoints · Participative modeling

1 Introduction

To gain valuable knowledge and insights, we can learn from models in two manners: By constructing new models, or by manipulating existing ones [1]. In both learning tasks, we usually focus on particular fragments (views) of the model, from the perspective of specific concerns [2]. To address these concerns, we use multiple viewpoints [3], which establish the conventions for constructing, interpreting and analyzing a view [2]. For instance, when using the ArchiMate language [4], we can choose the relevant viewpoints (e.g. Capability Map Viewpoint, or Value Stream Viewpoint) for modeling certain fragment of an architecture.

The construction of a model from scratch demands a considerable effort, but the reward is that the modeler ends up with extensive knowledge of the model. However, given the advances in **Participative Modeling** [5], as well as a concerted effort to expand the reach of enterprise modeling to non-expert modelers [6], it is increasingly common that enterprise models have several authors, and address different stakeholders. Model exploration is critical for ensuring model quality, learning from unfamiliar parts of the model, and transmitting this knowledge to larger audiences. However, tool support for these tasks is insufficient for collaborative modeling sessions, as current tools are tailored for

© Springer Nature Switzerland AG 2021
B. Shishkov (Ed.): BMSD 2021, LNBIP 422, pp. 306–316, 2021.
https://doi.org/10.1007/978-3-030-79976-2_19

traditional (individual) modeling and have several limitations when dealing with large models and multiple views.

In this paper, we argue that we can take advantage of structural and semantic information to offer better support for view-based model navigation and the selection of appropriate views to a group of different stakeholders in a collaborative modeling project. For this purpose, we propose an approach for reconstructing a cross-reference model that describes the relationships between ArchiMate views, offering a *map* for navigating the model, as well as an analysis method for discovering the viewpoints that can be associated to every view.

This paper is structured as follows: First, we give a short theoretical background and introduce the problem to be addressed. Then, in Sect. 3 we describe our approach. Section 4 illustrates the approach with a widely used Case Study. Afterwards, Sect. 5 offers the results of our analysis, and Sect. 6 provides related and future work.

2   View-Based Navigation in Participatory Modeling

The complexity of large models gets in the way of obtaining global and detailed understanding of the systems that they represent. This complexity is tamed by separating models into manageable fragments (**views**), and knowing how these fragments are related (**cross-reference view**). The ISO 42010 standard [2] offers a method for modeling and analyzing an architecture through views that address particular concerns of stakeholders. In particular, a viewpoint describes the element and relationship types allowed in a view, as well as the *"languages, notations, model kinds, design rules, and/or modelling methods, analysis techniques and other operations on views"* [2].

While the ISO 42010 standard establishes a common conceptual framework, it does not offer guidance on which viewpoints should be used. To obtain this guidance, we can make use of several architecture frameworks, e.g. TOGAF, which suggest a collection of viewpoints as first-level mechanisms –and a starting point– for modeling the architecture of a company. Many modeling languages (e.g. ArchiMate) already suggest useful viewpoints in their documentation, and modeling methods such as 4EM [7] offer a method for organizing views by the refinement of goal models to produce process, resource, and technical sub-models, with clear relationships between them. An important aspect of 4EM is that it is a participatory approach where stakeholders are included in the modeling process.

Approaches to **Participatory Modeling (PM)** [5,7] consist of Group Modeling Sessions, where expert modelers act as facilitators, and stakeholders are the real creators and owners of the model [8]. To avoid losing interest and commitment of stakeholders, PM sessions require additional setup and planning [8], with tasks such as selecting an appropriate modeling language, identifying stakeholder background and needs, and creating views of the model that are appropriate for the problem at hand. In large PM projects, the use of a preliminary model can speed up the collaborative modeling process and raise critical discussion topics [9]. Navigation of existing models is done with the aid of modeling tools, which can be employed for browsing views, selecting reusable fragments, as well as creating user-defined views [5].

2.1 Problem Statement

Nowadays, views are the main way for model navigation and manipulation. To preserve model quality and completeness, current approaches to multi-view modeling focus on consistency checks [10,11], and current modeling methods and tools offer several aids for this purpose. However, when envisioning multi-view modeling in 2020, von Hanxleden et al. [12] acknowledge that the modeling community is too much focused on consistency, while neglecting pragmatic aspects that are also important. More recently, Sandkuhl et al. [6] call into attention that Enterprise Modeling needs more lightweight approaches that do not focus on traditional qualities like completeness and coherence, but on usefulness and impact of models. The authors underscore that the scope of models must be managed to ensure that the right content is represented in the right way for each actor of the modeling process, and research is needed on how to automatically derive and maintain model views tailored to particular purposes.

Right now, the problem is that *session facilitators* and *tool operators*, two critical roles in PM sessions [5], have **inadequate support for browsing existing views and deriving new views that are appropriate to session participants**: Navigation mechanisms offered by current modeling tools are made for traditional (individual) modeling, and are not as effective for PM sessions [13]. Furthermore, these tools have several limitations when visualizing, navigating, and interacting with large models [5,14], and each tool has its own mechanisms for organizing and aggregating views, as externalized metadata that is not part of the model [15]. Sandkuhl et al. argue that tool-related research should investigate which types of concerns of which stakeholder groups can typically be supported by which types of models [6]. In this regard, viewpoints are useful for producing views that are tailored to particular stakeholders. However, a consequence of the heterogeneity of stakeholders in PM sessions implies that traditional viewpoints offered by languages such as ArchiMate might not not sufficient, or even too overarching (e.g. the Layered Viewpoint).

3 Proposed Approach

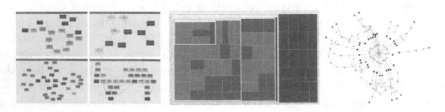

Fig. 1. Extracted views (left), view tree (center), and view model (right).

In order to create a model of all views, we propose a structural analysis in three steps: First, we parse the entire model and extract all the views therein. Then, we match the dependencies between views, and generate a hierarchical structure. Finally, we enrich the model with cross-references of elements and relationships embedded in each view (see Fig. 1).

View Extraction. Several modeling tools provide mechanisms for exporting a model as interchange files that employ well-known formats, e.g. XMI, KM3, or XML. Tool-dependent **metadata** is embedded in these files, containing additional information, such as the structure, names, and contents of individual views. We can process the model file to find isolated clusters of model elements and relationships that can be interpreted as views. This is done by generating a graph structure of the model, with model elements as nodes, and relationships between elements as edges. Nodes are enriched with additional information, such as View name, creation date, and other *metadata*.

View Tree Generation. Most modeling tools have a mechanism for organizing views, either by describing them as independent sub-models, or aggregated by tool constructs such as Folders. We can extract, also from tool metadata, these organizing criteria. In some cases, tool vendors provide the Tool Metamodel that describes these constructs. In the worst case, when no metamodel is available, it is possible to do a reverse engineering of the model file to identify aggregating constructs. This processing generates a hierarchical structure (a tree) of views.

Cross-Referencing. Finally, the View Model is enriched with additional relationships between views that are inferred from tool metadata. This is done when the model contains *navigation views*, which are a special kind of views that do not contain model elements or relationships; instead, they reference other views.

3.1 Viewpoint Analysis

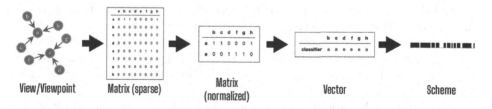

View/Viewpoint   Matrix (sparse)   Matrix (normalized)   Vector   Scheme

Fig. 2. Summary of the transformation from view/viewpoint to scheme

In order to identify which views are relevant to particular stakeholders, we create diagrams for the joint comparison of views and viewpoints. We start by creating

Schemes, which are vectorized representations of views and viewpoints. The translation from View to Scheme is done in an automated manner (see Fig. 2). Then, we apply a series of production rules for stacking and sorting Schemes. This can be seen as something akin to playing *Tetris*.

The idea behind Schemes is that any disjoint classification or partition of model elements and relationships has a hierarchical structure that can be represented as an adjacency matrix. A feature of these matrices is that they are fairly sparse, and can be represented in a more succinct manner using a simple visual notation that we call **Schemes**, which are vectorized representations of (meta)model fragments. Each dimension of the vector (i.e. the index of the array) corresponds to a particular concept of the metamodel, and a solid color inside each position corresponds to the presence of such concept.

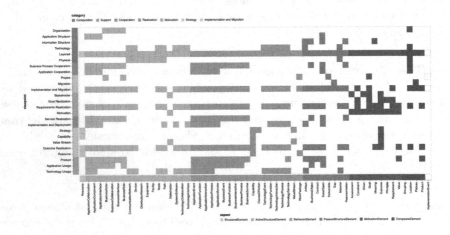

Fig. 3. Left: standard viewpoints matrix.

Viewpoints can be represented as Schemes by indexing all the concepts of the metamodel, with a solid color for concepts that are present in the viewpoint. For example, Fig. 3 shows the matrix for all 25 example viewpoints that are in the ArchiMate standard. We applied two classifiers that apply orderings to the matrix: For sorting rows, we consulted the viewpoint classification of the standard that offers seven categories. For sorting columns, we classified ArchiMate concepts by their Aspect, also from the standard. Views can be represented in the same manner, by inserting solid squares if there are elements in the view that are instances of the concepts.

After having a Viewpoint Matrix and a View Matrix, we can calculate the similarity between views and viewpoints by applying a cross product between both matrices. The result of this product is a **Similarity Matrix** (see Fig. 5) that contains views as rows and viewpoints as columns. Each cell of the matrix has a shade of grey: The darker the color, the more compatible is a view to a viewpoint. The similarity value is calculated by applying vector multiplication.

4   Illustration

To illustrate our approach, we employ ArchiMate, a widely used Enterprise Modeling language. In particular, we make use of the ArchiSurance Case Study [16], but this approach can be applied to any ArchiMate model. The model for the case study is provided by The Open Group as an XML exchange file[1] that can be imported to different modeling tools. The entire model, which consists of 315 elements and 467 relationships, is embedded inside a larger one that includes view metadata. This data describes, among other things, tool-specific information and visual attributes of the diagrams. We use this complete model as a starting point for extracting view information.

4.1   View Reconstruction

First, we obtained the tool metamodel from the source code repository of Archi, a popular tool for ArchiMate models. This metamodel has visualization information for displaying the different views of the model with the visual Archi-Mate notation. Inside this metamodel we found the following concepts that are relevant to extract view information: An **ArchimateModel** contains **Folder** elements, and each folder has **ArchimateDiagramModel** elements that represent each diagram. Each one contains **DiagramModelArchimateObject** instances, which can be either **ArchimateElements**, or **DiagramModelReferences**.

4.2   Viewpoint Analysis

According to the tool metadata, the ArchiSurance model only employs 7 (out of 25) standard viewpoints, and just 9 views (out of 54) have an assigned viewpoint. The lack of viewpoint information for most views emphasizes the need of a Viewpoint Analysis, as views with unassigned viewpoints don't impose restrictions on which concepts are allowed. In order to analyze the similarity of a view to all viewpoints, we create the Similarity Matrix using the construction process of Sect. 3 (see Fig. 5). As stated, the darker the color of a cell, the more appropriate is the respective View to its respective Viewpoint.

5   Results

The extraction process yielded 75 distinct views. Figure 1 shows a small sample of extracted views, the View Tree and the View Model for the ArchiSurance model. Figure 4 shows two close-ups of the View Model. After examining each view, we tried to make sense of the organization scheme used by the original modelers. However, folder names were not descriptive, and their hierarchy was too shallow. As a next step, we studied the architecture description document [16], and

---

[1] See: https://publications.opengroup.org/more-categories/archimate-models/y194m.

Fig. 4. Details of the view model.

identified all the views that appear in the document. Contrasting these diagrams with the 75 views extracted from the model led us to divide views into three categories:

- **Navigation Views (21):** These views do not contain any ArchiMate element, they just have links to other views.
- **Document Diagrams (33):** These views appear in the Architecture Description document.
- **Miscellaneous Views (21):** The rest of the views (including empty ones).

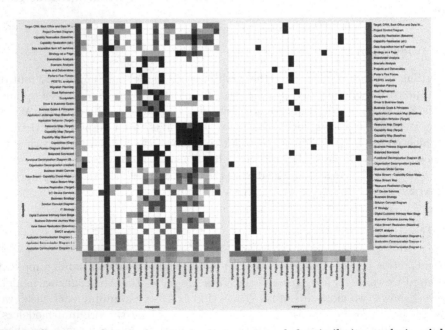

Fig. 5. Coverage of views by standard viewpoints. **left:** similarity analysis. **right:** chosen viewpoints

With our method, we discovered that most views have **total coverage** by standard viewpoints. There are 5 views with exactly one match (ignoring the Layered viewpoint), so it is safe to assign the matched viewpoint to the view. However, there are 21 views that have two or more matched viewpoints with 100% coverage, so we sorted standard viewpoints by their size, and picked the smallest matched viewpoint.

Furthermore, there are 15 unassigned views that have **partial coverage** by viewpoints. We proceeded to examine the differences between the concepts used by the view and the viewpoints with best match. In most cases, the difference is just one concept: *Grouping.* This concept does not change the semantics of any of the suggested viewpoints, so it is safe to ignore this concept and pick one of the best matches. There are three courses of action for the remaining views:

- Assign them to the Layered viewpoint
- Enrich one of the matched viewpoints with the additional concept(s)
- Create custom viewpoints

For simplicity, we opted for the first case, but we suggest taking any of the other two courses of action, depending on the context and usage of the views. Figure 5 shows to the right the chosen viewpoints.

5.1 Discussion

In View Reconstruction, we identified 42 views that were not part of the Architecture Description Document of the case study. Furthermore, we identified the main point of entry of the model, a Navigation View that links to other views. Finding this view in the Archi modeling tool is more difficult, as the tool operator needs to expand several folders and possibly open each view to make sense of the organization scheme of the modelers. Conversely, by reconstructing a View Model, we can visually inspect the organization of views and choose the ones that are more relevant.

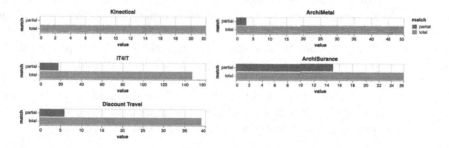

Fig. 6. Partial and total matches for five enterprise models.

In the Viewpoint Analysis, we found that in most cases the ArchiSurance modelers tried to employ the example viewpoints from the standard. We did not expect the appearance of so many partial matches (12) so, for comparison, we applied our method to other four ArchiMate models[2], and discovered that on average 92% of unassigned views can be assigned to a standard viewpoint (see Fig. 6). The outlier was the ArchiSurance model, which has more partial matches, but the reason behind this larger number is that modelers introduced one or two additional concepts to these views, and provided three valid courses of action. Some views, e.g. *Business Model Canvas*, probably need custom viewpoints.

6   Conclusion

Even medium-sized models (such as the ArchiSurance one) can have a large number of views. Navigating among these views using the mechanisms offered by modeling tools is a daunting task that needs better assistance in PM sessions. Our method allows the reconstruction and visualization of all views and their cross-references, providing a map for model exploration. Furthermore, our Viewpoint Analysis allows the automated classification of views with 100% coverage, and informs the best matches for views with partial coverage, as well as the difference in concepts. With this information, Session Facilitators can select the views that are most appropriate to a particular stakeholder, by selecting the relevant viewpoints that best represent their concerns.

This approach makes part of a larger endeavor for providing assistance to *Tool Operators* and *Facilitators* of PM Sessions. This assistance is provided in tasks such as model exploration and (re)design of alternative solutions, as well as the preservation and explanation of the rationale behind design decisions. Currently, we are designing an experiment to evaluate the effectiveness of the whole approach for addressing *Wicked Problems*.

6.1   Related Work

Approaches for recovering view information and facilitating model navigation [15,17], while valuable, introduce additional complications, e.g. they require specialized knowledge and careful planning, or access to the source code of the modeling tool for annotating metamodel concepts. A limitation of our approach is that View Extraction needs depends on the modeling tool that produced the model. In most cases it can be very similar to a reverse-engineering effort of the model file produced by the modeling tool. An advantage of our approach is that it does not need a modification of the tool internals, and that it provides a visual and interactive visualization of the view model. To date, we could not find similar approaches for discovering compatible viewpoints of a view.

Acknowledgment. This work was supported by the COLCIENCIAS grant 727 for doctoral studies.

---

[2] We excluded navigation views and empty views from this analysis.

References

1. Morgan, M.S., Morrison, M. (eds.): Models as Mediators: Perspectives on Natural and Social Sciences. Ideas in Context. Cambridge University Press, Cambridge, New York (1999)
2. ISO: ISO/IEC/IEEE Systems and software engineering: Architecture description. ISO/IEC/IEEE 42010:2011(E) (Revision of ISO/IEC 42010:2007 and IEEE Std 1471–2000), pp. 1–46, December 2011
3. Lankhorst, M.M., van der Torre, L., Proper, H.A.E., Arbab, F., Hoppenbrouwers, S.J.B.A., Steen, M.W.A.: Viewpoints and visualisation. In: Enterprise Architecture at Work, pp. 171–214. The Enterprise Engineering Series, Springer (2017). https://doi.org/10.1007/978-3-642-01310-2_7
4. The Open Group: ArchiMate 3.1 Specification. Tech. rep. (2019)
5. Stirna, J., Persson, A.: Enterprise Modeling: Facilitating the Process and the People. Springer International Publishing, Cham (2018)
6. Sandkuhl, K., et al.: From expert discipline to common practice: a vision and research agenda for extending the reach of enterprise modeling. Bus. Inf. Syst. Eng. 60(1), 69–80 (2018). https://doi.org/10.1007/s12599-017-0516-y
7. Sandkuhl, K., Stirna, J., Persson, A., Wißotzki, M.: Enterprise Modeling: Tackling Business Challenges with the 4EM Method. The Enterprise Engineering Series, Springer, Berlin Heidelberg, Berlin, Heidelberg (2014)
8. Persson, A.: Enterprise modelling in practice: situational factors and their influence on adopting a participative approach. Ph.D. thesis, Stockholm University, Department of Computer and Systems Sciences, Kista, Sweden (2001)
9. Renger, M., Kolfschoten, G.L., de Vreede, G.-J.: Challenges in collaborative modeling: a literature review. In: Dietz, J.L.G., Albani, A., Barjis, J. (eds.) CIAO!/EOMAS -2008. LNBIP, vol. 10, pp. 61–77. Springer, Heidelberg (2008). https://doi.org/10.1007/978-3-540-68644-6_5
10. Reineke, J., Tripakis, S.: Basic problems in multi-view modeling. In: Ábrahám, E., Havelund, K. (eds.) TACAS 2014. LNCS, vol. 8413, pp. 217–232. Springer, Heidelberg (2014). https://doi.org/10.1007/978-3-642-54862-8_15
11. Awadid, A., Bork, D., Karagiannis, D., Nurcan, S.: Toward generic consistency patterns in multi-view enterprise modelling. In: Bednar, P.M., Frank, U., Kautz, K. (eds.) 26th European Conference on Information Systems: Beyond Digitization - Facets of Socio-Technical Change, ECIS 2018, Portsmouth, UK, 23–28 June 2018, p. 146 (2018)
12. von H, Reinhard, Lee,·E.A., Motika, C., Fuhrmann, H.: Multi-view modeling and pragmatics in 2020. In: Calinescu, R., Garlan, D. (eds.) Monterey Workshop 2012. LNCS, vol. 7539, pp. 209–223. Springer, Heidelberg (2012). https://doi.org/10.1007/978-3-642-34059-8_11
13. Ghidini, C., et al.: Collaborative enterprise integrated modelling. In: Proceedings of the 5th Workshop on Semantic Web Applications and Perspectives (SWAP2008), p. 10. CEUR-WS.org, Rome, Italy (2008)
14. Naranjo, D., Sánchez, M., Villalobos, J.: Evaluating the capabilities of enterprise architecture modeling tools for visual analysis. J. Object Technol. 14(1), 3–1 (2015)

15. Jakob, J., Königs, A., Schürr, A.: Non-materialized model view specification with triple graph grammars. In: Corradini, A., Ehrig, H., Montanari, U., Ribeiro, L., Rozenberg, G. (eds.) ICGT 2006. LNCS, vol. 4178, pp. 321–335. Springer, Heidelberg (2006). https://doi.org/10.1007/11841883_23
16. Jonkers, H., Band, I., Quartel, D., Lankhorst, M.: ArchiSurance Case Study Version 3.1. Tech. rep., The Open Group (2019)
17. Jiménez-Pastor, A., Garmendia, A., de Lara, J.: Scalable model exploration for model-driven engineering. J. Syst. Softw. **132**, 204–225 (2017)

What to Do When Requirements Are Changing All the Time?
A Control System Example

Bert de Brock[⊠] [iD]

Faculty of Economics and Business, University of Groningen, PO Box 800,
9700 Groningen, AV, The Netherlands
E.O.de.Brock@rug.nl

Abstract. In our earlier work we sketched an approach to developing software systems. The goal of this paper is to further illustrate the applicability and use of that approach. Via the practical example of the development of a control system, we illustrate the applicability of our approach to another type of system (other than the usual information system) and the **manoeuvrability** ('agility') of our *textual* System Sequence Descriptions. We discuss how to deal with situations where requirements are changing all the time ('agility' during requirements analyses). We also want to sketch the **mental process** of going from a simple, naïve software solution towards various more subtle ones, probably inspired/ guided by brainstorms with customers. In this case, it even ends up in a **generic system** (so, not for one particular user organization only).

Keywords: Changing requirements · Agility · Textual System Sequence Description · Controller · Controlled system · Generic system · System scope

1 Introduction

When the requirements change all the time, the question is: How to deal with all those changes concretely in practical situations? We will zoom in on that problem. In order to really understand the problems when requirements are changing all the time and how to master them, we have to show the nitty-gritty details as well, because managing them in such constantly changing circumstances makes it all so difficult. The manoeuvrability of our *textual* System Sequence Descriptions (tSSDs) turns out to be very helpful when the requirements are changing all the time ('agility' of our textual SSDs).

This paper is also meant to illustrate and work out the mental process of going from a simple, naïve solution towards various more subtle ones, probably inspired/guided by brainstorms with the customer ('agility' during requirements analysis).

In our earlier work we sketched an approach to developing software systems [1, 2]. Comparisons to other work are already made in [2], in this volume. But the used examples might suggest that the approach applies to 'information systems' only: There was little to no interaction with other systems in those examples. So the question arose whether our approach is applicable to other types of systems as well, e.g., control systems. Yes, it is, as we will explain and show in this 'companion' paper.

© Springer Nature Switzerland AG 2021
B. Shishkov (Ed.): BMSD 2021, LNBIP 422, pp. 317–329, 2021.
https://doi.org/10.1007/978-3-030-79976-2_20

A **control system** (*controller* for short) is a system that has to manage the behaviour of other systems. So, a controller typically has (much) interaction with other systems. Our running example concerns thermostats, being classic examples of control systems. The running example also illustrates the phenomenon that the data structures of a system are usually more stable than the processes that system has to support.

With this paper we also want to discuss and illustrate the 'scope issue': What should be inside and what outside the scope of the system? Finally, we want to illustrate the development of a *generic* system, not a system for one particular user organization only.

The rest of the paper is organized as follows. Section 2 presents the preliminaries needed for understanding the rest. Section 3 gives an initial, simple, concrete description of our running development example. Section 4 introduces more than ten extensions, variants, and/or alternative options (except Sect. 4.3, which zooms in on the data needed). Section 5 gives an overview and the paper ends with a contribution section. For the reader's convenience, the Appendix shows the finally resulting textual SSDs.

2 Preliminaries

In [1] a grammar for textual SSDs is proposed. It is similar to the grammar for a programming language, except for the atomic instructions. We recall a part of that grammar below. The terminals are written in bold. The nonterminal $\underline{A}$ stands for 'atomic instruction' (or *step*), $\underline{P}$ for 'actor' (or *participant*), $\underline{M}$ for 'message', $\underline{S}$ for 'instruction' (or *SSD*), $\underline{C}$ for 'condition', $\underline{N}$ for 'instruction name', and $\underline{D}$ for 'definition':

A ::= P $\rightarrow$ P: M   /* *where* 'X $\rightarrow$ Y: M' *means:* 'X sends M to Y'
S ::= A | S ; S | S , S | **begin** S **end** | **if** C **then** S **endif** | **for each** <set element> **do** S **end**
    | **do** N
D ::= **define** N **as** S **end**

where 's1; s2' means 'first do s1, then do s2', 's1, s2' means 'do s1 and s2, in any order'. The construct '**do** N' is known as an *Include* or a *Call*. Definitions can be parameterized (see Sects. 4.7 and 4.8 for examples). The values for nonterminals P, C, M, and N are application dependent ('domain specific') and will appear naturally during the development of the specific application. We will sometimes use the terminal **System** for P to represent the system under consideration.

In order to avoid ambiguity, we use the binding rule that ',' binds stronger than ';'. We can break through this standard reading by using the 'brackets' **begin** ... **end**.

For atomic instructions we can distinguish the following four situations:

(a) Actor → **System**: i   Indicates the <u>input</u> messages the system can expect
(b) **System** → **System**: y Indicates the <u>transitions</u> (or <u>checks</u>) the system should make
(c) **System** → Actor: o   Indicates the <u>output</u> messages the system should produce
(d) Actor → Actor2: x   A step outside the system (maybe useful for understanding)

where Actor ≠ **System** and Actor2 ≠ **System** (but Actor and Actor2 might be the same). If the participant before and after the ' → ' are the same, the atomic instruction indicates what that participant has to do himself/herself/itself. We call step (a) an *input* step, (b) an *internal* step, (c) an *output* step, and (d) an *external* step.

The question arose whether our approach with textual SSDs only works in the context of 'information systems' or also in the context of control systems, for instance. In an 'information system' it is not uncommon that during a session (or Use Case) there is one fixed actor (role) interacting with the system. In other words, a 'dialogue' (bilateral conversation) between the actor and the system only.

A **control system** (*controller* for short) is a system that has to manage the behaviour of other systems, often triggered by signals coming from outside. A controller typically has (many) interactions with other systems, both on the input side as well as on the output side. In the context of controllers, typical atomic interactions are:

Controller → Sensor: Request
Sensor → Controller: Signal
Controller → Controlled System: Command
Controlled System → Controller: Feedback

A sensor might send a signal to the controller all by itself, without a previous request. The interaction steps shown in a picture (with several sensors and controlled systems) (Fig. 1):

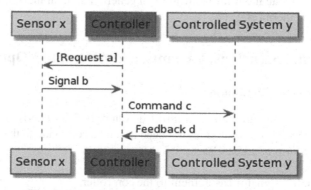

Fig. 1. Typical atomic interactions with a controller

3   Initial Description of the Running Development Case

Suppose we have a building with several rooms (e.g., an office or a school). Rooms have sensors for measuring the temperature ('temp.' for short) and might also have heatings and air conditioners (aircos). The systems to be controlled in this example are the heatings and aircos. The system to be developed (simply called 'the system') must be able to receive temp. measurements from the sensors and, when needed, start or stop the heatings or aircos in that room. (So the system is a type of 'distributed thermostat'.)

To be more precise, the heating(s) in a room must be started when the temp. in that room drops below 19 °C and must be stopped when that room temp. comes above 21 °C and, similarly, the airco(s) in a room must be started when that room temp. comes above 25 °C and must be stopped when that room temp. drops below 23 °C. In that case, a simple (even naïve) version of the main Use Case, *Handle Measurement*, might be:

1. A sensor sends a measured temperature to the system.
2. If that temp. is below 19 °C then the system starts the heating(s) in that room.
3. If that temp. is above 21 °C then the system stops the heating(s) in that room.
4. If that temp. is below 23 °C then the system stops the airco(s) in that room.
5. If that temp. is above 25 °C then the system starts the airco(s) in that room.

So, for any measured temp. one or even two of the steps 2–5 apply, as depicted below:

Heatings:	Step 2: Start		Step 3: Stop	

Heatings: Step 2: Start   ⋮........⋮ Step 3: Stop
Aircos: Step 4: Stop   ⋮........⋮ Step 5: Start
                        19°C   21°C   23°C   25°C

We note that in this example the sensors are not considered part of the system to be developed. In other words, they are outside the *scope* of the system.

In Sect. 4 we introduce many extensions, variants, and/or alternative options. Usually we first try to formulate them for controllers in general and then make it more specific for our distributed thermostat.

4   Subsequent Extensions, Variants, and Alternative Options

4.1   No Unnecessary Commands

If upon receipt of a measurement, a controlled system (CS for short) is already in the desirable state then the controller does not need to send a command to that CS anymore. Expressed in the form of a Use Case:

1. A sensor sends a signal/measurement to the controller.
2. If that signal might call for action *and the relevant CS is in undesirable state* then the system sends the proper command to that CS.

And schematically in the form of a textual SSD:

1. Sensor → Controller: Signal;
2. **if** signal might call for action **and** CS is in undesirable state
    then Controller → Controlled System: Command **endif**

We note that the combination of Step 1 and Step 2 constitutes a so-called ECA-rule for our controller (Event, Condition, Action): *Triggering Event; if Condition then Action.* Expressed as a textual SSD:

1. X → System: Signal ;   /* *Triggering Event*
2. **if** Condition **then** System → Y: Command **endif**   /* *if Condition then Action*

The idea of no unnecessary commands leads to the next version of *Handle Measurement* for our distributed thermostat from Sect. 3. In the form of a Use Case:

1. A sensor sends a measured temperature to the controller.
2. If that temperature is below 19 °C *and heating(s) in that room are 'Off'*
    then the controller starts those heating(s).
3. Similarly, if above 21 °C *and heating(s) are 'On'* then stop those heating(s).
4. Similarly, if below 23 °C *and airco(s) are 'On'* then stop those airco(s).
5. Similarly, if above 25 °C *and airco(s) are 'Off'* then start those airco(s).

And schematically in the form of a textual SSD (using variables instead of pronouns):

1. Sensor x → Controller: Temperature t ;
2. **if** t < 19 °C **then for each** heating h in the room of x that is 'Off'
    do Controller → h: 'On!' **end endif** ,
3. **if** t > 21 °C **then for each** heating h in the room of x that is 'On'
    do Controller → h: 'Off!' **end endif** ,
4. **if** t < 23 °C **then for each** airco a in the room of x that is 'On'
    do Controller → a: 'Off!' **end endif** ,
5. **if** t > 25 °C **then for each** airco a in the room of x that is 'Off'
    do Controller → a: 'On!' **end endif**

The commas between steps 2, 3, 4, and 5 say that those steps can be done in any order.

4.2 Constants Should Become 'Adjustable'

System requirements might contain constants which, as might turn out only later, should be adjustable. That means that those constants should be replaced by (system) variables.

4.2.1 Variable Thresholds

As presented now, the concrete threshold temperatures (19, 21, 23, and 25 °C) might end up 'hard-coded' in the thermostat, our control system under development. However, as a new user requirement, these thresholds should become adjustable. Therefore we introduce the four variables Hmin, Hmax, Amin, and Amax representing the minimum and maximum thresholds for the heatings and aircos, respectively. We also add the condition that Hmin $\leq$ Hmax $<$ Amin $\leq$ Amax.

In Step 2 of the most recent textual SSD, t $<$ 19 °C must be replaced by t $<$ Hmin; similarly, t $>$ 21 °C by t $>$ Hmax in Step 3, t $<$ 23 °C by t $<$ Amin in Step 4, and finally t $>$ 25 °C by t $>$ Amax in Step 5. The temperatures 19, 21, 23, and 25 °C could serve as *default values* upon installation.

4.2.2 Variable Thresholds Per Room

On hindsight, not all rooms do need the same threshold temperatures. E.g., a corridor might have a minimum threshold of 17 °C instead of 19 °C. Now we need these four threshold values *per room*, each with the condition that Hmin $\leq$ Hmax $<$ Amin $\leq$ Amax. The advantage is that the thresholds can now be set per room.

4.2.3 Variable Thresholds Per Room Type

That the thresholds must be set per room turned out to be a disadvantage in case of large buildings. Another variant is that the thresholds only depend on the *type of room* (e.g., classroom, gym hall, corridor, etc.), not on the individual room. In that case we need those four threshold values *per room type*, now of course with the condition *per room type* that Hmin $\leq$ Hmax $<$ Amin $\leq$ Amax. The advantage is that the thresholds can now be set uniformly for all rooms of the same type.

4.3 Which Data Does the Controller Need?

It is time to see which data (structure) the controller needs. In general, the controller needs to 'know' the *configuration*: the sensors, the controlled systems, and their state.

4.3.1 Configuration Data and State Data

In our running example: The thermostat needs to 'know' the sensors, the heatings, the aircos, their states, the rooms they are in, and the type of rooms (see Sect. 4.2).

Concretely: Suppose that each sensor has a unique sensor ID (SID), each heating has a unique heating ID (HID), each airco has a unique airco ID (AID), each room has a unique room ID (RID), and each room type has a unique room type ID (RTID). Furthermore, the controller needs to know the *state* of each heating and of each airco. Moreover, the controller needs to know the *room* of each sensor, heating, and airco. The controller also needs to know the *room type* of each room. And, in case of Sect. 4.2.3, the controller needs to know those four thresholds for each room type and also needs to know the condition Hmin $\leq$ Hmax $<$ Amin $\leq$ Amax per room type.

For Sect. 4.2.3 this leads to the following concepts and attributes (where we indicate the identifiers by a '!' in front and the referencing attributes by a '^' in front):

Sensor: ! SID, ^ RID

Heating: ! HID, ^ RID, State ('On' or 'Off')

Airco: ! AID, ^ RID, State ('On' or 'Off')

Room: ! RID, ^ RTID

Room Type: ! RTID, Hmin, Hmax, Amin, Amax

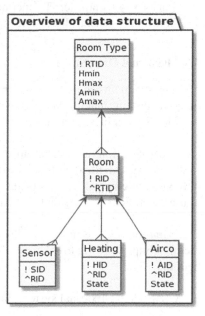

with the condition per room type that
Hmin ≤ Hmax < Amin ≤ Amax (Fig. 2).

Fig. 2. Overview of needed data

4.3.2 Keeping the Data Up-to-Date

The controller must keep its data up-to-date. So, when it changes the state of a controlled system, the controller has to update that state in its own registration as well. E.g., with variable thresholds per room type, Step 5 in the tSSD in Sect. 4.1 now becomes (with the update step underlined):

if t > Amax of the type of room sensor x is in
then for each airco a in the room of x that is 'Off'
        do Controller → a: 'On!' ;
            Controller → Controller: Register a as 'On'
    end
endif

4.3.3 Remembering the Measurements Too?

Controllers handle an incoming measurement by taking the appropriate actions. After that, the system can 'forget' that measurement. But, after all, the user organization (and the producers/installers of the controlled systems) wanted to be able to look at the past measurements. In that case, the incoming measurements must be remembered too, together with a timestamp. Then we need one more concept, say 'Measurement'.

For our running example this implies the following attributes for 'Measurement' (where the underlined combination *SID, Timestamp* is uniquely identifying):

Measurement: <u>SID, Timestamp</u>, RID, Temperature.

We did not indicate SID or RID as *referencing* attributes because they might refer to 'old' sensors or rooms that do not exist anymore.

Our main use case *Handle Measurement* now gets an extra step: Step 1 is replaced by

1. A sensor sends a measured temperature plus timestamp to the controller.
2. The controller stores the info of the sensor, its room, measured temp., and timestamp.

And schematically, as a textual SSD (where r_x indicates the room sensor x is in):

1. Sensor x → Controller: Temperature t plus timestamp s;
2. Controller → Controller: Store sensor x, room r_x, temperature t, and timestamp s

4.4 External Data Store

The measurements could be stored inside the system under development or in a separate external system (making the architecture less monolithic).

There could be several reasons for that:

- the organization/installer/producer already developed a system for that
  or has a system filled with measurement data with which 'our' data must be combined
- the measurement data must be integrated with other external data (e.g., weather data)
- the controller gets overloaded in case of heavy trend analyses on its measurement data

Whatever the reasons are, in this way we move more towards a micro-service architecture (https://www.guru99.com/microservices-tutorial.html). The new Step 2 would become:

2. Controller → External system: Store sensor x, room r_x, temp. t, and timestamp s

4.5 Simple Sensors Cannot Provide a Timestamp

In the example until now, it was the sensor that provided the timestamp (the time of *measurement*). If the sensors are so simple that they cannot provide a timestamp, the system itself could add a timestamp (say, the time of *receipt*) by using its internal clock. In that case, the first two steps in the use case become:

1. A sensor sends a measured temperature to the controller.
2. The controller stores the sensor info, its room, measured temp., and time of *receipt*.

And schematically, as a textual SSD (where s' is the time of *receipt*):

1. Sensor x → Controller: Temperature t;
2. Controller → Controller: Store sensor x, room r_x, temperature t, and timestamp s'

So, now the timestamp pops up in the second step, provided by the controller itself.

In case of an external data store, the second occurrence of 'Controller' in the second step can be replaced by 'External system' (cf. Sect. 4.4).

4.6 Synchronous Feedback from a Controlled System

It turned out to be a flaw that the controller adapts the registered state of a controlled system as soon as it issued such a command to that controlled system, without knowing whether the intended state actually changed. An extension/improvement/option is that the controlled system gives feedback about its status to the controller. Only then, the controller would change the registered state of that controlled system. In that case, the last four steps in the tSSD in Sect. 4.1 must be adapted. E.g., with variable thresholds per room type, Step 5 in the tSSD now becomes (with the new parts underlined):

> **if** t > Amax of the type of room sensor x is in
> **then for each** airco a in the room of x that is 'Off'
>   **do** Controller → a: 'On!' ;
>   a → Controller: NewState(a) ;
>   Controller → Controller: Register NewState(a) as the new state of a **end**
> **endif**

4.7 Asynchronous Feedback from a Controlled System

Often it takes a (tiny) while before a controlled system gives feedback. Meanwhile, the controller has to do other things as well... So, another option is that the controller does not wait for an answer and only adapts the registered state once the status feedback from the controlled system comes in. That leads to another UC, say *HandleStatusFeedback*:

1. A controlled system sends its status to the controller.
2. The controller adapts the registered status of that controlled system accordingly.

And the corresponding tSSD, cast in the form of a parameterized definition:

> **define** HandleStatusFeedback(y) **as**
>   y → Controller: State(y) ;
>   Controller → Controller: Register State(y) as the state of y
> **end**

The last four steps in the main UC (*Handle Measurement*) should be without these two instructions now. Step 3, for instance, now becomes:

> **if** t < Hmin of the type of room where sensor x is in
> **then for each** heating h in the room of x in state 'Off'
>   **do** Controller → h: 'On!' **end**
> **endif**

We note that it is easy to go back from the asynchronous to the synchronous situation, since we can just call *HandleStatusFeedback* within this most recent version of Step 3:

> **if** t < Hmin of the type of room where sensor x is in
> **then for each** heating h in the room of x in state 'Off'
>   **do** Controller → h: 'On!' ;
>   **do** HandleStatusFeedback(h)
>   **end**
> **endif**

4.8 Scheduled or Even Dynamic Threshold Changes

The user organization subsequently indicated that it is useful to have lower threshold temperatures for the heatings at night than during daytime. For example, in an office say 21 °C from nine till five from Monday till Friday, and 15 °C during the other time periods. And such schedules can be much more subtle, of course. It could be a wish that the controller changes the thresholds automatically in such cases. This could be realized if the controller 'knows' the schedule and has an internal clock. Then the question came up: Which type of schedules for threshold changes should be possible? E.g., based on the combination of weekday and time during the day only (as in the example above)? And thereafter the (internal) discussion in the organization advanced even more: Ideally, threshold changes might be determined dynamically, e.g., based on external conditions or events. For instance, in order to have a temp. of 21 °C at 9:00, it might be necessary to start the heatings (much) earlier, but how much earlier can depend on the inside temperature at hand, the outside temperature, the size (and isolation) of the room to be warmed, etc. Gradually the question arose whether the controller itself should know the schedule or that an (intelligent) external system should trigger the system with new threshold temperatures at the right moments. This idea was partly inspired by the rise of systems such as Homey (https://homey.app/en-gb/) where its users can constitute all type of rules to turn down (or off) the thermostat. This option is more flexible and, moreover, that external system could easily be replaced by a more subtle/advanced/ sophisticated one (provided that it keeps the same type of interface-mechanism with our controller). Where the development started with a concrete controller, by now they are thinking of a **generic** COTS-system (*Commercial off-the-shelf*) to be sold on the market, not meant for one particular customer anymore...

We will work out this generic option. So in other words, the scheduling/scheduler will be considered outside the *scope* of the system under development.

In conclusion, an external system - but also a human being - should be able to trigger our system with new threshold temperatures. We will use the term 'thresholder' here (instead of 'user'). For a change, we suppose that the threshold adaptions are on the level of individual rooms, not on the level of room types. So, Sect. 4.2.2 applies, not Sect. 4.2.3. Consequently, the attributes Hmin, Hmax, Amin, and Amax move from Room Type to Room in the model in Sect. 4.3.1, now with the condition *per room* that Hmin $\leq$ Hmax $<$ Amin $\leq$ Amax. The use case *AdaptThreshold* could run as follows:

1. A thresholder sends a (new) value for a threshold of a certain room to the controller.
2. The controller adapts the value for that threshold for that room.
3. The controller asks the sensor in that room for the current temperature.

The UC does not need to continue any further here, because once the controller gets the temp. from the sensor, the 'old' UC *Handle Measurement* starts and the controlled systems will be commanded accordingly if necessary, based on the new threshold value.

Note that there are four types of thresholds per room: Hmin, Hmax, Amin, and Amax. With A $\in$ {Hmin, Hmax, Amin, Amax}, we define a parameterized *AdaptThreshold*:

define AdaptThreshold(A, r, t) **as**
　　Thresholder → Controller: Update threshold A in room r to temperature t ;
　　Controller → Controller: Update threshold A in room r to temperature t ;
　　for each sensor x in room r **do** Controller → x: SendTemperature **end**
end

As explained before, hereafter the controller will receive the temperature from the sensor(s), then *Handle Measurement* starts and the controlled systems will be started or stopped accordingly (if necessary).

If threshold adaptions were on the level of room types, as in Sect. 4.2.3, then we should have to change '*in room r*' by '*for room type r*' in the first two steps of the tSSD and by '*in a room of type r*' in the last step of the tSSD.

5 Interactions Overview: Our Controller and Its Environment

We end with a general overview of the typical interactions between our controller and its environment. Instead of the earlier terms 'External System' or 'External Data Store' we use 'Data Store' because it might or might not be part of the system to be developed. The variables x and y in the overview indicate that there can be several such actors (Fig. 3):

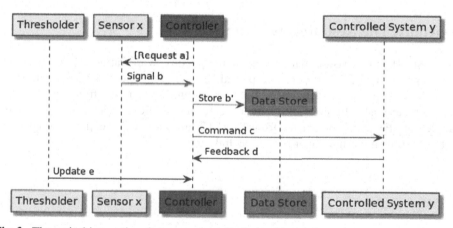

Fig. 3. The typical interactions between our controller and its environment
(This figure is not meant as a sequence diagram)

6 Contribution

As promised in the abstract, the paper discussed and illustrated the following topics:

– When system requirements are **changing all the time**: How to deal with that? As illustrated throughout the paper, by usually writing down only the (small) differences with a previous solution, and not writing out the new situation completely. Writing out the situation completely might be done once you have a good overview - that is why Sect. 4.3 came so late – or, contrarily, when you lost your overview.

- The **(mental) process** of going from a simple, naïve software solution towards various more subtle ones, probably inspired/guided by brainstorms with customers, was richly illustrated by the (>10) extensions, variants, and/or alternative options we introduced
- What should be inside and what outside the system scope? The **scope issue** was illustrated by the Data Store issue and the scheduling/scheduler discussion
- The development started with a concrete controller but ended with a **generic** COTS-system, not meant for one particular customer anymore (Sect. 4.8)
- **Agility** during requirements analyses was shown over and over again with all those extensions, variants, and/or alternative options we discussed
- The feasibility of our approach to another type of system, a **control system**, was illustrated throughout the paper
- The **manoeuvrability** ('agility') of our textual SSDs was shown during the many discussions of all types of variants ('textual SSDs in operation')

Acknowledgment. The author wants to thank Wilco Wijbrandi from TNO Research for the fruitful discussions we had about the many possible variants concerning thermostats.

Appendix: The Resulting Textual SSDs

The tSSD HandleMeasurement below is the version with variable thresholds per room type (Sect. 4.2.3), sensors that provide a timestamp (Sect. 4.3.3), a data store for registering measurements (Sect. 4.4), synchronous feedback from the heatings (Sect. 4.6), and asynchronous feedback from the air conditioners (Sect. 4.7). The tSSD HandleStatusFeedback originates from Sect. 4.7 and the tSSD AdaptThreshold from Sect. 4.8. (Blue underlined words serve as links too.)

define <u>HandleMeasurement</u>(x, t, s) **as**

○ Sensor x → Controller: Temperature t plus timestamp s ;

○ Controller → Data Store: Store sensor x, room r_x, temperature t, and timestamp s ,

○ **if** t < Hmin of the type of room sensor x is in

    then for each heating h in the room of x that is 'Off'

        do Controller → h: 'On!' ;

           do <u>HandleStatusFeedback</u>(h)

        end

    endif ,

○ **if** t > Hmax of the type of room sensor x is in

    then for each heating h in the room of x that is 'On'

        do Controller → h: 'Off!' ;

           do <u>HandleStatusFeedback</u>(h)

        end

    endif ,

○ **if** t < Amin of the type of room sensor x is in

    then for each airco a in the room of x that is 'On'

        do Controller → a: 'Off!' **end**

    endif ,

○ **if** t > Amax of the type of room sensor x is in

    then for each airco a in the room of x that is 'Off'

        do Controller → a: 'On!' **end**

    endif

end

define <u>HandleStatusFeedback</u>(y) **as**

    y → Controller: State(y) ;

    Controller → Controller: Register State(y) as the state of y

end

define <u>AdaptThreshold</u>(A, r, t) **as**

    Thresholder → Controller: Update threshold A in room r to temperature t ;

    Controller → Controller: Update threshold A in room r to temperature t ;

    for each sensor x in room r **do** Controller → x: SendTemperature **end**

end

References

1. De Brock, E.O.: On system sequence descriptions. In: M. Sabetzadeh, et al. (eds.) Joint Proceedings of REFSQ-2020 Workshops, etc. Pisa, Italy (2020)
2. De Brock, E.O.: From Elementary user wishes and domain models to SQL-specifications. In: Shishkov, B. (eds.) Business Modeling and Software Design. BMSD 2021. Lecture Notes in Business Inf. Processing, vol. 422, pp. 97–117. Springer, Cham (2021)

Value-Based Fuzzy Approach for Non-functional Requirements Prioritization

Khush Bakht Ijaz[1], Irum Inayat[1], Maya Daneva[2(✉)], and Faiza A. Bukhsh[2]

[1] NUCES, Islamabad, Pakistan
{i171097,irum.inayat}@nu.edu.pk
[2] University of Twente, Enschede, The Netherlands
{m.daneva,f.a.buksh}@utwente.nl

Abstract. Non-functional requirements (NFRs) are often addressed late in a project and, in turn, can get less attention in the requirements prioritization (RP) process. For various reasons, RP may happen based on functional requirements (FRs) only. While many approaches for prioritizing NFRs have been published, these are known also for some limitations, e.g. not being scalable, being domain-specific and not able to cope with changing requirements. In this paper, we proposes a value-based fuzzy approach for prioritizing NFRs together with FRs. Our proposed approach takes into account (1) the relationships of NFRs with FRs using experts' evaluations and fuzzy logic, and (2) the dependencies among both types of requirements and also the interdependencies that particularly exist among the NFRs themselves. We evaluated our proposal by conducting a real-world case study of an ATM system. We also compared the list of prioritized NFRs with the list of NFRs prioritized by different stakeholders on the basis of classification factors. The results of applying the proposed approach on NFRs of ATM system show that the approach produces a conflict-free and consistent list of prioritized NFRs.

Keywords: Non-functional requirements · Requirements prioritization · Fuzzy logic · Value-based requirements engineering · Design science · Empirical study

1 Introduction

Non-functional requirements (NFRs) are often addressed late [3] in requirements prioritization (RP) that happens early in the life cycle. One reason for this is that NFRs are rarely well-understood early in a project. Plus, variation of the perceived importance of the NFRs might well be possible due to various stakeholders' perspectives on them [31]. Systematic literature reviews on RP (e.g. [30, 31]) indicate that many approaches have been proposed for prioritizing NFRs as part of all requirements in a project, however these often lack scalability and pay only insufficient attention to requirements dependencies, be it dependencies between functional requirements (FRs) and NFRs, or NFRs interdependencies [33]. To counter these issues, recent efforts of the RE community focused on the application of fuzzy logic based techniques (e.g. [30]). While these proposals have been demonstrated to work in the specific contexts of the authors designing

© Springer Nature Switzerland AG 2021
B. Shishkov (Ed.): BMSD 2021, LNBIP 422, pp. 330–342, 2021.
https://doi.org/10.1007/978-3-030-79976-2_21

them, no generalizable and conclusive evidence has been produced so far regarding the strong and weak points of these approaches in real-world contexts. This paper contributes to the exploration of the application of fuzzy logic techniques for RP purposes. Drawing on previously published research [6, 7] on fuzzy logic in RP, we propose an approach named Value-based Fuzzy Requirement Prioritization that accounts for the relationships and interdependencies between NFRs and FRs [33] as perceived by experts in requirements engineering. Our proposal for a NFRs prioritization approach has been developed and evaluated by using Design Science [2] as our research method. Our work extends the application of fuzzy logic techniques [6, 7] to prioritize NFRs which so far has not been investigated in published literature. The proposed approach aims at helping requirement engineers in prioritizing large number of NFRs through a two-stage prioritization accounting for both stakeholders and experts. To evaluate this approach, we conducted a nearly real-world experimental study. The rest of the paper is organized as follows: Sect. 2 provides background on RP. Section 3 describes our research process. Section 4 proposes our RP approach. Section 5 is on its first experimental evaluation. Section 6 discusses this evaluation and the implications of this research. Sections 7 is on limitations and Section 8 concludes.

2 Background and Related Work

NFRs such as performance and security, can be considered as the constraints on a software system [8] that describe aspects such as how the system is performing and how secure it is to use, respectively. These aspects help software architects understand the architecture designs that best match the NFRs and the order in which they would be scheduled for implementation.

In the literature in the field of Requirements Engineering (RE), some approaches for NFRs prioritization exist. Examples are the CEP (Capture Elicit Prioritize) [11, 13] automated approach, the $\alpha\beta\gamma$ framework [12] for prioritizing NFRs, and the NERV methodology [14]. Next, an approach [19] leveraging the Analytic Hierarchy Process (AHP) [5] that focuses on interrelationships present between candidate NFRs has also been put forward. Moreover, other proposals include the hybrid approach that prioritizes FRs based on NFRs [15], the HAM (Hybrid Assessment Method) [16] that defines criteria for prioritization and also performs pair-wise comparisons of NFRs as used in [15] for defining trade-offs, simultaneous and separate prioritization approaches for NFRs and FRs [17], the NFR planning method for agile processes (NORPLAN) [18] which is a part of the NORMAP methodology discussed in [13]. Most of these approaches were demonstrated to work for only relatively small number of requirements. Moreover, studies show (e.g. [31]) that the proposed RP approaches are not guaranteed to be flexible and able to deal with ever-changing requirements (be it FRs or NFRs). This motivated our work on defining an approach that is both flexible and scalable in prioritizing NFRs.

Our work draws on published research by other authors on intelligent value-based approaches to NFRs prioritization. To the best of our knowledge, four studies [6, 7, 26, 27] have been published on such approaches. Ramzan et al. [7] proposed an intelligent value-based technique for RP based on fuzzy logic and expert systems. Kukreja et al. [26] presented a method concerned with providing verification to show that value based RP frameworks are effective and can help software development organizations to implement the most important requirements in earlier phases of software development life cycle. Next, the approach presented in [6] attempts to overcome the limitations present in existing RP approaches and suggests an intelligent-value-based approach able to produce the list of requirements prioritized based on the value assigned to the requirements. Finally, Padmanabhuni [27] deals with identifying a suitable framework for value-based RP. The selection of this framework is based on the nature of requirements. The work of these researchers [6, 7, 26, 27] inspired us in including the value-based perspective on software engineering, in the development of our approach.

3 Research Methodology

Our research process was inspired by the Design Science methodology [2] which aims at creating artefacts (methods and techniques) to solve real-life problems in information systems development and in software engineering. A design-science-based research process starts with goal-setting, and then proceeds with the creation of a method proposal and its evaluation in a realistic context. In the next sections, we first present the proposal of a RP method for NFRs and then we use an example of its application in a real-world case of an ATM system. The overall goal for using design science is to create a RP approach that accounts for the interdependencies among NFRs in a project as well as the interdependencies between NFRs and FRs.

4 Our Proposed Approach

This section provides a brief description of the concept of value-based fuzzy RP and then it elaborates on our proposed approach (called Value-based Fuzzy Requirement Prioritization).

As already said, our approach is grounded on the fuzzy logic theory and the value-based perspective. The fuzzy logic theory served as the foundation to create method of reasoning that resemble human reasoning. In the case of RP, generally fuzzy logic emulates the way of human decision making that involves the range of possibilities between digital values YES and NO. Our method also draws on the Value Based Intelligent RP technique of Ramzan et al. [7], which promotes iterative and multilevel prioritization and classification of NFRs from the perspectives of (i) stakeholders and (ii) experts in software projects. The iterative nature of the prioritization process makes sure that requirements are evaluated and re-evaluated by different actors and a more realistic priority ranking is achieved. In the technique of Ramzan et al. [7], assuming a set of elicited requirements has been documented and made available for RP, a *two-fold prioritization* takes place: first, the requirements are prioritized by the participating stakeholders and then by RE experts. Plus, the stakeholders themselves are prioritized by the experts. A priority assigned to a stakeholder is called a stakeholder profile. The experts rank stakeholders profiles on a scale of 1–10, where 1 means the least important, and 10 means the most important. The experts use this scale also for ranking the requirements. Using the stakeholders' profiles, the experts identify the importance of requirements provided by the particular stakeholder. Experts assign prioritization values to the requirements on the basis of requirement classification factors (RCFs) – these are prioritization criteria that are chosen by the RE experts specifically for the project as a whole, or for particular groups of requirements within the project. Examples of prioritization criteria are: importance, risk, requirement dependencies, development time, cost and technical debt. For a specific project and requirement in this project, these RCFs are assigned a score in the range of 0–5. The lowest value i.e. 0 indicates that particular factor is not present in a particular requirement and 5 indicates the high involvement of a classification factors in requirements. The requirement value (RV) is then estimated by using the formula [7] below:

$$RV = 0.35 + 0.02 \left\{ \sum_{i=1}^{n} pRCFi + \sum_{i=1}^{n} rRCFi \right\}$$

where *pRCF* stands for 'project-specific Requirements Classification Factor' and *rRCF* stands for 'requirement-specific Requirement Classification Factors. We note that the RV value is in the range of 0.35 (when all RCFs are scored to be 0) to 1.35 (when all RCFs are scored to be 5). We note that the constant 0.35 has been determined by Ramzan et al. [7] and we borrowed it in our method for the reason of assuring consistency of terminology.

Second, a fuzzy logic based algorithm (namely, the *fuzzy c mean algorithm* [21]) is then applied. This means that requirements are grouped by applying fuzzy membership value. Furthermore, we use the concept of intelligent value-based RP to the area of NFRs. And finally, our proposed approach aims at achieving two goals: (1) it should account for the dependencies between FRs and NFRs, and (2) it should account for the inter-dependencies of the NFRs themselves.

Below we describe the steps of the approach. Assuming a list of FRs and NFRs exists for a project, our approach includes:

Step 1. Determine the importance value of each NFR with respect to given FRs. Based on this importance value, the preliminary list of ranked FRs and NFRs is obtained.
Step 2. A decision matrix is constructed by placing the NFRs in a column and putting the corresponding FRs in rows.
Step 3. In the matrix, an ordinal scale is used to assign importance value to NFRs with respect to FRs. These values are put in the cells of the matrix. The values are assigned on a scale of 0–1, where 1 means 'most important' and 0 means "not important".
Step 4. NFRs final ranking is calculated by taking the weighted average of all the values belonging to NFR against all FRs. The NFR which gets the highest weight is given the highest priority.
Step 5. In order to account for the interdependencies among NFRs and to assure that the NFRs are conflict-free, we employ the NFRs conflict resolution method that was first presented by Dabbagh and Lee [28]. It identifies conflicting NFRs and then offers strategies to experts to resolve the NFRs conflicts before prioritization takes place. Because of space limitation, we do not present this approach in detail. Instead, we refer interested readers to the articles of Dannagh and Lee [28].
Step 6. The list of conflict-free NFRs is given to the experts. They assign prioritization values to the NFRs on the basis of the RCFs (i.e. importance, risk, requirement dependency, development time, cost and penalty). As indicated earlier, each of these factors is assigned a score in the range of 1–5.

Step 7. Requirement value (RV) is then estimated by applying the formula below. As indicated earlier, RV is in the range 0.35 to 1.35.

$$RV = 0.35 + 0.02 \left\{ \sum_{i=1}^{6} RCFi \right\}$$

Step 8. The *Fuzzy c mean algorithm* [21] is then applied to the final list of requirements prioritized using RVs and the initial prioritized list of NFRs. This ultimately leads to final priority ranks.

5   Our First Evaluation

The proposed approach has been evaluated by conducting an experimental study using real world data in a case of an ATM system. A real set of requirements has been obtained from the software requirement specification document of this ATM system. Both FRs and NFRs were defined. The total number of requirements is 40, including 20 FRs (see Fig. 1) and 20 NFRs (see Fig. 2).

FUNCTIONAL REQUIREMENTS OF ATM SYSTEM:

FR 1.1	If no cash card is in the ATM, the system shall display message on the screen.
FR 1.2	If the ATM is running out of money, no card shall be accepted. System displays an error message.
FR 1.3	The ATM has to check if the entered card is a valid cash card.
FR 1.4	If the cash card is valid, ATM shall read the serial number and bank code.
FR 1.5	System shall ask the user to enter his password. ATM shall verify the bank code and password with bank computer.
FR 1.6	The bank computer gets a request from the ATM to verify an account.
FR 1.7	If it is not a valid bank code the bank computer shall send a message to the ATM.
FR 1.8	The bank computer checks if the password is valid for a valid cash card.
FR 1.9	Bank computer shall process a transaction from the ATM if the details are valid.
FR 1.10	System shall display error message to the user if password and serial number are incorrect.
FR 1.11	If the password and serial number are correct authorization process is finished.
FR 1.12	If a card is entered more than three times and each time wrong password is entered then the card is kept by the ATM and system displays error message to the customer.
FR 1.13	System shall offer different kinds of transactions i.e. withdraw and deposit.
FR 1.14	System shall re initiate transaction dialogue if the amount entered by the user is not within the pre defined transaction policy.
FR 1.15	System shall perform valid transaction and wait for response from bank computer.
FR 1.16	System shall dispense the money if transaction is successful.
FR 1.17	Bank computer shall update the account of customer after processing the transaction.
FR 1.18	After dispensing the money, system shall log the amount with serial number of card. Notification is sent to the bank about dispensed money.
FR 1.19	If the transaction is not successful an error message should be displayed and the card should be ejected.
FR 1.20	ATM shall allow the customer to re login the account.

Fig. 1. FRs of the ATM system

The experiment started by first prioritizing the NFRs based on the six prioritization criteria (these are the RCFs) as shown in Fig. 3 (see columns B to G) with the participation of 7 stakeholders. This is **Step 1** in our approach. In Fig. 3, the criterion in column B reflects how much each NFR is important to be implemented for the stakeholders. The requirement dependency criterion (Req-dep, see column D) shows the extent to which particular NFRs is dependent upon a FR. Development time is the time required to implement the requirement. Cost of implementing the requirement has been calculated by adding Requirement dependency and development time. Penalty value is assigned

NON FUNCTIONAL REQUIREMENTS OF ATM SYSTEM:

NFR 1.1	The card verification time must not exceed 0.8 seconds under normal server workload and 1 second under peak server workload.
NFR 1.2	The pin number verification time must not exceed 0.3 sec. Under normal server workload and 0.5 sec. under peak server workload.
NFR 1.3	Cash withdrawal transaction time must not exceed 4 sec. under normal server workload and 5 sec. under peak server workload.
NFR 1.4	Receipt printing time after must not exceed 3 sec. Under normal server and peak server workload.
NFR 1.5	The product shall have a backup power supply in case of power failures.
NFR 1.6	Any abnormal operations shall result in the shutting down of the system.
NFR 1.7	After abnormal shutdown of the ATM, the system shall have to be manually restarted by maintenance personnel.
NFR 1.8	The system shall be compatible with AIMS security standards.
NFR 1.9	If there is no response from the bank computer after a request within 2 minutes the card is rejected with an error message.
NFR 1.10	User should be provided with only three attempts for login failing which his card needs to be blocked.
NFR 1.11	The ATM network has to be available 24 hours a day.
NFR 1.12	Only maintainers are allowed to connect new ATM's to the network.
NFR 1.13	The system should have the mechanism of self monitoring periodically in order to detect any fault.
NFR 1.14	Passwords shall not contain name of customers as they are easy to be hacked.
NFR 1.15	The memory system of ATM shall be of non volatile type.
NFR 1.16	The data communication protocol shall be such that it ensures reliability and quality of data and voice transmission in a mobile environment.
NFR 1.17	The system should inform the main branch automatically as soon as it detects any error. The kind of fault and the problem being encountered should also be mentioned by the system automatically.
NFR 1.18	Touch screen and button response time must not exceed 5000ms.
NFR 1.19	All functionality of ATM system shall be thoroughly tested.
NFR 1.20	There shall be a secured cash vault with a combination locking system.

Fig. 2. NFRs of the ATM system

when a required feature is not implemented. The values corresponding to each NFR and each criterion (also called RCF) are assigned by the 7 different stakeholders on a scale from 1–5. The two rightmost columns indicate the prioritized NFRs based on these 6 RCFs. Fig. 3 shows that NFR 1.13 and 1.18 are assigned highest priority values. In contrast, the least values are assigned to NFR 1.1 and 1.4. This means that NFR 1.13 and 1.18 are required to be implemented first and NFR 1.1 and 1.4 should be implemented the last.

Req id	Importance	Risk	Req-dep	Devp-Time	cost	Penalty	Priotity %	Priority
NFR 1.1	4	1	2	2	4	5	0.09	9
NFR 1.2	5	4	2	3	5	5	0.14	14
NFR 1.3	4	4	1	3	4	5	0.12	12
NFR 1.4	3	2	2	2	4	4	0.09	9
NFR 1.5	5	4	5	5	10	5	0.19	19
NFR 1.6	1	4	4	2	6	2	0.11	11
NFR 1.7	2	4	4	4	8	2	0.14	14
NFR 1.8	5	4	4	2	6	4	0.15	15
NFR 1.9	2	4	3	1	4	1	0.1	10
NFR 1.10	3	4	3	3	6	1	0.13	13
NFR 1.11	5	5	4	5	9	4	0.19	19
NFR 1.12	4	4	4	4	8	5	0.16	16
NFR 1.13	5	5	5	5	10	5	0.2	20
NFR 1.14	5	5	4	3	7	5	0.17	17
NFR 1.15	2	3	3	3	6	3	0.11	11
NFR 1.16	4	5	4	4	8	2	0.17	17
NFR 1.17	4	4	4	4	8	2	0.16	16
NFR 1.18	5	5	5	5	10	2	0.2	20
NFR 1.19	4	2	2	2	4	5	0.1	10
NFR 1.20	3	3	4	5	9	1	0.15	15

Fig. 3. Prioritized list of NFRs based on RCFs selected for the project

In order to assign an importance value to each NFRs with respect to FRs, a decision matrix was created (**Step 2**) by placing all 20 NFRs in columns and all FRs in rows (see Fig. 4).

	NFR 1.1	NFR 1.2	NFR 1.3	NFR 1.4	NFR 1.5	NFR 1.6	NFR 1.7	NFR 1.8	NFR 1.9	NFR 1.10	NFR 1.11	NFR 1.12	NFR 1.13	NFR 1.14	NFR 1.15	NFR 1.16	NFR 1.17	NFR 1.18	NFR 1.19	NFR 1.20
FRI.1	0.25	0.25	0.25	0	0.5	0.75	0.25	0.75	0	0.25	1	0.5	0.75	0	0.75	1	0.75	1	0.5	0.5
FRI.2	0.5	0	0	0.25	0.75	1	0.25	0.25	0	0.5	0.75	0.5	1	0.25	0.5	0.5	1	0.5	0.75	0.75
FRI.3	1	0.75	0.25	0.5	0.75	0.75	0.25	0.5	0.25	0.25	0.75	0.5	1	0.5	0.75	0.5	0.75	1	0.5	0.75
FRI.4	0.25	1	0.25	0.25	0.25	0.25	0.25	0.25	0.75	0.25	0.25	0.25	0.75	0.5	0.75	0.25	0.75	0	0.25	0.25
FRI.5	0.75	0.25	0.75	0.5	0.75	0.5	0.5	0.5	0.75	0.5	0.5	0.75	1	0.5	0.5	0.5	0.75	0.5	0.5	0.5
FRI.6	0	0.5	0	0.75	0	0	1	1	0.25	0.75	0.75	0.25	0	1	0.75	1	0	0.5	0.25	0.75
FRI.7	0.25	0.75	0.25	0.75	0.25	0.25	0.75	0.25	1	0.75	0.75	0.25	0	0.75	0.5	0.25	0	0.25	0.75	0.25
FRI.8	0.5	0	0.5	0.75	0.5	0.5	0.75	0.25	0.75	0.25	0.25	0.25	1	0.5	0.25	0.25	0.75	0.25	0.25	0.25
FRI.9	0.5	0.25	0.75	0	0.25	0.75	0.5	0.5	0.75	0.5	0.5	0.5	0.75	0.5	0.5	0.5	0.75	0.5	0.5	0.5
FRI.10	0	0.5	0.25	0	0.75	0.75	0.25	1	0	0.25	0.75	0.75	0.5	0.25	0.25	0.75	1	0.75	0.25	0.75
FRI.11	0.75	0.75	0.75	0.25	0	0.25	0.25	0.25	0	0.75	0.75	0	0	0.75	0.25	0.25	0	0.75	0.75	0.5
FRI.12	0.75	0.75	0	0.5	0.25	0.75	1	0.25	0.75	1	0.25	0	0.75	0	0.25	0.25	0.75	0.25	0.25	0.25
FRI.13	0.75	0.75	0.25	0.25	0.5	0.75	0.25	0.5	0.75	0.5	1	0.5	0.75	0.5	0.75	0.5	0.75	0.25	0.5	0.5
FRI.14	0	0.5	0.5	0.5	0.25	0.5	0.25	0.75	0.5	0.25	0.75	0.5	0.25	0.5	0.75	0.75	0	0.75	0.25	0.75
FRI.15	0.25	0.25	0.75	0.75	0.25	1	0.25	0.5	0.75	0.75	0.75	0.25	0.5	0.75	0.75	0.25	0	0.75	0.25	0.25
FRI.16	0.75	0.25	1	0.75	0	0.25	0.5	0.25	0.75	0.25	0.25	0.25	0.75	0	0.25	0.25	0.75	1	1	1
FRI.17	0	0.25	0.25	0	0.25	0.25	0.5	0.5	0.75	0.5	0.5	0.5	0.75	0.5	0.5	0.5	0.75	0.5	0.5	0.5
FRI.18	0.25	0	0.75	1	0.5	0.75	0.25	0.75	0	0.25	0.75	0.5	0.5	0.25	0.5	0.75	0.25	0.75	0.5	0.75
FRI.19	0.5	0.25	0.5	0.25	1	0.5	0.5	0.25	0	1	0.75	0.25	1	0	0.75	1	1	0	0.75	0.75
FRI.20	0.75	0	0.75	0.5	0	0.25	0.25	0.5	0.75	0.25	0.5	0.25	0.75	0	0.25	1	0.75	0.25	1	0.75
WAvg%	43.75	40.0	39.75	42.5	41.25	38.8	47.5	45	46.25	48.75	58.75	36.25	62.5	50	51.25	56.25	52.5	60	53.75	57.5

Fig. 4. Importance values assigned to NFRs with respect to FRs (**Steps 2, 3 and 4**).

In Fig. 4, using the scale of 0 to 1 defined in [29], the following values are assigned: 1 (being very highly important), 0.75 (highly important), 0.5 (low important), 0.25 (very low important) and 0 (not important). This is **Step 3** in our approach. The NFRs final ranking (**Step 4**) is calculated by taking the *weighted average* of all the values belonging to NFR against all FRs, see the last row in the table of Fig. 4. The NFR which gets highest weight is given higher priority.

To acknowledge for NFRs interdependencies, conflicts between NFRs are identified and resolved (**Step 5**) by using the technique of Dabbagh and Lee [28]. We note that in the case of the ATM, its application led to the elimination of two NFRs as throughout the conflict resolution they were found unimportant for the project. The list of remaining 18 conflict-free NFRs is then given to the group of ten experts (**Step 6**) tasked with assigning prioritization values to the NFRs based on the selected RCFs for the project as shown in Fig. 3: importance, risk, requirement dependency, development time, cost and penalty. Fig. 5 shows the scores assigned to all NFRs by the experts, in regard to these six RCFs.

For each NFR, the requirement value is then estimated by applying the formula for RV:

$$RV = 0.35 + 0.02\left\{ \sum_{i=1}^{6} RCFi \right\}$$

This is **Step 7** of our approach. The RV value against each NFR is shown in Fig. 6, left. Those NFRs having higher RV value are given higher priority. In line with this, the highest priority is assigned to NFR 1.13 (see the top row in Fig. 6, left).

The fuzzy c mean algorithm [21] is then applied (Step 8) to the final list of requirements that are prioritized using the RV values as shown in Fig. 6, left. In this study, the

RCFs					
	Importance	Risk	Req-dependency	Dev-Time	Cost	Penalty
NFR 1.13	5	4	5	4	9	5
NFR 1.18	4	4	5	4	9	4
NFR 1.11	4	3	4	4	8	4
NFR 1.20	4	5	2	2	4	5
NFR 1.16	3	2	1	1	2	4
NFR 1.19	3	1	4	2	6	4
NFR 1.17	3	2	3	3	6	3
NFR 1.15	2	2	1	2	3	2
NFR 1.14	1	4	4	4	8	1
NFR 1.10	1	4	4	4	8	4
NFR 1.7	2	2	3	4	7	2
NFR 1.9	3	3	2	2	4	1
NFR 1.8	3	3	2	3	5	1
NFR 1.1	2	3	1	4	5	3
NFR 1.4	2	1	2	3	5	1
NFR 1.2	2	2	2	3	5	2
NFR 1.3	1	1	4	1	5	1
NFR 1.6	1	3	5	4	9	2

Fig. 5. Scores assigned to the NFRs by 10 field experts (**Step 6**)

NFR 1.13	RV=0.99
NFR 1.18	RV=0.95
NFR 1.11	RV=0.89
NFR 1.20	RV=0.79
NFR 1.16	RV=0.61
NFR 1.19	RV=0.75
NFR 1.17	RV=0.75
NFR 1.15	RV=0.59
NFR 1.14	RV=0.79
NFR 1.10	RV=0.85
NFR 1.7	RV=0.75
NFR 1.9	RV=0.65
NFR 1.8	RV=0.69
NFR 1.1	RV=0.71
NFR 1.4	RV=0.63
NFR 1.2	RV=0.67
NFR1.4	RV=0.63
NFR 1.3	RV=0.61
NFR 1.6	RV=0.83

NFRs	Priority value	C1	C2	C3
NFR 1.1	(14,11)	4.95	8.03	11.9
NFR 1.2	(16,13)	7.49	10.7	14.7
NFR 1.3	(17,17)	10.6	13.8	18.1
NFR 1.4	(15,15)	7.73	11.0	15.2
NFR 1.6	(18,5)	10.1	11.8	13.9
NFR 1.7	(11,10)	1.83	4.89	8.91
NFR 1.8	(13,12)	8.56	7.62	11.7
NFR 1.9	(12,14)	4.96	8.17	12.5
NFR 1.10	(10,4)	5.98	5.15	5.90
NFR 1.11	(3,3)	9.27	6.06	1.75
NFR 1.13	(1,1)	12.1	8.86	4.37
NFR 1.14	(9,6)	3.92	3.04	5.16
NFR 1.15	(8,18)	8.16	10.2	14.2
NFR 1.16	(5,16)	7.37	8.29	11.7
NFR 1.17	(7,9)	2.36	1.19	5.47
NFR 1.18	(2,2)	10.7	7.45	3.16
NFR 1.20	(4,7)	5.94	2.74	2.65
NFR 1.19	(6,8)	3.71	0.61	4.11

Fig. 6. The RV values for the NFRs (left) and the final cluster values after 4th pass (right)

number of clusters has been selected as c=3. Thus, each cluster contains 6 NFRs (as the total is 18). Randomly three centroid values have also been given to these clusters i.e. for cluster 1, value 9 has been given as initial prioritization value and 10 is given as RV-based prioritized value. Similarly, random values have been assigned to other clusters as well. The distance from a point to cluster center has been defined as the Euclidean distance. The fuzzifier value "m" – which is the parameter controlling how fuzzy the cluster will be – is assumed to be 2 in this study. The number of centroids has been set as 3. Fig. 6 (see the right side) shows the final cluster values after the 4th pass.

The final prioritized list of NFRs is shown in Fig. 7. Therein, the highest priority is assigned to NFR 1.13 and least priority is assigned to NFR 1.15. To sum up, by applying value based fuzzy prioritization approach to the NFRs of the ATM system, we obtained

Final prioritized list of conflict free NFRs	
NFR	**Priority**
NFR 1.13	1
NFR 1.18	2
NFR 1.11	3
NFR 1.10	4
NFR 1.6	5
NFR 1.14	6
NFR 1.20	7
NFR 1.19	8
NFR 1.17	9
NFR 1.7	10
NFR 1.1	11
NFR 1.8	12
NFR 1.2	13
NFR 1.9	14
NFR 1.4	15
NFR 1.16	16
NFR 1.3	17
NFR 1.15	18

Fig. 7. Final prioritized list of NFRs (the result of Step 8)

a conflict-free list of prioritized NFRs. This list accounted for both the dependencies between NFRs and FRs and the interdependencies among the NFRs themselves.

6 Discussion

We compared the list of prioritized NFRs obtained by applying our value-based fuzzy prioritization approach (Fig. 7) with the list of NFRs prioritized by stakeholders on the basis of RCFs i.e. the prioritization criteria (Fig. 3). The prioritization criteria have been kept same for both the RP processes (i.e. for the value-based NFRs prioritization (our proposed approach) and the prioritization based on values assigned by stakeholders as shown in Fig. 3). The results of our experimental study show that the proposed approach produces better outcome in three regards: (i) our approach produced a *ranking* (as opposed to the percentages indicated in the column "Priority %" in Fig. 3), (ii) we obtained a prioritized list of *conflict-free* NFRs, and (iii) we implemented the *two-stage* RP by involving 10 experts in addition to the 7 stakeholders (Fig. 3). Our research has some implications for practitioners and for researchers. First, the proposed method keeps the requirement engineers focused on the prioritization of NFRs during early software development phase. As earlier research suggested [32], often the NFRs are treated late and then approached by software architects, developers, and even testers. Second, having a method for RP of NFRs helps project managers including NFRs in the estimation of effort of their projects. As Kassab et al. [34] indicate, project estimation is better, if it accounts for the NFRs' interdependencies and if it is aware of the NFRs conflicts. To RE researchers, the proposed fuzzy logic based approach opens up some interesting research directions First, the method assumes that stakeholders will assign priorities to the existing requirements. If stakeholder's involvement is not possible at that stage, what heuristics the RE specialist responsible for the project, could adopt in order to be able to create the inputs for the matrix that is created in the first steps of our method? Second, it is good to know if the applicability of the method depends on the characteristics of the application domain and the size of the project. Finally, we note that our evaluation study included 40 requirements in a realistic project (ATM). Although, this is more than what is included in the demonstrations of other published RP proposals, we can no claim for certain the scalability of our approach to contexts in which thousands or hundreds of thousands of requirements are to be prioritized. We think that researchers together with practitioners may conduct an empirical research on large-scale requirements repositories to explore the scalability, the accuracy and the efficiency of the proposed approach. Also, a comparative study may also be conducted to explore how our method compares with other techniques.

7 Limitations

This research has some limitations. As Hevner et al. [2] suggests, an important validity concern is the generalizability of our proposal. We did a very first evaluation of the RP method on a realistic project in experimental settings. This included 40 requirements. Clearly, most projects would have more. We however think that if the steps of our approach are fully automated, dealing with long lists of requirements would not be a problem. Would the approach be suitable to all project contexts? We think that the approach is more suitable for projects in which diverse NFRs are to be considered and their dependencies must be analysed in detail. This would be for example in contexts of large scale online systems, such as gaming software, social network software or e-commerce sites that are concerned with scalability, performance, privacy, security, usability, learnability and ease of use. In contrast to this, we think that certain types of applications such as administrative software systems (e.g. in human resources, in accounting) where the number of users is limited, would not benefit vastly from our approach. This is not to say that the projects developing such applications can not employ our method; they certainly could, however they might find no big difference between using our method and any other RP technique available in the marketplace. In this kind of contexts, there are usually a very small number of NFRs [32] and they are well understood and the trade-offs among them might well be known to the software architects.

8 Conclusions

This paper proposed an approach that employs intelligent value based fuzzy prioritization to NFRs. We made a step towards a RP solution based on fuzzy logic by extending the earlier work done on value based fuzzy requirement prioritization [6, 7]. Using a realistic case, an ATM system and its FRs and NFRs specifications, we have demonstrated that if a requirements engineer has a specification at his disposal, he/she would be able to prioritise the NFRs early in the development process by taking into account the NFRs interdependencies and also the dependencies between NFRs and FRs.

Manually performing all steps and computations is time consuming and requires a lot of efforts. Moreover the computations may also be prone to errors as they have been performed manually. Therefore, our immediate future work is to build a tool support for this approach so that all these limitations can be overcome. Plus, we plan to use this tool in other realistic contexts in order to evaluate the strong and weak points of our proposed method. Specifically, we expect to start more evaluation studies in the Netherlands in those companies that are RE research partners in the research projects of the last co-author). The proposed approach will be applied on larger set of non-functional requirements i.e. more than 20, and the results will then be compared with other existing approaches for NFR prioritization. More subjects will be involved to get larger number of functional and non-functional requirements of any real software system in order to give stronger foundation to the results.

We before, our future work also includes empirical studies in companies in order to evaluate the acknowledge that our experimental study was applied to relatively small set of NFRs (20). Ther applicability, the usefulness and the utility of our approach in real-world projects. Only then, we could make firmer conclusions about the qualities of our proposed method.

References

1. Yin, B., Jin, Z.: Extending the problem frames approach for capturing non-functional requirements. In: IEEE 11th International Conference on Computer and Information Science, pp. 432–437 (2012)
2. Hevner, A.R., March, S.T., Park, J., Ram, S.: Design science in information systems research. MIS Q. **28**(1), 75–105 (2004)
3. Nguyen, Q.L.: Non-functional requirements analysis modeling for software product lines. In: ICSE Workshop on Modeling in Software Engineering, pp. 56–61 (2009)
4. Gupta, V., Chauhan, D.S., Dutta, K.: Exploring reprioritization through systematic literature surveys and case studies. Springerplus **4**(1), 1–15 (2015). https://doi.org/10.1186/s40064-015-1320-0
5. Kassab, M., Kilicay-Ergin, N.: Applying analytical hierarchy process to system quality requirements prioritization. Innovations Syst. Softw. Eng. **11**(4), 303–312 (2015). https://doi.org/10.1007/s11334-015-0260-8
6. Ramzan, M., Jaffar, M.A., Iqbal, M.A., Anwar, S., Shahid, A.A.: Value based fuzzy requirement prioritization and its evaluation framework. In: 4th International Conference on Innovative Computing, Information and Control (ICICIC), pp. 1464–1468 (2009)
7. Ramzan, M., Jaffar, A., Ali Shahid, A.: Value based intelligent requirement prioritization (Virp): Expert driven fuzzy logic based prioritization technique. Int. J. Innov. Comput. Inf. Control (2011)
8. Baskaran, S.: A survey on prioritization methodologies to prioritize non functional requirements. Int. J. Comput. Sci. Bus. Inform. **12**(1), 32–44 (2014)
9. Dabbagh, M., Lee, S.P., Parizi, R.M.: Functional and non-functional requirements prioritization: empirical evaluation of IPA, AHP-based, and HAM-based approaches. Soft. Comput. **20**(11), 4497–4520 (2015). https://doi.org/10.1007/s00500-015-1760-z
10. Phillips, L.B., Aurum, A., Svensson, R.B.: Managing Software Quality Requirements. In: 38th Euromicr, pp. 349–356 (2012)
11. Maiti, R.R., Mitropoulos, F.J.: Capturing, eliciting, predicting and prioritizing (CEPP) non-functional requirements metadata during the early stages of agile software development. In: SoutheastCon, pp. 1–8 (2015)

12. Aasem, M., Ramzan, M., Jaffar, A.: Analysis and optimization of software requirements prioritization techniques. In: International Conference on Information and Emerging Technologies, pp. 1–6 (2010)

13. Maiti, R.R., Mitropoulos, F.J.: Capturing, eliciting, and prioritizing (CEP) NFRs in agile software engineering. In: SoutheastCon pp. 1–7 (2017)

14. Domah, D., Mitropoulos, F.J.: The NERV methodology: a lightweight process for addressing non-functional requirements in agile software development. In: SoutheastCon pp. 1–7 (2015)

15. Garg, U., Singhal, A.: Software requirement prioritization based on non-functional requirements. In: 7th International Conference on Cloud Computing, Data Science and Engineering, pp. 793–797 (2017)

16. Dabbagh, M., Lee, S.P., Parizi, R.M.: Application of hybrid assessment method for priority assessment of functional and non-functional requirements. In: ICISA 2014, pp.1–4 (2014)

17. Chopra, R.K., Gupta, V., Chauhan, D.S.: Experimentation on accuracy of non functional requirement prioritization approaches for different complexity projects. Perspect. Sci., **8**, Supplement C, pp. 79–82 (2016)

18. Farid, W.M., Mitropoulos, F.J.: NORPLAN: non-functional requirements planning for agile processes. IEEE Southeastcon, pp. 1–8 (2013)

19. Fellir, F., Nafil, K., Touahni, R.: System requirements prioritization based on AHP. In: 3rd IEEE CIST, pp. 163–167 (2014)

20. Paucar, L.H.G., Bencomo, N.: ARRoW: tool support for automatic runtime reappraisal of weights. IEEE 25th RE, pp. 458–461 (2017)

21. Bezdek, J.C.: Pattern Recognition with Fuzzy Objective Function Algorithms (1981)

22. Thakurta, R.: A framework for prioritization of quality requirements for inclusion in a software project. Softw. Qual. J. **21**(4), 573–597 (2013)

23. Kassab, M.: An integrated approach of AHP and NFRs framework. In: RCIS 2013, pp.1–8 (2013)

24. Singh, P., Singh, D., Sharma, A.: Rule-based system for automated classification of non-functional requirements from requirement specifications. In: ICACCI 2016, pp. 620–626 (2016)

25. Dhingra, S., Savithri, G., Madan, M., Manjula, R.: Selection of prioritization technique for software requirement using fuzzy logic and decision tree. In: IC-GET, pp. 1–11 (2016)

26. Kukreja, N., Payyavula, S.S., Boehm, B., Padmanabhuni, S.: Value-based requirements prioritization: usage experiences. Procedia Comput. Sci. **16**, 806–813 (2013)

27. Padmanabhuni, S.: Selecting an appropriate framework for value-based requirements prioritization. In: Proceedings of the 2012 IEEE 20th RE, pp. 303–308 (2012)

28. Dabbagh, M., Lee, S.P.: A consistent approach for prioritizing system quality attributes. In: 14th ACIS International Conference on Software Engineering, Artificial Intelligence, Networking and Parallel/Distributed Computing, pp. 317–322

29. Dabbagh, M., Lee, S.P.: An approach for integrating the prioritization of functional and nonfunctional requirements. Scientific World Journal (2014)

30. Bukhsh, F.A., Bukhsh, Z.A., Daneva, M.: A systematic literature review on requirement prioritization techniques and their empirical evaluation. Comput. Stand. Interfaces **69**, 103389 (2020)

31. Alsaqaf, W., Daneva, M., Wieringa, R.: Quality requirements in large-scale distributed agile projects – a systematic literature review. In: Grünbacher, P., Perini, A. (eds.) REFSQ 2017. LNCS, vol. 10153, pp. 219–234. Springer, Cham (2017). https://doi.org/10.1007/978-3-319-54045-0_17

32. Daneva, M., Herrmann, A., Buglione, L.: Coping with Quality Requirements in Large. Contract-Based Projects. IEEE Softw. **32**(6), 84–91 (2015)
33. Martakis, A., Daneva, M.: Handling requirements dependencies in agile projects: a focus group with agile software development practitioners. In: RCIS 2013, pp. 1–11 (2013)
34. Kassab, M., Ormandjieva, O., Daneva, M.: Scope management of non-functional requirements. Euromicro 2007, pp. 409–417 (2007)

Towards Augmented Enterprise Models as Low-Code Interfaces to Digital Systems

Hans-Georg Fill$^{(\boxtimes)}$ ⓘ, Felix Härer ⓘ, Fabian Muff ⓘ, and Simon Curty ⓘ

University of Fribourg, 1700 Fribourg, Switzerland
{hans-georg.fill,felix.harer,fabian.muff,simon.curty}@unifr.ch
http://www.unifr.ch/inf/digits

Abstract. Traditionally, enterprise models have been used for representing knowledge on all aspects of an organization. This aided not only in composing a holistic picture of the different layers of an enterprise in terms of its business model, products and services, business processes and IT architecture, but also for describing the inter-dependencies between the layers. Depending on the degree of formalization, algorithms may be applied to the models, e.g. for simulations. With the upcoming of low-code approaches in software engineering, we regard in this position paper how similar concepts may be integrated in enterprise engineering. In particular we regard augmented enterprise models as interfaces to digital systems and illustrate this view with approaches for semantic technologies, data analytics and blockchain platforms. It is envisaged that such approaches will aid domain experts in integrating digital technologies in their daily work practices.

Keywords: Enterprise modeling · Low-code development · Digital systems

1 Motivation

With the constant technological advancement and the permanent introduction of new technologies, enterprises need to react quickly to new developments and analyze potential effects on their business operations [7,28]. For that purpose, new technologies have to be rapidly understood and adopted through integrating them in existing environments if necessary [10]. In order to assess the potential of a new technology, a systematic approach is required that considers all necessary business and technological aspects [23]. This can be achieved through enterprise modeling which takes an engineering-oriented approach for representing all relevant aspects of an organization including its business model, products and services, business processes and organizational structures, IT services and workflows, as well as the IT and physical infrastructure [17,39,40,42]. Some approaches in enterprise modeling take a holistic perspective in the form of complete frameworks, e.g. MEMO [3], 4EM [41], ArchiMate [43], whereas others focus on partial aspects, e.g. just on business models [48] or process-related aspects in BPMN [34].

© Springer Nature Switzerland AG 2021
B. Shishkov (Ed.): BMSD 2021, LNBIP 422, pp. 343–352, 2021.
https://doi.org/10.1007/978-3-030-79976-2_22

In addition, enterprise modeling has been regarded on different levels of formalization [4]. Whereas some approaches can be characterized as partially formal or semi-formal as they provide an unambiguous definition of the syntax of a modeling language and describe its semantics in natural language, e.g. as found in the iStar framework [29] or related approaches for goal modeling, others operate on a level where both structure and behavior are formally specified, e.g. the Semantic Object Model (SOM) [11] or Heraklit [13]. Furthermore, formal specifications may be added during run-time, e.g. via annotations [14,15], which serves the purpose of adding further processing capabilities such as semantic reasoning or for realizing simulations.

From the perspective of software systems development, the concept of so-called *low-code development platforms* recently gained attention [8]. Low-code platforms can be regarded as the next step in the evolution of techniques for creating software applications with less effort for writing programming code. This has been addressed previously in model-driven engineering and model-driven architectures (MDE/MDA) [12] and computer-aided software engineering (CASE) [45]. Today, these platforms are run in cloud environments and make use of dynamic graphical user interfaces, visual diagrams and declarative languages for realizing fully operational applications [8]. Whereas model-driven engineering and CASE went into similar directions, low-code adds a new perspective by not aiming for a complete elimination of the need to write code (no-code), but stresses the possibility of adding code segments where necessary. In addition, the topic of low-code approaches is characterized by recent increased interest from the side of industry [7].

As both enterprise modeling and low-code development often revert to graphical models, we will discuss in the following how the concepts of low-code development may be joined with enterprise modeling. The main idea thereby is to create enterprise modeling platforms that are capable of directly interacting with digital systems. Whereas some areas in enterprise modeling have followed such ideas early on, e.g. for executing business process models using workflow [22] or simulation engines [2], or the introduction of MDE approaches for dedicated business applications [27] and the derivation of requirements for software systems from enterprise models [49], most types of enterprise models today do not target the interaction with technical systems but stay on a conceptual level. The augmentation of enterprise models with interfaces to digital systems has the potential to enhance the productivity of domain experts and decision makers by combining the conceptual capabilities of enterprise models with machine-processing features.

The remainder of the paper is structured as follows. In Sect. 2 we will review the main characteristics of low-code software development approaches. This is followed by a discussion on how augmented enterprise models can act as low-code interfaces to digital systems and illustrating the idea with examples from the areas of semantic technologies, data analytics, and blockchains in Sect. 3. Subsequently, requirements for augmenting enterprise models are derived in Sect. 4 and a conclusion and outlook are given in Sect. 5.

2 Characteristics of Low-Code Software Development

Whereas *no-code software development* aims at creating software applications entirely without writing any code in a programming language [8], *low-code development* takes a slightly relaxed perspective and is directed towards simplifying software development with *less* coding effort [44]. That means that low-code platforms may still require some coding knowledge or specialist skills, e.g. for entering mathematical formulas, but have the objective of shifting programming tasks from software engineers to domain experts [6]. For that purpose they revert to cloud-based architectures for the easy versioning, deployment and monitoring of applications via SaaS or PaaS, visual and domain-specific languages, and machine-learning techniques for assistance functionalities [6,44]. A particular advantage of both no-code and low-code approaches is seen in the possibility of enabling domain experts to create software applications and thus address the rising demand for software that so far required extensive coding skills [6,8].

Examples of no-code and low-code platforms can today be found across many domains. A recent survey showed a number of approaches for the visual encoding of blockchain applications and smart contracts [25], and from an industrial perspective, low-code approaches are investigated today especially for intelligent business process management, robotic process automation, or citizen automation and development [21].

3 Augmented Enterprise Models as Low-Code Digital Interfaces

When applying the idea of low-code software development to the realm of enterprise engineering [24,46], the following analogies can be found. Similar to the field of software engineering and the coding of software applications, also the interaction with state-of-the-art digital systems in enterprise engineering requires highly specialized knowledge. Consider for example the complexity of configuring a data analytics engine for applying machine-learning algorithms to sales data, the interaction with a blockchain platform for the realization of a decentralized autonomous organization, or the use of semantic technologies for classifying textual information.

In recent years, several efforts have thus been made for enabling domain experts in enterprise engineering with no or little coding knowledge to use such digital systems using no-code or low-code approaches. In contrast to software engineering it is thereby not aimed at creating arbitrary applications but rather at configuring and interacting with existing software systems. Examples include visual configuration platforms for machine learning and data analytics such as Knime, Azure Machine Learning Designer or RapidMiner Studio [1,31,36], the visual specification of semantic rules [35], or visual languages for production automation in Industry 4.0 scenarios [5,47].

However, these approaches have been mostly treated separately and were not integrated with enterprise models [46]. Such an integration would permit

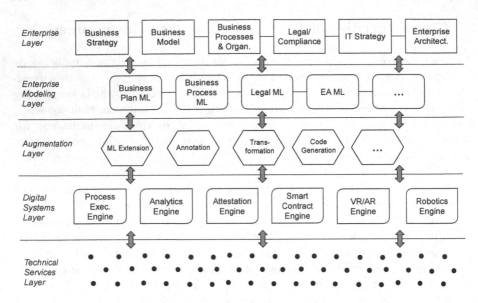

Fig. 1. Layers in augmented enterprise modeling

the seamless derivation of requirements for example in data analytics from the business strategy and the direct provision of according data.

For achieving this integration, we propose the following layers as depicted in Fig. 1. On the *Enterprise Layer*, the business aspects are shown that are relevant for enterprise engineering. Subsequently, the *Enterprise Modeling Layer* contains formal and semi-formal modeling languages (ML) for formalizing the business aspects. This permits for example to transform descriptions of business plans or business processes into machine-processable representations. Thereby, the degree of formalization determines the applicability and types of algorithms to be used. Whereas models whose behavioral properties are formally specified may be easily processed by algorithms, semi-formal models will permit only the application of selected algorithms [4]. For joining enterprise models with digital systems, we further propose an *Augmentation Layer*. This layer serves for the augmentation of enterprise models towards enabling a low-code interaction with digital systems. This can be achieved for example via the extension of modeling languages, the annotation of models, their transformation or the generation of code from models. The goal of this layer is to abstract from the technical details required for the interaction with the digital systems and embed their functionalities within the environment of the domain experts. The results of this augmentation then permit the interaction on the *Digital Systems Layer* with systems such as process execution or analytics engines, novel forms of attestation or smart contract engines or engines for the interaction with physical hardware such as VR/AR equipment or robotics to name some examples. Finally, the *Technical Services Layer* stands for the concrete implementations behind the digital systems, which typically follows today the paradigm of service orientation [9].

For illustrating how augmented enterprise models can be used in practical scenarios, we discuss in the following three examples where this approach has been already successfully applied. The first example presents the use of annotation models for enabling reasoning with semantic technologies, the second example the integration of functionalities from a data analytics platform in a business process improvement approach and the third example the integration of a blockchain-based attestation engine for enterprise models.

3.1 Example: Reasoning with Semantic Technologies

With semantic technologies, different kinds of classification and reasoning tasks can be accomplished. In particular, ontology and rule models permit to define formal conceptualizations of domains based on axioms. Subsequently, reasoners and rule engines can be applied for deriving new facts or classifying existing information. In the SeMFIS approach, enterprise models are augmented through annotation models that reference concepts in ontology and rule models [15,35] - see Fig. 2. The thus enriched models are then transformed into formats that can be processed by reasoners and rule engines. The resulting classifications or new facts are subsequently fed back into the enterprise models or may be used for interactions with digital systems. Thereby, all information is expressed visually without the need for coding.

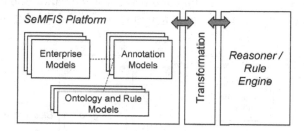

Fig. 2. Architecture of the SeMFIS annotation approach

3.2 Example: Integrating Data Analytics

For the integration of data analytics functionalities in enterprise modeling, the RUPERT approach for business process improvement reverted to the architecture shown in Fig. 3 [20,30]. Through linking enterprise models to so-called statistical interface models and from these to according data sources, code for the R analytics platform is generated. In the statistical interface models it can be chosen from different kinds of pre-defined data analyses with the optional specification of parameters. The results generated by the R platform are then delivered back to the modeling platform and represented graphically.

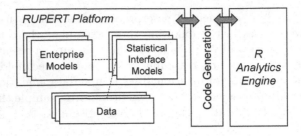

Fig. 3. Architecture of the RUPERT approach for integrating data analytics

3.3 Example: Attestation Using Blockchains

In enterprise engineering, digital artifacts in the form of enterprise models are at the core of planning the behavior and structure of processes, decisions, and any other domain-specific reality captured by models. For allowing the integration of models with digital systems to a greater degree, attestation permits the creation of dependable and binding models possessing a contractual character [26]. Building on smart contract technologies and blockchains, the attestation of process steps, business services, or other artifacts can certify their exact state, timestamps, instance-level changes, and author information. In contrast to the traditional way of certifying documents with a trusted third party (TTP), blockchains here permit the immutable recording and decentralized validation of models and instances through an attestation engine acting as TTP - see Fig. 4.

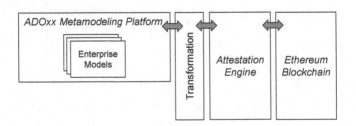

Fig. 4. Attestation architecture for ADOxx

In this way, the certification of information such as the recording of processes and instances becomes possible in a distributed setting. When using technical systems such as for process execution, other engines can dependably rely on the state and progression of artifacts. Further applications include the verifiable issuance of certifications on the domain level - e.g. issuing degrees from universities to students [26] - and the attestation of technical artifacts such as machine learning algorithms, ontologies, or abitrary types of enterprise models [16,18,19].

4   Requirements for Augmenting Enterprise Modeling

When aiming for an augmentation of enterprise models towards their use as low-code interfaces to digital platforms, we can formulate the following three requirements based on the experiences gained with the implementations shown above.

First, the parts of enterprise models that shall act as interfaces to digital systems respectively the extensions of enterprise models need to be *sufficiently formally specified* [4]. This is necessary to have a clear view on the required behavior and ease the design of algorithms for processing the contained information [24]. The degree of formalization is thereby inter-dependent with the algorithms - i.e., for an algorithm that shall execute a process-oriented model, a more elaborate formal specification is necessary than for an algorithm that shall just derive the graphical representation of a model or that extracts some parameters for configuring a system.

Further, the digital systems that shall act as the target of the interaction need to have well-accessible and well-specified interfaces. Ideally, they provide an *openly-accessible API* or *well-specified exchange formats*. Today this is typically accomplished using REST interfaces and standardized exchange formats such as XML or JSON [37]. The behavior of the APIs needs to be well-documented and endpoints have to be accessible in a granularity that is suited for the interaction with the modeling tools. In case the granularity is not adequate for a direct coupling, interfaces or even separate engines for transforming the content of models have to be added separately.

Finally, a major challenge is to find a good trade-off between an adequate *user experience* for interacting with the technologies from the perspective of the domain experts, the scope of the provided *functionalities* and the *technical efficiency* of the interaction in the form of algorithms. Whereas users require a certain redundancy in the encoding of information for reducing interpretation errors, c.f. [32], algorithms require unambiguous, mathematical specifications in formats that are efficient for processing. Such design decisions therefore require engineering-oriented approaches and can hardly be achieved through purely scientific approaches [46].

5   Conclusion and Outlook

In this paper we discussed how enterprise models can be augmented in a way that is similar to low-code approaches in software engineering. The goal is to enable domain experts to directly interact with digital systems without requiring extensive coding knowledge.

One field that we will target in the future are enterprise modeling applications in the field of VR and AR where first approaches for displaying ER models and legal models using augmented reality are available [33,38]. With the help of the Augmentation Layer and the Digital System Layer, AR-based enterprise modeling tools can be designed, in which the underlying language from the Enterprise

Modeling Layer is extended or annotated and automatically transformed and represented in VR or AR with the help of a VR/AR engine. This would permit to create direct interfaces between enterprise models and the physical or virtual world, e.g. for displaying the content of enterprise models in the physical space of the user or for immersing users in the knowledge space of enterprise models.

References

1. Berthold, M.R., et al.: KNIME - the Konstanz information miner: version 2.0 and beyond. SIGKDD Explor. **11**(1), 26–31 (2009)
2. Bocciarelli, P., D'Ambrogio, A., Giglio, A., Paglia, E.: BPMN-based business process modeling and simulation. In: 2019 Winter Simulation Conference (WSC), pp. 1439–1453 (2019)
3. Bock, A., Frank, U.: Multi-perspective enterprise modeling—conceptual foundation and implementation with ADOxx. Domain-Specific Conceptual Modeling, pp. 241–267. Springer, Cham (2016). https://doi.org/10.1007/978-3-319-39417-6_11
4. Bork, D., Fill, H.: Formal aspects of enterprise modeling methods: a comparison framework. In: HICSS 2014, pp. 3400–3409. IEEE (2014)
5. Bork, D., Fill, H., Karagiannis, D., Utz, W.: Simulation of multi-stage industrial business processes using metamodelling building blocks with ADOxx. Enterp. Model. Inf. Syst. Archit. Int. J. Concept. Model. **13**, 333–344 (2018)
6. Bucchiarone, A., et al.: What is the future of modeling? IEEE Softw. **38**(2), 119–127 (2021)
7. Burke, B.: Top Strategic Technology Trends for 2021. Gartner (2020)
8. Caballar, R.D.: Programming without code: the rise of no-code software development. IEEE Spectrum (March 11, 2020) (2020)
9. Demirkan, H., Kauffman, R.J., Vayghan, J.A., Fill, H., Karagiannis, D., Maglio, P.P.: Service-oriented technology and management: perspectives on research and practice for the coming decade. Electron. Commer. Res. Appl. **7**(4), 356–376 (2008)
10. Denning, P.J., Lewis, T.G.: Technology adoption. Commun. ACM **63**(6), 27–29 (2020)
11. Ferstl, O.K., Sinz, E.J.: Modeling of business systems using SOM. In: Bernus, P., Mertins, K., Schmidt, G. (eds.) Handbook on Architectures of Information Systems, pp. 347–367. Springer, Heidelberg (1998). https://doi.org/10.1007/3-540-26661-5_15
12. Fettke, P., Loos, P.: Model driven architecture (MDA). Wirtschaftsinformatik **45**(5), 555–559 (2003)
13. Fettke, P., Reisig, W.: Modelling service-oriented systems and cloud services with HERAKLIT. In: Zirpins, C., et al. (eds.) ESOCC 2020. CCIS, vol. 1360, pp. 77–89. Springer, Cham (2021). https://doi.org/10.1007/978-3-030-71906-7_7
14. Fill, H.-G.: Using semantically annotated models for supporting business process benchmarking. In: Grabis, J., Kirikova, M. (eds.) BIR 2011. LNBIP, vol. 90, pp. 29–43. Springer, Heidelberg (2011). https://doi.org/10.1007/978-3-642-24511-4_3
15. Fill, H.: SeMFIS: a flexible engineering platform for semantic annotations of conceptual models. Semant. Web **8**(5), 747–763 (2017)
16. Fill, H.: Applying the concept of knowledge blockchains to ontologies. In: Martin, A., Hinkelmann, K., Gerber, A., Lenat, D., van Harmelen, F., Clark, P. (eds.) Proceedings of the AAAI 2019 Spring Symposium on Combining Machine Learning with Knowledge Engineering (AAAI-MAKE 2019) Stanford University. CEUR Workshop Proceedings, vol. 2350. CEUR-WS.org (2019)

17. Fill, H.: Enterprise modeling: from digital transformation to digital ubiquity. In: Federated Conference on Computer Science and Information Systems. Annals of Computer Science and Information Systems, vol. 21, pp. 1–4 (2020)

18. Fill, H.G., Härer, F.: Knowledge blockchains: applying blockchain technologies to enterprise modeling. In: Proceedings of the 51st Hawaii International Conference on System Sciences (2018)

19. Fill, H.G., Härer, F.: Supporting trust in hybrid intelligence systems using blockchains. In: Proceedings of the AAAI 2020 Spring Symposium on Combining Machine Learning with Knowledge Engineering (AAAI-MAKE 2020), Stanford University, Palo Alto, California, USA, vol. 2600. CEUR-WS (2020)

20. Fill, H., Johannsen, F.: A knowledge perspective on big data by joining enterprise modeling and data analyses. In: Bui, T.X., Sprague Jr., R.H. (eds.) Hawaii International Conference on System Sciences, pp. 4052–4061. IEEE (2016)

21. Gartner: Gartner forecasts worldwide low-code development technologies market to grow 23% in 2021 (2021). https://www.gartner.com/en/newsroom/press-releases/2021-02-15-gartner-forecasts-worldwide-low-code-development-technologies-market-to-grow-23-percent-in-2021. Accessed 30 Mar 2021

22. Geiger, M., Harrer, S., Lenhard, J., Wirtz, G.: BPMN 2.0: the state of support and implementation. Future Gener. Comput. Syst. **80**, 250–262 (2018)

23. Gong, Y., Janssen, M.: Roles and capabilities of enterprise architecture in big data analytics technology adoption and implementation. J. Theor. Appl. Electron. Commer. Res. **16**(1), 37–51 (2021)

24. Grüninger, M., Fox, M.S.: The role of competency questions in enterprise engineering. In: Rolstadås, A. (ed.) Benchmarking—Theory and Practice. IAICT, pp. 22–31. Springer, Boston (1995). https://doi.org/10.1007/978-0-387-34847-6_3

25. Härer, F., Fill, H.G.: A Comparison of Approaches for Visualizing Blockchains and Smart Contracts. Jusletter IT Weblaw, February 2019 (2019). ISSN 1664-848X

26. Härer, F., Fill, H.: Decentralized attestation of conceptual models using the ethereum blockchain. In: Becker, J., Novikov, D.A. (eds.) 21st IEEE Conference on Business Informatics, CBI, pp. 104–113. IEEE (2019)

27. Henkel, M., Stirna, J.: Pondering on the key functionality of model driven development tools: the case of mendix. In: Forbrig, P., Günther, H. (eds.) BIR 2010. LNBIP, vol. 64, pp. 146–160. Springer, Heidelberg (2010). https://doi.org/10.1007/978-3-642-16101-8_12

28. Hopkins, J.L.: An investigation into emerging industry 4.0 technologies as drivers of supply chain innovation in Australia. Comput. Ind. **125**, 103323 (2021)

29. Horkoff, J., Elahi, G., Abdulhadi, S., Yu, E.: Reflective analysis of the syntax and semantics of the i* framework. In: Song, I.-Y., et al. (eds.) ER 2008. LNCS, vol. 5232, pp. 249–260. Springer, Heidelberg (2008). https://doi.org/10.1007/978-3-540-87991-6_31

30. Johannsen, F., Fill, H.G.: Meta modeling for business process improvement. Bus. Inf. Syst. Eng. **59**(4), 251–275 (2017)

31. Microsoft: Azure machine learning designer (2020). https://azure.microsoft.com/de-de/services/machine-learning/designer/#product-overview. Accessed 31 Mar 2021

32. Moody, D.: The "physics" of notations: toward a scientific basis for constructing visual notations in software engineering. IEEE Trans. Softw. Eng. **35**(6), 756–779 (2009)

33. Muff, F., Fill, H.: Towards embedding legal visualizations in work practices by using augmented reality. Jusletter IT (2021, forthcoming)

34. OMG: Business process model and notation 2.0.2 (2014). https://www.omg.org/spec/BPMN

35. Pittl, B., Fill, H.: A visual modeling approach for the semantic web rule language. Semant. Web **11**(2), 361–389 (2020)

36. RapidMiner: Rapidminer studio (2020). https://docs.rapidminer.com/latest/studio/. Accessed 31 Mar 2021

37. Reitemeyer, B., Fill, H.: Future research directions for improved service modeling. In: Koschmider, A., Michael, J. (eds.) Enterprise Modeling and Information Systems Architectures 2021 (2021, forthcoming)

38. Ruiz-Rube, I., Baena-Pérez, R., Mota, J.M., Sánchez, I.A.: Model-driven development of augmented reality-based editors for domain specific languages. IxD&A **45**, 246–263 (2020)

39. Sandkuhl, K., et al.: Enterprise modelling for the masses – from elitist discipline to common practice. In: Horkoff, J., Jeusfeld, M.A., Persson, A. (eds.) PoEM 2016. LNBIP, vol. 267, pp. 225–240. Springer, Cham (2016). https://doi.org/10.1007/978-3-319-48393-1_16

40. Sandkuhl, K., et al.: From expert discipline to common practice: a vision and research agenda for extending the reach of enterprise modeling. Bus. Inf. Syst. Eng. **60**(1), 69–80 (2018)

41. Sandkuhl, K., Stirna, J., Persson, A., Wißotzki, M.: Overview of the 4EM method. Enterprise Modeling. TEES, pp. 75–86. Springer, Heidelberg (2014). https://doi.org/10.1007/978-3-662-43725-4_7

42. Shishkov, B.: Designing Enterprise Information Systems - Merging Enterprise Modeling and Software Specification. Springer, Heidelberg (2020). https://doi.org/10.1007/978-3-030-22441-7

43. The Open Group: Archimate® 3.1 specification (2019). https://pubs.opengroup.org/architecture/archimate3-doc/

44. Tisi, M., et al.: Lowcomote: training the next generation of experts in scalable low-code engineering platforms. In: Bagnato, A., Brunelière, H., Burgueño, L., Eramo, R., Gómez, A. (eds.) STAF 2019 Co-Located Events Joint Proceedings. CEUR Workshop Proceedings, vol. 2405, pp. 73–78. CEUR-WS.org (2019)

45. Tolvanen, J.P., Rossi, M.: Metaedit+ defining and using domain-specific modeling languages and code generators. In: ACM SIGPLAN Conference on Object-Oriented Programming, Systems, Languages, and Applications, pp. 92–93. ACM (2003)

46. Vernadat, F.: Enterprise modelling: research review and outlook. Comput. Ind. **122**, 103265 (2020)

47. Vještica, M., Dimitrieski, V., Pisarić, M., Kordić, S., Ristić, S., Luković, I.: An application of a DSML in industry 4.0 production processes. In: Lalic, B., Majstorovic, V., Marjanovic, U., von Cieminski, G., Romero, D. (eds.) APMS 2020. IAICT, vol. 591, pp. 441–448. Springer, Cham (2020). https://doi.org/10.1007/978-3-030-57993-7_50

48. Wieland, M., Fill, H.G.: A domain-specific modeling method for supporting the generation of business plans. In: Modellierung 2020. GI LNI (2020)

49. Zikra, I., Stirna, J., Zdravkovic, J.: Bringing enterprise modeling closer to model-driven development. In: Johannesson, P., Krogstie, J., Opdahl, A.L. (eds.) PoEM 2011. LNBIP, vol. 92, pp. 268–282. Springer, Heidelberg (2011). https://doi.org/10.1007/978-3-642-24849-8_20

Bridging the Gap Between Structural and Behavioral Models in a Software-Centric Environment

Noël Hagemann$^{(\boxtimes)}$ and Bernhard Bauer

Software Methodologies for Distributed Systems, University of Augsburg,
Universitätsstraße 6a, 86159 Augsburg, Germany
noel.hagemann@informatik.uni-augsburg.de

Abstract. Induced by the last evolutionary step of systems, the virtualization and decentralization of systems is thriving leading to more complex systems. This causes the system behavior described by models to be split into additional models, creating gaps.

As a result, we present a novel approach that combines model artifacts describing the architecture of a system to recover the complete view of a system's behavior. Our design relies on model transformation to create a consistent model basis to enable cross-model connections. The combining process is carried out in two phases. First, an expert defines cross-model connections mapping behavioral models onto structural models. Second, these connections are used to derive direct connections between behavioral models to bridge the gap that emerged.

Keywords: Cyber-physical systems · Model-driven software development · Model transformation · Systems modeling

1 Introduction

Advances in communications technology and global interconnectivity have led to the next evolutionary step of systems. As a result, technologies such as cloud computing (CC), the Internet of Things (IoT) and cyber-physical systems (CPS) have emerged. As defined by the NIST, "Cloud computing is a model for enabling ubiquitous, convenient, on-demand network access to a shared pool of configurable computing resources (e.g., networks, servers, storage, applications, and services) that can be rapidly provisioned and released with minimal management effort or service provider interaction" [15]. While CC widens the gap between software and hardware by focusing on virtualization and decentralization, the IoT and CPS close the gap between the cyber and the real world. The IoT is defined in [1] as "a global infrastructure for the information society, enabling advanced services by interconnecting (physical and virtual) things based on existing and evolving interoperable information and communication technologies". CPS addresses several concepts also present in IoT but more focused in an industrial environment [17]. As a result, IoT devices are mostly used to monitor the real world [14] while CPS are designed to actively shape the world [8].

© Springer Nature Switzerland AG 2021
B. Shishkov (Ed.): BMSD 2021, LNBIP 422, pp. 353–362, 2021.
https://doi.org/10.1007/978-3-030-79976-2_23

2   Problem Statement

The ongoing trend towards virtualization, decentralization and real-world integration is adding complexity to systems. In case of virtualization and decentralization, components of a system often no longer interact directly with each other but must first overcome hidden behavior to reach other system components. In a software-centric environment, we assume that each such component is controlled by software which results in its behavior being set by programming language. In this context, hidden behavior describes software without available source code. Cloud computing is a prime example of highly virtualized and decentralized systems as it allows companies to outsource the hosting of their IT infrastructure making it a matter of cost [13]. In comparison to traditional distributed systems, a fundamental difference in architecture is that software in distributed systems is tied to a specific physical machine while software in cloud computing is tied to a specific virtual machine [16]. This results in the software being fully abstracted from the hardware leading to new challenges. [12]. One of these challenges is reliability [11]. However, there are several approaches that address this challenge on the architectural level [9]. Anyhow, cloud computing significantly adds complexity to systems which creates new points of failure. In recent years, there was effort to apply the concept of cloud computing to the concept of the IoT to cope with its problems [7]. The IoT allows systems to react and interact with the real world introducing physical processes to systems. This applies to CPS as well since the IoT and CPS follow a similar approach as described in Sect. 1. Physical processes add uncertainty to systems [18]. Uncertainty describes the lack of knowledge about a physical process i.e. state of the parent physical system, timing and nature of inputs. As a result, virtualization, decentralization and uncertainty are heavily adding complexity to systems.

A system, in general, is defined as a set of at least two components where each component has to affect at least one other component and has to be affected by at least one other component of the system [4]. Consequently, a component consists of properties which describe its behavior and connections to other system components. As stated in the specification of UML [10], UML model elements are categorized either as structural or behavioral. Structural Model Elements (SMEs) represent the static properties of a system that describe what the system is composed of. Behavioral model elements (BMEs) describe the dynamic features of a system that characterize how the components behave. Therefore, SMEs are used to model the properties of a system at a particular point in time while BMEs are used to model how they change over time. However, this categorization applies not only to the model elements but also to the models themselves. A structural model may contain BMEs but these are only used to request a particular behavior. In turn, a behavioral model may contain SMEs showing properties that do not change over time. As a result, we assume that models can be roughly categorized in either being structural or behavioral. Structural models often show the connections between system components such as UML component diagrams which show the interfaces of components and their structural connection. Behavioral models, in contrast, are often tied to a system component such as UML state machine diagrams that represent the internal behavior of a particular system component. As a result, the behavior of a system is usually described by several models, each representing a particular aspect of the system. As system complexity increases, these models become more complex as well. Subsequently, the number of models to describe a system potentially increases.

As the number of models to describe a system increases, we see a strong need to regain a complete view of the behavior of a system. Since structural models usually focus on representing the connections between components and behavioral models usually describe the internal behavior of a component, there is no model that sufficiently contains the behavior of the entire system. To derive the behavior of the system as a whole, the behavioral models describing a system need to be connected or merged.

3   Bridging the Gap

In this section, we propose a novel approach for using structural models to connect the behavioral models of a system. First, the structural and behavioral models that represent the architecture of a system are reduced to mixed graphs. This is detailed in Subsect. 3.1. Thereafter, the models are merged and transformed to a directed graph to enable cross-model connections which is described in detail in Subsect. 3.2. Finally, cross-model connections are defined that link structural models to behavioral models, from which additional cross model connections are derived to directly link behavioral models. This is detailed in Subsect. 3.3. In this section we focus on the syntax of the approach while the semantics are addressed in more detail in Sect. 4.

3.1   Reduction of Structural and Behavioral Models

In the context of models, dependency is often expressed by directed edges. A dependency induces some kind of order when it is included in a structural model as for instance inheritance in class diagrams. A directed edge as part of a behavioral model, in turn, enables the formation of paths that characterize the behavior of a component or the interactions between components. An example of behavior models that describe the behavior of a component in detail are UML state machine diagrams or activity diagrams. As behavioral models describe the behavior of the system, their edges are directed. However, behavioral models may contain edges that are undirected as described in Sect. 2. In addition, structural models may contain directed edges but they are usually undirected. As both types of model contain directed and undirected edges, we aim at reducing both types of model to mixed graphs. A mixed graph $M = (V, A, E)$ consists of a non-empty finite set $V(M)$ of elements called vertices, a finite set $A(M) = V(M) \times V(M)$ of ordered pairs of distinct vertices and a finite set $E(M) = V(M) \times V(M)$ of unordered pairs of distinct vertices as defined in [6]. We call $V(M)$ the node set of M, $A(M)$ the set of directed edges of M and

$E(M)$ the set of undirected edges of M. As the edges in $A(M)$ are directed, the edge $(a, b) \in A(M)$ represents a source-to-target connection where the node a is the source and the node b represents the target.

Let the set $X(S)$ contain all models that describe the system S structurally. In addition, let the set $Y(S)$ contain all models that describe the behavior of the system S. We reduce the behavioral and structural models of the system by transforming them into mixed graphs. Each structural and behavioral model is thereby transformed into exactly one mixed graph. This results in the sets $X_M(S)$ and $Y_M(S)$. The set $X_M(S)$ contains all mixed graphs derived from the structural models. In addition, the set $Y_M(S)$ consists of all mixed graphs derived from the behavioral models. The nodes of the behavioral model $x \in X(S)$ are thereby added to the node set $V(x_M)$ of the mixed graph $x_M \in X_M(S)$ that represents the model x. The nodes of the structural model $y \in Y(S)$ are added to the node set $V(y_M)$ of the mixed graph $y_M \in Y_M(S)$ representing the model y. The edges of the behavioral model $x \in X(S)$ are categorized as either directed or undirected and added to their respective set of the corresponding mixed model x_M. The edges of the structural model $y \in Y(S)$ are categorized and added in the same way.

3.2   Merging of System Architecture

To enable cross-model connections, the mixed graphs representing the system architecture are merged to form a consistent model basis. Therefore, the undirected edges of the mixed graphs are transformed into directed edges and the mixed graphs are merged into a single directed graph holding the whole system architecture. A directed graph $D = (V, A)$ consists of a non-empty finite set $V(D)$ of elements called vertices and a finite set $A(D) = V(D) \times V(D)$ of ordered pairs of distinct vertices as defined in [6]. We call $V(D)$ the node set of D and $A(D)$ the set of directed edges of D. As the edges are directed, the edge $(a, b) \in A(D)$ represents a source-to-target connection where the node a is the source and the node b represents the target.

As undirected edges can be considered bidirectional [6], undirected edges can be transformed to directed edges. The function $T : E(M) \rightarrow A(M)$

$$T(E(M)) = \bigcup_{(k,l) \in E(M)} (k, l) \cup (l, k) \tag{1}$$

transforms every bidirectional edge $(k, l) \in E(M)$ into the directed edges (k, l) and (l, k).

Let the consistent model basis be the directed graph $S = (V, A)$. Consequently, we define the set

$$V(S) = \bigcup_{s \in X_M(S)} \bigcup_{b \in Y_M(S)} V(s) \cup V(b) \tag{2}$$

as the union of all nodes of the mixed graphs that describe the system S. In addition, the set

$$A(S) = \bigcup_{s \in X_M(S)} \bigcup_{b \in Y_M(S)} T(E(s)) \cup A(s) \cup T(E(b)) \cup A(b) \tag{3}$$

of ordered pairs holding the edges included in the mixed graphs that describe the system S. The model thus consists of several independent model artifacts.

3.3   Directly Connecting Behavioral Models

In context of the consistent model basis, we define a cross-model connection as an edge between two nodes contained in the consistent model basis that originated from two different model artifacts that described the same system. Therefore, let the nodes a and b be contained in the set $V(S)$. Let the nodes a and b originate from two different models x and y. Let the models x and y be contained in $X(S)$ or $Y(S)$ and describe the system S. The node a can be paired with the node b resulting in the edge (a, b) being added to the edge set $A(S)$ of the consistent model basis S. As the edges are directed, the node b can be paired with the node a resulting in the edge (b, a) being added to the set of directed edges $A(S)$. The semantics are addressed in the following Sect. 4.

As the concept of transitive closures applies to directed graphs, we can use this property to directly connect behavioral models by deriving cross-model connections from walks. As defined in [6], a walk in D is an alternating sequence $W = x_1 a_1 x_2 a_2 \ldots x_{k-1} a_{k-1} x_k$ of vertices x_i and arcs $a_j = (x_i, x_{i+1})$ from D such that $\forall x_i \in W(D) \; \exists v \in V(D) : x_i = v$ and $\forall a_j \in W(D) \; \exists a \in A(D) : a_j = a$ with $i = j = 1, \ldots, k - 1$. Consequently, if a path exists from $x \in V(S)$ to $z \in V(S)$, then the edge (x, z) can be formed without violating the model. This allows the behavioral models to be directly connected by transitivity, bridging the gap.

4   Case Study: Smart Home

In this section, a case study is performed, design decisions are discussed and semantics for this approach are defined. The case study is performed on a simple system measuring the outside temperature and sending the information to a device called the *Smart Mirror*. The device capturing the temperature is called *Thermometer*. It reads the outside temperature every minute and sends the result to the smart mirror over a TCP connection. Since a TCP connection acknowledges the receiving of packets, both components influence each other and therefore fulfill the constraints of the definition of system. After receiving a packet, the smart mirror processes the message and displays the temperature.

The system architecture is composed of structural and behavioral models. Figure 1 shows the system structurally as an UML component diagram. The component *Thermometer* provides the interface *Temperature* which is required

Fig. 1. Component diagram illustrating the system structurally

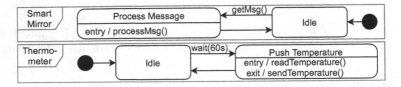

Fig. 2. State machine diagrams visualizing the behavior of each system component

by the component *Smart Mirror*. We chose UML for our representation because, despite a declining trend in its use, UML is still widely used [5].

In Fig. 2, the behavior of the components is described by UML state machine diagrams. They are framed by their respective name and are defined by two states. The smart mirror consists of an idle state and a state in which the temperature is collected from an internal sensor and transmitted to the network connecting both components. The device starts in the idle state and switches to the transmit state every sixty seconds. After the temperature is pushed to the network, the device changes its state to idle.

The thermometer includes an idle state and a state in which messages are processed and the new temperature value is displayed. This device also starts in the idle state and switches to the process state after a message is received. After the message is processed and the temperature is displayed, the device returns to idle mode.

As described in Sect. 3, cross-model connections need to be enabled to bridge the gap. For this purpose, the behavioral and structural models are merged in this approach. To derive the behavior of the system as a whole, undirected edges are considered bidirectional and cross-model connections need to be formed. In Sect. 3.3, the formation of cross-model connections is defined syntactically. In the following, the semantics of such connections are briefly discussed.

A cross-model connection describes an edge between two different models resulting in the possibility to connect structural with structural, behavioral with behavioral, behavioral with structural or structural with behavioral models. Since the approach is designed to extract the behavior of a whole system, connections from structural models to structural models are ignored as we assume that there is always a structural model that covers the structure of a system in its entirety. Connections from behavioral models to behavioral models are relatively difficult to derive directly since they usually describe the behavior of a specific system component or a directed information flow between components. If a behavior model describes the behavior of a component like state machine diagrams, then it can be linked to a system component but usually does not include information identifying that component. In this case, an expert for this system is needed to link a behavioral model to a node of a structural model. If a behavioral model, in turn, characterizes the communication between components like sequence diagrams, there are nodes that can be directly associated with components of the system and thus with other nodes of structural models. In this case, the connections can be formed automatically. However, the formation of cross-model connections need to be further refined as our goal is to establish cross model connections between nodes of behavioral models. For this purpose, nodes of behavioral models are identified as valid candidates for cross-model connections between such models. They can be marked as either input or output nodes to implicitly define the direction of connections. An input node requires stimuli from other system components enabling the formation of incoming cross-model connections. An output node provides stimuli to other system components enabling the formation of outgoing cross-model connections. Based on this information, cross-model connections between structural and behavioral models are formed.

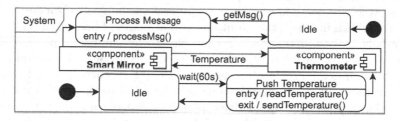

Fig. 3. Consistent model basis with cross-model connections defined

Figure 3 shows the behavioral and structural models representing the architecture of the case study in their merged form. The expert associated the behavioral models shown in Fig. 2 with their component in the structural model shown in Fig. 1 and marked the state *Push Temperature* as an output node and the state *Process Message* as an input node. Consequently, the edges *Push Temperature* to *Thermometer* and *Smart Mirror* to *Process Message* were formed.

The cross-model connections involving nodes of structural models are only used to derive the behavior of the system as a whole. In more detail, they are used to help the formation of direct connections between behavioral models to prevent unnecessary steps as SMEs do not infer behavior. To enable the formation of such connections, the modeler needs to add semantic information for every cross-model connection that link nodes of behavioral models to nodes of structural models. Based on these information, direct connections between behavioral models are derived. A cross-model connection between behavioral models is valid if a mapping exists that maps the properties of a node of a behavioral model to properties of a node of another behavioral model. In case of the case study, the function `sendTemperature()` is mapped on the function `processMsg()`.

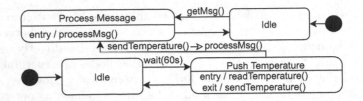

Fig. 4. Cross-model connection between behavioral model elements

Figure 4 shows the connected behavioral models of the case study. Note that all nodes of the structural models, their edges and cross-model edges between the structural and the behavioral models are not shown in the figure. They remain in the consistent model basis. Since there is a path from the *Push Temperature* state to the *Process Message* state in the consistent model base, the edge from the former to the latter is formed, directly connecting the two behavioral models and thus bridging the gap.

This two-phase decision approach has several advantages over a single-phase decision approach in which the input and output nodes of behavioral models are directly linked. By splitting the decision phase, the number of possible direct links between behavioral models is reduced as the inclusion of structural models significantly limits the possibilities. Furthermore, if the expert intends to directly connect nodes of different behavioral models, he needs to exactly know how the system behaves. In turn, if the modeler intends to associate a node of a behavioral model with a node of a structural model, then all he needs to know is whether the behavioral model details the node of the structural model as the node represents a system component. Consequently, mapping a node of a behavioral model to a node of a structural model is easier to accomplish than mapping a node of a behavioral model to a node of another behavioral model because less knowledge is required.

5   Related Work

The topic of systems modeling has been discussed for quite some time. There are several modeling languages and methods to capture the behavior of a system. One approach is SysML. SysML is a modeling language that reuses a subset of UML 2.5 [3]. It is particularly designed to specify requirements, structure, behavior, allocations and constraints on system properties. Cross-model connections are established by a matrix whose format is not prescribed. It can be used to loosely connect model elements of any SysML model. Our approach follows a similar technique but we aim to establish connections between nodes of different behavioral models and additionally connect their properties to validate the connection.

ArchiMate Enterprise Architecture is another modeling language [2]. It is designed to visualize and describe different architecture domains and their dependencies and relations. As it is not intended to model the behavior of a system component in detail, a complete view of the system's behavior is not derivable. However, an ArchiMate model is organized in layers. Connections between layers can be compared to cross-model connections. Cross-layer connections follow a specific rule set and therefore are syntactically restricted. We take a more general approach where cross-model connections between all nodes of different models are allowed but they are only valid if the properties of the nodes are mapped.

6 Conclusion and Future Work

The system architecture is often captured by models. In general, models can be categorized as either structural or behavioral. A behavioral model describes either the behavior of a system component or the communication between components. As decentralization proceeds, the behavior of a system is distributed away from one component to many components working together in a system. As a result, the overall behavior of the system is divided among an increasing number of models. As these models are not directly connected, they open a gap making it harder to derive the behavior of the system as a whole.

In this paper, we presented a novel approach to bridge the gap that has resulted from the last evolutionary step of systems. To simplify the idea behind the approach, the structural and behavioral models are first transformed to mixed graphs. These graphs are then merged and transformed into a directed graph to form a consistent model basis that enables the formation of cross-model connections. The behavioral models as part of the consistent model basis are connected by a semi-automatic two-phase decision approach. First, the behavioral models are connected with the structural models of the consistent model basis by an expert. Second, if the derivation of a direct connection results in more than one edge, the expert decides which edge is valid. In contrast to direct linking of behavioral models, this approach requires less system knowledge and significantly reduces cross-model linking possibilities.

In future, we want to further refine the approach and conduct various studies to prove our assumption that this approach is in fact a valuable way of combining models to derive the behavior of a system as a whole. Therefore, we want to apply this approach to a more complex case study and proof that the two-phase decision approach is in fact superior to the one-phase decision approach. We also see the possibility of using this approach in deriving models that describe communication between system components.

Acknowledgment. Electronic Component and Systems for European Leadership (ECSEL) supported the development of this approach within the project CPS4EU (Grant Agreement Number 826276).

References

1. Y.2060: Overview of the Internet of things. https://www.itu.int/rec/T-REC-Y. 2060-201206-I/en
2. Archimate 3.1 specification. Standard, The Open Group, November 2019. https:// pubs.opengroup.org/architecture/archimate3-doc/
3. OMG systems modeling language (OMG sysml) version 1.6. Standard, Object Management Group (OMG), November 2019. https://sysml.org/.res/docs/specs/ OMGSysML-v1.6-19-11-01.pdf
4. Backlund, A.: The definition of system. Kybernetes (2000)
5. Badreddin, O., Khandoker, R., Forward, A., Masmali, O., Lethbridge, T.C.: A decade of software design and modeling: a survey to uncover trends of the practice. In: Proceedings of the 21th ACM/IEEE International Conference on Model Driven Engineering Languages and Systems, pp. 245–255 (2018)
6. Bang-Jensen, J., Gutin, G.Z.: Digraphs: Theory, Algorithms and Applications. Springer, Heidelberg (2008). https://doi.org/10.1007/978-1-84800-998-1
7. Redha Bouakouk, M., Abdelli, A., Mokdad, L.: Survey on the cloud-iot paradigms: taxonomy and architectures. In: 2020 IEEE Symposium on Computers and Communications (ISCC), pp. 1–6. IEEE (2020)
8. Chaâri, R., et al.: Cyber-physical systems clouds: a survey. Comput. Netw. **108**, 260–278 (2016)
9. Cheraghlou, M.N., Khadem-Zadeh, A., Haghparast, M.: A survey of fault tolerance architecture in cloud computing. J. Netw. Comput. Appl. **61**, 81–92 (2016)
10. Cook, S., et al.: Unified modeling language (UML) version 2.5.1. Standard, Object Management Group (OMG), December 2017. https://www.omg.org/spec/UML/ 2.5.1
11. Dai, Y.S., Yang, B., Dongarra, J., Zhang, G.: Cloud service reliability: modeling and analysis. In: 15th IEEE Pacific Rim International Symposium on Dependable Computing, pp. 1–17. Citeseer (2009)
12. Dillon, T., Wu, C., Chang, E.: Cloud computing: issues and challenges. In: 2010 24th IEEE International Conference on Advanced Information Networking and Applications, pp. 27–33. Ieee (2010)
13. Lin, G., Fu, D., Zhu, J., Dasmalchi, G.: Cloud computing: it as a service. IT Prof. Mag. **11**(2), 10 (2009)
14. Mahmoud, R., Yousuf, T., Aloul, F., Zualkernan, I.: Internet of things (IoT) security: current status, challenges and prospective measures. In: 2015 10th International Conference for Internet Technology and Secured Transactions (ICITST), pp. 336–341. IEEE (2015)
15. Mell, P., Grance, T., et al.: The NIST definition of cloud computing (2011)
16. Mishra, S.K., Sahoo, B., Parida, P.P.: Load balancing in cloud computing: a big picture. J. King Saud Univ.-Comput. Inf. Sci. **32**(2), 149–158 (2020)
17. Pivoto, D.G., de Almeida, L.F., Righi, R.D.R., Rodrigues, J.J., Lugli, A.B., Alberti, A.M.: Cyber-physical systems architectures for industrial internet of things applications in industry 4.0: a literature review. J. Manuf. Syst. **58**, 176–192 (2021)
18. Zhang, M., Selic, B., Ali, S., Yue, T., Okariz, O., Norgren, R.: Understanding uncertainty in cyber-physical systems: a conceptual model. In: Wąsowski, A., Lönn, H. (eds.) ECMFA 2016. LNCS, vol. 9764, pp. 247–264. Springer, Cham (2016). https://doi.org/10.1007/978-3-319-42061-5_16

A Heuristic Technique for Project Time Analysis in Conditions with High Uncertainty

Maksim Goman$^{(\boxtimes)}$

Johannes Kepler University, Altenberger Street 69, 4040 Linz, Austria
Maksim.Goman@jku.at
http://www.jku.at/ie

Abstract. Project completion time evaluation under uncertainty is still a problem in project management. It is most acute in the areas of large uncertainty in activity estimations and fast changing environment, where only stochastic approaches are possible. We propose an analytical technique for managers that produces a worst case approximation of the project end time. This is an operationally simple heuristic that needs only one network traverse, with realistic model and assumptions, simple mathematical calculations and probability distribution types. The technique considers merge event bias that causes a delay in the stochastic project network. Additionally, end time of all activities and likely critical activities are found. To show the application of the technique, we analyzed time of a real construction project and obtained good accuracy.

Keywords: Stochastic PERT · Project completion time · Project time estimation · Merge event bias

1 Introduction

Evaluation of project end time is still a problematic area of project management (PM) [1,6,9]. A project model is usually a stochastic network also traditionally called PERT network (PN). Task times in the model are random numbers with such distributions that the problem can be easier resolved analytically, and usually without consideration how to obtain initial data for it. However, the analysis is based on initial activity durations obtained from experts.

The paper has practical focus and we consider *analytical approaches*. The literature contains mostly project evaluation and review technique (classical PERT) and its extensions with the main assumptions of independence and existence of a single critical path (CP) in the PN. It is considered the only established analytical probabilistic method for project managers to estimate project time [1,6,9]. Other analytical developments include mainly techniques of approximate analytic solutions [18,26] or derivation of exact bounds [18]. We refer to reviews of research in stochastic analytic techniques for PM in [4,9,18–20,24].

© Springer Nature Switzerland AG 2021
B. Shishkov (Ed.): BMSD 2021, LNBIP 422, pp. 363–373, 2021.
https://doi.org/10.1007/978-3-030-79976-2_24

Deficiencies of the classical PERT and its extensions based on the same principles and assumptions have been well understood, and they underestimate project time even in the theory [4,11,16,24–26]. The cause is merge event bias (MEB) in each node where several paths collapse [1,3,5,9, p. 346]. By construction, it exists *every time* when two or more activities merge before the next activity in the PN, which can begin only after all its preceding activities are completed. But MEB has been mostly omitted in literature. The effect of MEB was investigated or just shown by some scholars [1,3–5,7,11,14,16,23]. The attempts to mend the issue are hard to find in textbooks today, but they were discussed in the 20th century, e.g. [8,17, ch. 9].

CP has become a fundamental notion in PM [18,19,23]. It was shown that CP is problematic in probabilistic analysis due to MEB existence [1,4,7]. Clearly, consideration of only separated paths or presumption of a unique CP guarantees underestimation of the maximum project time, and the error can increase with larger number of parallel paths. Usage of a single CP, independent paths, or multivariate path distributions can not obtain the maximum PN time larger than a certain maximum time of a path with the longest duration.

An efficient way of PN analysis is simulation. However, managers assert that they do not have enough skills and merit to use that [9,23]. Thus, management requires a simple and reliable analytical technique providing a better estimation of maximum time, and the technique should be not more complex than the classical PERT [4,23], and [9, p. 346].

Activity durations are random values, and their realizations are not known until the activity ends. There is an operational issue with estimation of time distribution parameters for activity durations. Although there exist a lot of techniques for that (e.g. O'Hagan et al. [21]), practitioners in industry are hardly aware of them, for techniques for parameter estimation are not regularly taught and thus, are not used everyday in PM. Lindley [15, p. 318] wrote "...there is a real gap in our appreciation of how to assess probabilities – of how to express our uncertainties in the requisite form". Existing techniques for PM operate with distribution types with convenient properties like normal, exponential or beta time distributions. However, parameters of simpler distributions like uniform and triangular seem more feasible to obtain from experts (e.g. [13, ch. 5]). And there are circumstances of large uncertainty, where it seems not possible to find a trained expert or provide an acceptable or unbiased activity time estimation due to lack of knowledge or historic data.

We suggest to work with project duration (PD) and consider the whole PN structure that makes it possible to estimate PD realistically. Therefore, our analytical approach grounds not on paths, but rather on approximation of the MEB effect, and on the chance constraint method to measure stochastic dominance between time distributions of activities converging in each node of the PN.

Our aim is a heuristic technique that can be applied by project managers in practice. The work is primarily oriented at circumstances of high uncertainty in estimation of activity durations. We assume uniform time distributions in this work as a realistic choice in situations of high uncertainty. We design how to traverse the graph, and suggest how to approximate the distributions of delay in each node where several activities are collapsing (MEB effect) during PN traverse. Then, we perform analysis of a real project.

The technique enables evaluation of the upper part of probability density function (PDF) of activity times and PD in nodes. We compare our estimation to the real project outcome, and outcomes of PERT and M-PERT. Our results are more revealing for a decision maker (DM), so that DM can consider realistic outcomes for given input activity time estimations. The technique is built on a correct model, and the complexity is comparable to one of the classical PERT but it does not need path enumeration. Our algorithm determines both critical activities and completion time approximations in each node during a single forward pass through the PN.

The rest of the paper is organized as follows. First, we formally define the problem, give relevant definitions and introduce the technique in Sect. 2. The application of the technique to a real project is given in Sect. 3. The conclusion summarizes the work.

2   The Proposed Heuristic Technique

The model of a project is a directed acyclic graph without parallel arcs, where nodes are events between the activities, and arcs represent project activities with random duration $X_{i,j}$ (from node i to node j) with uniform distribution and known parameters. There are a start node 0 and an end node N. We begin PN traverse from the node 0 with PD $= 0$, navigate through all transitional nodes analyzing dependencies when arcs collapse, and end in the node N, with the estimated PD of the project. By construction, several arcs may collapse in nodes, where activities that end earlier are waiting for all other activities that finish later (due to their uncertain execution time) in order to proceed with activities right after the node. We will roughly estimate the time distribution in each node and determine likely CPs, and critical activities on them.

In nodes where several incoming arcs collapse, the start time distribution of the following activities is a distribution of maximum of end times of the preceding activities (the highest order statistic). Thus, the PD and sub-path distributions are changed by every consecutive activity in the PN (convolution), and by the MEB effect in nodes of the PN where arcs collapse. This means the delay due to activities with longest time realization in such nodes. Distributions of all subsequent activities are *dependent* right after the first merger of any previous activities in the PN.

Durations of sequential activities can be added together with convolution operation. Subtraction can be represented through addition of the original value reversed in sign. An analytical expression of exact PDF $f_n(s)$ of the sum of n uniform random variables $X_k \sim U(0, a_k)$, $k = 1, 2, \ldots, n$ is given in several sources, e.g. [22]. A symmetric triangular random variable can be represented as a sum of two equal uniform random variables. This property allows us to convolute in closed form parts of the current PD (sub-paths) represented as sequential uniform and symmetric triangular random variables (hereafter – convolution).

To compare distributions of random variables of arcs incoming into a node k, we use a chance constraint (see [2,12] for details) with a given threshold α. We will call it comparison operator (CO) "$>_\alpha$":

$$X_{ik} >_\alpha X_{jk} \Leftrightarrow Pr(X_{ik} - X_{jk} \geq 0) > \alpha, \tag{1}$$

where
X_{ik}, X_{jk} are random variables;
$\alpha \in [0.5, 1]$ is a reliability threshold.

If the expression (1) is true, then we say that the sub-path from i to k is sufficiently dominating the sub-path from j to k due to X_{ik} dominates X_{jk}. In this case, we will continue with only X_{ik} after the node as the resulting PD of the node. We use convolution to compute the difference between two sub-path durations in CO, and to find the PDF of a sub-path, if the sub-path contains more than one sequential activity.

To determine the PN delay in a node with collapsing arcs, we perform a substitution of a resulting theoretical PDF of the maximum order statistics with a symmetric triangular distribution (hence – approximation). This delay is explained by the fact that maximum order distribution cuts a certain lower part of the overlapping support of several initial PDF, but leaves the upper part intact.

Because all activity distributions are finite, we always know the minimum and maximum of the support of the target maximum order PDF in each node. The lower bound is the maximum among the minimums the PDF arguments of incoming arcs (end times of preceding activities), and the upper bound is the maximum of the maximums accordingly. We build the required symmetric triangular distribution between the points, and assign it as PD in the node.

There are two exceptions. If two uniform distributions are collapsing or if one of the compared PDF is right triangular, then a better approximation is a right triangular PDF built on the support of the maximum order distribution.

Currently the technique operates with the following distribution types:

1. Uniform PDF is the default type for initial activity durations.
2. PDF of the sufficiently dominating random variable determined with (1).
3. Symmetric triangular PDF. This is a default type after approximation of PD in nodes with arbitrary PDF of end times of two or more merged activities.
4. Right triangular PDF (the mean equals mode). This occurs if two uniform distributions are collapsing in a node, or if one of the compared PDF is right triangular.

If one PDF is right triangular, a definite convolution operation is required to obtain the resulting PDF. This is a commonly used operation and we do not give here its expression for the sake of space.

The technique sequentially computes PDF of each activity start and end times and PD in nodes. It starts in node 0 and ends in node N. Activity start time PDF is determined as either the end time PDF of the previous sequential activity or PD of the preceding node. The end time PDF of activities are convolutions of its start time PDF and duration PDF. PD in PN nodes are assigned to end times of the predecessor activity (sequential sub-path). In case of more than one collapsing predecessor activity in the node, it is determined applying dominance expression (1), and if no dominating sub-path exists, by approximating the PDF in the node with a symmetric triangular distribution. It can be generalized to a PN with multiple start and end nodes.

The technique consists of the following steps:

1. Set the end-time of activities without predecessors to X_{ij}, PD in node 0 is 0, and PDF of PD in all other nodes, start and end time PDF of the rest of activities to unset.
2. Compute and set the PDF in nodes where all preceding activities have already known end times using convolution or, if certain arcs collapse in the nodes, then using CO equation (1) and approximation, if required. Only two arcs with largest random variables measured with equation (1) are required for approximation [5]. Common parts of sub-paths from node 0 are omitted for comparison and CO approximation.
3. If the end node N is reached, return its PDF as the project PD and stop.
4. Set start time PDF of immediate subsequent activities to PD of the preceding nodes where it is already set (from the step 2).
5. For activities with computed start-time PDF find and set end time PDF by adding its duration using convolution.
6. Go to step 2.

After reaching the end node, a correction of the final PD is required, if CO operations were applied during PN traverse. This is done by approximating the last node PDF with a symmetric triangular distribution with support between the minimum argument value of the PDF, and the maximum of the PDF argument reduced by $(1 - \alpha)\%$ and after applying floor operation.

3   Application Example

We applied the technique to the data from a real construction project from [10] kindly provided by the authors. The PN consists of 74 arcs and 63 nodes. The adapted trimmed PN of the project is given in Fig. 1. Dashed arcs are dummy activities with zero duration, and continuous arcs are real activities. Estimated initial distribution parameters of activity durations in weeks are specified above each arc. The parameters were provided by experts for application with classical PERT. We utilize only minimum and maximum values to build uniform distributions of activity durations. All nodes are AND nodes, i.e. subsequent activities must wait until all preceding ones end, incl. dummy activities. Notice some activities having fixed duration, i.e. some following activities begin with a constant time latency after the preceding ones.

Application of the technique is given in Table 1. For several iterations, we show node number (column "Node"), its analyzed incoming random arc variables

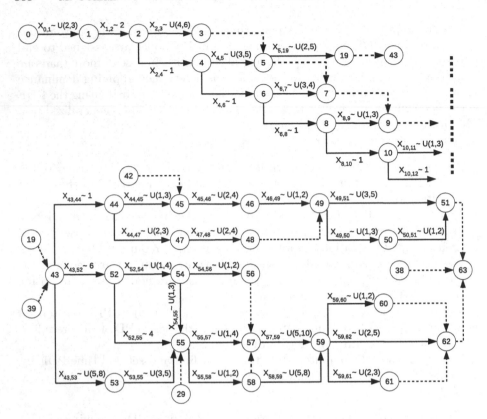

Fig. 1. The PN of the project. Dashed lines denote dummy activities.

and previous node PD variables (column "Comparison"); the column "Dominate" shows if dominance of any arc was identified (using CO (1)); and the column "Approx." specifies if approximation was performed. The last column "$PD_{<Node>}$" gives the final PD prototype for the node. PD of nodes are denoted as $PD_{<node\,number>}$, and PD of some *common* nodes are in brackets meaning that they are not participating in PD computations for the given node. The PD in node 63 is the approximated distribution of project duration, and is given in the bottom of the table.

For example, comparison in node 5 evaluates durations of two sub-paths starting from the node 2 (having common known network segment $PD_2 \sim U(4,5)$) with CO formula (1): $X_{2,3} >_\alpha X_{2,4} + X_{4,5}$. If one of them were sufficiently dominating, then we would continue with this random value as the PD in node 5. But they are probabilistically equal, so we apply approximation and obtain the (right) triangular distribution in node 5: $PD_5 \sim Tri(4,6,6)$. We use

PD_5 in the next nodes 7 and 19. In the same vein, four sub-paths are incoming into the node 55. Leaving their common node (PD_{43}) for the first two comparisons and (PD_2) for the last comparison, we reveal in the last comparison that sub-path through node 29 is well dominated and may be dismissed, and find the need to apply approximation for the rest three incoming sub-path durations in the node 55. As there were approximations with CO (see "Approx." column in Table 1), we apply correction of the final PD. It becomes $PD'_{63} \sim Tri(32, 42, 52)$, with the mean value 42.

We can compare our result to outcomes of the classical PERT, M-PERT, and real project duration from the original paper with the example problem [10]. The real project duration was 38 weeks that is very close to our mean value. Classical PERT determined the mean of the project duration as 38.34 weeks, but the distribution is narrow with the variance 2.72 weeks. This is a natural property of the classical PERT that gives an optimistic result, and it underestimates the area of possible outcomes above the mean (see also discussion in [7]). And the upper part of the final PD should provide the DM information about the possible worst cases. The M-PERT method was not applicable to the PN due to large number of parallel paths from node 0 to node N, and published M-PERT descriptions can be applied only to problems of much smaller complexity [10].

Classical PERT can determine only one CP. In contrast, our technique assumes those activities critical, that lie on PN segments where no domination of certain sub-paths was identified using (1), and also absolutely dominating parts of the PN. For the considered PN, these are activities: $X_{0,1}$, $X_{1,2}$, $X_{2,4}$, $X_{4,6}$, $X_{5,19}$, $X_{6,8}$, $X_{8,10}$, $X_{10,12}$, $X_{12,14}$, $X_{13,17}$, $X_{13,39}$, $X_{14,15}$, $X_{14,16}$, $X_{16,17}$, $X_{16,18}$, $X_{17,19}$, $X_{18,19}$, $X_{43,52}$, $X_{43,53}$, $X_{52,54}$, $X_{52,55}$, $X_{53,55}$, $X_{54,55}$, $X_{55,57}$, $X_{55,58}$, $X_{57,59}$, $X_{58,59}$, $X_{59,61}$, and $X_{59,62}$. All these activities are important, because any delay above their estimated upper bound can delay the whole project, or change dominance of sub-paths in the rest of the project.

Obviously, our mean is larger than the real outcome. However, the real outcome is unpredictable and random for us given so uncertain initial estimations and lack of certainty. Our technique shows what can *likely* happen, i.e. it gives a pessimistic prognosis. And although our technique is simple in comparison to M-PERT, it can process projects of any complexity and size using uncomplicated mathematical operations. Although the approximation of the project PD is very rough, it gives a good reference point to DM of what can the worst case be. Based on that, the obtained outcome is encouraging.

Table 1. Project analysis, $\alpha = 0.9$.

Node	Comparison	Dominate	Approx	PD$_{<\text{Node}>}$
5	$X_{2,3} >_\alpha X_{2,4} + X_{4,5}$	No	Yes	$(PD_2) + Tri(4,6,6)$
7	$X_{2,4} + X_{4,6} + X_{6,7} >_\alpha PD_5$	No	Yes	$(PD_2) + Tri(5,6,6)$
17	$X_{2,4} + X_{4,6} + X_{6,8} + X_{8,10} + X_{10,12} + X_{12,14} + X_{14,16} + X_{16,17} >_\alpha PD_{15}$	No	Yes	$(PD_2) + Tri(8,9.5,11)$
	$PD_{13} + X_{13,17} >_\alpha PD_{15}$	No	Yes	
19	$X_{2,4} + X_{4,6} + X_{6,8} + X_{8,10} + X_{10,12} + X_{12,14} +$ $+ X_{14,16} + X_{16,18} + X_{18,19} >_\alpha PD_{17} + X_{17,19}$	No	Yes	$(PD_2) + Tri(9,11,13)$
	$PD_5 + X_{5,19} >_\alpha PD_{17} + X_{17,19}$	No	Yes	
20	–	-	-	$(PD_2) + 8 + X_{18,20}$
39	–	-	-	$PD_{13} + X_{13,39}$
43	$PD_{39} >_\alpha PD_{19}$	No	Yes	$(PD_2) + Tri(9,13,17)$
45	$PD_{43} + X_{43,44} + X_{44,45} >_\alpha PD_{42}$	No	Yes	$(PD_2) + Tri(11,17,23)$
55	$X_{43,52} + X_{52,54} + X_{54,55} >_\alpha X_{43,52} + X_{52,55}$	No	Yes	$PD_{43} + Tri(10,11.5,13)$
	$X_{43,52} + X_{52,54} + X_{54,55} >_\alpha X_{43,53} + X_{53,55}$	No	Yes	
	$PD_{43} + X_{43,52} + X_{52,54} + X_{54,55} >_\alpha PD_{29}$	Yes	No	
57	$PD_{54} + X_{54,55} >_\alpha PD_{55} + X_{55,57}$	Yes	No	$PD_{55} + Tri(1,2.5,4)$
	$PD_{55} + X_{55,53} >_\alpha PD_{55} + X_{55,57}$	No	Yes	
62	$X_{59,62} >_\alpha X_{59,61}$	No	Yes	$PD_{59} + Tri(2,3.5,5)$
	$X_{59,62} >_\alpha X_{59,60}$	Yes	No	
63	$PD_{62} >_\alpha PD_{51}$	Yes	No	PD_{62}
	$PD_{51} >_\alpha PD_{38}$	No	Yes	

$PD_{63} \sim U(4,5) + Tri(9,13,17) + Tri(10,11.5,13) + Tri(1,2.5,4) + Tri(6,10,14) + Tri(2,3.5,5)$

4   Conclusion

We developed a simple and robust heuristic that enables more accurate result than similar analytical methods of today, for it uses the correct model that assumes stochastic dependence among activities and paths. Moreover, the technique is less complex than any known to us analytical techniques of project time analysis for managers, except the classical PERT. It requires only one passage through the PN, allows for MEB, applies simple mathematics, and needs unsophisticated input information from experts that is feasible to obtain. The output gives all critical activities and approximate start- and end-time PDF of all activities.

The assumption of very uncertain activity duration estimates justifies uniform distribution for estimation of initial activity durations. The technique allows flexible adjustment of risk tolerance to subjective perception of the DM with the reliability threshold α. As we can see, the heuristic technique produces a good approximation of the real project duration including MEB, i.e. it shows possible time realizations beyond duration of any separated path. Thus, it reveals, what can the maximum duration be in the form of PDF for given circumstances and uncertainty. The most important is the PDF part above the mean, for it reveals the possibilities of the worst case time realization.

Application of the technique to time analysis of a real-life project shows useful information for PM and matches well the real project end time. Comparison with the classical PERT and M-PERT is self-explanatory: our technique provides much more useful information about possible project outcomes and can work with PN of any structure and size.

The future work includes multiple verification of the technique in real-life projects, comparison with actual outcome of the project duration, and with other techniques, including simulations. This can show success of our technique relative to other methods in the practical area, and reveal limitations of practical applicability. The technique can be expanded to apply other useful time distributions for initial task estimations and approximations in PN nodes. These are primarily the triangular distribution and discrete distributions. Another focus area is the effect of PN structure on the final distribution of project duration. Finally, the approach will need addition of resource constraints into its model.

References

1. Ballesteros-Pérez, P., Larsen, G.D., González-Cruz, M.C.: Do projects really end late? On the shortcomings of the classical scheduling techniques. J. Technol. Sci. Educ. 8(1), 17 (2018). https://doi.org/10.3926/jotse.303
2. Birge, J.R., Louveaux, F.: Introduction to Stochastic Programming. Springer Series in Operations Research and Financial Engineering. Springer, New York (2011). https://doi.org/10.1007/978-1-4614-0237-4
3. Chu, W.M., Hsu, C.M., Tseng, H.E.: Using an path-comparison tracing algorithm to solve the most k critical paths problem of stochastic networks. World Acad. Sci. Eng. Technol. **56**, 545–554 (2009)

4. Cohen, Y., Zwikael, O.: A new technique for estimating the distribution of a stochastic project makespan. Int. J. Inf. Technol. Proj. Manag. **1**(3), 14–27 (2010). https://doi.org/10.4018/jitpm.2010070102

5. Douglas, D.E.: PERT and simulation. In: Highland, H.J., Nielsen, N.R., Hull, L.G. (eds.) Proceedings of the 10th Conference on Winter Simulation, WSC 1978, Miami Beach, FL, USA, 4–6 December 1978, pp. 89–98. ACM (1978)

6. Fernandes, G., Ward, S., Arajo, M.: Identifying useful project management practices: a mixed methodology approach. IJISPM - Int. J. Inf. Syst. Proj. Manag. **1**(4), 5–21 (2013). https://doi.org/10.12821/ijispm010401

7. Goman, M., Pecerska, J.: Merge event bias in project evaluation techniques - problems and directions. In: 61st International Scientific Conference on Information Technology and Management Science of Riga Technical University (ITMS), p. 1–6. IEEE (2020). https://doi.org/10.1109/ITMS51158.2020.9259326

8. Gong, D., Hugsted, R.: Time-uncertainty analysis in project networks with a new merge-event time-estimation technique. Int. J. Proj. Manag. **11**(3), 165–173 (1993). https://doi.org/10.1016/0263-7863(93)90049-S

9. Hall, N.G.: Research and teaching opportunities in project management. In: INFORMS, pp. 329–388 (2016). https://doi.org/10.1287/educ.2016.0146

10. Handoko, J.R., Gondokusumo, O.: Comparison of PERT and M-PERT scheduling for a construction project in Malang, Indonesia. In: IOP Conference Series: Materials Science and Engineering, vol. 508, pp. 1–10 (2019). https://doi.org/10.1088/1757-899X/508/1/012034

11. Hartley, H.O., Wortham, A.W.: A statistical theory for PERT critical path analysis. Manag. Sci. **12**(10), B469–B481 (1966)

12. Henrion, R.: Chance constrained problems (2009). https://www.stoprog.org/sites/default/files/tutorials/SP10/Henrion.pdf

13. Hubbard, D.: How to Measure Anything Workbook Finding the Value of "Intangibles" in Business, 2nd edn. Wiley, Hoboken (2014)

14. Klingel, A.R.: Bias in PERT project completion time calculations for a real network. Manag. Sci. **13**(4), B194–B201 (1966)

15. Lindley, D.V.: The philosophy of statistics. J. R. Stat. Soc. Ser. D (The Statistician) **49**(3), 293–337 (2000)

16. MacCrimmon, K.R., Ryavec, C.A.: An analytical study of the PERT assumptions. Oper. Res. **12**(1), 16–37 (1964). https://doi.org/10.1287/opre.12.1.16

17. Moder, J.J., Phillips, C.R., Davis, E.W.: Project Management with CPM, PERT, and Precedence Diagramming, 3rd edn. Van Nostrand Reinhold, New York (1983)

18. Möhring, R.H.: Scheduling under uncertainty: bounding the makespan distribution. In: Alt, H. (ed.) Computational Discrete Mathematics. LNCS, vol. 2122, pp. 79–97. Springer, Heidelberg (2001). https://doi.org/10.1007/3-540-45506-X_7

19. Monhor, D.: A new probabilistic approach to the path criticality in stochastic PERT. CEJOR **19**(4), 615–633 (2011). https://doi.org/10.1007/s10100-010-0151-x

20. Neumann, K.: Stochastic Project Networks. Lecture Notes in Economics and Mathematical Systems, vol. 344. Springer, Heidelberg (1990). https://doi.org/10.1007/978-3-642-61515-3

21. O'Hagan, A., et al.: Uncertain Judgements: Eliciting Experts' Probabilities. Wiley, Hoboken (2006)

22. Sadooghi-Alvandi, S.M., Nematollahi, A.R., Habibi, R.: On the distribution of the sum of independent uniform random variables. Stat. Pap. **50**(1), 171–175 (2009). https://doi.org/10.1007/s00362-007-0049-4

23. Schonberger, R.J.: Why projects are "always" late: a rationale based on manual simulation of a PERT/CPM network. Interfaces **11**(5), 66–70 (1981). https://doi.org/10.1287/inte.11.5.66
24. Soroush, H.: The most critical path in a PERT network: a heuristic approach. Eur. J. Oper. Res. **78**(1), 93–105 (1994). https://doi.org/10.1016/0377-2217(94)90124-4
25. Soroush, H.: Risk taking in stochastic PERT networks. EJOR **67**(2), 221–241 (1993). https://doi.org/10.1016/0377-2217(93)90063-S
26. Williams, F.E.: PERT completion times revisited. INFORMS Trans. Educ. **6**(1), 21–34 (2005). https://doi.org/10.1287/ited.6.1.21

ChainOps for Smart Contract-Based Distributed Applications

Willem-Jan van den Heuvel[1]($\boxtimes$), Damian A. Tamburri[2], Damiano D'Amici[3], Fabiano Izzo[3], and S. Potten[4]

[1] Jheronimus Academy of Data Science (JADS), Tilburg University, Tilburg, The Netherlands
w.j.a.m.vdnheuvel@tilburguniversity.nl
[2] Jheronimus Academy of Data Science (JADS), Eindhoven University of Technology, Eindhoven, The Netherlands
d.a.tamburri@tue.nl
[3] Smart Shaped Software Ltd., Pescara, PE, Italy
{damiano.damici,fabiano.izzo}@smartshaped.com
[4] D-VISOR, Eindhoven, The Netherlands
s.potten@d-visor.nl

Abstract. Three of the key impediments that need to be addressed to unlock the true potential of smart contract-based applications include: (i) a lack of operational capabilities to leverage trustworthiness, (ii) limited ability for reuse in volatile and heterogenous application contexts, and (iii) inherent coding complexity that hinders not only involvement of non-technical business experts but also widely used DevOps practices.

This paper reports on the core intermediate results of the development of a model-driven DevOps approach -labelled ChainOps- that ultimately will enable involvement of non-experts, promote reuse and allow for automatic semantic model checking and reasoning to ascertain improved trustworthiness. In addition, a preliminary architecture of an experimental prototype -that is currently under development- is discussed. Finally, this paper plots a roadmap for much needed future research to further explore, validate and extend our initial findings.

Keywords: Smart contracts · Blockchain · Domain specific languages · Model-driven engineering

1 Introduction

Automating business transactions across networks of untrusted business eco-systems is increasingly challenging due to the vastly distributed nature of parties within and the inherent lack of mutual trust between parties.

Blockchain entails a promising solution to facilitate business transactions in a trustworthy manner - in untrusted, heterogeneous and distributed business environments.

Part of this work is supported by the Next Generation Internet ONTOCHAIN initiative under grant agreement No. 957338.

In essence, blockchain constitutes a collective ledger that leverages a trusted, privacy-preserving, immutable data repository, enabling increased democracy, transparency and traceability. In addition, it also enacts decentralized execution of computations in the form of executable code, shortly referred to as smart contracts. In this way, smart contracts may simplify trade in ecosystems where parties may remain anonymous, departing from the costly and time-consuming need for brokers such as banks and/or notaries without compromising on authenticity, confidentiality, accuracy and credibility.

By now, blockchain-enabled smart-contracts have received much attention in literature. However, they suffer from three key impediments that seriously impede their successful uptake in industrial settings.

The first key challenges that needs to be overwon is their lack of operational capabilities to leverage trustworthiness [18]. Similarly to trustworthy AI in electronic marketplaces [19], trustworthiness of blockchains refers to the quality to operate in a manner that is (1) explainable and transparent, (2) responsible and auditable, (3) robust and reliable, and (4) safe and secure. Infusing these qualities basically implies that blockchain-enabled applications have to be able to consistently and reliably process inputs and deliver outputs, while safeguarding security and privacy. In addition, the next generation of blockchain-enabled applications should at the same time be transparent, tractable and open to inspection to its users.

The second key challenge is to enable non-expert and non-technical end-users (e.g., process owners, legal staff, etc.) to collectively help blockchain architects, programmers and system managers developing and evolving applications [20]. There is currently an acute lack of low-code support environments to effectively model, develop, deploy, and manage distributed apps in a collaborative, simple and predictable manner. Today's lack of such support environments seriously hampers the effectiveness and uptake of such technologies, especially in light of DevOps practices that assume such collaborations.

Thirdly, and lastly, current blockchain-enabled technologies often implicitly assume a closed, rather stable and homogeneous environment (e.g., a complete Ehtereum environment) [2] whilst the reality is that enterprises want to employ various blockchain environments simultaneously and wish to abstract away from the blockchain technology of choice to be able to better deal with changes, prevent lock-in, and reuse knowledge and application code over time and in various (project) contexts. One proven way to achieve this is by treating models as first-class citizens, and mapping them to code, while evolving them collectively over time.

This paper first briefly summarizes the results of an initial literature survey on the development, execution and maintenance of trustworthy smart contracts running on the blockchain and/or distributed ledger computing technologies. This paper then continues with introducing a novel model-driven DevOps framework for smart-contract governed, distributed applications, shortly referred to as ChainOps. Next, we outline an experimental prototype -that is currently under development- and that serves to demonstrate the implementability and feasibility of the framework. Lastly, we will outline a research roadmap to realize the vision of ChainOps and the corresponding low-code platform as part of the OntoChain approach.

2 Related Works

In this section we will briefly review the current state-of-the-art (SotA) in subsequently the domains of smart contracts, blockchain ontologies, and model-driven development of distributed applications.

2.1 Smart Contracts, DApps and Oracles

Recently blockchain-based smart contracts have attracted massive attention of industry practitioners and academic scholars. Whilst blockchain technology is subject to some healthy skepticism, according to industry watcher Gartner, organizations using blockchain-enabled smart contracts will increase overall data quality by 50% [3].

In [1], a structured multivocal literature review on the state-of-the-art in blockchain is reported that has been reported that briefly overviews smart contracts emphasizing the exploitative potential in the areas of business and legal. A recent and comprehensive overview of smart contracts may be found in [5].

Smart contracts hold the promise of providing compelling benefits to public- and private organizations and for society at large in fostering network collaborations, removing the necessity of a trusted third party, reducing risks of transactions being tampered with, whilst significantly lowering transaction costs due to less administrative settlement-, monitoring- and contract enforcement efforts. Notably, smart contracts may offer a near certainty of trusted exchange between trading and/or community partners [6, 7].

Given the fact that the smart contract runs on top of blockchain, her outcomes are immutable and irreversible through unmodifiable code [4]. One of the main programming platforms to code and deploy smart contracts is Ehtereum, which offers the Solidity programming language that resembles the OO Eiffel language with extensions for transaction management. Blockchain-enabled programming languages such as Solidity do not only enable the development of stand-alone applications but also leverage back-end functionality - popularly referred to as decentralized applications (DApps).

Typically, however, such DApps rely on- and off-chain functionalities. A common approach to lift the implicit assumption of many blockchain applications that all functionality is executed on chain, are oracles. Oracles are typically provisioned by third-party providers and inject external data and functionality on the blockchain [8].

Unfortunately, DApss developed in such smart contract programming environments suffer from serious vulnerabilities, including reentrancy, integer over- and underflow, timestamp dependencies, and revert-based DoS [12]. This implies semantically powerful approaches are needed to reinforce (continued) smart contract testing. In addition, they assume intimate knowledge of- and experience with the underpinning programming environment, hindering involvement of much-needed expertise from legal- and business experts.

2.2 Blockchain Ontologies

Semantic web technologies, and notably ontologies, have been recently studied in the academic literature to allow for formal specification and conceptualization of smart contracts, and advanced reasoning about their structural and dynamic properties.

In [11] a smart contract source code ontology has been suggested that allows to issue queries as semantic triple stores to check on various types of vulnerabilities. Interestingly, this research contribution also introduces a transaction run-time ontology to allow verification of smart contracts, prior and post execution.

Another relevant work [10] addresses a language-agnostic semantic framework that is capable of directly handling smart contracts coded in different high-level programming languages exploiting semantic extensions. In this way, it accommodates the formal verification of (security) properties with the generated semantics in the abstract, without the need to transform contracts in EVM bytecode or intermediate languages.

Semantic web technology in general, and ontologies more in particular, have been already applied successfully in smart contracts. However, there has been put little emphasis on how semantic reasoning may help dApp developers to take decisions on i. whether or not smart contracts can be composed, ii. which data and logic to store on- and off-chain, and iii. logically infer impacts of code modifications and version updates.

2.3 Model-Driven Engineering Distributed Applications

Model-driven engineering is an off-spring from the UML modeling flamework, with at the center court the Meta Object Facility, promoted by the Object Management Group in the late 90s. From its beginning, the MDE's DNA encompasses the following three nucleotides [9]: (a) domain-specific languages, (b) model transformation, and (c) model management facilities. The model-driven approach avoids vendor- and programming-language/platform lock-in, encourages implementation of proven good/best practice, promotes reusability across various technologies and applications, thereby harnessing trustworthiness of smart contract development.

Particularly, in [13] a model-driven engineering approach is presented and illustrated for developing (a) collaborative business processes and (b) registries for non-fungible assets. Several model-driven approaches for developing smart contracts have been introduced by now in literature, including [14] based on the DEMO-inspired DasContract language, [15] revolving around mapping UML Statecharts to Solidity, and [16] introducing a ontology-based model engineering approach for commitment-based smart contracts.

Unfortunately, however, most of the suggested methodologies for model-driven smart contracts at the one hand side remain conceptual, brittle, and rudimentary in nature, providing f.e. incomplete mappings to underpinning platform-specific models only. On the other hand, they lack serious, and end-to-end tool-level support, backed up with serious, real-world applications and use cases.

3   Model-Driven Round-Trip Engineering of Smart-Contract Enabled Distributed Applications

A disciplined, transparent and repeatable, model-driven development and management methodological framework of typical smart contract enabled applications and services lies at the heart of our vision. This methodological framework assists to deliver trustworthy knowledge and information exchange in collaborative and transactional business processes and data marketplaces, especially in light of their necessity to interoperate and easily integrate.

This will enable round-trip engineering of distributed applications, ensuring to continuous monitor and improve their operations, exploiting continuous feedback loops and testing/verification, while protecting them from vulnerabilities and anomalous behavior. In particular, we aim to leverage our model-driven and ontological models and reasoning, to address these challenges. The ontological foundation will allow multiple blockchain-oriented and domain-specific ontologies to be used in domain-specific scenarios for both semantic reasoning (e.g., for situational awareness, or smart services adaptability) and smart and trusted data transaction brokering. The model-driven oriented approach could also guarantee the ability for smart-contract enabled distributed applications developed thusly to natively integrate and interoperate both with one another.

We envision that the round-trip engineering process to be positioned along the perimetry of an ecosystem such as OntoChain. In short, OntoChain is the foundational cornerstone of the Next Generation Internet initiative, kick-started by the European Commission in 2018, that aims to shape the development and evolution Internet of Humans, promoting transparency and trustworthiness through the application of blockchain and distributed ledger technologies, including trustless oracles and decentralized ontologies [17].

3.1 Methodological Round-Trip Engineering Framework Leveraging OntoChainOps

The methodological round trip engineering framework has been designed to ensure that distributed applications come with high resilience, trustworthiness, and security, while fostering dynamic operations through continued semantic knowledge extraction and evolution driven by domain-driven models learning directly from the operational data. Specifically, and following current engineering practices, we propose a DevOps-inspired framework to help multi-disciplinary teams implement smart software featuring a service-based architecture, where smart contracts can be executed partially off-chain with containerized microservices (e.g., a function that contains a deep neural network for detection of anomalies in crowds). The framework will also be open and standards-friendly leveraging pre-existing support in its baselines (e.g., TOSCA-based customization and orchestration of smart contract blueprints). In particular, the framework will benefit from DevOps style fast-feedback loops to cater for round-trip engineering with continuous *automated* testing, composition, deployment and monitoring. In each loop, models are the central vehicle to capture application semantics, and reason about issues such as correctness, compliance, and, consistency. This will pave the way for realtime adaptations to ascertain the smart contracts to become more trustworthy and stay within the boundaries of policies, including those with respect to QoS and regulations, norms and directives including the GDPR. In this way, the framework will allow for a new strand of DevOps, shortly referred to as ChainOps.

In the below we will further explain the nine steps that embody the Dev and Ops cycle, and their interaction (see Fig. 1).

ChainOps Development

Coherently with the low-code paradigm, the framework encompasses a (meta) modeling environment (step 1 in Fig. 1) where smart-contract distributed applications can be visually modelled. To speed and ease this model-based application development, we will rely on predefined blueprints: domain specific, visual modeling skeletons that capture common business objects, logic and constraints (e.g., security policies).

Blueprints can be selected, configured, and then chained (step-2) into dApps. The *blueprint models* are grounded on a formal ontology (metamodels) that specifies their operational semantics. These metamodels can be defined and stored in the metamodel repository (step-3). For the purpose of this work, we have defined an OntoChain language that can define application semantics as well as compliance requirements, is easy to use, and general-purpose to impose constraints on control and data flow, and resource requirements (e.g., access/control).

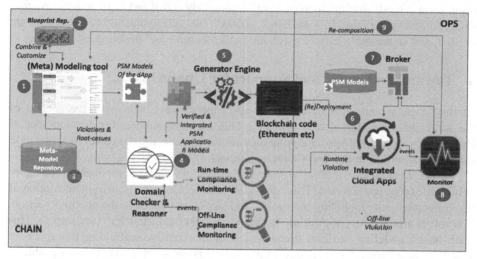

Fig. 1. ChainOps cycles, tools, and (automated) steps

In the next step (step-4), the abstract domain models are packaged and mapped into platform specific models (PSMs), e.g., specifically geared toward Solidity. The Domain Checker and Reasoner matches the PSMs models against policies, including QoS and compliance policies, detects root-causes, and reasons about solutions that it may feed back into the modeling tool.

Once the models have been synthesized and automatically verified against composition rules, and compliance and QoS policies executable code can be automatically generated (e.g., in Solidity/Ethereum) with the Generator Engine (Step 5).

As the DomainBuilder relies on a formal ontology built for the very purpose of defining OntoChain compliant applications, this allows for the instantiation of various domain specific models, like a domain model of a data marketplace, defining key objects, processes and policies that can be typically expected.

ChainOps Operations

Consequently, the deployment of dApps within our framework is also going to be greatly facilitated and rigged for an advanced DevOps/DataOps lifecycles. This will indeed advance the state of the art by furthering not only the theoretical but also the technical foundations behind facilitating blockchain logic development and continuous deployment, defining a radically novel fashion of ChainOps, intended as advanced DevOps-enabled blockchain-oriented and ontology-driven smart software operations.

In particular, the framework allows for the execution of the generated code of the Dev cycle as fully integrated, functional cloud apps (Step-6). A runtime broker is foreseen that ingests the ontological, platform specific domain models for the purpose of their runtime (re-)composition (Step-7). Assisted by a monitor (Step-8) that continuously observes and verifies the behavior of the integrated cloud dApps, any (potential) deviation could be detected, leading to potential re-composition at runtime (Step-9).

This interplay of tools allows for continuous code integration: novel code implementing add-on or modified functionalities are continuously coded and fused with the existing smart contract code base. In some cases, second order adaptation and deep changes are needed, and an anomaly may be escalated to the design-time modeling environment.

4   Toward Prototype Tool Support for ChainOps

At this stage, we are developing end-to-end support for ChainOps in the context of the aforementioned OntoChain project[1]. This includes support for development of OntoChain compliant dApps, meaning they conform to specific standardized application semantics specified in the OntoChain metamodel.

Figure 2 provides a high-level snapshot of the "physical" component architecture behind the proposed solution. This "physical" architecture entails an implementation of the conceptual one, including the cycles, and steps, introduced in the previous section. It revolves around the pre-existing AstraKode Blockchain Modeler[2] (see step 1). This SaaS-based modeling platform already provides an extensive scaffolding to implement a wide range of models/ontologies. In practice, this means that the platform is able to provide the logic necessary to render the blueprints at the frontend, both with respect to their graphical representation and means of configuration.

Coming to the actual architecture, as one can see in the above figure, the IDE will support a graphical notation that complies to the OntoChain metamodel and allows to specify dApps in an implementation-agnostic, standardized and low-code style (step-1). dApp models can then be fed into the Domain Modeler (step-2) that supports automatic verification of the models with respect to composition constraints, security policies, and other QoS-requirements. Verified models are issued back to the modelers so they can be checked by a non-technical dApp developer and then redirected to the AKB Rest Layer (step-3), which represents the boundary for the DEV perimeter of the architecture, stores all OntoChain PSM models, and is called upon at runtime to access the Engine layer.

The AKB Generator Engine (step 4) constitutes the workhorse of the architecture, as it provides the logic to turn the (configured) blueprints/models into source code as well

---

[1] https://ontochain.ngi.eu/.

[2] https://www.astrakode.tech/.

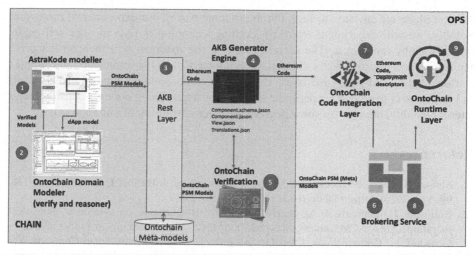

Fig. 2. Physical DomainBuilder platform architecture

as access most other platform verification services, such as notably QoS and compliance rules checking (Step-5). We have chosen RuleML to drive this verification.

Once the code has been verified, generated, the brokering layer will take care of brokering for runtime (re-)composition (step 6), as well as provide access to ChainOps code integration services (step-7). Lastly, code will be deployed on the runtime layer that will provide services such as continuous automated testing, deployment, and monitoring (step-8 and 9).

5   Conclusions and Future Research

This position paper introduces a framework that is ultimately designed to deliver (more) trustworthy smart software through the well-disciplined DevOps of smart-contract enabled distributed applications, that run on- and off- the blockchain. This approach -labeled ChainOps- assumes a low code, feedback-loop, and semi-automatic environment, allows involvement of- and co-design by non-technical end-users, and will promote reuse.

We have outlined the key workings of the ChainOps methodological framework, and plotted the physical architecture underpinning our experimental prototype. We have grounded our prototype on the AstraKode platform as it is one of the only commercial low-code IDE platforms currently available, but in principle, similar (forthcoming) tools could also be used.

Indeed, the results presented in this paper are core in nature. We have structured extensions and refinement along a three-phased R&D oriented roadmap as part of the H2020 OntoChain project efforts, in conjunction with academic research. In particular, during the first phase we wish to further elaborate the theory underpinning composable smart contracts, and verification of their operational semantics. This will involve formalization of the (meta-)models, and approach introduced in this paper. Also, during the first phase we envision to flesh out the runtime part of our experimental prototype. Notably, we will experiment with self-learning technologies (AI) to offer self-repair capabilities by the broker. The second phase of the roadmap will then further drive extensions and improvements through applying the ChainOps framework and support platform to five real-world use cases. The third phase consolidates phase-I and phase-II, and targets to converge the experimental validation ascertaining not only construct- and internal validity, but also (to some degree) the external validity of our approach.

References

1. Maesa, D., Mori, P.: Blockchain 3.0 applications survey. J. Parallel Distrib. Comput. **138**, 99–114 (2020). https://doi.org/10.1016/j.jpdc.2019.12.019
2. Butijn, B.-J., Tamburri, D.A., Heuvel, W.-J.V.D.: Blockchains - a systematic multivocal literature review. ACM Comput. Surv. **53**(3), 61 (2020). https://doi.org/10.1145/3369052
3. Goasduff, L.: Gartner Predicts that Organizations Using Blockchain Smart Contracts Will Increase Overall Data Quality by 50%, Gartner. https://www.gartner.com/en/newsroom/press-releases/2020-01-30-gartner-predicts-that-organizations-using-blockchain Accessed 2 Apr 2021
4. Zheng, Z., Xie, S., Dai, H., Chen, X., Wang, H.: An overview of blockchain technology: architecture, consensus, and future trends. In: IEEE International Congress on Big Data (BigData Congress), pp. 557–564 (2017)
5. Hu, B., et al.: A comprehensive survey on smart contract construction and execution: paradigms, tools, and systems. Patterns **2**(2), 100179 (2021).. PMID: 33659907; PMCID: PMC7892363. https://doi.org/10.1016/j.patter.2020.100179
6. Sillaber, C., Waltl, B., Treiblmaier, H., et al.: Laying the foundation for smart contract development: an integrated engineering process model. Inf. Syst. E-Bus. Manage. (2020). https://doi.org/10.1007/s10257-020-00465-5
7. Bedin, A.R.C., Capretz, M., Mir, S.: Blockchain for collaborative businesses. Mob. Netw. Appl. **26**(1), 277–284 (2020). https://doi.org/10.1007/s11036-020-01649-6
8. Wöhrer, M., Zdun, U.: Design patterns for smart contracts in the ethereum ecosystem. In: IEEE International Conference on Blockchain, pp. 1513–1520 (2018). https://doi.org/10.1109/Cybermatics_2018.2018.00255
9. Bucchiarone, A., Cabot, J., Paige, R.F., Pierantonio, A.: Grand challenges in model-driven engineering: an analysis of the state of the research. Softw. Syst. Model. **19**(1), 5–13 (2020). https://doi.org/10.1007/s10270-019-00773-6
10. Jiao, J., Lin, S.W., Sun, J.: A generalized formal semantic framework for smart contracts. In: Wehrheim, H., Cabot, J. (eds.) Fundamental Approaches to Software Engineering. FASE 2020. LNCS, vol. 12076, pp. 75–96. Springer, Cham (2020). https://doi.org/10.1007/978-3-030-45234-6_4
11. Petrovic, N., Tosic, M.: Semantic approach to smart contract verification. Facta Univ. Ser. Autom. Control Robot. **19**, 21–37 (2020). https://doi.org/10.22190/FUACR2001021P
12. Feng, X., Wang, Q., Zhu, X., Wen, S.: Bug searching in smart contract, pp. 1–8 (2019). https://arxiv.org/abs/1905.00799
13. Lu, Q., et al.: Integrated model-driven engineering of blockchain applications for business processes and asset management. CoRR abs/2005.12685 (2020). http://arxiv.org/abs/2005.12685
14. Skotnica, M., Klicpera, J., Pergl, R.: Towards model-driven smart contract systems - code generation and improving expressivity of smart contract modeling. EEWC Forum Doctoral Consortium (2020). http://ceur-ws.org/Vol-2825/paper1.pdf

15. Garamvölgyi, P., Kocsis, I., Gehl, B., Klenik, A.: Towards model-driven engineering of smart contracts for cyber-physical systems. In: 2018 48th Annual IEEE/IFIP International Conference on Dependable Systems and Networks Workshops (DSN-W), Luxembourg, Luxembourg, pp. 134–139 (2018). https://doi.org/10.1109/DSN-W.2018.00052
16. de Kruijff, J., Weigand, H.: Ontologies for commitment-based smart contracts. In: Panetto, H., et al. (eds.) OTM 2017. LNCS, vol. 10574, pp. 383–398. Springer, Cham (2017). https://doi.org/10.1007/978-3-319-69459-7_26
17. Kochovski, P., et al.: Smart contracts for service-level agreements in edge-to-cloud computing. J. Grid Comput. 18(4), 673–690 (2020). https://doi.org/10.1007/s10723-020-09534-y
18. Teng, Y.: Towards trustworthy blockchsains: normative reflections on blockchain-enabled virtual institutions. Ethics Inf. Technol. (2021). https://doi.org/10.1007/s10676-021-09581-3
19. Thiebes, S., Lins, S., Sunyaev, A.: Trustworthy artificial intelligence. Electron. Mark. (2020). https://doi.org/10.1007/s12525-020-00441-4
20. Iansiti, M., Lakhani, K.R.: The truth about blockchain. Harv. Bus. Rev. 95(1), 118–127 (2017)

A Stakeholders Taxonomy for Opening Government Data Decision-Making

Ahmad Luthfi[1,2(✉)] and Marijn Janssen[1]

[1] Faculty of Technology, Policy and Management, Delft University of Technology, Jaffalaan 5, 2628 BX Delft, The Netherlands
{a.luthfi,m.f.w.h.a.janssen}@tudelft.nl
[2] Universitas Islam Indonesia, Yogyakarta, Indonesia
ahmad.luthfi@uii.ac.id

Abstract. Stakeholders can have different views on the opening of data, and conflicts may arise between them. Several causes of disputes may arise during the decision-making process due to the diverse objectives, interests, and needs among the stakeholders that perceive their desires. Yet, no stakeholder taxonomy exists to guide this decision-making process. Direct and indirect stakeholders include open data providers, software developers, data scientists, privacy experts, decision-makers, users, open data evangelists, software developers, policy-makers and politicians. Using an iterative process, a stakeholders taxonomy was developed by classifying stakeholders based on their varying levels and views on openness. The taxonomy includes unaware, unknowledgeable, resistant, risk-averse, neutral, supportive, expert, champion, and leading roles. Each stakeholder proposes a unique mix of expertise, legitimacy, sense of urgency, perceived possible benefits, and risks. The stakeholder's taxonomy can help to improve the adoption of the decision-making process to open data.

Keywords: Stakeholder · Taxonomy · Open data · Open government data · Decision-making

1 Introduction

Varying stakeholders' interests in the decision-making process about whether to open or not disclose the data can be burdensome and challenging [1]. In government organisations, the challenges might be that stakeholders like decision-makers, civil servants, open data evangelists, software developers, and privacy analysis officers all have their different views and objectives [2, 3]. These stakeholders play diverse roles in the decision-making process of disclosing data ranging from setting goals, agendas, and ambitions to the actual opening of data [1]. Direct stakeholders are those who are involved in the decision-making process, but also indirect stakeholders might influence the ability to open datasets. For example, if indirect stakeholders like software developers adhere to transparency-by-design principles [4], then relevant datasets can be automatically opened or with less effort.

© Springer Nature Switzerland AG 2021
B. Shishkov (Ed.): BMSD 2021, LNBIP 422, pp. 384–391, 2021.
https://doi.org/10.1007/978-3-030-79976-2_26

The different backgrounds of stakeholders in terms of their roles and interest, politi-cal views and institutional framework, economic constraints and pressures, risks-adverse cultures, and technical knowledge are all influencing factors in the decision-making pro-cess of opening data [5]. Therefore, the decision-making process becomes cumbersome, and the merits of opening data like creating transparency, accountability, and improve citizen engagement are not accomplished. Also, the stakeholders' heterogeneous roles and interests in opening government data might create inconsistent decision-making and initiate conflicts.

For example, data privacy analysis officers should be risk-averse and protective against opening the datasets. At the same time, decision-makers might have the author-ity whether to release or keep undisclosed datasets. In contrast, other open data stake-holders, such as politicians, administrative officers, and civil servants, might preferably release datasets without having insight into the possible far-reaching consequences of data sensitivity, misuse and misinterpretation of the data. They might only think and believe about the advantages of opening datasets to the public domain. The more dataset opened, the open data stakeholders will perceive the higher merits. Hence, these pros and cons of opening data to the public domain can create conflicts among the stakeholders and delayed the decision-making process.

The objective of this paper is to develop a taxonomy of Open Government Data (OGD) stakeholders. First, we review the stakeholder theory. Thereafter, we conduct a case study to identify the main stakeholders and mapping them using a power-interest matrix. Based on their varying levels and views on openness, the stakeholder's taxonomy was developed consisting of nine categories: unaware, unknowledgeable, resistant, risk-averse, neutral, supportive, expert, champion, and leading. The use of the taxonomy was illustrated by revisiting the case and mapping the stakeholders on the taxonomy. This classification can help understand the decision-making process better and balance the interests and conflicts among the stakeholders when disagreement in the decision-making process is found.

2 Theoretical Background

Stakeholder theory defines the specific stakeholders and then investigates these stake-holders' treatment by looking at their salience [6]. Managing stakeholders consists of identifying people and key actors, groups, or organisations that may positively and negatively impact the decision-making process [7]. The different types of stakeholders might be difficult to manage, yet their engagement can be managed by identifying their actual attention and needs [8]. Therefore, stakeholder analysis is often used to under-stand concerns among stakeholders, capture their roles and interests, and select the best decision-making that might impact their organisation's objectives and agendas [3, 9].

In the OGD domain, the backgrounds of different stakeholders in the decision-making process are often heterogeneous [10]. Opening of data is often advocated by politicians for ensuring transparency, accountability, participation and innovation [11]. Several key actors like decision-makers, executive boards, and policy-makers can veto decisions and set the policy on opening data's decision-making process. Whereas other types of stakeholders, such as civil servants and public managers can manage the progress of the current state of the decision-making process, the best time to make a decision, and the possible outcome of the decisions made. Indirect stakeholders might set the conditions like software developers by ensuring software support for opening data, while others set the policy like privacy officers by determining rules of which data can be opened. Some stakeholders set the policy and weigh the estimated advantages and disadvantages of opening data, while others tend to focus on providing input and technical analysis to make decisions.

Classifying the stakeholders of OGD enables the decision-makers and policy-makers to manage stakeholder's interests and needs strategically [7, 8, 12, 13]. There are three main benefits of classifying stakeholder engagement to develop a management strategy in the decision-making process, as follows [3, 7, 8]: (1) Manage time to spend with each stakeholder. Decision-makers and policy-makers naturally manage decision-making process scope, timeline, possible investment, and other attributes while managing the stakeholders. The decision-makers should decide how much time to invest in each decision-making process to open data ranging from setting objectives, selecting the dataset, analysing the estimated advantage and disadvantage consequences, and time to decide whether to open or not to open the dataset. (2) Understand the most important roles and interests of each stakeholder. Classifying stakeholders by their level of positions for each role and interest may be very useful to the decision-makers. Every stakeholder in the OGD field indicates a unique mix of expertise, legitimacy, sense of urgency, perceived possible benefits, and potential risks-adverse. Therefore, classifying the stakeholders should define each stakeholder's essential roles, interests, and needs. (3) Determine the level of importance of each stakeholder's concern. In this situation, the decision-makers should prioritise stakeholders' level of importance based on the potential impacts on their concern on the decision-making process.

One of stakeholder management's key processes is defining and designing influential stakeholders' engagement agendas and plans [12]. The need to enhance stakeholder engagement is to help translate stakeholders' interests and needs into organisational goals and create an effective strategy in the decision-making process [1, 5]. Discovering the importance of consensus and intensive discussion among the OGD stakeholders should help stakeholders to reach a decision and ensure a time allocation and investment in a profitable outcome. There is a need for a stakeholder taxonomy to be able to understand the stakeholder positions and to improve the decision-making process of opening data.

3   Case Study Background

In this paper, we use electronic procurement (e-procurement) case study in Indonesia to capture stakeholders' context in the decision-making process to OGD. We employ a case study to the stakeholders, consisting of 25 participants derived from government institutions. The stakeholder included the member of the executive boards, politicians, decision-makers, policy-makers, civil servants, open data evangelists, and privacy analysis officers. Using the power-interest matrix of [12], the power and interests of the stakeholders in the decision-making process to open data were mapped, as shown in Fig. 1. The matrix shows that stakeholders have varying power and interest.

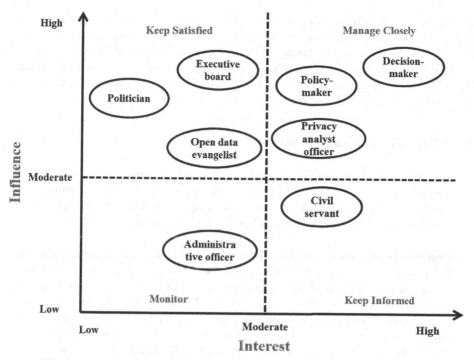

Fig. 1. The power-interest grid of stakeholders (based on the matrix from [12])

The decision-makers, policy-makers, and privacy analyst officers have a powerful influence and high interest in the decision-making process. The policy-makers established the policy-making objectives and agendas and translated the ideas into the policies. The decision-makers are responsible for setting decision alternatives and high interest to re-use the datasets to make better decisions. The decision-makers should adhere to the policies provided by the government institution. However, the procedures and policies are often ill-defined for a given dataset. Furthermore, policy-makers and decision-makers may have adequate knowledge and resources to create decision alternatives. Privacy analyst officers and open data evangelists are responsible for analysing and weighing the estimated risks and benefits of disclosing data; they all have high roles and interests in the decision-making process.

Thereafter, the politicians and executive boards have high roles and fewer interests in the decision-making process. The politicians, furthermore, can manage both contextual risks and the presence of open data legislation at the parliamentary level. Nevertheless, some politicians might not be interested in using the datasets for their personal advantages due to the cognitive constraint in analysing the datasets. At the same time, executive boards can contribute to the decision-making process to open data to support resources and policies. Yet, executive boards have limited time to re-use and analyse the datasets because they focus on the strategic programs and agendas. The civil servants have a moderate role and moderate interest level in the decision-making process. The civil servants can play a role in controlling the harmonisation among the stakeholders.

Simultaneously, the civil servants have enough attention to re-analyse the impact of published datasets. In addition, the administrative officers have a moderate role and lower interest level in the decision-making process administrative officers regularly maintain the OGD portal and provide valuable information to the public related to the dataset. The administrative officers also have soft attention to re-use and re-analyse the dataset to predict the consequence's opening datasets.

4   A Stakeholder Taxonomy

Our stakeholders' taxonomy was developed using an iterative process based on the stakeholder's overview, power, and interest (shown in Fig. 1). The stakeholders are classified based on their varying levels and views on openness. The stakeholder taxonomy consists of 9 roles. One stakeholder can have one or more roles.

a) *Unaware (UW).* These stakeholders are unaware of the decision-making process to open data & their potential impact can be taken lightly. In the OGD domain, it is possible that the decision-making process to open data in the low-level roles of stakeholders like administrative officers may be unaware of the decision-making consequences. Besides, they are not experienced in the benefits and estimated risks of opening data in the larger scale scheme. In our case study, the role of administrative officers is classified as an unaware stakeholder. Therefore, we suggested to this stakeholder can be classified as the supportive classification as the desired state.

b) *Unknowledgeable (UK).* Stakeholders having a lack of knowledge and expertise about the open data domain nor insight into decision-making methods are means for opening data. Our case study found that administrative officers are also facing some barriers to understanding the decision-making process and which approach should be taken in analysing the datasets. Therefore, we expect that this stakeholder can improve their cognitive and technical skills in the decision-making process.

c) *Resistant (RS).* These stakeholders are resistant to the decision-making process to open data & potential impact but resistant to change. Stakeholders classified at this engagement level can take jeopardise the decision-making process deliverables. Therefore, we should seriously take into account the need to be adopted the engagement level of such OGD stakeholders from the current state level to a more desired level. Hence, the government's top management level should devise an appropriate recognition system and reward for the potential stakeholders in this classification. In our case study, civil servants are classified as a resistant stakeholder. In the future, we expect that civil servants can improve their role as supportive stakeholder.

d) *Risk-averse (RA).* These stakeholders are unwilling to take risks as many as possible. The estimated risks of opening data can be derived from privacy violation, misuse, and misinterpretation of the dataset. In our case study, civil servants operated in a risk-averse culture and might embrace this attitude. This results in the decision to keep data closed by default to avoid the taking of any disadvantages.

e) *Neutral (NT).* The third classification is neutral to the decision-making process to open data. Stakeholders having this level of engagement are aware of the decision-making processes, yet neither supportive nor resistance can be taken lightly but cannot be ignored. Stakeholders classifying under this level have been identified as having a high role and power of significant influence over the decision-making. Therefore, in this third level, a particular endeavour approach across the top-level management like politicians should be expanded to take such stakeholders to a more desired engagement level.

f) **Supportive (SP).** The stakeholders falling under this classification are aware of the decision-making process to open data & potential impact and support the changes. Therefore, the stakeholder classifying in the supportive classification should be given high priority to continue to get the desired help by defining and providing agreement with other stakeholders. Our case study shows that executive boards, open data evangelists, and privacy analysis officers are potential supportive stakeholders. Still, we expect that these stakeholders classification can move to the leading cluster to help a better decision-making process of opening data. Simultaneously, we stimulate that several other stakeholders such as civil servants and administrative officers can also move their current states to the desired supportive classification.

g) **Expert (EX).** These stakeholders have in-depth knowledge to analyse the opening data decision-making process, including the way to release and which factors adopt the decisions. In the current situation, our study found that open data evangelists and privacy analysis officers require to improve their knowledge and practical-based experience to reach the expert's stakeholders. Thus, these stakeholders are in substantial comprehension of the technical parts and have sufficient knowledge to adopt the prior decisions.

h) **Champion (CH).** These types of stakeholders promote and stimulate the use of open data. They might not be involved in the actual opening data but advocate the benefits and provide support for opening data. Our study found that several strategic actors of the OGD stakeholders like politicians, policy-makers, and decision-makers are the most potential stakeholders to implement this champion's classification.

i) **Leading (LD).** The stakeholders in this engagement level are aware of the decision-making process to open data and its potential consequences. The stakeholders also actively engaged in ensuring the success and the best decisions are made. Therefore, stakeholders with high power and influence on the decision-making should ideally reach this level of engagement. In this classification, policy-makers and decision-makers are counted as the leading stakeholder. Nevertheless, we expect these stakeholders to stay focused on the decision-making process's objectives and help other stakeholders open more a selected dataset.

5   Illustrating the Use of the Stakeholder Taxonomy

For our case study, the stakeholders are mapped based on the stakeholder's engagement levels. Based on grid position in Fig. 1 and the stakeholder's taxonomy, we derive classifications of stakeholders' current state and desire state, as presented in Table 1. The table shows that, for example, privacy analysis officers can be risk-averse (RA) to the datasets, but they also able to aware of the decision-making process to open data & potential impact and support the changes (SP). This shows that one actor can have multiple stakeholder roles. Combining some roles is not possible as these are conflicting, like neutral and champion.

Table 1. Mapping the stakeholder Using the Taxonomy

Stakeholder name	UW	UK	RS	RA	NT	SP	EX	CH	LD
Executive board	–	–	–	–	–	C	–	–	D
Politician	–	–	–	–	C	–	–	D	–
Open data evangelist	–	–	–	–	–	C	D	–	–
Policy-maker	–	–	–	–	–	–	–	D	C/D
Decision-maker	–	–	–	–	–	–	–	D	C/D
Privacy analysis officer	–	–	–	C	–	C	D	–	–
Civil servant	–	–	C	C	–	D	–	–	–
Administrative officer	C	C	–	–	–	D	–	–	–

*C= Current state of the stakeholder classification
*D= Desired state of the stakeholder classification

6 Conclusion

In the case study, we found different interests and several tensions among stakeholders, which result in a reluctance to open the dataset. Each stakeholder has different roles, concerns and interests in the decision-making process of disclosing the dataset. The merits of enhancing transparency, accountability, and citizen participation were in strong contrast to the difficulty of the opening data by the stakeholders in reality.

Therefore, we developed a taxonomy consisting of 9 roles based on their their varying levels and views on openness, e.g., unaware, unknowledgeable, resistant, risk-averse, neutral, supportive, expert, champion, and leading. One stakeholder can have one or more roles, although it is unlikely that some roles are combined like champion and resistant. With our stakeholder taxonomy, stakeholder's roles and interests can be mapped to determine their positions and analyse the situation. Classifying the stakeholders can help government institutions and researchers better understand the importance of their roles and interests. This study contributes to providing a stakeholder engagement level to change the current state of the stakeholder's position to the desired state in the future agendas. The classification of the stakeholders in this study should be generalised with care as only a single case was studied. We recommend using different case studies and empirical settings to discover a deeper understanding of stakeholders' roles and interests in further research.

References

1. Luthfi, A., Janssen, M., Crompvoets, J.: Stakeholder tensions in decision-making for opening government data. In: Shishkov, B. (ed.) BMSD 2020. LNBIP, vol. 391, pp. 331–340. Springer, Cham (2020). https://doi.org/10.1007/978-3-030-52306-0_23
2. Scholl, H.J.: Applying stakeholder theory to E-government. In: Schmid, B., Stanoevska-Slabeva, K., Tschammer, V. (eds.) Towards the E-Society, vol. 74, pp. 735–747. Springer, Boston (2001). https://doi.org/10.1007/0-306-47009-8_54

3. Mascia, S.D.: Managing difficult stakeholders. Proj. Manage. World J. **4**(9) (2015)
4. Matheus, R., Janssen, M., Janowski, T.: Design principles for creating digital transparency in government. Govern. Inf. Q. **38**(1), 101550 (2020)
5. Moura, H.M., Teixeira, J.C.: Managing Stakeholders Conflicts. Construction Stakeholder Management. Blackwell Publishing (2010)
6. Mitchell, R., Agle, B., Wood, D.: Toward a theory of stakeholder identification and salience: defining the principle of who and what really counts. Acad. Manag. Rev. **22**(4), 853–886 (1997)
7. Ramirez, R.: Stakeholder analysis and conflict management. In: Conflict Collaboration in Natural Resource Management (1999)
8. Roeder, T.: Categorizing stakeholders. In: Managing Project Stakeholders: Building a Foundation to Achieve Project Goals (2013)
9. Kamal, M., Weerakkody, V., Irani, Z.: Analyzing the role of stakeholders in the adoption of technology integration solutions in UK local government: an exploratory study. Gov. Inf. Q. **28**(2), 200–210 (2011)
10. Gonzales-Zapata, F., Heeks, R.: The multiple meanings of open government data: understanding different stakeholders and their perspective. Gov. Inf. Q. **32**, 441–452 (2015)
11. McDermott, P.: Building open government. Gov. Inf. Q. **27**, 401–413 (2010)
12. Bryson, J.M.: What to do when stakeholders matter. Public Manage. Rev. **6**(1), 21–53 (2004)
13. Eliot, G.: What is a stakeholder? In: Managing Project Stakeholders: Building a Foundation to Achieve Project Goals (2013)

Towards IoT-Based Transport Development in Smart Cities: Safety and Security Aspects

Ivan Garvanov[1]([✉]), Magdalena Garvanova[1], Daniela Borissova[1,2], Bojan Vasovic[1,3], and Denislav Kanev[1]

[1] University of Library Studies and Information Technologies, Sofia, Bulgaria
{i.garvanov,m.garvanova,d.kanev}@unibit.bg
[2] Institute of Information and Communication Technologies, Sofia, Bulgaria
dborissova@iit.bas.bg
[3] Academy of Vocational Studies Southern Serbia, Blace, Serbia

Abstract. Innovative functioning models featuring smart cities are currently receiving much attention and this often concerns the notion of Internet-of-Things (IoT). Complex systems are considered in this regard, that are about the merging and processing of large volumes of data, aiming at quality-of-life-driven decision making. Safety and security aspects are considered in that perspective. Here, technology pros and cons are to be established as well as the potentials for combining different technologies, such that human-harmful effects are reduced and overall benefits are achieved. Addressing smart cities in general, we propose in the current paper a method that concerns the IoT-based transport development. The proposed method is about the detection of ground and air vehicles. In particular, we suggest using the forward scattering effect principle. On that basis, we suggest crossing the baselines formed between the numerous transmitters and receivers concerning corresponding IoT sensors. Finally, the proposed method is expected to enable electromagnetic pollution reductions, by limiting the number of emitters of electromagnetic waves.

Keywords: Smart cities · Internet-of-things · Air traffic management · Wireless technologies

1 Introduction

The design of smart cities is based on technologies and paradigms, such as the Internet-of-Things (IoT), satellite and ground communications, processing and analysis of large volumes of data (often obtained by numerous parameters sensors) [1]. We argue that a challenge in this regard is the establishment of smart transport involving both ground and air transport. In recent years, numerous systems have been set up to facilitate ground transport, supported by video surveillance, GPS navigation, autonomous driving, and so on. Some developments concerning drone technology concern service provisioning innovations aiming at improving quality of life. At the same time, drones can be dangerous (as it concerns security) and they may appear in situations challenging

© Springer Nature Switzerland AG 2021
B. Shishkov (Ed.): BMSD 2021, LNBIP 422, pp. 392–398, 2021.
https://doi.org/10.1007/978-3-030-79976-2_27

the air traffic management. Hence, it is not surprising that drone usage is banned in close proximity to airports, critical infrastructure points, and so on [2]. Some drones are very small, drones may be in different forms, built from different material, and they often have a high maneuverability potential – this all could pose difficulties in detecting and tracking them [3, 4].

There are various drone detection technologies [5] such as: 1) Video surveillance – it is effective during day time and in direct object visibility; 2) Microphone-related technical solutions featuring the detection of the sound generated by drones' engines – this can be effective in small distances only; 3) Frequency transmission between the drone and its ground station may be captured (using radio receivers) – even though this is effective in general, there are non-radio-controlled drones that hence cannot be detected using this technology; 4) Radar technologies for monitoring the airspace – only applicable for large-sized drones; 5) Doppler radar in particular, could enable detecting the presence of the drone's blade rotation – this is also limited to large-sized drones only; 6) Forward Scattering Radar (FSR) is an option as well, offering the possibility to also detect objects produced using stealth technology; 7) Combined usage of more than one of the abovementioned technologies could certainly be useful as well.

This all aligns well with some (recent) IoT developments (and also developments featuring wireless technologies), such as radio, television, terrestrial/space communication, and so on. This is all about millions of users and concerns hundreds of wireless communication channels (baselines) that are obtained in real time. They can be used not only for their intended purpose but also minding a secondary application featuring the detection of mobile and flying vehicles [6, 7]. Connection channels are used to create radio barriers. As the number of transmitters and receivers increases in smart cities, it becomes more convenient to implement such technologies.

Addressing smart cities in general, we propose in the current paper a method that concerns the IoT-based transport development. The proposed method is about the detection of ground and air vehicles. In particular, we suggest using the forward scattering effect principle. On that basis, we suggest crossing the baselines formed between the numerous transmitters and receivers concerning corresponding IoT sensors.

Our proposed method is expected to enable electromagnetic pollution reductions, by limiting the number of emitters of electromagnetic waves.

The remaining of the paper is organized as follows: Sect. 2 focuses on smart cities, taking an IoT perspective. Section 3 elaborates on the approach for target detection (concerning an IoT system) for air traffic management in urban conditions. Section 4 describes target detection in a passive forward scattering system based on IoT sensors. Finally, we conclude the paper in Sect. 5.

2 Smart Cities Based on the Internet of Things Concept

A smart city integrates information and communication technologies using different types of devices and sensors connected to an IoT data collection and processing network in order to optimize the efficiency of city management and improve urban operations and services. The technologies used in the smart city allow automatic monitoring and management of urban infrastructure, help reduce costs and consumption of resources, improve the quality of life and security of citizens (Fig. 1).

Fig. 1. Air target detection in smart city by using available communication channels

The economic and technological development of the smart city is based on IoT, which changes the way of life by transforming various business activities and technologies, managing things in our homes and offices, managing traffic as well as our cars [8]. IoT is based on the global network and provides communication and interaction between different physical objects, buildings, belongings, vehicles and others. IoT influences economic, societal and technological processes by minimizing human intervention. Challenges for the development of IoT are yet to come and are very much at stake for the development of smart cities, transport and industry.

For the development of transport in smart cities and in particular air transport, consisting of various (unmanned) aerial vehicles, it is necessary to build air traffic control centers [9, 10]. They should establish rules for the use of aircrafts and create different technologies for securing flights. A successful approach to air traffic control is the use of systems similar to current aircraft control systems, namely the use of obligatory transponders in individual flying objects. Due to the small size of some air vehicles and hence the use of low-power transmitters, as well as their movement in urban conditions with reduced communication capabilities with the control center, there could be problems with communication with air traffic control radars. At the same time, the presence of a large number of base stations and IoT sensors in the urban environment would usefully support the communication with air vehicles. No matter what rules are created for managing air vehicles and/or what technical means are used, there would always be stakeholders who would not be using the established infrastructure and/or would not be complying with the rules. For this purpose, similar to the primary airspace surveillance radars for detecting all aircraft, in our case it is proposed to use a multi-sensor radar system for detecting unmanned aerial vehicles based on Forward Scatter (FS) principles.

Smart technologies must be constantly evolving and improving to meet the challenges of the new age. If at the moment there are many and various technologies for land traffic management, then with the advent of unmanned aerial vehicles it is necessary to create new technologies and improve old ones [11, 12]. At the same time, some negative effects of the implementation of the new technologies, related to the safety and the security of the environment, should be taken into account.

3 Problem Elaboration for Air Traffic Management in Urban Conditions

There has been a rapid development of drones for the past few decades, this in turn leading to difficulties as it concerns the air traffic management in smart cities. Specifics and dimensions of drones make it difficult to detect, identify, track and control them. This requires the development of effective methods, algorithms and technologies for the detection of these aircraft.

This article proposes a method to improve transport management in new generation smart cities based on existing IoT sensors. We pose the following hypothesis: The continuous increase of the number of wireless communication devices (such as IoT sensors, radio, TV, mobile and satellite communication devices, and so on) would lead to the formation (in smart cities) of radio barriers that could be used not only to detect objects but also to improve urban transport management [7].

For example, while working on the Internet with our mobile device or making a phone call, we create a temporary radio barrier between us and the base station. If the radio signal we receive is processed by an algorithm that monitors the change in the amplitude of the received signal, an object crossing this radio barrier can be detected. At the moment of intersection, the amplitude of the received signal will change, which will be a sign that there is an obstacle in the path of the signal [11]. This information in turn can be submitted to a data pooling center by many sensors as a result of which the object can be tracked and recognized. Applying this additional processing to the communication signal will not change the performance of the IoT sensors. Their users will not be affected as well. The advantage in this case is that in parallel with solving the main task of a sensor, additional information will be obtained about the presence or absence of mobile objects between the transmitter and the receiver.

The use of existing wireless technologies for a secondary application is an up-to-date strand in science and finds more and more followers offering different solutions and applications [6]. For the processing of information in such a dynamic IoT system, rich of sensors, it is necessary to have a center or centers for data collection and processing. Pooling information obtained from many sensors operating in a given area will allow detection, classification of targets and determination of their trajectories. The size of the objects that can be detected with the proposed FS system depends significantly on the wavelength. The smaller the wavelength (the higher the bearing frequency of the signal) the diffraction of the signal will be more pronounced and smaller-sized objects can be detected [5]. In recent years, the frequency range of radio devices has expanded and many of them already operate in the GHz range, allowing the detection of objects with an effective reflecting surface of less than 10 cm^2. As an additional advantage of the secondary application of wireless technologies is the reduction of electromagnetic pollution of the environment [6].

The most appropriate technology for moving targets detection, including those that use stealth technology and at the same time do not pollute the radio broadcast, are Forward Scattering systems that apply radio signals in the space.

4   Target Detection in Passive Forward Scattering System Based on the Internet of Things Sensors

Forward Scattering Radar is a special type of bistatic radar, where the target is close to the transmitter-receiver baseline as shown in Fig. 2 and the bistatic angle is equal or near 180° (β ≈ 180°) and the target dimensions are larger than the transmitted wavelength [12, 13]. In this scenario, the radar system uses the diffraction phenomenon and is called the Forward Scatter. FSR presents a conservative class of systems that have a number of fundamental limitations, including the absence of range resolution and operation within narrow angles, and therefore require the target to be very close to the transmitter-receiver baseline. On the other hand, FSR offers a number of peculiarities that make it a viable interest. Its most attractive feature is the steep rise in the target Radar Cross Section (RCS) compared to traditional monostatic radar, which improves the sensitivity of the radar system. Target RCS at forward scattering is bigger than in the monostatic case by 30–40 dB, depending on the frequency band [9, 14].

Diffraction of wave can be divided into two classes: Fresnel diffraction (when the target is close to the transmitter or the receiver) and Fraunhofer diffraction (when the target is far from the transmitter and the receiver) (Fig. 3).

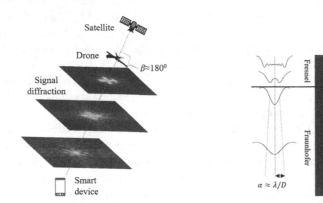

Fig. 2. Forward scattering radar system   **Fig. 3.** Types of diffraction

In this paper, a small omnidirectional commercial GPS antenna and GPS recording system, developed by the Colorado University for drone detection, is used. During the experiment, the drone is located near the baseline "satellite-receiver", which means that the bistatic angle is close to 180° (Fig. 4). The navigation message at the output of the Code&Carrier loop received from the GPS satellite at the time of crossing the radio barrier GPS satellite – GPS receiver from a drone is integrated with a sliding window of 300 ms and the results are shown in Fig. 5. From this figure it is seen that during the passage of the drone, the intensity of the information signal reduces and forms a FS signal with the certain geometry and form. From the results, it is evident that we can apply a signal processing algorithms for detection and classification of drones, using their FS signals.

Fig. 4. Topology of the experiment   **Fig. 5.** Target FS signal

The occurrence of FS signal is a physical phenomenon, which can be applied to extract some useful information about the objects that create it. The information obtained can be used in various applications like those in the classic radar, including radio barriers, security, classification and identification of moving and stationary objects.

Using the signals available from many different transmitters in the smart city and the millions of receivers of wireless users, millions of radio barriers are created, filling the airspace around us. These barriers are a source of rich information that can be used to detect both ground and air vehicles. At the same time, our proposal featuring the usage of FS technology for improving the transport management in smart cities, would lead to less pollution of the radio broadcast with additional radio signals.

5   Conclusions

We argue that our IoT-based proposal (concerning the transport development in smart cities) can be useful in various systems as it concerns security and/or surveillance. In addition, the considered technology can be used to create a passive FS radar network for detection of air targets based on their radio shadows. It is also a passive system using signals from available IoT sensors and different satellites that cover the entire globe with signals. Thus, the proposed FSR system could be widely used. We have considered an example of detecting an aircraft using a GPS software receiver, fulfilling the conditions for FSR. With the increase in the number of communication satellites, as well as the operating frequency of the signal, it becomes possible to detect relatively small unmanned aerial vehicles. We plan as future research to test our air vehicle detection algorithms, using signals from IoT sensors.

Acknowledgement. This work is supported by the Bulgarian National Science Fund, Project title "Synthesis of a dynamic model for assessing the psychological and physical impacts of excessive use of smart technologies", KP-06-N 32/4/07.12.2019.

References

1. Talari, S., Shafie-khah, M., Siano, P., Loia, V., Tommasetti, A., Catalão, J.: A review of smart cities based on the internet of things concept. Energies **10**, 421 (2017)
2. Alhaji Musa, S., et al.: A review of copter drone detection using radar systems. Defence Sci. Technol. Tech. Bull. **12**(1), 16–38 (2019). ISSN 1985-6571
3. Shishkov, B., Hristozov, S., Verbraeck, A.: Improving resilience using drones for effective monitoring after disruptive events. In: Proceedings of the 9th International Conference on Telecommunications and Remote Sensing (ICTRS 2020). Association for Computing Machinery, New York (2020)
4. Shishkov, B., Hristozov, S., Janssen, M., Van den Hoven, J.: Drones in land border missions: benefits and accountability concerns. In: Proceedings of the 6th International Conference on Telecommunications and Remote Sensing (ICTRS 2017). Association for Computing Machinery, New York (2017)
5. Raja Abdullah, R., et al.: Passive forward-scattering radar using digital video broadcasting satellite signal for drone detection. Remote Sens. **12**(18), 3075 (2020). https://doi.org/10.3390/rs12183075
6. Garvanova, M., Garvanov, I., Kashukeev, I.: Business processes and the safety of stakeholders: considering the electromagnetic pollution. In: Shishkov, B. (ed.) BMSD 2020. LNBIP, vol. 391, pp. 386–393. Springer, Cham (2020). https://doi.org/10.1007/978-3-030-52306-0_28
7. Garvanov, I., Kabakchiev, C., Behar, V., Daskalov, P.: Air Target detection with a GPS forward-scattering radar. In: XVIII-th International Symposium on Electrical Apparatus and Technologies SIELA 2016, Bourgas, Bulgaria, pp. 1–4 (2016). https://doi.org/10.1109/SIELA.2016.7543000
8. Shishkov, B.: Tuning the behavior of context-aware applications, using semiotic norms and Bayesian modeling to establish the user situation. In: Shishkov, B. (ed.) Business Modeling and Software Design BMSD 2019. LNBIP, vol. 356, pp. 134–152. Springer, Cham (2019). https://doi.org/10.1007/978-3-030-24854-3_9
9. Pavlova, K., Ivanov, V.: Application of information systems and technologies in transport. In: Fidanova, S. (ed.) WCO 2019. SCI, vol. 920, pp. 173–182. Springer, Cham (2021). https://doi.org/10.1007/978-3-030-58884-7_9
10. Boneva, Y., Ivanov, V.: Improvement of traffic in urban environment through signal timing optimization. In: Dimov, I., Fidanova, S. (eds.) HPC 2019. SCI, vol. 902, pp. 99–107. Springer, Cham (2021). https://doi.org/10.1007/978-3-030-55347-0_9
11. Kabakchiev C., et al.: Experimental parameter estimation of vehicles GPS shadows by forward scattering systems. In: International Radar Symposium 2017, Prague, Czech Republic, pp. 1–7 (2017). https://doi.org/10.23919/IRS.2017.8008216
12. Kabakchiev, H., et al.: Multi-channel target shadow detection in GPS FSR. Cybern. Inf. Technol. **19**(1), 116–132 (2019). https://doi.org/10.2478/cait-2019-0007
13. Lazarov, A., Kostadinov, T.: 3-D SAR geometry and LFM waveform for ship target imaging. In: 21st International Symposium on Electrical Apparatus & Technologies (SIELA), pp. 1–4 (2020). https://doi.org/10.1109/SIELA49118.2020.9167159
14. Kostadinov, T., Simeonov, S.: Acquisition and processing of navigation parameters. In: 21st International Symposium on Electrical Apparatus and Technologies (SIELA), pp. 1–5 (2020). https://doi.org/10.1109/SIELA49118.2020.9167140

Author Index

Printed in the United States
by Baker & Taylor Publisher Services